Consciousness

Consciousness

Philosophical, Psychological
and Neural Theories

David Rose

OXFORD
UNIVERSITY PRESS

OXFORD

UNIVERSITY PRESS

Great Clarendon Street, Oxford OX2 6DP

Oxford University Press is a department of the University of Oxford.
It furthers the University's objective of excellence in research, scholarship,
and education by publishing worldwide in

Oxford New York

Auckland Cape Town Dar es Salaam Hong Kong Karachi
Kuala Lumpur Madrid Melbourne Mexico City Nairobi
New Delhi Shanghai Taipei Toronto

With offices in

Argentina Austria Brazil Chile Czech Republic France Greece
Guatemala Hungary Italy Japan Poland Portugal Singapore
South Korea Switzerland Thailand Turkey Ukraine Vietnam

Oxford is a registered trade mark of Oxford University Press
in the UK and in certain other countries

Published in the United States
by Oxford University Press Inc., New York

British Library Cataloguing in Publication Data
Data available

Library of Congress Cataloging in Publication Data
Data available

Typeset by Newgen Imaging Systems (P) Ltd., Chennai, India
Printed in Great Britain
on acid-free paper by
Antony Rowe Ltd., Chippenham, Wiltshire

ISBN 0–19–879294–8   978–0–19–879294–9

10 9 8 7 6 5 4 3 2 1

For Richard and Priscilla,
and for Dora

■ CONTENTS

■ PREFACE

This is a book full of theories – theories about the philosophy, psychology and neuroscience of consciousness. It deals in theories because knowledge is stored in the form of theories, and to understand consciousness we need a great deal of knowledge. They say that mathematicians and physical scientists have their brightest ideas while young, but biologists need to be older because of the greater complexity of their material; yet for consciousness this is likely to be even more the case. For just as the question 'What is life?' requires us to know genetics, chemistry, anatomy, physiology, ecology . . ., so the query 'What is consciousness?' demands in addition to these an understanding of philosophy, phenomenology, psychology and neuroscience. In one sense, then, this has to be an *advanced* textbook; there just is not enough space here to present all the evidential bases from which the theories in these various fields have been derived. As such, this book is most suitable for final year undergraduates, postgraduates and researchers who have already covered most of the basic facts about how the brain works. These relevant foundations can be found in the many excellent introductory textbooks of biopsychology and neuroscience, and in the literature on consciousness studies listed in the Recommended Reading below.

In particular, after much deliberation, I chose to focus the book towards students of psychology and neuroscience. Rather than explaining the basics of cognition, nerve cell firing and brain structure, I have assumed that readers are familiar with ideas such as working memory, brain scanning, the conical shape of pyramidal cells, the limited speed of action potentials and the location of the occipital lobe (though reminders of many of the basics will be included at several points in the text). Given that target audience, I have therefore included an elementary introduction to philosophy, a vital topic that is not often taught alongside courses in science faculties. Students who have completed a year or more of philosophy can therefore skip part one of this book without missing anything they don't already know. But others should begin there, because the vehicle that is this book follows particular philosophical paths: for instance, it takes consciousness to be a matter of representation, and so the search for neural events relating to consciousness can begin with the (already well-developed) study of the neural bases of representation.

Nowadays, how one names the problem carries implications about what one thinks one is doing, and for how readers interpret the whole exercise. For example, the title of this book, at draft stage, was variously 'Function, brain and mind', 'The neural bases of consciousness' and 'A textbook on consciousness'. Yet all of these expressions seemed to mean various things to different people, whose prejudices and expectations were aroused, often inappropriately. The final form, 'Philosophical, psychological and neural theories', is designed to reflect my central themes: that to understand consciousness we need to know what is happening at all the relevant levels, that these can be integrated into a coherent picture and that at the present time such a theory is very much what we need.

Now, since most current theorizing about consciousness revolves around the activities of nerve cells in the brain, much of the book is devoted to neural theories (particularly the second half). The relationship between consciousness and neural firing is not, however, one I think can be treated as a single step that bridges some mysterious gulf. Instead, multiple levels are involved and have to be incorporated into the process of inquiry. The reasons for this will be elaborated in chapters 3 and 4, which begin my depiction of the complex – but soluble – task before us all. Thus, in later chapters, I try to return as often as possible to the philosophical aspects of the neural theories that I discuss there in depth, with the aim of tying these levels together. The comparison also enables us to reflect on the theories' logical strengths and weaknesses as revealed by philosophical analysis, as well as on their empirical and rational bases. For at the moment, isolated facts on their own have limited benefit and we need coherent theories to help us interpret experimental outcomes and guide our future studies.

Accordingly I have included extensive cross-references between topics and sections in the book, so as to tie the ideas into a network of knowledge, rather than just presenting a series of atomistic bite-size chunks strung together as a single narrative. Although there is, of course, a clear and, I hope, logical sequence to the topics in this book, which can indeed be read through in the order presented, this thread is not the only one that could be drawn. The many cross-connections I give should later assist in seeing alternative themes, and in noticing the props of support and the clashes of inconsistency where these exist.

The materials covered also include some that might be described as historical; but these are valuable because old ideas are often forgotten and rediscovered, they are the source of much currently common terminology and they certainly influence the theories that are now being proposed. The study of old ideas should not be eschewed because they must be wrong, given that newer and putatively more correct theories have come along.

In fact, the belief in the existence of a single Right Answer to our problems is one I want to wean you away from. As Side-box 0.1 explains, understanding the world proceeds through three stages (roughly analogous to childhood, adolescence and maturity!). You have to get beyond the belief that all you need to do is memorize the correct facts, and then beyond the idea that all ideas are equally valid. Instead, adopting a position on the mind–body problem involves a commitment to a particular point of view that cannot be proved absolutely correct but nevertheless is the one you think the best available at this time (and, moreover, changing circumstances can alter the optimal choice). All positions have their pros and cons, their advantages and disadvantages, and you have to make a judicious decision after weighing all the evidence and arguments on each side. In short, it is *thinking skills* that you need most if you are going to investigate consciousness, not just facts. To this end this book contains many sections where arguments for and against particular points of view are listed and contrasted. Then, most of the major neural and cognitive theories described in the later chapters are followed by evaluative critiques. Each chapter also begins with an 'Objectives' section that gives guidance as to the (meta-) cognitive skills that are emphasized within it. Given the plethora of fascinating but conflicting claims and counter-claims currently swarming around the field of consciousness research, the point is to learn how to be a critical judge rather than someone who accepts and memorizes proposals at face value. It is important to be able to recognize theories which have no justification other than that their author has 'seen the light' – and to beware of making this mistake yourself.

SIDE-BOX 0.1 KNOWING ABOUT KNOWING ABOUT KNOWING

Individual development can be divided into stages: true or false? Studies of the stages of understanding through which university students progress have actually shown that belief in single true answers to questions such as these is a relatively immature position (Perry, 1970). As students progress, they normally move on to adopt first a more open-minded, relativistic outlook. Finally, they should reach a stage where they recognize the complexity of the world, but realize they must choose to adopt a particular theory and act upon it, which involves personal commitment and responsibility for the consequences of one's choice.

To elaborate: given a conflict between several theories, novice students assume that one and only one must be true. To quote Perry's summary (1970, pp. 9–10): 'The student sees the world in polar terms of we-right-good vs. other-wrong-bad. Right Answers for everything exist in the Absolute, known to Authority whose role is to mediate (teach) them. Knowledge and goodness are perceived as quantitative accretions of discrete rightnesses to be collected by hard work and obedience.' Next, as the student progresses, diversity of opinion and uncertainty are perceived and are first ascribed to 'poorly qualified Authority' and are then interpreted as 'legitimate but still temporary in areas where Authority "hasn't found The Answer yet".' Later, disillusion sets in and conflicting theories are described as the mere (but equally valid) opinions of whoever proposed the theories; 'anyone has a right to his own opinion'. Thus, 'the student perceives all knowledge and values (including authority's) as contextual and relativistic'. Still later, in developing students, it comes to be understood that there must be 'some form of personal Commitment (as distinct from unquestioned or unconsidered commitment to simple belief in certainty)', and that we have multiple responsibilities that unfold and change over time. Thus all theories have pros and cons; accepting one theory means accepting its disadvantages as well as its benefits, and means losing the potential benefits of the alternative theories. In the final stage, 'mature' students are aware of the practical and moral consequences of having to choose a theory to guide their actions, and are prepared to accept the responsibility if things go wrong! This last is most easily understood in fields such as medicine, where introducing a new treatment might cure some patients but make others worse or introduce harmful side-effects.[a]

Kitchener (1983) and Salner (1986) then modified the conception of a three-stage progression, calling the successive phases cognitive, metacognitive and epistemic. In the first, people memorize facts and solve problems. In the second they learn how they learn, and can monitor their own progress at (first-phase) learning, altering their method if necessary. At the third stage people can think about what knowledge is, how best to get it, how to recognize and use it when it is found, how reliable their knowledge is and which strategies are best for carrying out the first- and second-phase cognitive tasks under different circumstances. Thus the higher levels feed back to modulate the lower. For further information see ⟨http://www.perrynetwork.org⟩.

In conclusion, knowledge is of three types: knowing about the world, knowing that you know and knowing what knowing is. This suggests how we might understand consciousness; replace 'knowing' in the previous sentence with 'consciousness' and we have a hypothesis that there are three types or levels of awareness. Indeed, in chapter 11 we will see how philosophers have already drawn analogous distinctions between lower-order, higher-order and self-consciousness.

Yet our understanding of these processes is not advanced, and before we can come to terms with the full structure of consciousness we will spend most of this book dealing with the processes by which the most basic stage arises: how do we become aware of the world around us?

[a] There is also a striking analogy here between Perry's stages and the history of the philosophy of science in this century: (1) positivist empiricism, (2) relativism (the sociology of knowledge programme) and (3) competing research paradigms and programmes; see Side-boxes 3.2 and 3.6.

Of course, successful teaching requires that we start with simple ideas and then build up to the complex. Inevitably, then, there are simplifications in this book that are placeholders for later elaborations. The aim throughout, however, has been to avoid persistent oversimplification and misleading shorthand. One of the problems is the terminology; first, this differs between disciplines (so we have to learn the languages and jargon of several), with concomitant risks of misunderstanding when the same word is used in different technical senses in different contexts, so translation misfires. Second, the new concepts being developed do not have names, so metaphors or analogies are often used, and these run the risk of confusion with their original meanings. Nevertheless, this is an enterprise that must succeed; we have to be able to talk to one another – philosophers, psychologists and neuroscientists – in order to build an understanding of consciousness that is comprehensive, integrated and avoids the tunnel vision that obtains in most individual specialities. It is to this end that the present volume is dedicated, and even if it constitutes only a small step in that direction, I hope it inspires you all to move forward on this project, just as the theories contained here have inspired and infuriated me.

■ RECOMMENDED READING

General introductions to consciousness studies are appearing with increasing frequency nowadays. For lay readers, Blackmore's Consciousness: A Very Short Introduction (2005a) is the most compact, while Ramachandran's The Emerging Mind (2003a), based on the BBC Reith Lectures, gives a neurological point of view, and Zeman's Consciousness: A User's Guide (2002) also introduces much of the background needed. Freeman's Consciousness: A Guide to the Debates (2003) and Blackmore's Conversations on Consciousness (2005b) both explain the issues in more depth but very readably. Some further entertaining arguments are given in a series of New York Times reviews involving John Searle, published as The Mystery of Consciousness (edited by Searle, 1997).

As for books suitable for set courses at university level, Blackmore's Consciousness: An Introduction (2003) is the standard first year text, while Koch's The Quest for Consciousness (2004) then gives the neuroscientific evidence you need; the present text follows next in that sequence.

For background reading, there are numerous anthologies of relevant papers, both classics and modern summaries, and some of these also contain valuable reviews and commentaries by the editors. These include Two Sciences of Mind (Ó Nualláin et al., 1997), The Nature of Consciousness (Block et al., 1997), Minds, Brains, and Computers (Cummins and Cummins, 2000), Philosophy and the Neurosciences (Bechtel et al., 2001), and Essential Sources in the Scientific Study of Consciousness (Baars et al., 2003). For the neural theories, see especially Metzinger's Neural Correlates of Consciousness (2000), The Cognitive Neuroscience of Consciousness (Dehaene, 2001), Osaka's Neural Basis of Consciousness (2003), Gazzaniga's, The Cognitive Neurosciences III (2004) and The Boundaries of Consciousness: Neurobiology and Neuropathology edited by Laureys (2005). For reference, see Arbib's The Handbook of Brain Theory and Neural Networks, 2nd edn (2002) and Gregory's The Oxford Companion to the Mind, 2nd edn (2004).

Current research articles appear in the periodicals Consciousness and Cognition, Journal of Consciousness Studies, Consciousness and Emotion, and increasingly in many mainstream psychology and neuroscience journals (especially **Trends in Cognitive Science**). Freely available electronic journals also exist on the web, such as **Psyche, Psycoloquy** and **Science and Consciousness Review**. Links to these and to many other sources of information can be found on my web pages: ⟨http://www.psy.surrey.ac.uk/staff/d.rose/drpage325.html⟩, and, for the more elementary level, ⟨http://www.psy.surrey.ac.uk/staff/d.rose/drpage345.html⟩ and at the Oxford University Press Online Resource Centre ⟨http://www.oxfordtextbooks.co.uk/orc/rose⟩.

There are two main series of conferences on consciousness. One is organized by the Center for Consciousness Studies and meets biennially in Tucson, but with intervening meetings in Europe; the Tucson conferences lead to anthologies of papers edited by Hameroff et al. and called **Toward a Science of Consciousness** (1996), II (1998), III (1999) (and presumably so on). The second series is organized by the Association for the Scientific Study of Consciousness. Links to both their websites can be found on my pages.

■ ACKNOWLEDGEMENTS

This book would not have existed without my students and their need for a long overdue overview of this topic. The bulk of my assistance throughout its six-year growth came from Dora Brown, while invaluable comments were also contributed by Jolanta Opacka-Juffry, administrative and technical help by John Cusack and Nigel Woodger, and welcome relief from some of my teaching load by Bart De Bruyn; thanks to you all. The work could not have been completed without the patience of the editors at Oxford University Press, particularly Jonathon Crowe, and I should also thank the Press's reviewers for their comments – even those who told me there was too much material in it and then complained I hadn't included their own work (I've cited nearly 1400 references, yet still I feel the need to apologize to everyone whose work is not in here!). Finally, for their support, enthusiasm and inspiration, I must thank Sue Blackmore and Richard Gregory, pioneers both in this enterprise of putting mind to paper.

■ FIGURE ACKNOWLEDGEMENTS

Copyright material was reproduced by kind permission of the following:

Figure 3.1 from M. Arbib, *Handbook of Brain Theory and Neural Networks*, published by MIT Press, © 1995 Massachusetts Institute of Technology.

Figure 3.3 from *Fundamental Neuroanatomy* by Walle J.H. Nauta and Michael Feirtag, © 1986 by W.H. Freeman and Company.

Figure 3.4a, © 1971 from F. Valverde, 'Short axon neuronal subsystems in the visual cortex of the monkey', reproduced by permission of Taylor and Francis Inc., ⟨http://www.taylorandfrancis.com⟩.

Figure 3.4b reprinted from A. Fairén and F. Valverde, 'Specific thalamo-cortical afferents and their presumptive targets in the visual cortex. A Golgi study', *Progress in Brain Research* 51, 419–438 (*Development and Chemical Specificity of Neurons*, C. Cuénod, G.W. Kreutzberg and F.E. Bloom, eds.), © 1979, with permission from Elsevier.

Figure 3.5a from H. Braak, *Journal of Comparative Neurology* 166, 341–364, © The Wistar Institute Press 1976, reprinted with permission of Wiley-Liss, Inc., a subsidiary of John Wiley & Sons, Inc.

Figure 3.5b from J. Szentágothai, 'Synaptology of the visual cortex', *Handbook of Sensory Physiology* VII/3/B, 1973, p. 316, Fig. 24, © Springer-Verlag Berlin Heidelberg 1973, with kind permission of Springer Science and Business Media.

Figure 3.5c from chapter 'Chemical soup' by A. Sillito from *The Artful Eye* (1995) edited by D. Rose et al. By permission of Oxford University Press.

Figure 3.6b from Rodney Cotterill, *Enchanted Looms*, 1998 © Cambridge University Press reprinted with permission.

Figure 4.2 from chapter 'A portrait of the brain' by D. Rose from *The Artful Eye* (1995) edited by D. Rose et al. By permission of Oxford University Press.

Figure 4.6 reproduced with permission from D. Rose and J. Harris, 'Perception', in *Psychology*, pp. 156–179 (M.R.C. Hewstone, F.D. Fincham, and J. Foster, eds.), Blackwell, Oxford.

Figures 4.8a and 4.8b, © Nature Publishing Group, reproduced with permission.

Figures 6.7 and 6.9 reprinted from B.L. McNaughton and R.G.M. Morris, 'Hippocampal synaptic enhancement and information-storage within a distributed memory system', *Trends in Neurosciences* 10, 408–415, © 1987, with permission from Elsevier.

Figure 6.10 from S. Kauffman, *Origins of Order*, Fig.5.6, © 1995 by Stuart Kauffman; used by permission of Oxford University Press, Inc.

Figure 7.2 reproduced with permission from D. Rose and J. Harris, 'Perception', pp. 156–179 in *Psychology*, (M.R.C. Hewstone, F.D. Fincham, and J. Foster, eds.), Blackwell, Oxford.

Figure SB 8.2.1 reproduced with permission from D. Rose and J. Harris, 'Perception', pp. 156–179 in *Psychology,* (M.R.C. Hewstone, F.D. Fincham, and J. Foster, eds.), Blackwell, Oxford.

Figure SB 8.8.1 from S. Shipp, 'The functional logic of cortico-pulvinar connections', *Philosophical Transactions of the Royal Society of London, Series B* 358, 1605–1624 (2003), p. 1610, Fig. 10, published by the Royal Society of London.

Figure 9.1 from E. Rolls, *Hippocampus* 10, 380–388, © 2000 Wiley-Liss Inc.; reprinted with permission of Wiley-Liss, Inc., a subsidiary of John Wiley & Sons, Inc.

Figure 9.3 reprinted from T.S. Lee, D. Mumford, R. Romero and V.A.F. Lamme, 'The role of the primary visual cortex in higher level vision', *Vision Research* 38, 2429–2454, © 1998, with permission from Elsevier.

Figure 9.4 from G.M. Edelman, *Bright Air Brilliant Fire,* © 1992 by Basic Books, Inc.; reprinted by permission of Basic Books, a member of Perseus Group, L.L.C.

Figures 9.5 and 9.6 reprinted from S. Grossberg, 'The link between brain learning, attention, and consciousness', *Consciousness and Cognition* 8, 1–44, © 1999, with permission from Elsevier.

Figure SB 9.1.1 reprinted from A.J. Marcel, 'Conscious and unconscious perception: experiments on visual masking and word recognition', *Cognitive Psychology* 15, 197–237, © 1983, with permission from Elsevier.

Figure SB 9.1.2 reprinted from A.J. Marcel, 'Conscious and unconscious perception: an approach to the relations between phenomenal experience and perceptual processes', *Cognitive Psychology* 15, 238–300, © 1983, with permission from Elsevier.

Figure 11.1 from G.M. Edelman, *Bright Air Brilliant Fire,* © 1992 by Basic Books, Inc.; reprinted by permission of Basic Books, a member of Perseus Group, L.L.C.

PART ONE

Thinking about Mind and Brain

In the first part we will examine the philosophy behind the methods that have been developed for studying the mind. This strategy is not only of interest to philosophers, because just as the current methods used in science generally are the result of philosophical debates that took place centuries ago, so our approaches to the mind are similarly influenced by philosophical arguments that have grown from the time of Descartes up to the present day. After some terminological introductions and a survey of the field in chapter 1, we follow in chapter 2 the progress of philosophers in understanding how the mind can be approached, with particular regard to its relationship with the physical world of brains and nerve cells. These chapters form part of any standard introduction to philosophy of mind, and can be skipped by anyone who has already studied this topic at university level. They take us from the time of Descartes up to about the last quarter of a century, which is as far as most introductory textbooks currently go (though we will go further in part two!).

In chapter 3, I approach the mind–body problem from the other side, by looking at what philosophical presuppositions underlie current practices in neuroscience. What are workers in that area trying to achieve, and what do they think are the best methods for achieving that aim? The core issues are not just about their understanding of the mind and its relationship to the brain, but also their implicit assumptions about philosophy of science. The latter deals with such basic questions as: what is knowledge and how can I get some, and what is truth and how can I recognize it? The methods used by scientists to gather data, draw inferences and test hypotheses all depend on answers to these questions that were developed a long time ago. Although I cannot go into detail here, a case can be made that obsolete methods are still in use, and these match equally obsolete assumptions about mind–body relationships. These deliberations set the scene for part two, in which it will be demonstrated that the use of current opinion in philosophy would enable more realistic and satisfactory conclusions to be obtained.

1 **Philosophical approaches**

1.1 **Definitions**

1.1.1 **Mind and consciousness**

It is important to begin with some definitions, since it is often unclear what people mean when they use words like 'mind' and 'consciousness'. These terms are used widely and have broad connotations. For example, 'consciousness' can refer to awareness of the world, self-awareness, subjective experience, being awake, knowing, understanding, being attentive or the possession of free will (for an in-depth analysis, see Lycan, 1996, chapter 1).

Let us look at the word 'mind', which is used in many different ways. The narrowest sense would be equivalent to: immediate ongoing consciousness. Asking someone 'What is on your mind?' or 'What is in your mind?' means, 'What are you thinking of *now*?, or 'What is the exact content of your ongoing thoughts and experiences?' But one can also use the word 'mind' to include various unconscious (or immediately unconscious) processes. These can include:

1. All the memories you have that you are not actually recalling at this moment in time. If these could in principle be recalled, they may be considered part of the mind.

2. Various other unconscious processes as well: cognitive mechanisms such as those involved in speaking grammatically, understanding sentences, recalling the capital of Cuba, recognizing a face and many other kinds of processing task. The modern consensus seems to be that vast numbers of psychological processes proceed subconsciously.

3. One can also argue that the kinds of repressed memories or thoughts postulated by Freud, if they exist, are part of the mind.

4. Then there is also the issue of what happens during sleep – when you are asleep, what has happened to your mind? If we are not conscious then, do we still have minds? Similar questions arise as to other putatively unconscious states: adults lying inert following a blow to the head or suffering severe illness; babies or foetuses; and animals – do each of these have minds, and if so are they conscious minds? Where does one draw the boundaries? These are issues we will be coming to in the next chapter.

5. And what about the imagination: thoughts you make up like unicorns, stories or lies? In some situations there can also be false memories: things you think you remember but that are actually false. Are these thoughts or ideas part of the mind even though they are untrue? Do false ideas, thoughts about nonexistent states of affairs, delusions, hallucinations (e.g. schizophrenics hearing voices), imagining the future and planning actions you have not carried out yet comprise part of 'the mind'?

Perhaps the most fundamental schism is between whether 'the mind' comprises all thoughts that are potentially conscious, including memories and imaginings, or whether it also includes unconscious processes that can never become conscious, as for example the mechanisms which analyse grammar or create visual illusions. This is a matter of definition, and I am not saying that only one meaning is 'correct'. I am only saying that when people (including you) use the word 'mind' you must be careful what is meant, because there are a number of different ways of drawing the boundary between mind and non-mind.

1.1.2 Mental state

'Mental state' is a phrase used in philosophy to contrast with 'brain state' or 'physical state'. It's used often by philosophers on the (apparent) presupposition that you are in one mental state at any one time – that your entire mind is engaged in whatever one thing you are doing. The examples they give are typically are about specific conditions like 'seeing red' or 'believing that Havana is the capital of Cuba'.

Some philosophers have categorized mental states into two or more types. One type comprises sensory states, also known as awareness, 'raw' feelings or 'qualia' (see below). These include experiences such as seeing something that is red, being in pain, being frightened, being depressed and so on. This group of mental states is characterized by *qualitative* characteristics: there is a certain raw, basic feel to what red looks like that is different from what green looks like, that is different from what a cuckoo sounds like or from a pain in your toe. These are elements of conscious experience.

The second group incorporates thoughts or beliefs, including attitudes, abstract thoughts, conceptual knowledge and all the things you think – thinking *that* it is raining, believing *that* the walls of this room are green, 'knowing' *that* Havana is the capital of Cuba or not liking the weather. These are often characterized as being 'propositional' in the sense of having a verbal or linguistic format to them – as opposed to the analogue, imagistic format of the states of feeling or sensory awareness. They are often described as 'propositional attitudes'. Propositions are statements of the kind 'this table is solid' or 'the walls of this room are cream'. The meaning of 'attitude' is not quite like 'attitude' in social psychology. In this context attitudes are internal, personal reactions that include not just liking or disliking (e.g. liking the fact that it is sunny today) but also more general kinds of cognitive thinking such as believing that the weather is sunny, wanting the weather to be sunny, thinking that the weather is sunny and so on. There is thus a two-part composition to propositional attitudes: the idea or 'content' and your reaction or stance towards it, what you think about it (the 'vehicle' that carries the content). There is a school of philosophy which assumes that all psychological processes involve propositional attitudes, and these are central to all of mental life and everything we do.

We have talked about two kinds of mental state so far, feelings/senses and beliefs/thoughts/propositional attitudes. Some people also add a third type of mental state that involves self-awareness and some kind of internal scanning or monitoring process. This is broadly known as introspection, but can be defined a bit more precisely than that. It involves being aware of yourself: knowing what *you* think, knowing what you are feeling and knowing your own mind. The idea is that you must have some special extra mechanism to generate this third kind of mental state.

So we have the beginnings of a scheme for categorizing what types of mental states there are: raw feelings, propositions and self-awareness. It is often not clear which one someone is talking about, and for general purposes philosophers often lump them together and talk about mental states in general: about what mental state someone is in and how this relates to the physical state of the brain. The same applies in much of recent neural theorizing, where 'consciousness' is treated as a single, unitary phenomenon. For much of this book we will need to take advantage of this simplification as well, but we will return to the issue of the multiplicity of types in later chapters (especially in chapter 11).

1.1.3 Intentionality and qualia

'*Intentionality*' and '*qualia*' are a couple of technical terms that refer to what some philosophers of mind regard as the Big Problems of recent research. Let's start with the issue of '*qualia*' because we've already introduced it under sensory awareness. Qualia (singular '*quale*') are elements of sensory awareness, qualitative feelings such as red or pain. In its original meaning, 'qualia' refers to an experience of, say, red, in a pure form devoid of any other quality such as spatial location or object identity – just the simple concept of red. Other examples would be the pure concepts of distance or pain or a high-pitched tone. In contrast, complex percepts, such as that of an armchair, can be broken down into subcomponents such as colour, location, surface texture, etc. The latter are the qualia, the minimal atomistic elements of experience that cannot be broken down or analysed further. They have no substructure, and thus are sometimes described as 'homogeneous'. Qualia have a *qualitative* feeling to them which is central to the issue.

There is, however, a broader use of the term which has crept in, which is to apply it to all sensory experiences – not just the simple elements but also the whole complexity of sensory input: of stimulus objects and even the entire context, so long as we are referring to the qualitative aspects. There is in fact a debate about whether we can actually experience sensations as isolated elements or whether we always experience the whole world as a complex (e.g. Barlow, 1972, 1995, Dennett, 1988, and Lycan, 2001, deny that sensory experience is atomistic). In its wider use, the term is applied to all aspects of conscious experience. For example: 'We will call the space of all possible conscious experience qualia space' (Stanley, 1999, p. 49). Typical examples of more complex stimuli are the sound of your mother's voice, the smell of a rose, or the taste of Marmite (or Vegemite). They are difficult to describe in words or to analyse into simpler components. Seager's (1993, p. 353) description of 'being slightly drunk' as a quale would also come under this category.

These uses all reflect the view that 'the mental' is to be defined in terms of its experiential qualities. (However, I will not be following that usage here.)

'*Intentionality*' is another important technical concept. The original definition comes from Brentano (1874), and it is not strictly related to intentions or actions or how will-power works. Instead, intentionality refers to 'meaning' or 'aboutness': mental states are about something. For example, typical mental states are your belief that Havana is the capital of Cuba, or your thought that the walls of this room are green. In other words, your mental states refer to something in the world outside you – the capital of Cuba, the colour of the walls. If you think something about yourself, the mental state refers to you, but there is still referring or referencing, a meaning[1] to your mental state. Another way to express intentionality is to say that mental states point to (literally, 'aim at'), indicate or symbolize something.

The problem of intentionality is understanding how it is that mental states can have meaning and be about something, in contrast to things like stones. A stone is not about anything: it does not refer to or point to anything else, in the way that your mental state is about something else. Now consider, if your brain is just full of neurons, glia, and so on, how can those neurons (or their activity) be about anything else? How can an action potential be about the colour of the room or your belief in the Prime Minister? How is it that activity in certain parts of your brain has meaning? In what way is it different from a stone? This is the problem of intentionality.

In its broad use, intentionality becomes a defining characteristic of 'the mind' – all and only mental states have intentionality. (Contrast this with the definition of mental states as those which have experiential qualities – qualia. Do these definitions coincide in

1. Note that in philosophy the word 'meaning' itself can have several meanings, and under some definitions only a subclass of intentional states have meaning. This will be explained in more detail in chapter 5; but for now, note that I often use 'meaning' and 'intentionality' interchangeably, since most of the book is about the basis of representation (see section 2.5), which for simplicity is treated as a unitary concept (until chapter 11).

identifying states of the world which are 'mental', or are they rival theories? We will discuss this in chapters 9–11.)

Intentionality and qualia are the two Big Problems in a sense, in that both concepts are very difficult to solve. There has been quite a lot of progress recently on intentionality, and we have several ideas now about how mental states could have meaning; we will cover these below (e.g. chapters 4 and 5). However, there has been very little progress on qualia: we are still up in the air about how the activity of nerve cells could possibly give rise to sensory experiences with particular qualities. Indeed, some philosophers have partitioned this question off, calling it 'the hard problem', and one which some of them think is insoluble (however, we will not be so pessimistic).

1.2 **Ontology**

Ontology is the study of what there is, of reality, the nature of the world: what are atoms and brains really made of; what is really out there? Ontology of mind broadly divides into two positions: monism and dualism.

'*Dualism*' is the idea that mind and matter are different in some way. There is a qualitative difference between the nature or composition of mind and that of material objects like the brain. Mental processes differ from material processes either in that those processes run on mechanisms made of fundamentally different substances, or in that they are distinct properties of certain types of substance. (I will present more detailed discussion in chapter 2.)

In '*monism*' (short for 'mono-ism'), everything is just a single kind of entity, material or substance; there is a single reality of which everything is composed. There are various positions within monism. The first, '*materialism*', refers to the idea that everything is made of matter: everything is physical – and that includes the mind. So if you are a materialist you think that not only brains but also mental states and the contents of your mind are in some way physical or material at base, whether objects, entities, events or processes.

The word '*physicalism*' is often used pretty much synonymously. It has a slightly different connotation in that it emphasizes the laws of physics: everything in the physicalist universe has to conform to the laws of physics. So according to physicalism your thoughts and mental life are explicable purely in terms of physical laws. This is obviously tied up with materialism, and also with '*naturalism*', the belief that the mind is part of nature and is not a separate entity or substance that is in any way 'supernatural', as dualism would suggest.

The extreme opposite of materialism is 'idealism'. The 'ideals' here are not what we normally mean by the word (though you can probably get away with thinking of it as 'idea-ism'). The term actually derives from Plato's theory that there is no such thing as a perfect (ideal) circle – in the real world there are always irregularities – yet we can conceive of a perfect circle very easily in our imagination. Well, according to idealism, everything is (made of) mind: everything is mental and only the human mind – or only your own mind – is real. The rest of the world is a construct of our minds (or, in some versions of idealism, of God's mind). To caricature it, the world is a figment of our imagination; atoms and tables and chairs are not real – we think they are real, but it is only our thoughts that are actually real. Bishop Berkeley (1707) was the most famous advocate of this idea. That's all I'm going to say about idealism. It's not discussed a lot nowadays.[2]

There is in a sense a third monist position, *'dual aspect monism'*, which states that what is real is neither mental nor material as we normally understand them; instead, it's something else (which we can't get at). Mind and matter are different aspects of this fundamental underlying something. In just the same way that in physics there was an argument about whether light is particles or waves, and they ended up with the theory that light is both particles and waves at the same time, mind and matter and atoms and thoughts could in some way be different aspects of some underlying substance. What that 'substance' is cannot, of course, be established easily, since we have no direct access to it.[3]

In sum, then, there are several monistic positions. As most people know, in modern science the fundamental assumption is materialism, and the belief that minds are in some way related to brains. Hardly anyone supports idealism, while the dual aspect theory is very difficult to prove or disprove.

1.3 **Semantics**

The topic of semantics is broadly concerned with meaning and the issue of intentionality already mentioned: how is it that our thoughts have meaning, how can thoughts refer to anything outside themselves, and how are they linked to those external objects? There are analogies here with linguistic theory and philosophy and the question of how words have meanings.

Two important words are 'extension' and 'intension'. Notice the 's' in intension – it's different from the 't' in intention and intentionality. They are two different concepts. Intension is the opposite of extension, which is a word you are more familiar with. Extension refers to the idea that there is some kind of causal link between your thoughts and the outside world; the occurrence of an event in the outside world can lead you to think of it, or your thoughts can cause you to do something to the object in the outside world. There is an external reference, some sort of connection between the contents of the mind and the external reality.

---

2. One reason for the demise of idealism is the lack of explanation for how mind conceives the material world, and why it conceives it to be that way in particular. Another problem is the lack of correspondence between our mental 'common-sense' understanding and the empirical discoveries of science. For example, our intuition that the geometry of the world is Euclidean is at odds both with general relativity and with quantum mechanics. The power of science is that it can demonstrably prove the material world to be constructed in ways that are counter-intuitive or that go beyond anything we can or did imagine beforehand.

3. Something that Chalmers (1996), Seager (1999), and Hiley and Pylkkänen (2001) suggest is that the underlying something is information. It is not a new idea that 'information' spans both the mental and physical realms (e.g. MacKay, 1956), but one of the theories that is currently arousing interest is that information or structure (or geometry?) is some kind of fundamental aspect of the universe that can reveal itself in minds and in material. How it works, though, is, of course, still a mystery.

'Intension' refers to the relationship between two thoughts or two words. The meaning of each thought or word is given by its relationships to all the other thoughts or words in a complex extensive network. All your thoughts are linked to one another by intensions – they are associated in some way so the occurrence of one such thought influences certain others. For example, thinking 'cat' can bring up other thoughts, of 'dog', 'meow', 'milk', 'claws', 'mammal' and so on. In its extreme form, then, the theory is that the meaning of the concept 'cat' is given by its relationships to these other concepts. Moreover, all these concepts tie into one another and form a *holistic* entity – an entire semantic network. All the concepts, ideas and thoughts we have are related to one another in some way, and they are thus mutually defining. A strength of this idea is its ability to account for the meaning of abstract concepts such as truth (or intension) and other nonexistent entities such as Superman and Santa Claus.

Now, many studies in cognitive psychology have demonstrated that there is a structure to semantic memory, and concepts are not associated with one another at random (Lindsay and Norman, 1977, chapter 10). At the least, we can say that every word usually has an obvious meaning (like cat, for example) but it also has connotations and overtones; so 'black cat' is associated with 'good luck' (at weddings), 'bad luck' (if owned by a witch) or sneezing (if you are allergic); while 'red' is associated with danger, blood, heat, ripeness (of fruit), communism, guilt, etc., depending on context. So each word or thought, even if it does have external reference, certainly also has internal connections and relationships to other concepts within the mind. These are the intensions.[4]

In sum, at one extreme you have the argument that all meanings are given by their relationships to other concepts in a complex network, and at the opposite extreme is the idea that words get their meanings strictly by their relationships to the things they refer to in the outside world. These principles apply to the meanings of thoughts generally ('psychosemantics') as well as to words.

1.4 Epistemology

Epistemology is the study of knowledge: what is it and how would we recognize it if we met it? In this context, how is it that we can know anything about minds? The issue divides into two categories.

4. The narrow, technical meaning of 'intension' is the relationship between the content and the attitude in a propositional attitude. Thus *the meaning of 'Santa Claus exists' is given by that phrase's extension (if any!), and the link between it and 'I believe' is an intension.* This is designed to explain how the content can be changed without changing the truth value of the proposition. For example, I can *truly* believe that 'Santa Claus exists' or that 'the morning star is not the evening star', even though the extensions of those phrases are false. The most extreme form of holism says that thoughts have no meaning without such intensions. By analogy, the word 'dog' means dog in English but it has no meaning in French. A thought (or a quale) has no meaning outside the context of a whole, unified system of thought, and could in principle change meaning if placed in a different context (just as *the word 'burro' means 'donkey' in Spanish but 'butter' in Italian*). Breidbach (2001) traces this idea back to the ancient Greeks' method of memorizing long speeches by using spatial imagery: all ideas have their topological place, or 'topic'. I most commonly use 'intension' in this book to refer to the links between concepts in a semantic network; this is a sufficiently general interpretation of the underlying concept and is not too far from being acceptable to philosophers (e.g. Bechtel, 1988a, uses it in this way), I hope.

1.4.1 **Knowledge of your own mind**

How do you know what is happening in your own mind? There are some philosophers who think that we just plain know what we are thinking; we have direct knowledge of our minds and cannot be mistaken about our own thoughts or motives. However, going back to Freud, if not earlier, there is a great deal of evidence for unconscious processing, showing that there are mechanisms that affect, if not control, our behaviour and actions and thoughts, and to which we don't have introspective access. The issue then becomes: how do we come up with explanations for behaviour and thinking, given that we only have indirect knowledge of our own minds, and we can't be sure of our own motives and reasons?

1.4.2 **Knowledge of other minds**

The second issue is not just the obvious question of: how do you know what other people are thinking, how their minds work, what their psychology is, and what makes them behave the way they do? It is also the more fundamental question of: how do you know that they have minds at all? How do you know that other people really do have any kind of mental life or experience? Philosophers use the word 'zombie' to refer to a (hypothetical) entity or person who looks and behaves just like an ordinary person as far as anyone can tell, but who has no consciousness. Zombies are by hypothesis functional but entirely non-conscious. This idea derives from the theory that it is possible for *all* the mechanisms which underlie psychology, mental life, thinking and behaviour to be unconscious mechanisms, and that consciousness is just not necessary at all. This is an old theory (and may or may not have any truth in it), but the epistemological issue is: how do you know whether people are 'zombies' – whether any person you meet in the street is conscious? How can you prove or even attempt to test your answer?

This is of obvious philosophical and theoretical interest, but there are also practical issues of (literally) life and death importance here. For example, how should we treat people with schizophrenia or brain injury, and most obviously people in a coma or persistent vegetative state? Imagine a patient lying in a bed after sustaining a head injury: the family are saying to you 'What's happened? They're not the same person as they were before', while the man from the insurance company is saying 'They're just faking, we don't have to pay out millions in compensation'. You are the neuropsychologist who has got to make a decision (and to justify it in court) as to whether this patient really is conscious as normal or whether their consciousness is degraded, and if so by how much, if not completely. How do you tell? (See Side-box 1.1.)

Similar issues arise in relation to animals (Do they suffer in battery farms? Is it morally acceptable to kill animals for food? Do cows and sheep even have minds at all? What about spiders or bacteria?) and to human babies (At what age are foetuses able to feel pain? At what age is it morally acceptable to perform abortions? At what age do babies have minds at all?).

Another classic example is aliens – particularly those intelligent enough to have built space ships and travelled to Earth. A modern equivalent is computers: can computers have consciousness – indeed, can you deliberately build artificial consciousness as well as intelligence? Igor Aleksander (2000) claims he is building a computer that will be

---

SIDE-BOX 1.1 KNOWLEDGE OF ANOTHER'S STATE OF MIND

A twenty-two year old woman suffered severe brain injury after a road traffic accident, losing large areas of frontal and temporal cortex, and perhaps even more widespread cell loss due to anoxia. Almost completely immobilized and unresponsive to the world around her, eighteen months later she was considered so barely and inconsistently conscious that her quality of life was too low to be worth maintaining. The prospects for any recovery were slim, and the required intensive health care would be expensive (and the costs could continue for decades). Moreover, she had, before the injury, expressed the view that she would not wish to be kept alive if she ever sustained severe brain injury of this type. The decision was therefore taken to withhold intragastric feeding and allow her to die.

To remove any remaining doubt about her mental condition, the solicitors called in a neuropsychologist to assess the patient's level of awareness and her will. A schedule of questions was devised, with carefully counterbalanced repeated items, and statistical analysis was made of the responses she could make (small movements of her hand). This diligent testing revealed a significant degree of sentience, particularly in autobiographical memory and new learning (though not in self-awareness), and a desire to live.

As a result, the planned euthanasia was dropped. Gratifyingly, her condition improved over the next few years. She became able to eat and speak, albeit not perfectly, and now shows awareness of her own condition. Although still needing care, she engages in social activities and continues to wish to live. (For details, see McMillan, 1997, 2000, and McMillan and Herbert, 2000, 2004.)

What can a philosopher make of this? McMillan's technique involves asking someone to respond to external stimuli with behavioural responses. Such tests are not limited to verbal exchanges, either as stimulus or response. (Although in this case the stimuli were verbal, this is not necessary in principle.) Consciousness is not restricted to language. The technique involved the person 'telling' the interrogator nonverbally what she felt, thought or believed, and as such revealed both knowledge of the requirement of the task (i.e. awareness of the situation; she had to respond to the incoming stimuli) and the ability to respond appropriately, i.e. to process information intelligently. She also possessed and could express her desires (not just her will to live, but she chose willingly to engage in the task). The techniques are, however, merely a careful formalization of the normal processes by which we interact with people every day, and by which we attribute consciousness to them. There is no hermetic method that solves the problem of other minds.

---

conscious when complete. How could you tell if he has succeeded? Would it be ethical to unplug a computer that is conscious, or would that be murder?

These then are the epistemological questions: how do you know what kind of consciousness there is or whether there is consciousness at all? How could you tell – what are the characteristics, signs and symptoms? What difference does consciousness make that is detectable to an external observer?

1.5 Methodology

1.5.1 Relevant evidence

The first issue in methodology is what kind of evidence you should collect and what carries most weight. One important question is whether it should be first or third person evidence. A cornerstone of the traditional scientific method is that everything has to be open to public scrutiny, and if you do an experiment somebody else has to be able to replicate it (at least in principle) and achieve exactly the same result. The observations you make and the data you use have to be available to outsiders and everything must be verifiable by other people ('third persons' – he or she). But with mental life, subjective awareness and consciousness, the observations are all private: the knowledge is only first person. I know how I feel, but you do not know how I feel. You are not telepathic; you have no direct access to my thoughts and feelings. Although I can tell you how I feel, and you can observe my behaviour, these are indirect measures which do not necessarily give you a correct or reliable picture of my personal experiences.

This problem gives rise to the old chestnut: how do we know that if I am looking at a red tomato and you are looking at the same tomato we are both experiencing the same qualitative colour (Locke, 1690)? Perhaps if I could see through your eyes I would say 'That tomato is green' and you would say 'No, it is red', because you have always called that sensation 'red'. How can you prove that other people have the same sensations as yourself?

To cope with this problem, there is currently a swing towards accepting that first person evidence must be included as part of science. Such data have to be used in our studies, and we can't just stick to using third person evidence, as traditional science demands we should. '*Phenomenology*' is the study of subjective experiences,[5] and so phenomenological evidence must be considered. Some people put it this way: first person data are what we are trying to explain – how is it that people experience colours and thoughts? This is the subject of our studies, so to deny first person data is to reject the very material of consciousness. The whole point is to explain why we have these experiences. To do this you need to describe the experiences properly, and this can only be done by accepting first person evidence as valid (e.g. Searle, 1992). Indeed, whole areas of modern academic psychology (such as psychophysics) can be construed as having developed methodologies to measure first person experience scientifically, so the solution may not be as remote as some philosophers think it is.

1.5.2 Level of description

Another issue in methodology is: what level of description gives appropriate evidence? Obviously, we must study the subjective level and first person data, and we must also study the material world, particularly the brain. But the brain can be described at many levels: the activities of nerve cells, waves of electrical potential, concentrations of chemicals, genetics and so on. Some physicists say that we should study the brain not just at the molecular or atomic levels but deeper – at the quantum level. These people suggest that consciousness arises in quantum interactions within the molecules that form microtubules, which are protein structures within nerve cells (see section 6.2.3).

At the other extreme, there are people who analyse interpersonal behaviour and social situations who say that consciousness arises through social interactions between individuals. What I think of myself is in some way related to what I think you think about

---

5. Don't confuse this with the (more extensive) philosophical movement called phenomenology. Some people suggest we should use the term 'phenomenality' to refer to subjective experience, but this is not universal practice yet.

me. I need to know what you think about me so I can predict your behaviour, and I must also take account of what you think I think you will do, and so on! Such processes of reflection and social construction go on within societies and families all the time, and have a major, if not exclusive, determining effect on the contents of the mind, including conscious experiences. Such social-anthropological levels of description are believed by these schools to provide the most appropriate data on the origins of consciousness (we will return to this in section 6.2.2).

In fact, there are many levels of description and many kinds of evidence (all of human life!), and maybe all are relevant to consciousness. While anthropologists think in terms of anthropology, physiologists in terms of neuronal physiology, physicists in terms of physics, and so on, in my view the full picture will require all levels of description and none can be omitted (see chapter 4).

The question then arises: which level should we start at? We might begin by studying the high levels and then try to work out what underlies the phenomena we discover at those levels (top-down reasoning). Conversely we might begin with the most basic levels and then try to figure out how the higher levels arise from the processes and mechanisms that exist at the low levels (bottom-up reasoning). Philosophers are generally thought to begin with abstract principles and to draw out the logical consequences of those ideas (rationalism), whereas scientists are generally understood to follow bottom-up methods of making generalizations from observations (empiricism). As we will see, there are debates about which is the best method, but all these types of reasoning have their place.

1.6 **Metaphysics**

The word 'metaphysics' is often used similarly to 'ontology', but it also has more general or fundamental connotations, in that it deals with the most basic characteristics of the physical world (and of the mental world, if there is a separate one).

1.6.1 **Cause and effect**

One basic question is: which causes what? Are the thoughts in your mind *caused* by events in your brain? Does consciousness arise purely from activity in the brain and do the interactions between nerve cells *determine* what is happening in your mind? Conversely, how does what is happening in your mind – your thoughts, your will – influence the physical world? If you decide to move your hand, how does your subjective decision actually cause the physical movement of your body? If you decide to pick up a coffee cup, how does your mental decision influence the movements of atoms and molecules in your brain, and hence in your muscles and ultimately in the outside world?

One can also wonder about cause and effect within the same level. Are your thoughts caused by the thoughts that you had a moment ago? In the stream of consciousness, the continuing chain of thoughts that you have (for example, when you are thinking a problem through logically and arriving at a conclusion), is the conclusion you reach caused by the chain of thoughts that you had, by the rational, logical argument that went through your head at a mental level? Or do you need to engage the neural level to explain how you arrived at the conclusion: one of your thoughts caused certain nerve cells to fire and these activated other nerve cells (via the physical mechanisms of synaptic connectivity) that gave rise to the next thought?[6]

1.6.2 Religion

Mind and consciousness are tied up with religious concepts – life after death, for example. When speaking about life after death most people actually mean consciousness after death. (A tree is alive, but few people think that when we enter heaven we will all be standing around like trees.) Obviously if you believe in life after death you are likely to adopt a position on the philosophy of mind which is dualistic in the sense that mind is different from matter, hence mind can survive the death of the body. On the other hand if you are a materialist your position is less compatible with life after death. Thus, for example, Foster (1991) has emphasized that dualism is required for religious belief, whereas at an opposite extreme Varela et al. (1991) and Blackmore (2003) explain how eastern religions (particularly Buddhism) can be related to western philosophy of mind.

Metaphysical issues also apply to the origin of mind. Does the mind grow and develop slowly in the body or is it created fully formed at a particular instant in time? Do you have a soul which is infused into you at some early stage in your life, and if so, when? Is your consciousness somehow related to this soul?

1.7 Conclusion

The discipline of 'philosophy' is a broad one, and ranges from the fundamental logic of reasoning to the gut feelings of religious beliefs. It infuses all aspects of psychological, and indeed scientific, endeavour. We all need to know our philosophical position (What are you doing? Why are you doing it? How are you doing it? How will you know whether you have succeeded?) and we cannot leave these issues to a few specialists in 'neurophilosophy'. The jargon introduced in this chapter seems daunting at first, but provides useful and precise tools for specifying more exactly what we will be talking about. (A common form of 'progress' or 'discovery' in philosophy is that people have been confused in the past because they were using the same word to mean two different things, without realizing it.) It is therefore worthwhile becoming familiar with the terminology if we are to approach the mind–body relationship in a scientific (i.e. systematic and precise) manner. In the next chapter we begin by looking at the course of recent philosophical history, in which the origins of the concepts used in the field will be explained.

---

6. These questions are of much concern to current philosophers (e.g. Heil and Mele, 1993; Sperber et al., 1995; Kim, 1998; Juarrero, 1999; Andersen et al., 2000) and we will discuss them again in chapters 2, 4 and 5.

▧ RECOMMENDED READING

For a quick overview of the issues in philosophy of mind, it may be worth starting with some chapter-length articles. I recommend Lycan's 'Philosophy of mind', which appears in **The Blackwell Companion to Philosophy** (Bunnin and Tsui-James, eds, 1996, 2nd edn 2001) and **The Blackwell Guide to Philosophy of Mind** (Stich and Warfield, eds, 2003). The **Routledge Encyclopedia of Philosophy** has a good introductory paper, 'Philosophy of mind', by Jackson and Rey (1998). If you find these too technical, then perhaps you should begin with some popular books, such as **Matters of the Mind** (Lyons, 2001) or **Introducing Consciousness** by Papineau and Selina (2000). An excellent introduction to epistemology and its importance in studies of the mind is given in **Knowledge and Mind** by Brook and Stainton (2000). For reference, and in particular for looking up definitions of the technical terms you will encounter in philosophy, check out **A Companion to the Philosophy of Mind** (Guttenplan, ed. 1994); also useful are **The MIT Encyclopedia of the Cognitive Sciences** (Wilson and Keil, eds, 1999), **A Companion to Cognitive Science** (Bechtel and Graham, eds, 1998; especially chapters 9 and 47–52), and Honderich's **The Oxford Companion to Philosophy**, *2nd edn* (2005).

2 The history of the mind–body problem

OBJECTIVES

In this chapter, we will be looking through the modern history of attempts to solve the mind–body problem. By the end of the chapter, you should have acquired knowledge of the course of progress in the field, as well as learning many new technical terms. The ideas you encounter will in many places be surprising or even counter-intuitive, and it is important to see where these ideas came from, and how they have been defended and attacked. The changes of opinion over the years have taken place against a background of progress in academic philosophy and method more generally, and you should be aware of how these fundamental (and often unspoken) attitudes have influenced understanding of the mind–body problem. You should also become familiar with the various styles of argumentation that take place within philosophy, such as the 'thought experiment', deductive reasoning, *reductio ad absurdum* and the use of everyday (and often lurid) examples to make a point of abstract logic. The subject material bridges the gaps between religion, science and everyday life, so its broad range makes it seldom boring. However, there is still a seeking after technical precision that proceeds in a manner different from that of conventional science, and which it will be very useful for you to understand and to be able to utilize.

2.1 Introduction: The ontological problem

The story of how modern views on the mind–body problem developed centres on the onto-logical problem, which concerns the nature of mind and body: what are they and what is the relationship between them? (We won't go into whether the relevant material entity is the brain or body; the point is how the mind relates to the physical world.) There are a number of possible relationships between mind and brain which can be categorized according to the assumed directions of cause and effect (Figure 2.1).

2.1.1 Interactionalism

The first position assumes that there is some kind of causal interaction between mind and brain. In the physical world P at time t_1, physical events cause other physical events, so there is a chain of cause and effect within the brain. At the same time, mental events M at time t_1 cause mental events at time t_2, giving another chain of events (Figure 2.1 a). Interactionalism assumes that physical events at t_1 also give rise to or cause mental events at the following instant in time, so there is a causal interaction between the physical world and the mental world. Meanwhile mental events also have a causal effect on the physical world, so that any decision that you make in the mind will influence the flow of electrical activity through nerve cells in the brain. Thus there is a two-way interaction between the different levels of the mental and the physical.

2.1.2 Epiphenomenalism

Second is the idea that everything that is relevant to explaining the sequence of events happens at the physical level (Figure 2.1 b). The mind is just an epiphenomenon, a useless

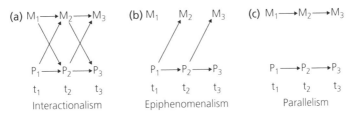

Figure 2.1 Possible causal effects over successive instants in time t_i between mental states M_i and physical states P_i. **a.** Interactionalism. **b.** Epiphenomenalism. **c.** Parallelism.

by-product or side effect of the processes which go on in the brain. An epiphenomenon is something that just accompanies the activity of a system, like the heat emitted by a car engine or the exhaust fumes given off. It is something that is produced but is not in any way important for the normal functioning and purpose of the system. So the epiphenomenalist position is that mind does not have any causal effect. Our subjective awareness is similar to watching events on a screen: we are just passively observing what our bodies and the world do. We *imagine* we have some kind of causal control but in fact we don't – or at least at the mental level we don't: all the causal control we have is happening unconsciously. The processes of decision making and action control all occur perfectly well on their own and conscious awareness just comes riding along on the back of this animal, our body, that is moving around on its own. We are not actually controlling the animal. We are only observing what happens – maybe accurately or maybe not accurately – but certainly not accurately if we imagine that we have any say in what actually happens.[1]

2.1.3 Parallelism

Finally, there is an old idea to the effect that there is no cause and effect between levels. Physical events cause other physical events, mental events cause other mental events, and there is no interaction between the physical and the mental levels (Figure 2.1c). It *appears* that there is, in the sense that if you bash somebody in the head then their consciousness is affected, but this is really not cause and effect; these events are merely occurring in parallel, and God just set everything up so things happen at the same time on the two levels (Leibniz, 1710). We don't need to worry about how the mental and physical levels are related, they just run synchronously.

2.1.4 Summary

There are several variations on how the mental and physical might be related; however, parallelism and epiphenomenalism do not explain much and thus are not very satisfactory. Most research goes on within the interactionalist position, assuming that there are some kinds of causal interaction between the mental and physical levels of description.[2]

2.2 Dualism

Let's now look at dualism in a bit more detail. There are various kinds of dualism, so let's start by looking at the main subcategories.

---

1. Carpenter (1990) is one of the rare modern supporters of this theory.
2. The question of how the interactions occur is, however, proving difficult to answer. One alternative is identity theory, which says there is no need to worry about cause and effect because the two levels just are one and the same thing (see section 2.4). Another solution is to limit cause and effect to horizontal interactions within a level (MacKay, 1980; Rose, 2000a, 2002).

2.2.1 **Substance dualism**

Substance dualism divides into two kinds: popular and Cartesian. Both postulate that there is some kind of material basis for the mind, but it is not the normal physical material. The mind is an entity which is on a par with matter, with atoms and molecules, but there is some special kind of mental 'substance' which is qualitatively different from those kinds of physical substance.

2.2.1.1 **Popular dualism**

The 'popular' variations on this are many and various, and begin with the everyday feeling we have that we have a mind, a subjective life, and that this is something unique, special and different about us. Many people think it could survive death, or it could be reincarnated. Various religions believe in a spirit or essence or soul. Indeed, people sometimes report 'out-of-the-body experiences' (in which they feel themselves floating free of their body, and can look down upon their reclining body), memories of past lives or, after revival from near death due to anoxia, that they felt they had been moving down a tunnel towards a light. So it is an everyday, common idea that we each have (or are) some special life-force within us. In fact many people think of it rather like a 'ghost in the machine', a spiritual entity that rides around inside the head. Remember too those old pictures of Victorian seances showing 'ectoplasm' coming out of people's mouths in trances. The idea that there is some kind of spirit is widespread in many cultures in the world – that there is something natural yet supernatural, that is different from atoms or brains and other material things. So the theory is that each person has a spiritual soul which is a unique, singular, indivisible entity and its attachment to the body is only temporary or contingent, i.e. it can survive the death of the body. Mental states are states of this mental substance.

2.2.1.2 **Cartesian dualism**

The Cartesian philosophy of dualism is that developed by René Descartes (1637, 1641). He is the triggering point of modern philosophy of mind and some people blame all of our modern problems on the mistakes he made! But his philosophy is the cornerstone of the issues that currently go on in thinking about the relationship between mind and body. The basic notion of Cartesian dualism is that there are two different entities or substances, material and mental, that are defined in particular ways. There are two main characteristics that differentiate between them. One is that of physical location and size. The idea is that material objects in the physical world always have a location and a size; in other words, they have physical extent and occupy a certain amount of space. In contrast, mental events like thoughts or beliefs don't have a size or extent. It is meaningless to try to apply that concept to them. They are rather like truth or justice or other abstract concepts: where is truth or where is justice? Where is my thought that Havana is the capital of Cuba? Thoughts don't have a spatial location or size: how big is my thought that Havana is the capital of Cuba? How big is my experience of red? Thoughts do not have a size; it is a silly question, it seems totally inappropriate to ask. So, one of the characteristics of the mental level is that spatial notions just don't apply within it. The mind does not have a spatial location; it is not that the mind has zero size, but it is in a different universe, the mental.

The other distinguishing characteristic of the mental is the ability to think. In Descartes' original conception, thoughts can be rational, logical, reasonable, true or false. We see evidence of this in language, which only humans possess. Material objects like stones and atoms obviously cannot think or talk. Yes, nowadays we have material things like computers that can be said to reason and use logic, so this argument is not so strong as it was in Descartes' day, but this was one of his original defining distinctions: people can think and they can use language, which proves them clearly distinct from stones and atoms. Even animals cannot talk, so they too are without minds/souls.

2.2.2 Property dualism

An alternative idea is that there is no special mental 'substance', but there are just two kinds of material: those that have consciousness, of which the brain is one, and other kinds of matter that don't have consciousness. There is a property that some kinds of matter have and others don't (versus the alternative that all kinds have it). Such property dualism is also sometimes called 'non-reductive materialism' (a less contentious term). It divides into two kinds: emergent and elementary.

2.2.2.1 Emergent property dualism

In order to explain this idea, I need to introduce a number of further concepts which describe the ways in which mind and brain might relate to one another. These are '*emergence*', '*reduction*', and '*supervenience*' (see Figure 2.2).

'Emergent' properties are properties which are possessed by a *system*. A system consists of various parts and these parts interact with one another in various ways, e.g. nerve cells, parts of a radio, parts of a complex machine, organs within the body – they all interact with and influence one another to give the whole system its overall emergent properties. I define an emergent property as '*a property of a system which is not possessed by any of its constituent parts in isolation*'. Each part of the system, e.g. each nerve cell in the brain, does not have the property of being able to think and to generate consciousness, whereas the entire system of the brain, all the nerve cells working together in the right way, can generate consciousness, thinking, language and all the other psychological phenomena we are familiar with.

This idea, that mind is an emergent property of the brain, is a simple, straightforward, eminently reasonable proposal, according to John Searle (1992, p. 14): 'Consciousness is a higher-level or emergent property of the brain in the utterly harmless sense of "higher-level" or "emergent" in which solidity is a higher-level emergent property of H_2O molecules when they are in a lattice structure (ice), and liquidity is similarly a higher-level emergent

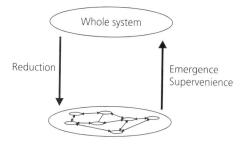

Figure 2.2 A system is composed of several interacting parts or subsystems, to which it can be *reduced*. The system's properties *emerge* from the properties of the parts and the ways they interact. The system's properties are determined by the lower level, i.e. they *supervene* on it.

property of H_2O molecules when they are, roughly speaking, rolling around on each other (water).'[3]

Because these properties are not possessed by any of the parts, they are described as not being '*reducible*' – hence this is a 'dualism'. The notion of '*ontological reduction*' is one which comes from science in general. It refers to the idea that scientific progress involves first identifying entities, objects, phenomena and things in the world which we think are separate, but then discovering they are in fact the same entity, object, etc. For example, lightning just is electricity – these are the same substance or physical event. Another example is heat in fluids, which just is the kinetic energy of the molecules – in liquids and gases, the velocity of molecular movement is the same thing as heat. (See further: 'Reductive materialism', section 2.4).

One of the standard ways of proceeding in science for the last several hundred years has been '*methodological reductionism*', which says that to understand something you have to take it apart into its bits. Then you look at the bits (the elements, the constituents, the molecules, the cells, or whatever) and at the properties of those bits. The idea is that once you have investigated those parts thoroughly you will be able to understand how, when those parts are put back together again, they would interact with one another to re-form the original system. With emergentism, that system displays some new overall property (or performs some new overall function) that is not displayed by any of the parts in isolation. Any such new properties which are possessed only by the system are the emergent properties, arising from cooperative integration between the parts.

In general, there are many examples of emergent properties. I have already mentioned water, which is liquid, wet, transparent and can refract light, unlike any individual H_2O molecule on its own. Similar arguments can be made about the molecules that form a cell, the cells that form a bodily organ, the organs that form a body and the bodies that form a society. Thus in social grouping, emergent properties like mob behaviour or consensus politics are not possessed by individuals but arise once a group of individuals comes together and interacts in a certain way. There are also more abstract examples, such as in geometry: by simply having four lines forming a square you get emergent properties of enclosure, area and so on that are not possessed by any of the four lines on its own – they have to be arranged in the right way.[4] As the Gestalt psychologists said: the whole is greater than the sum of its parts.

So the idea is: mind is an emergent property of the brain, and so too consciousness is an emergent property of the brain. There are two crucial aspects to a system – the elements of the system and the way they are arranged. *Both* must be specified to explain and understand the system. The emergence of new properties depends on the way the parts of the system are organised, and this is the crucial point that I think a lot of philosophers have not taken on board (e.g. Kim, 1998). (We will come back to this later under 'Homuncular functionalism' in chapter 4.)

---

3. Yet many philosophers dispute this, for example on the grounds that it assumes narrow content and local supervenience; see sections 2.4.3.1 and chapter 5.

4. More examples are easy to think of: unlike any of its parts in isolation, a car can accelerate uphill. The properties of water are very different from those of hydrogen and oxygen, and of table salt from those of sodium and chlorine!

The idea of emergence can in fact be subdivided into two logical types (which I think is where some confusion has arisen in the past). The subdivision is between whether or not emergent properties can be *predicted*. Given that you have complete knowledge of the properties of all the individual parts or constituents, when they are fitted together to form the new system, can you predict what the emergent properties of the entire system will be – how it will behave as a whole? Some philosophers think that the answer is no, that emergent properties by definition are unpredictable ('radical emergentism'; see Silberstein, 2001). So when it comes to consciousness, they claim that even if you had complete knowledge of everything physical about the brain, or some individual's brain (even if you knew what every nerve cell was doing, how every nerve cell was connected, where they were, and so on), you would not be able to predict what that person was experiencing, what their consciousness was. This idea fits with that of a group of philosophers called '*mysterians*', because they say it is a mystery – you'll never be able to explain consciousness by studying the physical brain (this group includes McGinn, Jackson, Nagel, Levine and Chalmers; see more in section 2.4.3). Most famously, Chalmers (1996) has described the question of how experience relates to the brain as the 'hard problem', which contrasts with the 'easy problems' of how the brain functions (problems that can at least be studied using the normal scientific methods).

However, there are, of course, other people, from a biological background, who are used to the notion of emergent properties in nature generally,[5] and who say that emergent properties are nothing mysterious: they are in principle predictable. We have already met some obvious examples (the area of a square, the movement of a motor car, etc.) and another will be given in sections 3.5.5.1 and 6.4.1 (neurons forming a loop: Figures 3.2a and 6.2a). *In practice*, of course, it is often very complicated to predict the behaviour of a complex system such as the brain. But there is no *logical* division between predictable and unpredictable (forever mysterious) systems.[6]

Finally, the word '*supervenience*' was introduced by philosophers to specify the materialist mind–body relationship in a more technical way. 'Supervenience' literally means 'coming above', and is nothing to do with supervising, intervening or interfering. It is suggested that the mind supervenes on the brain (see Kim, 1993).[7] The notion of supervenience is first that the mind comes with the brain, and you cannot have a mind without a brain. In particular, the mind *depends* upon the brain; it is necessary to have a brain in order to have a mind, and the mental is determined by the physical. Second, identical brains (if they

5. The concept of emergence (and its associated ideas of multiple levels, system dynamics and non-deterministic causation: see chapter 4) may not be understood intuitively; it requires appropriate training and experience to develop the necessary conceptual background (Penner, 2000; Jacobson, 2001; Charles and d'Appolonia, 2004).

6. A standard example in biology is the way complex protein molecules fold up; there are typically several hundred amino acids in a protein molecule and the way in which the overall shape of the protein is determined is very, very difficult to predict, simply because it is extremely complicated. Each connection between adjacent amino acids is flexible, and the number of ways the protein molecule can fold and bend is enormous; yet the same kind of protein always adopts the same shape. However, although we know everything physical about the molecule, we can't predict how the molecule will fold up. This is a classic example in biochemistry of how emergent properties should be predictable but in practice they are just computationally too complex.

7. This is local supervenience; for global, see below under broad content: chapter 5.

existed) would give rise to identical minds. Third, you can't have a change in your mind unless there is a change in your brain. So there is a kind of causal link, but it's asymmetrical: it is not that change in the brain necessarily causes change in the mind (though it may), but you can't have a change in the mind without having some change in the physical brain. This precludes any supernatural properties at the mental level.[8] (See Van Gulick, 2001, for a comprehensive survey of the variations on emergence and reduction, and the tension between these positions.)

In sum, with the emergent property theories we have the idea that the mind emerges from brain properties and cannot be reduced to them. The big question, of course, is *how*. We will return to this in part two.

2.2.2.2 Elementary property dualism

Elementary property dualism ('*elemental*' might be a better word) is a different kettle of fish, and should not be confused with emergent property dualism. The idea is that consciousness is in some way an elementary or elemental property of nature, which ranks alongside electromagnetism, gravity and so on. Consciousness is a fundamental property of the physical world. This contrasts with substance dualism: the mind and consciousness are here seen as subject to natural physical laws, the same as quarks, atoms, planets and so on (hence it can be called 'naturalistic dualism': Chalmers, 1996). Mind is just some kind of entity or force, a natural phenomenon, but one that has not been 'discovered' by physics yet. A few hundred years ago people didn't know about electromagnetism, the strong force and so on – the basic forces of nature. So people suggest there may be a new one, not yet discovered, that is responsible for (or just is) consciousness.

This philosophy perhaps shades across into '*panpsychism*', the theory that mind is everywhere. For example, Lotze (1879) suggested that atoms are souls and have a minimal degree of consciousness – an interesting if extreme position. The recent revival of panpsychism is discussed by Seager (1999), and Skrbina (2003) demonstrates that it is not just a recent or rare idea (e.g. many cultures do or did worship the 'natural spirits' of streams, woods, stars and so on).

2.2.3 Arguments against dualism

How do they interact? If mind and matter are different substances, then how does mind influence matter and vice versa? The same question arises with property dualism: if mind is a property and matter is a substance of which the mind is one of the properties, how does change in the mind cause change in the brain? For example, how does deciding to pick up a cup of coffee make the atoms in your hand move? What makes nerve cells alter their firing when you make a mental decision? Conversely, how does the smell of coffee coming in from the outside manage to affect the mind; how does the mind become aware?

The problem of interaction is a major stumbling block for dualism. People did throw this question at Descartes at the time and he tried to come up with answers, but the answers he produced were not satisfactory. This problem has never been solved, which is probably the main reason why Cartesian dualism is not accepted nowadays. The same applies to other

---

8. You may also see a converse term, 'subvenience', which is occasionally used and refers to the possession of properties at the base level.

kinds of substance dualism: if you have some kind of immaterial spirit, how does it interact with the physical matter of the brain and vice versa?

With emergent property dualism, it is also not obvious how the emergent properties will influence the activity of the parts of the system. How can a particular emergent property have a sort of 'downwards causation', so that the events happening at the higher level of description, the mental level, can influence events at the lower levels, of nerve cells and atoms? How does the whole system control its parts? This is the big question. (In fact there have now been attempts to answer it: see under 'Homuncular functionalism' in chapter 4 and 'Teleological functionalism' in chapter 5.)

With elementary property dualism, there is also the question of interaction. If mind or consciousness is an elemental force, why has it not been discovered before, intervening in the behaviour of the physical universe? Well, some phenomena in quantum physics may indicate that there are just such interactions; however, this proposal is highly contentious. (More on the interaction between observer and observed will be given under 'Quantum level theories', in section 6.2.3; see also Seager, 1999.)

In summary, the notion of how mind and matter interact is the major stumbling block with the dualisms. In recent research the property dualisms have been most successful in coping with it. But before we can see how, we need first to trace the route philosophy has followed in reaction to substance dualism. This we do in the rest of this chapter, before we can examine again the issue of emergent properties in chapter 4.

2.3 Philosophical behaviourism

In the first half of the twentieth century, behaviourism was the extant philosophy in psychology, and associated ideas in science generally. Only observable facts were to be accepted as true, and observable things and events as real; hypothetical entities (such as gravity, atoms and extraversion) that no one has ever observed, while convenient fictions, are nevertheless not real (see chapter 3 for more details). Similarly, in philosophy of mind there was philosophical behaviourism, which represents a radical reaction to the substance dualisms, and is summarized by the crucial works of Ryle (1949) and Wittgenstein (1953). Behaviourism, as you know from psychology, is based on the premise that we should get on with doing science without worrying about unobservable fictions like minds. In fact one of the originators, Watson (1925), said that talking about the mind is equivalent to talking about the soul, and Ryle (1949) described the mind as a 'ghost in the machine'. Instead of involving such religious or supernatural concepts, we should restrict ourselves to the scientific study of overt, publicly observable behaviour. The behaviourists thus repudiated any study of mentality or subjective feelings as not scientifically acceptable.

2.3.1 Mental states as dispositions to behave

The philosophical behaviourists had a related but slightly better defined approach. Their idea was that mental states, what we call subjective feelings or beliefs, can be defined in terms of behaviour, and that mental states are just what they called 'dispositions' to behave.

There is an analogy with certain materials that have dispositions to behave in certain ways in certain contexts. For example, sugar dissolves when placed in water, so sugar has a disposition to dissolve in water; it is one of the properties of sugar that it can dissolve in water. Similarly, porcelain vases have the disposition to shatter when you hit them. So there are physical properties that can be revealed under certain circumstances, that tell you what will happen to that physical system given certain contexts. Since the brain is a physical system, in certain environmental contexts it will do certain things, because built into it is a set of dispositions. These dispositions are part of the material world, and they are what we are really referring to when we talk about mental states. Desires, thoughts, feelings and so on are just tendencies to behave in certain ways in certain circumstances. For example, Churchland (1988) uses the example of wanting to go on holiday. If somebody wants to go on holiday, say to the Bahamas, this means that given the right circumstances they *will* go on holiday there. This is how to define, categorize and circumscribe the mental state of wanting to go on holiday.

2.3.2 Arguments for philosophical behaviourism

2.3.2.1 The mind–body problem is a category error

This is one of Gilbert Ryle's (1949) arguments, based on the notion of different levels of description, of different categories. One of the examples he used concerned the University of Oxford. If you show somebody round Oxford, you can show them the Bodleian Library and New College and the physiology laboratories and the Sheldonian Theatre, and at the end of the visit your visitor might then say 'Well, this is very interesting, but where is the University of Oxford?' Ryle replies, well, the University is actually a kind of high-level administrative structure, so it's a different category of entity from the physical buildings and structures that constitute the University of Oxford. So in the same way he distinguishes between the mind and the body: these are just different categories of description. The mind is a high level description of brain events and organization. It is not that there are two different entities which have to be related in some way, as in the dualistic positions where you assume that there is a mind and that there is a body, and you have to say what is the relation between them. Dualism implies that mind and body are in some way the same kind of thing: things you can count. There are two of them: mental stuff and body stuff, mind and matter. Ryle claims that this is a mistake: whether you argue that these are two things or one thing, it still implies that they are both (for dualism) or it is (for monism) 'things' or substances – and this is wrong. Psychology is just a high-level description of events, structures and organizations of material. It is not a different kind of entity but just a different way of describing the one.

2.3.2.2 The term 'mental states' is circular

How do we know that people have mental states? We know people are in certain mental states because they behave in particular ways, i.e. they react in characteristic ways in experiments, do particular things. So, why do they behave in those particular ways? Because they have mental states that make them behave in those ways. That is a circular argument (you know people have mental states because they behave in a certain way, and they behave in a certain way because they have mental states), so, therefore, talk about mental states is vacuous, meaningless and unhelpful. Only publicly observable events and things are real.

2.3.3 Arguments against philosophical behaviourism

There are counter-arguments to the arguments for, but I will leave these to you to reconstitute, and instead mention three further arguments against.

2.3.3.1 Qualia do exist

We do have subjective sensations, of red, pain and so on, and it's silly to deny it. The whole point (see chapter 1) is to explain why we have these sensations, beliefs, wants and all the other psychological experiences that we have. It's obvious you can't just ignore them.

2.3.3.2 The definitions need to be indefinitely long

To define any given mental state purely behaviourally, such as the mental state of 'wanting to go on holiday', you end up having to list all the kinds of behaviour that are or could be manifestations of that mental state. However, the number of ways in which you can go on holiday is extremely large: you could fly to Jamaica, or take a ship, or go to the Bahamas, etc., etc. So the list of behaviours which constitute and define the mental state ends up being indefinitely long; maybe not infinitely long but for all practical purposes it might as well be. And the problem does not end there. Logically, if you apply the scientific method properly (Bacon, 1620), you have also to list the negatives: you have to say what behaviours are *not* constitutive of that mental state (but are parts of other mental states). Obviously, that list is going to be pretty much infinite in length! You will have to say that sitting at home in bed is not an example of wanting to go on holiday, and nor is going to work and everything else you could do instead of going on holiday. So the definition becomes so unwieldy, so ridiculously long, that you can't actually define any given mental state purely in terms of overt behaviour, because there are just too many kinds of behaviour that are, and too many kinds of behaviour that are not, constitutive of that mental state.

2.3.3.3 The definitions must include other mental states

When you do something your behaviour is not determined by one mental state alone and no other mental state. For example, if you want to go on holiday you are only going to go in reality if you hold certain other mental states. These include beliefs that you can afford it; you have the time; you'll enjoy going to that particular place; it will be safe; there is no other place in the world that you prefer to go to instead; and so on. You must also not hold beliefs that might prevent you from expressing that behaviour, such as that you need to stay home to look after your grandmother. The point is that if you want to define a mental state in terms of what you would actually do, you inevitably have to make reference to other mental states. But then you have to be able to define each of those states, and then each such definition itself ends up making reference to other mental states, not just behaviours. Of course this goes on and on – an endless list of connections between mental states. Whether a particular mental state expresses itself in behaviour is contingent on the other mental states that you need to be in or need not to be in. To define any mental state you have to list all those other mental states, so you end up with infinitely long descriptions of behaviour. In the end, there can be no purely behavioural definition of 'wanting to go on holiday' or any other mental state.

2.4 **Reductive materialism**

2.4.1 **Identity theory**

This theory is also known as 'type–type identity theory', or 'central state materialism', and arose in the 1950s (Place, 1956; Smart, 1959). The idea was not simply that the mind is identical to the brain – this had been suggested many times before. No, the theory is that each *type* or category of mental state is identical to a *type* of brain state. For example, consider the mental state known as 'feeling a pain'. The exact state that you are in each time you feel pain is not exactly the same. Nevertheless, if you are going to categorize what you experience each time as 'feeling pain', you are saying there is a certain type of state that is the experience of feeling pain. The same is true for the experiences of seeing the colour red, believing that you want to go on holiday and so on. Mental states are circumscribable – definable, categorizable – into particular types. Similarly, states of the brain can be categorized in particular ways, according to certain crucial parameters that define these particular types of state. For example, certain types of stimulus induce firing in a group of small-diameter axons called 'C-fibres'. These fibres are often activated by noxious tissue damage, and if they are cut there is a (temporary) loss of pain sensations. The early identity theorists therefore used this example to propose not just that a pain is nothing but the firing of C-fibres, but that all pains are instances of C-fibre firing and vice versa. (I'll return to this example with more details in section 2.4.3.4.)

So the identity thesis states that you can map the mental and the physical categorization schemes onto one another in one-to-one fashion: each particular kind of mental state will correspond to a particular kind of physical state (see Figure 2.3). The category boundaries are identical: the pain/no-pain boundary at the mental level matches the C-fibre-firing/no-C-fibre-firing boundary at the physical level; and so on for all the other types of state.

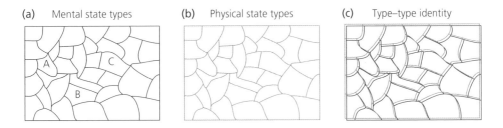

Figure 2.3 Venn diagrams of state types. Each rectangle circumscribes the entire set of all possible states. **a.** Mental states can be divided into a number of types (for example, type A might all be pains, type B seeings of the colour red, type C beliefs in God, etc.). **b.** Physical states can be similarly divided. **c.** Type–type identity theory says that the type boundaries at the mental and physical levels coincide exactly (they have been offset slightly here simply to reveal the two levels, shown as black and grey, more clearly).

Within those categories, each of these mental–physical match ups will be identical in the sense that the mental state *is* the physical state: there is no difference. Thus it is not that there are different kinds of substance or property that are attached to or associated with different kinds of brain state, as dualism postulates. Instead, there is simply an identity, in the sense that when you talk about a mental state and about the corresponding physical state you are talking about one and the same thing.

2.4.2 Arguments for identity theory

2.4.2.1 Scientific progress involves theory reduction

I have already described ontological and methodological reduction, but let me here explain '*theory reduction*'. A scientific theory is normally constructed first to explain phenomena within a particular domain, such as psychology, genetics, light, and so on. The theory is designed to account for a certain set of data within that domain. So a theory of short-term memory should account for data from numerous experiments on the retention of information over periods of several seconds, while a theory of long-term memory accounts for another set of data, on retention over longer periods of time.

What it means to 'reduce' a theory is to subsume it into a larger, broader and more fundamental theory that explains a wider range of phenomena – and explains them more simply or at a more fundamental level. For example, in physics, a theory of light would be subsumed into a theory of electromagnetic radiation, that would also explain X-rays, microwaves, infrared, ultraviolet and radio frequency waves. Thus the theory of electromagnetism is broader and explains a wider range of phenomena; it is therefore more powerful than a theory which applies only to visible light. This model of how science works certainly applies in the history of physics and chemistry: it has been the course of progress in those areas to see progressive theory reduction, e.g. from electricity and magnetism to electromagnetism, which was then linked in with the strong and weak forces and (perhaps soon) with gravity to give Grand Unified Theory, i.e. the most broad and fundamental explanation. Similarly, the theory of genetics can be subsumed into the molecular biology of DNA and chromosomes, and this covers a broader range; it explains data at the molecular level as well as the genetic level of description.

By inference, then, the future of psychology might include theory reductions as follows. The theories of short- and long-term memory, for example, might be reduced to a single, all-embracing theory of memory which applies to retention over all periods of time. Such a theory of memory might then be absorbed into a more general theory of information processing, or of intelligence. And these theories in turn would be integrated into even wider theories of a more fundamental nature. Ultimately, psychology in general would be subsumed into a theory of brains or neuroscience. This theory would have a broader range and explain not only psychological phenomena but also how brains work, how peripheral nerves work and even how nervous systems work in simpler organisms that do not have any mind or consciousness (if there are such creatures). It will thus have a broader domain of influence and explanation and therefore be preferable to psychology on its own.

So the argument is that, if theory reduction goes ahead in psychology–neuroscience as it has done in physics, we will in future be categorizing psychological and mental states in terms of brain states. The lower level of description has the broader realm: it's not that brain research will be reduced to psychology but the other way round.

2.4.2.2 It obviates cause and effect across levels

If in reality there's just the one level, and all the apparent levels are in fact the same level – there is just one system that is the brain and the mind – then you don't have to explain the relationship between levels. You don't have to explain how they interact or which causes which: how changing your mind causes the cells in your brain to fire in particular ways, or vice versa – it's all the same single event. It is like being able to say that lightning does not cause electricity and electricity does not cause lightning, they are the same event or thing. So a mental state, such as thinking that you want to see your grandmother, is a particular state of your brain and there is no problem of how you relate the two together; they are just the same thing and it is meaningless to ask in what way they are different.

2.4.3 Arguments against identity theory

Despite its intuitive appeal to materialists, since the 1960s identity theory has been a central subject of attack by philosophers. There are now lots of convincing arguments against the reductionist position outlined above, and I will present a few of them here.

2.4.3.1 It assumes 'narrow' intentionality

Remember, intentionality was defined in section 1.1.3; see also the discussion of supervenience in section 2.2.2.1.

The classical reductive position presumes what is known as '*narrow content*' (as opposed to 'broad' or 'wide content') in the source of intentionality – the meaningfulness of mental states. The theory of narrow content is simply that what a mental state is about depends on, and only on, the state of the (physical) brain. If brain states and mental states are the same then the content of a mental state (i.e. what it is that you are thinking about: a unicorn or red or the capital of Cuba) is in some way identical to the brain (or, at least, part of it; for example, C-fibres in the case of pain). This means that, if you open up someone's head and look inside their brain, then in principle, you could tell what they are thinking. So if you could monitor their physical states you could discover what their mental states are: what they are thinking and experiencing.

This idea is referred to as 'narrow content' because it means that the content of the mental state is determined by a narrow range of physical things, i.e. those things that are in the brain. Identity theory is therefore a theory of narrow content, since it suggests that the contents of the mind are entirely determined by the contents or state of (part of) the brain.[9]

The rival position, '*broad content*', implies that what we think, the content of our mental states, depends also on the environment, i.e. on the outside world. It depends only partially on what is in the brain. There are many reasons to believe that what we think – our understanding of the outside world – depends on the state of the outside world. Obviously,

---

9. Of course, there are arguments in favour of narrow content, which for brevity I did not include in section 2.4.2. These will be given in more detail in section 5.3.4, and for now I will continue with the arguments for broad content, because these count against identity theory, which is the purpose of this section.

if you want to understand how a particular mental state can be about horses or unicorns or grandmothers or Volkswagen cars or Superman or whatever else, you have to know whether these things exist in the real world (or have ever existed).[10]

Our thoughts are largely about the outside world. The theory of extensional psycho-semantics (section 1.3) states that they are determined by the state of the outside world because there is a causal connection between the properties (e.g. the shape) of the object in front of us and the mental state. So to that extent, our mental state (e.g. experiencing a shape) is not determined purely by our brain state. The object in the outside world, you could argue, causes (at least logically, if not mechanically) your brain to go into a certain state, which thus means the mind is in a certain state. It is not just that the mental state is caused by the brain state (as dualism says), and not just that it is identical to the brain state (as identity theory says), but that the mental state is caused by the state of the outside world.

So to ascertain the meaning of a mental state you have to know what is happening in the outside world. If you open up a man's head and look in at his brain state and you conclude that this person is seeing red, then it may be that there is something red in front of him, but maybe there isn't something red in front of him. Whether there is or not determines whether the mental state has meaning and the content is valid, or whether he is having a hallucination or suffering a visual illusion. Identity theory would not distinguish between those various situations; it posits that the mental state is identical to the brain state and this would not tell you whether the meaning of the mental state is correct or not, valid or not – indeed whether it has any meaning at all, because the meaning depends on causal links with the outside world beyond the brain.

Philosophers make this point with the 'twin-earth' argument, after Putnam's (1975) paper asserting 'meanings ain't in the head'. Imagine an atom-for-atom duplicate being made of your brain. According to the thesis of narrow content, the meanings of the physical states of the two brains must be identical. However, Putnam asks us to imagine that one of these twin brains is located on a twin Earth, which is an exact duplicate of Earth except in one respect, namely water is not made of H_2O. Instead, it is made of some-thing else that looks and behaves just like water, but is actually XYZ. One brain is therefore misrepresenting the state of the world when it 'thinks' of water; the brains (and, under identity theory, the minds) have different intentionality despite having identical physical composition.[11]

Thus identity theory is too limited: even if it were true that a mental state is identical to a brain state, this would still not be enough to give us a full *understanding* of mental experi-ences and events. These depend also on the *context* in which the brain state exists.

10. One can also argue that the physical constitution of the brain depends on what is in the environment, but we will defer discussion of this idea to chapter 5 on teleological functionalism.

11. This example can be very misleading. Anyone who has studied chemistry knows that H_2O is a unique and unusual molecule (for example, it forms a liquid at room temperatures, unlike the heavier molecules ammonia, propane, etc.), and if something behaves exactly like water then it can only be H_2O. As philosophers would say, XYZ breaks the conventions of modal logic in that it can only exist in a world in which the laws of physics are different from those in the H_2O world. However, we must keep in mind Putnam's aim, which even if badly made was merely to demonstrate that intentionality depends on the world outside the brain (as well as the brain's inner state).

2.4.3.2 **The knowledge argument**

Complete knowledge of the material world would not tell us 'what it is like'. This is sometimes known as the *'knowledge argument'* and originates from Nagel (1974) and Jackson (1982, 1986). Nagel's paper was actually entitled 'What is it like to be a bat?' and it centres around the issues of understanding the phenomenology of mental experience. How do we explain mental experience, given knowledge of the material world? Imagine, for example, that we had complete knowledge of the brain of a bat: that physiology, anatomy, biochemistry and neuroscience had completely discovered every factual thing there is to know about bat brains. Now, bats have a kind of sonar sense that allows them to fly around in the dark. They emit ultrasounds that bounce off flying insects and the environment and come back to the bat's ears. Bats use this sonar sense of navigation to fly in the dark, avoid obstacles and catch prey. Well, Nagel says that even if we had this complete knowledge of the physical structure of the bat's brain, it would not tell us what it is like to be a bat. It would not give us any kind of experience or understanding or even the ability to imagine what the bat experiences when it is flying around using its sonar sense. Because this is a different sensory modality from the ones which we have, we could not possibly know the bat's subjective sensations.

So the argument against identity theory is that even if we were given knowledge of all the brain states of a bat (or a human or a Martian or any other animal or organism), we still would not have an explanation, understanding or knowledge of what the subjective mental world of that organism is. Therefore there is something left to learn over and above the facts about the physical world: facts about what experience is like.

Another thought experiment, of the type of which philosophers are so enamoured, is generally referred to as 'what Mary knew'. Jackson (1982) asks us to imagine a situation where there is a wonderful neuroscientist called Mary. She learns everything there is to know about the neurophysiology of the human brain, and even, if you like, of the entire material world: she possesses all knowledge about physics, biology, biochemistry, neuroscience, everything there is to know – she learns complete, perfect science, in which all the facts have been discovered. But the crucial idea is that Mary has been brought up in isolation, in an environment that lacks colour and only contains black, greys and white. Mary has never seen colour for herself. Jackson's first point is not simply that, despite all her knowledge about the physical world, she cannot imagine what colours look like – she may well have some imagination. The point is that when she comes out of her environment and sees a coloured object for the first time, like a banana or a tomato, she *learns* something new: she learns what the colour actually looks like, what the experience is; something she did not know before. However, given that the hypothesis was that she did know everything before, at least about the physical world, how can she have learned something new? Therefore, either (a) she did not have complete knowledge before – so physical facts are not all the facts there are – or (b) what she has learned is not about the physical world or based on physical knowledge. In either case, identity theory therefore cannot be correct, because mental states cannot be identical to physical states. If identity theory were true and if she knew everything there is to know about the physical states, she could not learn something new about her own mental state, i.e. the mental state she goes into when she looks at something red.[12]

---

12. Lest you find this example too bizarre (for some nice parodies see Lodge, 2001, chapter 16), let me rephrase it in some more everyday terms. One alternative might be Georgina, the world's leading

There has been a lot of discussion about Jackson's argument (see Ludlow et al., 2004). One of the counter-arguments derives from the distinction in psychology between declarative and procedural memory (though philosophers have not used those terms). Thus Nemirow (1980) and Lewis (1988) suggested that what Mary learned in her black and white environment was all 'factual knowledge', i.e. it was what psychologists call semantic and episodic memories (declarative, explicit memories). These are distinct from procedural memories, which are what the philosophers call 'knowing how' to do something, as opposed to 'knowing that' something is the case. So beforehand, Mary knew that the brain was made of this and that action potentials work like that, and so on – all the facts about what the neural mechanisms of colour perception do – but she did not know what it was like to experience colour: she did not know *how* to experience colour. The argument was that what she learns is a procedural skill – how to go through a particular experience, or how to generate a particular mental state within her own mind. It postulates that seeing is like riding a bike or swimming, rather than memorizing facts.

Whether this argument is acceptable is dubious, I reckon, if only because procedural knowledge is not conscious, whereas experiences such as seeing red are within the realms of awareness. (Do you know 'how' you move your arm? No: you just do it.) Jackson himself (1986) replied that Mary does learn a new fact, but it is about other peoples' mental states: she learns what they experience when they look at something red (assuming this is the same as her own experience). Since other people are part of the physical world, not her own mental world, she learns third person factual knowledge.

Another answer to the knowledge argument runs as follows (e.g. Churchland, 1985; Dennett, 1991). If you really did know everything about the material world, or even just about the physical nature of the brain, you would know a vast amount – because there is such a vast amount to learn. But we cannot imagine what it would be like to know everything about the physical world (or even about the brain); there is so much to learn, so many details and it's so complicated that we can't even picture to ourselves what we would feel like knowing that amount of information. Therefore we cannot decide whether Mary would or would not learn something new when she leaves the room and sees red; the whole scenario is beyond our imagination. So therefore we cannot make a judgement or come to any conclusion based on Jackson's thought experiment. The same applies to Nagel's bat: the outcome is imponderable. Dennett claims that if somebody did have complete knowledge of the physical world they would be able to understand, know and predict what it would be like to experience a colour they have never seen before (and what it would be like to be a bat). Jackson and Nagel cannot disprove this – it falls to being just a matter of intuition. Dennett says, well, Nagel and Jackson's intuitions are wrong. If we knew

---

obstetrician, who knows every fact there is to know about having a baby, but does not know 'what it is like to have a baby' until she actually has one. Or there is her colleague George, who knows just as much but can never 'know'. Or there is the psychopharmacologist who has never taken drugs. Or John Locke, sitting in England in 1690 wondering what a 'pine-apple' tastes like. Or young Lolita and Hubert, who have read up all about sex, but when they reach adulthood and try it themselves.... Perhaps you will find it easier to imagine obtaining 'complete' factual knowledge followed by personal knowledge in one of these cases than in the case of Mary's colour vision. But remember it is the abstract logical point that matters, not the realism of the example!

everything we would be very different people; we would have much greater knowledge and we would not come to the conclusion they come to.[13]

2.4.3.3 Why is it like what it is like?

The knowledge argument implies that if we knew all the physiology it would still leave a gap. Levine (1983) calls this the '*explanatory gap*': what we still lack is an explanation of 'why it is like what it is like'. McGinn (1989, p. 349) put the problem as: 'how can techni-colour phenomenology arise from soggy grey matter? . . . Somehow, we feel, the water of the physical brain is turned into the wine of consciousness'.

There is a certain intuitive appeal to this. Perhaps we could extend this argument, for instance within our own sensory modalities. Seeing, for example, does not seem at all like hearing, smelling, tasting, touching or feeling pain. Each of these experiences is qualitat-ively different: there is something unique to each of them. (Unless you have synaesthe-sia, where you get a sort of cross talk between the different sense modalities, like associating colours with sounds and so on.) So if we were to know everything there is to know about the human visual system, for example, this would, first, not give us any understanding of the subjective experiences of vision, and second, even if it did, it would not give us any insight into the mechanisms of hearing – or smell or any other sensory modality. This is true even though, at least superficially, the visual cortex and the auditory cortex have many physical similarities: they have neurons, columns and layers of cells, synapses and dendrites, the same as in all regions of the cerebral cortex. Even though there are some small subtle differences between them, these seem to be relatively minor: matters of cell density and exact connection patterns. So it is not obvious why activity in the visual cortex gives rise to visual experience that is so different from the effect of activity in the auditory cortex, which gives such a qualitatively different subjective sensation.[14]

Conversely, we could use the argument about people whose brains are not like ours. What is the visual world of a colour-blind person like? Some people in fact have four cone pigments instead of three (Jordan and Mollon, 1993): what is their colour experience? More dramatically, brain damage can radically alter one's physical state; understanding how such people feel is important for many reasons, not least being the design of appropri-ate treatment (Brown et al., submitted). According to Nagel, however, we cannot make predictions from the nature of the damage to the subjective state.

13. I am reminded of the adage that any sufficiently advanced science is indistinguishable from magic (Arthur C. Clarke). Thus a caveman would consider a car, an aeroplane, a computer or a cellphone as drop-jaw incomprehensible. Yet we know there is nothing magical or non-physical about these devices. They operate on predictable, learnable principles – just very complicated ones, and there are a lot of things we need to know in order to understand their workings. By analogy, we are in the position of cavemen when it comes to consciousness.

14. It is in fact an old issue in neuroscience as to how the senses differ in quality: vision is not like hearing, touch and so on. Müller (1826) suggested there is either a characteristic 'specific nerve energy' in each of the different sensory nerves, or the places in the brain where they arrive must differ in some way. However, no such energies have been found (see Rose, 1999a). The physiology of nerve cell firing (action potentials) seems to be the same in all mammalian nervous systems, as well as in different parts of our own brain and in different sensory nerves, just as Helmholtz (1866) said it was.

2.4.3.4 **The chauvinism argument: multiple realization**

This criticism of identity theory is nowadays regarded as the original killer argument, having been put forward by Putnam (1967) and Fodor (1968). It states that identity theory is too specific. This arises partly because the originators defined the theory in too narrow a way, one that seems to apply only to humans. The kind of identity that they suggested defined the physical states in terms of the biology of the human brain and the mental states in terms of human mentality. One of the examples they used is pain (section 2.4.1), which, as a mental state, they suggested is identical to the firing of C-fibres.

This is slightly out-of-date physiology, but it is worth explaining here. Nerve axons running into the nervous system from the body were originally categorized according to their size: A (the largest), B (medium) and C (very small fibres, which were thought to carry pain signals). So in the 1950s when identity theory was put forward, this was the standard example they used: pain is identical to the firing of C-fibres, i.e. action potentials coming up C-fibres and entering the central nervous system. (More details are given in Side-Box 2.1.)

SIDE-BOX 2.1 PAIN AND C-FIBRES

When early researchers applied electric shocks to nerves and measured the responses some distance along the nerve, they discovered there was no single answer to the question: how fast do nerves conduct impulses? Instead, the evoked responses came in three waves, which the researchers called A, B and C; the fastest, the A wave, was further subdivisible into four groups, named $A\alpha$, $A\beta$, $A\gamma$ and $A\delta$ (Erlanger and Gasser, 1937; Table SB 2.1.1). These waves were attributed to the fact that nerves are bundles of axons, which form several different groups based on their size: the largest diameter axons conduct the fastest. Tracing these into the spinal cord and brain, the groups segregate out into different tracts, and therefore become liable to differential damage. Loss of the C-fibres results in the loss of the slow aching pains that we experience when deep tissues are damaged (the 'guts-ache' type of pain). Loss of $A\delta$ fibres knocks out the burning and prickling pains we get from skin damage. The other fibres mediate such functions as sensations of touch and temperature, and the unconscious monitoring of joint position and movement, muscle tension, and the 'autonomic' control of hormone release, digestion and the cardiovascular system.

Table SB 2.1.1. Types of nerve fibre

Fibre group	Conduction velocity (m/s)	Function
$A\alpha$	90–120	Proprioception
$A\beta$	70–90	Touch, temperature
$A\gamma$	30–70	Muscle spindles
$A\delta$	12–30	Fast pain
B	2–15	Autonomic
C	0.5–2	Deep pain

Subsequent research has shown that pain cannot simply be equated with C-fibre activity, however. For one thing, deep pain sensations return a few weeks after the C-fibres are cut. For another, the effects

continues

SIDE-BOX 2.1 continued

of their activity within the brain are complex, dividing at minimum into processes mediating their unpleasantness and their perceived location and strength (Dennett, 1978, chapter 11; Rainville, 2002).

The point that functionalism makes in attacking identity theory, however, is not that it is an over-simplification to say that pain equals C-fibres firing (the principle of identity remains valid even if this particular example is misleading). No, the point is there is no obvious reason why pain should be conveyed by fibres conducting at less than two metres per second. It is perfectly conceivable that in another taxon, in Martians or in robots, pain could be carried in fibres of, say, ten metres per second. But these are B-fibres. As long as the functions subserved by B-fibres in vertebrates are mediated somehow, there is no reason why B-fibres should not convey pain instead (or as well).

Some might say that it is the central connections that define the function subserved by the afferent fibre activity. Quite probably. Nevertheless, this example still illustrates the possibility that there could be multiple physical realizations of pain, which is the point that functionalism seeks to make against identity theory.

Now, the issue is that structures like C-fibres, whose firing supposedly just is 'pain' in the human brain, may not be identical to the structures which subserve pain in other brains. For example, in another species it is entirely conceivable that pain is identical to the firing of fibres 3 micrometres in diameter, which in humans would be B-fibres. So we would have to define pain as 'the firing of C-fibres in humans and B-fibres in species X'. A few more examples like this (differences between species, and between functions – pain, seeing red, feeling sad) and the whole identity theory soon unravels.

This is not just a thought experiment: while monkeys may have brains that are similar to ours, when it comes to creatures like spiders or octopuses there are major differences between their brains and ours. Yet our intuition is that all these creatures can feel pain. Presumably (if more contentiously), if there are intelligent aliens, these would have certain mental states that are similar to ours. For example, any functioning organism must have an ability to sense the environment, to react and respond to it and to understand the meaning of the objects which are in the environment – including 'pain' reactions to bodily damage. So they must have intentionality and perhaps qualia; so they possess mental states. Yet the physical instantiation or realization of those mental states may be different in each of the different organisms. This could be true even within the terrestrial kingdom of 'higher' animals, and it is certain likely to be true of aliens and robots (assuming you could build a robot that felt pain or at least saw red). OK, it is debatable whether or not computers could have mental states, but we still have a feeling that mental states and minds do occur in at least higher animals. So because there are (or even may be) differences in the physical structures underlying those same mental states, the criticism arises that identity theory is too chauvinistic because it delimits too narrowly the structures which can subserve any given mental state.

2.4.3.5 The generation question

The fifth argument is that identity theory does not give an *explanation* as to why some brain states generate consciousness and other brain states do not (Seager, 1999). This assumes that there are unconscious neural processes, and functions in the mind that are non-conscious. Whether or not you accept this depends on your definition of mind and consciousness, as we discussed in chapter 1, but in chapter 7 we will see that there is a great deal of evidence that there is much activity going on in our brains that, it is fairly safe to say, does not enter consciousness. For example, we can drive a car while talking to a passenger, stopping when the traffic lights are red and steering perfectly correctly. Or put more commonly, you can walk and chew gum at the same time. So there can be many processes going on in a brain at the same time, not just the one which produces (somehow) consciousness.

Yet if mental states are just identical to physical states, the question remains why some of them are conscious states and some of them are not. This is one of the big questions now, what Seager calls the *'generation question'*. Identity theory, by simply saying that mental states and physical states are identical, does not answer that basic question (though I am not sure that other theories do either). Why are some of the physical states associated with (give rise to, generate) consciousness, while other physical states are not; what is the crucial difference? Identity theory does not provide an answer – and indeed does not come anywhere near to supplying an answer to this crucial question.

2.4.3.6 Reductionism is obsolete or inappropriate

In contradiction to the view that scientific progress consists of theory reduction (section 2.4.2.1), alternative models of science now exist. Scientists (and not just philosophers of mind!) need to keep abreast of what is happening in philosophy of science (see, for example, Chalmers, 1999; Losee, 2001; Ladyman, 2002). For instance, one alternative discussed in this area is the co-evolution model. Here, theories pertaining to phenomena at two levels are not seen as temporary, with one level claiming to be the 'lower', hence the more fundamental, and thus seeking to replace the 'higher-level' theory. Instead, both proceed as valid descriptors of their respective domains. The aim of science is not, however, just to maintain their independent existence, but to explain how they are related. It is understanding we seek, not reduction and simplification (Bechtel and Richardson, 1993).

If there are general laws of nature to discover, these include 'bridging laws', which explain how the fields are related. For example, genetics proceeded as a progressive discipline for more than fifty years before the hypothesis was formulated that DNA is the physical basis of the gene. Even today, the molecular biology of DNA has not replaced genetics as a science; both levels of theory coexist and are linked by laws which explain their relationship (Darden and Maull, 1977; Darden, 1980). Similarly, neuroscience and psychology can be seen as coexistent bodies of study. New discoveries in one have implications for the other, where they stimulate further research; the new work in the second discipline then throws up yet more ideas for the former. Over time, the two levels of study help guide one another towards more accurate theories (Churchland, 1986; Bechtel, 1988b). One of the best examples of this type of progress happened in the study of vision. First, neurophysiology discovered orientation-selective cells in the visual cortex (Hubel and Wiesel, 1959). Then, psychophysics established the presence of similarly orientation-tuned mechanisms in human vision (Campbell and Kulikowski, 1966) that also turned out to be specific for the spatial frequency of the grating stimuli that were being used (Campbell and Robson, 1968; Pantle and Sekuler, 1968). This in turn led to the discovery that cells in the cortex possess the same property too (Maffei and Fiorentini, 1973).

Thus the prediction now is that studies of mind and brain will not collapse via reduction to a single global theory. Instead, both domains will proceed in tandem, each feeding ideas to the other, thus stimulating their mutual growth and consistency.

2.4.4 **Eliminativism**

The aspiration of identity theory was to find a one-to-one match between categories at the mental and physical levels, and then to conclude that there is ontological identity between them. However, some philosophers doubt whether our mental categorization scheme is good enough for this. What we think of now as 'mental states' are really just confused and inaccurate concepts derived over the course of history in our everyday attempts to under-stand human behaviour, which eliminativists derogatorily call 'folk psychology'. Folk psychology is useless, however, as witness for example its inability to explain the changes of behaviour seen in schizophrenia, brain damage, sleep, dementia, violent crime, drug addiction and so on. Folk psychology has not progressed over thousands of years, and does not enable us to make quantitative predictions, since mental states are qualitative and cannot be measured. Therefore we should abandon any attempt at finding mental equivalents of physical state types (e.g. Churchland, 1988).

In the extreme, eliminativism involves the removal of any idea of 'the mind' and replacing it with ideas from the theory of neuroscience, couched in terms of brain states and neurophysiology. So instead of saying 'I hate you', you would say something like 'Oh, you make cells fire in my left ventro-medial amygdala'; instead of saying 'I'm seeing red' you'd say 'My long-wave cones are overactive relative to my middle-wave cones'; instead of saying 'Maggie is insane' you would say 'Maggie has excess dopamine D2 receptors in her mesolimbic system'; and so on. We would learn a new vocabulary and a new interpretation of our minds in terms of neuroscience, that would eventually replace our folk psychological terminology and provide us with a more accurate understanding.

Eliminativists draw analogies from science in general, saying that mental states are like formerly theorized entities such as demons, phlogiston, caloric, crystal spheres, the ether and so on, which were once believed to exist but in whose existence we no longer believe. For example, women schizophrenics at times in the past may have been called witches. However, nowadays we don't believe witches exist, either in reality or even as a theoretical possibility. It is not a category which exists any more. In the same vein, people who behaved bizarrely were thought to be possessed by evil spirits or demons which had taken them over. But such demons have now been eliminated from our understanding of the universe. So too, the theory that possession by evil spirits causes bizarre behaviour has been eliminated.

So by extension, mental categories will one day be shown not to exist as ontologically real. The only reality is physical states and types of state, and we may as well use the nomenclature of neuroscience to describe our psychology as well as our brains. (This contrasts with identity theory in which mental categories are seen as real but identical to their corresponding physical categories.)

2.4.5 **Arguments against eliminativism**

2.4.5.1 **Qualia and intentionality do exist**

Subjective experiences such as qualia do exist and you can't eliminate mental states. Intentionality also exists: mental states do have meaning – thinking about tomatoes means tomatoes, in a way that the firing of nerve cells doesn't. So we can't eliminate mental states and the mental level because it is obvious that they exist.

2.4.5.2 **We need mental (folk psychological) terms**

We cannot do away with mental terms to describe the way we interact with each other and with the environment. First, to explain any given mental state in neural terms, you would have to come up with a description that is very complex and long. The brain is very complicated and to characterize its state at the neuronal level you would have to describe the activity of all 10^{12} nerve cells, plus their connections, at each relevant instant of time (e.g. Flanagan, 1992; Harth, 1993). If you wanted to characterize the brain's state at a lower level (e.g. the atomic), then you would have to include a vastly greater number of items in your description. Such descriptions would be so unwieldy and unhelpful that we need, if only for shorthand, to be able to say 'I feel' or 'I hate her' or 'I thought the lights were green, officer, honestly'. Those kinds of mental state terms are necessary for us to function as people (as well as to work as psychologists); we need to use these terms, and it is silly to think we can eradicate them.

In principle, Fodor (1987) argues, explanations of behaviour require more than just a description of the brain's state. For example, to understand 'When he went out he took an umbrella because he thought it was going to rain', it is difficult to see how the behaviour of taking an umbrella can be explained in terms of physical nerve firings.

A second argument, allied to this, is one against the possibility of zombies (Moody, 1994; see Sutherland, 1995, for discussion). Zombies are putative people who function perfectly but not consciously – without mental states (section 1.4.2). The counter-argument is that a lot of our speech includes reference to mental states and terms, and our actions depend on them. Thus people frequently say things like 'I am not revising because I feel bored', 'I want to go partying', 'I came because I thought you wanted to see me' or 'I think I can see red'. To come up with an objective explanation of this verbal behaviour we need to be able to account for such self-ascriptions of mental states. But these ascriptions only mean anything if mental states are real and mean what we normally assume them to mean. Importantly, the behaviour of a listener is affected by such speech acts, in ways consistent with the listener understanding what the speaker's words mean, that is, as though the listener believes the speaker's mental states are real. A lot of the social interaction and other behaviour we engage in revolves around mental states in such ways. So to explain all of behaviour you have to use the terminology of mental states and you have got to have theories that explain why we talk about mental states at all. Therefore mental states must be real.

2.4.5.3 **Which level of description is the single relevant one?**

If you eliminate or reduce psychology, what do you replace it with: neuronal physiology? But you can reduce neuronal physiology to (or eliminate it in favour of) the actions of biochemical molecules in the brain. And you can eliminate/reduce the activity of biochemical molecules to the electrostatic forces between the atoms of which they are composed, and you can reduce electrostatics to the basic forces of the universe. Such 'reductive eliminativism' operates down a series of levels from one to another. But which level should you reduce mental states to? Do you describe mental states in terms of the activities of whole areas of the brain like the visual cortex or the amygdala, or do you say that particular cells are active in those structures, or that particular neurotransmitters are being released, or that particular ion channels are opening in parts of the brain, or that the quantum states of the microtubules are resonating at particular frequencies? Which level of description is the relevant one? It seems there is an infinite regress: once you start eliminating one level and reducing it to a lower level then you may just as well keep going and say, well, we can explain human psychology in terms of Grand Unified Theory and the Big Bang – the most basic levels of physics – but that is obviously stupid, a *reductio ad absurdum*.

So you need to keep all levels of description and you can't eliminate them. You even need sociology, ethics and politics beyond the individual human being; you can't reduce sociology to psychology, for example.

2.4.5.4 **Unclear: reinterpretation or elimination (epistemological or ontological)?**

It is not clear whether eliminativism postulates that the mental level just doesn't exist, because mental states don't exist, or whether such states exist but we just reinterpret what they are. Thus talking about the elimination of caloric, phlogiston, ether, crystal spheres and demons during scientific progress implies that what is eliminated are ontological entities. The stars are not really supported by crystal spheres that surround the earth and rotate daily; there are no such things.

However, eliminativists at other times say it is a matter of theory change: the phenomenon still exists (e.g. the stars appear to move) but we learn to interpret it differently (the earth is rotating, not the heavens). All observations are made within a framework of theory, and we need to change our background theory (e.g. from folk psychology to neuroscience) to explain better the phenomena (of human mental life). The application of eliminativism to schizophrenia does not actually enable us to deny that schizophrenics exist as entities. What we do is reinterpret their behaviour in the light of a new theory – neuroscience – which has a broader remit than any psychological level theory.

So, it seems that with respect to schizophrenia and schizophrenic mental states, we have eliminated devil possession as an *explanation*, and devils as ontological *entities*, but we have *not* eliminated the existence of schizophrenia (and its mental states) as a real category of behaviours and experiences. Indeed, the Churchlands (1988, 1996) say with hindsight that they should have called it 'revisionary' materialism, not eliminative.[15]

2.4.5.5 **Unclear: eliminate some or all mental states?**

It is unclear how reinterpreting mental states as nonexistent is different from just saying they are nothing more than brain states. In other words, eliminativism can itself be reduced to identity theory.

On the other hand, if eliminativists are saying that mental states are (ontologically) real, but we simply have the wrong (epistemological) categories and types at the moment, and future science must find the right way to interpret and categorize them, then under that future science there will be no difference between the predictions of eliminativism and identity theory. But this is not surprising: science makes progress all the time by refining and clarifying its category boundaries. Eliminativists are merely calling for a revolution in psychology; but revolutions happen all the time (e.g. from behaviourism to cognitivism)

15. Bickle (1998) describes revisionary materialism as falling along a continuum between identity theory and eliminative materialism. The revised concepts at the higher level (revised as a result of the co-evolution of theories, à la Churchland, 1986) are altered from their original formulations (hence, there can be no identity reduction), but they are still in some way equivalent or analogous to the concepts in the old theory, and they still exist (hence, no eliminative reduction).

and are not philosophically novel to the extent that eliminativism can be considered a separate philosophy from identity theory. [16]

Finally, eliminativists sometimes predict a mixed outcome in which, in the future, some mental states will be eliminated but others reduced (Churchland, 1988). This too does not seem a revolutionary philosophy.

2.4.5.6 Folk psychology is not a theory

Folk psychology reflects the functioning of our cognitive modules for interpersonal behaviour (see section 6.2.2.1). It is part of our evolved human nature for empathizing with and understanding other people, so that, for example, we can predict their behaviour, manipulate them, or give or seek help. Folk psychology is not a scientific theory; so talk of beliefs and desires cannot be eliminated by neuroscience in the way that epistemological reductionism can lead to a whole field of academic enquiry being subsumed into another, broader domain of knowledge (Davies and Stone, 1995).

2.5 Computational functionalism

Given the problems known to affect dualism, behaviourism, identity theory and eliminativism, what do philosophers believe is a sound theory? The dominant theories in philosophy of mind at the moment (i.e. the theories with the most followers) form the functionalist group of theories. Here I will outline the original theory, and in chapters 4 and 5 I will come back to talk about two further developments. The main originators of this theory include Fodor (1975), Putnam (1975), Pylyshyn (1980) and Stich (1983).

The central idea of functionalism is that the categorization or definition of a mental state is based on its *functional and causal role*: what it actually does. To a certain extent there is an abutting here with behaviourism, in that it places emphasis on functional output, purpose and cause, and how mental states affect behaviour and action. But unlike behaviourism, there are mental states in functionalism: these are allowed and their categorization depends on what they are doing. The difference between red and green is not simply that you experience red and green differently but that red and green have different roles in affecting your behaviour, your train of thought and your mental life.

Let me elaborate first by using the two big analogies. One of the primary analogies is with Chomsky's (1957) linguistic theory. In language, there are words that have meanings or '*semantics*', and there is grammar or '*syntax*'. Within the grammatical system are '*rules*' which can be applied to sentences to transform their structure. The idea of 'transformational grammar', as Chomsky called it, is that there are various processing devices, the rules of

16. The Churchlands' description of 'folk psychology' as not making progress over thousands of years ignores the very real, scientific advances made in what we might call 'academic psychology' over the last hundred years or so. And one could also argue that 'folk psychology' has actually made progress: concepts such as unconscious motivation (since Freud), intelligence, extraversion, short-term memory, SSRI, caffeine high, autism, ADHD, Alzheimer's disease, epilepsy and so on are common currency as explanatory causes of behaviour and its disturbances (and are not just redescriptions of behaviour). These constructs are used in everyday discourse alongside explanations in terms of beliefs and desires.

grammar, which can be applied to change, for example, an active into a passive sentence or a positive into a negative sentence and vice versa (Figure 2.4a).

The '*language of thought*' hypothesis is part of this analogy. Different parts or modules of any complex system must communicate with one another: they send messages and pass information to one another. This process is analogous to people speaking to one another, using language. Some philosophers use the word '*mentalese*' to refer to this hypothetical inner language. It's as though there is a language in the mind and the different parts of the mind communicate with one another in a language of thought.[17]

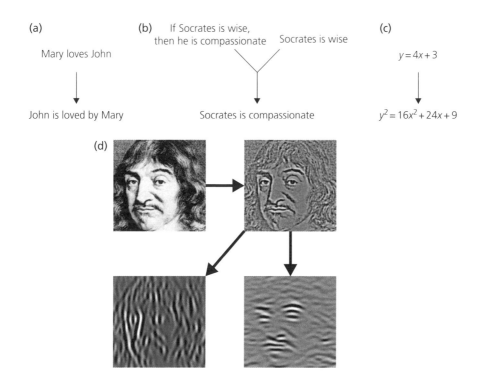

Figure 2.4 a. Transformational processing of sentences (after Chomsky). The truth value of a sentence is preserved while an active-to-passive operator is applied. **b.** Functionalist processing of logical propositions (after Chrysippus, 280–206 BC). Two premises are combined using the *modus ponens* operator to give a conclusion that retains the truth value of the premises. **c.** Functionalist processing of mathematical propositions. Application of a squaring operator to both sides of an equation preserves the truth value of the equation. **d.** Computational functionalist processing of images (after Marr): the successive application of operators to a representation. The original (top left) is first subject to a Laplacian filter that selects the edges (top right). The resultant representation can then either be passed through a vertical (bottom left) or horizontal (bottom right) Gabor filter, to make explicit selectively the locations of vertical or horizontal energy, respectively, in the original image.

17. Be careful to envisage this inner language as a relatively impoverished medium of communication, compared to English, French and so on. It does not have all the qualities of a full-blown language; mentalese is merely analogous to language. (It is also important not to confuse this idea with the behaviourist hypothesis that thought equals language, and just is inner speech, like 'talking to oneself'.)

Thus, the reasoning continues, within mentalese there are processes analogous to transformational grammar. First, you have *'representations'* which are equivalent to sentences; they are meaningful units or elements. The information which is being processed inside the system represents things in the outside world, so it has intentionality. What is represented becomes the content of consciousness. (Hence this whole approach is also known as the *'Representational theory of mind'*.)

Second, the representations can be processed by various grammatical-type *'rules'* to combine them and to transform them into other meaningful units and to use them to follow through an argument and arrive at some rational *meaningful* conclusion (Figure 2.4b). Both representations and their processing have to be present. The research programme of functionalism aims to explain the existence of the representations – what they are, how they have meanings – and to explain the processing rules.

The other analogy is with maths, i.e. computation. The idea is that the elements you are processing are *symbols*, like numbers, or *x* and *y* in an equation. They are units which have some meaning, i.e. they represent something, and then you can operate on them. Processes like addition, subtraction, division, integration, differentiation and a whole range of *operators* are the equivalent of the transformational rules in Chomsky's grammar. For instance, you can take an equation such as $y = x^2$, take the square root of both sides and you get $\sqrt{y} = x$. Thus you apply a transform, an operator, which in this case is the square root operator, to both sides of the equation. Note that this preserves the truth value of the equation; if the facts that you start with (the premises) are correct, then the conclusions will be too. Figure 2.4c illustrates the converse operation, squaring.

There is also a good analogy between this functionalist approach and visual image processing: for example, Marr (1982) explains the necessary mechanisms as the application of operators to an image. Thus any image analyser must first use an operator to find edges in the image (Figure 2.4d), and by successive application of a series of various operators transform the image through a series of 'sketches' that ultimately can lead to identification of the stimulus.

Finally, let's consider another psychological example: reading words aloud. The visual system first extracts the edges in the stimulus, as just explained (Marr, 1982), operates on those features to group them into letters (graphemes), and then into words. For reading aloud, these have to be translated into representations of speech sounds (phonemes), via either the grapheme-to-phoneme route or, for irregular words such as 'yacht', the whole word, lexical-to-phoneme route (Ellis and Young, 1996). Finally, the phonemes are re-coded into articulatory representations that can run on the motor output system. Here, the latter are translated into individual organ (lung, jaw, etc.) movements and then into patterns of muscle (diaphragm, tongue, etc.) contractions for speaking. Meanwhile, the reader may simultaneously come to understand what is being read, by interpreting the stage of word representations via another process to create representations of the words' semantic meanings (Craik and Lockhart, 1972). Thus several stages of representation are involved in carrying out the task, with different operations carried out to 'translate' the representations at each stage.

A corollary of functionalism is that the internal symbols may be arbitrary, in the same way that words are arbitrary (why should a dog be represented by the word 'dog', as opposed to the word 'suz', for example?). In maths, too, calling a variable *'x'* tells us nothing about what that real-world variable actually is. The rules of grammar and of maths then operate on the symbols regardless of what the symbols mean (although within certain interesting constraints, for example of grammatical class – nouns versus verbs).

SIDE-BOX 2.2 TWO ASPECTS OF REPRESENTATION

Vehicles and contents

We can break a representation down into two aspects: the '*vehicle*' and the '*content*'. The information that is contained within the representation must possess meaning; this is the content of the mental state, for example, 'grandmother's armchair' or 'a red patch'. The vehicle is the medium that is conveying or carrying the content.

One well used example contrasts a picture of a castle and a verbal description of that castle: same content, different vehicles. Dretske (1995, pp. 34–38) has another nice analogy, between experience and stories. The story is the content, perhaps of a book, while the story's vehicle is the words in the book. If we ask: 'Where is the story of Harry Potter's adventures?', the answer has two parts: the vehicle is in the books written by J.K. Rowling and the content is in Hogwarts School. Similarly, if we ask where is experience (qualia) or meaning (intentionality), it is not where the representation is: the representation is a vehicle and is in the head, while the content is (assuming it is about the world) in the world. [a]

The linguistic analogy posits that the vehicle is like the structure of a sentence, while the content is given by the particular choice of words. Grammatical processes are supposed to operate on the sentence structure, independently of the particular words – or at least, independently of their meanings. [b] In fact, the central supposition of computational functionalism is that 'rules' can be applied regardless of the particular symbols they are applied to. This is what gives cognitive systems their flexibility (Fodor, 1975).

In computers, the vehicle/content distinction is not necessarily equivalent to that between hardware and software. There are typically two levels of information within the software. This works as follows: the content of a software word stored in the random-access memory (RAM) can be another address in the RAM; it does not have to be a number that represents something about the outside world. [c] Every location in RAM has a numerical 'address'. In running a program, the computer processor is often required to take a number from the hardware location that has address A and place that number in the location of address B, which itself is found in a third address, C. The content of address C is literally called a 'pointer' to a location B inside the machine, and thus has internal intentionality (because the literal meaning of 'intentionality' is 'aiming at', which means the same here as 'pointing at'). The number that was originally in address A might represent something outside the machine, such as the location of Professor Snape's classroom, and is thus content at a higher level than the number in address C.

The point is that *what we are aware of is the content; we do not become aware of the vehicle*. You are not aware that cells are firing in your head. Similarly at higher levels: you are not aware of the syntactic mechanisms that underlie language (e.g. how to convert a statement into a question), generate visual illusions (e.g. make lines look different lengths when they are the same) or retrieve a memory (e.g. what is the capital of France?). These mechanisms are processes that operate on vehicles that convey content.

Propositional attitudes

The linguistically influenced philosophers of mind regarded the mind as filled with what they called 'propositional attitudes'. An example of such an attitude is: 'I believe that I am looking at a red armchair'. In this example, there is a vehicle (also known as a 'mode of presentation'), which is the belief state I am in, while the content is 'I am looking at a red armchair'. The link between the vehicle

continues

SIDE-BOX 2.2 continued

and its content is an intension, while the link between the content and the world is an extension (cf. chapter 1).

A corollary of this is that the vehicle is only revealed when it is used; the processing of the content entails that the syntactic structure of the representation engages with (or 'is read by') some mechanism or operator. A propositional attitude can thus be treated as a symbol plus the rule or computation that is being applied to it. We cannot *experience*, say, the sight of a red armchair unless we believe/think/know that we are seeing a red armchair. Thus the explanation of how we are conscious is that underlying our 'experiencing' a red armchair is our processing (believing, knowing, etc.) of a certain information-bearing content ('red armchair').[d]

a. See section 11.3 for what happens when the content is about the self or one's own thoughts.

b. Consider such sentences as Chomsky's 'Colourless green ideas sleep furiously', or Lewis Carroll's 'All mimsy were the borogoves', which can be converted unproblematically to the negative or interrogative form despite their semantic dubiousness.

c. For a computer to 'know' the address in RAM is like having a Turing machine in which the computer knows the absolute position of the read/write head along the tape, not just how many steps to move the tape relatively left or right. This knowledge is built into the hardware of modern computers.

d. And note that the processing is a particular kind of processing, not just 'associating' (see section 2.5.1.2)!

The study of how representations can have meaning is known as 'psychosemantics'. The principle is that the representation is a 'vehicle' that carries a 'content' (Side-box 2.2). These are analogous to syntax (grammar) and semantics (meaning) in mentalese: syntactic operators can transform sentences regardless of the particular meanings of the words (provided these are the same grammatical category). For example, the operator that transforms 'Mary loves John' into 'John is loved by Mary' can cope equally with 'Tom hates Sally', 'Pauline admires the psychologist' and so on. Thus semantics can be reduced to (explained in terms of) the mechanical operations of symbol processing, and the mystery of intentionality is solved.

Functionalism is also sometimes known as 'token–token identity theory'. This emphasizes that functionalism is still a variety of materialism. The identity theory that we discussed above was 'type–type' identity theory, because the categories of mental and biological levels of description were supposed to overlap exactly. With token–token identity, the categories don't necessarily coincide. The idea is that mental states exist and can be divided into certain kinds (seeing red, being in pain, wanting to do things and so on). Physical states also exist and can be categorized (C-fibres firing, amygdala underactive and so on). However, these categories are not necessarily going to be identical to or match the mental ones. Yet if we take any individual case or 'token' of a mental state and a physical state, these are identical in the ontological sense that mental states are just physical states of the brain. So it is not a dualism: there is an identity but the categories may be different. One type of mental state could be instantiated by several types of physical state, while one physical category could be subserving several psychological types (Figure 2.5).

In sum, the idea of functionalism is that in the mind there is some kind of computing going on, transforming the meaningful units by various kinds of operations – a process that preserves their logical sense or meaning, and indeed develops the meaning of the symbols towards a conclusion, decision or goal. The essence of mental activity is a series of mentalese or computation-like processes.

Token identity

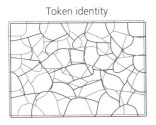

Figure 2.5 Following the convention of Figure 2.3, mental state categories are demarcated by the black lines and physical types by the grey. Under functionalism these do not necessarily correspond.

2.5.1 Arguments for computational functionalism

2.5.1.1 Multiple realization

The categorization of objects according to what they do leads us to group together things that are not necessarily physically identical. Consider a clock, for example. Clocks can be digital or analogue, powered by electricity or a wound spring, use a balance wheel, pendulum or quartz crystal to keep time. They may even be candles or sundials. In other words, there are multiple ways in which the function of a clock, namely to keep time, can be made manifest. Functionalism says the same is true of mental states. Just as with clocks, calculators and boats, the functional categories that are pains, seeings of the colour red, beliefs in Santa Claus and plans for dinner, can each include a variety of types of entity. Yet within each category, each token fulfils a similar function.

One analogy commonly used in functionalism is between the hardware and software of a computer. You can run a given program on many different computers. The internal logic of the computer program determines what it does, and indeed, what it is. Yet that logic is not dependent upon any particular type of hardware, and can be run on a desktop computer, a mainframe, a hand calculator, an abacus, a brain, or whatever passes for a brain in a Martian. Moreover, that logic can be studied independently of the hardware. Likewise, psychology and mental states can be studied independently of the brain; the internal principles upon which the mind operates are autonomous. Searle (1980) named this field '*strong AI*' (artificial intelligence) to contrast it with 'weak AI', which is psychology studied with allowance for constraints imposed by the underlying machinery of the brain or computer.

In fact, it is important, as we shall see, that the hardware analogy is not restricted to computers. Robots, humans, animals and aliens are all similar, to the extent that they are all complex systems, they have to analyse a large amount of data and they have to make decisions about what to do in the world about them. Thus they all necessarily have beliefs, sensations and so on. Such processes are common to all these kinds of system and can be treated autonomously, and it does not matter whether they are physically instantiated or realized as human brains, animal brains, Martian brains, computers or robots.

We can therefore allow our intuition that animals (at least higher ones) and intelligent aliens might be conscious. Since consciousness depends on the functional organization of the brain, and since this organization can be realized in many hardware forms, consciousness is not restricted to any particular physical form, such as the human brain. Functionalism thus avoids one of the problems with identity theory (section 2.4.3.4).

2.5.1.2 **It is more powerful than behaviourism**

Like behaviourism, functionalism concentrates on what mental states do, rather than on the creation of representations for no apparent purpose (so the dualistic mind can contemplate and admire them?). Additionally, inner states are allowed under functionalism, which as we have seen is vital for a convincing account of the mind. The functions of the representations can include their effects on other mental states, not just on overt behaviour.

One of the important differentiating points between functionalism and behaviourism is that functionalism does not involve *associations*. In many areas of psychology, the idea of 'associative' links is central, e.g. when I say the word 'cat' you think of 'milk', 'meow', 'dog', etc. This is part of folk psychology now too: what is the first word that comes into your head when I say 'mother'? In functionalism, however, Fodor (1994a, 1998a) makes the very important point that the relationships between different concepts in the mind are not simple associative links. Associationism has never worked because it is basically inadequate: it is not enough to say that the relationships between concepts in semantic networks, minds, or AI structures are ones of simple association. Instead, the links are of various, particular kinds.

Consider Figure 2.6. There are various inputs and outputs to the whole system, and various types of functional connection between the mental states. But some of these connections are negative or antithetical; for example, 'cats and dogs hate one another', and 'black is the opposite of white'. Or: 'cats possess claws'; it is not simply that cats are associated with claws but there is a particular *kind* of relationship between the two concepts: cats *possess* claws. Similarly, there are specific types of relationship between the concepts of 'cat' and 'dog', 'cat' and 'meow', and 'cat' and 'mammal' – cats are not dogs, but cats are a subset of the kind 'mammal', and so on. Figure 2.7 shows some examples of this idea as used in research in cognitive psychology.

Or consider a mathematical problem. If $4(x^2 - 3) = 24$, then $x^2 - 3 = 24/4$ and $x^2 - 3 = 6$, so $x^2 = 6 + 3$, therefore $x^2 = 9$ and $x = 3$. At each step in the chain of reasoning a different operator is applied to the symbols: division of both sides of the equation by four, division of the numerator by the denominator on the right side, addition of three to both sides, addition of the terms on the right side and taking the square roots of both sides.

So to understand thought, you have to know the particular kind of link, operator or transform that is applied when moving from one meaningful functional unit to the next. It is not simply an associative link, where all the links are of just the one kind. So the pathway through which thought proceeds depends on the particular kinds of transform applied – *it is not simply a matter of the passive spread of activity through a network of associations, where every association is simply a connection which is equivalent to every other connection.* Under associative theories some connections may be stronger than others, but they are all qualitatively identical. However, Fodor (1994a, 1998a) contradicts this, and I think he makes a very interesting point.

Functionalism

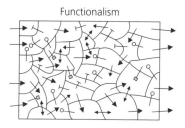

Figure 2.6 The interactions between states are not all of the same kind (e.g. 'associations') but involve several types of relationship (e.g. 'implies', 'is the opposite of', 'is a subset of', 'belongs to', etc.) as indicated by the different types of connective between states in this diagram.

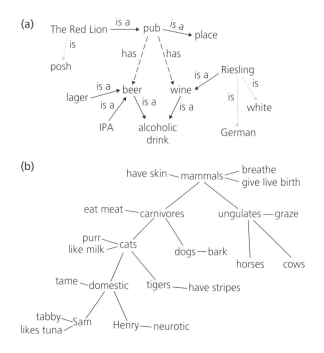

Figure 2.7 a. Organization of a fragment of semantic memory, showing three kinds of connective. Based on Rumelhart et al. (1972). **b.** Structure in semantic memory. It takes longer to answer the question 'Does a cat breathe?' than 'Does a cat purr?' (Collins and Quillian, 1969). How many types of connective are there here?

2.5.1.3 **It explains reasoning, imagination, creativity and counterfactuals**

In addition to the ability to make logical inferences (Figure 2.4b) and thus explain human rationality and decision making (Clark, 2001), functionalism can account for other aspects of our mental life that lower-level theories (behaviourism, neural nets) do not. For example, Chomsky's transformational grammar is '*generative*': it explains how an infinite number of sentences can be constructed from a limited number of words. (Speech is not limited to those sentences we have heard others using.) Thus by analogy our minds can construct an infinite number of ideas out of a limited number of representations, by repetitive and/or recursive application of the limited set of rules we possess. Previous philosophies have either ascribed our powers of creativity and imagination to unexplained mechanisms within a mysterious dualistic 'mind', or to random stimuli disturbing the normal process of a deterministic mechanism (or perhaps to random failures of such a mechanism). With symbols and rules within the mind, the individual has a mental life that is autonomous from the environment (as Fodor puts it), freeing it to imagine alternative outcomes of potential future actions, and thus giving a choice between those outcomes (Craik, 1943; MacKay, 1956), rather than being a passive victim of whatever stimuli are entering from the immediate ongoing environment, reacting deterministically only to the present in a reflex fashion.

For example, by using a rule for combining two representations, one can generate a representation of some nonexisting state. A simplistic example would be to combine the concepts 'man' and 'horse' to generate 'centaur', but the whole range of counterfactuals (nonexistent states), including models of how the future might be, can be accounted for by the limitless internal combination of meaningful units.

2.5.2 Arguments against computational functionalism

Numerous criticisms have been aimed at computational functionalism since its appearance in the mid 1970s, and I will begin with two that concern its treatment of qualia.

2.5.2.1 The inverted spectrum argument

Basically, this simply means that the colours each of us sees may not be the same as the colours that other people see. This is the old chestnut I mentioned above, that when I look at a ripe tomato and you look at a ripe tomato we both say it is red – but if I could look through your eyes, say if I were telepathic, then I might say 'Hey! That's not red, that's green' – and the sky looks yellow and the grass pink and so on. But with functionalism there is no reason why we should experience the particular qualia that we do – why do colours appear in the particular way they do? By extrapolation, why do all the other mental states or subjective experiences feel the way they do to us? What matters in functionalism is merely whether the mental state functions. The symbols in our heads are arbitrary in the same way that, in language, words are arbitrary symbols.

So some functionalists simply reply, well, so what, it doesn't matter; as long as we behave and function in exactly the same way in response to the tomato, what difference does it make whether or not we do have different experiences? It is quite possible that we do. This is a very interesting possibility – that it does not make any difference in practice and you can't prove it one way or the other. Even if we do experience different colours, our minds still work the same. The actual functional symbols stand for certain things – the experience of red has certain meanings and its functional roles are going to be the same whatever the actual subjective experience. As we grow up, we assign arbitrary symbols to the different kinds of sensory experience that we have, and it doesn't matter whether different individuals assign different symbols to them. Maybe when you look at a tomato you experience a colour which qualitatively is completely different from any of mine, but there is no reason at all to suppose that there is uniformity of experience between us. Now, this argument is obviously one which comes down to your intuition, and whether you buy it or not depends on your attitude towards functionalism in general.

An associated response is that the definition of qualia (as of all mental states) is functional. Their 'function' is what they do – what role they play in affecting our behaviour, thoughts and decisions. So if a quale-in-me and a quale-in-you fulfil the same functional role then they *are* the same mental state, by definition. You can say that, if that mental state involves a subjective sensation, the sensation will be the same because the functional role played by the mental state is the same. So we do have the same experiences if they fulfil the same functional role, because it is the functional role that determines that the state is a mental state, and what particular mental state it is, and that distinguishes it from other mental states.

A third answer which functionalists come up with is to fall back onto biological determinism. The functionalist position does assume that individual cases of mental state and brain state are identical, that particular incidences (tokens, as they call them) of mental states are tokens of brain states. The issue then is just one of categorization: if we have similar brains, similar physiology (e.g. 'red' cones, 'green' cones and 'blue' cones), and our neural pathways are connected up the same way, then we will have similar mental states, because our mental states are determined by, or in fact are identical to, our brain states. So to the extent that we can say that we have similar physiology, we can say that we have similar minds. And so, given that we know that cones with 'red' pigment, ganglion cells and so on are connected up in most of us in similar ways, we can conclude that we do have similar subjective experiences. Colour-blind people would have different experiences, which would be pretty much what we would expect. So that argument says that the inverted spectrum is not possible – it is not possible for people to have rainbow colours all swapped around.

Now, the final argument touches on the issue of whether qualia are actually atoms – isolated, individualizable elements of experience – and whether we can say that the feeling of red or pain or wanting to go on holiday is a pure experience, and can be treated as such independently of the other qualia. The traditional idea of qualia (Locke, 1690; Hume, 1739; etc.) is that these are basic elements that are then linked together through associations and experiences to form complex concepts. However, one can argue that we have more Gestalt-holistic experiences and we never experience, or we cannot (either in principle or in practice) experience, isolated sensations or raw feelings. Experience is always a very complex whole and is based on a mass of information coming in all the time. The perception of one element, e.g. one part of the visual scene, is always relative to the other elements present there.

For example, when it comes to colour, it is easy to show that red and green are opposed to one another, and blue and yellow are opposed to one another (Hurvich and Jameson, 1957). We can say that pink is in-between red and white, and we can see how orange is in-between red and yellow. There is a structure to our colour experiences (remember from perception: the colour circle and the layout of colour space; e.g. Gregory, 1998). Some pairs of colours are more similar than others; for instance, orange is more similar to red than it is to blue. Experimentally one can measure the structure of people's colour space by mapping out how similar the various colours are to one another (Clark, 1993). You always find that red and green are opposed, blue and yellow are opposed and white and black are opposed to one another, and this occurs in everyone who has physiologically normal colour vision. This complete integrated structure means that individual bits of it cannot be isolated – you cannot swap red and green around without causing some disruption to the map or web of relationships between the other colours.

So when you say 'inverted spectrum', what do you mean? If you think through how we could rotate the whole of colour space, you realize it is not just a one-dimensional thing like the rainbow. Each colour has its degrees of saturation, hue and brightness. This forms a three-dimensional space and there are several ways you could 'invert' a three-dimensional space – inverting one axis or several, or rotating the whole sphere around one or more axes. Most critically, it turns out that human colour space is not exactly isotropic: it is not a perfect sphere, and the three axes are not quite at right angles to one another. Thus the topology of an individual's colour phenomenology cannot be altered without causing some noticeable difference to their observable behaviour. However, the empirical evidence is that this does not happen (unless the person has a particular colour vision defect or problem): humans are consistent in their colour-related behaviour. Since it is extremely unlikely that an alternative set of colour qualia would give the same relational colour space, the conclusion is that people do have similar kinds of absolute (not just relative) experiences of colour, and therefore people do not experience inverted spectra (Clark, 1993, 2000; Palmer, 1999a).

2.5.2.2 Absent qualia, zombies and the Chinese nation argument

Why do we have qualia at all? Given that mental states are defined by their functional role, surely they can perform their function without being accompanied by subjective experience. Do the subjective experiences have any functional role, given that vast amounts of our psychological and cognitive processing occur subconsciously, and consciousness we now think seems to illuminate a relatively small amount of our information processing machinery? Surely the whole thing could just as well be going on unconsciously, e.g. I can walk up and down without having to think where to move my feet – it all happens automatically – so why not the rest of what I am doing? Why could not everything else be automatic? (If there are people like this, they are referred to as 'zombies': see chapter 1). Functionalism does not give any reason why we need qualia, nor does it give any functional definition of qualia.

One of the classic caricatures that uses this idea is Block's (1978) 'Chinese nation' argument. It begins with the idea that if function is the crucial factor in determining consciousness, then any system which has the same organizational, functional structure as the brain will have consciousness. Now, the Chinese nation example takes as premise the idea that the brain has 10^9 nerve cells in it (we know now that there are more than that, perhaps 10^{12}, but let's pass that over for the moment) and it happens that in China there are (or there were when Block was writing this) 10^9 people, roughly. So, Block says, suppose that the people of China were organized in an identical fashion to the way that a human brain is organized: that each person fulfilled the role of an individual nerve cell and received messages in some way from the particular right set of other Chinese people, and as a result of those messages then transmitted other messages on to other Chinese people in just the same way their own particular equivalent nerve cell would transmit messages on to other nerve cells. If you set the whole Chinese nation up with all the connections, etc., in exactly the same way as the brain, then, according to functionalism, the Chinese nation would be conscious. Block then says: well, this is ridiculous, so therefore functionalism is ridiculous.

Now, there are a number of replies to this. One of the most obvious is: who says the Chinese nation would not be conscious? How do you know? It is just a matter of opinion whether the Chinese nation would or would not be conscious. The functionalists could say: yes, it would be conscious, so there, you can't prove otherwise. It is just a matter of opinion – you are just throwing up your hands and saying 'the idea that it could be conscious is ridiculous'.

My view is that you can't just attribute consciousness to a system. We discussed in section 1.4 what is called 'the problem of other minds', when we raised the issues of whether consciousness arises in animals, people with brain damage, robots and so on, and if it does, how you would tell. We concluded that this is an imponderable thing, a very difficult problem to solve. In a sense, what Block has given us here is another problem of other minds: how would you know whether or not the Chinese nation is conscious? You have exactly the same problem as you would knowing whether any other person, animal, Martian or robot is conscious, and you cannot solve it just by just throwing up your hands and saying 'Of course they are/they are not conscious'. So it is not that clear cut an example, when you look at it in that light. Suppose we continue the example by setting up the people of India and Russia to form another system that mimics a brain in its functional organization. We instil into this brain the question: is the Chinese nation conscious? How is the Indian plus Russian brain supposed to know?

Another argument against zombies is that qualia do have a functional role and they do do something. We do make discriminations and decisions based on our qualia – for example, we stop at red lights and go at green lights, and we avoid situations that would give us pain. We make decisions based on these subjective experiences, so therefore these subjective experiences have a real functional role in our minds, and therefore they can be defined and included as part of functionalism. We cannot ignore them and we could not function the way we do, both in making decisions and in talking about qualia (e.g. 'I don't like that colour'), if there were no such a thing as subjective feelings. We talk about qualia and feelings and mental experiences all the time, so even from a behaviourist point of view, how do we account for that behaviour if we have no qualia? (This latter point is the same argument given in section 2.4.5.2.)

The final argument is that the absent qualia and Chinese nation arguments assume narrow content, which I defined above. They assume that the contents of the mind depend purely on the physical structure of the brain, and that the presence or absence of awareness and feelings and so on is determined purely by the functional organization internal to the brain. But you have to ask: what is the environment within which the Chinese nation exists? The mental states the Chinese nation would have if it were conscious would depend upon the sensory inputs and the effects of its movements, if it is really like a person. The environment does play a role, as we discussed above, in determining intentionality – and indeed mental states in general. Block's Chinese nation ignores the idea that the environment plays an important role in determining mental states. So if you accept broad rather than narrow content, the Chinese nation argument does not hold water.[18]

2.5.2.3 Multiple realization is too liberal

As we discussed above, identity theory was set up in such a way that only people with human-type brains could have mental states. Martians, robots or octopuses would not have mental states, or might have completely different ones from humans. The functionalist theory has the opposite virtue: it allows 'multiple realization'. Given that the functional organization is what counts, then you can have consciousness in humans, monkeys, chimpanzees, dogs, cats, Martians, robots and whatever – just as long as their functional organization is the same, and as long as the relationships between the different mental symbols and the rule-like transformations that link them are the same, in whatever is the crucial way for consciousness.

But since it is only the organization that counts, you can have consciousness in the Chinese nation, in the economy of Bolivia (another example that is often used: philosophers

---

18. Another argument, of a more empirical/contingent nature, is given in section 4.3.2.

talk about the mental 'economy' as a complex system full of interactions) or in a construction made out of tin cans linked together by pieces of string.

The fault is thus that functionalism is too liberal, because there are no limits, in principle, on how far you can go. It does seem that allowing consciousness in the Chinese nation, the economy of Bolivia or in tin cans is being a bit too broad. There are no restrictions on what kind of organism or structure could have consciousness.

Block in fact points out that between these two extremes, identity theory and functionalist theory, there is, in principle, no way to draw the line defining what we allow as consciousness: in humans only or in everything that is organized in the right fashion. This may or may not be a serious problem – it is a matter of fashion as to how far down you think consciousness can go. In the past many people have thought that only humans have minds, souls and consciousness, but nowadays most people seem to think that monkeys, chimpanzees and so on have some kind of mind at least (we've discussed this above). But the problem is still: where do you draw the boundary between conscious and unconscious entities? The extreme positions defined by these two philosophical positions (identity and functionalism) are not satisfactory, and any intermediate position seems arbitrary.

2.5.2.4 Processing can be done by neural networks

For the last twenty years, much hype has centred on this idea, which is also referred to as parallel distributed processing (PDP), connectionism or parallelism. The debate is over which paradigm to adopt in information science: traditional functionalism or PDP. We will go into more detail about neural nets in section 6.4.3, where the arguments for and against will be described.

But for now, first beware that the word 'network' is often used in two different senses. The functionalists' model is based on the *semantic* network. These are nets that contain systems of relationships between meaningful units or 'nodes' (as they are commonly called in cognitive psychology: e.g. Collins and Quillian, 1969; Rumelhart et al., 1972; Bruce and Young, 1986). For example, we have talked about 'cat' and 'dog', 'cat' and 'meow', and 'cat' and 'mammal'. Each of these words refers to a concept – 'cat', 'dog', 'meow', 'mammal' – and there are various relationships between them. They are linked in a semantic network, that is to say, there is a systematic pattern of meanings between them: cats hate dogs, cats make the sound 'meow', cats are a subset of mammals and so on (Figure 2.7). In addition, cats are nothing whatsoever to do with clouds – cats and clouds are completely different, unlinked concepts. The physical instantiation of these nodes is unspecified; some theorists assume they are like single nerve cells, but this position has many problems (see section 6.2.6.1). Instead, most semantic network theorists take nodes to be higher-level entities, more like the folders on your computer desktop.

With *neural* networks the idea is that concepts or representations are held or carried in a set of units that at the most fundamental are very similar to nerve cells. Although the basic analogy is with nerve cells, functionally you can generalize to any mechanism which has relevantly similar properties (of which the most obvious is the property of either being 'on' or 'off', which is analogous to a nerve cell either firing or not firing, or a semiconductor gate in your computer being open or closed). The idea, then, is that you have a large number of units responding to their inputs, and at any given instant the inputs set up a '*pattern of activity*' across that set of nerve cells. One way to picture this is to think of the cells in the retina. If you are looking at the letter A or the letter B, a cat, a dog or a red tomato, each of these stimuli sets up a different pattern of activity in the retina. Some cells in the retina fire and some cells in the retina don't fire. Each of the individual objects in the outside world is represented in the set of retinal cells by its own unique pattern of activity. This pattern of activity just is the crucial information or representation that is related to the object in the outside world.

The set of cells then sends action potentials out along its axons to carry that information to another set of cells. A simple analogy is with the set of one million ganglion cells in each retina, whose axons run up to the lateral geniculate nucleus (LGN). In the LGN another set of a million cells transmits to the hundred million cells in primary visual cortex. In each of these loci visual stimuli evoke complex patterns of activity that represent each stimulus. As each pattern is transmitted from one set of cells to the next, there is some kind of transformation in the pattern. For example, if you recall, individual cells in the LGN respond best to spots of light whereas cells in the visual cortex respond to lines or edges at particular orientations – there is a transformation in the way the information is encoded as it passes between these two locations (see also Figure 2.4d).

The point here about functionalism is that these neural networks work: they perform functions in that they transform representations of the stimulus. In some cases they transform them in a way which is suitable for output – for controlling behaviour or for categorizing stimuli into different types. Although there is a lot of argument about how well these networks mimic real people's behaviour and whether they show the same kinds of anomalies, errors and generalizations that people do, neural nets are quite successful. So the implication is that functional networks of this type may be the neural basis of mental life. (See section 6.4.3 for further discussion and details.)

Now, there are two ways in which these networks operate differently from the processing postulated in functionalist theory. First, is the question of symbols. In functionalist 'mentalese' the idea is that the symbols are arbitrary, in the same way that the words 'cat' and 'dog' are arbitrary symbols for cats and dogs. With connectionism the symbols are not arbitrary, to the extent that the pattern of activity set up in the retina by a stimulus is not arbitrary: it is linked in some fashion, perhaps an isomorphic fashion, or certainly in some kind of deterministic fashion, with the stimulus. In principle, if you recorded from all the cells in the optic nerve you could tell what the stimulus was. The shape and structure of the representation, of the pattern of activity in the brain, is in some way linked with the pattern of sensory input. So the patterns are not arbitrary; there is some sort of tie, e.g. isomorphism.

This suggestion has led to a lot of argument about how arbitrary the patterns are, especially when you go up into higher regions of the brain, where the patterns represent, for example, words in the human language system. How is the word 'cat' actually represented in our minds? It does not have to be a cat-shaped pattern of activity! Perhaps in the visual system it is, or possibly when we imagine a cat, but does thinking of the word 'cat' mimic the auditory pattern of the word, or the motor control system's command pattern for saying or writing the word, or for stroking the cat, or some amodal (non-sensory) encoding, or what? This is called the '*grounding problem*'. It refers to the question of how you can have symbols at a high level of description that are arbitrary, in the sense necessary for the functionalist mentalese theory, yet that can be grounded, i.e. related to the physiology of the brain, in a way that allows the arbitrariness of the higher level of description while still being a matter of real nerve cells firing deterministically at the lower level. A number of people have been arguing about how this can possibly happen (I won't go into details here: see Smolensky, 1988; Harnad, 1990; Barsalou, 1999; Marcus, 2001). This is one of the issues that functionalists have to resolve to defend their theory: they have to solve the grounding problem of how arbitrary symbols could be implemented in the brain.

The second issue, and perhaps the more crucial one, is about rules. According to functionalism there are transformational rules, analogous to Chomsky's transformational grammar or operators in mathematics such as addition, Fourier transforms and so on. However, in the connectionist, PDP models, there is no kind of rule in that global sense. There is no overall rule that says, for example, that the transformation going from the LGN to the visual cortex is the application of rule X. What you have instead is a whole lot of nerve cells which release neurotransmitter onto another lot of nerve cells. There are just units in the neural network that activate or inhibit other units in the next set of nerve cells along. Now, within those connections there are what are called 'local rules', that are limited to the synapses (or the equivalent of the synapse). These local rules determine what effect each synapse has on the probability of discharge of the receiving cell, and how many inputs are necessary for the cell to become activated, etc. Other local rules apply to learning, for example, the Hebb rule for plasticity, that determines how the strength of each synapse changes after each message passes through it (we will return to this idea in section 6.4). But these are all local rules, applying to what is happening in each individual synapse. Given that you may have a million nerve cells in one set transmitting information to a million cells in the next set, and each cell can contact several thousand other cells, you have thousands of millions of local rules in operation at the synapses. But at the physical level, there is no single overall rule of the type proposed in the functionalist theories for describing the relationships between symbols (like 'cat hates dog', or 'cat is different from dog', or 'cat and dog are both mammals'). These rationalistic logical rules don't exist. So this is the argument which the connectionists put forward that casts doubt on whether functionalism is correct.

Functionalists can counter-argue that the brain is not a single neural network: the brain is a collection of neural networks. Thus there is the retina, the LGN, the visual cortex, many different areas of cortex and so on. Each of these is a separate functional neural network. How these neural networks interact with one another and affect one another's overall function or performance may instantiate a completely different set of rules. All the local rules are for the elements *within* a network, a set of individual nerve cells interacting with other individual cells, but if you have a set of a million nerve cells then maybe they have some kind of emergent collective behaviour. You can treat them as carrying a pattern of activity, which is a symbol. That pattern of activity can affect the activity in another set of nerve cells in a way that is best described as implementing a rule that transforms the pattern of activity in the receiving set of nerve cells in a particular way. The rule exists as the pattern of connections between the two sets of nerve cells. So it might just be a matter of level of description: you may still have functionalism at a higher level of description than PDP, while PDP applies at the lower level of implementation. Pattern activity is a slightly higher level than nerve cells, and functional symbols and rules are a higher level still, and maybe awareness is another level above that (we will develop this idea further under 'Homuncular functionalism' in chapter 4).

2.5.2.5 Intentionality: the Chinese room argument – syntax does not determine semantics

The functionalist picture assumes representations are like sentences – not words. These sentences have units arranged in a structure. The meaning of a sentence, its 'content', is different from its structure or syntax, the 'vehicle' which carries the content (Side-box 2.2). The latter is mechanical and can be operated on by deterministic rules implemented by physical processes. This implies that intentionality or meaning is determined by the rules applied to the symbols, which entails that the (holistic) structure of the network of interacting representations determines meaning. However, at dispute is how syntactic rules can determine the meaning of a sentence/representation.

The notion in grammar is that you can put meaningful words into a slot within the functional structure of a sentence. For example, if you can say or understand 'John likes Mary', you can fathom 'John likes Helen' or 'Helen likes Mary'. You can just replace one meaningful unit with another. The syntax is exactly the same, although the sentences have different meanings since they involve different people. So the meaning of the sentence is not determined purely by the syntactic structure – you've got to know the meanings of at least some of the actual symbols themselves. Yet functionalism states that meaning is derived purely by application of syntactic rules to arbitrary (intrinsically meaningless) symbols; rules can be applied whatever the content. Thus functionalism would mean accepting Chomsky's sentence 'colourless green ideas sleep furiously' as meaningful, just because it is grammatical.

Or consider $y = x + 3$, hence $y^2 = x^2 + 6x + 9$. The syntax determines that true premises lead to true conclusions, i.e. functionalism explains how thought is rational and proceeds through chains of logical reasoning (see introduction to section 2.5, above). But functionalism does not say how the symbols themselves acquire their meanings (and their truth or falsity) in the first place. What does x represent in the above equation? It could be anything. Functionalism does not account for where the 'original' intentionality comes from.

There must be a mechanism for fixing the meaning of at least some of the basic representations, that can then slot into the higher-level representations of mentalese 'sentences'. But the mechanisms by which such fundamental, elemental meanings are assigned is not part of functionalism. (Indeed, it is not until the recent developments covered in chapter 5 that we will see how this issue is being addressed.)

To make this point, the classic thought experiment is Searle's (1980) Chinese room. Imagine that there is a room and inside there is a person, and coming in through a slot in the wall are a lot of pieces of paper with Chinese symbols written on them. The person in the room does not speak or understand Chinese, but what he or she does have is a grammar book – a big book of rules that says: when you see this symbol or set of symbols, write the following symbols on a piece of paper and push them out through the (other) slot. Searle invites us to imagine that this is the functionalist picture of how the brain works: that you receive sensory inputs which are arbitrary symbols, in the sense that they don't have any meaning for the sub-parts within the system. (A cell in the visual cortex cannot speak Chinese or even mentalese; all it knows is that some kinds of transmitters are being released onto its dendrites. It does not know that this transmitter release has been caused by looking at a dog rather than looking at a cat, or whatever.) If you just have the syntax transforming the input symbols into output symbols (i.e. motor behaviour), Searle asserts that such a room could behave in the exactly the same way as a real Chinese person would behave. People outside would not be able to tell the difference between the Chinese room and a real Chinese person – the Chinese room could simulate a Chinese person (i.e. pass Turing's test[19]). Searle then says: nothing in the Chinese room understands Chinese and therefore the functionalist picture does not explain intentionality. If you have arbitrary symbols there is no explanation of how those arbitrary symbols have the particular meanings that they do.

There has been a lot of debate about this (Searle, 1997, says more than a hundred responses have been given to his argument). Many people have taken it too literally and missed the general point. Some people say: well, maybe the person inside the room does not understand Chinese but the room plus the person plus the rule book plus the pieces of paper, i.e. the system as a whole, understands Chinese. Another answer is that when it comes to real people you don't just have arbitrary symbols as inputs: you also have interactions with the real world, e.g. you bump into things if you move about. You learn what the connections are between the (initially arbitrary) symbols, and thus infer you are interacting with real objects in a real outside world. So when you produce an output this produces non-arbitrary feedback through the environment to affect your inputs and give them meaning, and the whole fits together in some way. The Chinese room does not have this process within it as a model, and thus real people are not like Chinese rooms. Yes, Searle states, this is the point: functionalism ignores the environment by positing that the internal symbols and rules are arbitrary and thus have no intentionality.[20]

In conclusion, computational functionalism has many strong points, but also several shortcomings. Nevertheless, the idea that computation is what the brain does is well entrenched within neuroscience, following the influence of Craik (1943), Marr (1982) and many others (see Harnish, 2002, for a historical review). In the next chapter we will look at which philosophies neuroscientists actually use (if implicitly), before returning to the nature of functionalism in chapter 4.

2.6 Conclusion

The positions discussed in this chapter can be neatly summarized by relating them to their attitude to reduction (Table 2.1). Only identity theory asserts that mind will reduce to brain, because they are identical. The other theories disagree, but for different reasons.

---

19. Alan Turing (1950) asked whether a machine could be built that could fool a human being into thinking he or she was communicating with another human being instead of with a machine. The subject of this experiment would be in a room sending and receiving messages via a computer console. The test actually required the subject to decide whether the entity generating those messages in another room was male or female. Only a real human, Turing thought, could express the qualities that distinguished male from female messages, and that therefore would not be detectable at all in messages from a machine.

20. This is again the narrow content versus broad content argument (see section 2.4.3.1). The meaning of mental states depends on the environment, whereas functionalism, as Block's Chinese nation and Searle's Chinese room illustrate (sections 2.5.2.2 and 2.5.2.5), is couched purely in terms of functional relationships within the structure of the mind. This is narrow content – meaning is determined within the system without having to relate to the environment.

Table 2.1 Attitudes of four major philosophies towards the reduction of mind to brain

Theory	Reduction?	Why?	Best method[a]
Identity	Yes	They are identical	BU and TD will converge
Dualism	No	Mind is not physical	Autonomous sciences
Eliminativism	No	Psychology of mind is inaccurate	BU best
Functionalism	No	Mind is multiply realizable	TD best

a. BU = bottom-up, TD = top-down

Moreover, the methods that best suit each theoretical stance vary. For example, with functionalism, the top-down method is essential: we need to know psychology before we investigate the brain.

As we have seen, each of these theories have their pros and cons, their supporters and detractors and their strengths and weaknesses. Note how, over the years, theorizing in philosophy has advanced, just as it has in science. We will update the philosophy further in chapters 4 and 5, but in the next chapter we will look at what neuroscientists actually seem to think when they study the brain. Advances in one field always take decades to make themselves felt in other disciplines, and you may recognize some old philosophical and psychological ideas when we examine what happens currently in neuroscience. Moreover, although a few brain researchers have studied philosophy and psychology, most have not, and it is important for us to understand how neuroscientific practices are affected by the practitioners' attitudes towards the mind (and how their results in turn affect the empirical and philosophical studies of mind).

■ RECOMMENDED READING

There are many excellent introductory textbooks on the philosophy of mind. The modern source-book and inspiration is Churchland's (1988) Matter and Consciousness, which set the standard – and has been obviously influential upon my own organizational style. Among the more recent works which have been found useful by my students, the most readable are Cunningham's What is a Mind? (2000, chapter 1 and the first half of chapter 6) and Maslin's An Introduction to the Philosophy of Mind (2001, especially chapters 1–6); see also Ravenscroft's Philosophy of Mind (2005). More detailed coverage can be found in Goldberg and Pessin's Gray Matters (1997, especially chapters 2, 7), Bem and Looren de Jong's Theoretical Issues in Psychology (1997, chapter 4), and Heil's Philosophy of Mind: A Contemporary Introduction, 2nd edn. (2004a, chapters 1–9, 12–15). A very brief summary can also be found in Appendix I of Clark's (2001) Mindware.

There are also several texts that present the material in a different layout from that used here, but make many relevant points clearly, such as Brook and Stainton's Knowledge and Mind (2000, chapters 1, 4, 5), Crane's Elements of Mind (2001, sections 9, 10, 13–30, 36, 37) and Cockburn's An Introduction to the Philosophy of Mind (2001, especially chapters 5, 6).

Readers with some background in philosophy might like the following slightly more advanced introductions: Kim's **Philosophy of Mind** (1996, especially chapters 1–4, 7–9), 'The Philosophy of mind' by Davies in **Philosophy 1** (Grayling, ed., 1998, pp. 250–335), **The Philosophy of Psychology** (Botterill and Carruthers, 1999, chapters 1, 2, 9), Lowe's **An Introduction to the Philosophy of Mind** (2000, especially chapters 1–3), and **Understanding Consciousness** by Velmans (2000, chapters 1–5).

Finally, many of the classic papers in this field have been reprinted in anthologies. These also contain useful introductions and comments from the editors, which are well worth reading in their own right. The best include **Mind and Cognition**, *2nd edn* (Lycan, 1999), **Minds, Brains, and Computers** (Cummins and Cummins, 2000), **Philosophy of Mind: Classical and Contemporary Readings** (Chalmers, 2002), **Philosophy of Mind: Contemporary Readings** (O'Connor and Robb, 2003) and **Philosophy of Mind: A Guide and Anthology** (Heil, 2004b).

3 The philosophy of neuroscience

OBJECTIVES

In this chapter you will learn how important it is to know about the philosophy of science and how it applies in practice within neuroscience. All scientific fields have methods and aims that are the result of prior (philosophical) debates about the nature of knowledge and how best to obtain, recognize and test it. We will discuss the recent history of such debates and whether their conclusions are implemented in current neuroscientific research. The debate in this chapter centres on whether the methods used in neuroscience are as current as they should be and whether they can be improved in the light of recent advances in the philosophy of science. You should become aware of the fact that progress in one field often does not transfer across into neighbouring fields for decades, and also that both philosophy and scientific method are not set in tablets of stone but progress in the same way that any academic field does as new ideas are generated during the course of research. You should develop a critical eye towards scientific practice, which depends upon implicit assumptions about scientific method and the aims of the research. Disagreements in science often stem from hidden differences in such background assumptions, of which you need to be aware.

3.1 Introduction

In this chapter I will discuss the philosophical assumptions behind current neuroscience. These include the philosophies of both science and mind. I will suggest that many areas are stuck in an obsolete paradigm that really should be updated. For example, much of our theorizing attempts to explain psychology in terms of neural firing, on the assumption that the neuron is the appropriate unit of analysis and can account for all of 'higher' mental and brain function. While theories based on this 'neuron doctrine' are obviously important and must not be ignored (e.g. Barlow, 1972, 1995; Crick, 1994), I will suggest that the neural level should not be the *only* one at which we couch our explanatory theories. A warning should also be given about the insidious assumption which may follow, namely that neurons are the only *real* entity within the mind, and that psychological and phenomenological events are in some way unreal (with obvious implications for our understanding of the nature of mentality).

I will also point out that many researchers build models of brain function that are explicitly behaviourist, in that they incorporate reflex-like stimulus–response connections that account only for overt performance, while leaving out any explanation for the subjective aspects of brain activity. Hence, putting this together with the emphasis on generating explanations for behaviour at the neural level, we arrive at the term 'neuronal behaviourism' to describe this field.[1]

3.2 Scientific method

It would not be controversial to say that modern practices in neuroscience broadly follow three principles: materialism, reductionism and empiricism.[2] These presuppositions about the 'correct' way to do science are deeply imbued into the modern world-view, particularly in biology. Although there are exceptions, these broad principles describe how most scientists see themselves and their discipline as working. This is not the place to review

---

1. While 'behaviourism' means to some people the eschewal of any attempt at providing internal explanations for behaviour, the term is here taken in the more positivist context of excluding unobservables such as mental states but allowing publicly testable empirical data about nerve cells. Interestingly, the similar term 'neuro-behaviourism' has been independently coined by Panksepp (2005) to describe the same philosophy.

2. Here, 'empiricism' means the opposite of rationalism, not of nativism.

the philosophy of science *in toto* (see, for example, Chalmers, 1999), but a few words on this topic are needed to set the scene for the next two chapters.

First, 'materialism' is the assumption that everything is made of matter (see chapter 1); the main point here is that science should exclude supernatural forces – and thus substance dualism.

Next, 'reductionism' refers to the preference for broader, more all-encompassing theories that account for the widest range of data (as detailed in section 2.4 on 'theory reduction'). Such theories tend also to be those phrased at the lowest (most molecular) level of description possible (a principle known as 'Lloyd Morgan's Canon'; for more on levels, see section 4.2.3). For example, explanations couched in neuronal terms are preferred to those that postulate psychological and 'mental' entities, such as short-term memory or subjective pain. Implicit in this view is an assumption of bottom-up causation: for example, the phenomenon we call pain is caused by a certain pattern of events and structures at the neuronal level; indeed, pain is merely a side effect of those events. Only real physical events can cause other real physical events, in accordance with the laws of physics, and neurons are somehow 'real' and 'physical' whereas memory, qualia and so on are not.[3]

Finally, by 'empiricism' I mean the principle that '. . . in science, only observation and experiment may decide upon the acceptance or rejection of scientific statements, including laws and theories' (Popper, 1963, p. 54). Typically, a set of empirical data is collected, that is then generalized by induction to obtain a universal law of nature, i.e. one with unlimited applicability. Predictions as to the expected results of further empirical tests are subsequently obtained from this law by deduction (Oldroyd, 1986). In practice, however, scientists have to use additional, blatantly rationalist principles to guide their progress, although they may not admit it (Maxwell, 1984, 1985; Rose and Dobson, 1985, 1989). For example, the criterion of simplicity is commonly used to assess and compare theories. The preference for the simplest possible theory is often (mis-)attributed to Occam ('thou shalt not multiply hypotheses needlessly') and calls for adoption of the simplest of all available theories that is consistent with the evidence. Yet this tactic is not something one can prove empirically. (See also Side-box 3.1 for another widely used criterion.)

Now, these three principles (materialism, reductionism, empiricism) were core aspects of the dominant view of what science is and should be, known as 'positivism', that flourished between about fifty and a hundred years ago. Its dominance among the official institutions of science was such that it is often referred to as the 'Received View' (e.g. Bechtel, 1988b) or – in view of its mythical status – 'Legend' (Kitcher, 1993a). (See Side-box 3.2 for historical details.)

The general assumption of positivist empiricism in science tied in very well with the psychological movement of 'behaviourism', which operated upon very similar principles. Thus in behaviourism, talk of mental phenomena, particularly consciousness, was not allowed, and only publicly observable events such as behaviour were acceptable as data. Theories were seen merely as convenient summaries of the empirical data rather than descriptions of real psychological entities, and such non-observable constructs as memory,

---

3. Even philosophers assume physical level interactions have priority over the mental level in explaining causation: it seems less controversial to say that one nerve cell causes another to fire than to say that one thought causes another thought directly, although we may wish to find an explanation for how this can happen (see Kim, 1998; sections 1.6.1 and 2.1).

SIDE-BOX 3.1. CRITERIA FOR RECOGNIZING TRUTH

The two main criteria for assessing the truth of scientific theories are '*coherence*' and '*correspondence*'. The first of these is the assumption that, since the universe is self-consistent and logical, true theories will turn out to be self-consistent and logical as well. Thus we can judge a system of hypotheses in terms of how well-integrated a whole is produced; in other words, there should be no logical contradictions between the various parts of a theory. In this book I rely a great deal on this criterion.

This contrasts with the correspondence criterion, which sees true statements as those that accurately describe the real world; empiricism holds that observational data are true in this respect.

The reasons one might downplay empirical data – although of course not ignoring them – are many and controversial! They include, for instance, the unreliability of experiments and observations taken individually, and their usefulness only in historical overview: it takes decades before a consensus is reached about which data are reliable, and which were crucial proofs or disproofs of a particular theory (Lakatos, 1970).

SIDE-BOX 3.2. THE HISTORY OF POSITIVISM

The tenets of the first positivist school of empiricism that flourished in the decades around the beginning of the twentieth century were that, from publicly repeatable observations, descriptions can be induced that are general rules for summarizing the relationships between observed events; these rules are nothing but descriptions of those relationships.

A second school of positivism grew out of the first, from attempts to solve the problem within positivism as to whether mathematics has any validity. It differed from positivism mainly in its formal incorporation of theory as well as observation. The usual names for the movement are '*logical positivism*' or '*logical empiricism*', and its heyday was in the late 1920s and 1930s, particularly among a group of philosophers known as the Vienna Circle. Summaries of logical positivism are given, for example, by Churchland (1986, 2002), Oldroyd (1986), Smith (1986), Bechtel (1988b), Losee (2001) and Ladyman (2002).

Logical positivism accepted the basic tenets of the first school of positivism, that observational data are the ultimate arbiters in decisions as to what counts as knowledge, and that induction from the data leads to general laws. However, they added to this the idea that theories could be accepted as valid knowledge, provided that they were derived from observational data by sound steps of logic. Statements of theory and equations could be expressed in symbolic form and converted by formal rules into other statements. Ultimately, all such statements could be linked to 'basic' statements about observational data. The truth of these basic statements could be verified by shared experience. Thus there was a clear distinction between observation statements and theory statements, in that only the former could be verified and thus constituted certain knowledge about real states of affairs.

Statements that could not be logically linked to observations were described as meaningless. Words were defined in terms of procedures, actions and events ('operational definitions'). Theories could thus consist of elaborate hierarchies of concepts, but all had to be ultimately reducible to statements about observations.

Moreover, the laws of psychology could be reduced to biological laws, and biology to chemistry and physics; all branches of science, indeed all enquiry that was rational, obeyed the same principles of logic and formed a connected unity. The most successful scientific discipline, physics, was held up as the model that all the other disciplines should try to emulate in their methodology.

SIDE-BOX 3.3. BEHAVIOURISM IN PSYCHOLOGY

There were two main phases of behaviourism (see, for example, Baars, 1986, Leahey, 2000, and Brennan, 2003, for historical reviews). The first was the original movement led by Watson from 1913 to 1920. The methodological proposals of this programme included the eschewal of postulates about unobservable entities (such as purely mental processes) and the adherence to the mere description of publicly observable events. Thinking was regarded as sub-vocal speech, and consciousness as 'merely another word for the "soul" ' (Watson, 1925, p.1).

The neobehaviourist school flourished in the 1930s and 1940s. These workers realized that there was a need for theory in addition to observations, but would only accept theories that were closely linked to observable phenomena. They used operational definitions of their terms, and Hull (1943) in particular attempted to develop formal mathematical laws to describe the relationships between the concepts in his theory and the behaviour he observed in his experimental animals.[a]

There was thus a close similarity between the approach of the neobehaviourists and their contemporary philosophers in the 'logical positivist' school (Side-box 3.2). There was indeed some cross-fertilization of ideas here, but the conclusion that Smith (1986) reached from a detailed study is that the general principles of neobehaviourism developed largely in parallel with those of logical positivism. Both movements grew out of the general background of positivism that had been extant in physics and biology earlier in the twentieth century. It was only after their initial positions had been adopted that each school discovered and became interested in the other.

[a] Later, Skinner's behaviourism returned to the pure positivism of Watson, in which theoretical terms were not accepted at all (e.g. Skinner, 1987).

---

perception, reward and so on had to be defined 'operationally', in terms of the empirical events that corresponded to them (see Side-box 3.3 for details).

It is nowadays a common thesis that these empiricist principles are the central tenets of neuroscience research; they describe and determine how it works (Bickle, 1998, 2003a,b) or should work (Bennett and Hacker, 2003).[4]

3.3 What neuroscientists do

I will not present fully detailed case studies here, but will just briefly mention some examples to give the flavour of what I am referring to. Some detailed accounts of how neuroscientists think and work in this way have been given by Bennett and Hacker (2003) and Bickle (2003a,b).[5]

4. Bennett and Hacker (2003) complain that neuroscientists are not positivist enough – or at least that they do not apply positivism consistently. I think it still valid to say, however, that many are trying to use this philosophy, even if implicitly.

5. Neuroscientific practices have also been described from other points of view: by sociologists such as Latour and Woolgar (1979), Lynch (1985) and Star (1989), by neuroscientist Jacobson (1993) and by philosophers Bechtel and Richardson (1993).

3.3.1 **Meaning**

First is the reduction of representation and intentionality to the level of individual neurons. Thus the representation of objects by the sensory systems has been postulated to be realized by firing in individual cells (section 6.2.6.1) or small groups (section 3.3.2). Meaning is reduced to neural coding (section 5.3.8) – especially to 'labelled lines' (for reviews see Harris and Jenkin, 1997; Rose, 1999a); and empathy to the firing of 'mirror neurons' (section 6.2.2.1; Gallese et al., 2004; Keysers and Perrett, 2004). Neurons 'make decisions' (Cohen and Blum, 2002; Hernández et al., 2002; Shadlen and Gold, 2004) and dopamine release means 'novelty' (Gray et al., 1997) or 'error in the prediction of reward' (Cohen and Blum, 2002). Perception is reduced to stimulus–stimulus associations (Barlow, 1985; Singer, 1985; Toet et al., 1987) or stimulus–response associations (e.g. Cotterill, 1998; section 8.4).

3.3.2 **Learning**

Consider next work on the neural basis of learning. The dominant theory in this area is that of Hebb (1949; see section 6.4.1): representations consist of collections of cells firing in assemblies, thinking involves the successive activation of cell assemblies that have become linked to one another, and cell assemblies (and their interconnections) form when synapses increase their strength under situations of associative conditioning. This entire view is founded upon the behaviourist view of the brain as a collection of associations and the early twentieth-century telephone switchboard as the metaphor for the brain. Modern improvements to this theory take into account the massive parallelism of the brain by postulating neural networks as the relevant level of analysis, in which the information is encoded in the pattern of activity across many nerve fibres and memory is stored in a pattern across many synapses, rather than along simple reflex-like pathways (see section 6.4.3). However, these models nevertheless still function as nothing more than telephone switchboards (even if they are digital switchboards!) – they represent a return to the associationist approach (Pinker and Mehler, 1988). Particularly, the theory of tensor networks (Pellionisz and Llinás, 1979) sees the brain as nothing more than a hierarchy of reflexes. Claims that memory has been reduced to long-term potentiation (i.e. enhanced transmission through Hebb synapses) are common (for example, Bickle, 2003a,b; Side-box 3.4) and also assume associationism and reductionism.

3.3.3 **Psycho/neuropathology**

In addition, it is common (though perhaps more so among non-clinicians) to see neuroscience as reducing mental diseases to abnormalities of neurotransmission (and/or genes): schizophrenia is just excess D_2 receptor concentration, depression is low 5-HT, and so on. Similarly for the interpretation of brain damage: hemineglect follows right parietal lesions, therefore people conclude that paying attention is just the right parietal lobe functioning properly; blindsight studies are taken to show that V1 generates visual awareness; and so on (for criticisms see Uttal, 2001, and section 4.3.6). Finally, synaesthesia is explained as being caused by mis-wired connections between brain areas (Ramachandran, 2003a; Gray, 2004), and Capgras syndrome by disconnection of the amygdala (Ramachandran, 2003a; Side-box 11.1).

SIDE-BOX 3.4. THE REDUCTION OF LEARNING?

A common claim one hears among neuroscientists is that learning and memory have been 'explained' as being long-term potentiation at synapses. This assertion has been analysed in impressive detail by the philosopher Bickle (2003a, b), who supports the conclusion and characterizes it as a reduction in which the higher-level terms have been eliminated. He also concludes that representational content is narrow in that it is determined entirely by processes within the head (see sections 2.4.3.1 and 5.3.4), and says that people who think otherwise do not understand evolution (2003a, pp. 332–333)! High-level theories act as useful frameworks to guide neuroscientific research but should be dispensed with once the empirical facts are known. People who continue to assume the ontological reality of those high-level concepts are labelled pejoratively as 'dualists' (Bickle assumes emergent properties are only of the unpredictable variety; see section 2.2.2.1) and as 'consciophiles' – as if we should not believe consciousness exists!

Bickle seems to think that just because there are some changes in neural firing or synaptic strength under certain circumstances, this is *all* that happens in reality, and describing those changes is not just necessary but also sufficient for a complete ontological account. He is also unclear as to whether the neuronal or the molecular is the level to which reduction should[a] aspire, since neuroscientific accounts of 'learning' have been put forward at both levels. Moreover, there are alternative non-associative paradigms for memory (as reorganization and restructuring) that Bickle does not consider; see, for example, Mandler (2002).

While his motivation to counter the 'mysterian' school (who deny the possibility of any explanation of consciousness; sections 2.2.2.1 and 2.4.3) is laudable, Bickle simply goes to the opposite extreme. He dismisses (computational) functionalism on the grounds that multiple realizability has not been proved (e.g. 2003b, pp. 131–136), and in his attack on externalism (e.g. 2003b, pp. 206–212) he ignores the diachronic explanation put forward by teleological functionalism (chapter 5).

In conclusion, claims that neuroscience has reduced learning[b] simply to synaptic strengthening seem rather premature at this time.

---

[a] To be fair, he claims he is merely describing what neuroscientists think, and is not being prescriptive himself as to what they should think. I would not be so trusting of others to get things right, however!
[b] The reduction actually applies only to memory consolidation, just one component of the memory/learning system.

3.3.4 Interim summary

In general, explanatory models are reduced to their simplest conceivable components. The rule seems to be: if a schematic diagram of a psychological mechanism can be drawn, for example in the form of black boxes with connections between them, these should simply be replaced with neurons and axons respectively. This gives a minimalistic neural circuit which (at least superficially[6]) appears capable of performing the same task as the original, symbolically represented, cognitive mechanism. In each such case, the neural explanation is then interpreted as having replaced (and hence eliminated) the psychological concept

---

6. Quantitative verification of the functionality can later be carried out with neural network simulations. Note, however, that these always assume certain properties are built into the neurons and axons involved, and the networks are not always very biological (section 6.4.3).

SIDE-BOX 3.5. REDUCTION OR METAPHOR?

It is often unclear how literally neuroscientists take reduction. One issue is the use of metaphors. A claim to have shown that neural firing enhancement is the basis of attention (Side-box 8.6), or that long-term potentiation is memory (both examples given by Bickle, 2003a), or that we have internal scanners that perceive our internal states (Crick, 1984; Blakemore, 1990; Baars, 1997; see also section 11.2.2.3) is to claim reduction of a metaphorically described entity to the neural level. For to use words such as 'attention', 'memory' or 'perception' to describe the function of part of the brain is to use such terms as metaphors.[a]

Now, metaphors have a long and useful history in brain research (Stevens, 1971; Daugman, 1990), cognition and consciousness (Barnden, 1997; Watt, 1997; Farber, 2005), but their application to neuroscience has recently been challenged by Bennett and Hacker (2003). These authors take a hardline positivist stance, in which there should be a clear separation between 'matters of fact' (and 'explanatory theories' about them) that can be tested empirically, and 'conceptual questions', such as the nature of (and relationships between) mind, memory, consciousness or thought, that can only be analysed logically by philosophers (2003, p. 1). They abjure and abhor any sub-personal use of words normally applied to whole persons. Their reasoning is Wittgensteinian in that these words cannot be defined at those levels, only in terms of the behaviour of a whole person (via ostensive definition: p. 97). They give accounts of how scientists such as Blakemore (1990) use and defend metaphorical descriptions of the function of various parts of the brain. Bennett and Hacker claim that this is inappropriate, first in that the words are undefined and so lack sense, and second because neuroscientists typically forget their own aim to use the words metaphorically and instead start to think that brain parts indeed literally perceive, think, remember and so on.

From the point of view of Bickle's (1998, 2003a, b) analysis of neuroscientists as commonly using reductive or eliminative theory, this would mean not just that sub-personal functions such as that of the parietal lobe or hippocampus come to be regarded as either identical to, or eliminated in favour of, descriptions of neural firing, but also that the whole person's abilities in seeing, remembering, making decisions and so on are so reduced to the neural level too (cf. Figure 3.2b on page 73: reducing the square to the circles – via or skipping over the triangles – is like reducing (whole person) learning – via or skipping over the computational/physiological functions of the hippocampus – directly to long-term potentiation of Hebb synapses).

Bennett and Hacker (2003, p. 77) also challenge the use of words such as 'symbols', 'representation' and 'meaning' at the intra-cranial level. They argue that all internal events are 'natural signs' or indicators rather than semantic symbols. This is not the place to discuss this important issue, but note that opposite views will be presented in section 5.2.5.

This is also not the place to discuss Quine and Wittgenstein's disagreement over semantic holism versus atomism; Bennett and Hacker support the latter, but it is true to say that the majority of philosophers do not. It is an a priori metaphysical presupposition whether you believe in the reality of sub-personal functions that can be metaphorically described in psychological terms, or whether you wish to reduce everything to language games. In this book I will be taking the former position, for reasons to be elaborated in chapters 4 and 5. Just as Fodor (1975) was able to propose a 'language of thought,' provided we remember it is an impoverished type of language compared to English or French (section 2.5), so we can talk about the interactions between brain areas in terms of communication, messages, talking, monitoring, believing, deciding and so on, providing we remember these are impoverished functions compared to their referents at the inter-personal level. The various parts of the brain can

continues

SIDE-BOX 3.5 continued

safely be treated as semi-intelligent homunculi, each with restricted knowledge, ability and awareness, and this applies at many levels (chapter 4).

Consider the opposite: if we cannot use metaphors, how should we describe events at these levels? (Indeed, the linguists Lakoff and Johnson, 1980, said that all concepts, including thoughts and linguistic terms, are metaphorical! Meaning is given by conceptual structure.) Within any brain area there are too many neurons doing too many clever things for descriptions at the single neuron level alone to suffice for summarizing an area's function (section 3.5.5).

[a] Essay topic: Is the statement 'consciousness is nerve cells firing' a reduction or a metaphor?

and its underlying functions and algorithms (Side-box 3.5). Presumably, the assumption is that the neural circuit by itself comprises a *complete* explanation.

In some cases, the function of a whole cognitive mechanism may even be compressed into a single component such as a nerve cell, or a small assembly of them. Although sometimes this process may create a correct model, Gregory (1985) warns that often it proves to be a *premature reduction* of the characteristics of the whole system to its parts. If accepted, such a move then leads to the myth that those parts have seemingly magical high-level powers of their own.

3.4 In support of the current approach

3.4.1 It works

Neuroscience is obviously an expanding and successful research endeavour. It generates neural explanations for an increasingly wide range of phenomena, relates these to the empirical evidence and predicts the results of new experiments designed to test the hypotheses severely and in detail. It drives advances in medical and pharmaceutical treatments such as drug intervention and rehabilitation, and is solving (or dissolving) the mind–body problem bit by bit. There are many instances of such successes, such as the ability to create particular phenomenal experiences by microstimulation of small groups of cells (Salzman et al., 1992) or the treatment of 'mental' diseases by the alteration of neurotransmitter action at specific receptor protein sites by the administration of deliberately designed drugs (e.g. Rang et al., 2003; Smith, 2005) or by genetic engineering. Theories generated by using the current philosophical/scientific method thus have explanatory, heuristic and pragmatic power.

3.4.2 Simplicity is a successful heuristic

This is demonstrably true in science generally, and it should therefore be promoted, both by seeking intertheoretic reduction and by applying Occam's razor in the making of choices between theories. Simple theories have the benefits of being more concise summaries of the data, being more easily communicated to other scientists and the general public, and reducing the redundancy of theoretical terms and concepts.

There is also an ontological assumption behind simplicity, namely that a theory should mirror reality and the world is in fact built upon simple physical principles.[7] The brain's functions have to be carried out somewhere within it, and if a simple circuit will do the job, why elaborate unnecessarily? In many experiments a stimulus arrives and a short time later a response is emitted; it is a common situation both in the laboratory and in natural environments. We know much about what nerve cells can do, and if a relevant chain of processing can be traced at the neuroanatomical level – and can be simulated by a set of model neurons to mimic and predict the system's behaviour with quantitative accuracy – then we have good reason to assume we have a complete explanation of how the stimulus and response are functionally connected to one another within the brain.

3.4.3 Methodological reduction is the only way to go

Faced with an incomprehensibly complex system such as the brain, the only way we can make progress is to break the problem into smaller ones and try to solve each of these separately (section 2.2.2.1). If any such problem is still intractable, we must break it down again and again until we have a system that is analysable successfully using the methods we have available to us (i.e. empirical methods). Once we understand how the various small parts work, we are able to see how they fit together to make the more complex system that we started with function the way that it does.

3.5 Problems with the current approach

3.5.1 Empiricism is an imperfect description of science

In response to the argument in section 3.4.1, the fact neuroscience works *does not mean it works as well as it might* (Maxwell, 1985). Nor does it mean the philosophy of empiricism *accurately* describes what goes on; for example scientists also use rationalist methods in their work (see Side-box 3.6 for details). Empiricism is an obsolete, irrational, unreliable and misleading philosophy, for reasons that should be familiar to all philosophers, and to scientists too.

3.5.2 Behaviourism is an obsolete paradigm

The reasons are familiar to all psychologists; for historical reviews see Baars (1986), Smith (1986) or Leahey (2000). Psychology abandoned behaviourism because it failed to account

---

7. Some have argued that the universe is constructed according to a few basic principles, whether created by God or generated in a Big Bang. Others have argued that natural selection would have ironed out through evolutionary history any unnecessarily complicated organisms, since these would be likely to contain conflicting, redundant, energy-expensive, genetically demanding or informationally noisy mechanisms, and hence have been less efficient than simpler organisms. For reviews, see Dobson and Rose (1985) and Rose and Dobson (1985).

SIDE-BOX 3.6. PROBLEMS WITH LOGICAL POSITIVISM

The reasons for the rejection of logical positivism by philosophers are summarized by, for example, Maxwell (1984, pp. 205–218), the Churchlands (1986, pp. 259–271; 1988; 2002, pp. 262–269), Bechtel (1988b), Losee (2001) and Ladyman (2002). Briefly, here are ten arguments:

1. The method of induction cannot generate certain knowledge. Patterns of data are frequently found that turn out not to generalize beyond their immediate domain. Moreover, this sequence of events repeats itself again and again. Therefore, by induction, the method of induction is false. The method is thus self-contradictory (Hume, 1739).[a]

2. Science does not proceed from randomly made observations to theory. How do scientists decide which data to collect? In practice, theory tells us which observations to make. Further, theory specifies which data are relevant to the theory and which are epiphenomenal. Theory comes first.

3. Empiricism tells us nothing about how theories and ideas are generated. It restricts itself to the testing process, and leaves the creativity of scientific hypothesizing as a mystery whose explanation is outside science.

4. The dichotomy between empirical facts and conceptual theories is unsustainable. There is no clear division, and each is defined in terms of the other. Words are defined in terms of one another, forming a holistic semantic net (section 1.3). Therefore, neither the words we use to describe observations nor those we use to define concepts express independent atoms of truth.[b] All observations are theory-laden and statements about theoretical states of affairs are not necessarily clearly either significant or meaningless (Quine, 1951; Hanson, 1958). Although Quine's critique applied to the semantics of theory-terms, consider also the methods used to collect data. For example, data on the memorization of three-letter 'nonsense' trigrams only make sense within an associative theory of learning, and the false alarm rates measured in a psychophysical task only mean something under signal detection theory. Even hardware tools such as electron microscopes, fMRI scanners and SSRI drugs rely upon complex theories as to how the physical world works (with respect to how the apparatus functions, what the properties of the object of study are and how the apparatus and object interact). Instruments are often designed and built following a prediction from theory that there is something there that the instrument will be able to measure and manipulate (Hacking, 1983).

5. Any given hypothesis is supported by almost any datum. For instance, the idea that 'all schizophrenics have excess DA receptors' has as corollary that everyone with normal or deficient DA receptors is not schizophrenic. Therefore, finding anybody who is normal in all respects 'confirms' or 'verifies' the hypothesis. Such an observation is also 'consistent' with and therefore 'supports' all the more complex theories that include the original hypothesis, such as: 'all schizophrenics have excess DA receptors and the moon is made of green cheese'. Finally, hypotheses such as 'schizophrenia is always caused by excess DA receptors' and 'schizophrenia is currently caused by excess DA receptors, but after the year AD 2378 it will be caused by excess 5-HT receptors instead' are equally supported by observing a schizophrenic with excess DA receptors today.

6. Defining something (such as schizophrenia) by listing relevant examples of observable behaviours generates, in many cases, indefinitely long lists. In addition, one needs to list all the negative examples (e.g. behaviour that is not characteristic of schizophrenia) and also all the *ceteris paribus* clauses (specifying the conditions that must be absent for the behaviours to manifest themselves, such as the person not being asleep, drugged and so on). This all leads to infinitely long definitions (see section 2.3.3.2).

continues

SIDE-BOX 3.6 continued

7. Theories are too complex and flexible to test empirically (the 'Duhem–Quine thesis'). Any observation that is problematic for a theory can be explained by adding an ad hoc subsidiary hypothesis to the theory to account for the deviation of the new data from prediction. Theories rapidly turn into complex structures, with many interlocking hypotheses. Moreover, many are built upon metaphysical presuppositions that are irrefutable and untestable empirically (Lakatos, 1970), such as whether the mind is dualistic or monistic, complex or simple, or whether our aim is to account only for behaviour or for phenomenology.

8. In practice, scientists actually use non-empirical criteria for comparing theories, such as their elegance, simplicity and so on (Maxwell, 1984). They have to assess which is the more logically consistent, both within its own structure as well as with the available data (Kuhn, 1962).

9. Theories are often 'incommensurable', that is to say, they cannot be compared using a common yardstick to assess their relative merits. This is because each has different aims, experimental methods and metaphysical presuppositions (Kuhn, 1962; Feyerabend, 1970). Empirical testing will therefore never convince opponents which theory is 'right', or even better than another.

10. Social and psychological factors affect science. The social and political context within which scientists work affects their attitudes and opinions – not just towards their colleagues but also towards theories and data, and in ways that are no different from those at work in any other aspect of life (Bloor, 1976; Latour and Woolgar, 1979; Lynch, 1985; Star, 1989; Jacobson, 1993; Shadish and Fuller, 1994). This has been established by observation of scientists, so if you believe in empiricism you must believe that empirical data do not determine – at least not exclusively – which theories are accepted as correct. As a description of how science works, empiricism is thus logically inconsistent.

Of course, the above arguments do not deny the importance of empirical methods and data. What is at stake here is the philosophy of 'empiricism', which attributes to observations a particular role within science. Other philosophies of science exist, however, that respect experimental and observational data but use them in a more sophisticated way (e.g. Chalmers, 1999).

[a] One proposed solution is falsificationism, which suggests we can disprove theories unequivocally, i.e. we can be certain about which ideas are wrong (Popper, 1934). However, this still relies on empirical observations to establish the facts. Given the unreliability of individual observations, the method still leaves the unresolvable question of how many repeated disconfirmations of a theory it takes to establish a conclusive disproof. (It also falls foul of problem 7.)
[b] Facts (if such things exist) are states of the world, not Wittgensteinian human language games.

for the constructive nature of memory (Bartlett, 1932; Neisser, 1967), Gestalt completion phenomena in learning and perception (Köhler, 1940; Gregory, 1970), memory organization and meaning (see Mandler, 2002), the generativity of language and imagination (Chomsky, 1957, 1959; see also sections 2.5.1.3, 5.3.4 and 6.4.3.1) and the ability to plan for the future and choose alternative actions (Craik, 1943; MacKay, 1956; Miller et al., 1960) – not to mention the phenomenology of experience in general. Philosophy abandoned its version of behaviourism for reasons which include those given in sections 2.3.3 and 2.5.1.

3.5.3 We need to know why as well as how

Empirical science was originally designed to uncover the universal laws of nature that underlie the physical universe. Biological systems, however, were not designed according to universal laws; they evolved through millions of years of changing environments, chance events and dynamic 'arms races' against multiple interacting competitors (e.g. Gould, 1980; Dawkins, 1982; Dennett, 1995). Applied to biological organisms, empiricism may be of use to elucidate the *mechanisms* by which particular systems work: the parts of which they are made and their dynamic interactions. However, it does not shed any light on the *functions* of these systems and the reasons for their being the way that they are. In other words, empiricism addresses the question of 'how' things work but not that of 'why' they work – why they exist in the first place. Both questions must be answered in the biological, psychological and social sciences, including neuroscience (Breakwell and Rose, 2000; Craver, 2001; section 4.2.4). See Bechtel and Richardson (1993), Machamer et al. (2001) and chapters 4 and 5 of this book for more on how a non-reductive neuroscience is needed to answer both questions.

3.5.4 Specialism

Against the ideas in section 3.4.3 is the argument that methodological reductionism leads to 'specialism', that is to say, to the progressive fragmentation of scientific disciplines, each of which studies some small phenomenon in detail (Staats, 1983; Maxwell, 1984; Midgley, 1989). When the analysis fails there is a division into yet finer sub-disciplines studying different aspects of the problem. Scientists thus seem to be always seeking answers at lower and lower levels of description: to understand the mind they may first study psychology; then to understand the mechanisms they discover at that level they examine brain scans or EEGs, then single neuron firing; then to understand how neurons work they may look at transmitters, intracellular biochemistry, genetics . . . and even quantum physics (Rose, 1987; Cahill et al., 2001). Eventually they may find or construct 'facts' which they regard as nuggets of truth, but these are isolated (semantic atoms) and cannot be related to findings in other fields or to the big picture of how the overall system works.[8]

3.5.5 Oversimplicity

Contra the argument in section 3.4.2, neuronal behaviourism presents too simple a picture. Although simplicity is a valid (if rationalist) criterion for assessing theories, the brain itself is complicated. A 'correct' theory will therefore be correspondingly complicated.

Overly simple neuronal behaviourist theories, however, abound within neuroscience. For example, Cahill et al. (2001) point to the common mistake of interpreting the phenomenon of learning a new stimulus–response pairing as the acquisition of a single association (section 3.3.2). Even the simplest conditioning task is actually complex and always involves many associations. It is also too simple to explain conditioning in terms of any unitary mechanism such as 'reward', the activation of a genetic 'consolidation switch' or the strengthening of Hebb synapses. Even spinal reflexes are actually complicated. (For instance, Figure 3.1 shows part of the circuitry underlying a simple eye-blink reflex; it is not just a monosynaptic arc!) Analogously, Pribram (2003) points out that regarding direct cortico-cortical connections as mediating synaesthesia (Ramachandran, 2003a; Gray,

---

8. Bickle (2003a, pp. 346–347) also describes evidence that neuroscientific sub-disciplines work in isolation and hold outdated ideas about what is happening in neighbouring fields.

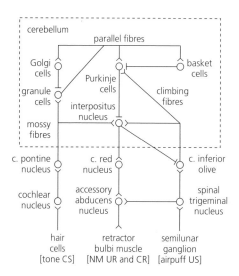

Figure 3.1 Anatomical circuitry underlying the blink reflex to a puff of air into the eye in the rabbit. From Bartha and Thompson (1995).

2004; section 3.3.3) is a return to a simplistic hundred-year-old theory of 'association cortex' and the philosophy of logical positivism.

In perception, most neuronal models have assumed vision to be an almost reflex-like, automatic, serial analysis of the input, rather than synthesis with memory. This process was supposed to convert an input into an invariant output that represents one aspect of the scene such as an object (Young, 2000).[9] Yet in vision, hearing and touch, as deCharms and Zador (2000) point out, even the simplest stimulus activates over a hundred thousand neurons in primary sensory cortex, with an intricate spatio-temporal pattern of excitation and inhibition (while Freeman, 2000, p. 13, gives ten million as a more typical number). At threshold there may be fewer cells involved (Krauskopf, 1978; Watson and Robson, 1981), but the identity of the stimulus is actually encoded by comparing the firing of different cells: meaning comes from the 'frame of reference' (Harris and Jenkin, 1997; Mandler, 2002; see also section 6.4.3.3, critique).

Most critical for the simplification paradigm, minimally sufficient or merely adequate models only account for the limited range of functions and behaviours designated as explananda within the methodologically reduced situations that have been selected for study. The most obvious explanation omitted is of the phenomenology accompanying the operation of the modelled system. If additional circuitry is needed to explain what it feels like to experience 'reward' or to see the colour red, then the model cannot be claimed to be complete. If, on the other hand, the model is put forward as a complete account, then there has to be some philosophical justification for asserting the model generates consciousness as well as behaviour – even if it is only by fiat (they are type-identical, for example, or dual aspects of the same thing). Neuronal behaviourism, however, does not even consider the need for such an explanation, instead merely ignoring the phenomenal aspects of brain function.

9. Since the turn of the millennium there has been a shift of consensus away from such simple bottom-up processing models, however, as explained in Side-box 7.6. See also chapters 8–10 for more integrative models.

In all these cases, then, what happens in the brain is actually more complicated than neuronal behaviourist research would lead us to believe.

3.5.5.1 On complexity

Do not be put off, however, by thinking that if theories are not simple they must be incomprehensibly complicated. There is a structure to the brain that allows us to break the problem into parts and to get a grasp on each section at a time. For one thing, there are many levels of description within the account we must give, and we can arrange our conceptual models accordingly.

To demonstrate the complexity of the brain, and to get us started on the scope of what we have to cover in the rest of the book, I would like to conduct an exercise of the imagination (or what Dennett, 1988, would call an 'intuition pump'). First, revise the concept of an emergent property, that is, the fact that a group of interacting entities can form a 'system', and this may have properties not possessed by any of its parts in isolation (see section 2.2.2.1 for the basics; a fuller account will be given in chapter 4). For example, Figure 3.2a shows two nerve cells connected to form a loop. This circuit possesses the ability to resonate, which does not exist unless the cells are connected together in this way. Resonance is thus a new property of the system formed by the two cells.[10] Figure 3.2b gives a more schematic exercise on emergence.

Starting at a fine scale, consider now Figure 3.3, which shows an electron micrograph of a synapse. See how much structure there is within it. Imagine what must be going on in there: vesicles, mitochondria, membranes, microtubules, all interacting dynamically to give the synapse its overall function.

Next, Figure 3.4 shows some whole nerve cells and axonal arborizations. Zoom your imagination in on one of the many dendritic spines and synaptic boutons, which show as small dots here. Remember each forms one side of a synapse that contains all the machinery visible in Figure 3.3. Now expand your focus of attention to embrace a whole cell. Notice that the 'thousands' of synapses are part of a structure that has its own level of complexity. Imagine the signals flowing around this structure, the electric fields generated and the changes in chemical and ionic composition of the media which compose it.

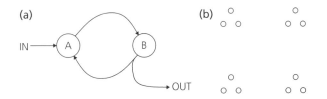

Figure 3.2 a. The simplest system: two interacting units. **b.** Three circles form a triangle, and four triangles form a square. Question 1: Do the circles form a square? Question 2: The circles are 'real' but are the triangles and the square 'real'? Question 3: (i) Can the square be (ontologically) reduced to the triangles and each triangle to three circles? (ii) Can the square be reduced to the circles? Are (i) and (ii) both possible (hint: see section 4.3.3)?

10. Other typical functions able to emerge predictably from neural circuits include gain control, low and high pass filtering, noise reduction, logic gating and so on (e.g. McCulloch and Pitts, 1943; Koch, 1998).

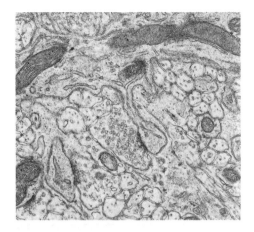

Figure 3.3 Electron micrograph. In the centre is a typical synaptic bouton (with about 80 vesicles visible) synapsing with a dendritic spine, which descends from the dendrite crossing the upper part of the figure horizontally. Two smaller synapses are visible in the lower left quadrant. Tissue from rat cerebellar cortex. The overall width of the figure is 3.26 μm. From Nauta and Feirtag (1986, p. 7).

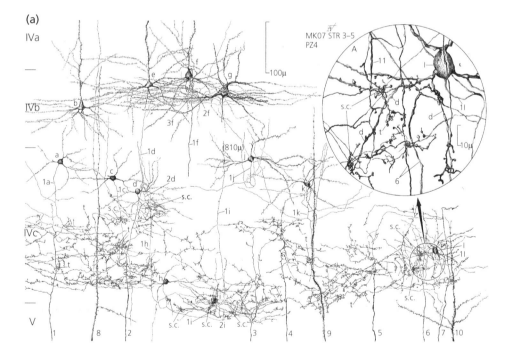

Figure 3.4a Camera lucida drawings of the middle layers of Golgi stained cortex (monkey area V1). Scales are included in each part of the figure. Fibres 1–7 are LGN afferent axons and 8–10 are apical dendrites of layer V pyramidal cells. Note the zoomed section on the right. From Valverde (1971).

(b)

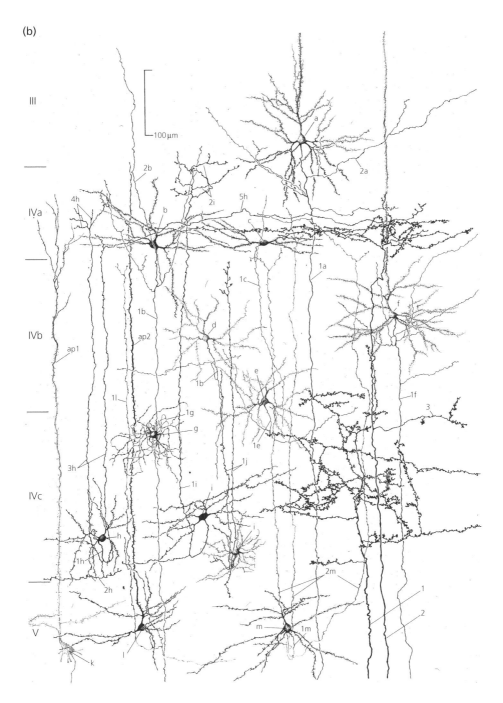

Figure 3.4b Axons 1 and 2 are LGN afferents. From Fairén and Valverde (1979).

Figures 3.4 and 3.5 give a hint at the local circuitry formed by the thousands of neurons which interact over distances of a fraction of a millimetre. Note first the variety of cell shapes and sizes (and remember too that there are many neurotransmitters involved at different synapses). What properties emerge from the fact that the cells are arranged in this fashion?[11]

Finally, Figure 3.6 (which will be discussed again as Figures 8.3 and 8.13) shows some diagrams of the circuitry joining whole areas and nuclei of the brain. As in the previous examples, zoom your focus of attention between micro and macro scales. Again, it takes the whole of one's imagination to grasp the changes in functional properties that might arise with each such change of scale.

Recall Figure 3.2a, which shows two nerve cells connected to form a loop. This loop possesses the property of resonance, which is not possessed by either cell alone. Such resonance can function as memory (persistence), selectivity (tuning to input at the resonant frequency) or as a rhythm generator or clock (giving regular output pulses) – which of these functions the loop performs depends on the neighbouring systems with which it interacts. If a system this simple can generate novel, interesting and functionally useful emergent properties, what can those illustrated in Figures 3.1 and 3.3–3.6 do?

How many such levels of emergence are there between matter and mind? Well, it depends where one starts (quanta, atoms, molecules, synapses, neurons . . .) and finishes

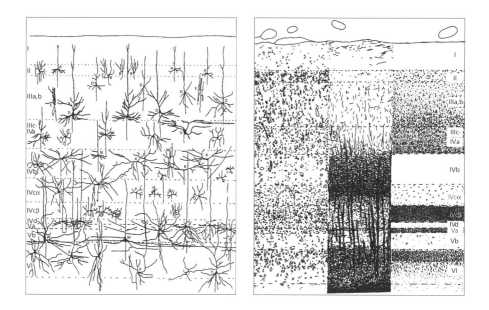

Figure 3.5a Cell and fibre distributions through the whole depth ($\approx$ 2 mm) of the human cortex (area V1). From Braak (1976).

---

11. For reasons given in section 5.3.2, we should rather ask: what properties must be brought into being that necessitate the circuits be arranged the way they are?

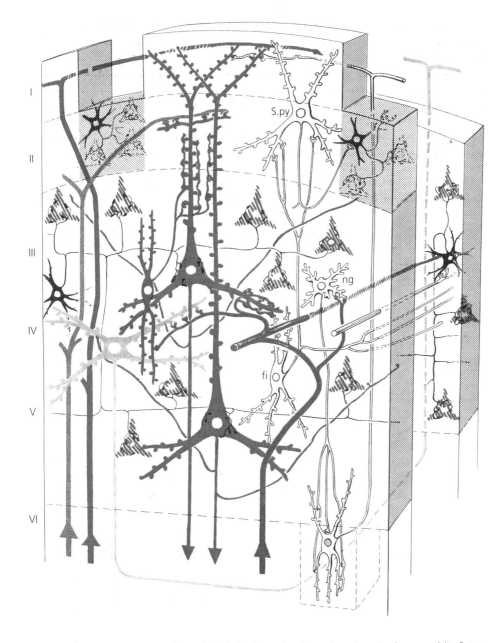

Figure 3.5b Graphic depiction of a cortical mini-column showing rudimentary circuit connectivity. From Szentágothai (1973).

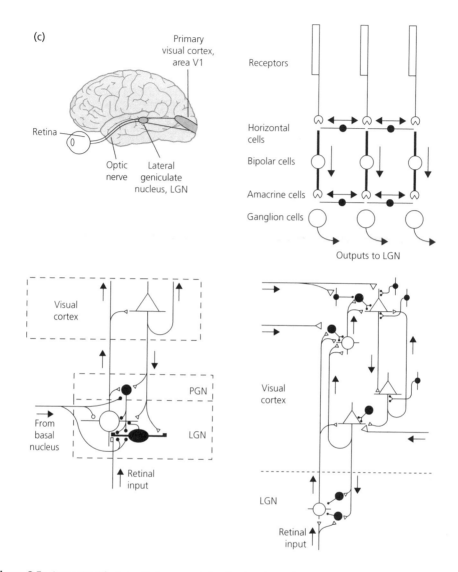

Figure 3.5c Some simplified circuit diagrams of the visual pathway from retina to V1. From Sillito (1995, p. 296).

(local circuits, areas, dynamic state transitions, whole brain networks, embeddedness in the environment . . .). And correspondingly in mental terms (sending messages, information coding, symbol transformation, belief fixation, representation of the environment . . .): there could be at least a dozen such levels in both realms. One question our research programme must solve is how many steps bridge the intermediate zone between mind and brain. This theme will be taken up again in section 4.2.

The point is that any given activity in the brain takes place at many levels simultaneously: as synapses are releasing transmitters, so the circuits they are part of are performing a calculation and you are perceiving your grandmother. A full explanation requires all levels to be described: the neuronal level is not the only relevant level.

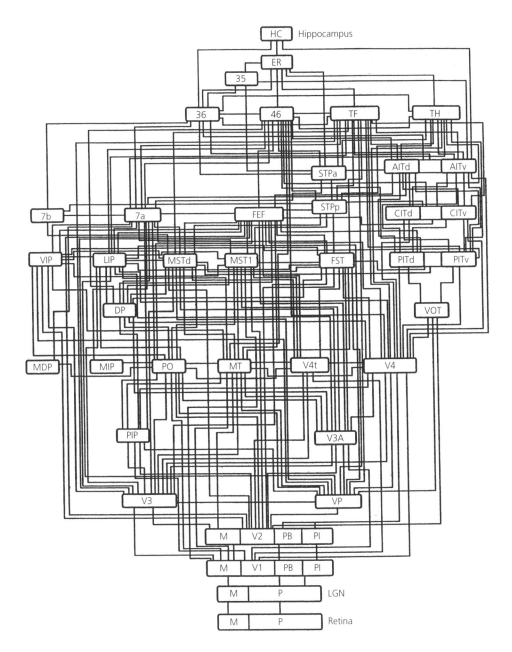

Figure 3.6a The visual cortex of the macaque monkey. The retina (RGC) and LGN (at bottom) feed up into 11 successive layers of cortical areas (rectangles), with the hippocampus (HC) at the top. About 40% of the entire cerebral cortex is involved. Two-thirds of the connections shown are reciprocal (i.e. information passes in both directions). From Felleman and Van Essen (1991).

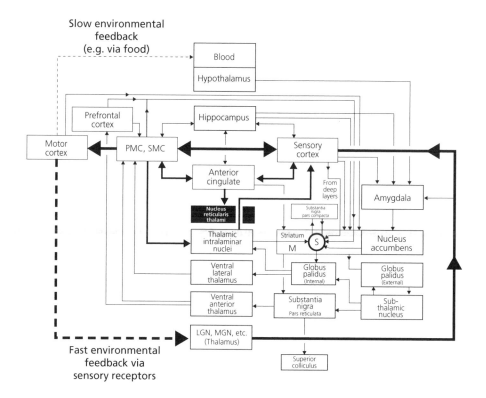

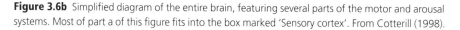

Figure 3.6b Simplified diagram of the entire brain, featuring several parts of the motor and arousal systems. Most of part a of this figure fits into the box marked 'Sensory cortex'. From Cotterill (1998).

3.6 Implications of the current approach for philosophy of mind

Now, as translated into philosophy of mind terminology and applied back to neuroscience, the extant principles of neuronal behaviourism dictate that neuroscientists do not base their work on dualism, but preferably use identity theory or possibly eliminativism (Bickle, 1998). Occasionally computational functionalism rears its head (e.g. following Marr, 1982) but tends to be treated as behaviourism with internal states (cf. Side-box 3.7) – though it is ignored by anyone who has not studied psychology, philosophy, linguistics, cybernetics or engineering, and mathematics.

However, the complexity of the brain, as emphasized in this chapter, demonstrates that under any of these two-level approaches the mind–body problem is not going to be solved – just as suggested by the mysterian group (hence their 'explanatory gap': sections 2.2.2.1, 2.4.3.1 and 2.4.3.3). But the argument I have presented does not establish this gap is unbridgeable. Indeed it suggests just the opposite. There are more than two levels, and understanding the relationship between each is a problem – but it is a mini-problem in comparison to the whole. And solving a series of mini-problems is easier than solving one big 'hard' problem.

SIDE-BOX 3.7. FUNCTIONALISM VERSUS REDUCTIONISM ACCORDING TO GRAY

The neuroscientist Gray (2004, chapter 10) has rejected functionalism in preference for more reductive neural explanations on the basis of his studies of synaesthesia (e.g. seeing colours when you hear or read words). First, he defines a function as an input–output connection, mediated via some kind of intermediate processing (p. 132); this is akin to computational functionalism as described in section 2.5. However, he then seems to assume that this applies to the whole organism, and thus he takes stimulus–response associative learning as an example of functionalist processing. He then shows empirically that such learning cannot account for the observations on synaesthesia, and therefore concludes that qualia are not explained by functionalism.

Second, Gray specifies that, under functionalism, qualia must have a beneficial functional role, and this is not the case in some kinds of synaesthesia. Moreover, the role played by colour qualia is equivalent whether they are activated via normal visual input or via the auditory system (seeing colours when hearing words). Therefore Gray concludes that different functions are linked with the same qualia.

Note, however, his definition of a (computational) function as including the whole input–output connection. Yet under an alternative paradigm, the 'functional role' of a mental state is determined purely by its downstream causal effects, that is, by what effect its output has (see chapter 5 for some debate on this issue). Therefore the fact that a given subjective state such as experiencing the colour red can be evoked by many different inputs (including a mistake in the brain's wiring that connects the speech areas to the colour area – or stimulating the brain directly: Penfield, 1958) does not bear on the validity of functionalism.

What is interesting for the present chapter is Gray's equating of associationism with functionalism, his regarding of explanations couched in terms of neural connections between brain areas as incompatible with both and his conclusion that the neural theory provides the better explanation.

So, yes, the brain/mind is complicated. But you must not run away from the complexity: *you've got to love it!* Only by embracing the problem will you solve it (or at least, understand how it can be solved). The so-called 'explanatory gap' exists only in our own imaginations (a point made also by Churchland, 1985, and Dennett, 1991, in another context: section 2.4.3.2). Although the relationship between neurons and subjective experience will be a 'hard problem' to solve, this means it is difficult to grasp as a whole, not unsolvable in principle (section 4.2.3).

3.7 Conclusion

Neuronal behaviourism (or neural behaviourism) is the term I use to describe the flavour of research that dominates much of current neuroscientific thinking, in which the brain is described purely in terms of neural activity without worrying about phenomenology (and in many cases even cognition). The mental and psychological levels are ignored, or assumed eliminated or reduced by the neural explanations. This philosophy has roots that run deep within the history of science[12] and it is part of the problem in understanding the relationship between mind and brain.

In place of the standard reductionist approach that leads to neuronal behaviourism, in chapter 4 I present an alternative philosophical theory that accepts the emergence of real and causal entities at multiple levels. Not only does it break the mind–body problem down into smaller, more manageable chunks, but it is more compatible with other non-reductive (or at least non-eliminativist) philosophical analyses of how neuroscience actually works (e.g. Bechtel, 1988b; Bechtel and Richardson, 1993; Machamer et al., 2001).

▨ RECOMMENDED READING

There are several good introductions to the philosophy of science, with What is This Thing Called Science? (Chalmers, 1999) being the standard text, while Ladyman Understanding Philosophy of Science (2002) and Losee A Historical Introduction to the Philosophy of Science (2001) are also very readable. Bechtel Philosophy of Science: An Overview for Cognitive Science (1988b) is the most directly addressed to the issues in the neuroscience of mind. Chapter-length summaries are given by Papineau (1996), Bem and Looren de Jong (1997, chapter 4), Breakwell and Rose (2000) and Machamer (2002), while more in-depth chapters on various aspects can be found in A Companion to the Philosophy of Science (Newton-Smith, ed., 2000).

Excellent advanced treatments of the philosophy of neuroscience are given by Bechtel and Richardson in Discovering Complexity (1993), and in Theory and Method in the Neurosciences (Machamer et al., eds, 2001). Churchland (e.g. Neurophilosophy, 1986, Brain-wise, 2002) also covers much appropriate ground. For overt support of positivist positions the main texts are Bickle Philosophy and Neuroscience: A Ruthlessly Reductive Account (2003b) and the commendably readable Philosophical Foundations of Neuroscience by Bennett and Hacker (2003). For additional readings at an accessible level, Philosophy and the Neurosciences (Bechtel et al., eds, 2001) presents a variety of relevant points of view.

12. It may be the source of much of the antagonism towards science shown by many researchers into consciousness (Whitehead, 2004). However, this should not be so, because science is not actually what most people, both insiders and outsiders, think it is (e.g. Kitcher, 1993; Chalmers, 1999)

Function and Brain

Under the discussion of intentionality in part one, we examined the theory that some kind of meaningful representation exists in the mind as to what is happening in the world (see also, for example, Sterelny, 1990; Rey, 1997; Seager, 1999; Clapin et al., 2004; Kolak et al., 2006). We began to divide this concept up into the notions of the 'content' of the representation (the meaningful information within it), the 'vehicle' that is carrying that content, and the 'processes' that operate upon the representations to transform them into other meaningful representations, units or symbols.

In part two, the theme will be the physical undercarriage or mechanics of representation. For simplicity I will first treat representations as a single class of being, and thus include the neural foundations of concepts, beliefs, thoughts, attitudes, feelings, experiences, ideas and so on, in an all-embracing fashion (if only because the neural theories rarely make distinctions between these types of mental state).[1] The issue of whether all representations have the same underlying structure, for instance whether they are all intentional and whether they all have subjective correlates such as qualia, will be reintroduced later (e.g. in section 11.2.1.1).

Chapters 4 and 5 will first update philosophical ideas about representation, in particular how functional units are organized in the mind and the origins of their intentionality. The relationship between representational content and the world around us will be a principal issue as we endeavour to connect philosophical and psychological theories of mental function with brain physiology and the wider world of biological science.

In chapter 6 the possible physical bases of representation will be introduced and reviewed, and some examples will be given of the kinds of proposal that have been put forward by neuroscientists and psychologists. These range from sub-cellular theories to those involving complex networks of nerve cells, and even to those requiring informational exchange between the whole brain and the environment (including other brains). We will also introduce theories of brain dynamics, which emphasize

1. I often use the word 'ideas' in a cover-all sense to refer to the contents of any representation, but this is a broad everyday use and does not imply any particular philosophical definition such as that of Ideas (versus Impressions), or simple versus complex ideas, found in the works of Locke (1690) and Hume (1739).

the flow of information and neural activity around the brain rather than treating representations as static pictures.

In chapter 7 the issue under debate will be whether all representations underlie consciousness, and if not, what the difference is between them, at a physical level. What neural distinctions may there be, and what similarities, between thoughts that are conscious (i.e. of whose content we are aware) and thoughts that are unconscious? Is the distinction between conscious and unconscious thoughts a sharp one or is there a continuum of degrees of consciousness? Is the border static or is it shifting? For example, some psychologists equate conscious thought with serial, logical language-like processing, perhaps in the left hemisphere, and this contrasts with unconscious, parallel, holistic, right hemisphere processing. On this theory, conscious thoughts are ones which involve chains of logically connected representations.

Chapter 8 then introduces a more dynamic picture of brain function, with the distribution of neural activation forming an ever-changing pattern. We delve into the circuitry and flows of activity in some detail, to give a better understanding of how elaborate the brain really is. The processes underlying selective attention and the internal effects of motor output will be used as examples where this type of analysis is unavoidable.

The next chapter examines the dynamics on a longer timescale, in our investigation of learning and memory. We concentrate on the role of the brain's inbuilt structure in analysing sensory input, since this is a well-researched area and the interaction between inputs and the fabric of the brain is, according to empiricist philosophers at least, foundational for all knowledge. Moreover, it is often proposed that the recognition of stimuli involves recurrent cycling of information between parts of the brain, providing another illustration of the dynamic nature of brain function. Further, the recall of memories often involves sensory imagery, thus providing another example of the bidirectional flow of activity. Finally, the creative nature of memory suggests how representations may not be perfectly faithful depictions of the states of the world that they purportedly represent.

In chapter 10 we then return to the attack on how and where consciousness arises by studying visual representation, first anatomically and then temporally. The dynamics of representation entail (on the hypothesis that consciousness is a matter of representation) that consciousness should also have a temporal dimension. The attempt to map the timing of phenomenology onto the dynamics of the brain's responses to stimuli promises to yield useful information on and tests of at least some of the theories of consciousness.

Chapter 11 then returns to the possibility that there are various types of representation and consciousness. For instance, we ask whether the mechanisms underlying sensory and conceptual awarenesses are the same, or, put another way, whether qualia and intentionality are 'generated' in (or supervenient on) different parts of the brain (or if instead they are inseparable). This question will lead on to further suggested subdivisions between kinds of representation and consciousness. Another topic of note in chapter 11 will be whether the representation of the self is different in kind from other representations, and whether it plays a crucial role in generating awareness per se.

Recent advances in functionalism I. Homuncular functionalism

OBJECTIVES

Given that much of neuroscientific practice is implicitly based on obsolete and problem-riddled philosophies (chapters 2 and 3), we need to find a better way of thinking about the mind. As it happens, academic philosophy has made a lot of progress since the days when neuroscience was founded, and there are modern developments that relate much better to the issues at hand and that would form a far sounder basis for brain research. In this chapter and the next, therefore, we look at two recent movements in functionalism in detail, since these are important theories and they figure prominently in the current philosophical literature. By the end of the chapter, you should have deep understanding of another way of approaching the functionality of the brain, and be able to see how this relates to research already going on in the brain sciences and how it can promote the closer integration of neuroscience, psychology and biology.

4.1 Introduction

Chapters 2 and 3 illustrate that many problems exist in our current understanding of the relationship between mind and brain. Many simple solutions have been proposed, but all fall short. In this chapter, we will look at a philosophical movement that (1) avoids some of the philosophical problems seen with the earlier analyses (chapter 2) and (2) is more up to date than those currently in use in neuroscience (chapter 3) and in some parts of psychology (although it is consonant with some areas of cognitive and clinical neuropsychology).

Homuncular functionalism involves looking at the brain/mind as an organized collection of semi-intelligent, semi-autonomous *modules*. A 'homunculus' is classically described as a little man in the head.[1] Homuncular functionalism embraces the idea that we each contain not just one but many such creatures, and by combining this with a new meaning of the word 'functionalism', comes up with some surprisingly useful solutions. The originator was Attneave (1961) but it has been taken up and developed by Fodor (1968), Dennett (1987), Lycan (1987, 1996), Bechtel (1988a) and many others.

Let me explain step by step.

4.2 Arguments in favour of homuncular functionalism

4.2.1 Homuncular functionalism avoids the man-in-the-head problem

One of the oldest issues in psychology is how to avoid the 'man-in-the-head problem' – you can't solve the problem of how the mind works by postulating that inside the mind there is another little person, a homunculus, who has all the abilities of a full human being. For example, in the case of vision, it explains nothing to suppose that the visual system is simply projecting the visual scene onto a screen in the brain and that there is a little person in the head who looks at the screen and interprets what it sees there. If there were such an internal person, we would still have the question of how that little person could 'see' the screen; in other words, nothing about consciousness would have been solved or explained (Ryle, 1949).

Instead, the idea with homuncular functionalism is that there can be lots of little people in the head, a whole group of them – but this is acceptable as long as each of those individuals on its own is more stupid than the whole mind or organism. Here, 'stupid' means: it does

---

1. Notwithstanding the fact that we should now say 'person' rather than 'man', the terminology remains resolutely derived from the masculine gender.

less and it knows less. Each is only part of the system, and the whole person only operates or functions successfully because those little homunculi cooperate with one another appropriately. They interact with each other to give the whole system some new, global, *emergent* properties. Emergent properties are those not possessed by any individual part of a system. (They were introduced under 'property dualism' in section 2.2.2.1 and elaborated upon in section 3.5.5.1.) The individual parts are stupid on their own, but they coordinate with one another to give the whole system more sophisticated functional abilities.

This is the basic argument; but the next clever point is that you can then carry this on and say, well, each of these parts, subsystems or homunculi is itself a functioning system. So having broken the whole person into sub-parts, then you can then break each of the sub-parts down into further sub-sub-parts; and then similarly, carry on breaking each of the sub-sub-parts down into further components, constituents or subunits. The principle is illustrated in Figure 4.1.

For example, in the case of vision the modules might include subsystems for colour vision, motion, distance and direction perception. Each subsystem carries out one particular function, and each of them has within it several other sub-subsystems which are implementing its function (Figure 4.2).

Now, the next important idea is that as you go down and down the levels in the system you eventually arrive at a level in which the functional units are so dumb, i.e. the function they perform is so simple, small or trivial, that it is not difficult to see how it can be performed by a physical system, such as a collection of neurons, or even an individual nerve cell. So, for example, at one of the low levels all that may be needed is components sending messages from one module to another, and you can say, well, sending messages is something that axons do: they transmit action potentials, and action potentials are messages. There can be a simple identity, in that the function 'sending a message' is the same as the mechanical process 'an action potential travelling down an axon'. Similarly, performing a mathematical transform (addition, division, etc.) or a logical operation (AND, NOR, etc.) is something that small groups of nerve cells can do, or even the current flows within a single nerve cell (McCulloch and Pitts, 1943; Koch, 1998). This gives the possibility of seeing how there is a link between functional activity and physical structures within the brain, and thus solving the problem of how the mind and body are related.

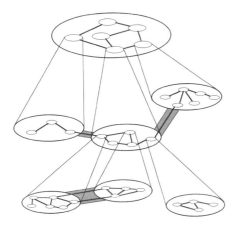

Figure 4.1 Biological systems have nested structures. Each system consists of a number of subsystems that interact with each other to give the system its overall properties. The interactions comprise the 'causes' that produce 'effects', i.e. activity within the system. The overall system is simultaneously interacting with other complete systems at its own level (grey links).

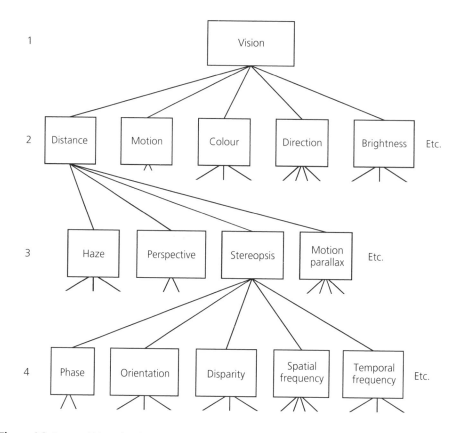

Figure 4.2 A nested hierarchical analysis of the visual system. Only the psychological and psychophysical levels are shown here; further levels below this include channels, networks and cells (not shown). This particular analysis is for illustration and should not be taken to imply that this is 'the' way the visual system is organized. From Rose (1995).

In sum, homuncular functionalism solves the man-in-the-head problem. It breaks the mind down into subunits, and as long as these are more ignorant and stupid than the whole then we don't get into the logical problem of proposing an infinite regress of little people within little people, like a Russian doll, within the head.

4.2.2 Homuncular functionalism simplifies the mind–body problem horizontally: modules

Homuncular functionalism simplifies in that it breaks the mind into separate, but interacting, 'modules'.[2] Each of those should be easier to understand than the entire mind as a

2. There are various definitions and uses of the word 'module' (for a review see Coltheart, 1999). Here, I will be using it in the general sense of a functional unit, or any mechanism that performs some function (under any of the three definitions of function covered in this book: computational – section 2.5, homuncular – chapter 4 and/or teleological – chapter 5). This is a broader use than that adopted by some (Fodor, 1983; Pylyshyn, 1999), who, while accepting that such parcellations of processing exist

whole. Obviously the mind and brain are horrendously complicated systems, but if we break them into subunits that can be analysed one at a time, we can perhaps solve the problem of how each subunit is working without having to worry about how the other subunits work. This is a basic scientific method: breaking a system up into parts and studying each individually ('methodological reductionism'; see section 2.2.2.1).

For example, just as we can analyse someone's vision without worrying about their hearing (or their general intelligence or personality), and we can study their stereopsis independently of their sensitivity to linear perspective, so we can measure the conduction speeds of their magno cell axons independently of the speeds of their parvo axons, and so on.

4.2.3 Homuncular functionalism simplifies the problem vertically: multi-levellism

At the same time, it is widely considered that there are *multiple levels* at which a system can be described and analysed (Oppenheim and Putnam, 1958; Wimsatt, 1976; Scott, 1995; Lycan, 1996; see Side-box 4.1 for more about the concept of levels).

SIDE-BOX 4.1 LEVELS OF DESCRIPTION

On 31 March 1990 a mob of angry demonstrators rioted in Trafalgar Square in the centre of London, in protest against the introduction of a new poll tax. How should we describe this event? Well, haven't I just done so? A large number of people rampaged through the square smashing the windows of police cars and setting fire to neighbouring buildings. But consider this event in more detail. There were in fact many thousands of people, and not all of them smashed the windows of police cars. Some of them threw pieces of wood at the police, others just stood and shouted, and others held up banners. So to describe the riot accurately, I should give an account of the actions of every one of the thousands of people present. But also, each person did not perform the same action throughout; some may have smashed a police car window then run across the square then hidden behind some other rioters while shouting abuse at the police. So I need to describe the actions of each person present throughout the entire duration of the riot. But consider one of those people as he ran across the square. How many steps did he take, and where did he place his feet? And now consider any one of those steps: which of the muscles in his leg contracted, with what strength, and through what trajectory did his leg bones move as a result? And then, any one of those bones was made of molecules and atoms that traversed their own arcs in space and time. So for a really full and accurate account, don't I need to give equations that describe the courses followed by each atom of each person who was in the square that day?

Clearly, I can describe this 'event' at many levels: the political (a protest), sociological (a riot), psychological (anger and desire to change the future), physiological and anatomical (movements of the body), chemical and physical (the trajectories of atoms). Each of these accounts will be correct in its

continues

(Fodor, 2000, pp. 56–57), instead reserve the term 'module' for a functional unit that also contains its own proprietary database of (innate) knowledge to which only it has access. Fodor regards such modules as rare, but they may in fact be commoner than he supposes (see Nakayama, 2001).

SIDE-BOX 4.1 continued

way, though varying in precision and detail. The higher-level accounts are briefer but lack detail, while at lower levels they gain accuracy but are longer and more cumbersome.

Which is most useful? The answer depends on the context in which the question is being asked. An answer to the question: 'Why did the riot take place?' would not be much use if couched in terms of the movements of the atoms in the Queen's arm as she signed the tax into being.

Many people have the intuition that the lowest level, that of physics, is in some way 'real', in a way that the levels of sociology and politics are not, the latter just being constructs of our imagination and of convention and consensus. However, social scientists can reason that for practical purposes the high-level concepts are necessary, not just as convenient shorthand descriptions of reality, but also because they have independent causal powers of their own. The rioters were there because the tax had been introduced, not because an atom moved in the Queen's hand. The tax was real, just as was the rioters' anger and the movements of their legs. Multi-levellist philosophers believe all levels of description are real and have causal powers; the lower levels indeed contain many more events, but these together are identical to a high-level event.

The mind–body problem can be characterized as how to bridge the gap between subjective mental life and material events such as the firing of neurons. Philosophers in the past have been trying to make one big leap between these levels, and have found it beyond human comprehension how to do so (e.g. McGinn, 1989, and the 'mysterian' school described in sections 2.2.2.1, 2.4.3.1 and 2.4.3.2). However, under multi-levellism we can break the problem into several smaller, and hence more easily solved, problems, namely those of how to relate each adjacent pair in the series of levels. All we need to do then is create a series of such smaller solutions and use them to bridge the whole mind–body 'gap', like walking across river by using a series of stepping stones, or climbing a ladder rung by rung.

It is like a mathematical or scientific proof: proceeding in a series of small, logical, comprehensible steps allows us to prove something that is intuitively beyond our immediate grasp as a whole. Thus we may not see at once how the energy in an object can possibly be equal to its mass times the speed of light squared, but a physicist who has been through all the steps in the proof has no doubt that the equation is correct. So too, one day, will be the situation with regard to the mind–body problem.[3]

Another analogy: a word is a pattern of letters, and has properties greater than the sum of those of the individual letters. A sentence is a pattern of words, and a discourse or text is a pattern of sentences. At each level (if the writing is appropriate), new and more profound meaning emerges.

For example, we know what happens when a nerve cell fires. Ion currents flow through channels in the cell membrane to create a self-perpetuating wave of activity that travels along an axon. At the next higher level, we can imagine a million nerve cells firing in this way, and then that there is a *pattern* of activity across them. We can understand how that pattern can be described at a higher level than the level of individual action potentials. (Section 6.4.3 will include further details of this step.) Moreover, the pattern obviously has properties not possessed by individual action potentials (e.g. see Side-box 6.4)! Thus we can

---

3. Another analogy or 'intuition pump': which is the better explanation of how human beings came into existence on this planet, a single act of creation or a long series of small evolutionary steps?

easily see how it is possible to go from one level of description to the next, and how new properties may *emerge* with each step upwards.

We already know a lot about the higher levels of the mind: these are subjective awareness and mental life, and just below those are the levels of functional modules such as vision (Figure 4.2), memory and language that psychologists have also studied extensively. We also know much about the very low levels: of atoms, cells and patterns of activity across neural networks. As we build down from the higher levels and up from the lower, somewhere in between there should be a meeting place where the levels of description coincide. Previous thinkers have suggested such words as 'information', 'symbols' or 'patterns' to characterize such a level, but since these intermediate levels are at present beyond our familiar knowledge we as yet have only metaphors to describe the functional units that exist there. Nevertheless, once that series of steps between levels is complete, we will be able to say we have an explanation of how mind and body are related.

4.2.4 The mind is a biological structure: nested hierarchies

Homuncular functionalism shows how mind could fit within the natural world. A common way of understanding Nature is as a *'nested hierarchy of systems'* (e.g. Koestler, 1967; Polanyi, 1968; Ayala and Dobzhansky, 1974; Salthe, 1985; Bechtel, 1986; Kirsh et al., 1993; the modern philosophical analysis is usually attributed to Cummins, 1975; see also Hatfield, 1991; Craver, 2001; and for applications in neuroscience, see Machamer et al., 2001). Thus atoms fit together to form molecules, and molecules fit together to form cells, and cells fit together to form organs, and organs fit together to form a body, and bodies fit together to form a society, and societies form a species and multiple species form an ecosystem. The whole general picture is of Nature as composed of parts which interact with one another. Each of those parts has sub-parts, which itself in turn has sub-sub-parts, and so on. We can follow the hierarchy right down to molecules, atoms and quarks in one direction (towards the 'molecular' or 'atomistic'), while in the opposite direction (towards the 'molar' or 'holistic') the hierarchy leads up to societies and ecosystems.

According to *'general systems theory'*, the principles upon which the hierarchy is organized and functions are in many ways the same at all levels, whether of atoms, molecules, brain cells or societies (Bertalanffy, 1968; Miller, 1978). Nowadays, general systems theory has been supplanted by *'dynamic non-linear systems theory'*, which we will deal with in section 6.4.3.3 (e.g. Capra, 1996), but the point is the same.

One benefit of this approach is that it explains how minds can be part of Nature's hierarchical structure, or in other words how they can be *'naturalized'*: seen as part of biology rather than as a mysterious extra supernatural thing that is in some way special or peculiar, and beyond the rules which apply to the rest of the natural world. Minds are the overall functions of brains, which are merely organs of the body. Just like any other biological system, the brain contains subsystems (e.g. cells) that interact with one another, and the brain also interacts with other organs in the body – the heart and the glands and so on – to give the overall physiology of the whole organism.

One helpful analogy is with large organizations (Dennett, 1983). A company has a board of directors, which contains someone who is in charge of personnel, someone in charge of manufacturing, someone in charge of sales and so on. Each of these people knows their own section of the company but does not necessarily understand the whole company. Consider next the situation within one of these subdivisions. The director of manufacturing has working immediately under him or her several other people, who are in charge of procuring raw materials, operating the machines, maintaining the machinery, quality control and so on. And then under each of them there are people who actually operate the machinery: oiling the wheels, shovelling the coal, pushing the pens and so on. The point is that there are many different individuals within a company, but none of those individuals knows how the whole company works. Under them are various people of still lower rank who know even less; they do simpler jobs. As we continue down into the lower ranks the jobs become simpler and simpler, until it becomes a matter of people just tightening nuts on items moving along the manufacturing line – performing a simple task over and over again in a mechanical and 'mindless' way.

The analogy with brains is clear: at the lower levels, the functions performed will be so simple even a single nerve cell or protein molecule could do them. Yet at the highest levels the functions could be as complicated as to generate consciousness. But at no stage is there any magical transformation or change of principle: all levels are merely performing *functions* that are the same in kind throughout. The hierarchy of Nature is not, however, simply one of scale, like some giant fractal. Emergent properties arise at each level. For example, different organs within the body interact to give a whole functioning organism that can move around, reproduce and do things that the individual organs can't do on their own.

One of the points I want to make within this notion of hierarchy is the relativism of terms between levels (Figure 4.3; cf. Figure 2.2). When examining any particular unit there are two questions that you can ask. These call for either 'functional' or 'mechanistic' explanations (Breakwell and Rose, 2000; Craver, 2001). The first asks about the *function* of the unit: what is it doing, *why* is it there? And the other asks: *how* does it do it, what is the *mechanism* by which that unit achieves its goals and functions; how are they implemented or made real ('realized')?

What does the word *'function'* mean; what does it involve? *The function of any given subunit is to interact with other subunits at the same level* – with other components or modules within the system of which the subunit is a part – *to generate the properties of the whole system.* These interactions mostly occur within the system, although in the case of some

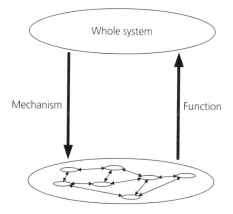

Figure 4.3 A system is able to perform its function because it necessarily contains sufficient mechanism to implement or realize the function. That mechanism comprises an organized structure of several subsystems, at the next lower level. The function of any given (sub-)system is to play a role in mediating the action of its superordinate system.

modules it is possible to have direct interactions outside the system: with the outside world, so to speak. For instance, a sensory system can interact with the environment by receiving stimulation onto some of its specialized subunits that function as transducers. Also, the neural motor system can interact with part of the brain's environment, namely the musculoskeletal system, via specialized motoneuron subunits. However, most mental systems will be interacting with the other systems that exist in the mind, to give the mind its overall functional organization.[4]

The point is that these functional interactions must be such as *to give an emergent property at the next higher level*. This property must be such that the higher level is also able to operate in some useful functional role: in some way that it is of benefit to its own metasystem as a whole.[5]

So to know what the function of any individual part of a system is, you've got to know (1) how it interacts with its neighbouring parts at the same level and (2) what the emergent property is that the system needs to have arise out of those interactions between its parts: what the beneficial function of the emergent property is, and why the system must have it. To understand function you have to look *upwards* from the level of description you are talking about, to the overall, containing metasystem.

For instance (according to the simple schema illustrated in Figure 4.2), the function of distance perception is to enable the whole visual system to operate – to know what is going on in the outside world, including what objects are around and where – and the distance module does this by interacting with the direction, motion and colour modules. Then, the function of the whole visual system is to enable the whole mind to operate, which vision does by interacting with hearing, memory, attention and so on. Similarly, the brain interacts with other bodily organs to enable the whole person to interact successfully with the environment.

What about the flip side of function, namely mechanism? Like function, the notion of mechanism is also relative, but it involves looking *downwards* from one level to the next (Rose and Dobson, 1989; Craver, 2001). The unit can perform or achieve its function because within it there are various subunits that interact with one another in a certain way; there have to be these components – and the right kinds of interactions between them (not shown in Figure 4.2).

Each component's properties are in turn given by mechanisms within that component. So, for example, the distance perception module works by having various cue-extraction modules (stereopsis, perspective, haze, etc.) within it. None of these work very well on their own, but together they can give a highly accurate estimate of stimulus distance (Ramachandran, 1985). And the stereopsis mechanism, for example, has its properties by virtue of having within it certain mechanisms that match features in the two eyes, work out the disparity between them, and so on.

4. Here, 'interact' implies a causal connection of some kind: mechanical, informational, intentional, intensional – the appropriate word varies with level.

5. In general, such 'benefits' may simply be persistence or stability over time; the red spot on Jupiter would not exist without having the particular constituent mechanisms that it does. Self-organizing orderly states occur very widely throughout the universe (Bohm, 1980; Prigogine and Stengers, 1984), the biological world (Simon, 1962, 1996; Thom, 1975; Kauffman, 1993; Mingers, 1995) and the brain (Ashby, 1952; MacKay, 1956; von der Malsberg, 1973; Kohonen, 1984).

4.2.5 **Homuncular functionalism defines the relevant properties**

There are two ways of doing research, 'bottom-up' and 'top-down'. Bottom-up research is the kind of thing that reductionists do. They take one little part out of a system and study its properties. Then they do the same for another part, then another, generalizing as much as possible about the remaining unstudied parts (section 2.2.2.1). Then they try to fathom how the parts fit together, how they work together, and thus to understand how the system as a whole works. They look first at the parts and their 'intrinsic' properties and then try to imagine reconstructing the whole.

However, if this does not work, the temptation is to continue it indefinitely. Thus reductionists actually end up doing research at quite low levels, in terms of studying smaller and smaller units. For instance, there are many psychologists who have gone into neurophysiology, but then having studied nerve cells they discover we don't understand fully how neurons work – so they have then gone down to molecular levels, into molecular genetics and pharmacology. So over time there are more and more people, even in psychology departments, doing more and more molecular-level research. They've gone down and down levels of description, ending up with specialized research on tiny parts of the system that they don't, and indeed can't, relate to the whole (Staats, 1983; Maxwell, 1984, 1985; Rose, 1987; Midgley, 1989).

One of the problems with that approach is that there are no guidelines on how to break a system up into appropriate parts. Second, you don't know whether what you observe is *relevant* or not – whether it is *epiphenomenal*. For example, when studying a nerve cell in the brain you can measure various aspects of it: size, structure, physical and chemical properties and behaviour, and so on, but you don't know which ones are important for the system's function. In other words, you don't know why those structures and properties are there, why their particular behaviour occurs, or what their purpose is. Some phenomena that you come across might be functionally irrelevant – such as the amount of heat produced by the chemical machinery of the neuron during its metabolic activity, for example. Also, in a physiological experiment you can measure how often sensory cells fire when you don't stimulate them (their spontaneous activity), how large a response they give to a particular kind of stimulus, how variable those responses are, how they fluctuate with the animal's waking or sleeping state and so on. There are an enormous number of variables that can be measured and you don't know which ones you should spend your time quantifying and how precisely they need to be measured. To put it bluntly, you need to know, or at least suspect, what the function is *before* you collect any data (to be sure the data are relevant).

In contrast, with the top-down, homuncular functionalist approach you start by knowing, or at least hypothesizing, what the function is; then you deduce what mechanisms *must* exist within the system in order to perform that kind of function. Sometimes you might be able to think of several different mechanisms that would perform the function perfectly well (or at least adequately). If so, then you go in to do experiments to see which of those mechanisms actually occurs. But the point is that you need what Gregory (1959) calls a 'functional hypothesis' – an idea about what the function is – in order to interpret the data and understand what they mean (see also Marr, 1982). Gregory has a caricature that illustrates this argument: a Martian comes to Earth, observes a motor car and discovers that hot gases come out of the exhaust pipe. The Martian thinks: 'Oh! This must be a kind of hair dryer; not a very efficient one, but it is giving out a lot of hot air so that must be what its function is'. Simply observing the exhaust gas of a car (which we know is epiphenomenal), the Martian thus infers this is the main function of the system: to generate hot gas. If you haven't got a proper functional hypothesis about what the system does, you too might make similar mistakes. Consider in contrast, a Venusian who reasons top-down. It would think: 'Well, Earthlings need a method of transport; wheels are good for transport, so they might well build things with wheels. This device has wheels, so presumably this is a transportation machine'. Thus the Venusian would interpret the car properly. The moral is that you need functional hypotheses to *interpret* observational data and to understand which are the *relevant* aspects of the physical structure of the brain, when you find them. Homuncular functionalism provides functional hypotheses by reasoning from a given system's functioning as to what mechanisms *should* exist at the next lower level.

Further arguments in support of this strategy of applying 'top-down' epistemology can be found in, for example, Gregory (1974), Dennett (1978), Marr (1982), Rose and Dobson (1985, 1989), Jacobs (1986), MacKay (1986) and Hatfield (1999).

4.2.6 Homuncular functionalism has evolutionary plausibility

Simon (1962) made the point that the evolution of organisms happens in a piecemeal fashion. Each time there is a mutation or change, the organism which results has to be viable and functional as a whole. Given that the mutations are random (or that the changes in the environment which cause evolutionary pressures to change are random), any new functional modules which evolve can disappear (and even reappear later) – there can be mutations where particular abilities are lost, not just ones which produce new modules. When Simon worked out the probability of a complex organism evolving purely by chance over the course of time, he found it is much more likely to evolve if its functional modules are very small and there are lots of them, rather than if the organism contains very few or only one complex mechanism. The chance of a human being or a conscious mind evolving in one step is obviously very low, whereas the chance of evolving via piece-by-piece development is much higher. Even though sometimes a species may go backwards (there is no systematic direction: Dawkins, 1976), in the long run, evolution towards complexity still happens (Nitecki, 1988; Gould, 1996). It is much more plausible to believe that complex systems will evolve if they are modular in this fashion, such that if they lose one bit, the organism as a whole does not fall apart completely. For example, if a species loses its vision its members can still feel their way around and hear; perhaps they cannot do quite as well, but they may still be sufficiently viable in terms of survivability. There is more adaptability and flexibility than if everything needed is subserved by a single, holistically functional unit.

Another argument in favour of modular architecture is that modularity helps in searching for information in our memory. If we had a single holistic database it would take too long to search because of a combinatorial explosion in the number of possible connections between ideas. Many arguments for the evolution of modularity can be found, for example, in Cosmides and Tooby (1992), Pinker (1997), Spector (2002), Carruthers (2004) and Clarke (2004); though for contrary views see Fodor (1998b, 2000), Woodward and Cowie (2004) and sections 4.3.4 and 4.3.7. This whole movement is thus sometimes called 'evolutionary psychology' (Buller, 2005a), and the idea that the mind is entirely modular is commonly called the 'massive modularity thesis'.

4.2.7 Empirical evidence for modules

4.2.7.1 Neuropsychology

First come the arguments from brain damage. When people sustain localized damage to parts of their brain, then in many cases they suffer particular, restricted changes in their behaviour or their mental experiences, or both, rather than a general deficiency across all their mental and behavioural faculties.

To draw convincing conclusions about modularity, investigators need next to find a *'double dissociation'* between two types of case. In one type, damage to physical system A leads to some mental change B; and in the other type damage to a different physical system X leads to a different mental change Y. Most importantly, the damage to the physical systems A and X must *only* affect B and Y respectively. In other words, damage to system A does not affect function Y and damage to system X does not affect function B (Figure 4.4). This is a double dissociation: the kind of evidence which enables us to conclude that B and Y are separate functions, rather than just one function that can be used in two or more different circumstances. B and Y are underlain by separately damageable mechanisms and constitute separate functional modules.[6]

Such double dissociations have been found many times. For example, one can have an aphasic subject who does not have visual problems or a visual agnosic subject who does not have language problems. Thus we can say with confidence that language and vision are separate functional systems: each can be altered without altering the other. Another often cited example is the distinction between short-term and long-term memory: each can be affected in isolation by lesions – to the parietal and medial temporal lobe respectively (Side-box 4.2).

A complementary technique to studying the effects of lesions is that of brain stimulation (Bechtel and Richardson, 1993). Thus when small electrical currents are injected into parts

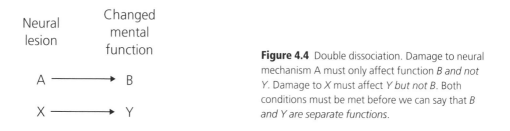

Neural lesion

Changed mental function

A ⟶ B

X ⟶ Y

Figure 4.4 Double dissociation. Damage to neural mechanism A must only affect function *B and not Y*. Damage to *X* must affect *Y but not B*. Both conditions must be met before we can say that *B and Y are separate functions*.

6. This does not mean that functional modules can *always* be discovered and separated out by lesion studies. First, most lesions affect millions of neurons, and even if only a few millimetres of brain tissue are damaged, there could still be different cells within that area mediating different functions. Second, even if one particular cell type is destroyed, that type could have been carrying multiplexed information subserving several purposes. Third, a given physical structure might be used to carry out different functions at different times, depending on context.

SIDE-BOX 4.2 DOUBLE DISSOCIATION

The textbook case of a double dissociation is that between short- and long-term memory (STM and LTM). Damage to the hippocampus bilaterally leads to anterograde amnesia. In such cases, it is possible to retain information for short periods (several seconds), longer with active rehearsal, but as soon as attention is diverted the contents of STM are lost. There is no retention over a longer period. However, it is still possible to recall information that was acquired before the damage to the hippocampus, even years before, and indeed as far back into childhood as people with an intact brain can recall. The conclusion is that the transfer of information from STM to LTM requires the hippocampus. Scoville and Milner's (1957) patient HM is the classic case study; for an update see Knott and Marslen-Wilson (2001).

In contrast, damage to the parietal lobes can induce an impairment of STM, such that its normal capacity is decreased, for example from seven to two or three items (Warrington and Shallice, 1969). However, there is no problem in laying down new long-term memories based on the information that does exist in STM (nor in recalling information that had been stored in the pre-injury period). More recent work has tended to locate the STM store(s) in frontal as well as parietal areas (section 7.2.2.3) but the principle of a dissociation remains (see chapter 9 for more on memory processes).

The conclusion is that the laying down of information for long periods is a different function from the retention of information for short periods; and we may therefore say that the memory system has at least two sub-modules within it.

(Note that this does *not* mean that we can conclude that the functions are actually carried out in the brain areas affected by the lesions: see section 4.3.6.)

of the brain, subjects may report particular experiences. This technique was pioneered by Penfield and Rasmussen (1950), who stimulated conscious patients' brains during surgery. For example, upon stimulation of area V1 of the cerebral cortex, the patient said 'I see flashes of light'. This is the converse report to that given by a person who has sustained damage to the same area of cortex, who says 'I can't see anything; I have gone blind'. Recent developments also allow us to stimulate the brain in intact, normal people, by applying transient magnetic fields from the outside of the scalp, with similar results (Cowey and Walsh, 2001; Walsh and Pascual-Leone, 2003).

So there is a convergence of evidence from two different kinds of study, both supporting the idea that one area of cortex is important for one particular function. The same procedure has been applied to many other functional systems, supporting the localization of functions.

4.2.7.2 **Anatomy and physiology**

Next, there are findings from anatomy and physiology that show first that there are separate regions in the brain. These include not just the various nuclei (basal ganglia, thalamus, raphe nuclei and many others), but also divisions within the cortex. For example, the Brodmann areas are anatomically distinct regions of cortex (see Side-box 4.3). Although the existence of anatomical differences does not by itself prove that there are functional differences, the evidence is suggestive to say the least (especially since research into brain plasticity shows that anatomy is affected by function, at least partially).

Moreover, physiologists have placed electrodes in these areas to record their gross electrical activity ('evoked potentials') and the activities of individual cells in them. As is well known, it has been clearly demonstrated that visual cortex is visual, somatosensory is somatosensory and so on. Although the functions of the areas in-between remain to be fully characterized, and there are many areas of functional overlap (a few cells in visual cortex respond to other

---

SIDE-BOX 4.3 CYTOARCHITECTURE OF THE CORTEX

The cytoarchitecture or cytoarchitectonics of the brain (its structure at the level of cells) is as fascinating as it is complex. A common procedure is to take thin slices of brain and stain them so that their inner components can be seen in a microscope. Some stains mark the cell nuclei while others reveal the entire soma and dendrites, for example. By using several types of stain, a complete picture can be built up. We saw several examples in Figures 3.4 and 3.5a. Here, we consider how the cortex was divided into areas based on its cytoarchitecture.

Figure SB 4.3.1 shows a slice of cortex that has been stained to show cell bodies. It is about two millimeters from top to bottom. There is a clear change in the pattern of cell density at the arrows, which reveals the border between areas V1 and V2 (also known as areas 17 and 18 respectively: Brodmann, 1909).

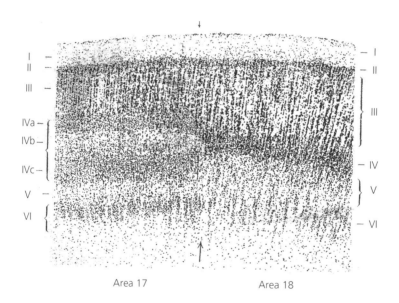

Area 17   Area 18

Figure SB 4.3.1 Brodmann's (1909) picture of the change in structure between the primary and secondary visual areas.

Brodmann studied all areas of the cortex and counted the number of different types of architecture. Although more sophisticated analyses have since been made (e.g. Zeki, 1993), the overall distribution and numbering of the areas that Brodmann drew up is still used. It is shown in Figure SB 4.3.2.

continues

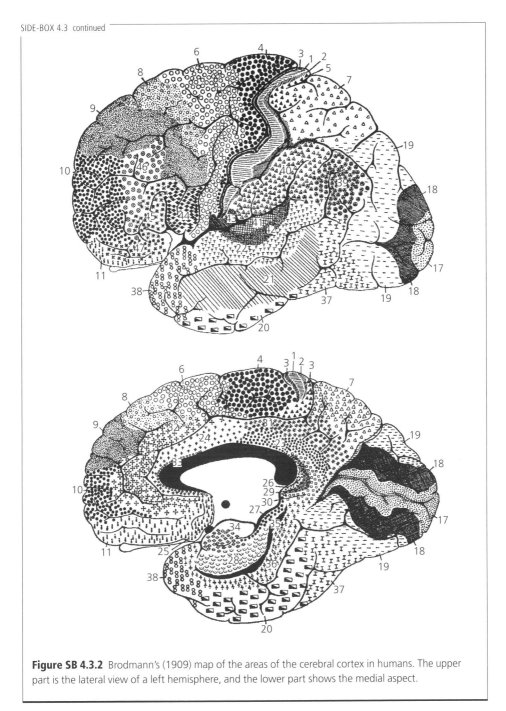

Figure SB 4.3.2 Brodmann's (1909) map of the areas of the cerebral cortex in humans. The upper part is the lateral view of a left hemisphere, and the lower part shows the medial aspect.

modalities of stimulation, for example), the basic principle is indisputable. In addition, modern PET and fMRI studies have confirmed these fundamentals in living humans: not all areas of the brain light up in every task, and those that do are consistent with expectation from the previous physiological and brain damage studies.[7]

Most interesting for the hierarchical theory of functionalism is that if you go down to compare groups of cells within any of these gross regions you find more detailed functional differences. For example, there are both anatomical and functional columns and mini-columns in the cortex (e.g. Buxhoeveden and Casanova, 2002), and in some columns there are even individual cells that perform various different sub-functions (e.g. Mountcastle, 1957; Hubel and Wiesel, 1962, 1968). So there are as well various scales at which functional divisions can be discovered both anatomically and physiologically.

4.2.7.3 Cognitive impenetrability

By using a criterion they call 'cognitive impenetrability',[8] Fodor (1983) and Pylyshyn (1999) have supported the existence of separate modules, whose function is independent of what is going on in other parts of the brain (see section 4.2.2). One obvious case of such isolation is visual illusions. As visual information comes in, some of it may be subject to processes that introduce various kinds of distortion, leading to illusory perception, e.g. of the relative lengths of lines in Müller-Lyer illusions (there are hundreds of these effects on record: for examples, see Figure 4.5, and Robinson, 1972). The point is that the observer may *know* it is an illusion; you can get a ruler and measure the physical dimensions of the stimulus yourself, or other people may tell you it is a visual illusion, yet the stimulus still looks distorted. So even though people may know cognitively what the stimulus should look like, they still experience the illusion. This implies that whatever mechanisms are causing the illusion are not 'penetrable': they are not modifiable by cognitive, conscious will, desires or knowledge. So there must be at least two separate functional parts of the mind, the part that is generating the visual illusion and the part that has the knowledge that it is an illusion. The latter cannot influence the former.

There are other examples as well, such as language: the syntactic mechanisms of speech comprehension and production are unconscious. The point is that these unconscious or preconscious processes are not modified by knowing that they are there. You cannot become aware of the mechanisms by which you construct a sentence with proper grammar – you just produce it. In the same way, you are not aware how you ride a bicycle or how you recall a memory – you just do these things.

4.2.7.4 Phenomenology

There is also, I suppose, an even more obvious phenomenological case for modularity. Compare, for example, vision versus hearing. These just don't seem the same – there is such

---

7. Caveats abound, in that more areas tend to light up than expected, but nevertheless the fundamental divisions, for example into language, sensory and motor cortices, have been confirmed. However, see section 4.3.6.

8. Also known as 'informational encapsulation', the knowledge stored within a module is not accessible to other parts of the cognitive system; see Coltheart, 1999; Fodor, 2000, especially pp. 62–64; Clarke, 2004). This constitutes a narrower meaning of the term 'module' than the one I use elsewhere in this book (see section 4.2.2); but this merely strengthens the present argument.

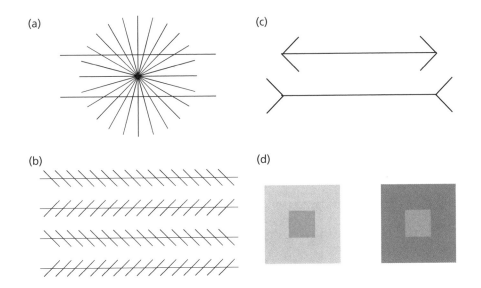

Figure 4.5 Some visual illusions. **a.** The Hering fan: the two parallel, straight lines look curved. **b.** The Zöllner: the four horizontal lines are parallel but look tilted. **c.** The Müller-Lyer: the two horizontal lines are equally long but the lower looks longer. **d.** Simultaneous brightness contrast: the two central squares are equally bright but the one on the right looks brighter.

a qualitative difference between what things look like and sound like (and smell like, and between movement and thinking and memory and being depressed and so on) that it is obvious that these are separate systems. Consider experiences like seeing red, green, blue and yellow: there is a certain similarity between them although they are qualitatively different – yet still they are massively different from the sound of your mother's voice or the smell of new-mown grass.

4.2.7.5 Psychophysics

In addition, it is possible to *adapt* each of these systems independently. If you expose someone to an intense stimulus for a period of time, it desensitizes them to that stimulus, and an after-effect is commonly observed. Well-known examples are adaptation to a dark room after exposure to bright light, or adaptation to colours, loud noises and so on (Figure 4.6). However, when you adapt somebody in this fashion, you modify their sensitivity only to a restricted range of sensory stimuli. First, adapting to a bright visual field not only does not affect hearing, it also does not affect colour perception or movement perception. Conversely, adapting to lights of different colours does not affect sensitivity to movement or to distance or to brightness perception. Second, adapting to red does not affect sensitivity to blue, adapting to vertical lines does not affect horizontal and so on. So even within the visual system there are modules and sub-modules that can be selectively adapted out while leaving other modules functionally normal. Similar principles apply within hearing and other areas of sensory psychology.

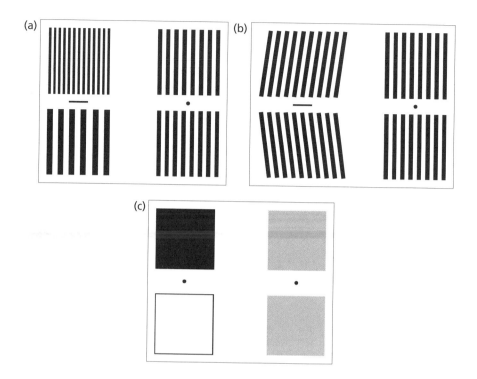

Figure 4.6 Some visual after-effects. In each panel, the right-hand pair of stimuli is the test field, and the left-hand pair is the adapting field. Before adapting, gaze at the central black dot between the upper and lower stimuli in each test pair and note that they appear identical. Then adapt by gazing at the spot or running your eyes slowly back and forward over the bar between the upper and lower adapting stimuli. After about thirty seconds, switch your gaze back to the spot between the two test stimuli, and note any difference in their appearance. **a.** The size after-effect. After adapting to fine stripes (upper stimulus), medium stripes appear coarser, and after adapting to coarse stripes (lower stimulus), medium stripes appear finer. **b.** The tilt after-effect, in which it is the perceived orientation of the test stripes that is affected. **c.** The luminance after-effect. Adapting to a dark patch (upper stimulus) makes a mid-grey patch appear lighter, while adapting to a white patch (lower stimulus) makes a grey patch appear darker. (After Rose and Harris, 2005.)

4.2.7.6 Cognitive psychology

Next is a whole set of evidence from cognitive psychology. You should certainly be familiar with the distinctions between short-term and long-term memory, the visual-spatial scratch pad and the phonological loop within working memory (Baddeley and Hitch, 1974), semantic and episodic memory, procedural and declarative memory and so on (see chapter 9 for more details). One technique for demonstrating such modularity is the 'dual-task paradigm'. If you can do two tasks at once without detriment to your performance on either, you must be using independent parallel functional systems. Given that most people can walk and chew gum at the same time, talk and drive, count the corners on an imagined outline letter F while detecting changes in the brightness of a light (Baddeley and Lieberman, 1980) and so on, then we have such modules within ourselves.

4.2.7.7 Conclusion

There is empirical evidence for homuncular functionalism from a variety of sources. Conversely, homuncular functionalism provides a philosophy that fits well with current research in much of modern biology, cognitive psychology and neuropsychology.

4.3 Arguments against homuncular functionalism

4.3.1 Homuncular functionalism still doesn't explain qualia/experience

Homuncular functionalism does not explain subjective experience, so it is no improvement on the original functionalist position. (Well, no theory explains qualia at the moment, but still, that doesn't invalidate the point.) Put another way, homuncular functionalism is about intelligence, not qualia/awareness (remember, consciousness is not necessarily the same as intelligence). There is a distinction between what Block (1995) calls 'access' consciousness (which can be explained by functionalism) and 'phenomenal' consciousness (which remains mysterious: sections 2.4.3.1–2.4.3.3); see also section 11.2.2.1.

The issue, however, hinges on what exactly qualia are. For instance, one reply is that the traditional idea of qualia is rather simplistic. Although they were originally defined as basic elements of awareness, in practice what we really experience are very complicated wholes. We are actually aware of all of our current sensory input from the environment to some extent (though some parts more intensively than others, depending on attentional focus). We never in practice experience a single quale: we always have complexes. Learning to perceive involves the breakdown of those wholes into meaningful units or categories, not building them up from a set of basic elements (Gibson and Gibson, 1955). In principle, there is no end to how fine the discriminations are that we can learn to make, for example as we develop connoisseurship at wine tasting, or come to hear the harmonics in a note played on a guitar (Dennett, 1988), or classify trees into elms and beeches, or chicks into males and females (Biederman and Shiffrar, 1987).

Another way of putting this is that our experiences are multi-layered: there are lots of levels within perception (Lycan, 1996, chapter 7).[9] One example is seeing a stimulus which might be, at the lowest level, a patch of red: it has the simple qualities of being red and being in a particular location. But at the next higher level the stimulus is a patch of textured red leather, and at the next higher level it is the arm of a red leather armchair, and at the next higher level it is grandmother's armchair. And one can go further: it is a very expensive antique (rather like its owner); to the touch it will feel crinkly and give way under your finger slightly; if sniffed it will smell a certain way (like leather); if viewed under sodium light it will look black, and so on. So you are capable of mentally 'focusing' in and out to experience that particular stimulus at many different intentional levels. There are things you know that are relevant to different levels of that stimulus complex.[10] So one can analyse

---

9. Similar depictions of phenomenology as structured have been given by Metzinger (1995), O'Brien and Opie (1999) and Brown (2002).

10. The sizes of the (relevant) modules in your knowledge base vary with level; see the summary of horizontal problems in section 4.3.7.1.

any particular real-world experience into many levels and break each level into a large number of elements that are simpler (and more numerous) at lower levels and more complex at higher.

Perception is actually very complicated, and so the functional mechanisms and structures that underlie it must be similarly complex. Homuncular functionalists can thus argue that once we find out enough about the structures underlying perception – about all the hierarchical arrangements within the sensory and cognitive systems – we will see how these match the phenomenal aspects of experience.[11] There is an identity between the hierarchical structure of the functional systems and the complex structural layers of awareness (including those traditionally called 'qualia'). Homuncular functionalism addresses the complexity of the brain and world in a way that simple, two-level (mind versus matter) philosophies do not.

One analogy that might be of help here is with vitalism. A couple of centuries ago it was widely held that there is a dichotomy between living and non-living things (all-or-none possession of some 'vital spirit'). However, we now believe that what we think of as living things are alive because they contain within them millions of chemical reactions, all going on simultaneously. The studies of physiology, anatomy, biochemistry and molecular genetics all have to be mastered if we are to understand in what way living things differ from non-living things. Similarly, then, we may suggest that the difference between conscious and non-conscious things will turn out to depend upon millions of complicated interactions between nerve cells (and, under broad content theories, the external world too) in multi-level, deeply embedded, recursive, dynamic, hierarchical systems. Homuncular functionalism is an appropriate step towards drawing that picture.

Vertical problems

Next are a couple of counter-arguments to the idea of vertical division into multiple levels. How sharp are the boundaries between different levels? How precisely are we going to be able, as scientists, to analyse the mind–brain system into separate functional levels?

4.3.2 Level independence and radical emergence

Homuncular functionalism contradicts the arguments from the 'strong AI' school of computational functionalism that you can study functional systems regardless of whether they are implemented as human brains, computers or Martians – in other words, that there is an independence between different levels. The sciences of psychology and neuroscience, for example, can therefore proceed autonomously (Fodor, 1975, pp. 9–26; 1998b, chapter 2). Thus according to Block (1978), computational functionalism implies that the people of China might be able to form a conscious system, and so might a collection of tin cans connected by pieces of string. As long as a system is functionally organized in the right way it does not matter what the lower level constituents are (section 2.5.2.2).

However, homuncular functionalism assumes that the properties of high-level systems emerge from the interactions between their lower-level constituents. Moreover, these

11. This argument is similar to one given by Churchland (1985) and Dennett (1991) that if we knew everything there is to know about the brain and the world we would be able to see how phenomenality is generated (see the 'what Mary knew' argument: section 2.4.3.2).

interactions depend on the intrinsic properties of those constituents. Biological systems are self-organizing, that is to say, the particular interactions have come to be, in part, the way they are *because* the intrinsic properties of the parts are what they are (see also section 6.4.3.1). To that extent, then, it is not possible in reality to replace those constituents with tin cans, transistors or the people of China without losing the overall function.

At root is the issue of which type of emergence is assumed by homuncular functionalism. As we discussed in section 2.2.2.1 under property dualism, emergent properties can be defined as unpredictable in principle ('radical emergence') or not ('weak emergence'). I have defined emergence here in 'weak' terms, which I think fits better with the way biologists see Nature as a whole. As such, the independent levels criticism carries little weight, since it depends on the assumption of radical emergence.

4.3.3 Homuncular functionalism leads to a vertical infinite regress

Homuncular functionalism follows conventional reductionism in positing a downwards drift in the explanation of *mechanism*,[12] but homuncular functionalism adds a new problem, that of seeking ever higher levels from which to derive functional hypotheses in the first place. For if we have to know the higher purposes of a system before we can study any of its subsystems, and if all systems are part of a metasystem or context, then where do we start? In physics it appears we would have to propose first a function for the whole universe, in biology for the ecosphere and in psychology for all humankind.

Many would say this is too broad (e.g. Buller, 1998). It seems odd to say the ecosphere has a function, and that clouds exist to water your garden (Millikan, 1993, p. 20). One answer is to embrace panpsychism (Skrbina, 2003), or at least the Gaia hypothesis (Lovelock, 1982), and to merge science with religion. We need not be afraid of this: religions are just hypotheses about the function of the universe and of humanity's purpose within it, from which all our understanding stems. However, the ramifications of this viewpoint may not be acceptable to all. Religion is normally excluded from the conventional picture of science followed by most neuroscientists (chapter 3). It seems to the working neuroscientist to be a long way up to the religious level, so much so that religion seems remote from the everyday problems of neural mechanisms, pharmacology and genetics. Do we really have to begin right up at the highest level and then work our way down? Surely that is going too far. However, just as the explanatory gap in the mind–body problem is less of a chasm than it seems (section 4.2.3), so too is the separation between religion and science – in fact, all levels of enquiry are part of our combined attempt to find a unified, coherent and comprehensible explanation of life, the universe and everything.

In practice, of course, we begin in the middle by studying the world of everyday objects of medium size, and we have over the millennia worked our way up to the cosmos and down to atoms and beyond. For practical purposes we can make scientific progress by

12. This leads to the problem of how far down one should go: there seems to be an infinite regress such that effects we see at human scales are supposed to be caused by processes at smaller and smaller scales as we go down the levels, without any end in principle as to how fine a scale provides the 'ultimate' bedrock of 'real' causation. This is not the place to discuss causation, but one response is that of Salthe (1985), who advocates restricting explanation to adjacent levels only. Thus events at one level are to be explained in terms of the next lower level only. See Figure 3.2b for an analogy.

beginning at the well-established middle levels. Strictly, all that homuncular functionalism requires is that we look for function at the one level immediately above the system we are studying, and for mechanism at one level below (Figure 4.3; Salthe, 1985).

Horizontal problems

The next four sections (4.3.4–4.3.7) cover counter-arguments to the idea of horizontal division into modules. How sharp are the boundaries between different modules? How precisely are we going to be able, as epistemologists, as scientists, to decompose or analyse the system into separate functional modules? There are arguments that things are going to be more complicated than the theory requires.

4.3.4 Homuncular functionalism assumes perfect and complete hierarchical organization

One problem with homuncular functionalism is to what degree the brain/mind really can be decomposed universally and neatly into functional homunculi. How should the system be divided up, and are the resulting module boundaries sharp or fuzzy? Homuncular functionalists recommend that the way you define a module should be based on its functions, which are deduced top-down. Hence, circumscribing the boundaries of a module and knowing its functional connections comes prior to studying the module itself. However, an awful lot of work in science does not operate in that top-down fashion (chapter 3). Instead, experimentalists make observations on certain systems and then postulate what those systems do. Often there may be more than one plausible hypothesis, with supporting evidence.

For example, let us take stimulus localization: knowing where something is in the outside world. If you start by breaking the mind down into a visual system and an auditory system, say, then within the visual system there will be subsystems which analyse colour, movement and so on, but also the location of the object. Within the auditory system there is also at least one system for discovering the location from which the sound is coming. So this analysis would imply that each of those modules, the visual and the auditory, has within it a sub-module which is performing spatial localization. But there are lines of evidence, both empirical and theoretical, that suggest that there may be what is called an 'amodal' system. In the case of location, such a module would be registering or keeping track of an object's location regardless of the source of information – whether you are seeing the object, feeling it, hearing it, or however. As long as you know where it is, if, for example, you are going to reach out and pick it up, your motor system does not really need to know whether you learned about the location of the object through sight, sound or touch (Andersen and Buneo, 2002). So there may be a shared system of spatial information used by all the higher systems that require maps of extrapersonal space. In principle, such sharing could be a general phenomenon, and there could be many functional subsystems that are each used by several higher-level systems.

Another example is the existence of mechanisms that recognize shape from any cue (colour, motion, luminance, motion, etc.: Cavanagh, 1989; Lennie, 1998).

Such a possibility does not fit into the pure hierarchical structure that I showed you in Figure 4.1, where each system has its own subsystems. One response may be to say that if such shared subsystems are discovered, we must have construed the hierarchy wrongly: for example, it is quite likely that localizing objects in the environment is actually the higher level, and vision and hearing are both subservient to that function. Similarly, shape recognition is superordinate to cue extraction.

Alternative, more complex hierarchical structures have been proposed, for example by Sloman (2001) and Wimsatt (2002). However, these involve layers of control rather than or as well as levels (see Side-box 4.4 for further details about layers versus levels). It is difficult

---

SIDE-BOX 4.4 WHAT IS A 'LEVEL'?

It is important to define 'level' since much confusion arises from conflation of several entirely different concepts which may be given that name. Side-box 4.1 explains what is meant by 'level of description,' but one often hears about levels of analysis, processing, Nature and so on. What do they mean? More particularly, are these all synonyms or do they refer to different underlying principles, and if so, how many are there?

Let's start with the relationship between scientific disciplines, and their associated levels of the natural world (Oppenheim and Putnam, 1958). These are (typically) physics, chemistry, biology, psychology, sociology, ecology and so on, and count as our first example of 'levels'. In brain science we often see a division drawn between the neural and cognitive levels, or between the physical levels of stimuli, movements and neurons and the 'higher' levels of perception, cognition and awareness (for several examples of such usage, see Harris and Jenkin, 2003). The hardware/software distinction is another attempt to express this division. In the philosophical literature we find similar dichotomies, between body and mind, or the brain and its function (chapter 2). But there are also schisms between the ontological or 'real' and the levels of semantics and epistemology (chapter 1). Thus some 'thing' (e.g. cell firing) may have a meaning (sense or reference, intentionality), in other words an additional presence in the semantic level, or it may not. Likewise for epistemology: we may distinguish what is real from what is virtual, a simulation, model or theory. As Newell (1982) puts it, there has to be a distinct 'knowledge level' (for an update on the levels theory of Newell and other cognition theorists, see Roelfsema, 2005). Thus 'levels' can be interpreted as levels of reality or of epistemology.

When we consider the ontological levels (as described by the physics . . . . biology . . . psychology . . . sociology . . . dimension), there is obviously a difference in scale (atoms . . . neurons . . . people . . . societies). Entities at the 'higher' levels contain those at lower, and there are part–whole ('mereological') relationships between them. The elements of the higher-level descriptions are composed of those at lower levels. Events at the higher levels also progress more slowly: the time constants are longer. Indeed, the differences in rate and duration may be what *cause* the levels to segregate (Haken, 1978; Allen and Starr, 1982; Salthe, 1985, pp. 72–75).

The corresponding epistemological levels are more akin to levels of description. The differences between them can be conceived as forming a dimension between the nitty-gritty details and the overall summary, big picture or gist; between the local and the global. The higher levels can be categorizations, generalizations or abstractions of the lower. They are arrangements, patterns, summaries or interpretations of the multitudinous items of factual knowledge that exist at the lower levels.

Within the ontological realm, too, the inter-level contrasts may be of several kinds. Because the events at higher levels are of larger scales, they are also more complex, if only because they comprise multiple lower-level items. However, complexity need not follow from such increases in size and

continues

number of items. Complexity is also a matter of interaction between the parts. The way the parts are organized makes the difference between a system and a mere aggregate: a house is more than just a pile of bricks. Although complexity can be quantified (e.g. Tononi et al., 1996, 1998) what is relevant is not just its amount but the sudden qualitative shifts that occur in a system's pattern of internal organization as it develops and 'self-organizes'. These transitions may create what we can call boundaries between 'levels'. As the system crosses a boundary, new properties arise: Gestalt patterns or emergents, which make the whole greater than the sum of its parts.[a]

Now, one of the commonest expressions we encounter in the study of sensory and cognitive systems is 'levels of processing'. It is important to note that this confuses two notions. First is the presumption of serial processing. Incoming information is analysed through a series of what I will call *stages*, i.e. a sequence of steps, at each of which some different process is applied to the representation (e.g. Marr, 1982; see Figure 2.4d). It is presumed also that the purpose of all these stages is to analyse the stimulus, in other words to categorize it, recognize it, or find out what it 'means', and to react appropriately. For instance, in experimental investigations of verbal information processing (Craik and Lockhart, 1972; Conway, 2003) written material is postulated to be analysed and encoded according to its sound (or appearance), phonological composition, syntactic structure or semantic content, depending to what 'level' the processing proceeds. The further the stimulus is analysed, the 'deeper' and more meaningful the understanding of it (hence 'depth of processing' is an alternative term). Thus there is conflation with the second notion, namely level of description. For example, the semantic content of a word such as 'riot' is obviously at a higher level of description (the sociological level) than the lines or sounds that form the word (the physical level). Once the reader or hearer understands the word, there have arisen intentional and connotational layers of additional sense – implications and shades of meaning, evocations of past experiences and analyses of riots, and overlaid feelings, prejudices and expectations.[b]

However, we can explain this confusion of stages of processing with levels of processing as follows: (1) As researchers, we can describe the brain and the events within it at many levels of description, from the physics of neurons to the phenomenology of understanding. (2) The brain (the mind, the self, the person, the visual system or whatever) itself, however, is trying to understand the world around it, and can also do so to many levels or depths. Thus putting together these two premises, *we are trying to describe how the brain describes the world*. Note that there are two occurrences of 'describe' in this conclusion, and hence the ambiguity about which we are referring to when we talk about 'levels of description'.

Thus sensory systems work as follows (according to serial processing models). As analysis proceeds through successive stages, the brain describes the world at increasingly higher levels. But we (as scientists) can describe each and every stage at many (all?) levels. A system of physico-chemical processes in an optic nerve fibre may be described as an action potential (at the physiological level of description), and also as one small part of the act of recognizing your grandmother (at the psychological level), and also as one (relatively even smaller) part of 'behaving politely at a party' (at the social level). An identical action potential in the same optic nerve fibre, at some other time, might be part of reading the word 'riot' (at the cognitive level), and of understanding the political message in *Doctor Zhivago* (at the sociological level). Each event at each stage fits within a hierarchy, which has many levels, and is separable into fewer, larger/longer 'events' at higher and higher levels. (See also Rose, 2000a; Figure 10.1.)[c]

Two more concepts need to be clarified before we are finished. One is that some terms for 'level' are actually *relative* to the 'real' kinds of level I have been talking about. An example is the distinction

continues

SIDE-BOX 4.4 continued

between function and mechanism introduced in section 4.2.4 and Figure 4.3. In principle, the distinction between function and mechanism recurs at all levels. There is thus not just one functional level and one mechanistic; these terms are relative, and refer to the relationships between adjacent *pairs* of levels (upwards versus downwards). The dichotomy of why versus how recurs at all levels. In similar vein, we can assimilate the well-known conceptual trichotomy between problem, algorithm and implementation (Gregory, 1961; Marr, 1982; Pylyshyn, 1984; Hatfield, 1988). According to this view, there are three 'levels' to any system: purpose, plan (blueprint) and practice. Within the strict multi-levellist programme, we can see that these are also relative terms that can be applied to each of the multitude of levels. I'm tempted to suggest yet another new term here, such as 'strata'.[d] Hence we could say that there are three strata at every level: why the system exists, how its parts are organized and what the parts are made of ('the parts' being the subsystems at the next lower level).

The second issue is the notion of 'levels of control'. Many models in cognition and AI posit executive modules or routines that function by turning subsidiary 'slave' routines on or off as the ongoing task demands. For example, Baddeley and Hitch's (1974) model of working memory has an executive that can use an articulatory loop and a visuo-spatial scratch pad as temporary stores for information. Some models of cognition have a hierarchical structure, with routines calling subroutines that in turn can call sub-subroutines and so on (just as occurs in most computer programs). I suggest we use the term '*layers*' of control to refer to such structures, rather than levels. This is because within such hierarchies the modules or subroutines may all be at the same level, in the sense outlined above (Figure SB 4.4.1). For example, Baddeley and Hitch's (1974) central executive operates as a higher layer above the layer

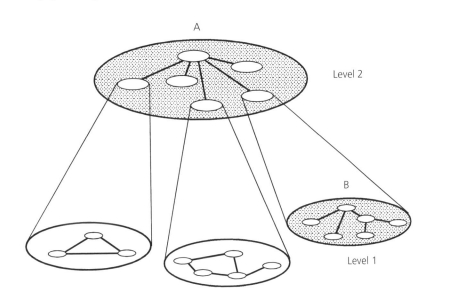

Figure SB 4.4.1 A hierarchy of systems, like that in Figure 4.1, except that in this case only two levels are shown, and the systems A and B have a *layered* internal structure, indicated here by the presence within each of a master subsystem that controls or mediates the activities of the other subsystems at its own level. Such master subsystems may act as 'central executives' or as 'bus controllers' (cf. Schachter, 1989; Baars, 1997; Baddeley, 1997).

continues

containing the articulatory loop and the visuo-spatial scratch pad. However, one area in the frontal lobe might be (contain, implement) the executive, one area in the right parietal lobe the visuo-spatial scratch pad and part of Broca's area the articulatory loop. These three are all anatomical areas at the same level of description; they might be of similar size and internal complexity, and interact with each other functionally at the same horizontal level in the hierarchy that is the entire brain.

These terms can easily be confused if processing is assumed to be serial.[e] *Ex hypothesi*, as the representation of a stimulus ascends a serial processing chain, it comes to more 'central' stages and then to more 'motor'. At the same time the stimuli are 'analysed' or interpreted to greater depth. For both reasons, one can say there is an increase in 'control' – the control over behaviour becomes more direct at the later stages, and the deeper the understanding of the stimulus, the wiser and more flexible the response to it can be. However, the meaning of 'control' that I am using, within a hierarchical model (Figure SB 4.4.1), refers to internal control of the system and its many sub-units, not to control over behaviour. The latter is, of course, affected by the way higher layers use lower layers, but indirectly. The control of higher layers over lower may occur throughout the system, but it is a matter of the internal organization and structuring of the system, not how directly or powerfully each part affects the final output.

So do higher levels control lower levels? Here, the word 'control' refers to top-down causation, and this is not defensible (see section 5.3.2 and Rose, 2000a). For example, Haken (1978) described subsystems as becoming 'slaved' to their containing system, meaning their state's propensity to fluctuate in response to local inputs is nullified by the feedback that ensures the global system's stability over time. At strongest, the term 'constraint' should be used to describe top-down relations, rather than causation. See also Sperry (1980, 1984) and Salthe (1985, pp. 53–65).

In *conclusion*, to clarify the confusion between (1) what happens as information is processed in the brain and (2) the information processed by science, we need to distinguish *stages* from *levels*. (1) is best referred to as stages of processing and (2) as levels of description. The latter is supposed to reflect something of the levels of reality. We must also be careful to distinguish how information processing is structured in the brain, i.e. (3) the concept of *layers* of control. Such terms as 'levels of analysis' and 'levels of processing' are vague and should be abjured without proper definition.

[a] Cf. Ryle's (1949) division between the 'categories' of a university (an organizational structure) and the list of its buildings and people (section 2.3.2.1). For more on the complexity of Nature, see Godfrey-Smith (1996) and Mitchell (2003).
[b] There may be variable depths of understanding, perhaps increasing with one's degree of wisdom, rather than understanding being all-or-none; but this does not obviate the point I am making here about what levels are.
[c] Serial processing models can also be hierarchical (e.g. Hubel and Wiesel, 1962, 1965; see also grandmother cells: section 6.2.6.1), which makes them *sound* as though they involve processing through successively higher levels. However, this is deceptive. The serial processing hierarchies are of successive convergence (plus lateral inhibition and other local processing) between stages of a heteroassociative neural network (section 6.4.3.1), and thus exist within a single level (anatomy).
[d] Churchland and Sejnowski (1992) make a similar point; in their terminology there are three levels of 'analysis' at each level of 'organization'. (They also define a third dimension, between levels of 'processing', which are akin to my 'stages'.)
[e] For example, Sloman (2001) confuses stages, layers and levels, and Feinberg (2001a) groups stages and layers, particularly in his misunderstanding of Sperry (pp. 123, 127). Feinberg assumes that stages generate awareness via 'radical emergentism' (p. 132) while levels are the outcome of 'weak emergentism'.

to keep the concepts of level, layer and stage separate, since in some cases there is a broad correlation between them (for example, as sensory inputs are analysed, one sees higher stages, levels and layers all becoming engaged or generated). Thus, much care is needed in defining functional systems, both bottom-up and top-down.

Another complication to the pure hierarchical scheme postulated by homuncular functionalism is that there may be flexible reorganization of subsystem usage, depending on task, the internal needs of the organism and the environmental context. The cognitive theory of a central executive states that it can allocate tasks to its 'slave' subroutines on an as-needed basis. Thus the purpose for which any given subsystem is used – the functional role that it fulfils – can change from time to time. One obvious example is the visual module: sometimes you use vision to look for danger, while at other times you use it to walk along without tripping, to search for a mate or to look for food. Also, the working memory stores can be used to hold information about many different things. So there are different functional roles which can be implemented by a particular module. Therefore, dividing the functions of a system into neat little packages, each of which fulfils a specific role, is futile, because the functions can change from time to time.

An allied point is that the uses may also change with learning. Skill acquisition involves automatization of processing, and this may engage different parts of the brain (e.g. Haier et al., 1992).

Another problem may be that, as Fodor (2000) has recently argued, we have only a limited number of modules, and each of these is limited in what it can do. The rest of the cognitive mind is much more extensive and important than the modules and works on different principles. Beyond the sensory and linguistic syntactic modules there is still a massive amount to explain; separating off these modules is not really helpful for under-standing rational thinking and the stream of consciousness. For example, people can draw globally on all the information they know in order to solve any given problem (this is known in AI as the 'frame problem'); a broad background of contextual knowledge often turns out to be relevant to a task, and in unexpected ways. (For example, when Köhler's (1925) apes wanted to get some bananas hanging from the ceiling by a thread, they had to realize that the boxes lying around the room could be piled on top of one another so the ape could then climb on the boxes, without the boxes collapsing, to reach the bananas.)[13] This leads us to 'holism': the entire semantic knowledge base must and indeed can be accessed virtually instantaneously. This has to be beyond the scope of computational functionalism, whose mechanisms for rational processing (symbols and rules) must therefore be restricted to the (small) modules. Therefore Fodor doubts to what extent modularity continues deeper into the system – whether the modularity principle can be generalized to all aspects of mental states. (Fodor's arguments will be taken up again at the end of section 4.3.7.)[14]

13. I suspect the frame problem is overstated by Fodor. Yes, we sometimes solve it, but this does not mean we have unlimited access to all our memories. Any student sitting in an exam knows we cannot access our whole inner database instantaneously! It is clear we do not have holistic memory. Those occasions when we do manage to come up with a solution, by using 'lateral thinking' or creativity (Side-box 5.2), may just be lucky strikes in a random search through conceptual space (however, intelligent heuristics are also most probably built in to the search system). Nevertheless, we cannot conclude that holism is generally true on the basis of a few instances where solutions pop into our minds instantaneously. (For further discussion, see Clark, 2001, chapter 8.) Our reasoning processes similarly often lead to conclusions that are incoherent and irrational; in other words, we do not possess a unified belief-structure that has been thoroughly checked for internal consistency (Millikan, 1993; Clarke, 2004).

14. Fodor (2000, p. 71) says that the problem of a combinatorial explosion of possible search paths through the database (memory) arises only if the holistic part uses classical computations. He implies that computational functionalism cannot therefore apply for most of our rational thought processes. (However, he doesn't say what other mechanism thought might be based on.) But Spector (2002)

However, note that Fodor's definition of a module is restrictive in that it only includes processing systems with an impenetrable database. The overall structure of the mind as a homuncular system of information processing modules is not challenged by Fodor (2000, pp. 56–64). It is only for searching through and utilizing memory that, he says, limitations apply and the number of modules is small.

4.3.5 Holism

The previous argument leads us towards the extreme idea that you can't decompose at all: that the mind is holistic. At the neural level, too, the brain is one big functional system – one 'neural network'. Every part is connected to every other part, even if indirectly, and all the parts talk to one another. So in practice there is no isolation and no obvious boundary between modules. Although there is anatomical structure within the brain, information can still go through the barriers or across the gaps between the various parts.

For instance, one of the methods used by neural network theorists to prove their position is to consider what happens when a system breaks down. In 'black box' systems, which have separate functional modules connected by neat connections (as in most computers), the kind of breakdown that you get is catastrophic: any small malfunction – such as one little bit going wrong in one of the registers in your computer, or one wire coming loose – and the whole thing either freezes or churns out garbage; the whole system collapses. If there is an error then there is a complete cessation of correct function across the entire system. It is one of the defences of holistic models that both neural networks and brains don't do that. Instead they show 'graceful degradation', i.e. a partial and progressive deterioration of function that is proportional to the amount of damage. If there is a small injury to part of the system it doesn't collapse catastrophically (in most cases); therefore the brain is working holistically. (More details on neural networks will be given in section 6.4.3.)

But even if there are modules there is still the problem of '*diaschisis*'. This is an idea, developed in the context of clinical neuropsychology, that localized brain damage can have widespread effects on the whole system. Although there can be some mechanical reasons for this (such as local swelling causing compression of the whole brain within the skull), the actual principle of diaschisis is a functional one. Basically, it is that different parts of the brain communicate with or 'talk' to one another. Each part of the brain, or of the mind, or of any functional system, receives messages from one or several other parts. It is in some way 'listening' to those messages and on the basis of the information in them it then 'makes a decision' (or at least 'processes the information') and gives out its own message. It passes on its conclusion to certain other parts, of which there may be one or several. This process continues right round all the parts in the system.

Now if any one of these parts is damaged then the messages it sends to other parts will be either absent or garbled in some way (Figure 4.7). Because those parts will then be receiving meaningless messages, or not receiving any message at all, they will not be able to fulfil

---

presents a counter-argument: with hierarchical organization (of layers!), the combinations only grow with log N, so the problems are tractable computationally (see also section 5.3.7). Another counter-argument is that the 'central' mechanisms of reasoning are themselves modular and domain-specific, and there are more modules than Fodor recognizes (e.g. Nakayama, 2001; Clarke, 2004).

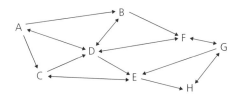

Figure 4.7 Diaschisis. The network of interconnected functional modules malfunctions whenever any one of them is damaged. For example, if module A is damaged then modules B, C and D will malfunction, because they have each lost one of their inputs. In turn, modules E and F will then be affected, and finally G and H too. Similarly, if H is lesioned then G will suffer, then E and F, then C and D, and then A and B.

their functions properly. Therefore they will malfunction as well, and they will in turn send on garbled, incorrect, absent or inappropriate messages to the next subsystems. This carries on right round the whole functional system or network. So if the parts of any functional system are densely connected and interacting, then in practice any one malfunctioning part can lead to a widespread deviation of function from the normal or 'proper' functioning of all the parts. It is then difficult to pinpoint the primary source of the malfunction. This weakens the usefulness of the theory that multiple modules with neatly circumscribable functions exit.

4.3.6 Empirical evidence

How do these arguments square with the empirical evidence given in section 4.2.7 above? This showed that, for example, different areas of the brain subserve different functions. Well, first, there is some controversy over to what extent the physiological studies (Zeki, 1993, 2004) support such a simple interpretation. Instead, several workers have found that the cells are almost always selective for several stimulus features within each visual area, not just for one (e.g. Lennie, 1998; Gegenfurtner and Kiper, 2003, 2004; Tootell et al., 2004), and the differences between the areas are just a matter of emphasis (Zeki, 1978) rather than all-or-none. Certain roles seem to be fulfilled by several areas, or several areas seem to be fulfilling the same function in parallel (albeit with subtle differences between them).

Logically, lesion studies, even those with double dissociations, do not provide unequivocal conclusions about the localization or even about the modularity of function (Young et al., 2000; Uttal, 2001, pp. 172–181). Other models, such as those involving complex, dynamic, non-linear networks of interacting parts, are also consistent with the loss of specific functions after local lesions.

Further evidence comes from brain scanning studies showing that several areas light up when performing any given task and any given area may be involved in several tasks (e.g. Howard, 1997; Beck et al., 2001; Friston and Price, 2001; Corbetta et al., 2002; Naghavi and Nyberg, 2005). Examples are shown in Figure 4.8. However, these do not show that the whole brain lights up, merely a network of areas, so this evidence does not support the *extreme* holistic position described in section 4.3.5.

Finally, there is disagreement about how impenetrable the modules really are. Recall that Fodor and Pylyshyn (1981, 1988) gave as a criterion for the existence of modules their

(a)

(b)

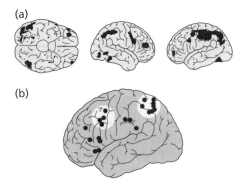

Figure 4.8 **a.** Brain areas activated during one task, in this case, change detection. Several areas are involved (shown here as black patches of cortex) but not the whole brain! From Beck et al. (2001). **b.** Summary of five studies (including Beck et al., 2001) showing foci of the areas whose activation correlates with changes in visual awareness (black spots). Two prominent clusters are highlighted by the pale circles. From Rees et al. (2002).

imperviousness to cognitive knowledge and expectation (section 4.2.7.3). An allied notion was that of 'pre-attentive' processing, in which the early stages of sensory analysis were said to proceed automatically and fully, whereas later processing was selective and required (or just was) attention (Neisser, 1967; Treisman and Gelade, 1980; Julesz, 1981). Recent studies, however, have revealed that what were thought of as early modules can in fact be influenced by attention (Chaudhuri, 1990; Driver and Frackowiak, 2001; Paradiso, 2002; Rose et al., 2003; see chapters 7–10 for more details). Moreover, brain scanning methods reveal that even the LGN can be affected by visual attention (Vanduffel et al., 2000; O'Connor et al., 2002). Where does this leave the concept of modules? These no doubt exist, but their boundaries currently appear more flexible and permeable than was previously thought. Alternatively, attentional and informational penetration might be operating between sub-modules within certain parts of the hierarchy – such as within the modules for visual object recognition, face recognition, reading, and understanding speech – but not between those modules (Coltheart, 1999).

In sum, the debate about how neat the decomposition is continues at the moment. Although there is empirical evidence that there are functional modules, the boundaries are not always sharp. In some cases this may be because there is some kind of cross-talk between the modules: interactions and conversations are going on continually between the parts of the system. Let me next elaborate on this a little.

4.3.7 **The binding problems**

When dealing with an object or situation that is complex (the way such things normally are), homuncular functionalism posits that information about that situation or object is analysed by separate functional modules. But if the information is broken down and separated out into parallel modules that operate independently, then how is the knowledge or information that those different bits of information come from the same object, or pertain to the same situation, maintained? How is information from a single source 'bound' together when that information has been split up into separate modular chunks within the mind or brain?

Now the original, proper meaning of 'binding' arose within vision, in the context of feature analysis. For example, the colour, movement, direction and position of a seen object may be analysed by separate functional modules (Zeki, 1993; Figure 4.2). But if the information is split up in that way, how does the brain maintain the fact that this information all comes from the same object? This is the point of Treisman's feature integration theory (note that Treisman and Gelade, 1980, did cite Zeki's work). Treisman's theory is that attention *is* the process of binding together information from these different modules to form a representation of an object. If there are several objects in the visual scene, you have to bind the correct features of each object with each other. Treisman showed that if you do not pay attention you can make errors in that process and get misperceptions of objects, such as illusory conjunctions of features (e.g. seeing a red triangle when presented with a red circle and a green triangle). We'll talk about the neural models later on (chapters 8 and 9).

The concept of binding also arises for representations of real-world objects whose features cross modalities. For example, the perceived sight and sound of an external event may be integrated via the so-called 'multimodal' areas of cortex (Bushara et al., 2003). Actions too may become bound with perceptual representations (Hommel, 2004).

Some people have also used the term 'binding' in a more general sense, to describe the unity of the self. They talk about binding between hearing, vision, memory, 'gut feelings' and so on: just the fact that you seem to be a single independent individual.[15] How do all the different bits of information, experiences, feelings, qualia and thoughts that you have all seem to be linked together into one person, one unified self? The theory that there is such a unity is important, because it contrasts not just with theories that there is no such unity (bundle theories; see section 11.3.4.4) but also with evidence that there can be people with multiple personalities, that schizophrenics can hear internally generated thoughts as coming from outside themselves, and that people with hemineglect may deny possession of the contralateral side of their own body (see Side-box 4.5). Obviously this meaning of the

---

SIDE-BOX 4.5 BINDING THE SELF

How does the unity of 'the self' arise? We may get some clues by looking at the many cases in which this process seems to break down.

In multiple personality disorder, for example, there may be restricted access to parts of the episodic memory base at certain times, such that there is intermittent switching between two or more views that the person has of him- or herself. This most commonly occurs in cases of child abuse. In adulthood, the ability to remember the abuse leads the individual to assume that other people normally indulge in immoral behaviour, and thus it may be permissible to follow their example. However, when these memories are unavailable, the person thinks, talks and behaves far more conventionally. The memories of the abuse are present but dormant, and are thus not binding with the person's other ongoing mental states to form a more complete 'self'. Humphrey and Dennett (1989) give a philosophical discussion, and Taylor (1999, chapter 11) and Forrest (2001) give neural ones. The implication is that we normally need access to all our memories.

continues

---

15. For example, Zeki (2003) uses the term for two 'levels' of processing: binding between attributes (e.g. for vision: colour and motion) to form percepts of objects, and binding to form the unified consciousness of self. Llinás (2001, p. 126) also equates the self with the binding of synchronous oscillatory activity between the whole thalamus and cortex.

SIDE-BOX 4.5 continued

In schizophrenia there can also be dissociations between what one knows and what one believes about oneself. For example, sufferers may behave in a certain fashion but deny it is their willed choice to behave in that way. They may, for example, claim that aliens are beaming rays at them that cause their limbs to move. Their internal mechanisms that make the decision to act are not binding to the mechanisms that generate or enable self-awareness. Similarly, internally generated thoughts may be heard as externally generated voices, without the person being aware that these are internally generated. For more details see, for example, Frith and Gallagher (2002).

Another bizarre example occurs in the condition known as hemineglect or contralateral neglect. In typical cases (which usually involve right parietal lobe damage) the left side of the body is affected, particularly the limbs. These are not moved when the person is asked to move them, and they are ignored when dressing, washing and so on. The person not only may fail to recognize that they have a left side, but may also deny that there is anything wrong with them at all (Side-box 11.1). Yet the syndrome can be relieved temporarily by drawing attention to the neglected limbs, or by increasing the general arousal level of the right hemisphere. Thus information about the left side of the body is present, but is not integrated with the rest of the information processing in the brain. Detailed studies of this syndrome can be found in Robertson and Halligan (1999), Leclercq and Zimmermann (2002) and Karnath et al. (2002).

Although these cases (arguably with the exception of schizophrenia) involve localized brain damage, and may therefore be explained simply as the result of disconnection of one module from another, they show that in normal cases there is, first, a multitude of functional modules, and second, tight integration between these modules. The effects of disconnecting (or 'unbinding') these various aspects of the 'self' are dramatic and devastating.

'binding problem' is different from the one in vision; we will return to it under the issue of self-awareness (section 11.3).

Binding implies some kind of physical tie or reunification. However, it is arguable as to whether you need to reunify the information (for one thing, this implies there is a 'Cartesian theatre' where the information all comes together so the little man-in-the-head can look at it; see more in chapters 8 and 10). One alternative is that the binding problem is solved by adding some extra quality to all the information from one object, and this quality is the same for all that information whichever module it is being processed by. At the same time, all the information coming from a different object must have a different quality, and this can coexist within the same module as the first quality. This enables one module to process information from two or more objects without confusing the information about each. Treisman's original theory was that the common quality is the spatial location of the various features of the object (given by links to a 'master map' of space). Another (neural) theory is that the common quality is the rate of oscillation of cell firing (see section 6.4.2).

Summary of horizontal problems

What all these issues (sections 4.3.4–4.3.7) have in common is semantics. The modules need to talk to one another, but in what language do they communicate? Remember, we discussed the issue of semantics in section 2.4.3.1, where we compared broad and narrow content – the issue of whether the meaning or intentionality of systems derives from their inner constitution or from their relationships with external systems. Fodor (1975) introduced the notion of a 'language of thought', but more recently (2000) he has questioned the universality of such a language. If modules exist as distinct entities, he argues, each performs a specialist task, and therefore has a specialist terminology, i.e. its own particular knowledge base, represented in its own proprietary way. So how can one module possibly communicate with another, given that each has its own specialized terminology and knowledge, and by definition does not possess the terminology and knowledge of the other module(s)?

Note that Fodor allows that information-processing and computational modules form a hierarchical system (2000, pp. 56–57). The problem of communication arises only for a certain type of module, namely those that contain innate and idiosyncratic knowledge bases. These include the modules for perception and for language.[16] Let us consider how communication could occur between modules in general, given the problem Fodor poses.

I am not so pessimistic as Fodor. The members of a Board of Directors (section 4.2.4) do manage to say something to one another! We need to find languages that mediate communication between modules (for example, Side-box 4.6 introduces some of the possible

---

SIDE-BOX 4.6 COMMUNICATION BETWEEN MODULES

Consider the common computer, which contains many modules (for input, output, memory, central processing, interfacing with disks and external media, a modem and so on). These are all connected via what is known as a 'bus', which is basically a bundle of wires that runs between all the modules. Messages sent from one module to another are preceded by the address of the module to which they are being sent, and the message takes over the bus for as long as necessary by using a system of built-in 'interrupts' that assign priorities to messages and ensure that only one module can use the bus at a time.

Now, how do these modules 'talk' to one another, given that they each have separate built-in knowledge? The answer is that they communicate via a simpler system (of interrupts and simple commands such as 'transmit this message from place A to place B' and so on), and the contents of the (higher-level) messages are independent of the housekeeping functions. The low-level addresses are built in to the hardware (Dennett's, 1987, 'tacit' knowledge). (The internet carries packets of information whose addressing poses similar problems and these too seem to be solvable.) Is this analogous to the distinction between syntax and semantics, or between vehicle and content, or between low- and high-level functions? Does it solve the problem that Fodor (2000, pp. 77–78) raises about how specialized modules can communicate and how particular representational contents come to be processed by the appropriate module(s)?

Of course, the bus solution is interesting because it is analogous to the model proposed for the brain by Baars (1997) in his 'global workspace' theory (see section 7.2.3). In that theory, there is a system for 'broadcasting' messages universally throughout the brain. Does this theory fall foul of Fodor's problem? Or does it prove that there is no problem (since the brain obviously does work)? Is it consistent with homuncular functionalism? To the latter question I suggest that the bus (aka the global workspace) is a module at the same level as the other modules (the relevant level of modules, that is: in psychology,

continues

---

16. Fodor does not explain how those modules communicate with the rest of the cognitive mind, which presumably they do, despite having their own separate, specialist knowledge bases!

SIDE-BOX 4.6 continued

these are vision, working memory, attention and so on; and in brain research they are the visual system, hippocampus and so on). It is a separate layer rather than a separate level (in the terminology given in Side-box 4.4).

One way of looking at the bus/global workspace is as a module that specializes in communication between the other modules. It is a universal translator as well as transmitter, or perhaps it uses some lingua franca that is understood by all the modules. (In principle it could generate a different language as appropriate for each module that is being addressed at the time, but that would probably be imputing too much cleverness to it.) Another putative solution is that the human language module does the integration (i.e. the module that enables the whole person to speak); it must 'understand' what is happening in all the other modules so that the person can communicate the relevant information in the form of external speech (Carruthers, 2004; see also section 7.2.2.3).

In conclusion, the problem of communication between modules is undoubtedly soluble – in principle in several ways.

---

mechanisms). Here are several more ideas. First, in some systems there are specialized 'boundary mechanisms'. A general exemplar is the cell membrane (Salthe, 1985), but functional modules could similarly encapsulate specialist sub-mechanisms for mediating the interactions between the module and others at the same level. Nerve cells communicate by releasing transmitter molecules onto each other; each cell contains a specialist subsystem to generate and release transmitter, and other subsystems (receptors and allied machinery) to receive messages. Since translation and transduction are common processes in biology, it is likely that informational or semantic translation can happen at many levels, including the more sophisticated, mental levels. Even people communicate, despite having (at least partially) different knowledge bases. They can do this by virtue of containing a variety of specialist subsystems for producing and receiving speech, facial expression, 'body language', vocal intonation and timbre, and so on. At the level of intracranial modules, the patterned neural networks connecting brain loci can also be seen as performing just such a translation function (Mumford, 1992). Cognitive (mental) modules could thus be communicating in an analogous fashion.

Another suggestion is that the communications that pass between modules are mere summaries of what is going on in each module: compact, low-bandwidth packages of information rather than fully detailed downloads of the entire contents (Spector, 2002).

Third, there may be a lot of redundancy in the language of thought. Thus modules communicate by understanding only a few of the 'words' they receive and by making intelligent guesses to fill in the gaps in their understanding. Just as our visual system uses its inbuilt knowledge to interpolate between the fragmentary parts of an incomplete stimulus (as in, for example, the Kanizsa triangle: Gregory, 1998; Figure 9.2), so modules have rudimentary imagination and experience that they can call upon.[17]

---

17. An allied notion is that the homunculi form 'mental models' of each other. (The inverted commas in this paragraph indicate the terms are being used metaphorically to represent more impoverished abilities than those held by a whole human.) By 'conversing', in whatever language they use, the

Finally, we could move away from the old understanding of functionalist processing as like running a serial computer program, and instead take a new analogy from modern object-oriented programming (Mather, 2001; see also Shallice, 1972; Cooper, 2001). Here, programs are both hierarchical and modular (and the modules may run simultaneously and in parallel). For the present argument, note that each subroutine usually possesses 'local' variables, i.e. values of x, y, and so on which are restricted to that subroutine (and, under object-oriented programming, to all sub-subroutines that run under it in the hierarchy). These contrast with 'global' variables that are accessible to all the subroutines in the whole program. A subroutine may set one of its local variables equal to one of the global variables, then perform all sorts of local processing using its various local variables as (interim or permanent) data stores, and then give output by setting the global variable (or another) to some new value. There is thus communication (via globally accessible variables) at the same time as there is local module-specific information, which can include permanently stored specialist 'knowledge'.

Contrariwise, like Dennett (1995, pp. 412–422), we may reject the whole problem of internal languages and say that each module derives its semantics from interactions with the same, real world, and thus communication is no problem. In general, Fodor's problem seems to arise only if the mind is a single level. But in a fully hierarchical, multi-level system, the behaviour of a module shows itself in the behaviour of its containing metasystem (one level up), which may affect in turn all the other modules within that metasystem. As an illustration, consider changes at the organism–environment level; these create feedback loops through the individual and the environment. In other words, a module's activity affects the organism's behaviour in the world, which affects the inputs to (potentially all) the modules within that organism. Analogous processes operate within an organism at the levels of modules and sub-modules.

We also need to bear in mind that at different levels in the hierarchy there will be different languages – different kinds of language, even (at some level, 'language' has become more like 'code'). At lower levels the languages will be simpler, and there may be many more of them (in principle, each pair of modules or subsystems may have its own unique 'language' to convey meaningful information). However, I suspect they will become more similar at lower levels: action potentials are more homogeneous as a group than are thoughts or scientific theories (just as atoms of hydrogen are more similar to each other than are action potentials). There must be a hierarchy of intentionality (as well as the hierarchy of qualia as described in section 4.3.1 above). At lower levels modules become

---

homunculi learn about their companions (at the same level) with whom they interact. Each may store knowledge internally in some proprietary or idiosyncratic terminology, but the homunculus can interpret the meanings of those terms and use them to direct its own output functions. Its 'colleagues' may also pass on information about their world in general (i.e. facts about the system they are all part of, couched at their level of description). This process is analogous to the way individual people learn about each other (and about the world) through social communication. By taking this as a metaphor for events at lower levels, we may postulate that homunculi have an impoverished kind of social life (even generating, perhaps, the equivalents of rumours and social consensus as to the states of affairs that apply across wider domains). Most significantly, if we accept the view that consciousness arises from social interactions (section 6.2.2.1), then we can see how homunculi could have genuine if impoverished consciousness (see also chapter 12).

smaller and more numerous; hence intentionality points over shorter distances, figuratively speaking (Rose, 2000a), and is more primitive (Dennett, 1995, pp. 205–206). But how intentionality arises at all is still not clear. We will deal with this in chapter 5, where a solution to the problem of intentionality and a new theory of semantics will be proposed.

4.3.8 Function is purpose

According to homuncular functionalism, if a system is malfunctioning it will not contribute to the overall function of its containing system. So a diseased heart may not pump blood and thus does not help the body to live, or a representation of a tiger might be misinterpreted as that of a tabby cat and thus lead us to try to stroke the tiger behind its ears. So according to homuncular functionalism, the diseased heart is not a heart because it does not pump blood, and the misrepresentation is not a representation because it is not contributing correctly to our understanding of the world.

However, surely the diseased heart is still a heart, and the misrepresentation is still a representation, even if neither of them is working properly.[18] But that is the point: how do we know what their proper work is? Homuncular functionalism requires us to go up a level and deduce what the lower-level function should be. It says that if a person is being kept alive by an artificial heart machine then that machine is now their heart, since it is fulfilling that necessary functional sub-role at this moment in time, whereas the anatomical diseased so-called heart in the chest is not.

By looking only at current function, the critics say, homuncular functionalism is defining function merely as 'function as', as in: the artificial heart machine functions as a heart, even though it is not actually a heart (Millikan, 1993, chapter 1). It misses the fact that systems may have functions in the sense of 'purposes' (the purpose of the heart is to pump blood). A diseased heart still has the purpose of pumping blood, despite the fact it is not doing so. Such functions may be attributed to systems on the basis of how they have performed in the past, how they might perform in the future, the particular characteristics (shape, composition, etc.) that they have at the moment and how they acquired them. These assignations of function as purpose are instead better accounted for by the next development, teleological functionalism.

4.4 Conclusion

Homuncular functionalism provides a way of looking at the brain that promises to solve the man-in-the-head problem by breaking it down into manageable chunks. It suggests how the diverse range of mental functions and experiences can be segregated and approached one by one, and as such is consonant with much of the research techniques already practised in perception, cognition and clinical neuropsychology. It does, however, try to

---

18. Millikan (1993, p. 21) also mentions mating displays that do not always attract a mate, yet are still mating displays. A chat-up line may not lead to someone getting pulled, yet it is still a chat-up line.

impose an idealized theoretical structure onto the brain/mind, and its strict parcellation of functions may not always depict accurately the way actual minds are organized (partially for reasons to be explored in the next chapter). Nevertheless, despite these problems it provides a useful way of looking at the brain/mind and how its systems are an integrated part of the natural world.

■ RECOMMENDED READING

A classic introductory text on these topics is Bechtel's **Philosophy of Mind** (1988a, chapter 7), while Lycan's **Consciousness** (1987, chapters 4 and 5) is also very readable (mainly). Quick overviews of the principles can be found in **Stairway to the Mind** by Scott (1995, chapter 9) and Pinker's **How the Mind Works** (1997, pp. 27–31, 77–81, 92), while a more extended treatment is given by Feinberg in **Altered Egos** (2001b, chapter 8). Among the more recent textbooks, an introduction to levels can be found in Heil's **Philosophy of Mind**, 2nd edn (2004a, chapters 7–8 and 13–15), while Botterill and Carruthers (**Philosophy of Psychology**, 1999, chapter 3) are good on modularity. For readings, see Lycan's **Mind and Cognition** (1999), especially section 4 and the Introduction on pp. 8–13.

The recommended readings for chapter 5 also cover many of these topics as well as the subject matter of that chapter.

5 Recent advances in functionalism II. Teleological functionalism

OBJECTIVES

In this chapter we look in detail at another recent movement in functionalism. You should obtain from this chapter further understanding of how the brain may acquire its functionality and how the brain/mind is integrated with the world around it. The question to bear in mind is whether or not this theory genuinely provides a solution to the problem of how intentionality arises, as its proponents claim it does. As with the previous chapter on homuncular functionalism, you should try to see to what extent this philosophy relates to research already going on in the brain sciences, and how it suggests an alternative way of integrating neuroscience, psychology and biology.

5.1 Introduction

Teleological functionalism is the next development in functionalism and provides various benefits. It is often combined with ideas from homuncular functionalism (such as multi-levellism) to form a powerful and comprehensive theory. Van Gulick (1980), Millikan (1984, 1993), Dretske (1988, 1995), Neander (1991a,b, 1995) and others have developed this theory as an explanation for intentionality; see Allen et al. (1998) and Buller (1999a) for collections of classic papers, and Hardcastle (1999a) and Ariew et al. (2002) for more recent reviews.

The overall strategy is that consciousness is explained (grounded, reduced) as intentionality, intentionality as function (see chapters 1 and 2), function as teleology and teleology as evolutionary history (this chapter). Darwinian evolution is proposed to provide an account of teleological function that does not depend on any prior intentionality or consciousness, hence obviating any infinite regress or circularity of argument as to where and how consciousness arises.

5.2 Arguments in favour of teleological functionalism

5.2.1 Teleological functionalism explains function

The first and crucial question we should ask is: what is a function? Teleological functionalism takes its answer from recent advances in the philosophy of biology, and particularly that field's strides in defining function. The word 'function' has a different meaning here from in its previous contexts. These were first the computational functionalism of strong AI and mentalese (section 2.5). There, the analogy with computation meant that a function was a mapping system or operator that related one thing to another, and translated or transformed one (meaningful) representation into another. This function is like the mathematical function 'y is a function of x'. Here, y depends on x in some way which can be specified in a formula. Second, the teleological meaning differs from that used under homuncular functionalism, where the function is to subserve the immediate metasystem at the next higher level in the hierarchy.

Instead, in the evolutionary biological context, the word 'function' is used to mean purpose, goal or aim. '*Teleological*' functionalism ties the states of the brain and the mind to their role of subserving the needs of the organism in an evolutionary context. Just as the function of the heart is to pump blood, and the function of the stomach is to aid digestion, so the function of the brain is to generate or subserve consciousness, or just to *be* conscious. Being conscious is what the brain does.[1] This is a quite different meaning of 'function' from the computational one (although, as we shall see, it can be reconciled with the homuncular usage).

1. Why the brain should generate consciousness is a higher-level question that we may also approach teleologically. Although I will not be going into details of this question, note here that it is one that is not easily raised at all under other philosophies.

5.2.2 Teleological functionalism is consistent with evolution

In terms of evolutionary history, a property, characteristic, ability or trait fulfils some functional role if, at some time in the past, the possession of that property actually helped the ancestors to survive, by enabling fulfilment of some beneficial outcome (leading ultimately to reproduction). Thus if the individual organism we are talking about has an evolutionary history in which possession of a particular ability helped that organism's progenitors to survive and to reproduce, and if the same property or ability is possessed by or built in to the present organism, then that property can be said to be functional, and its function is to help the organism (and, under some theories, the species, or the genes!) to survive and reproduce. The property has been established through evolutionary history; that is a core tenet of Darwinian theory.

These are nowadays sometimes called Wright functions, after Wright's (1973) analysis of biofunctions. They contrast with Cummins functions (1975), which are the types described by 'functional analysis' under homuncular functionalism.

In philosophy of mind, teleological functionalism ascribes functions to our representations, faculties and skills by taking the Darwinian view of the world.

5.2.3 Teleological functionalism includes the environment

The ability to survive depends not just on the individual but also on the environment. Individuals and species may or may not survive in different kinds of environment, and when the environment changes, so the kinds of organisms that survive may change as well. Thus the ability to survive is context-relative.

Teleological functionalism assumes mind fits into the ecosystem, which it matches or mirrors. The mind and the environment fit each other like a lock and a key – except the interaction is informational rather than mechanical (as, at a lower level, is the interaction between the brain and the environment). Under '*teleosemantics*' the lock 'represents' the key. The mental lock is the shape it is because previous encounters with environmental keys led to evolutionary selection of the right shaped lock (see further in section 5.2.5).

As with all the functionalisms, the meaning of a mental state is its function. So for philosophy of mind, what we have here is an explanation of '*broad content*'. Remember, one of the criticisms of the original, computational functionalism is that it involves only narrow content: like identity theory it assumes the contents of the mind depend solely on the brain and it ignores the environment (section 2.4.3.1). Here, however, an explanation is given as to how the contents of the mind are related to the environment, and thus how they have intentionality.

Some theorists take 'meaning' to be grounded in what actions are 'afforded' by the environment (e.g. Gibson, 1979), i.e. which behaviours are suggested by the stimulus. Teleological functionalism is consistent with this approach but explains the mechanism of intentionality in more detail, as we shall see in section 5.2.5.

5.2.4 Teleological functionalism is naturalized

Teleological functionalism sees the mind as '*naturalized*' in that it is part of the natural world where it has evolved and developed in the context of the biosphere (rather than being parachuted in from some 'supernatural' world of souls).

Technically, the converse of naturalized explanation is *'normative'*. Under the old positivistic philosophy developed for the physical sciences (chapter 3), to explain a phenomenon means to state which causal process accounts for it, where causal processes are understood to be laws of Nature. For example, the speed at which the apple fell onto Newton's head is explained quantitatively by Newton's laws of gravity and motion. One corollary of normative accounts is that there is a single correct way that an organism should be, which is: in exact conformity to the laws. In biology and the social sciences, however, the way people are now is not a matter of their obeying universal laws of nature, but of their individual evolutionary and learning history (e.g. Millikan, 1993, p. 280).

5.2.5 Teleological functionalism explains intentionality

The biggest advantage claimed for this approach is that it explains the intentionality or meaningfulness of mental states. The idea is that the meaning derives from the state's evolutionary history in fulfilling a functional role or achieving a goal. Mental states are adaptive: they help us to survive and to achieve aims and they subserve the needs of the organism.

Let me try to give some flavour of the argument. Remember from the old computational functionalism the concept of representation; this is maintained within this branch of functionalism. States of the mind *'represent'* the environment: they have a meaning that pertains to particular objects and events going on in the environment. These representations are generated within the system, and they are then *used* within the system. Thus there are a number of stages that have to be explained. One is how a representation is *generated*. Second is what the nature of that representation is. Third is how the representation is used – or *'read'*, given the mentalese metaphor that sentences in the mind's language have to be *'interpreted'* by other mental mechanisms.

Now, Dretske (1988, 1995), for example, says that the first things that are generated are what he calls *'natural signs'* or *'indicators'*. He draws an analogy here with signs or symbols in the natural world that indicate that something has happened, such as a footprint in the snow. This is a natural sign that indicates a bear (or a person or whatever has made the footprint) has been there (Grice, 1957). These signs are, in a sense, infallible: they have a direct relationship to their origin, and they cannot mis-indicate. The source or the cause of this sign is some event in the natural world. Dretske's argument is that sensory systems are there to construct natural signs within the brain or mind that are indicators of the presence of features or properties of the outside world. These signs are the bases of qualia, the raw experiences we have of the world.

These natural signs are rather like the speedometer in a car (although without the labels which say what the values are!). An internal homunculus must then 'look at' the speedometer and interpret it. Thus, the internal representations or signs have to be used: read or interpreted by other mechanisms. These interpreters process the information in the signs and generate beliefs, thoughts and other kinds of representation that have intentionality, i.e. they are *meaningful* interpretations of the information contained within the natural signs. These functional information-processing mechanisms give rise to mental representations at a higher level.

Dretske (1988, 1995) suggests that learning involves changes in the way that representations are used or read. Learning is a matter of adjusting how to interpret the qualia and other representations rather than learning new signs or new representations. Instead, learning is actually learning to process representations in different ways.

Side-box 5.1 illustrates in simplified form how Dretske and many others see the structure of the mind: as a combination of primary and secondary representations.

Controversy arises, of course, because other people have made alternative emphases within their theories. For example, Millikan (1984) says there are no natural signs: all the mechanisms and representations have to *co-evolve*. (Co-evolution involves two entities developing mutually, like pollinating insects and flowers – neither would ever have existed without the other.) There has to be evolution of the mechanisms that generate representations, but also evolution of the mechanisms that process those representations and interpret them to form higher-order representations and to control behaviour. The former mechanisms are 'producers' of representations and the latter 'consumers'. Both types of mechanism have to co-evolve in such a way as to achieve the overall functionality of the organism.

This contrasts with Dretske's picture, in which natural signs may sit there unused. A frog may hear a trumpet but not know it is hearing a trumpet (see section 11.2.2 for more). Millikan, however, believes that all representations are fallible and all internal signs are the same: they all need interpretation and there are no 'natural' signs (for more on this, see section 5.3.5).

5.2.5.1 Teleosemantics as the explanation of meaning

Since intentionality is supposed related to meaning, this whole theory has given rise to some wonderful neologisms: psychosemantics has transformed into '*biosemantics*' and '*teleosemantics*'. Remember from chapters 1 and 2 that the old psychosemantic theories distinguished between 'extension' and 'intension' as sources of meaning (see also Side-box 5.1).[2] Extensions are the connections between thoughts and their real-world content. There is a causal relationship by which the inner representation comes to correspond to something in the outside world. Intensions are the links between concepts within the mind. The idea is that the content of a representation is defined by its relationships with other meaningful concepts: that 'cat' is related in particular ways to 'meow', 'dog' and so on, and also, more closely to 'meow' and 'dog' than to 'cloud' or 'truth'. These links can also be referred to as logical connectives such as AND or NOT, or as processes of 'inference' or 'judgement'.[3] The entire network of these links should form a complex but unified whole.[4]

---

2. In philosophy of science, a similar distinction is drawn within epistemology as to the definition of truth. On the one hand, the 'correspondence' theory asserts that true statements match the state of the world and can be tested by empirical means. On the other hand, the 'coherence' theory recognizes that empirical evidence is unreliable and suggests that true statements would be logically consistent with each other. They should combine to form a unified whole, since reality (if it exists) is a single, integrated system. Theories can thus be tested by reasoning (rationalism rather than empiricism). See Side-box 3.1, and Chalmers (1999) for a good introductory textbook.

3. There are echoes of this idea going back to Aristotle and to Kant (1781/7), who reasoned that there are certain 'categories' or abilities (i.e. faculties) in our minds that we *must* have in order to be able to have any kind of knowledge at all. This is not the same as needing innate knowledge, but to say you must have certain kinds of logical processing abilities and thinking mechanisms – for example, to categorize and analyse the sensory input, to tell if one thing is larger than another, or if there is one or several things and so on. More recently, Fodor (1998a, p. 142) has suggested that mechanisms, rather than content, may be what is innate. For example, logical connectives (the mechanisms of inference) such as AND and NOT are necessary for our thoughts to have meaning, since the content of a concept in isolation is insufficient to carry semantic intentionality (Fodor, 1994b, pp. 76–77).

4. Millikan (1984, p. 324) suggests that a mechanism for detecting incoherence or contradiction is all that is needed to guarantee that our beliefs are true. However, she also points out that we do not in

SIDE-BOX 5.1 TWO-FACTOR SEMANTICS

Figure SB 5.1.1 illustrates how many workers envisage the structure of the mind. Several thinkers have suggested that there are two types or stages of representation (e.g. Locke, 1690; Hume, 1739; Block, 1986; Dretske, 1988; Sterelny, 1990; Neander, 1995). These thinkers vary widely in how they characterize the two types and their relationship, so we must be careful when lumping them together, but nevertheless there is clearly a common theme.

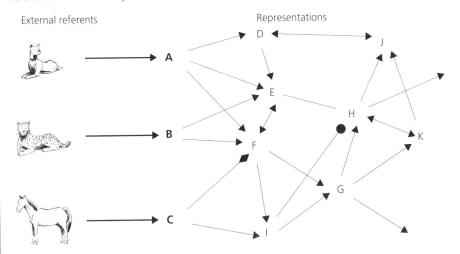

Figure SB 5.1.1 Two types of representation in psychosemantics.

Recall the explanations of extension versus intension, broad versus narrow content, informational versus inferential role and atomism versus holism in chapters 1, 2 and 4. Figure SB 5.1.1 illustrates how both are supposed to be combined. One stage of representation may be defined roughly as

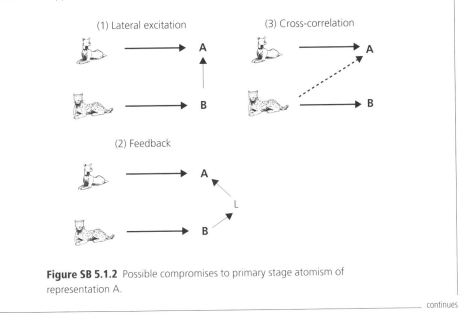

Figure SB 5.1.2 Possible compromises to primary stage atomism of representation A.

continues

SIDE-BOX 5.1 continued

extensional, broad, informational, naturalist and atomistic: these are representations A, B and C in this figure. The second stage is intensional, narrow, inferential, interpretative and holistic (representations D to K). The links between the second stage representations may all be similar in type (as befits behaviourism, connectionism or Dennett, 1991) or they may be of various types, as shown here and in Figure 2.6. The flow may be mainly serial, bottom-up, from the sensory end towards the motor outputs, or it may run in all directions to form a tangled web, as shown here.

Figure SB 5.1.2 shows three ways in which the pure atomistic character of a primary stage representation (in this case, representation A) might be compromised: (1) by direct cross-talk between primary stage representations (perhaps mediated by some form of lateral excitation), (2) by feedback from higher stages or (3) by imperfect tuning (perhaps a result of correlation between the stimuli).

Now, the teleosemantic theories we have been discussing (especially those of Dretske and Millikan) make use of the distinction between extension and intension in different ways. Dretske regards the extensions as infallible (natural signs). Both he and Fodor (1987) rely on the input side to give fundamental meaning (hence their theories are of 'indicator semantics' or 'informational semantics'), whereas Millikan places more emphasis on the output side of a representation – it is the consumers that define the representation's meaning (see Millikan, 1993, chapter 6, and Rowlands, 1999). These consumers are the intensional network and the motor outputs of the organism. Note that one representation can be consumed by many others on any given occasion, and these interact with each other. So extracting meaning is not just a matter of executing a serial process, a single knock-on chain of cause and effect, like a row of dominoes falling over (the serial processing model). Interpretations affect each other as well as behaviour (see also Dennett, 1991.) The grounding of meaning in this network is known as 'inferential role semantics' or 'causal role semantics' (because the representations have to have causal effects on other parts of the system, downstream).[5]

5.2.6 Teleological functionalism explains misrepresentation

As may have become apparent, one of the problems teleological functionalism is trying to solve is the issue of *mis*-representation: of how it is we often get things *wrong* (e.g. Millikan, 1993, pp. 3, 123). It is easy to imagine systems that could function perfectly, but what we also need to explain are those systems that are like humans to the extent that they make errors: for example, they misperceive things. Thus you can look out of the window and think that you see a horse in the distance when in fact you are looking at a cow. Another example is that of frog bug detectors. Remember from basic perception that the frog visual

practice check our belief structure comprehensively for logical consistency; hence our thoughts are often incoherent (Millikan, 1993, chapter 14).

5. Beware: informational semantics is confusingly sometimes also referred to as 'causal' because it postulates a 'universal-law-of-nature-obeying' causal link between the external object or stimulus and the existence of the representation.

system has cells that respond to small black moving spots in the visual field. Barlow (1953) and Lettvin et al. (1959) said, well, these are ideally suited as fly detectors, since frogs eat flying bugs and those are the stimuli that will excite the cells maximally. Because finding food is a major functional need, this may be the role those cells fulfil. Philosophers point out that, well, these cells are not strictly bug detectors, because the cells also respond to small black spots of light waved on a screen in front of the frog by physiologists, so they are not *exclusively* functioning in that role. You can't just ascribe the role of bug detector to them, because they actually respond to any small black moving object (Fodor, 1987, 1990).

So *how do you ascribe a function to those cells (or to any cells)?* As stated in the previous section, some functionalists emphasize the output rather than the input when defining function (Rowlands, 1999). Can we therefore look to the behavioural output and categorize the frog's cells as those whose firing leads to the frog's mouth snapping at the location in visual space where the stimulus is?

Teleofunctionalism is, however, more subtle than this. Millikan's definition of function is in terms of *'normal'* or *'proper'* function. The normal function of a mechanism is to do whatever it was that it evolved to perform (like detecting bugs in the case of certain cells in the frog). Its function is what it is *supposed* to do. A bad heart may not be able to pump blood, but it is still a heart; that is its proper function. A screwdriver can be used as a can-opener, but it is still a screwdriver. Perhaps on certain occasions the frog's visual system may malfunction, for example when a distant blackbird flies across the scene, or when the frog is ill, or held down by a physiologist who waves small dark pieces of paper in front of it, but that does not obviate the fact that the proper function of the mechanism is to detect bugs.[6] In the evolutionary past it was useful for frogs to possess such bug detectors, because these facilitated survival.

Millikan concludes that because individual mechanisms can misrepresent (for example, a distant blackbird as a fly), what have evolved are multiple redundant mechanisms, each of which is capable of building a representation. Each such mechanism is not particularly good at its job; the representational contents it produces are not necessarily accurate and reliable. But because we have lots of similar mechanisms trying to work towards the same goal, then the desired effect is achieved most of the time – or at least sufficiently often to enable us to survive (Millikan, 1993, e.g. pp. 362–363). As Millikan puts it: 'no actual person has a head that functions entirely properly' (1993, p. 361).

In summary, this viewpoint gives teleofunctionalists the ability to allow for the fact that we sometimes make errors. Our representational mechanisms work in a rough and ready fashion. However, at the same time it is valid for scientists to postulate what is (roughly) the normal proper function of any given mechanism. We can say that the mechanism has evolved for such and such a purpose, even if it does not fulfil that purpose *perfectly*.

---

6. Perhaps on most occasions there is failure of function. Reliable function is not necessary. Compare spermatozoa: only one in several million needs to reach the ovum for the species to be perpetuated, yet every sperm still has that goal as its proper function (Millikan, 1993, pp. 130, 362). The role of cognitive psychology is therefore not to study the average or the actual, but the *ideal* human functioning.

5.2.7 Teleological functionalism explains redundancy and inefficiency

The previous point was that teleofunctionalism can explain how we can sometimes come to misrepresent. But how do we come to have inefficient, imperfect, multiple and redundant systems? Because we have an evolutionary history that is very chequered, shall we say. The environments our ancestors had to survive in have changed many times in the past, in ways that are at least chaotic, if not random: climate changes, new predators arising, finding themselves in new environmental niches (for example, as they migrated into different parts of the globe) and so on. As we moved into each environment or each environment changed, so we had to adapt, in standard evolutionary terms. Now, such adaptation takes time, so the first point is that at any given instant in time, systems will still be evolving towards perfection. Moreover, before we have yet achieved perfect adaptation, the environment usually alters again: it changes frequently, if not continuously. As our context and situation change, so systems that have developed to cope with one environment may no longer be appropriate for the new environment. These systems do not, however, 'de-evolve' instantaneously: they often remain as evolutionary hangovers, persisting despite their redundancy and inefficiency in the new, current environment.[7]

So we may have redundant, inefficient systems because they were more efficient in the past, but in a different environment. A system may have an evolutionary history that has pushed it towards performing a function, but that function is never perfectly realized. The organism only survives as a whole because it has several mechanisms whose normal or proper function is to achieve some similar goal, either in parallel or as back-ups for one another (Millikan, 1993, pp. 360–363).

Now, a classic example in vision is depth perception, where we have several mechanisms for perceiving how far away things are: stereopsis, convergence of lines, haze, texture gradients, height, occlusion and so on (Gregory, 1998; see Figure 4.2). There are several different mechanisms in the brain, all of which are working towards the goal of discovering how far away from you a visual stimulus is. Each of these mechanisms on its own works best within a limited range of distances, or gives only an approximate estimate of distance. But because there are several of these mechanisms working in parallel, the total amount of information they gather altogether is enough to achieve the goal very well. If they interact to form a coherent system, their overall effect can even be greater than the sum of the parts. Ramachandran (1985) presented an analogy with two drunks staggering along the road. Consider two people, each of whom is too drunk to walk alone, yet by leaning against each other and giving mutual support they are able to make their way home. In this analogy, as with depth perception, the different modules on their own are pretty incompetent but the system they form has a new, emergent property (in this case, being able to move).

A variation on this theme is that systems that evolved for one reason in a particular environment sometimes get taken over and used for something different. One example from biology is the panda's thumb (Gould, 1980). Pandas eat bamboo, which they do by

---

7. Sometimes they persist because their cost is so low it is not worth de-evolving them; in other cases they may continue because their genes are physically adjacent to genes that are still very useful. Sometimes structures exist that may have been necessary during ontogenetic or phylogenetic development – like temporary scaffolding while constructing a building – but are not necessary now (Dennett, 1995, p. 217).

holding the bamboo shoot with their thumb – or what appears to be their thumb – while they chew the leaves. But what appears to be their thumb is not actually a thumb: it is one of the wrist bones that has grown protruding outwards and is now used in the same way a human might use a thumb. Although it did not originally evolve as a thumb, it works as a thumb now, i.e. its function has changed. Another example is (arguably) the use of feathers for flying. Feathers may have originally evolved in order to keep animals warm: as a way of trapping air near the body. Only later on did feathers become used for flight, i.e. become adapted for a new function. Some of our psychological functions may also have evolved in this way, such as language developing out of gesture and imitation (Rizzolatti and Arbib, 1998), and the use of secondary sexual characteristics as signals for attracting a mate.

A corollary of Gould's theory is that if the environment changes, then the mechanisms or modules available within the organism may change their functions without themselves changing internally. New circumstances do not always drive the evolution of new mechanisms to cope with the new situation, but may instead lead to the development of new uses for old mechanisms. A module's function is not a fixed 'essentialism' (i.e. defined immutably by God or genetics). There is no fact of the matter about what its function is – all functions are relative to whatever environment is current, or could be current (Dennett, 1995, pp. 401–412). A further corollary is that most if not all the systems we have currently have changed their functions during our evolutionary history (Millikan, 1993, p. 46; Dennett, 1995, p. 281).

In summary, teleological functionalism is thus unlike computational or homuncular functionalisms, which require or assert 'perfect' structures and processes.[8] It can account for our poor performance on many cognitive and behavioural tasks while still explaining why we are the way we are.

5.3 Arguments against teleological functionalism

5.3.1 Teleological functionalism is Panglossianism

Medieval Christian dogma was that God created the world, and everything in it. So Leibniz (1710) reasoned that since God is perfect, God could not have created an imperfect world. The world must therefore be perfect, and everything in it is as good as it possibly can be. (We are God's chosen creatures, He made the world for us to live in, and He did so benevolently, with our best interests at heart.) If we allow that the world is imperfect in any way, then this is a criticism of God. Also, it would mean that God is imperfect, which would be a contradiction since God is defined as the perfect being. So therefore we live in the best of all possible worlds.

However, Leibniz's conclusion was satirised by Voltaire (1759) in the story 'Candide'. Leibniz was cast in the form of a character called Dr Pangloss, who believed that we live in

---

8. There are some other isms that also assert perfection: meaning rationalism (the idea that our beliefs are consistent with one another, so there must be a coherent holism in our network of concepts: Millikan, 1984) and semantic atomism (concepts are univocal and unambiguous: each has an immutable, single referent: Fodor, 1998a).

the best of all possible worlds. He went around making defences of this belief that were, in Voltaire's hands, patently stupid. For example, he said we wear spectacles because our noses are perfectly designed to perch spectacles on top of them, and that legs are visibly designed for the wearing of stockings. When there was an earthquake in Lisbon that killed thirty thousand people, and Dr Pangloss was asked why, if this was the best possible world, there could be such a terrible disaster, he simply asserted that things cannot possibly be different from what they are, and everything is for the best.

The term 'Panglossianism' was later coined by Gould and Lewontin (1979) in a famous paper in the Proceedings of the Royal Society. In this article they criticized the idea of universal adaptation that they claimed was extant in biology at that time. Gould and Lewontin said that a lot of the Darwinians were taking an extreme, Panglossian view, in that they were assuming that biological species are perfectly adapted for their environments. We could explain the way all the different structures, functions and behaviours of every species are, as being perfectly consonant with their environment. But Gould and Lewontin said that this is not true, for some of the reasons I have mentioned already (the panda's thumb is one of Gould's examples; see section 5.2.7). The course of evolutionary history involves millions of years of complex, unpredictable factors, and the way that species are at the moment, the way that we are, is determined by this history. We have not been designed in any way to fit the current environment. What scientists actually find is that systems are not perfectly designed, and that there are inefficient functional modules that are bodged up, ad hoc, and not perfectly suited to any particular circumstances. Things that evolved to perform one function have been taken over and used for other functions, such as feathers being used for flying and so on. In sum, you are not going to find that the teleological, evolutionary story gives you any reliable or certain way of defining what the functions of any given system or mechanism are *now*.

One counter-argument is that for epistemology it makes more sense to assume perfect adaptation first, then look for deviations. This at least gives us hypotheses to test. If we assume all is chaotic and unpredictable, science will be left relying on random observations. Indeed, this is the simplest way to answer the Panglossian criticisms: assume perfect adaptation first (Maynard Smith, 1978; Ruse, 1986; Dennett, 1995, pp. 212–213) when formulating hypotheses, then test them and correct them by discovering how messy the biology actually is (Rose and Dobson, 1985, 1989; Eliasmith and Anderson, 2003, pp. 20–21). The other way round won't work: assuming evolution has been random, or at least imponderable, gives us no ideas about what to examine next, or what to make of each finding. At the very least, we must adopt the 'design stance' (Dennett, 1987), that is, behave as if there is design.

5.3.2 Teleological functionalism means backwards cause and effect

The argument that functions, mental and physical states of the brain are the way they are in order to achieve some desired goal in the future implies backwards cause and effect through time. However, there are several important counter-arguments here:

5.3.2.1 Cause and effect is an obsolete paradigm

Cause and effect analysis may be useful in the simple systems studied in chemistry and physics (e.g. in the billiard ball model of the universe explicit in Newton's first law of

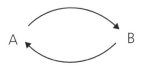

Figure 5.1. Mutual interaction between two entities, A and B. Since A affects B and B affects A, continuously and simultaneously, it is impossible to say what is 'cause' and what is 'effect'.

motion), but with biological systems there are a lot of feedback loops that render the notion irrelevant. If you have two entities A and B, where A affects B and B affects A (Figure 5.1), it is very difficult, perhaps inappropriate, to talk about cause and effect: does A cause B to change or does B cause A to change? Well, because they are mutually interacting, there is a cycle generating properties beyond those explicable on the basis of isolated causes and effects (see sections 2.2.2.1 and 6.4.1 for more on emergent properties). One should instead talk in terms of a dynamic, continuous, ongoing change in the whole system formed by A and B. The system is the appropriate level of description, and describing lower-level events as though they could be isolated from the whole system's dynamics is missing the point (Kant, 1790; Schrödinger, 1944; Sattler, 1986; Scott, 1998).

A more concrete example of this is to acknowledge that the individual and the environment interact, with mutual causality. Individuals act upon the environment, both deliberately and accidentally, often to bring about changes in the environment that suit the individual (e.g. Dawkins, 1982; Odling-Smee, 1988). Such changes include killing predators, building safe dwellings, storing food, wearing clothes, creating fire, making tools, etc. One should not analyse the individual organism as a passive recipient of inputs from an unchanging environment.

5.3.2.2 Evolutionary causes work normally

The evolutionary argument is that the interaction between the way your functional systems are now (the causes of behaviour) and the achievement of goals such as reproduction (the effects of behaviour) is due to feedback that has happened in the past. Some systems in the past 'caused' particular behaviour that achieved reproductive goals, and that goal achievement in the past 'caused' the genes for those systems to be passed on, which set up the current systems to be the way they are (which is, the same as they were before, in their direct ancestors). Through the evolutionary argument one can circumvent the idea that one has to talk about current states of the brain being caused by events in the future; this is not an appropriate way to describe the teleology involved here.

5.3.2.3 Constraint not causation

The functional role of higher levels in a hierarchical system is not to cause changes in the lower levels, but to *constrain* or prevent the wrong thing from happening at those lower levels. Natural selection demands that given a set of mutations or random changes at low levels, some will survive and some will not. The 'right' ones, i.e. the beneficial ones, will survive and the maladaptive ones will die out. We can phrase this as follows: the teleological effect of natural selection is killing off the variations that are not beneficial and that will not lead to that final goal of survival. The changes that survive are the ones that are permissible: they are not going to be killed off by the environment or by any internal inconsistency. So the action of natural selection is one of constraining, of preventing the wrong thing from happening, rather than causing the right thing to happen. It is causing the wrong things to die out. Meanwhile, the right things are not themselves 'caused' – *they happen spontaneously* (the metaphysics of Heraclitus: see Dobson and Rose, 1985) – as in the replication of genes, for example. Thus there is a subtle but important inversion in the meaning of 'causation' in the evolutionary context compared with that in the context of physics.

5.3.2.4 Structuring versus triggering causes

A fourth answer, which comes from Dretske (1988, 1995), is that what evolution creates is the *structure* of the mind. The environment induces a certain structure of information processing, decision making and choice selection within the mind. This means that what is selected is which of the particular kinds of possible behaviours you might emit – which ones are chosen and aid survival. (One can also use the evolutionary analogy in the context of individual learning as well.)

So the cause, in teleological 'cause and effect', is what Dretske calls a '*structuring*' cause rather than a '*triggering*' cause. The latter refers to the immediately ongoing stimulus that initiates behaviour now, at this instant. Previous stimuli and experiences have already structured your behavioural repertoire. Moreover, ongoing stimuli coming in from the environmental context and events are continuously modifying the structural connections within the mind and thus altering the range of possible behaviours that will be available to choose between in the future.

If we now incorporate the previous point (section 5.3.2.3) about constraints rather than causes, we can say: choosing which behaviours you actually *use* involves both doing those behaviours *and* not doing all the others that you could have chosen to do. What the evolutionary and learning history has set up is a system whereby you don't do the wrong things: the inappropriate behaviours are filtered out and the right kinds of connections are left intact within your mind between the context, the stimulus, your goals and the appropriate behaviours.

It is not just that the structuring causes select behaviour; they also select which stimuli in the environment control your behaviour – which stimuli you respond to and which you ignore. With experience you learn which stimuli are relevant, important or crucial and those particular stimuli or aspects of the context are the ones which are paid *attention* to and used as the basis for making decisions. So structuring affects the analysis of the input as well as the production of motor output.

5.3.2.5 Reasons versus actions

A further way of approaching the problem is to identify the causes of behaviour and decisions with our desires and wishes. I do something because I want to do it. That want can be treated as a traditional cause, since it precedes the behaviour in time. What past history gives is the content of our desires: it determines what the 'something' is that I want to do. In propositional attitude terms (Side-box 2.2), the vehicle is the immediate cause of behaviour, while it is the content that is teleological. The fact that my attitude (want, desire) represents a particular something (money, fame, another beer) is the fact that is accounted for teleologically (Buller, 1999b, p. 5).

5.3.3 **The definition of 'adaptive' is circular**

In the context of the theory of evolution and the notion of the fitness and adaptiveness of species to survive, the concept of function is central. The debate in biology centres on what makes one species survive and another go extinct. The usual, simple argument is that the species that survive have some abilities or functional properties that are adaptive and enable them to survive. But you then get into a circular argument: how do you know that *that* particular function helps them to survive? Well, because they do survive. So why do they survive? Because they have that particular functional ability.

This argument implies the whole of Darwinian evolutionary theory is unsatisfactory. Do you really want to abandon Darwinism? Most people would say not, but we still need some reasoned replies to the challenge.

One answer to the conundrum comes from retaining some of the useful ideas in homuncular functionalism. You can make an informed decision about what is adaptive and what is not in a top-down fashion. In multi-level hierarchical systems, it is possible to develop functional hypotheses about what the purposes or goals of systems are. (Indeed you absolutely need such functional hypotheses about what the system is doing or needs to be doing – see the story about the Martian and the hair dryer in section 4.2.5 above.) From the point of view of a higher-level metasystem, you can look down at a system to see whether it is achieving the functional goal that it should be achieving (to make the metasystem work). If it is, you can say, well, this is a well-adapted, efficient functional module. If it isn't, you can say that it is inefficient or that it is not adaptive – for example, it may be an evolutionary hangover or a mistake.

So that is how to get out of the circularity: go up to a different level of description and then come back down again. Only this manoeuvre will enable you to interpret whether or not the mechanism you are looking at is adaptive. How adaptive a system is, is relative to the context, which in hierarchical systems is the metasystem.

Conversely, Amundson and Lauder (1994) and Hardcastle (1999b) propose that circularity can be avoided by deriving function bottom-up, from considerations at a lower level such as the anatomy of the system. Parallels can be drawn with homologous structures in other species, for example. This is, these authors maintain, common practice among biologists. If it looks like a brain, wobbles like a brain and grows at the front end of what looks like a spinal cord, it is a brain! Thus their resolution of the problem is to step down a level or two to depict in detail the structure that is of unknown function, move sideways to find similar structures that, it is well-established, mediate a known function, and then assign the same function to the new structure under investigation.

A complementary notion is that of Fodor (1983, pp. 12–16). He suggests that to individuate functions without postulating a mysterious essence, we need to describe them in symbolic format. These can then always be made real in the form of computational machines. In other words, if a function can be described symbolically it can be implemented as a low-level mechanism (Turing, 1936).

We can construe all these manoeuvres as uses of the multi-levellist part of homuncular functionalism: by ascending or descending a level of description we can avoid proposing functions that have circular definitions. Indeed, Buller (1998, pp. 511–512) explicitly advocates the introduction of such Cummins functions to save teleological theories from just this problem of circularity.

5.3.4 Arguments for narrow content

'Narrow content' is the view that the meaning of our thoughts depends purely on what is in the mind/brain; I mentioned this before, under narrow versus broad content, internalism versus externalism, etc. (section 2.4.3.1). In contrast, teleological functionalism asserts that the meaning or intentionality of mental states and representations depends on the outside world (broad content) and not purely on what is in the brain. But obviously and as always there are some philosophers who counter-argue that narrow content is correct.

One reason is the intuitional argument. We just have a feeling that what is in the mind depends on what is in the brain. This is what Dretske (1995) calls the 'internalist intuition', the feeling that our thoughts depend on what is on our heads. After all, there is evidence that if you get bashed on the head then you may lose consciousness, see stars or perhaps undergo some (more or less lasting) change in behaviour if the brain is damaged. Dretske's reply is that this intuition is just an intuition and the arguments for broad content are more convincing (section 5.3.6). We need the outside world as well as our brains, and changes in either can lead to changes in our conscious experiences.

Another reason to believe in narrow content is the creativity and generativity of thought – the ability to construct an apparently limitless set of ideas. (An analogy here is with the generativity of language: we can construct an endless list of meaningful sentences, including many we have never encountered in the real world; see section 2.5.1.3.) Thus we can imagine the world as it might be if things were different and we can think of objects that do not exist such as unicorns and Santa Claus (i.e. counterfactuals). We can also conceive of things we cannot perceive or point to, such as quarks and truth. Therefore the meaning of each of these thoughts cannot be given by extension. Instead, it must be given by intension, in other words, by processes taking place entirely within our heads. Most obvious for the argument about teleology is that we can think about the future: this does not exist and never has, so how can evolved mechanisms refer to it?

Third is what is called 'systematicity', or the logical interrelatedness of our thoughts, which are organized into categories of states of similar type (Fodor, 1987, Appendix; 1998b, chapters 9 and 10; Fodor and Pylyshyn, 1988). For example, anyone who understands the meaning of 'Mary loves John' can also understand 'John loves Mary'; people just don't exist who cannot do this. Also, anyone who knows that 'Mary loves John and hates Bill' can deduce the truth of the individual components of that scenario, namely: 'Mary loves John' and 'Mary hates Bill' (and the same applies vice versa, from possessing both components to their combination). Our mental representations do not exist in isolation from each other. Having knowledge about the world enables us to draw inferences by combining items of knowledge in logical ways, giving us the ability to formulate arguments and draw rational conclusions. Yet those manipulations of our knowledge representations happen purely internally within the mind.

Fourth is an argument about the individuation of concepts. Just as synonyms may have different causal effects (compare the 'Bringer of War' and the 'Red Planet'; or 'E' and 3,4-methylenedioxymethamphetamine), so too may thoughts about the same external object. The point is made even more forcefully if you do not know they are synonyms. For example you would react very differently towards the person who stole your CD and towards your best friend, even if unbeknownst to you these are in reality the same person.

The fact that you are unaware these are the same person is purely an internal matter – a limitation in your knowledge. Yet the extension is the same in both cases. So the difference in your reactions and thoughts is not caused by the external object, as extensionalist theories of meaning would assert, since in each case the external object is the same.

Many people have argued that the answer may be a mixture of both: a bit of narrow content and a bit of broad content (e.g. Dretske, 1988; Sterelny, 1990; Neander, 1995, 1999; Garfield, 2000; see also Botterill and Carruthers, 1999, pp. 156–160, 180–181). External factors may determine the meaning of some terms, especially concrete nouns compared to abstract ones, for example. We don't need to go to one extreme or the other. Perhaps teleological functionalism gives the fundamental origin of meaning (via innate atomistic natural signs or simple primitives), which intensions then elaborate on (by giving the relationships, associations, inferences and so on that you learn or form between different ideas). The meanings of 'horse' and 'horn' may derive from the external environment, but putting them together to form 'unicorn' is purely an internal process. Side-box 5.1 describes this theory in more detail.[9]

5.3.5 Teleological functionalism is too broad: panpsychism?

The teleological argument, that the meaning of mental states depends on their evolutionary history, is one that can be applied to any kind of evolved system. Obviously, then, it applies to things like the heart, which has the function of pumping blood, and the leaves on trees, which have the function of synthesizing energy-rich molecules by using chlorophyll. Indeed, all biological systems that have evolved have a function. So, why are hearts and leaves not conscious? What is the difference between mental teleo-functions and other kinds of biological teleo-functions?[10]

Well, Millikan (1984, 1993) in one way welcomes this point and says: yes, these are all biological functions; this analysis proves that the mind is naturalized – it is part of nature, and has functions just like other biological entities do. There are functional (i.e. intentional) states in the mind in the same way that there are functional states in any other biological system. Hearts and so forth have representations – of blood pressure and so on.

The difference between a leaf or a heart and a brain is that in brains the meaningful representations that arise – the ideas, concepts, thoughts and so on – are *used* or consumed. In functionalist terms, symbols have to be *read* by something else. What generates meaning,

9. Millikan (1984, chapter 19) also presents a theory similar to this view. She distinguishes between basic 'concepts' that are teleologically derived in their semantics, and 'beliefs' that are inferentially derived from concepts and form an (imperfectly!) holistic network. However, she also argues against this being a sharp dichotomy, saying that signs have varying degrees of intentionality rather than all-or-none (1984, chapter 7). In contrast, Fodor (1998a) maintains that almost all concepts/representations are information-bearing atoms (and, moreover, he is opposed to their meanings having teleological origins). In addition, Perlman (1997, 2002) also argues against Neander's (1999) two-factorism; see section 5.3.8 for more details.

10. One could interpret this teleological argument more positively, as being consistent with the metaphysical position of panpsychism, that is, the theory that consciousness is everywhere and is not just confined to humans, higher animals or any such elite group of systems. Throughout history, this theory has in fact held wide support and might be worth reviving (Skrbina, 2003).

then, is the process of using the representations – of *interpreting* the symbols or concepts, or making *judgements* about them. Millikan (1984, pp. 320–324) depicts a holistic network of intensions between the beliefs or judgements. Intentionality comes in degrees, depending how many intensions are involved (p. 126). Dennett (1988, 1991) also uses the term 'judgements' to describe the processing within the mind. Millikan says these judgements concern 'concepts' that derive their intentionality from their historical origins in evolution and learning.

Under these theories there are thus two types of representation: low and high order. This is touching on a theory of consciousness based on '*higher-order thought*' or '*higher-order perception*' (which I will come back to in section 11.2.2.3). The idea is that there are, as it were, two successive stages of crucial processing within the mind. One stage gives rise to simple, information-bearing representations of the outside world (cf. Dretske's 'natural signs' or indicators; see section 5.2.5). Then there is a higher-order stage that processes that lower-order information to generate thoughts, beliefs and other meaningful mental states that are also conscious states (such as 'I know I am now looking at a red spot'). The contents of the first-order states are about the world, but the contents of the second-order states are the first-order states. Consciousness requires this two-stage mechanism and cannot exist without it. Trees and hearts are not conscious because they do not have a second stage of representation.[11] Teleological functionalism per se does not necessarily entail that all biological systems are conscious.

I will come back to this theory later; we need to go through the neural theories first, since some of these are two-stage too. I'll join the neural and philosophical theories together in chapter 11.

5.3.6 Teleological functionalism excludes new mutations and ideas: the swampman argument

Imagine a philosopher called Davidson. A perfectly respectable philosopher, to be sure, but one who has the strange hobby of wandering about in swamps during thunderstorms. One day, while indulging in this pastime, he is struck by a bolt of lightning that reduces him to ashes. At the same time, the lightning also hits a nearby dead tree, and purely by chance the atoms and molecules within that dead tree are rearranged to form an object identical to the way that Davidson was. This creature is 'swampman': it is identical to Davidson but has been formed by random chance from the lightning strike (Davidson, 1987; see also Millikan, 1984, p. 93). (In fact, the original Davidson does not have to be killed for the argument to work.)

The general idea is thus that an entity that is an identical, atom by atom, copy of an existing person could in principle arise purely by chance. Now, according to teleological functionalism, that entity would not have thoughts or consciousness or even functions, because it would have no functional history: it would not have evolved. (Millikan, 1984, p. 93, says it might have qualia but certainly no intentionality.) Yet the argument is that we would naturally assume swampman to have the same thoughts, consciousness and experiences as the original Davidson. Swampman would go to Davidson's home, recognize his wife and talk in exactly the same way that Davidson would have done were he still alive.

---

11. The same applies for nonbiological representational states; for example, thermostats represent the environmental temperature but have no higher-order states and so are not conscious.

Behaviourally, swampman would be indistinguishable from the original Davidson and, we assume, subjectively or internally indistinguishable too. So there is a contradiction, a paradox, between our intuitions (the dictates of common sense) and the principles of teleological functionalism.

A corollary of this problem is that if some new 'thing' does arise in evolution, whether it is a whole swampman or merely some tiny change from a common organism (as happens in normal evolution), how many times does it have to be selected for before it counts as having been selected for, and therefore adaptive, and therefore functional? How many critical situations, where the new type of organism might either survive or die, does the organism have to live through in order for us to be able to say: well, this is a functionally adaptive, beneficial change? How long does swampman have to live? How many times does his heart have to have beaten in order to say that his heartbeat is adaptive? How many times does he have to go through meeting and escaping from alligators in the swamp in order to say that his mental state or tendency to run away whenever he sees an alligator is adaptive? The answer is indeterminate. So therefore all teleological arguments are too vague: they don't say how many times something has to survive in order to count as being adaptive (cf. Kitcher, 1993b; Godfrey-Smith, 1994).

Well, one can argue that adaptation is not an on and off thing; as we said above (section 5.2.6), you can have inefficient systems that are evolving towards perfection. You can, as some do, also say that it is species that are adapted, not individual organisms; you can count their numbers as proof of fitness. But still the questions remain as to how many generations a trait has to reproduce itself for, or how many organisms must exist carrying the trait, before you categorize it as selected for.

However, the individuals argument is important because one extension of the debate concerns whether traits are selected for during individual ontogeny. Does learning proceed through similar principles of selective winnowing of a mass of randomly generated ideas, or of experiences encountered in a complex life history (see Side-box 5.2)?

There are a number of answers to the swampman argument. One (Dretske, 1995, especially pp. 141–149) is that the notion that swampman would have the same kind of consciousness as the original Davidson is just an 'internalist intuition' that what we are aware of depends *only* on what is in the head. This intuition keeps creeping into our arguments; but it is the narrow content theory again (sections 5.2.3 and 5.3.4).

Dretske also asks: how do you know that this entity is a perfect copy of Davidson? Maybe it is a copy of a Martian. It may be an imperfect copy of a Martian (or a perfect one for all we know), but in a Martian the thing that looks like a human brain may not be used for thinking – in a Martian, what looks like a human brain might be used for cooling the blood (after all, Aristotle believed this is what the human brain does). So the question of whether this entity's 'brain' is generating consciousness or not depends on whether you think it *should be* generating consciousness. You only think that it should be generating consciousness because you are making the prior assumption that it is a copy of a human being. But maybe it is not a copy of a human being; maybe it is a copy of a Martian, or of nothing at all (since it's just a random collection of atoms).[12]

---

12. Dretske actually talks about whether the lightning creates a Klingon space shuttle or a copy of his old car, but I have changed the example to make it more directly relevant. Millikan (1984) presents a similar argument about swampman's heart.

SIDE-BOX 5.2 CREATIVITY

How do we think of new ideas, and why do only some of those ideas survive? Many theories of creativity postulate that there is an almost 'random' churning around of ideas in your head, mainly subconsciously, to give continuous chance restructuring, recombination or reordering of concepts (Poincaré, 1908; Hofstadter, 1995). Every now and then this process comes up with something that is somehow deemed a '*good*' idea, and thus one worth entering consciousness. A good idea is a beneficial, new mental state. But now we should wonder what the difference is between a good idea and a bad idea.

The teleological functionalist would say that the good idea is adaptive while the bad one isn't. Well, how do you know it is adaptive until it has been through some kind of testing procedure? If you have an idea that has not been used yet, how does the awareness mechanism that gives us an 'aha!' experience 'know' that this is a good, beneficial idea? The fact is that we lose many bad ideas before they are even tested. So the same sorts of questions can arise within the issue of mental creativity as with evolutionary innovation. One answer is that good ideas show coherence with the rest of the knowledge base (Rose, 1999b; Mangan, 2001). This is analogous to the idea that the likelihood that a new species will survive depends on how well it fits into its environment.

See Heilman et al. (2003) for a discussion of which brain areas are important in generating new ideas.

So before you can know whether a given system is or is not conscious, you have to know whether it should be, and whether it should be depends on whether it *represents* anything, and whether (and what) it represents depends on whether (and for what purpose) it *evolved*. And it is only by knowing that certain entities, such as you and I, have gone through an evolutionary history that we know that we should have consciousness generated in our brains (because only evolution generates the intentionality and '*representativeness*' of the brain systems upon which consciousness is based). If one of us is a zombie, a Martian or a Klingon in disguise, then our brain's functions (where 'our brain' is defined by its anatomical appearance and location) may be completely different. So whether swampman is or is not conscious does not settle the issue about whether teleological functionalism is valid or not; the argument is not convincing because you have to have a prior decision about what swampman is supposed to be. If it is supposed to be a human then Davidson's (1987) argument is valid – but this is an arbitrary and unjustified assumption at least, and at strongest it is an incorrect assumption (because we know swampman has no evolutionary history and thus is not *supposed* to be anything).

Imagine that, instead of swampman, Davidson had been replaced by a tree. Now, in normal trees there are tree rings whose sizes 'represent' the climate in each year of the tree's growth.[13] But do swamp-tree's rings represent any such thing? No: swamp-tree is just a random collection of atoms, and so is swampman.

---

13. Dretske (1988, pp. 55 and 66) says tree rings 'indicate', rather than represent, but the argument presented here still holds.

Swampman's brain might be able to do pure maths but not applied maths. For example, given that A>B and B>C it can work out that A>C, but it does not know what the symbols A, B and C mean. It can work out that red is more similar to pink than to blue, but not what those qualia represent.

Another reply to the swampman argument is to alter the definition of function. One variation allows for the possibility that there may be structures within an organism that have never actually been used in the past to aid survival. This situation can occur if their use has never been demanded by the circumstances (either of the individual or of the species as a whole). Nevertheless, these structures might turn out to be useful in some future situation. Arguably, then, they should be defined as having a purpose (Bigelow and Pargetter, 1987). It's easiest to see this in examples from within an individual. There are structures in our bodies, such as the spleen, that are there to deal with emergencies that we may never have had. The spleen is useful if you have a haemorrhage, for example, but if you have never had such an emergency you have never used your spleen. Does this mean that your spleen does not have a functional role? Surely it is not just an evolutionary hangover: a useless thing like the appendix that may have been important at one time in your ancestry but is not important now? We must be able to distinguish your spleen from your appendix, even though both may never have helped you at any time (so far).

Now, in the swampman case, you could say: well, the swampman has a complete set of structures and mechanisms in its brain that have the *potential* to be of benefit. So in that way, Bigelow and Pargetter's 'forward-looking' definition of function is appropriate. If an alligator swims up to swampman, or if swampman meets Davidson's wife, then the appropriate kind of adaptive coping behaviour will be triggered. Therefore on that definition of function, swampman does have the appropriate functional (mental) states within it.

However, there are problems with Bigelow and Pargetter's view. For example, Enç and Adams (1992) ask how far into the future we need to, or are allowed to, look. Survival is always relative, depending on the fit between the environment and the organism. There is no obvious limit to what new environments we can speculate might one day be encountered, and when. So the argument is liable to fall into an infinite regress across time, or to be indeterminate. Bigelow and Pargetter's view really is no advance over the backward-looking accounts of Wright (1973), Millikan (1984) and others (Kitcher, 1993b; Godfrey-Smith, 1994).[14]

Dennett (1995) argues that there is no principled answer, and that ascriptions of function are all indeterminate in the sense that functions are relative to the environment at the time. However, Amundson and Lauder (1994) and Hardcastle (1999b) instead suggest that we can use morphology (i.e. descend to an anatomical level) to ascribe function (after all, this is what practising scientists do). Their analyses return to Cummins' (1975) definition of function, which we discussed above under homuncular functionalism (section 4.2). Amundson and Lauder claim this approach too has a historical dimension, in that the evolution of structure is a guide to what functional roles the structures have played through the evolutionary development of the present organism. Thus teleological function can be ascribed, at least to anatomically definable structures.

---

14. The infinite regress argument also operates backwards in time: exactly how long in the past did evolution set up the present meaning of the representation? For details, see section 5.3.8.

5.3.7 **Nature does not represent and representations did not evolve**

First, Fodor (1996) has argued (in response mainly to Dennett, 1995) that the grounding of intentionality in evolution is nonsense because mental states are representational, that is to say, they are about something. They play a functional role in causing things to happen within the mind and in behaviour, which they can do because they symbolize some state of affairs outside themselves. Their content has meaning. But none of these properties applies to Nature. Evolution may be described as a 'blind watchmaker' (Dawkins, 1976) but there is no representation of where Nature wants to go, what the final design should look like, or how to go about shaping the course of events so as to cause the desired end. She does not have foresight and cannot represent either where she does or does not want to go. Moreover, natural selection, unlike the mind, cannot represent counterfactuals, i.e. states that do *not* exist, or have *never* existed in the past, or cannot possibly exist at any time in the past or future. Therefore things selected by natural selection cannot have intentionality (at least not in the same way that our mental states have intentionality, can stand for nonexistent states or can misrepresent). Hence our mental representations did not (necessarily) evolve in the same way that humans, spiders, elm trees, brains and neurons evolved.

Dennett (1996) replies that Darwin's mindless designer explanation of evolution is exactly what we need to see how intentionality reduces to (or is grounded in) a mechanical process. Intentionality did not suddenly spring up in full-blown form at a single point in human development. It evolved gradually, by 'incremental steps', and so did representation (see also Dennett, 1995, pp. 201, 205).[15]

Second, Fodor (1998a, 2000) argues that concepts are innate but not teleological. How can this be? Surely if something has evolved it is innate, and vice versa. He attributes the answer to Chomsky (1980). Fodor states that the only innate true knowledge creatures have is about the minds of other members of the same species. In the human case, he particularly mentions the language and the 'theory of mind' modules (2000, pp. 95–97).[16] The knowledge (e.g. the universal laws of grammar) we have is the same in all members of our species. It does not matter what those laws are (so long as they work), so long as we all have the same laws (e.g. Chomsky's 'linguistic universals'). The environment we evolved in, and the moment or period in history at which we acquired those laws, does not matter. Thus the meaning of the particular knowledge we have innately is not determined by the (nonhuman) environment, so its truth value is not determined teleologically. What our knowledge represents is the insides of other peoples' minds, and so long as we all have the same kind of mind our representations hold content that is true, and our evolutionary history is irrelevant.

Okasha (2003) disputes this, however, saying first that people are part of our natural environment, so if we have innate knowledge of their minds, what we know are still facts about our environment. Further, when the genes for language first appeared they had to spread within the species until every individual had them, and Fodor does not explain that development. There are many cases in biology where fitness to survive depends on how

---

15. Millikan (1984, chapter 7) also makes the point that intentionality comes in degrees, not as an all-or-none property.

16. However, he rather contradicts this when he approvingly supports (Fodor, 2000, p. 118) the existence of a module for spatial orienting within the environment (Hermer and Spelke, 1996).

common a trait is within the species, and one of those traits must be the having of true beliefs about the language of others, for if we can understand one another's language we are better adapted for survival. Hence evolutionary theory does account for our possession of linguistic universals via the standard Darwinian principles of natural selection.

In general, Spector (2002) follows Simon (1962; see section 4.2.6) in arguing that computationally functional modules will evolve naturally, and that they will be organized in a hierarchy.[17] Moreover, many computer simulations have shown that this can occur, and indeed have generated completely original problem-solving mechanisms ('genetic programming').

Fodor instead sees the functions of our representations as determined by synchronic factors, that is, by what they do now. For instance, Fodor (2000, p. 85) asks: what if Darwin's theory were one day discovered to be wrong – would this mean the function of the heart is not to pump blood? Of course that is its function, he says, and we don't need to look to the past history of that organ to see so. Although he doesn't go into detail, Fodor instead suggests that function may be ascribed on the basis of 'if the heart didn't do this the organism would die' (pp. 86–87). This could be construed as a more Cummins-like functional analysis, of the type we described under homuncular functionalism in chapter 4.

5.3.8 Teleological functionalism leads to an infinite regress of function

In the classic studies by Barlow (1953) and Lettvin et al. (1959) of ganglion cells in the frog's visual system, some of the cells were ascribed the function of detecting flying bugs, since the cells respond maximally to stimuli that induce the same image pattern on the retina as a flying bug. In section 5.2.6, I discussed how this ascription has been challenged on the grounds that stimuli other than flying bugs can activate those cells. In this section I introduce an even more profound disquiet, namely that of how far away intentionality points. 'How far away' can be understood both spatially and temporally. In spatial terms, at one extreme we have the 'distal' stimulus, namely, the flying bug. At the other is the 'proximal' stimulus, namely the image on the retina; for it is possible to claim that the cells are actually responding to changes in the pattern of light and dark striking the matrix of receptor cells. For that matter, it is possible to come even more proximal and say that a ganglion cell is responding to changes in the activity of the small group of receptor cells that lie within (or just are) its receptive field, or to the activity of the bipolar and amacrine cells that synapse onto it or, even more proximally, to the concentration of glutamate released into the vicinity of its dendrites . . . .

In temporal terms, over what timescale does the alleged function of the cell operate? The purpose of the cell's activity might be to detect bugs (or shadows on the retina, or changes of glutamate concentration or whatever), but why should it detect bugs (or whatever)? Because bugs are food, and it is useful to detect food. Why? So food can be caught. Why does the frog need to catch food? To obtain energy and nutrients. Why does it need those things? To keep itself alive. Why does it need to do that? So it can reproduce. Well, here we have a whole chain of purposes, aiming at consequences at longer and longer times into the future. So which one is *the* purpose of the cell's firing? Is it to detect bugs, catch food,

---

17. I think Spector's hierarchies are of layers rather than levels, as I define these terms in Side-box 4.4.

obtain nutrients, extend the frog's life, help reproduce the frog, continue the species, help construct the biosphere, engage in the planetary carbon cycle . . .? The answer seems indeterminate, and any single assertion would seem arbitrary (Dretske, 1986; Perlman, 2002; Enç, 2002).[18]

Now, first, some authors conclude there is a logical slide towards one extreme or the other. For example, Enç (2002) despairs that all biological functions collapse to the very distal 'aids reproduction of the species'. This function is unhelpfully broad; for example, it is obviously of no use in explaining how my thought of a tomato differs from my thought of Harry Potter. In contrast, Neander (1995) thinks that all functions collapse towards the proximal. (However, although this is logical, she hopes there is a way it can be stopped, as we will shortly see.)

Neander's hope reflects the fact that, like most authors, she has the intuition that there should be only one answer to the question of what a given mechanism does, or of what its content means. My thought about Harry Potter should be about him and about nothing else.

For example, Millikan (1993, pp. 92–94, 222–224) argues for a (moderately) distal stimulus in cases similar to that of the frog's visual cells, namely a bug. This is what the cells are *supposed* to do, the function they have evolved to fulfil. The frog species has survived because it contains cells that (at least sometimes) detect flying bugs, *tout court*. Hence, the frog's representational systems refer truthfully if they refer to bugs, not to shadows on the retina. Hommel et al. (2001) also arrive at a similarly distal solution (in general cognitive terms, not just for frog vision). Crossmodal integration (the coordination of vision, touch and hearing) in the guidance of action demands that what happens inside the nervous system must be 'about' objects and events in the world, such as a bug flying past, not about the proximal stimuli on the receptors.[19]

In contrast, Neander (1995) suggests we stop the logical slide to the proximal at a slightly lower-level description of the stimulus, namely a small dark moving thing. This level of description is the lowest at which the meaning is 'unanalysed', and that is thus independent of context/environment. To reach this conclusion, Neander (1995, 1999) utilizes a two-factor theory of meaning, in which a distinction is made between simple and complex types of representation, that is, between natural signs (sensory primitives) and inference-based representations. Remember, we introduced this duality back in section 5.3.4, as a compromise solution to the debate between externalism and internalism, or broad versus narrow content. Look back to Side-box 5.1 to refresh your memories on this. Neander follows especially Dretske's (1988) analysis.[20] Neander says it makes sense to suggest that the

18. To fill in yet more detail: why should the cell detect glutamate concentration changes? Because this means the afferents to the cell have changed their firing. Or: why should the cell detect changes in the pattern of light and dark in the retinal image? Because this means there may be a bug out there. (For even more problems and putative solutions, see the recent reviews by Enç, 2002, Perlman, 2002, and Walsh, 2002.)

19. Sterelny (1990) also plumped for flies. So too did Dretske (1981).

20. Neander (1999) criticizes the idea that all representations are teleologically derived, innate and atomistic. Atomistic concepts cannot be about things that have never impinged on our senses, like unicorns and quasars. Concepts defined purely by their internal links inevitably become part of a holistic network; but such networks slide towards solipsism and the inability to communicate with

simple types indicate the presence of physical features of the environment (a conception that fits well with the way workers on 'early vision' such as Marr, 1982, describe function at this stage of processing). It is these physical features (of flying bugs, and so on) that are causally efficacious in affecting neural activity and hence have an evolutionary role. Next there arise more complex representations derived by inferences from the simpler type and from each other. These are more like 'frames' (section 4.3.4) or data structures than like sentences in mentalese.

Neander says that misrepresentation cannot occur in the simple stage (hence they are like Dretske's 'natural signs'; section 5.2.5), but it can at the higher stage, where errors of judgement can occur. This gives a natural boundary to stop the logical slide into proximal meaning. A representation must be able to misrepresent in order to have intentionality (e.g. so it can stand for counterfactuals). Events that are too proximal cannot therefore have intentionality because they are infallible. Hence she concludes that frog visual cells function to detect the physical features that flying bugs possess, namely the properties 'small', 'dark' and 'moving'. Anything more proximal could not be a misrepresentation.[21]

However, Neander's analysis has been criticized by Perlman (2002) on the grounds that at very proximal levels malfunctions can occur. (Neander states that there can be malfunctions following neural, genetic or embryological damage, so there is the possibility of misrepresentation in principle – just not in practice – in undamaged frogs.) However, it is not obvious what the difference is in kind between these and the errors in interpretation that Neander says can occur at the later stage. In general, all two-factor theories are weak because they have no principled, non-circular, objective way of deciding whether any given representation derives its meaning from external causes or from internal patterns of inference (Perlman, 1997). Moreover, Perlman (2002) challenges Neander's account of how errors occur at the higher stage of processing. How are the contents of the other representations determined, except via the same mechanisms of inference that are proposed to account for the misrepresentational content of the focal representation? But these mechanisms are also liable to error, so the argument is circular.[22]

others, since any difference (such as learning something new) changes the whole network (Quine, 1960; Fodor and Lepore, 1992). However, if some concepts are innate atoms, and other concepts are derived from them by inference, but there are boundaries on how far these inferences reach, then Neander says everybody can be happy.

21. Neander (1999) also says that the slide into holism can be prevented by the modularization of the mind. The choice of which other representations form the background 'frame' (that contains relevant information) is constrained by the module boundaries. Conversely, and perhaps better, we could define modules as the regions of the mind that contain intrinsic links that form mini-holistic networks. Of course, then there arise issues about boundaries and the communication between modules that were introduced in sections 4.3.4 and 4.3.7. Fodor (2000), for example, has recently argued against the global modularity thesis, and in favour of atomistic representations (Fodor, 1998a). However, among no doubt many other ripostes to Fodor, Neander might reply that she is concerned with perceptual representations in this instance, and Fodor does not exclude sensory modules (just modules throughout the whole mind).

22. Contra Perlman, the higher-level errors might occur in the process of determining which other representations should be involved in the inferences, not in the process of reading their contents. Errors in reasoning often occur when the wrong premises are included, or when vital information is omitted.

We can add some further points of our own here. First, contra Neander, even at low levels the representations are not atomistic and are prone to errors. If there are cross-correlations between representational activations, then they no longer hold a single meaning each (Dretske, 1988, pp. 151–153). Empirically we know that even at early stages of vision, cells do talk to their neighbours and form links where there is correlated firing (e.g. Barlow, 1985; Field et al., 1993; Gilbert et al., 1996; DeVries, 1999; Kourtzi et al., 2003; Schnitzer and Meister, 2003). They also receive feedback from later stages (Hochstein and Ahissar, 2002; Stettler et al., 2002; Freeman et al., 2003, 2004). So pure, isolated, atomistic, single-meaning representations are not a viable hypothesis even at the low levels of analysis. (Side-box 5.1, Figure SB 5.1.2, illustrates some of these possible confounds.)[23]

More profoundly, all these workers confuse proximal/distal meaning with low/high level and with early/late stages of processing. Serial-processing models of a system comprise a sequence of stages, but all of these stages have many levels of description, from high to low, that give accounts of the functions, algorithms and mechanisms of each stage (see Side-boxes 4.1 and 4.4).[24] Therefore Neander's idea of limiting the slide at a certain 'level' refers to a level of description, but this does not coincide with a stage of processing, from which point one can read off the distance on the proximal/distal dimension. Thus her analysis does not give a dichotomy between error-prone misrepresentations and infallible natural signs, and thus a single answer to the question of meaning.

Instead, the answer may come by accepting a pluralist solution. Nature is multi-levelled, and interactions occur within systems at these various levels. A corollary is that at higher levels the systems have intentionality that is broader (their content being about things in

23. The fact that I have given empirical evidence pertaining to area V1 (neurophysiologically, concerning single cells; psychophysically, concerning channels) should not be taken to mean that single units there 'represent', in the way that grandmother cell theory asserts that single units can represent (section 6.2.6.1). Atomistic representations could in principle emerge from the collective activity of units whose firing is partially correlated (section 6.4; Nirenberg et al., 2001). However, in the context of the present discussion about whether retinal cells could be bug detectors, and whether 'early' stages of processing could be innate atomistic indicators (as Neander suggests), the point is that descending to a level as low (or a stage as early) as feature detectors does not solve the problem of how representations can be univocal (having single meaning); the empirical evidence does not support this suggestion.

24. To understand psychosemantics fully, we need to follow through completely the implications of the multi-level model. One consequence is that intentionality points over distances that correlate with level. *A question we should ask is, 'meaning for whom?'* Many philosophers speak as if there were an implicit self for whom the representation has meaning. This is virtual dualism. Others emphasize the consumers of representations, but again these recipients should not be seen as whole people – they are processing mechanisms linking to other representations and to behaviour. If the meaning of a representation depends on its interpretation, then that meaning is given by whatever those consuming mechanisms are, whether a whole network or just a few output systems. Alternatively, the mechanisms downstream from the representation may be seen as passively receiving the meaning or content. (I am contrasting the views that the 'late' mechanisms are 'listening to' versus 'reading' the output of the representation; cf. Dennett's 1991 distinction between 'show' and 'tell'; Dennett prefers the latter.) In either case, what is most important is that these mechanisms comprise only a fraction of the rest of the brain. However, mechanisms at lower levels are more numerous than at high levels, the relevant (late, downstream) mechanisms form a physically smaller network that comprises a smaller fraction of the brain, and the content or information they process is more limited in scope (Rose, 2000a).

the environment, for example), whereas at lower levels system activity is about more proximal events (like mentalese vehicle syntax, nerve cell firing, and glutamate concentration) and is thus narrower in scope. This multi-level nature of events means that many meanings apply to any event (such as the firing of a cell in the frog's visual system), at all the various levels. A thought about dinner is not a simple thing, semantically speaking. It includes many connotations, defining conditions, implicit implications, images (visual, gustatory, olfactory, and so on), potential motor responses, emotional overtones and so on, at levels from autonomic gastroenteric responses up to anticipation of the satisfaction of feeling full. So, like Goode and Griffiths (1995), Lycan (1996, chapter 7), Walsh (2002, pp. 320–322) and Enç (2002, p. 311), we should reject the assumption there is only one true (essential) meaning or function of a representation. We can agree with Lycan (2001, p. 33) when he writes: 'Does the frog represent flies, food, small dark moving objects, or black blobs? I say, yes. (All of the above).'

5.4 Conclusion

Teleological functionalism constitutes a genuine attempt to solve the problem of intentionality, and may be considered to have made considerable progress towards understanding how our thoughts can have semantic content. Not everyone is convinced, and there are problems with the theory that continue to drive further research. Nevertheless, the core idea behind the movement is certainly an improvement over the supernaturalism of some previous philosophies (chapter 2).

Which is better, though: homuncular or teleological functionalism? In one sense, the tension and debate between these two continues. Yet aspects of both are often used and combined into a single theory, since there is much commonality in their assumptions of multi-levellism and modularity, and in the emphasis on functional role. (For an explicit example of how homuncular and teleological functionalisms can be combined, see Buller, 1998.)

Indeed it may be that these are not rivals but complementary aspects of the problem of scientific understanding. For example, homuncular theories are the basis of much of the 'functional analysis' that is actually carried out by neuroscientists to discover the mechanisms existing in the brain (e.g. Machamer et al., 2001), while teleological analysis can explain the origins of the structure of the mind/brain and the purposes of the various mechanisms and their organization. *The how and the why of a system both have to be accounted for.*

▓ RECOMMENDED READING

Brief introductions to teleological functionalism are given in the classic texts by Bechtel (**Philosophy of Mind**, 1988a, chapter 7), and Lycan (**Consciousness**, 1987, chapter 4). More detailed textbooks on psychosemantics and teleosemantics include Goldberg and Pessin's **Gray Matters** (1997, chapter 3) and Lowe's **An Introduction to the Philosophy of Mind** (2000, chapter 4). Also, Botterill and Carruthers

(The Philosophy of Psychology, 1999, chapters 6 and 7) are excellent on the origins of psychosemantics, while **Approaches to Intentionality** by Lyons (1995) contains a valuable introductory review of theories, and Jacob and Jeannerod, in **Ways of Seeing** (2003, chapter 1), apply teleosemantics to vision.

A gentle introduction to the current debates on the evolution of modules is given by Plotkin in **Evolutionary Thought in Psychology** (2004, chapter 7), while for hotter arguments see the volumes edited by Hitchcock on **Contemporary Debates in Philosophy of Science** (2004, chapters 15 and 16) and those on Darwinism edited by Ross et al. (**Dennett's Philosophy**, 2000) and Brook and Ross (**Daniel Dennett**, 2002). Some other readable monographs on the evolution of cognition and the modularity hypothesis are Sterelny's **Thought in a Hostile World** (2003) and Buller's **Adapting Minds** (2005b).

Some classic readings on functionalism are included in Lycan's **Mind and Cognition** (1999, sections 4 and 10; see especially the Introductions on pp. 8–13 and 195–198), while very good collections of papers are to be found in **Nature's Purposes** (Allen et al., eds, 1998), Hull and Ruse's **Philosophy of Biology** (1998), Buller's **Function, Selection, and Design** (1999a), Hardcastle's **Where Biology Meets Psychology** (1999a) and Ariew et al.'s **Functions** (2002). A very readable discourse on teleology is Dretske's **Naturalizing the Mind** (1995) and an update of Millikan's views is given in **Varieties of Meaning** (2004). For more advanced discussions, see **Dynamics in Action** (Juarrero, 1999), **Norms of Nature** (Davies, 2001), **Philosophy of Mental Representation** (Clapin, 2002), '*Thoughts and their contents*' (Adams, 2003), Margolis and Laurence's '*Concepts*' (2003) and Clapin et al.'s **Representation in Mind** (2004).

Representation and the physical basis of mental content

OBJECTIVES

According to the dominant functionalist programmes (chapters 2, 4 and 5), consciousness depends on symbolic representations that have intentional content (broadly speaking, they 'mean' or are about something). Inferential, computational processes may or may not have to operate on representations to make them conscious representations.[1] In this chapter, therefore, we will look at materialist theories of representation within the mind–body context. First, we discuss at what level such entities might exist and how many of them can coexist, and then three examples will be presented of common neuroscientific models of representation and associated processing. This will

---

1. The need for inferential processes would tie functionalism in with *indirect* theories of perceptual psychology.

prepare us for a comparison of the properties of conscious and unconscious representations in the next chapter.

You need to become aware that representations may exist at many different levels. Unfortunately the various possibilities are often not compared or even discussed as a group within the narrow disciplinary structure of research (that is, neuroscience departments tend to assume neural models are all there are, physicists like quantum theory, social scientists take interpersonal interactions to be the only relevant source of the mind and so on). It may or may not be a matter of picking which is the 'right' level at which to explain representation and consciousness. Under homuncular functionalism (chapter 4), for example, we need to know what is happening at all the levels at once. Additionally, as humans develop, the relevant level may shift as functions become built in, lower levels become restructured and new higher levels emerge.

Another important lesson is that old theories can be worth knowing about: modern workers often rediscover them, and are not aware of the problems that were raised first time round that, in many cases, had led to those models being abandoned.

6.1 Introduction: On representation

The word 'representation' can mean different things to different people, so I must begin by clarifying what I will be talking about. For the most part, I will be using the word in an everyday sense, to refer to what is going on in your head when you think about X, where X might be, for example, 'grandmother'. To understand this level of representation is in fact a core thrust of this book. I will be trying to analyse this level in the next few chapters and relating psychological to neural definitions – for example, treating representation as the physiological effects of a stimulus (*pace* Marr, 1982, for example, who used the word in this way). Whenever an event occurs in the outside world, the sensory receptors respond and messages travel along the sensory nerves and initiate a chain of events in the central nervous system. These central events presumably function to analyse the stimulus, identify it and so on, and may sometimes, somehow, lead to our 'conscious awareness' of the stimulus. Generalizing, maybe the same physiological principles of operation underlie all our thoughts and feelings as well as our sensory experiences. In later chapters we will consider the possibility that different principles may apply in these cases, but at first we will stick to the simplification that there is only one type of representation.

As we have seen, the representationalist thesis is controversial: a great deal of work has had to go on to defend it against attacks from numerous quarters.[2] One might think that the everyday notion we begin with here – what is going on in your head when you think

---

2. One such attack is that representations are the objects of study by a dualistic mind; they are literally re-presentations of the stimulus to the mind, or as Dennett (1998) puts it, second transductions (the first being from the outside world to the brain, and the second from the brain to the mind). They are therefore most consistent with Cartesian dualism.

about grandmother – is not vulnerable to such problems. However, even this everyday definition carries presumptions that we have both to be aware of and to beware of – for example, the common intuition of narrow content, i.e. that subjective experience depends *only* on what is in the head (section 5.3.4).

It is all too easy to slip across from using and understanding the word 'representation' in one meaning to another. Indeed, this may be the main reason we have such problems communicating with one another in the various disciplines of psychology, philosophy and neuroscience.[3] However, it is important to bear in mind these shades of meaning here. The issues are not simple, and the meanings do overlap to an extent: for example, all theories accept that sensory events cause central events that are specific in some way to the particular sensory event. Whether you call these central events 'representations' (as opposed to signs, indicators, and so on: section 5.2.5) depends what your underlying assumptions are about the nature of mind, and how precise you want to be. At the current state of thinking in this field, precision might be premature. For pedagogical purposes at least, we need to start simply. Hence I begin by treating representation as a single concept, using it to introduce us to theories that talk about the neural bases of 'consciousness' without subdividing types of representation. Later, I will return to the issue of the subdivision of representation – and indeed to alternatives to philosophical representationalism altogether.

6.2 **What are the relevant level(s) of description?**

The first issue is what level of description we need to look at. There have been numerous suggestions as to which 'crucial' level gives rise to consciousness. Note that these implicitly assume that there is only one such level, which contrasts with the conclusion of homuncular functionalism that many levels are relevant. Remember, under the discussion of multi-levellism in chapter 4, we outlined the view that complex systems such as the brain are nested hierarchies of systems and subsystems, with new emergent properties arising from the interactions between the subsystems. As was explained in Side-box 4.4, 'levels' have to be distinguished from 'stages' (along a serial processing pathway) and 'layers' (of control, which can take place between subsystems at the same level, e.g. an executive and its slave subroutines). Although the different levels often correlate with the scale or size of the systems under discussion, the distinction between levels is more the logical one of supervenience/emergence rather than whole/part encapsulation. (See Salthe, 1985, chapters 6 and 7, for a more detailed discussion.)

Now, the levels I will discuss can be ordered most simply by scale, from the smallest to the largest: they are the quantum, field,[4] sub-neuronal, neuronal, polyneuronal, mental, social

---

3. Some authors deal with such ambiguities by defining terms such as representation$_1$ and representation$_2$ to help distinguish their meanings. I have not done so here, since such terms are not universal and so readers constantly need to look up the definitions to remind themselves which meaning is which in the context of the current section of the book.

4. It's not clear how large 'fields' are envisaged to be by their protagonists, so my placing it next to the quantum level merely reflects a similarity between physics-based as opposed to cellular theories.

and environmental levels. However, for expository purposes I need to end up talking about the neuronal and polyneuronal levels, since these are the main topics in research on consciousness. I will therefore begin just above the neuronal with the mental level, move up to the largest levels, then leap right down to the smallest (the quantum) and move progressively up again until I arrive at the neuronal level.

6.2.1 Mental level

Homuncular functionalism presupposes that there are many levels within the mind as well as throughout nature. However, for the moment, I think that we are going to have to simplify and just talk about two 'mental' levels. One is the level (or set of levels) that concerns awareness of the outside, i.e. the non-mental, world. This includes (awareness of) seeing red, being in pain, inspecting a table, etc.

This contrasts with awareness of yourself, which some people construe as a second or higher level (or set of levels).[5] Some people use the term 'consciousness' only to refer to self-awareness: if you are aware of yourself then you are conscious, and if you are aware only of the outside world then you are not conscious. For example, you can operate on 'autopilot', engaging with the world – driving, eating and so on – while your attention is focused elsewhere.

Most of the content of chapters 6–10 is about the basic type: awareness of the outside world. This is, first, because, according to some, it is logically prior. For example, the empiricist philosophers Locke and Hume asserted that thoughts are built up out of experiences. (This view contrasts with the rationalism of Descartes and others, that thought takes priority.) Second, evolutionary theory implies that we need to represent the world before we need to know ourselves, so self-awareness is a later development and thus probably more complex (Churchland, 1988; but compare the social theories in section 6.2.2 below). Third, it is simpler in that we can get a handle on sensory and motor phenomena, by breaking them down into atomic 'qualia' and specific action plans, whereas 'the self' seems a very complex whole and is thus more difficult to analyse. Finally, neuroscientific research on animals pertains, many people assume, to their awareness of the outside world rather than of themselves. Thus most of physiology is about interaction with the outside world: how animals move, find food, maintain homeostasis and reproduce the species. Most neuroscientific theories of how the brain works have therefore arisen within the framework of studying how organisms deal with the outside world.

We will return to the notions of self-awareness and higher-order representations in more detail later, in chapter 11.

In general, theories of consciousness and representation at the 'mental' level include cognitive information flow models and diagrams of the interconnections between black-box modules subserving memory, language, visual perception and other specific functions. These show the relationships between different types of putative representation and the pathways mediating various processes of inference or association that must exist to create and transform one representation into another.

5. Others see this level rather as a higher 'stage' of processing, along the lines illustrated in Side-box 5.1. Again, this can be confusing, because it is not clear what they mean! In chapter 11 we will discuss these dichotomies of mental states again.

6.2.2 **Social and environmental levels**

'Above' the mental we may place models at the interpersonal and the environmentally 'embedded' levels (which are not mutually exclusive).

6.2.2.1 **Interpersonal level**

There are several positions attributing the origin of mind to social factors. One suggests that an important function of the mind is to predict events in the world – including the behaviour of others. Now, if others are assumed to be like us, they too are trying to predict what we will do. Cognitive psychology (following Craik, 1943) would suggest we build models in our heads of other people, so we can run the models in fast time to predict their behaviour. An individual (let's call him or her Gerry) therefore goes through a process of inference as follows: 'Each person around me possesses a mental model of me. Therefore I must put a model of me within my model of each person, in order to predict what that person thinks I am going to do, because that in turn is affecting what that person is about to do.' The assumption is that Gerry's models of others' models of Gerry give rise to representations within Gerry, not only of what Gerry is going to do, but also of what Gerry thinks and knows. This then is consciousness – or we might say it is what gives Gerry consciousness, or makes Gerry's representations conscious ones. By generalizing across the models that Gerry attributes to the many individuals around him or her, Gerry develops an idea of the contents of Gerry's own mind as unique, and this, it is proposed, is Gerry's self-consciousness (e.g. Humphrey, 1983; see also Bogdan, 2000).

Social interactionists (e.g. Cooley, 1902; Mead, 1934) tell a similar story, except couched mainly in terms of linguistic interaction: we tell each other what we think about each other, and our self-portraits develop from these interactions. What others tell us about themselves gives us our representations of them; and what they tell us about ourselves, and we in turn tell them about ourselves, is what we think we are. This view in fact forms part of a tradition, dating back at least to the 1830s, in which social forces are proposed to be dominant in determining what we believe and in creating the exact nature of the individual self and personality. This paradigm has been developed by Feuerbach, Marx, Harré, Foucault, Vygotsky and others (see Burkitt, 1991, for a clear review).[6] In all cases, the existence of consciousness per se is postulated to originate from social interactions rather from the intrinsic psychological or biological properties of the individual. For instance, Mead's (1934) 'social behaviourism' was an attempt to locate the origin of consciousness within the social realm rather than the individual mind. In adults, thinking could arise in the form of internalized or inner speech: a conversation between the active (executive, action-selecting) thinking process and the internalized model of the self-as-seen-by-others built from previous experiences of social interaction and stored in memory.[7] This tradition

---

6. For example, early versions of the theory saw the general social consensus as the crucial factor, while more recently the dictats of authority figures are acknowledged to have disproportionate influence. Prelinguistic influences (gesture, body language) on self-consciousness are also increasingly recognized.

7. With hindsight one can recognize here similarities to Miller et al.'s (1960) division of thoughts into plans and images, held in frontal and posterior parts of the cerebrum (Side-box 8.1). Essay topic: Compare this dichotomy with modern theories of the updating of cognitive models of the self by internal feedback mechanisms and their failure in various disorders (Side-box 11.1). In what ways are

emphasizes the importance of the individual's taking an active behavioural role in initiating and maintaining interactions with other people, rather than building awareness within the individual from passively received sensory inputs originating from an unchanging and objective external world.

One could perhaps categorize the recent concept of 'memes' as falling within the overall social/linguistic tradition. Memes are ideas that spread from person to person, occupy their thoughts and mutate so as to become more intrusive and persistent (Dawkins, 1976; Dennett, 1991, 1995; Blackmore, 1999). Much (if not all) of the mind is suggested to be filled with such ideas, including those expressing the social consensus (what is desirable, acceptable habits, 'cool' fashions) and the very idea of ourselves as conscious beings. Another recent strand of research connects nonverbal imitative behaviour to our mutual and hence self-understanding. Thus the control and perception of body movements seem to be intimately linked and, given that even newborn children can imitate maternal gestures, there may be innate mechanisms linking the expression and identification of gestures (e.g. Metzinger and Gallese, 2003; Gallese et al., 2004).[8] Another innate mechanism for social interaction we may possess is a 'theory of mind' module that enables us to grasp the contents of other minds – and even to conceive the idea that other people have minds at all (e.g. Frith and Frith, 2003). A more general notion is that consciousness arises from empathic communication between people: 'inter-subjectivity' based on an intuitive or emotional understanding of other people's feelings and states of mind (see Thompson, 2001; Whitehead, 2001; Thompson and Colombetti, 2005).

A wide range of views thus exists within this category of 'social cognitive neuroscience', and these ideas seem to be of increasing influence; see further in section 11.3.2.3. For reviews, see Ochsner and Lieberman (2001), Cacioppo (2002), Adolphs (2003) and Ochsner (2004); for readings, see Cacioppo et al. (2002), Frith and Wolpert (2003), Heatherton (2004) and Hurley and Chater (2005). Of especial interest is the way several of these theorists emphasize the need for multi-level analyses (see chapter 4), integrating the social, cognitive and neural levels, rather than seeing any single level as predominant in creating consciousness.

6.2.2.2 Environmental level

A perhaps more general group of theories stresses environmental 'embeddedness'. These are an extreme form of what we have been calling 'broad content' theories (section 2.4.3.1; see also sections 2.5.2.2 and 5.2.) They emphasize that consciousness arises from the interaction between the brain and its environment (which can be physical as well as social). The argument here extends not just to intentionality, however, but even to qualia. For example, 'colour' does not exist in the outside world (there are just photons of different wavelengths) nor in the brain (there are just nerve cells firing); colour is an emergent construct of the interaction between the world and the brain. The rocks on the surface of this planet were not 'coloured' before creatures with colour vision evolved, and conversely such creatures would not see colours without those rocks (and other things) to look at. The emphasis is on

---

theories of 'internal conversation' (Mead, 1934; Morin, 2005) different from Fodor's (1975) 'language of thought' (section 2.5)?

8. At the neural level such imitation might involve 'mirror neurons'; see section 11.3.2.3.

co-evolution; we evolved the mechanisms to experience colours because in our ancestors' environments there were physical arrangements that made such experiences useful (Varela et al., 1991; Thompson, 1995). Another example is the perceived colours of plants. Monitoring the ripeness of fruits has often been cited as a function for colour vision, and a pigment in the retina in some species of monkey has been found to match very precisely the spectral reflectance of the ripe fruits that the monkeys eat (Sumner and Mollon, 2000; Regan et al., 2001; Wolf, 2002). Both the monkey's retinal pigment and the fruit's skin pigment have co-evolved to match one another (cf. the co-evolution of flowers and pollinating insects.) By analogy, all conscious awareness of the world has arisen similarly. The mind matches the world; the mind is a model of the world; 'information' flows freely between the mind and the world, in both directions, and consciousness is an emergent property of that flow.

6.2.3 **Quantum level**

Now we leap to the opposite extreme, to quantum level theories. The idea that to explain consciousness you need to look at events at the quantum level actually has quite long roots (see Jibu and Yasue, 1995). One idea within quantum physics is that observing events in some way influences those events: there is an interaction between the observer and the physical world (see Side-box 6.1). From here it is not far to the idea that human consciousness, through acts of observation, interacts with the physical world at the quantum level (the 'Copenhagen interpretation' of Niels Bohr). Hence consciousness itself must be explained at that level.

One of the modern developments of this theory (Penrose, 1989, 1994; Hameroff, 1998) centres on the microtubules, long hollow tubes of protein running across the inside of nerve cells. One traditional theory about microtubules is that they hold the structures of the nerve cell in position and maintain its integrity and motility (together with microfilaments and intermediate filaments). There is evidence to suggest that they also transport proteins and other materials within the cell – synaptic vesicles, for example, move along microtubules towards the synapse. However, Penrose points out that there is an unusual mathematical structure to the microtubule molecules. Penrose's suggestion is that they can undergo a kind of resonance, such that quantum wave functions are generated within the microtubules. His theory, then, is that when you make a decision or have an experience, this involves the collapsing of the wave functions, resolving them into some particular state of the microtubule proteins.

Penrose also argues against our ability to simulate consciousness on computers. There are mathematical theories which state that certain problems are 'undecidable': some puzzles cannot be solved ever, in principle. Penrose (1989) suggests that we cannot even write, let alone solve, a mathematical description of consciousness, because this is one of those problems. You couldn't even simulate consciousness on a computer, because the mathematical problems at the quantum level are undecidable. Thus the idea of functionalism, that you can simulate consciousness on a computer (see section 2.5), is excluded.

In sum, the idea of quantum theories is that the origin of consciousness is in some way linked with really fundamental aspects of the physics of the universe. To understand consciousness we have to look right down to events at the quantum level.

SIDE-BOX 6.1 QUANTUM PHYSICS: THE 'DOUBLE-SLIT' EXPERIMENT

Figure SB 6.1.1a shows a plan view of a partition with two vertical slits in it, and a source of coherent waves, such as laser light. There is also a screen at the back. Light passing through each slit radiates out as though from an independent source. If there is only one slit, then the light illuminates the screen smoothly, with the peak intensity in line with the slit. The intensity profile created is like that in Figure SB 6.1.1b. But if there are two slits, then these both act as sources of light and the waves they give out interfere with each other, either cancelling out or adding together to give peaks and troughs of light energy. Thus what you end up with on the screen is a rhythmic intensity profile: a *'grating'* pattern (Figure SB 6.1.1c). The spacing between the peaks of light intensity varies with the spacing between the slits. This demonstration affirms the wave theory of light.

However, this phenomenon is not easily explained by the particle theory of light. When a particle goes through one of the slits it heads off towards the screen at the back – but why doesn't every

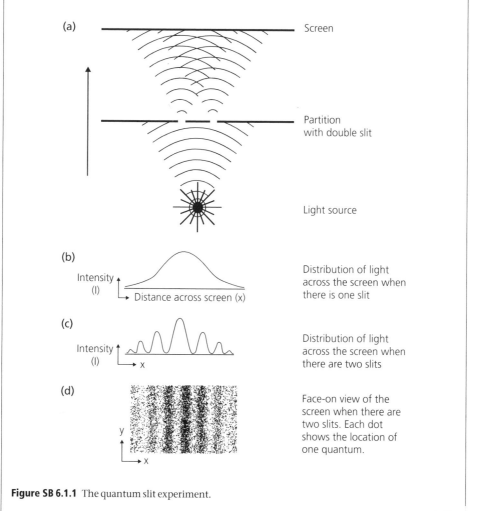

Figure SB 6.1.1 The quantum slit experiment.

continues

particle always go in the same direction? If you make the light source very, very dim so that you can actually monitor individual quanta (for example, you can put photocells or photographic film in place of the screen) then you can see where each quantum lands (Figure SB 6.1.1d). What is remarkable is, first, that the density (with two slits) is periodic. Second, when each photon reaches the screen it exists at just one spot on the screen, where a pulse or quantum of light is detected. One does not see a diffuse wave; one photocell only at a time lights up and registers each particle. By the time the quantum arrives at the screen it is a particle. But if it is a single particle, why should the second slit make any difference? If a single particle passes through one slit it should just carry on where its own momentum takes it; but why should the second slit have any effect on which direction the particle moves in? If you cover the second slit up, it makes a big difference to the distribution pattern of hits, and this is one of the basic puzzles faced by quantum physics.

Now, the resolution is that so-called 'particles' of light, photons, are actually little 'wave functions'. They are semi-localized but they also contain a wave of a particular frequency that is spread out and that potentially covers a very wide area (in theory, perhaps an infinite area). Certainly the wave function spreads over the entire apparatus including the observational mechanism (the screen). So where exactly is the photon? When the screen is present it resolves the event (the passage of the photon) to create a unique outcome, in which the photon becomes localized to a single point in space and time. This is what they call 'collapsing the wave function'. The wave is actually a kind of probabilistic wave that defines the probability of where the particle is in space. Thus the location is initially indefinite or unresolved, until you make an observation (i.e. you cause the wave function to interact with the screen). The act of making an observation causes the wave function to collapse to a single point, the position where the photon is when it hits the screen. But until that occurs, the wave function is widely spread out: its location and momentum are undetermined.

Schrödinger satirized the idea of 'indeterminacy until you observe' with a thought experiment. Imagine you have a cat in a completely sealed box, inside which there is some radioactive material that is decaying, i.e. giving out particles at unpredictable intervals. Also in the box is a detector of those particles. If the detector registers a particle of the radioactive substance coming off, then it triggers a mechanism that releases a poisonous gas that kills the cat. So if one of these particles has been emitted, then the cat will be dead, and if no particle has been emitted, the cat will be alive. Now, if you ask the question, as an observer outside the box: 'At *this* instant in time, is the cat alive or dead?', the observer can't tell, because no one knows what has happened (if anything) in the box. So what quantum physics postulates is that the cat is neither alive nor dead – the cat is in an indeterministic, unresolved state. That is to say, there is a probabilistic wave function inside the container. When you open up the container and look, the wave function resolves itself (collapses), and the cat instantly becomes either alive or dead, i.e. the probability of the cat being alive or dead reduces to either 0 or 1. Thus the suggestion is made that the observing instrument (whether a person or a mechanism such as a screen) is part of the wave function; all of the entities are initially linked together ('quantum entanglement'; for a tutorial review, see Woolf and Hameroff, 2001).

There are, obviously, caveats about this kind of theory. One can wonder about the validity of making such a very big leap between a very low level of description and a very high level of description (consciousness). What are all these intermediate levels: why do you need nerve cells and neural networks, why are nerve cells the shapes they are, why is the cortex anatomically different from the basal ganglia, and so on? The process of cause and effect seems to leap over these intermediate levels. Why does losing blood supply to the brain or giving someone a hallucinogenic drug affect their consciousness? There must be some relevant processes at the intermediate levels of synaptic neurotransmitters and anatomical structure, yet these are not specified by the theory.

Woolf and Hameroff (2001) have made a start on this question, suggesting that neurophysiological processes as conventionally studied are all preconscious. These, what I have been calling 'intermediate' levels, affect which neurons are involved in creating any given quantum wave function. By the activation of synapses, a chemical cascade is initiated within the dendrite, turning on or off the ability of microtubules to engage in quantum states, and thus whether that cell will generate consciousness. Woolf and Hameroff further posit that the quantum wave function relevant to consciousness is not (usually) restricted to the microtubules within a single neuron, but is normally spread throughout the brain, or at least a region of brain. By opening and closing 'gap' junctions[9] between dendrites, Woolf and Hameroff speculate, the spread of quantum waves between neurons is initiated and controlled. Once created, it is the collapse of a wave function that constitutes a conscious experience or a conscious decision. Thus, to explain consciousness fully, we still need to know about all the neuroanatomy, physiology and pharmacology. Yet the 'hard question' (section 2.2.2.1) remains unanswered: how is it that collapsing a wave function leads to phenomenal experience, i.e. qualia?

One can also wonder about the specificity of the theory, because microtubules are, in fact, a component of all cells, from amoebae upwards; certainly small single-celled organisms have microtubules in them. So does this mean that every organism that contains microtubules is conscious? Or is there something special about the microtubules in nerve cells, and if so, only in human brains or in animal brains as well? The theory comes close to panpsychism (cf. section 2.5.2.3); it seems too broad.

There are also important doubts about whether the relevant quantum states can be created at normal body temperatures. Such states normally require very low temperature conditions and isolation from other systems (see Woolf and Hameroff (2001) for the ongoing debate).

And, I suppose, equating consciousness with collapsing wave functions at the quantum level is a kind of identity theory. Do mental thoughts cause the wave functions to collapse or is it the collapse of the wave functions that causes the thoughts? Neither: they are the same. The theory has all the problems of two-level identity theory that we described in chapters 2–5.[10]

---

9. Gap junctions are close connections between cells that allow the passage of small molecules and electric currents directly between the cells through a tunnel-like aperture. Their functional roles are a matter of much debate at the moment. Although their conductivity decreases at high frequencies (it is reduced by more than 70% in the gamma frequency range), they have been linked to the genesis of synchronous oscillations at 40 Hz (but also at lower and higher frequencies). They connect cells of certain types, particularly GABA-releasing inhibitory interneurons (in the cortex), to form large networks. Several such networks may exist in parallel among different types of inhibitory cells and glia. Note that there are almost no gap junctions between pyramidal cells, as Woolf and Hameroff (2001) speculate there should be. Also, mutant mice lacking gap junctions show no obvious behavioural changes (are they zombie mice?). For reviews, see Galaretta and Hestrin (2001) and Connors and Long (2004).

10. It also has the problem of how intentionality is determined within a widespread area of activity of varying size; cf. Calvin's theory that there is spreading activation among the pyramidal cells of the cortex (section 7.3.3).

6.2.4 **Field level**

Several theories involve a brain 'field', which means a continuously graded physical variable spread over a region of brain tissue. The postulated size is usually unspecified; it might lie within a single cortical area, or it might fill the entire brain.[11]

For example, as mentioned in the previous section, Woolf and Hameroff (2001) posit a quantum wave field spread throughout the visual areas of the brain. This is supposed to explain the binding of the various features of a visual stimulus (its colour, motion, orientation, etc.) to form a unified percept (section 4.3.7).[12]

However, most field theories postulate electromagnetic gradients.[13] Since the brain is electrically active, and this activity can be detected even from outside the scalp by EEG and MEG recorders, it seems reasonable to wonder if the potentials inside the brain's volume might be affecting cell activity there in any functionally relevant fashion. One of the first theories was put forward by the Gestalt psychologist Köhler (1940). According to this idea, electrical field potentials across the brain represent objects. These potentials correspond to the particular objects they represent by resembling them: for example, seeing a triangle involves the formation of a triangularly shaped potential across the visual cortex. Intentionality is thus based on isomorphism.[14] In addition, the fusion of the images from the two eyes occurs because the electrical fields set up by each superimpose in the visual cortex to form a single field, the basis of single 'Cyclopean' vision (Marshall and Talbot, 1942). However, Köhler's approach to representation suffers from the man-in-the-head problem (who is looking at the potentials to recognize their shape?), so the isomorphism idea is omitted from the several recent revivals of electromagnetic field theory. These theories claim an explanation for consciousness in such fields (Pockett, 2000, 2002a; John, 2001; McFadden, 2002a,b).

Regrettably, recent proponents of these theories seem not to discuss the empirical evidence that led to similar theories being discounted more than fifty years ago. Researchers then first lacerated the visual cortex in cats and monkeys with deep cuts that would have disrupted any continuous field, and found this made no difference to the animal's visual functionality.[15] But these workers did not just content themselves with making a series of cuts crisscrossing the extent of the cortex. They even inserted metal pins into the cortex to short-circuit any electrical field, or conversely, inserted electrically insulating material

11. In addition, Libet (1994) has a dualistic theory of a 'conscious mental field' that is not physical, and Searle (2000) a monistic biological (non-reducible emergent property) theory in which consciousness is a 'unified, qualitative, subjective field' that is modified (rather than created) by sensory inputs.

12. In another dualistic theory, Eccles (1986, 1990; Beck and Eccles, 2003) proposed a set of about forty million independent quantum fields, each about sixty micrometres in diameter (see section 7.2.2.1).

13. So far, no one has speculated that the field underlying consciousness might be chemical or ionic, despite the empirical evidence for the existence of such fields (Syková, 2004; Vizi et al., 2004). Their functioning would be slower than for electric fields; but not all aspects of consciousness are instantaneous (section 10.3)!

14. See Barsalou (1999) for a recent argument in favour of analogue, imagistic (and in some cases isomorphic) representation, and arguments against arbitrary language-of-thought symbols.

15. Because cortical tissue is supplied with blood from vessels running across the outer surface of the brain, vertical cuts can be made into the depth of the cortex between the blood vessels to disrupt the continuity of the neural tissue with minimal damage to it.

(mica) to block the field. Any electrical current or field would thus have been completely disrupted or distorted. Yet no effects on behaviour could be observed (Lashley et al., 1951; Sperry et al., 1955; Sperry and Miner, 1955).[16]

Köhler (1958) himself pointed out two further problems for his theory: (1) how can visual after-effects (Figure 4.6) develop and persist despite eye or object movements (which should smear out the fields across the spatial extent of the brain), and (2) how can memory for a sequence of stimuli be upheld without the fields representing each event in the sequence forming a homogeneous whole? Köhler suggested the only possible explanation is that time is represented spatially in the brain – a theory for which no support has been forthcoming, certainly not in terms of electrical fields, and which has been rendered unnecessary by subsequent developments in neurally based theories of after-effects (e.g. the build-up of inhibition, reduced gain function, etc.) and of memory (e.g. following from the work of Hebb, 1949).

Pribram (1971, 1986) therefore suggested that electromagnetic fields might operate at a smaller scale: around the vicinity of local synapses and short-axoned interneurons, where local 'microwaves' would be created by neural activity and would in turn influence the function of the local junctions. As far as I can judge from Pribram's explanation of his theory, this would put the upper limit on the fields' size at about one millimetre. Thus such fields could not be functioning to unify or bind across modalities to form a single sense of 'self', nor even to bind visual features between areas of visual cortex, which can be spread over several centimetres in humans and monkeys.

Another problem is that of informational bandwidth. Any field potentials would be averaging the potentials generated by large numbers of neurons, and would therefore carry less data than the underlying neuronal activity does.[17]

One answer is that large amounts of information can be stored holographically, and a subcortical locus would not have been affected in the lesion studies just mentioned. O'Keefe (1985) indeed pointed out that two sources of input to the hippocampus generate field potentials at theta (4–7 Hz) frequencies when an animal is active. If these frequencies are closely spaced, then a holographic encoding might be possible, distributed across the hippocampus and the cortical, thalamic and hypothalamic centres with which it is closely connected. The hippocampus integrates and unifies information from wide regions of the brain, so this field might well be the neural basis of consciousness.

However, the general trend following the arguments described in this section was for field theories to be abandoned in favour of neuronal theories of brain function, which are much more flexible and powerful.

16. Köhler (1958) disputed these results on technical grounds. He said that Lashley's strips of gold would have carried little current, and would soon have become 'sealed up' as the tissues adapted. However, surely the latter would have created insulators, thus still disrupting the normal fields. Köhler (1958) also doubted Sperry's results, since some of the lesions were so extensive that they should have disrupted vision a great deal, but they didn't. Also, Sperry's behavioural methods were not described in sufficient detail to exclude all alternative explanations.

17. This might be construed as an advantage of the theories, because, as Baars (1988) points out, consciousness has a narrow bandwidth: there is a limited number of items we can be aware of at once (see section 7.2.3 for more on Baars' theory).

6.2.5 **Sub-neuronal level**

The fifth level I have labelled 'sub-neuronal', to refer to scales above quantal but below neuronal. Theories at this level have become more popular recently (Barlow, 1998; Koch, 1998). The point is that nerve cells are quite complicated structures (and should no longer be regarded as mere passive binary switches, as they have been since McCulloch and Pitts, 1943). As Barlow says, a single dendritic spine is about the same size as an amoeba – a whole single cell organism. Inside an amoeba there are enough biochemical processes to maintain life and reproduce the species. So within an entire nerve cell there must be an enormous amount of biochemical machinery. Thus the kind of information processing taking place within a neuron could be very complex. For example, representation could be mediated by a local increase in calcium concentration, or a voltage potential across a small part of the cell membrane, in one part of a dendrite, while another part of the same dendrite could be representing something else. Thus we could develop theories of representation, information processing, computation, symbol transformation, consciousness and so on that all happen within a single cell. For all we know, such theories could be correct. Remember that computational functionalists will say: fine, if the people of China can be a conscious system (section 2.5.2.2), then you can have a single nerve cell being conscious; just so long as the mechanisms inside it have the right kind of structure and organization to implement the necessary processes.

This theory has not been developed a great deal yet. Most neuroscience theory in the last fifty years has treated nerve cells as *relatively* simple structures that take in inputs on the dendrites and put out neurotransmitters through the synapses. Although we know quite a lot about the physics of nerve cells and the way electric currents flow through dendrites, there are as yet relatively few higher-level processing theories that take account of the complexity of what nerve cells do (see Rieke et al., 1997, Koch, 1998, and Eliasmith and Anderson, 2003, for recent exceptions). But it is possible that this may happen in the future – theorists will attribute cleverness to single nerve cells and regard them as quite sophisticated functional sub-mechanisms within the brain.

6.2.6 **Neuronal and polyneuronal levels**

This is the dominant theoretical paradigm, which takes nerve cells as the basic units of analysis and builds complex structures out of these. The 'neuron doctrine' is the name often given to the presupposition that we should treat neurons as the basic elements of any theory of the brain (e.g. Ramon y Cajal, 1906; McCulloch and Pitts, 1943; Barlow, 1972; Jacobson, 1993; Crick, 1994).

6.2.6.1 **The single cell theory: grandmother cells**

The simplest idea is that representation of a doorknob, a colour or whatever consists of the firing of a single cell. This is sometimes referred to as '*grandmother cell theory*' because one of the classic examples (Blakemore, 1973) suggests that when you see your grandmother there is a particular cell in your brain that fires. This cell is active whenever you see your grandmother and only when you see her. There are other cells that fire when you see your other grandmother, your grandfather, dogs, red and so on. You have individual cells to represent each of the possible thoughts you could have: for every object you recognize, every quale you can experience, there are different cells whose firing constitutes each of them.

Another exemplar used within this theory is the 'yellow Volkswagen detector', which responds only to combined inputs from generalized 'yellow' detectors and generalized 'Volkswagen' detectors. The point is that this is the culmination of a serial processing model, where cells respond more and more selectively to particular stimuli at successive stages of stimulus processing.[18]

The most fully explicit theory of this type is Konorski's neural behaviourist theory (1967; see also Gilinsky, 1984; Gross, 2002) According to this theory, the cerebral cortex is divided up into certain areas – the sensory areas, the motor areas and the emotion areas – and that is all: there is nothing else in-between. So the visual areas consist, for example, of the primary visual cortex, which contains cells that fire when you experience primitive elements of colour and brightness, and vivid images. Then the 'higher', surrounding regions of the visual 'analyser' area contain cells that respond to grandmothers and other complex objects, and the sight of those objects from different viewpoints. The sound of your grandmother's voice is stored in the higher areas of the auditory analyser region, and there are associative links – by which Konorski meant physical axonal connections – between these different areas. In that way, the sight of your grandmother would be associated with the sound of her voice and vice versa. This is thus the simplest possible model of association: each association consists of an axon running from cell A to cell B and releasing excitatory transmitter onto cell B.

Konorski's idea was then that thinking about grandmother, for example, would consist of activation of these higher cells. Imagery, particularly vivid images such as in dreaming, would occur when these higher cells activate their 'descending' axons to the primary cortex to arouse the cells in the primary visual and/or auditory cortex. This process would explain hallucinations, dreams and mental images of your grandmother. Such vivid experiences can only occur when the primary sensory cortices are activated, either by a sensory stimulus or by these descending connections. In the absence of activity in primary cortex, you can have abstract thoughts only.

Now, empirically there is some support for grandmother cell theory. Single-unit physiologists have recorded from parts of brains, particularly in monkeys but occasionally in humans, and have found (or claimed that they found) cells in the infero-temporal cortex which do behave a bit like grandmother cells. Thus Gross et al. (1972) claimed to find a 'monkey's paw detector': this was a cell in the monkey's brain that responded to the sight of a monkey's paw and to nothing else. Similarly, Perrett et al. (1982) reported face detectors in the monkey temporal cortex and Kreiman et al. (2000a) and Quian Quiroga et al. (2005) the same in the human medial temporal lobe.

There are a number of problems with the single cell theory (e.g. Barlow, 1972, 1995; Rose, 1996). An obvious one is that cells are dying off all the time in the brain. However, it is easy just to modify the theory and say: well, there is not going to be just a single cell but a dozen (or a hundred or whatever) cells, that may be scattered around the brain. In the course of a

---

18. The theory has roots also in the Pandemonium theory of Selfridge (1959), Hubel and Wiesel's (1962, 1968) model of visual analysis, serial processing models in general and the philosophy of Locke and Hume (chapters 1, 2, 11).

lifetime a few of these may die off, but lifelong memories can be maintained by this redundancy, by having multiple cells subserving the same function.

The serious problems are:

1. Firstly, one can argue as to how selective cells really are. In order to prove that a cell is a face detector or a monkey paw detector or whatever, you have to show that it (i) responds to the 'grandmother', and also (ii) does not respond to any other stimulus. But given that there are an infinite number of other stimuli, you cannot in practice test all those other stimuli to prove that the cell does not respond to any of them. So there is always that logical caveat accompanying any claim to have discovered grandmother cells. In practice, experimenters show a wide range of stimuli, and claim it is sufficiently convincing if they find cells that respond to only one or two of the stimuli. But others argue that the data show that most if not all cells respond to two or more objects and not just to one (e.g. Baylis et al., 1985; Young and Yamane, 1992; Tanaka, 2004; Tanifuji et al., 2004). There is thus an intermediate situation: the representation of any given object is actually a pattern of activity across several cells – although by no means all the cells in the area take part ('sparse coding'). For example, some cells respond to grandmother or grandfather, some to grandmother or mother, some to all old women and so on.[19]

The philosophical arguments over semantics also come in here. In section 5.3.8 we discussed the idea that frogs contain cells that respond to flying bugs. This raises similar issues to grandmother cell theory, since both posit that the activity of a single cell represents a single object. In that section we concluded that there is no single meaning, for example because bugs are also food and their presence means survival. If a bug has so many levels of meaning, then so too does grandmother!

2. Next is the issue of how you learn to recognize new objects. Does this require that in, say, the infero-temporal cortex there is a large number of unused cells lying around, waiting for new stimuli to come along and trigger a process of wiring up these cells in such a way that they come to respond to these new stimuli? Every time you meet a new person and learn to recognize that face, are you rewiring cells in the 'face area' of cortex which were previously quiescent? Or are you having to take over other cells: unwire cells of people you don't see very often and reuse those cells for the new peoples' faces? Or what other mechanism is used? These alternatives have not been specified.[20]

3. There are questions about to what extent you can treat objects and features as isolated stimuli. Are experiences composed of isolated qualia, or are experiences complex wholes that cannot be so atomized/modularized (as suggested by Dennett, 1988, and Barlow 1995)? The images you see are always very complex: you see grandma at a particular angle and in a particular light, in a certain room and so on. Experiences of the same object or person are different from occasion to occasion. So there is always an entire complex of cells firing to represent the entire complex situation. How can you specify that one cell is a grandmother cell and another is a grandmother's armchair cell and another is a

19. There may be cells that respond only within a class of stimuli, such as 'faces', but these are not selective for individual faces within the class, as 'grandmother' cell theory predicts they should be.

20. Empirical studies on learning in infero-temporal cortex suggest that the representation changes from one in which the stimulus activates many cells towards one involving fewer neurons ('sparse coding') – though the change does not go as far as the generation of single-cell representations (Tanaka, 2004).

light-coming-in-through-the-window cell? The theory all gets a bit ad hoc and resembles a construction by Heath Robinson (in Britain) or Rube Goldberg (in America); in other words, hundreds of little mechanisms have to be wired up, and the representation of the entire situation is extremely complicated. (Compare the arguments over holistic versus atomistic semantics in chapters 1–5.)

4. Another question is: where do the axons of grandmother cells go to? Konorski says that they just go across to cells in other regions of emotional, motor and sensory cortices, adding the associated information about whether you like your grandmother or not, or what the sound of her voice is like and so on. In the original theory, consciousness (to the extent it was mentioned at all) just was identified with the firing of a grandmother cell – so when you think of your grandmother or recognize her, then this cell is firing and that is all there is to the mind–body problem (Gilinsky, 1984).

But under other theories, we can ask whether the axon goes off to another part of the brain where consciousness is generated. Presumably the axon runs (if only indirectly) to the arousal systems, to the memory systems and so on. But is it valid to draw a boundary around the visual system and say that this is a visual module; grandmother cells lie within the visual system and their axons go out to other functional modules, such as the arousal systems, memory systems, a consciousness system (if there is a separate one) and so on, that are not visual? If so, it entails that there is a sharp boundary between the visual areas and the non-visual areas. This may be true for some modules, of which vision is a prime example, but it is contentious to what extent such sharply defined modularity extends throughout the system (Fodor, 2000; see section 4.3.4).

5. In addition, Konorski's theory excludes polymodal cells. Why can't there be there a cell that responds to the concept of grandmother? Such a cell would respond to your grandmother whether you hear her voice or see her. You still think, 'Oh, it's grandma' – you can still recognize her – regardless of the modality through which the stimulus comes in. So there may be even higher-order cells that are responsive to grandmother in an amodal sense (any modality). These also fire when you think of her in any way, including imagining her appearance or even recalling that she exists at all. (There are indeed regions of the cortex where polymodal cells exist: e.g. Baylis et al., 1987; Kohler et al., 2002.)[21]

6. And then you get on to abstract cells. Do you have cells for God, truth, justice and so on? And for people you know about but have never met, for fictional characters . . . for future events? If you have cells for abstract and counterfactual concepts, then how do they develop? There must be a difference in ontogeny between cells for acquired concepts, such as 'the President of the USA', and concepts that presumably might be genetically prewired, such as 'red'. So there must be two kinds of cell: those that are innately connected and those wired up through learning. What then is the physiological difference between them (Rose, 1996)?

7. And finally, there is the problem of occlusion. If grandmother is partly obscured, for example if she is trying to hide behind her armchair, but you can see enough to recognize it

---

21. There are also several areas where one modality modulates the responses of cells to another, although it is not always clear that individual cells respond to both modalities singly. There are also areas where more than one modality can produce gross responses (as seen in evoked potentials or blood flow measures), but it is not clear whether these regions merely contain a mixture of unimodal cells.

is grandmother, why don't your grandmother cells fill in the missing bits? You should be able to see the parts of her that are occluded – hidden behind the chair. If you have a grandmother cell that is activated by the sight of half or three quarters of her face, then you should be subjectively aware of the whole of her face (if your consciousness of the image of her face depends purely on your grandmother cell). If your imagery depends on some kind of feedback from memory back down to the primary visual cortex (as some theories suggest: section 10.2), then OK, but this is not grandmother cell theory, this is a modification of grandmother cell theory.

6.2.6.2 Whole-brain theory

At the opposite extreme is the idea that the physical basis of a representation or an idea is somehow related to the activities of every cell in the brain. Some people seem to assume this is entailed by identity theory, which posits the identity of one mental state with one brain state (section 2.4). Identity theory can thus be criticized on the grounds that to know what the physical basis of a mental state is, you would have to know the physical state of all 10^{12} neurons in the brain. This is far too many to measure, so it is just not practical to test identity theory, which is hence unfalsifiable (Flanagan, 1992; Harth, 1993). However, mental states need not be dependent on the whole brain, as we shall see below.

We know that, anatomically, the brain does have structure: it is not a homogeneous mass like smooth porridge. Not all nerve cells are the same, and there are different cytoarchitectonic structures in different regions of the brain. Surely there must be some functional reason why these different structures exist. Simply saying that we have to look at the whole brain in one go does not offer any guidance – it does not tell us what to do next. We need to reduce the problem slightly by breaking it up into smaller, more manageable units.

Another important point is that the problem is four-dimensional, with time as the fourth dimension. The activity in the brain flows, it is *dynamic*. Action potentials move down axons and electric currents flow through the dendrites of nerve cells. So we should not just imagine an instantaneous snapshot of the brain and look only at the three-dimensional pattern of activity; *the physical basis of representation is four-dimensional*. Also, at the mental level, the stream of thought flows – we move from one thought to another. Mental states are not static. There is a dynamic situation at this level, too, and we need to map (or identify or whatever) these dynamic mental states onto dynamic physical states. This idea will be elaborated in section 6.4, but first we need to ascertain the 'extent' of a representation.

6.3 The scale of representation

6.3.1 Psychological evidence for the multiplicity of thought

The issue of unity versus multiplicity of thought is important. If it is not the whole brain that is representing one thought, then we have to look at the possibility that multiple representations can occur simultaneously. Indeed, several lines of argument and evidence from psychology exist in favour of multiple simultaneous representations or streams of thought at the psychological level (e.g. Neisser, 1963; Kihlstrom, 1987, 1993). There is evidence, for example, that unconscious creative processes are important in generating ideas that then pop up into consciousness (Side-box 5.2), and 'implicit' perception and learning are well-known (e.g. de Gelder et al., 2001; Bowers and Marsolek, 2003).

The fact that we can do two tasks at once – walk and chew gum, hold a conversation while we are driving and so on – shows that we can perform multiple functions at the same time. Hence multiple representations must be being processed simultaneously. A large literature on cognitive psychology and attention supports the idea that multiple functional subunits within the mind process information in parallel. The conscious stream of thought is limited in capacity – it famously has 7 ± 2 units capacity, it is slow and serial – and to achieve anything at all it requires a lot of ancillary sub-processors or subroutines functioning in parallel subconsciously on various sub-tasks. One group of theories posits a 'central executive' that divides up the job that has to be done into these various sub-processes. This kind of model has been around at least since the 1970s: Shallice (1972, 1988), Lindsay and Norman (1977), Baars (1988), Schacter (1990), Baddeley (1997) and other theorists have it that consciousness is in some way related to only one of the several units in such a cognitive architecture (see section 7.2.2.3: frontal lobes). Yet other theories, while positing the existence of multiple functional homunculi, deny there is any central controlling unit or single centre for consciousness. For example, the philosopher Dennett (1991) uses a Pandemonium (Selfridge, 1959) metaphor in which multiple processors try to out-shout each other in a competition for control (over each other and over the functional behaviour of the overall system). Dennett's theory will be described further in section 10.3.2.3. To the extent that all these subroutines, modules or homunculi handle representations, many such representations must exist simultaneously.

There is also evidence from studies of selective attention that you can switch your processing from one task to another (see Side-box 8.5 for a reminder), and presumably from one thought to another. Imagine switching your attention from the words on this page to the colour of the walls of the room and back. In order to be able to switch back to an unattended stimulus, you have to be holding a representation of it. Otherwise, the switch of attention could go by chance to any one of the myriad of information streams that is arriving via the senses at every instant. This line of argument entails that the representations you are not paying attention to are not being dealt with in the particular way that generates consciousness. You are really conscious only of the things you are concentrating on – though this is contentious![22] Perhaps their representations have been moved to some crucial site in the brain, or there is something special about the properties of these representations that generates the consciousness of their contents. These are the issues we shall address in chapters 7 and 11.[23]

---

22. For example, many have suggested that a weaker or different kind of consciousness exists outside focal attention: e.g. 'fringe' (James, 1890), 'ambient' (Trevarthen, 1968) or 'preattentive' (Neisser, 1967; Julesz, 1981) awareness.

23. There is also evidence that as your alertness or overall arousal level varies, so the quantity of representations you can hold and process, or the depth of processing of a single representation, might change. Thus the general level of arousal may be influencing the breadth and the depth of your consciousness or your focus of attention. However, there is still an upper limit to how much information you can deal with (Kahneman, 1973).

So from now on, let us assume each of us has multiple thoughts or representations at any one time.

6.3.2 The neural scale of representations

If there are multiple representations, how can this be implemented physiologically? Well, we can think of a number of obvious possibilities and try to classify them a priori. The brain has many areas, lobes, columns of cells and little circuits. So first we have to consider the question of how *large* representations are: do they involve a few hundred cells, a few million, a thousand million? Are they locally restricted within a small region of the brain or spread out over a wide region – half the brain, three quarters or what? For the moment we can't pin this down, so I shall use the word '*region*' as a general term to imply something intermediate, that is, larger than a single cell and smaller than the whole brain. It is a vague term, but it reflects how imprecise our knowledge is at the moment. (The same considerations also apply to the dimension of time, but we won't go into that until chapter 10.)

So we will say that (the physical basis of) a representation exists within a particular region. Now:

1. There are theories that all the cells in a small patch of the brain are involved in a spatio-temporal pattern of activity that is whizzing around within this patch. It might, for example, represent 'grandmother'. Then there is another group of cells somewhere else which is representing 'armchair' (Figure 6.1a). Similarly, in Konorski's theory the visual representations of grandmother are in the visual cortex, and representations of her voice are in the auditory cortex.

2. On the other hand, it could be that the representations are intermingled. There is no reason, given the specificity of neural connections, why this could not happen even though the actual cells involved are physically in the same region (for example, the temporal cortex, the frontal lobe or wherever). Given a lack of any active connections between the two relevant sets of neural circuitry, these circuits can be independently carrying two different representations (Figure 6.1b).

3. In principle, this kind of scattering could be not just in a region, but across the whole brain (Figure 6.1c). In general, large anatomical regions of the brain could be involved in any single representation, but not all the cells in any region. Then if any region of the brain was damaged there would be equal effects on all the representations therein. In contrast, in the case of anatomically separated representations (theory 1), you could get lesions knocking out one representation but not the other.

4. However, complex concepts such as those for whole contexts and environmental structures, or very difficult abstract thoughts, might involve large regions of the brain. In those cases, brain scanning or lesion studies would fail to show any difference between the areas of brain involved with different representations.

The evidence for these various a priori possibilities for the size of a representation (sorry, René) will be considered in several places throughout this book. For example, Side-box 6.2

describes one ongoing debate about where visual stimuli are represented. But first we will look at three well-known theories that fit into these different categories.

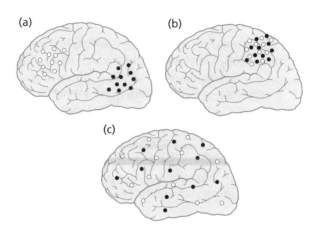

Figure 6.1 Some possible interminglings of cells carrying two representations. **a.** Two separate regions. **b.** One region, intermingled. **c.** Whole brain, intermingled.

SIDE-BOX 6.2 VISUAL CATEGORIZATION AREAS

Studies of single cells in monkeys and of brain damage in humans and monkeys have long suggested that visual objects are recognized using mechanisms located in the inferior and ventral parts of the occipital and temporal lobes. Recent brain scanning techniques have added to the confirmatory evidence, and thrown further light on the question of whether there is a single, general purpose mechanism for all stimuli, or whether different categories of stimulus are handled in different areas. The latter possibility has been suggested, for example, by the classification of some brain-damaged patients as 'prosopagnosic', that is, having a specific deficit in distinguishing different faces with no reduction in their ability to recognize other objects. This diagnosis has, however, been contentious, with some physicians finding prosopagnosics who also cannot distinguish buildings, animals, tools or other classes of object (for good introductory texts, see Groome et al., 1999, Farah, 2000, Stirling, 2002, and Banich, 2004; some relevant cases are described by Dixon et al., 2002, and Kolinsky et al., 2002).

In one PET brain scanning study, Damasio et al. (1996) showed that retrieving words activates separate areas along the anterior–posterior axis of the ventral surface of the occipital and temporal lobes, depending whether they pertained to faces, animals or tools. More accurate fMRI techniques have also emphasized the medio-lateral dimension, with scenes of places activating a region of cortex more medial than that responding to faces. (Nearer hippocampus means nearer to the spatial map of the environment: O'Keefe and Nadel, 1978!) This is taken to mean that at least some separate areas of cortex deal with specific categories of stimuli (Grill-Spector et al., 2001, 2004; Spiridon and Kanwisher, 2002) (cf. Figure 6.1a).

continues

SIDE-BOX 6.2 continued

However, Haxby et al. (2001) claim instead that all these regions respond to all stimuli. The areas do not all respond equally; some are activated more than others by a particular class of stimulus (faces, houses, chairs, etc.), and there is a different pattern of activity for each category. Thus the representations are intermixed, at the scale of regions (cf. Figure 6.1b).

A third theory is that the regions being studied are in fact specialized for distinguishing between stimuli that are very similar, regardless of what the stimuli are. Thus faces are much more similar to each other than are faces and buildings, vegetables and bent paper clips. As we experience a set of stimuli, we learn to distinguish them as individuals rather than as an amorphous category, and it is this learning that engages the ventral occipito-temporal cortex (Gauthier et al., 1999; Tarr and Gauthier, 2000).

One reason for the disagreements may be that the brain areas aroused in an experiment change if the subject's task is changed, for example between judging objects by their appearance versus semantically (Devlin et al., 2002). These authors did find evidence for the localization of general categories such as living things, but not for more specific subcategories such as animals, faces or fruit.

For recent reviews on this continuing debate, see Kanwisher and Duncan (2004).

6.4 Three 4-D theories of representation

In this section, I will present three important and generic examples of multi-neuron models of representation, whose influences will crop up repeatedly throughout the rest of the book. Historically, all are developments of neural behaviourism (chapter 3), and the third in particular is often proposed as the antithesis to computational theories of representation (section 2.5.2.4). Thus throughout this book you will repeatedly find theoretical tension between simple connectivity as the basis of brain function and more cognitive/mental views of processing and representation. The point of our journey is to bridge the gulf between the neural and mental levels, and to this end we will see whether the more complex models of neural dynamics can be (sensibly and coherently) merged into theories of (at least lower level) cognitive representation, semantics and intentionality. Let's start with one of the classic first steps in this direction.

6.4.1 Hebb's theory of cell assemblies and phase sequences

The fundamental idea behind this theory is that the neural basis of representation is a group of nerve cells connected together so activity will flow around in a cycle, sometimes called a *reverberatory* loop' (Figure 6.2a). So for each thought, idea, concept or percept, a particular loop, or 'cell assembly', exists.[24] The anatomical hard-wiring that defines the

24. The term 'cell assembly' is sometimes used nowadays to refer to any kind of cooperative action amongst an ensemble of multiple nerve cells functioning together. Historically, Lorente de Nó (1938) had considered persistence around a simple loop unlikely, so Hebb (1949) postulated the 'assembly' in which all cells may connect onto all others. The nodes and/or arrows in Figure 6.2b were then

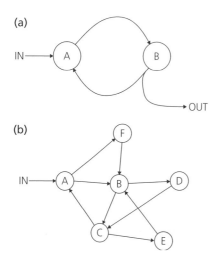

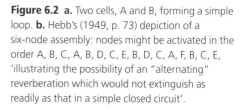

Figure 6.2 a. Two cells, A and B, forming a simple loop. **b.** Hebb's (1949, p. 73) depiction of a six-node assembly: nodes might be activated in the order A, B, C, A, B, D, C, E, B, D, C, A, F, B, C, E, 'illustrating the possibility of an "alternating" reverberation which would not extinguish as readily as that in a simple closed circuit'.

loop just is the neural basis of the permanent memory of the concept, and activity flowing round the loop is the physiological basis of the functional activation or use of that concept (and perhaps even of its existence in consciousness).

Note that certain '*emergent properties*' come out of this arrangement of nerve cells (sections 2.2.2.1, 3.5.5.1, 4.2). These are properties that individual nerve cells do not have on their own, such as the ability to store information by maintaining activity passing around the loop (assuming all these connections are excitatory). An input will initiate a continuing flow of activity around the loop. This one can call short-term '*memory*', for example, because this persisting activity is a trace of the occurrence of the stimulus that outlasts the stimulus and maintains the effects of the input over time. You can also see that the fading away of the trace would explain forgetting.

Such a loop also has another emergent property, '*resonance*', since it takes a constant amount of time for the information to flow around the circuit. This makes the loop sensitive to certain frequencies of input rather than others. For example, if the input consists of a repetitive train of action potentials coming in, and if it happens that the periodicity, the interval between these action potentials, coincides with the time it takes an action potential to go around the loop, then in the first, receiving cell A (see Figure 6.2a) the activity comes back round the loop to it at the same time as a new input is coming in. Therefore these two inputs to cell A arrive synchronously and act synergistically to reinforce one another, and thus enhance the magnitude of the signal sent round the loop by cell A. With repetitive inputs the activity level of the loop will build up progressively. On the other hand, if there is asynchrony – the relative timing of the action potentials' arrivals at cell A is mismatched – then the loop will not resonate. Thus there is '*tuning*' for a particular frequency: the circuit is highly active when there is a particular frequency of input and not other frequencies.[25]

assemblies (or assemblies of assemblies) rather than individual cells. But for our present purposes it is clearer to begin by considering the basic mechanism, that of cells connected together to form a simple loop.

25. There can be resonance to harmonic frequencies too.

Thus there are at least two emergent properties that arise from having cells connected in this way. Now, Hebb's (1949) original analysis was constructed partly as an account of learning. He was working within the behaviourist paradigm, and the idea then was that learning consisted of forming new connections from the input to the output in a stimulus–response way, analogous to conditioned reflexes. That kind of model, of inputs connected onto interneurons that connected into outputs, is fine for the simplest reflexes, but it always had a problem with memory. However, the anatomists at the time (Lorente de Nó, 1938) had observed that there are axons in the central nervous system that pass backwards to form recurrent loops. The presence of these axons running back towards their cells of origin suggested that looping could be one of the processes that was important within the nervous system, and so Hebb's theory incorporated the idea of recurrence. Figure 6.2a shows the simplest possible loop; Figure 6.2b shows Hebb's more realistic depiction, with multiple, redundant loops and an irregular cycle.[26]

Such assemblies of cells were the basic structures in Hebb's theory. They might represent, for example, simple visual features such as the corners of a triangle. Hebb then reasoned how these features could become linked to form the concept of a triangle itself: eye movements between the corners of a triangle create associations between the sight of each corner and vice versa in a self-reinforcing cycle. Internally, the three assemblies (one for each corner) would become linked by the growth of synaptic connections (by mechanisms I will describe in a moment). Their firing would thus occur successively in an irregular 'phase sequence', for example from the assembly representing one corner to that for another, then to all three at once and back to just one corner again, and so on.[27]

At an even higher level, associations may form between complex concepts, and their underlying phase sequences come to fire in what Hebb called a 'phase cycle'. For example, the sight of a triangle might become associated with the sound of the word 'triangle'. Or, to switch to an example of Pavlov's, the sound of a bell might become linked to the sight of food, which is already linked to the response 'salivate'.[28] Influenced partly by the work of Lashley (see Side-box 6.3), Hebb incorporated into his theory the idea that the cells in such higher successions of assemblies are distributed widely around the brain. The successions cannot just involve local circuits spanning a few hundred micrometres within small regions of the cortex (although those might be forming the low levels of feature representation). While the representation of, for example, the sight of food must extend over at least part of the visual cortex, it is not limited to that region.

26. Hebb was slightly unclear as to whether the nodes or the arrows in Figure 6.2b should be counted as cell assemblies; he described the arrows as both 'multiple pathways' and as 'functional units' (1949, p. 73).

27. This accounts also for our ability to attend selectively to different levels in the structure of a stimulus, for example to each side of a triangle in turn versus to the whole triangle. Depending on whether it is a single assembly or an organized complex of assemblies that is active, we are aware of a part of the stimulus or its whole.

28. Pavlov (1927, 1955) was a physiologist working on digestion in dogs. He noticed that his dogs would initially salivate when they saw food, but after some experience they would begin to salivate as soon as they were brought into the experimental apparatus. This provided a good paradigm for studying learning, and Pavlov found that if a bell was sounded before the meal was presented, the dogs would shortly come to salivate as soon as the bell rang. The question then arises as to what neural mechanisms underlie the new connection between the dog's auditory system and the pre-existing mechanisms connecting its visual and salivatory systems.

SIDE-BOX 6.3 IN SEARCH OF THE ENGRAM

In the 1930s and 1940s, Karl Lashley (Hebb's PhD supervisor) performed a series of experiments to try to find the location of the memory trace, the 'engram' – the writing-in of the memory connection (Lashley, 1950). The assumption was that a rat's memory for, say, running a maze would be located in a particular part of the brain, or along a particular pathway – but which part? After Lashley trained rats, he destroyed different parts of the brain (in different rats) and then tested whether they could still remember how to run through the maze. What he found, over the course of all his experiments, was that it did not matter where he made the lesions. Lesions in any part of the brain seemed to cause some deterioration in the rat's ability to run the maze after the operation. This gave rise to what Lashley called the 'Law of Equipotentiality': all parts of the brain are equally potent, capable and relevant to the storage of the memory trace, and the memory trace is distributed throughout the entire brain.

The other law Lashley came up with was the 'Law of Mass Action'. He observed that the larger the lesion, the worse the rat's performance. How bad the rat was, afterwards, was proportional purely to the amount of tissue damage, i.e. inversely proportional to the amount of brain left. The more brain the rat had the better it was at running the maze, regardless of which bits of brain it had. So the total, mass activity of the available brain tissue determined how good the rat was at remembering the maze.

Lashley's results are nowadays thought to be due to the fact that when a rat runs a maze it uses multiple mechanisms and multiple sensory cues. The rat looks around, sniffs, feels the walls of the maze, listens to noises and uses a whole range of parallel processing modules to discover cues to the route through the maze; and various kinds of motor output control module as well. As Lashley destroyed small parts of the brain, each time he knocked out the ability to use one or two of these cues: for example, if the rat was blinded by destroying the visual cortex, the rat could still feel its way through the maze, but obviously it was not going to run through the maze as quickly and as confidently as when it could see as well. The same applies vice versa: if Lashley destroyed the somatosensory cortex, the rat would not be able to feel so well but it could still see, so its performance would have deteriorated but it would still be able to perform the task. So the modern interpretation of Lashley's results is that the effects of his lesions in different areas were simply to knock out different cue-extraction processes, different subroutines operating in parallel, and it is not that the task was simply revealing the action of just one holistic process. Therefore, it is no longer accepted that the entire brain subserves each memory 'equipotentially'.

Let us consider in more detail what happens during Pavlovian conditioning. A dog learns to associate two different stimuli, such as the sound of a bell and the sight of food (Figure 6.3). Suppose that activity in phase sequence A has the particular function of representing the sound of a bell, while other loops in the dog's brain store or mediate other representations such as the sight of food (sequence B), or its smell, the thought of eating, or whatever went on in Pavlov's dogs' minds. According to Hebb, learning a new association ('conditioned reflex') must involve forming a physical connection between two (or more) of these sequences.[29] Through repeated instances of pairings of the sight of food and the

29. Pavlov's theory was quite different. It involved waves of excitation irradiating out over the cortex from the auditory area, initially in all directions (as the animal gave what we now call a nonspecific 'arousal' response to the new stimulus; see Side-box 8.4). With learning these waves became focused towards the target, salivary area (as the other directions of irradiation became inhibited).

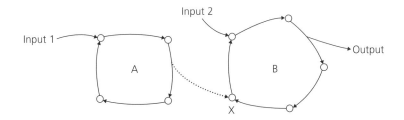

Figure 6.3 Two cell assemblies, A and B. Input to one of the four cells in assembly A sets up 'reverberatory' activity circulating around the loop. An 'associative' branch connection (dashed) may then activate assembly B, which can in turn activate further assemblies or generate motor output.

sound of a bell, connections form between the two relevant anatomical structures. These connections are the physical basis of a new association (see section 6.4.1.1 for more details of the mechanisms). Therefore, obviously, these sequences need to involve connections that spread between the visual and the auditory cortices, as well as the motor system that controls behaviour. The linking of A and B therefore forms a complex concept or phase cycle, underlying the fact that both the sound of the bell and the sight of food now *mean* 'food coming soon'.

The high-order phase cycles (successive activations of the phase sequences that represent concepts) can also explain the train or series of associated thoughts that people commonly experience. These may thus underlie what can be called the 'stream of consciousness' (for example: I am hungry, I need food, I have no food, I must go to the shops, I will need money, I must visit the bank first . . .).

In sum, there is thus a nested hierarchical structure in Hebb's theory. For higher and more complex concepts, the representation is itself an assembly of cell assemblies, each of which is an interacting group of single cells.

6.4.1.1 **For Hebb's theory**

On the positive side, there are a couple of ideas in Hebb's theory that have lasted. First is the idea that the synaptic connections are '*plastic*': malleable or changeable. Long term memory formation involves the alteration of the strengths of various synapses. During the processes of conditioning or learning, there must be a selective strengthening of synaptic connections. This occurs, according to Hebb, when there is synchronous activity in the pre- and the post-synaptic parts of the synapse. The basic idea is that these is a cell (or an assembly or a phase sequence) whose output leads to salivation (as in Pavlov's conditioning experiments on dogs; Figure 6.4). This cell has a synaptic input from a cell assembly representing the sight of food. The sound of the bell has then to affect this system (the bell that Pavlov rang before he showed the dog the food). Now initially, when the bell is rung the dog does not salivate, because it has not been conditioned to associate the sound of the bell with being fed. That is to say, the synapses onto the salivation cell from the auditory cell assemblies are initially ineffective. But then, when the visual and auditory stimuli are paired, consistently and in that temporal order, the visual system first depolarizes the dendrite in the salivatory system (see Figure 6.4). If auditory activity then arrives simultaneously or

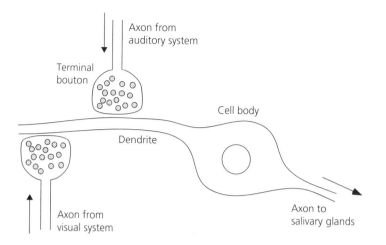

Figure 6.4 Synaptic connections postulated to underlie classical (Pavlovian) conditioning: formation of a new association between two stimuli (the sound of a bell and the sight of food). According to Hebb's rule, the synapse from the auditory system grows in strength whenever it is activated at the same time as the dendrite is depolarized; the latter is caused by an input from the visual system. Note that this is the simplest possible circuit that could mediate such learning (cf. chapter 3). Under Hebb's theory of representation (Figure 6.3) the inputs and output need not be so directly connected to the sensory receptors and motor effectors. For example, the 'cell body' in this figure could belong to any cell in loop B of Figure 6.3, perhaps cell X. The 'axon from visual system' shown here could be from any other cell in loop B and the 'axon from auditory system' would be from any cell in loop A.

soon after, so that the pre-synaptic bouton of the auditory input is depolarized at the same time as the dendrite is depolarized, then this synapse needs to be strengthened so that it becomes more effective. After repeated pairings of the stimuli in this way, the synapse progressively becomes more effective until ultimately a state is achieved where the auditory input alone will be capable of activating the behavioural response. At this point, the animal will have learned a new association, and the sound of the bell alone leads to salivation.

This mechanism implements what is known as '*Hebb's rule*': synapses strengthen their activity when both the pre-synaptic input and the post-synaptic dendrite are active – when they are both depolarized or excited. Researchers in neuroscience have spent a long time trying to establish that Hebb's rule actually applies in reality. We are finally at the point where there is sufficient empirical evidence from physiology that Hebb's kind of synaptic strengthening does occur in situations of conditioning in mammals – and not just in the hippocampus (Frégnac and Shulz, 1999; Song and Abbott, 2001). But even before we had such hard evidence, Hebb's rule was widely accepted as valid, and there was a consensus that this or something very similar must be going on.

The second positive side of Hebb's theory is the division between anatomy and physiology. The idea is that long-term memories are stored as – or consist of – anatomical changes in the synapses, and this is the right level at which to look for the physical basis of memory. When long-term memories are laid down, anatomical alterations occur that in turn require changes in the read-out from the genes to maintain the permanent state of the altered synapses.

One of the most convincing experiments is one in which rats were trained to run a maze. Their body temperature was then lowered to the point where electrical activity in the brain ceased (though not down as far as freezing). The rats' body temperature was then elevated back to normal. When the animals had recovered, they were put in the maze again, and it turned out that they could remember their way round perfectly well (Andjus et al., 1955). This established that long-term memories were not stored in the form of enduring patterns of activity passing forever around these loops (Figures 6.2 and 6.3). So long-term memory is not a matter of continuous reverberation throughout your life.

Instead, short-term memory might be mediated by this physiological process; evidence from blows to the head and from pharmacological or ECT (electroconvulsive therapy) intervention shows that it does take some time for the anatomical changes to take place and to be 'consolidated'. There needs to be continuing activity while those changes take place, and disruption of that activity, by a bash on the head, for example, can lead to retrograde amnesia for events that occurred within the few seconds or minutes before the blow.[30]

This idea of distinguishing between the anatomical pattern of connections, which is the basis of long-term memories, and the physiological activity pattern, which subserves short-term memory and current thoughts, is one which will recur frequently as we survey more modern theories.

6.4.1.2 **Against Hebb's theory**

Nowadays, behaviourism is regarded as obsolete, and this kind of simplistic association-formation model of everything is just not powerful enough (see arguments in chapters 2 and 3).

Lashley's results favouring the widespread nature of memory traces are also no longer credited (Side-box 6.3). Today we believe that specific memories are more localized, although exactly how localized remains at issue. In a recent use of Hebb's theory to describe the representations of words, for example, Pulvermüller (1999, 2001, 2002) posits that each word is subvened by a network of connections linking traditional language cortex with whatever parts of the cortex normally deal with the meaningful content of the word (for example, the representations of a word about a visual feature such as a colour contain links to the relevant visual areas in the brain).

Further, Hebb's theory presupposes that the synapses are already physically in place, even though silent, in order to explain how you can, for the most part, form connections/associations between anything and everything. This would imply that every cell assembly

---

30. In chapter 9 we will discuss memory in more detail. For now, let me preview briefly. Blows to the head or traumas often cause a degree of retrograde amnesia, in which you lose only your most recent memories. If you also lose your distant memories, these tend to recover, and of those, the most ancient memories tend to recover first (Ribot's law; 1881). This is believed to be due to the long time it takes while (1) a biochemical cascade of processes of progressively increasing duration alters the readout of DNA so as to implement a permanent change in the structure of the synapses, and (2) episodic memory is shifted from hippocampus to cortex (though there is some contention over this: Shastri, 2002; Side-box 9.2). But memory for events during the few seconds before the blow may never be recovered: short-term memories are completely labile.

must be connected to every other, anatomically, even if the synapses are not active. That is unlikely, and so a puzzle for the theory.[31]

The existence of synapses that augmented with use so as to create reverberatory loops was also criticized as liable to build up uncontrolled excitation. The brain would become more and more active and the oscillations would go out of control. Such fits occur in epilepsy, but not in normal brain function. Subsequent modifications of Hebb's theory therefore emphasized the need for a mechanism of inhibition (Milner, 1957), hypothesized an intrinsic slow decay of synaptic strengths (Rochester et al., 1956), or postulated that there must be nonlinear 'modulating' as well as strong 'driving' excitatory synapses within any given loop (Crick and Koch, 1998b).

6.4.2 The synchronicity of firing and 40 Hz oscillations

It seems intuitively obvious that a nerve cell is most likely to fire when lots of the excitatory synapses onto its dendrites are active at the same time; the excitatory post-synaptic potentials evoked by each synaptic input will summate, which probably will cause the recipient nerve cell to fire. The '*40 Hz oscillation theory*', as it may be called, takes that idea and puts it together with some empirical evidence that was obtained in the mid 1980s. Recordings of the activity of cells in the cat visual system revealed that their firing in response to a sensory stimulus was not simply a burst of action potentials as everybody thought. The bursts of action potentials were actually structured, and if you looked in close detail, consisted of a series of micro-bursts (Figure 6.5; see Engel and Singer, 2001, for a recent review). At the top is shown what happens if you wave a bar across the receptive field, and below, with an expanded timescale, you can see that there are micro-bursts within what seemed at the slower timescale to be a single burst. The micro-bursts occur at a periodicity of about twenty-five milliseconds, so they happen forty times a second. For different cells or stimuli, this frequency varies; it is somewhere between 30 and 80 Hz, in what is called the '*gamma band*' in EEG terms. (For brevity, it is also common to use '40 Hz' as a shorthand name for this range of phenomena.) You can also record the field potentials in the EEG or intracranially by using a large electrode. The same frequency of oscillation is visible (see Figure 6.5). This shows that many cells are firing micro-bursts in synchrony, so their extracellular potentials sum to give the field potential (if the cells were firing asynchronously, their extracellular potentials would cancel out). Indeed, when two cells were recorded simultaneously, their responses to the same stimulus did oscillate at the same frequency, in perfect synchrony. The theory is then that if there is convergence of these cells' outputs onto any other cell, that latter cell would be receiving a very strong instantaneous signal, and hence would be almost certain to fire due to summation of the excitatory post-synaptic potentials.

---

31. In fact, Hebb assumed that an axon passing anywhere near a dendrite could be effective in firing the dendrite, and if the firing patterns were consistently related, a new axonal thickening with a new synapse would then form there. See Stepanyants and Chklovskii (2005) for a recent update on this idea. For pairs of higher level representations, Hebb (1949, pp. 130–131) argued this problem would be less critical, as their neural systems were more likely to have a common subsystem that was already part of both of the higher-level 'concept complexes', and thus at least weakly connected synaptically to the remaining subsystems within each of them.

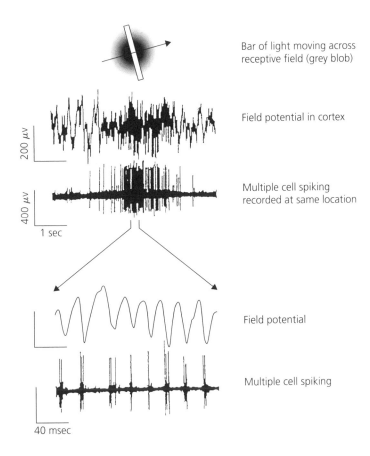

Bar of light moving across receptive field (grey blob)

Field potential in cortex

200 μV

Multiple cell spiking recorded at same location

400 μV

1 sec

Field potential

Multiple cell spiking

40 msec

Figure 6.5 Evidence for 40 Hz oscillatory activity in the visual cortex of the cat (from Gray and Singer, 1989, adapted by Kelso, 1995). The upper two traces are at a slower timescale than the lower two; each pair shows the electrical potential in the cortex, and below it the action potentials of a group of cells.

6.4.2.1 **For 40 Hz theory**

There are a number of arguments in favour of the 40 Hz theory:

1. The theory explains how the brain solves the binding problem, the issue of how information about a particular object is in some way linked together (section 4.3.7). Given that the different features of the object – for example, in the case of vision, its colour, movement, shape, location, etc. – are analysed in separate modules or areas of the cortex, how does the system keep coherent the information about each object? This is particularly problematic when there are several objects in the visual field (which is, after all, the normal situation). The idea here is that binding is implemented by having a particular frequency for each of the objects in the visual field. Thus if you are actually looking at three cows, each of those cows would be represented by cells bursting at a different frequency. These might be 41 Hz, 37 Hz and 53 Hz – the actual frequencies are

arbitrary.[32] The same frequencies would be found over all the relevant cortical areas, however widely separated in the brain. Indeed, empirical evidence shows that this can happen even for cells in opposite cerebral hemispheres (Engel et al., 1991).

2. Secondly, it has been claimed that 40 Hz oscillations correlate with consciousness. For example, in humans, gamma-band oscillations in the EEG have been reported to occur with enhanced amplitude when the subject builds a representation of an object (Tallon-Baudry and Bertrand, 1999), becomes aware of a stimulus (Meador et al., 2002) and, more generally, in situations of waking consciousness as opposed to sleep (e.g. Llinás and Ribary, 1993; Steriade, 2000). This model of representation has been central to several theories of consciousness, which we will return to in sections 7.3.1, 8.2.2, 8.3.1 and elsewhere (e.g. Crick and Koch, 1990; Zeki, 1993).

6.4.2.2 Against 40 Hz theory

On the other hand, there are several arguments against the 40 Hz theory:

1. The actual mechanisms by which each frequency is determined have not yet been discovered – we just know it is easy to generate repetitive bursts within a small neural network. Why the particular frequencies are used for the particular objects has not been specified in detail; it is very unclear.

2. Another problem is the physical one of how it is that nerve cell firings can possibly come to be so closely synchronized given that they are widely separated in the brain. The cells responding to aspects such as colour, shape, movement and so on may lie several centimetres apart in a human brain. Is there a master oscillator, somewhere down subcortically, perhaps, that sends impulses up, or is it some spontaneously emergent property of the network of connections between cells in different regions of the cortex? This problem still remains to be solved (e.g. Niebur et al., 2002).

3. Another problem is when and where these oscillations occur. Originally, they were recorded in anaesthetized cats, although subsequent experiments showed that in awake cats the oscillations were larger and easier to pick up, and more prominent. Nevertheless, there was still the question of why they occur in anaesthetized animals at all (e.g. Vanderwolf, 2000). And there are also species differences: they are much more difficult to find in monkeys (e.g. Young et al., 1992). Also, some laboratories find them more easily than others (reviewed by Shadlen and Movshon, 1999). And why do they sometimes occur in the retina and olfactory bulb? Are these locations sources of consciousness? So it is not clear yet how general and valid the phenomenon is.

4. Many experiments have shown that perceptual and behavioural measures correlate well with the magnitude of cell firing but not with the existence of 40 Hz oscillations in synchrony across cells (reviewed by Shadlen and Movshon, 1999). Among more than a

---

32. According to Freeman (2000), the frequency actually changes irregularly because the system dynamics are chaotic (see Figure 6.11c). Each representation is a unique spatial pattern of activity that is changing chaotically but synchronously across a whole patch of neural tissue (e.g. the olfactory bulb for a particular smell, or a set of ten million neurons in a part of the cortex). In sensory areas, each set of firing cells constitutes an emergent, meaningful classification of the stimulus, whereas the individual neurons within the set carry mere 'information' about the features of the stimulus.

dozen criticisms, Shadlen and Movshon suggest that much of the experimental evidence for oscillation arises from using imprecise cross-correlational methods on sparsely coded representations, in which brief bursts of neural firing are evoked by transient stimuli. Some of the cross-correlations could arise from common sources of variance; indeed Vanderwolf (2000) found 40 Hz oscillations to co-occur with slow frequency waves, which are a sign of general synchrony across large groups of neurons.[33]

5. Shadlen and Movshon (1999) also ask how flickering stimuli can be represented. How would the downstream centres distinguish an intrinsic from an extrinsic oscillation frequency? (Flickering stimuli should also sometimes create beats with the neuronal oscillation frequency.)

6. The empirical evidence from human EEG and MEG studies is also not consistent. In a recent study, 40 Hz power over the human visual cortex was found to be evoked by low but not by high spatial frequency stimuli, despite the equal subjective visibility of those stimuli (Adjamian et al., 2004).

7. Another problem is that objects are not atoms; they have structure, which is often hierarchical, with features and micro-features (Hinton, 1990). For example, consider face representation. A face has two eyes, a nose, mouth and hair, and each eye has a pupil, iris, eyelashes and so on; yet at the same time these are also parts of a face. If you have, let's say, the left eye represented by firing at one frequency and the right eye by firing at a different frequency, then how is the face represented, given that the left and the right eyes are both parts of the same face? You cannot have different frequencies representing different levels simultaneously in a hierarchical structure. For example, if grandmother's face is represented by 43 Hz oscillations in the visual system, then how can grandmother's left eye be encoded at the same time as 31 Hz, her right eye as 52 Hz and her nose as 47 Hz? This seems a logical problem: the theory leads to a contradiction. Perhaps as attention shifts from one feature or part to another or to the whole, the oscillations shift frequency; but this still leaves the problem of how unconscious, non-attended representations are maintained (the various features of non-attended objects still need to be bound[34]).

In sum, the exact functional role of these oscillations is still under debate. It is not clear whether this really is the mechanism for representation and for individuating and keeping separate particular representations, or just some artefact of the method, or an epiphenomenon generated by the brain's physiology as it processes information. More recently, the emphasis within the theory has tended to shift to the synchronicity of firing as the crucial property rather than the oscillations or their frequencies. Synchronicity is harder to detect empirically, so more studies are still needed to settle its role and importance. (Meanwhile I will continue to use the shorthand term '40 Hz' to refer to the theory, although bearing in mind that 'synchronized firing' might be a more appropriate label.)

33. Brief bursts of 40 Hz occur at intervals within slow-wave sleep (in cats at least; see Destexhe and Sejnowski, 2001) and even in anaesthetized rats (Vanderwolf, 2000).

34. Although there is a theory that binding only occurs between the features of attended objects (Sidebox 8.5), complex unconscious representations may still exist (section 6.3.1).

6.4.3 Neural networks

The theory of neural networks is also known as 'parallel distributed processing', or PDP for short. It has attracted much philosophical interest, as we discussed in section 2.5.2.4. The basic idea is that it is the *pattern* of activity across a large number of cells that carries the meaningful idea – the representation, the content of your thought (or, under identity theory, these activity patterns just are the meaningful representations). Each representation is held in an 'array' of cells.

'Heteroassociative' theories model one of two functions: either how two representations can become related or associated, or how one representation is transformed into a second. In these nets, the two representations are held in separate arrays, that are joined by a complex tangle of connections of variable strengths, mimicking the plastic synapses postulated by Hebb and growing according to Hebb's rule. After first describing these nets in more detail, we will contrast them with 'autoassociative' nets, in which the two representations are held in the same array, at successive instants in time.

An important caveat is that neural networks have to be distinguished from *semantic networks*, which we talked about under computational functionalism in section 2.5 and Figure 2.7. In the latter, connections (of particular types) form between 'nodes', which are bundles of information, like files on your computer desktop. (In Figure 2.4 we described the connectives as 'operators' or 'rules'.) An example would be the node representing 'grandmother', which coordinates (if it doesn't actually contain) a whole lot of gen on the old lady. Thus it is connected to the node 'woman' by the operator 'is an example of', to the node 'members of my family' by the operator 'is a', and so on (cf. Figure 2.7). This architecture is different from that described under neural net theories, in which simple units resembling on/off neurons, all of a single type, are connected by links, also all of a single type (although, with Hebbian synapses, these links vary in strength), and in which 'grandmother' is represented by the pattern of activity across the units (and her memory is embedded in the pattern of connections between them). Since both theories involve connections, they have both been called 'connectionism', but they are very different entities and should not be confused.[35]

6.4.3.1 Heteroassociative networks

In heteroassociative networks, axonal connections form between two separate sets of nerve cells. In each set there is a particular pattern of activity, that is, some of the cells are active and some inactive. One of the ways in which this field can be simplified is by treating each cell as being on or off – as either firing or not firing. This enables us to symbolize them as binary digits, such as 0,1,0,1, where 0 represents 'cell not firing' and 1 represents 'cell is firing' (see Side-box 6.4). Different patterns of activity represent different objects or entities.

---

35. Such confusion is seen, for example, in the works of Fodor, and is promoted by the predilection of some network theorists to attach high-level functional names (categories such as 'face', reward, novelty, motive and so on) to individual low-level units in an array of similar units. Such ascriptions are motivated by the simplistic presuppositions of neural behaviourism, but merely end up as premature reductions to Mickey Mouse theories. They are as unsatisfactory as dualism: one cannot stand outside a neural network and just parachute meaning into the firing of a simple unit, any more than one can parachute in consciousness or a soul. At best, we should treat them as a 'hybrid' class of nets.

SIDE-BOX 6.4 FUNDAMENTALS OF NEURAL NETS

Encoding and representation

In a classic paper, McCulloch and Pitts (1943) suggested that the behaviour of a nerve cell can be simplified as either on or off, at any instant in time. This led to a very fruitful analogy with digital computers. In such computers, numbers are coded in binary form (zero is 0, one is 1, two is 10, three is 11, four is 100, five is 101 and so on). Consider the one-dimensional array of six nerve cells shown in Figure SB 6.4.1; their state can be encoded by the binary number 010001 (which is the same as seventeen in decimal notation).

Figure SB 6.4.1 Six cells are indicated by the row of triangles. Two of them are firing (indicated as black) and four are not (white). Their states are symbolized by the binary digits underneath: '1' for active and '0' for inactive.

This way of encoding the state of the array enables us to appreciate the power of neural nets. Within each array, the number of possible patterns that can be held is larger than the number of cells: it is 2^N, if you consider each of the N cells as being either on or off. Imagine a net with only two cells; one may be on and one off, or vice versa, or both on, or neither on. In binary symbolism, these are 10, 01, 11 and 00 respectively; thus there are four possibilities, i.e. 2^2. If there are even a hundred nerve cells in an array there can be 2^{100} (over 10^{30}) possible representations or meaningful patterns of activity that can be handled or stored in that array. So there is a 'combinatorial explosion': the number of patterns that can actually be encoded doubles with every extra cell added to the array.

This compares very favourably with grandmother cell theory, where the number of representations is equal to the number of cells (or actually, less, given that you need several cells per representation, in case any die off).

An example of how an array can come to hold meaningful representations is in terms of the cells on the retina. If you shine the letter A onto the retina (Figure SB 6.4.2), then some of the cells become active, where the lines are; if you shine a different letter (such as Q), a different set of cells is activated. All these cells then send their axons in a bundle up to the brain. The point is that this is a *functional* pattern and that you then could, as it were, twist the axons randomly on their way to the brain. Yet at the other end you would still have a pattern uniquely representing each letter. It is an arbitrary pattern in that the spatial arrangement of the cells/axons is not relevant to the meaning.

Figure SB 6.4.2 A grid of cells on the retina is stimulated in a different pattern by the letters A and Q. For example, starting from the top left of the grid and counting across, the letter A is encoded as 001100001100... whereas Q is 011110010010....

continues

SIDE-BOX 6.4 continued

Another clear example of how symbols can be encoded in nets is the way digits are coded in the standard seven-bar LCDs so common in electronic equipment nowadays (Figure SB 6.4.3). Note, however, that in this case, of course, the meaning of the symbols is imposed by the human readers, rather than being intrinsic to the system as it must be in the brain.

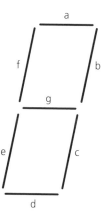

Figure SB 6.4.3 The international coding of seven segment displays. They are conventionally labelled in the order shown, so that the binary code 1101101 represents 2, 1110000 represents 7, and so on.

Thresholds and logic

In neural nets, the axonal connections from one cell may synapse onto any number of other cells, and conversely, any cell may receive any number of synaptic inputs. Whether a cell fires depends on how many inputs are active, and how sensitive the cell is (i.e. on its 'threshold'). For example, if a cell receives only two inputs, and each injects one unit of electrical current, then if the cell is so sensitive that it will fire whenever it receives a single unit of current, then obviously either input will activate the cell. The cell is thus implementing what is called a 'logical OR gate', which means it will fire if either one input or the other is active (or both together). On the other hand, the cell may be less sensitive, such that it will only fire when two inputs are active. In that case it requires simultaneous input from the first and the second synapse, so it is a 'logical AND gate'. Such logical functions are the bedrock of computers, where they are implemented in silicon chips. With neural systems, however, synapses can also be inhibitory. These give added potential for creating logical functions (for further details, see Koch and Poggio, 1985; Koch, 1997).

Now, the way in which the connections form between the two arrays transforms the activity pattern from the input layer to the output. The pattern in the output layer is not necessarily the same as the one at the input, because the connections are not on a one-to-one basis. Each axon can synapse onto two or three or even all of the output cells. Further, the strengths of these synaptic connections are not necessarily equal.

Let's consider how a (simulation of a) neural network is run on a computer. To begin with, you make up a pattern that you intend to teach the neural network to recognize, and an output pattern that you want the network to generate as a signal that it has recognized the input. First you put the network through a 'training' phase, where you force the output units to be in the desired pattern while the inputs are in the pattern to be recognized. The strengths of the synapses are then changed in accordance with Hebb's rule, depending on whether the post-synaptic cells and the pre-synaptic cells fire synchronously or not. (If they don't fire synchronously, the synapse weakens.) The result is that the next occurrence of the input pattern evokes an output closer (more similar) to the one desired. Repetitive training events eventually change the synaptic strengths throughout the net so it produces an output identical to the desired pattern.

The interesting point is that you can train each network to learn many different input patterns, and to associate these with many other arbitrary output patterns – in other words, the network can perform more than one pattern-to-pattern transformation with the same set of synaptic connections.

There are two fields to which this technique is commonly applied.[36] One is sensory input classification: disentangling a complex collection of patterns of receptor activation, so that, for example, there is one output that says 'it's the letter A' and another output which says 'it's the letter Q'. This is stimulus categorization or identification. Neural networks can form associations of any arbitrary type. For example, you could have five hundred input patterns and you could just associate them with only two outputs, i.e. just categorize the inputs into a small number of categories (e.g. grandmother present versus absent). Conversely, you can have a large number of output categories – as many as five hundred in this case, so that each input pattern is associated with one output pattern and only one output pattern. (Obviously, such a one-to-one matching would not be doing anything very clever, but you get the point about how many categories you can have; anything between one and five hundred is possible, provided you have at least $\log_2 500$ output units to carry that number of binary coded patterns.)

The other field to which neural networks are commonly applied is that of learning. As a general model of learning, we can simply say that one pattern of activity in the input array and one pattern of activity in the output array must be associated, that is to say, the presence of the input pattern must cause the output pattern to occur. These two patterns could represent, for example, the sound of a bell and the sight of food.

The early neural networks simply had an input pattern going directly into an output pattern. However, it was found that this was a bit limited: there were some logical functions that could not be performed at all, such as exclusive OR.[37] The recent revival of interest in neural networks, dating back to the 1980s, occurred when it was realized that if there are not two but three sets of cells then you could get the nets to work much better; you could form much more accurate, flexible and powerful models. So, conventionally, you construct an input layer and an output layer and what's called the 'hidden layer' (e.g. the middle layer in Figure 6.6). For example, in this diagram the particular (if rather over-simple) rule as to how cells become activated is that each cell fires if at least one of its inputs is active. (You

36. There is a third application of neural nets, the simulation of topographic maps in the brain. However, it is not clear whether such maps have any functional significance, or are merely by-products of the brain's anatomical machinery (Cowey, 1979); for recent work, see Lee et al. (2003).

37. The exclusive OR rule is that a cell fires if either of its inputs are active *but not both* (or neither).

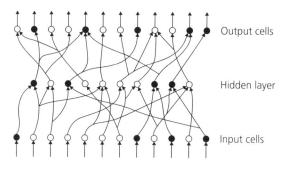

Figure 6.6 Three sets of cells forming a three-layer neural network. Active cells are shown as filled circles, and a cell in the hidden or output layers is activated if at least one of its inputs (arrows) is active. The spatial pattern of input activity is transformed at each transition into a different pattern.

have to have a '*local rule*' that determines how sensitive each of the cells is to its inputs; Side-box 6.4, 'Thresholds and logic') If you work through Figure 6.6, you can see how the particular input pattern (100000010101) will transform to a very different output pattern (010010010011), via the intermediate pattern (1010000110) in the hidden layer.

A much more realistic network is shown in Figure 6.7 (McNaughton and Morris, 1987). It has only two layers, but still transforms several simple patterns reliably. Six output layer cells (black circles) are contacted by axons (entering from top left) from six input layer cells (not shown). An inhibitory cell adjusts the sensitivity of the output cells so they are not overloaded if they have too much excitatory input. The table below shows four input patterns and the corresponding outputs to which they are transformed.

For neural networks

Several aspects of these networks make them attractive:

1. The simulations have shown that large numbers of patterns can be encoded very efficiently in a small number of nerve cells, and retrieved. Now, given that humans can store and remember enormous amounts of information in a lifetime, neural network theory provides an explanation for this basic human ability.

2. They have biological plausibility. They are modelled on the nervous system, in that they contain large numbers of independent elements that have properties similar to those of nerve cells – such as either firing or not firing, having a particular sensitivity to their inputs and being joined by one-way axon-like connections with plastic synapses at the ends.

3. The nets have certain properties that mimic those of human and animal learning.

i) First is 'noise resistance': sometimes there occurs an input that is similar to a well-known, previously trained input, but differs from it by only a small amount. What happens then is that despite the deviation from the learned input pattern, the net still produces the same output pattern. (You can call this deviation 'noise', in that it may be caused by missing activity, for example due to failure of one of the elements, or by extra activity in the input. Thus you can recognize a stimulus such as a letter A with dots or lines over it, or conversely with parts missing: Figure 6.8.) Put another way, the network reverts to the nearest known output.

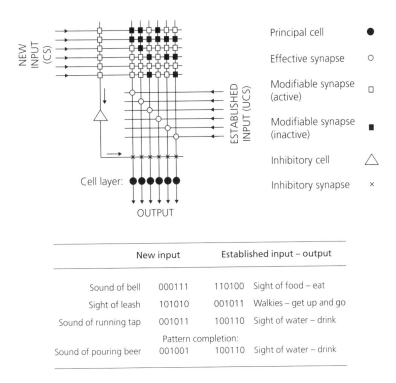

	New input		Established input – output
Sound of bell	000111	110100	Sight of food – eat
Sight of leash	101010	001011	Walkies – get up and go
Sound of running tap	001011	100110	Sight of water – drink
	Pattern completion:		
Sound of pouring beer	001001	100110	Sight of water – drink

Figure 6.7 The heteroassociative network of McNaughton and Morris (1987). At first, three well-established patterns ('unconditioned' stimuli, UCS) entering from the right activate corresponding behavioural outputs (right hand column of Table). After training, the synapses in the 6 × 6 matrix at the top have been modified in strength in such a way that three new input patterns ('conditioned' stimuli, CS) entering from the top left each come to evoke one of the available output behaviours. Further, when a new pattern 001001 is the input, 'completion' (generalization or categorization) to the most similar 'known' pattern occurs (bottom row of Table; see also Figure 6.8). Note that the circuit via the triangular cell is inhibitory and divides the firing rate of the output cells just enough to ensure that the output pattern does not saturate (i.e. become 111111) if the number of excitatory synapses activated by the input pattern is high. (Imagine, for example, there were a hundred input lines instead of just six – the outputs cells would be permanently depolarized.)

Figure 6.8 Demonstrations that the letter A can be recognized despite added noise (left) or missing parts (right).

ii) The second, similar, property is 'stimulus generalization'. If, for example, you train a pigeon to peck at a red key and not to peck at a green key, and then show it an orange key, the pigeon will tend to treat it as though it is a red key, that is, it will generalize the orange to the nearest stimulus which with it is familiar, namely red. The more different the stimulus is the lower the probability that the animal will respond in this fashion. A neural network is like this in that the more similar an input pattern is to one of those it has already learned, the more likely it is to give the output that is appropriate to that learned pattern. A specific example is given in Figure 6.7 ('pattern completion').

iii) In addition to stimulus generalization and noise resistance, some people claim that you also get certain features that are similar even to phenomena that are usually ascribed to symbol-level rule following in functionalist systems (section 2.5). One of the examples that is much discussed is the use of linguistic rules. Some researchers have formed neural networks that learn to 'talk'. These networks seem to give out errors of the same kind that children make when they are learning to speak – for example, sticking '-ed' at the end of all verbs to make the past tense, such as saying 'speaked' instead of 'spoke'. Children go through a phase of doing this and some neural networks do too (Rumelhart and McClelland, 1986; Sejnowski and Rosenberg, 1987).

For these reasons, the proponents of neural networks suggest that rather than having symbols and rules in the computational functionalist (Chomsky and Fodor) style, all we have in our brains are neural networks. Such nets can account for all aspects of the thinking and behaviour of real humans. This is important because symbols are central to functionalism, and eliminating them would constitute a major shift in our theorizing (Schneider, 1987; Palmer, 1988).

4. 'Graceful degradation' refers to what occurs when you damage parts of a network. If you simulate a brain lesion by destroying some of the units or some of the synapses, is the network still capable of functioning? Well, what happens is a progressive deterioration of function: the more damage you inflict, the less accurate the output and the more errors the network makes in categorizing the stimuli. You do *not* get a *sudden* degradation or stopping, wherein the network still works perfectly if the damage is mild, but the network suddenly stops when the damage gets beyond a certain degree of severity. Instead, performance tapers off gently as the damage increases. This is said to be the kind of effect that you get with humans (and it is what Lashley found in his experiments on animals; Side-box 6.3): damage to a small region in the brain does not completely wipe out all of human thought (unless the damage is to the arousal systems – but there are other reasons why that might be; see sections 7.2.1.3 and 8.2.2.3). With functionalist symbol and rule systems, on the other hand, and with cognitive 'black box' models of information processing, if any component or connection fails then the whole system fails catastrophically, i.e. the whole system just stops working.

This again is regarded as an argument for the idea that neural networks are the mechanism that explains human behaviour, rather than the existence of all-or-none symbols (which are either meaningful or nonsense), rules (which are either applied correctly or not) and modules (which either exist or not, and are either connected together appropriately or not) at a higher level.

Against neural networks

1. Some neural networks are not biologically plausible. To take just one example, some of the information used at each of the Hebb synapses is proposed to be made available through what is called 'back propagation'. However, this is a very unbiological postulate

(e.g. Arbib et al., 1997) in which the synapses are given information about what the output *should* be as well as what the finished output actually is, and the corrections to synaptic strengths are made accordingly. In multi-layer nets, the synapses are also given information about what the output should be when the output is several synapses downstream. There has been some controversy over whether we can think of a biological mechanism of back propagation or whether we should stick to networks that do not have it.

2. There are also disputes about to what extent neural nets do mimic the behaviour of humans. In particular, Pinker (1997) and Marcus (1999) have defended the symbol and rules functionalism paradigm, and argued that the kinds of mistakes that neural networks make are not exactly the same as those made by humans during learning (for example, of language rules) or after brain damage.

3. There are also arguments that some kind of symbolic level of description is necessary. We must have symbols to explain such things as generativity, creativity and the ability to behave in innovative fashions and not to be reactive in a purely deterministic fashion (to have autonomy from the environment, as Fodor puts it). Neural networks are predictable and mechanical in the way that they provide output, but they are no good for explaining problem solving, creativity, choosing between alternative possibilities or deciding amongst alternative courses of imagined action (section 2.5.1.3).

4. Neural network theorists often try to explain everything in terms of a single neural network. However, the brain is not a single neural network. If you look at the brain anatomically it is very variegated: there are nuclei and cortices and bits here and there. The brain is not a uniform mass of nerve cells – there are clearly distinct parts with different internal structures. So trying to mimic a complex human behaviour, like language learning or pattern recognition, in terms of a single or even a couple of layers of neural network is overly simplistic.

It might be, as a compromise, that neural networks are a mechanism that operates at a low level of description. Within each region of the brain is a neural network, but different regions of the brain are then connected to one another, and the principles that apply in the interactions between regions may be completely different from those that apply within a single neural network. The inter-regional interactions may more closely approximate the rules and processing of symbolic representations. Symbols and rules may be emergent properties of a network of neural networks.[38]

Another way of looking at it is that there is a hierarchy of systems in the brain (as we discussed in chapter 4). Thus we return to the question of the spatial scale of representation that we encountered in section 6.3: how big is 'a neural network'? Does a functional neural network exist throughout the occipital lobe, or in the primary visual cortex, or just one of

---

38. Smolensky (1988) proposed that the patterns of activity may act as symbols (and it is not far to propose that the patterns of connections between nets act as rules; they are applied whatever the particular content, i.e. activity pattern, filling the input array). Harnad (1990), in contrast, suggests that each symbol may be reduced to an individual cell in the hidden layers of multi-layer nets. These hidden layers often have very few cells (e.g. Lehky and Sejnowski, 1990, found their net could function well with as few as three, or, for simple stimuli, even one), and these cells typically become selective for particular features of the set of stimuli that the net is trained on – for example, bright versus dark images, vertical versus horizontal lines.

the columns of the primary visual cortex? How do you circumscribe each neural network, given that there are extensive connections between all areas and structures within the brain?[39] How many functionally distinct neural networks are there in total? Moreover, in a hierarchical system, are the principles of interaction the same at all levels?

In conclusion, it may be that the neural network level of description is an appropriate one to explain at least certain aspects of the mind, being, as it were, one level up from single nerve cells. There are indeed groupings of nerve cells, and the patterns of activity across the cells in those groups form an appropriate and important level of description. Nevertheless, there may still be higher levels of description, such as symbol levels, emerging from interactions at an even larger scale between local networks in different regions of the brain.

6.4.3.2 Autoassociative networks

In contrast to heteroassociative networks, in which one group of cells is connected to another group, '*autoassociative*' nets (also known as 'Hopfield nets', after Hopfield, 1982) basically involve a single group of nerve cells. These cells are connected to one another; possibly every cell is connected to every other cell in the group. They are 'autoassociative' because they have connections through Hebb synapses internally within the set of cells (Figure 6.9).

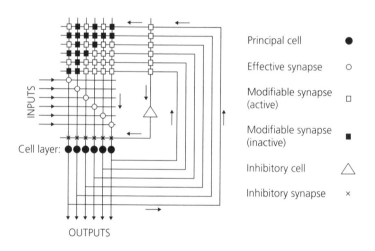

Figure 6.9 An autoassociative network. Six cells (black circles) are driven by six inputs (left), that can be active (1) or inactive (0). This network can handle three input patterns: reading from the top input line to the bottom, they are 000111, 101010 and 001011. The inhibitory circuit (triangle and crosses) adjusts the sensitivity of the cells according to the number of input lines active. Arrows show the direction of information flow. According to McNaughton and Morris (1987), 'this net can act as a pattern completion device with additional capacity to keep patterns active by reverberation. If this reverberatory activity is not explicitly silenced before presentation of new information, this network will store event sequences and recall them from a fragment of the initial event in a sequence.'

39. Rolls (2000) has recently argued that the synaptic links between networks must be much weaker than those within a net, by a factor of about a hundred.

How do these work? They process spatio-temporal patterns of activity, rather than just static patterns. Consider first the situation at one instant in time. There is a certain pattern of activity within the group: some cells are active and the rest are inactive. The cells that are active then, through their synapses, depolarize some of the other cells, after a short delay (determined by the time taken for action potentials to travel along the axons). Those depolarized cells may themselves fire, if the total amount of depolarization they receive is sufficient. Thus at the following instant in time there may be a different pattern of activity. This process then continues repetitively over successive instants of time: each instantaneous pattern of activity transforms itself into another pattern, then into another, and another and so on.

Now, when modelling associative learning, the aim is to transform the input pattern into a single, desired output pattern. In autoassociative nets, this happens by the changes settling into a single final pattern. The pattern held by the network may move through any number of arbitrary intermediate patterns on its way to the final state. But the final state needs to be one in which the pattern held transforms itself back into itself; the cycling activity passing along the axons does not change the pattern held in the cells.

As Figure 6.9 shows, this almost magical property can emerge from a system of simple, well-understood components (cells and Hebb synapses). Moreover, the processes required appear to be implemented in the hippocampus (McNaughton and Morris, 1987; Rolls, 2000).

6.4.3.3 Dynamic systems theory

In some cases, an autoassociative network may settle into a repetitive cycling pattern as its final state. For output purposes, it might be just one of the final patterns that is the crucial one, but it is more likely that the whole cycling set of patterns is the target state of the network – in other words, it produces a four-dimensional representation. The added temporal dimension makes such neural networks a subcategory of '*dynamic*' systems.

Dynamic systems theory incorporates chaos theory. It is a mathematical method for describing any kind of complex dynamic system, from the weather, through to sand falling down a sand dune, turbulence in water, activity patterns in neural networks or the expression of the genes. There is a whole range of systems that have many small (often identical) parts that interact with one another to give complex emergent behaviour. The development of that behaviour over time gives the dynamic aspect, and the study of how those systems proceed over time and how they develop is generally called 'systems theory'.

The example in Figure 6.10 is taken from Kauffman (1993, 1996). It depicts three nerve cells, all connected to one another (Figure 6.10a). Cell 1 only fires if both its inputs, from cells 2 and 3, are active at once (it thus forms what is known as an AND gate). Cell 2 has a different logic: it will fire whenever either of its inputs is active (it is thus an OR gate). Cell 3 follows the same logic as cell 2: it too is an OR gate. Cell firing is determined purely by those local rules. (AND and OR functions can easily be implemented in nerve cells; McCulloch and Pitts, 1943; see Side-box 6.4, 'Thresholds and logic').

Note first that at any instant there are eight possible patterns of activity, in which cells 1, 2 and 3 can each be either active (1) or inactive (0). There are thus eight (2^3) possible states of the system at any given time t (Figure 6.10b).

At the succeeding instant in time t + 1, what will be the state of the system? Look at what each of the cells would do, given what its inputs were at the previous instant in time (top

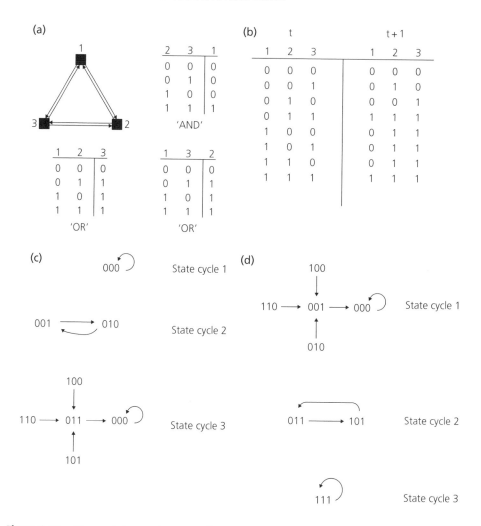

Figure 6.10 a. Three cells (squares) are mutually interconnected. Each can be firing or not. The three truth tables show how each cell's firing depends upon the prior activity of the other two cells: cell 1 only fires if both the other cells were active (i.e. it is an AND gate), but cells 2 and 3 will fire if either of the other cells was active (i.e. they are OR gates). **b.** Each of the eight possible states of the system at the initial time t is followed at the succeeding instant t + 1 by one of only five possible states, as listed here. **c.** The trajectories that the system can follow, given each of the eight possible starting conditions, lead to only three possible end-states. **d.** The trajectories and the three end-states that occur if, instead of cell 2 implementing an OR gate (as in a–c), it is mutated into an AND gate. From Kauffman (1993).

left). Sometimes the pattern will be the same, and sometimes it will transform (as listed in Figure 6.10b). Figure 6.10c summarizes each of these transitions. If the network starts off with all cells inactive (000) it will just remain with all cells inactive, and will continue in that state indefinitely. If it starts with only cell 2 active (010), or only cell 3 (001), then there is an '*oscillation*', a cycling between these two states. Any of the other five initial conditions will eventually progress through to a state where all the cells are active (111) and the net will then just sit there in that state from then on. It may take a few transitions to get there but eventually it settles down into a '*stable*' state.

So whatever the initial conditions, of the eight possibilities, the network will eventually settle down into one of just three possible final states: all cells firing, all not firing, or a regular oscillatory cycle. Some states are unstable, but these rapidly filter through into the all-cells-firing state.

By comparison, consider what happens in Figure 6.10d. Here, the local rule for cell 2 has been changed from an OR to an AND gate, so cell 2 will now fire only if both its inputs are active. If you go through the same process – working through the tables again – you find that there are again three possible final states. However, these are different from the previous ones. There can be a cycle, but between the firing of cell pairs 2 + 3 and 1 + 3, instead of 2 and 3 alone. The unstable states will default down to the non-firing condition with all the cells inactive. So there are again three final states, but these are different in terms of which patterns they originate from and which are the two oscillating states.

Figure 6.11a starts off by illustrating the idea of '*state space*'. The cube on the left has three dimensions which I have labelled 1, 2 and 3. You can regard these as representing the states of the three cells in the previous diagram. Each cell is either active or inactive, so the system as a whole can be represented by a single point at one of the eight corners of the cube. Each corner represents one of the eight possible states the system can be in. The various state transitions then involve changing from one corner to another. The system will end up in one corner (000) or the opposite corner (111), or oscillating between two other corners.

To obtain a more general picture of a dynamic system, in the next two cubes (Figure 6.11b), I have first removed the simplification that the cells are either firing or not firing. Instead, imagine that there is a continuum of rates of firing. Real nerve cells can fire at anything from zero up to several hundred times per second. So given that there is a continuously variable rate at which each of these cells is firing, the state of the system at any instant can be represented by a point within the volume of the cube-like state space. Changes can be represented by the point moving along a trajectory through the inner volume of the cube. Depending where it starts, it may spiral in and end up at one final resting

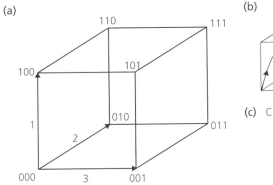

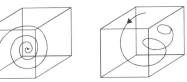

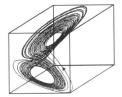

Figure 6.11 State space for a 3-vector network.

place, an '*attractor*' (Figure 6.11b, left). What happens is that, if you start within a certain region in the state space, the point that represents the state of the system will move towards this attractor and will settle down on to it. Starting from anywhere within a different region of state space, however, the net might settle onto a different attractor.

On the right of Figure 6.11b, I have drawn the trajectory of a system that ends up in an oscillating state; here, I have it going round in an ellipse (though it can be a torus or one of many other shapes).

The locations and types of attractors, whether they are stable or cycling, depends on the rules that determine how the cells interact with one another. The cube in Figure 6.11c shows a situation that can occur according to chaos theory, where the rules are such that the attractors are not attained in the way they are in Figure 6.11b. In chaotic situations, the movement is far more complex. The system may cycle around one of the attractors for a while without actually touching it, then flip off and cycle around another attractor. This behaviour is very difficult to predict; it looks random but it is still deterministic: there are fixed and sometimes very simple local rules that determine how the system moves from one state to another. Nevertheless, the statistical properties of how the system as a whole moves through the state space turn out to be very complicated.

Next, imagine that instead of three nerve cells we have several hundred million; perhaps as many as 10^{12}. Try to imagine a space that has that many orthogonal dimensions. The idea is that the brain is in a state space in which at any instant there are roughly 10^{12} cells which are firing to varying degrees. You could in principle plot the state of the brain at any instant as a point in this 10^{12} dimensional space. (Or if you want to consider only a thousand cells in one column in the cortex, then you'll have a thousand dimensions to your state space.) So the progress of thoughts through the brain, the stream of consciousness, the activity patterns in the brain – all these consist of movement along a trajectory through such a multi-dimensional state space.

In theory, the brain could settle down to a stable attractor. This may be what happens, for example when you identify a stimulus, remember something, come to the solution to a problem or decide what to do – you are settling on one single answer (in a convergent problem-solving task). There is a period of stability from which the brain is finally perturbed only by the arrival of an external stimulus, or by some internal noise. The stable state might be a regular oscillation – several such oscillations have been observed, for example in the EEG (such as the 40 Hz oscillations we discussed above), or in rhythmic motor activity such as walking and breathing. Or the brain could be in a chaotic state, in the sense that your physical state is never the same twice. We can thus describe many mental and physiological states in the terminology of dynamic systems theory (indeed, numerous examples will occur in subsequent chapters).

Critique

Dynamic systems theory can seem very abstract and mathematical, but a lot of people (though not all!) think it is a good way of looking at how the brain works. The brain is a complex network that is dynamically and continuously moving through various states.

1. There is a great deal of theoretical support for this approach. I won't go into the history, but nowadays there are numerous authors proselytizing for the world-view that systems are

dynamic and self-organizing and – to introduce you to some of the buzz words – autopoietic (literally, self-organizing!), embodied (in contact with the rest of the world), embedded (merged in with the flow of the entire universe) and so on. Tie-ins with Buddhist philosophy are also common. Good introductions are given by Varela et al. (1991), Kauffman (1996), Capra (1996) and Clark (1997).

2. There is also much empirical evidence for this approach. For example, it is common now to record simultaneously the activities of many cells with tens of microelectrodes – or to record gross potentials with dozens of EEG electrodes, or blood flow in thousands of voxels with fMRI machines – and to interpret the complex patterns as representations (Eichenbaum and Davis, 1998). There is evidence from the hippocampus, for example, that representations of the environment the animal is in are associated with particular locations in a multi-dimensional space, where the dimensions are the firing rates of different hippocampal cells and the animal's position in and movement through an environment is encoded in terms of different areas in the potential state space (Wilson and McNaughton, 1993).[40]

3. Whether this interpretation as representations can be related to the functionalist view of the brain, as an engine that manipulates symbols according to rules, remains a topic of hot investigation. Churchland, for example, has suggested that the meaning of a representation can be categorized into a type (such as 'red', 'pain' or 'grandmother') by dividing the neural state space into regions (e.g. Churchland, 1988). Remember each rectangle in Figure 2.3, which we can now interpret as a 2-D state space, divided into functional types. Now imagine the same principle applied to the 3-D space in Figure 6.11 – and then to even higher-dimensional spaces. Activity in each division of the n-dimensional volume represents a particular meaning ('red', 'pain', 'grandmother', etc.). However, Fodor and Lepore (1992) point out that this begs the question of how the dimensions (the axes of the cube in Figure 6.11, for example) acquire their meaning as semantic variables rather than neural variables. They are asking how the semantic symbols are grounded in (arbitrary) parts of the state space, a question that also arises with respect to neural network coding, as we saw above (section 2.5.2.4). Dynamic systems theory is on a par with neural network theory in this respect.[41]

4. Another interesting question is whether conscious states can be distinguished from unconscious states by partitioning state space into 'conscious' versus 'unconscious'

---

40. Proponents of dynamic network theory often cast it as an alternative to representationalism (e.g. Skarda, 1999). However, their definition of representation is narrower than the one I adopt here, where any deviation in a system's trajectory through state space is regarded as in some way representing the stimulus that caused the deviation. See Eliasmith and Anderson (2003, chapter 8) for a representationalist analysis of neural system dynamics.

41. This debate has been rumbling on for a decade without either side giving way. For example, Fodor and Lepore (1999) add that neural space is not the same as semantic space, and ask when a concept is represented by a point rather than a dimension of the state space. Churchland and Churchland (e.g. 2002) now call their position 'domain portrayal semantics' and support semantic holism over atomism. They emphasize that a similarity matrix between stimuli gives structure to the state space (see Clark, 1993, pp. 210–221, for a clear exposition of similarity matrices). However, as Margolis and Laurence (2003, pp. 200–202) point out, such matrices still need to be anchored and semantic atomism still cannot be excluded (i.e. the meaning of at least one representation must be grounded by its extension, otherwise the similarity matrix can be rotated or inverted).

sectors, or whether it is a matter of the stability versus the transience of the state. To answer this, however, we need to go on to the next chapter.

6.5 Conclusion

There are many levels within Nature, and each seems to have been the focus of one theory or another as to the origin and location of consciousness. Given, however, that the whole mind–body problem is about inter-level relationships, we need to understand how levels can possibly be integrated or mapped onto one another. Having established such a conceptual framework, it is surely applicable to all pairs of adjacent levels. The most fruitful theories, then, appear to be those that are not chauvinistic about the origins of consciousness but take an eclectic (open-minded?) approach and understand Nature as an organized and structured whole. We might then point to a (hyphenated) social-cognitive-neuroscience as the most promising field for the future.

For the present, however, the dominant paradigm is the neuronal one, in which the analysis of brain function centers on the properties of single cells and networks. The theories at this level are obviously a vital and intricate part of the picture we need to build up. As the latter part of this chapter began to demonstrate, there are already many neuronal theories that are complex, sophisticated and quantitative. Although brain dynamics are clearly important, they are difficult to test empirically. Nevertheless, they can be investigated by simulation, which provides an opportunity for mathematical analysis and prediction that will open the door to more precise comparisons of subtle differences between and within theories.

The well-developed state of research at these neural levels will become even more apparent in the next several chapters, since many people have now suggested relationships between consciousness and the neural levels of representation.

▪ RECOMMENDED READING

The philosophy of representation has been discussed in chapter 2. The neural underpinnings are, however, covered far less extensively in the literature, and tend to be classified as 'neural coding'. Some recent discussions can be found in Dayan and Abbott's Theoretical Neuroscience (2001), Pouget et al.'s 'Computation and Inference with Population Codes' (2003) and Olshausen and Reinagel's 'Sensory Coding in the Natural Environment' (2003).

The 'levels' approach was introduced in chapter 4; a useful, clear survey, ranging from quantum to social approaches, is given by Scott in Stairway to the Mind (1995); see also his chapter in Velmans (2000) and his recent article (Scott, 2004).

Brief introductions for beginners to neural nets and dynamic systems are given in many texts nowadays, such as Pinker's How the Mind Works (1997, pp. 98–131) or Cotterill's Enchanted Looms (1998, pp. 104–182). Several excellent textbooks on neural networks exist for those wishing to pursue the field in depth, such as Gurney's **An Introduction to Neural Networks** (1997), McLeod et al.'s **Introduction to Connectionist Modelling of Cognitive Processes** (1998), **Neural Networks and Brain Function** by Rolls and Treves (1998) and Rolls and Deco's **Computational Neuroscience of Vision** (2002, chapter 7). Some of the classic papers are reprinted in **Minds, Brains, and Computers** edited by Cummins and Cummins (2000, part II).

On dynamic systems, Juarrero's **Dynamics in Action** (1999, chapters 7–11) gives a stunning introduction that integrates the theory with the philosophies of homuncular and teleological functionalism, cause and effect, and semantics. Eliasmith and Anderson relate multi-level representationalism to neural system dynamics in **Neural Engineering** (2003), and in **Neurodynamics** (2000) Freeman provides evidence for intermediate-level, 'mesoscopic' scale, chaotic, spatio-temporal representation. Kelso's **Dynamic Patterns** (1995) is an oft-cited classic, but assumes you have mathematical skills, as does Kauffman's **The Origins of Order** (1993) – and Wilson's **Spikes, Decisions, and Actions** (1999), in spades! More qualitative expositions are found in Kauffman's **At Home in the Universe** (1996) and **Investigations** (2000), Holland's **Hidden Order** (1995) and **Emergence** (1998), and in Capra's **The Web of Life** (1996). An interesting application of dynamic systems theory to social interactions is given by Arrow et al. in **Small Groups as Complex Systems** (2000). Finally, several readable chapters sampling the range of relevant topics can be found in Morowitz and Singer's **The Mind, The Brain, and Complex Adaptive Systems** (1995), and a good collection of research papers on neural dynamics is that edited by Pawelzik (2000).

Conscious and unconscious representations

OBJECTIVES

Our goal is to understand the origin of consciousness, and as such we need to compare what is related to consciousness and what to unconsciousness within the brain. The strategy continues to be to narrow the search, adopting the premise that there are conscious and unconscious representations within the brain and seeking to discover the critical difference(s) between them. Following the dominant stream of research, we will begin by focusing in on the anatomical level, beginning with the view that to understand consciousness we need first to find where in the brain it arises. Then we will look at theories that consciousness is a property best described physiologically or informationally.

You need to become aware of the advantages and disadvantages of this approach. Is the search for consciousness one that can be 'narrowed down' and are we misguided in seeking a 'crucial difference' between what is conscious and what isn't? What implicit assumptions are there behind these strategies?

For example, is there a single 'Right Answer' that I should be leading up to and which I should finally reveal to you in the Conclusion? By now you should know that would be premature (see also the Preface).[1] At the present stage of research it is most important that you acquire *thinking* skills. As you will discover in this chapter, all too many people are happy to tell you what they think The Answer is, often without seeming to be aware of their philosophical presuppositions, flaws in their reasoning, contrary evidence and the existence of historical precedents and why these were rejected. For pedagogical reasons it is necessary to learn about some of these models, however absurd or outdated they might appear, or however misguided they seem when considered from your own philosophical point of view. You have to learn how to evaluate new theories: what to make of the many and various claims and suggestions, how to recognize speculation and bullshit, and how to reply appropriately to the often eminent authors of articles published in high-profile journals. What evidence and arguments are there for each theory, and what further tests need or can be applied?

7.1 **Introduction**

In the previous chapter we looked at some theories of the neural basis of representation. In chapter 1 (and section 6.3.1), however, we made the point that some information processing proceeds unconsciously, while other processing leads to awareness. Yet the notion of 'representation' can be applied to both types. Therefore, we come to the question of what the difference is between a representation that is part of conscious processing and one that isn't.[2] The natural temptation is to imagine that there is a miraculous and magical something that makes the difference (Figure 7.1),[3] and that the mind–body problem will be solved if we can only find what that something is. This assumption is of course dubious (essay topic: explain why!) but it is one that I think motivates and informs most theorizing within this area, and one at which most of the work has been aimed. I will therefore use this

1. For what it's worth, my view is that The Answer will turn out to be complicated and multi-stranded (a whole lot of little answers), much like the answer to 'what is life?' For the purpose of teaching, however, it is necessary to start with simple concepts, and once these have become familiar, to build further upon that knowledge base. Therefore you will find many models of consciousness here that were proposed some time ago but have since been elaborated or assimilated into other theories. This does not mean that the old theories are worthless or wrong; epistemological growth is not a linear accumulation of more and more 'true facts'. (A better model might be 'thesis–antithesis–synthesis'.) Instead, learning is a drive towards 'understanding' – a far deeper matter that involves respecting how the human mind works, so it can develop and apply wisdom and skill (e.g. Maxwell, 1984, 2001; Midgley, 1989). We need more holism and abduction, not atomism and induction.

2. For brevity I may sometimes use phrases such as 'representations that are conscious'. Of course, I do not mean that the representations are little homunculi that experience consciousness the way we do as whole persons (though homuncular functionalist theory and panpsychism might imply such partial consciousness!), but that we are aware of the contents of those representations. 'Conscious representations' are not conscious 'things' but 'representations of whose contents the possessor of the representation is conscious'.

3. This is a pitfall in science generally, but one that seems especially common in consciousness studies.

"I think you should be more explicit here in step two"

Figure 7.1 The present state of consciousness research?

assumption to organize the material in this chapter, which continues our survey of neural theories of consciousness.

Two further caveats: first, the 'miracle' theory implies that consciousness is all-or-none: a representation either has it or it doesn't. However, it is conceivable that there are degrees of consciousness of the contents of any given representation. When we consider the whole person, we know subjectively that there are degrees of consciousness, in that we may vary between full alertness and drowsy 'absent-mindedness'; however, this could reflect variations in the number of representations we possess, each of which has all-or-none consciousness, rather than the partial consciousness of each one.

Second, what is meant by 'consciousness' may differ from one theory to another. It is common to distinguish two concepts: (1) the general existence of consciousness per se, that is to say, most simply, the difference between being awake and being asleep or comatose; and (2) the contents of consciousness, i.e. what we are aware of when we are aware. The latter, as we have mentioned, may itself divide into the mechanisms of such various types of content as (i) qualia, sensory experiences, (ii) beliefs, complex or abstract ideas, secondary or higher order thoughts, (iii) self-awareness, introspective self-regarding and (iv) emotions. Some theories address only one of these (sometimes it is not clear which!) and some cover several or all.

Now, one way people have approached the problem of the neural bases of consciousness is to try to narrow it down, and the most obvious way is to try to pin consciousness to one specific anatomical location in the brain. If this can be done, it is assumed, we could then go on to find out what the crucial physical difference is between this and the other locations in the brain, and then exactly how that difference generates consciousness.

Another approach is to identify a particular quality that occurs only for conscious representational states. Such a property might result from a special type of processing that the representation undergoes, one that changes it in some way (possibly *in situ*, or while moving it), or that changed its precursors when they were used to create the representation.

We will deal with both approaches in turn, in sections 7.2 and 7.3. See also Side-box 7.1 for more on how the nature of representations and/or processing may differ between conscious and unconscious states.[4]

SIDE-BOX 7.1 REPRESENTATIONS AND PROCESSING

Given that there are conscious and unconscious representations or processes in the brain, what are the differences between them? This question may also involve that of how consciousness is generated. What is the key factor – or are there in fact several necessary factors? Let us look at representations first of all.

Representations

One possibility is that there are two types of representation: one an unconscious one and the other a conscious one. There is some crucial difference between these types of representation that makes one conscious and the other unconscious.[a]

Another possibility is that there is only one type of representation, but that there is something extra that can be added to the representation to make it conscious. In other words, there is some kind of quality or property (the meanings of these words themselves need to be thought through carefully) that is added to a representation and that converts it from an unconscious representation into a conscious one.[b] The nature of the extra quality is at present mysterious and our task is to discover what it is.

The difference between these two possibilities is that if you have a representation plus some extra quality you still have the original representation there, as opposed to the first alternative, which assumes there are two separate representations that differ in basic type.

For example, perhaps the simplest example of a quality that could be added to any representation is that of *quantity*: the amount of the representation, its size or strength. Now what this means depends on the nature of the representation. If it is a symbolic representation it is there or it is not there, i.e. it has an on or off existence. However, with other kinds of representation (e.g. analogue or imagistic), you can imagine the more intense, detailed or hi-fi (higher signal-to-noise ratio) it is, or the more the activity (of whatever kind), then the more conscious the (content of the) representation is, or the more likely it is to be conscious. Some specific theories are given in section 7.3.

A second example of a candidate quality that could be added to a (neural) representation is the synchronous oscillation of cell firing at around 40 Hz (introduced in section 6.4.2, and discussed again in section 7.3.1). These oscillations either exist or they do not, making an all-or-none change, or the numbers of cells involved (and/or the duration for which synchrony exists) could vary parametrically, making a graded change. Each possibility is conceivable.

Processing

The other issue in the functionalist approaches is that these representations are *processed* (cf. the various analogies to computation and to transformational grammar described in section 2.5).[c]

continues

---

4. Of course many theories involve a combination of both approaches: it could be that a special kind of activity in a special part of the brain has to take place, so that we need to solve both those problems – why is that area and only that area special, and what is the special something that happens there?

SIDE-BOX 7.1 continued

The difference may be, first, whether there is any processing at all. You are only going to be conscious of a representation if it is being processed, in the sense of being used to do something functional (section 5.2). Recall, for instance, Dretske's idea that a representation may sit there unused (a frog may hear a trumpet but not know it is hearing a trumpet; section 5.2.5). One can certainly argue that sensory systems generate representations all the time depicting what is going on in the environment, so that when awake we always possess a lot of representations; but we don't *use* all of them. '*Selective attention*' involves utilizing only a few of those representations, and these are the ones we become conscious of because we are actually processing them further in some way. We will see these possibilities exemplified in section 8.3.

Alternatively, the relevant difference may be the type of processing that occurs. There is something special about one (or several) of the types of processing that renders conscious the information being processed. This might be something qualitatively unique that we have yet to characterize. On the other hand, it might be some simple and quantifiable extension of a known process, like the duration for which the processing continues, the speed of processing (e.g. some processing is conscious because it is very rapid: Flohr, 1991), or the extent to which the information is spread within the mind or brain (as in Dennett's, 1991, idea that only some homunculi shout loudly enough to become influential or 'famous' in the brain; or in global workspace theory: section 7.2.3). Other theorists ascribe a special role to genuinely linguistic processing (i.e. not just impoverished 'language of thought'), or to categorical, symbolic or propositional (as opposed to analogue or imagistic) processing.

In sum, there are many a priori categories of representational theory within which researchers can look. These suggest that there may be something special about the representation or the processing or both that in some way underlies consciousness.

[a] Representations can be divided into content and vehicle, so in principle, it could be a difference between the type of content or the type of vehicle. However, differences in content are not prescriptive of awareness. Yes, there is a difference between thinking of a horse (or any other real object) and thinking of truth (or any other abstract subject; or a counterfactual), but this is a difference in type of content, not in whether there is consciousness or not. So the relevant difference must be in the vehicle: the difference that occurs when looking at two horses and attending to (being aware of) one of them but not the other, for example; there are two representations with similar contents, but they are treated differently.
[b] Logically it could be the other way around – the representation could lose something to make it conscious – but no theory that I know of postulates that.
[c] Special processing could generate a special kind of representation – so the two sets of theories could both be right.

7.2 Anatomical location theories

The '*anatomical location*' theories propose that there is a special structure or location in the brain where activity (in neural terms) or representation (in functional terms) is conscious (or becomes conscious or generates consciousness), purely by virtue of being in that location. Information may be processed through several stages in various parts of the brain and then transmitted across to that particular, key, crucial part of the brain. But it is not until the information reaches there that the information achieves consciousness (or reaches a state of consciousness or is transformed into conscious information).

These theories may be divided into (1) subcortical sites, (2) cortical sites[5] and (3) a group known as 'global workspace theories' that propose a common functional arrangement but place the crucial locus in various sites.[6]

7.2.1 **Subcortical sites**

Several theories attribute consciousness to subcortical loci, of which three will be mentioned here. The first arises within substance dualism, the second may do too,[7] and the third adopts dual-aspect monism.

7.2.1.1 **The pineal body**

In section 2.1 we described Descartes' substance dualism. His idea was that since we only have one soul, the point at which the soul or mind (soul = mind = consciousness) con-tacts the body has to be unitary. Looking anatomically within the brain, the only structure he could find that is unitary is the pineal body; all the other structures are paired, one each on the left and right sides of the brain. The pineal is the only structure that is single – it's on the midline, just below the back end of the corpus callosum.[8] The Cartesian idea is that information from the sense organs passes along the nerves and sets up vibrations in the fluids of the cerebral ventricles; these changes are then somehow transmitted to the pineal body, where the mind senses the activity ('the passions of the soul') and uses it to discover what is going on in the outside world. Motor 'actions' involve the opposite direction of transfer. Although this theory is not widely held today, for reasons we covered in chapter 2, Cartesian terminology is still used, as we will discover later (e.g. section 7.2.3).

7.2.1.2 **The centrencephalon**

In the brainstem lies the reticular formation, a structure that when damaged leads to coma and permanent loss of consciousness, but when stimulated wakes you up (or just increases your arousal level if you are already awake). This is the base of the reticular arousal system, which is central to consciousness (Morison and Dempsey, 1942; Moruzzi and Magoun, 1949). Now, this system may be an obvious candidate for a site for consciousness, but it is also obvious that it is not necessarily so. The general view of the arousal system is that it simply activates the rest of the brain. (Consider a piece of electronic equipment, such as a computer. Stopping or restarting the power supply will alter the level of information processing in the computer, but this does not mean it is the power supply unit that does the

---

5. It is worth noting, in anticipation of chapter 11, that there may be more than one type of consciousness, with correspondingly various anatomical bases. For example, primitive feelings such as nausea, fatigue, thirst and the basic emotions may be subcortically generated, while the more rational thinking and sensing processes are cortical (e.g. Bogen, 1995a; section 7.2.1.2).

6. Of relevance to the third group is the debate about whether a single module exists that integrates inputs from all the other modules (see sections 4.2.4–4.2.7, and Side-box 4.6). Such a module might be regarded as a candidate not just for the stream of cognitive reasoning but also for the seat of consciousness.

7. Penfield (1975) supported dualism but admitted he was tentative about this conclusion.

8. Nowadays we know that it releases melatonin and is important for diurnal rhythms, hence is sometimes called the pineal gland.

information processing; the logic chip, the memory chips, etc., do that.) If the reticular activation is cut off then the rest of the brain will just go quiet; hence you are not going to get consciousness because nothing is doing anything in the brain. The reticular formation is *necessary* for consciousness but it is not actually generating it itself. It is not *sufficient* for consciousness on its own: if you were to remove the rest of the brain apart from the reticular formation you would not have a conscious being (although this would be difficult to test!).

Thus when the neurosurgeon Penfield (1958) reviewed the effects of direct electrical stimulation of different parts of the brain, he concluded that consciousness is generated by activity in a central part of the brain that he dubbed the 'centrencephalon' – literally the middle of the brain. The structures he had in mind are anterior to the reticular formation, somewhere near the thalamus and the basal ganglia, in the central core of the cerebral hemispheres. (They didn't have the detailed anatomy worked out in those days, so Penfield was vague about the exact location.) Activity entering that region from incoming sensory stimuli or descending from the cerebral cortex is crucial in some way for generating consciousness. This region, deep in the cerebral hemispheres, is widely connected: there are axons running between there and all other regions of the brain, including all the major centres and the reticular formation, so it seemed to be a good, strategic location that might fulfil the necessary central integrative role.

Confirmation of a link between conscious awareness and the centrencephalon has been given recently by Balkin et al. (2002), who observed that increases in blood flow through the brainstem and thalamus are the first changes to occur during waking from sleep.

We now know more about the anatomy of this centrencephalic region (see Side-box 7.2), and several people have also based more detailed theories of consciousness there (e.g. Baars, 1988; Bogen, 1995a, b; Purpura and Schiff, 1997). For example, the *intralaminar nuclei* have the anatomical connectivity necessary to integrate and disseminate information from wide regions of the brain. Bogen (1995a) and Purpura and Schiff (1997) approach these nuclei from a clinical neurology point of view. Small lesions to intralaminar nuclei affect consciousness quite dramatically, in ways that cortical lesions do not. Bogen therefore proposes a direct connection between the intralaminar nuclei and consciousness. Purpura and Schiff, however, see these nuclei as vital for consciousness, but as just one part of a mechanism for integrating and switching the processes occurring across wide regions of the brain. In particular, they emphasize the coordination of visual awareness, attention and memory that must take place as we make saccadic eye movements. Damage to these nuclei accordingly leads to separated islands of activity in various regions of the brain, because these are differentially 'gated' on and off, rather than because they receive different amounts of arousal from the nonspecific systems (see also Schiff and Plum, 2000).

7.2.1.3 The brainstem

With regard to emotional experiences such as fear, rage, lust and panic, Panksepp (1998, 2005) has recently proposed that subcortical regions are the main centres of origin. In particular, the hypothalamic-periaqueductal grey axis integrates and coordinates the brain into the particular, global states that characterize each of these patterns of instinctive behaviour and emotional feeling. Panksepp adopts a 'dual-aspect monist' attitude towards the problem of consciousness (section 1.2): the underlying dynamics of the whole system can be viewed from complementary perspectives to analyse the twin manifestations of

SIDE-BOX 7.2 THE ANATOMY OF THE THALAMUS

The thalamus is often introduced as a 'relay' centre for messages passing from the senses to the cortex, and its role is described as that of controlling the flow and amount of information reaching the cortex – it is closed down during sleep, for example. However, the truth is, as ever, more complicated than that, and we need to have a much more detailed picture if we are to understand this region of the brain properly. Figure SB 7.2.1 shows some of these details.

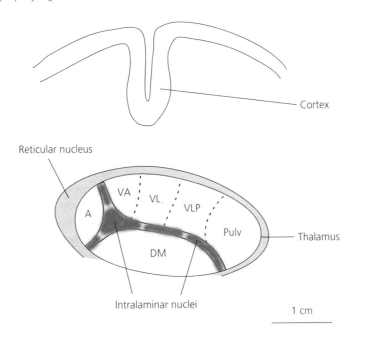

Figure SB 7.2.1 A horizontal slice through the brain showing the anatomical layout of the thalamus and a section of cortex. The reticular nucleus forms a shell around the egg-shaped thalamus, which contains various sub-nuclei (A = anterior, L = lateral, P = posterior, D = dorsal, M = medial, V = ventral; Pulv = pulvinar), and a chain of intralaminar nuclei forming a streak through the thalamus.

First, we can divide the thalamus into the core nuclei and a shell that surrounds it, called the 'reticular nucleus of the thalamus' (variously abbreviated as RNT, TRN, or similar; do not confuse it with the 'reticular formation' in the brainstem: the nomenclature reflects similarity of histological appearance but not necessarily of function). The reticular nucleus contains a network of inhibitory (GABA-releasing) neurons that connect to each other and to the 'relay' cells in the core of the thalamus. Because the axons of these relay cells send branches into the reticular shell as they pass through it on their way to the cortex, the reticular nucleus would appear primarily to provide negative feedback to cells in the relay nuclei (Scheibel and Scheibel, 1967). However, many other roles have been assigned to it, as described in chapter 8.

Next, the core nuclei can be divided into specific and nonspecific types. The former include the well-known relay nuclei such as the lateral geniculate nucleus or LGN (for vision) and the ventral posterior

continues

SIDE-BOX 7.2 continued

(for somatosensation). Almost all areas of cerebral cortex are connected with one of these nuclei, in reciprocal fashion (i.e. the thalamus not only sends information to the cortex, it also receives information back from the cortex – indeed, from the same area of cortex to which it projects). The thalamo-cortical axons terminate in the middle of the cortex (layer 4) and the cortico-thalamic axons originate in pyramidal cells in cortical layer 6.

Within the specific nuclei, a distinction can also be made between primary (first-order) and secondary (higher-order) types. The former are the main centres carrying sensory drive from the receptors to the cortex, such as the lateral geniculate that carries visual signals from the eye to the primary visual cortex, area V1. The secondary or 'higher' nuclei deal with non-primary areas of cortex. For example, visual areas V2, V3 and so on (Figure 8.3), and indeed much of the anterior occipital and posterior parietal lobes, are connected with the pulvinar – a large nucleus in the rear end of the thalamus, lying adjacent to the LGN. Nuclei such as the pulvinar are traditionally regarded as relaying information to the cortex from various subcortical sites, such as the superior colliculus, basal ganglia and/or limbic system, but they also receive inputs from the cortex – and not just from their 'own' area (i.e. the one to which they project) but also from neighbouring areas. For example, area V1 projects to the pulvinar (via layer 5 pyramidal cells) as well as to the LGN (from layer 6). The importance of this is discussed in section 8.3.2.

Finally, turning to the nonspecific core nuclei, there is a group commonly known as the 'intralaminar nuclei' (sometimes abbreviated as ILN, and including certain 'medial' or 'midline' nuclei), which lie scattered between the specific nuclei. These are traditionally regarded as projecting widely to the cortex – not as widely as the brainstem arousal systems, but more widely than the specific nuclei (hence, confusingly, they were once known as the 'thalamic reticular system': Jasper, 1949, 1954, 1960; do *not* confuse these with the reticular *nucleus*, which is an entirely different structure!). Their axons terminate in layers 1–3 and may run laterally for some distance in layer 1. (They also strongly innervate the basal ganglia.) Their cell bodies also receive inputs from wide sources. They have therefore been classed as 'nonspecific', and perhaps mediate what we might call 'moderately selective' attention (Kinomura et al., 1996; Minamimoto and Kimura, 2002). By 'moderately selective' I mean attention to, for example, visual rather than auditory input or vice versa – as opposed to highly selective attention to, for instance, red rather than pink, or one individual's voice at a cocktail party. Their role too has been the subject of further speculation, however (see, for example, sections 8.2.2.2 and 8.4).

Alternatively, Jones (2002) does not base the distinction between specific and nonspecific systems on their anatomical nuclei of origin, but instead finds the thalamo-cortical projection patterns correlate with the thalamic cell's histochemical properties (the densities of different calcium-binding proteins). Thus he finds specific projections originating from some of the intralaminar nuclei, and from only some parts of the specific nuclei (such as the main layers in the LGN). Nonspecific projections, in contrast, come from cells widely scattered throughout all the thalamic nuclei. He thus calls the specific cells the 'core' system and the scattered cells the 'matrix'. Whether this characterization of thalamic function proves more useful than the nucleus-based approach remains to be determined (cf. Sherman and Guillery, 2002, 2004, for ongoing debate, and Rodriguez et al., 2004, for a functional interpretation).

overt behaviour and subjective experience. Functional information processing may then arise at the 'higher levels' of consciousness that become organized around the basic emotions: cognitive knowledge about the stimuli and responses available, and introspective awareness of one's inner states and feelings. These forebrain-dependent functions are, however, orchestrated by the brainstem, via various neurochemically-characterized connections (e.g. section 8.2.2.3).

7.2.2 **Cortical sites**

The cortex is disproportionately large in humans, relative to other brain structures, so it is natural to postulate that our particularly human qualities (of which consciousness is assumed to be one) would arise from it. Many people have latched onto the cerebral cortex, or regions of it, as the site of consciousness (the first was Willis, 1664; a recent example is Fuster, 2003). I will cover the general theories first, then those that narrow the search further within the cortex, either within some of its substructures or within particular regions.

7.2.2.1 **The whole of the cerebral cortex**

Prima facie evidence arises within the tradition of clinical neurology, as witness the basic observations on brain damage. For example, if somebody's primary visual cortex is removed, they become subjectively blind. It is thus natural to assume that visual awareness 'arises', as it were, in the primary visual cortex. Similar thinking has been applied to all the other regions of the cortex; in the past, even areas whose functions could not be readily discovered were assumed to be mediating general 'associations' or meanings. This localizationist view about consciousness is common in medical textbooks, although it is not a logically sound conclusion from that evidence alone (see Side-box 7.3).

From an overtly dualist point of view, Eccles (a neurophysiologist who won the Nobel prize for his work on the spinal cord) developed a theory linking the mind specifically with the cortex. At first (Popper and Eccles, 1977, p. 363) the liaison between mind and brain was attributed to the left hemisphere, particularly the speech areas. Later (Eccles, 1986), the site where the mind controlled the body was identified as the supplementary motor area (SMA), a region of cortex just anterior to the motor cortex in the frontal lobe.[9] However, by 1990, Eccles had progressed to include in addition sensory consciousness and memory recall, i.e. situations where the body communicates to the mind. He concluded that all areas of cortex play a part in mind–body interaction. In general, he proposed that the cortex is divided into some forty million modules, each composed of a bundle of about a hundred pyramidal cell apical dendrites (what we nowadays call 'mini-columns': Buxhoeveden and Casanova, 2002). Eccles named these 'dendrons', and each was linked to a mental unit called a 'psychon', that physically overlapped with it. Psychons might interact with each other within the mental realm, but they could certainly influence, and were influenced by, the release of neurotransmitter at synapses onto the dendrites within each dendron. The mechanism of interaction operated at the quantum level via a probability field that

---

9. The reason for attributing mind–body control to the SMA was that this is where blood flow rises when a person is mentally rehearsing the execution of a sequence of movements without actually carrying them out (as measured using positron emission tomography: Roland et al., 1980). This implies that the SMA is the site where mental decisions are made (or at least conveyed to the brain), such as 'I am going to move my hand forward now'. Of course one could counter-argue that there certainly are axonal inputs to the SMA, but perhaps they arise in widespread regions of the brain. For this reason their activity is too slight to show up when you examine the gross activity in each of those other regions individually. Nevertheless, when their influence arrives at the SMA, the activity sums together to become large and easily detectable even by the relatively crude techniques available in the 1970s. There is thus nothing special happening in the SMA that cannot be explained by standard neurophysiological processes.

SIDE-BOX 7.3 ARE LESION STUDIES CONCLUSIVE?

Inferences from lesion studies are subject to the caveat that Gregory (1959) put forward, which is that if you lesion a part of the brain you cannot logically infer that the function of the damaged part of the system in normal brains is to generate the function that has now disappeared. The whole system may now be malfunctioning (chapter 4). Taking a condenser out of a radio may cause the radio to emit howling noises, but that does not mean the condenser had been put there to prevent howling noises. Damaging the primary visual cortex can result in subjective blindness, but this does not mean that that area is the one and only source of visual experience.[a] (After all, blindness can also result from damaging the retina; why is the cortex considered a generator of consciousness if the retina isn't too?) The same reasoning applies to emerging experience as well as to deficits: for example, right hippocampal degeneration can lead to excessive religiosity (Wuerfel et al., 2004), but this does not mean we have a right hippocampus in order to prevent religiosity. (For a critique of the localization of functions in general, see Uttal, 2001, especially pp. 172–181.)

   There are, however, some defences that can be made of the simple assumption that if a function is lost after a lesion then the lesioned area normally subserves that function. One is that it has led to a great deal of empirical success in predicting the results of further studies, including tests of some detailed and sophisticated theories based on the assumption (J.C. Marshall, in reply to a question by R.L. Gregory at the 50th Experimental Psychology Society conference, Cambridge, 1996). Applying the criterion for the success of research programmes put forward by Lakatos (1970), the localizationist programme is progressive (i.e. it is expanding and leads to empirically successful predictions) whereas the behaviourist alternative offered by Uttal is degenerate (i.e. it has led nowhere). Second, there is converging evidence for functional specialization from other techniques, particularly brain stimulation, single cell neurophysiology and neuroanatomy. These all, at least in some cases, confirm the conclusions based on lesion studies (see Bechtel and Richardson, 1993; Landreth and Richardson, 2004). Functional neuroimaging can also be used in this way (Henson, 2005). After all, the logic does not exclude that there is localization, it just does not prove it by itself. See also sections 4.2.7 and 4.3.6.

   Whatever the reasoning, theorists continue to ascribe consciousness to cortical mechanisms. We will meet many examples in later chapters, together with a broad range of arguments and evidence.

[a] Although destruction of visual area V1 abolishes normal visual phenomenology, if all the other visual areas are intact there can be some functional and perhaps subjective residuals ('blindsight'). For reviews, see Heywood et al. (2003), and for further discussion, see Side-box 10.1.

---

affected (and was affected by) the probability of exocytosis. For a clear summary, see Beck and Eccles (2003).

   Next is an important functionalist theory that also implicates the cortex. As we will discuss in chapter 9, one of the general roles of the cortex is to store long-term memories, particularly those of semantic and episodic information (e.g. Fuster, 1995, 2003). In semantic networks, concepts and representations are connected together in a hierarchy of 'nodes', which are like files where information about particular topics such as cats, dogs or the weather is stored (Figure 2.7; Collins and Quillian, 1969; Rumelhart et al., 1972). These nodes are linked together in a network, which explains the patterning of semantic associations (when I ask you what is the first thing you think of when I say 'France', your answer is not chosen at random from your entire memory store). Interestingly, Lindsay and Norman

(1977) proposed the metaphor that attention acts like a flashlight that at any instant is illuminating part of this semantic knowledge base. In other words, the long-term memory store is organized in a particular way, and when you think about cats, but not about dogs, there is selective activation of the part of the network where information about cats is stored, and no activity in the dog node. It is as though there is a searchlight moving around the network of concepts (which are interrelated to one another systematically) and this moving spot is the focus of attention – and thus the focus of consciousness. Thus, if the cortex is indeed the location of knowledge, then it may also be the site of origin of consciousness. (For comparable theories, see section 7.3.2, and Ruchkin et al., 2003. For reviews of the metaphor of information 'files', see Hommel, 2004, and Mitroff et al., 2005. For more on the searchlight metaphor see section 8.3.1.)

7.2.2.2 Particular cortical cell types and layers

The attribution of consciousness to the functioning of certain areas leaves open the question of how the cellular mechanisms within those areas actually generate consciousness. Attempts to narrow the search have focused on particular cell types (pyramidal versus stellate, for example) and/or particular layers.

Thus several workers have argued that since consciousness must *do* something, it must have outputs – perhaps outputs that connect more or less directly onto 'motor' centres. The layer 5 pyramidal cells in all areas of cortex, for example, project to the caudate nucleus and many to the brainstem; the cortico-spinal 'pyramidal tract' does not originate only from primary motor cortex. Indeed Diamond (1979) described layer 5 of the whole neocortex as being the real 'motor cortex'. Crick (1994, pp. 235, 251) thus considered it plausible that these neurons carry the results of 'neural computations', some of which correspond to consciousness.

Crick also speculated that thalamo-cortical loops involving layer 4 and 6 neurons may generate sensory consciousness by virtue of maintaining a reverberatory short-term memory. Harth (1993) similarly regarded thalamo-cortical connections as the source of visual experiences, while cortico-cortical connections carry out non-conscious processing (section 10.2.1.1). LaBerge (2001) narrows it down even further, suggesting that only the apical dendrites of pyramidal cells generate consciousness, while their basal dendrites function without direct relationship to consciousness (section 8.3.2).

Cortico-cortical connections originate, in general, from the upper cell layers 2 and 3, so theories of consciousness that take direct interactions between cortical areas as causative of awareness necessarily involve these layers. The most explicit example is Dehaene et al.'s (1998, 2003) global workspace theory (section 7.2.3.4), which postulates that areas participate in the workspace in proportion to the thickness of their layers 2 and 3. (However, Dehaene et al. do include thalamo-cortical loops as part of the workspace, so layers 4 and 6 are also involved.)

7.2.2.3 Particular sub-regions of cortex

The cerebral cortex contains the majority of human grey matter, and although there are commonalities of structure across the entire cortex, there are also regional variations. Several theories ascribe consciousness to some regions but not others. These touch on all the lobes, which I will deal with in turn.

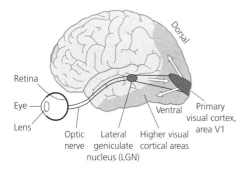

Figure 7.2 The visual pathway leading to the primary visual cortex and then on to the 'higher' visual areas (uniform grey shading). The dorsal and ventral streams run into the superior parietal and inferior temporal lobes respectively. From Rose and Harris (2005).

The occipital and temporal lobes

In a classic study, Milner and Goodale (1995) studied patients with localized damage to their visual systems. One sustained a lesion to the ventral parts of the occipital and temporal lobes and showed deficits in awareness of the objects she was looking at. For instance, she could not indicate whether an elongated, letter-box-shaped gap in a screen was horizontally or vertically oriented. However, she could reach out and post a letter through the gap with no problem. Other patients had lesions in the superior parts of the parietal lobe and had the opposite symptoms: they could not use vision to guide their reaching behaviour ('optic ataxia'), though they were fully aware of the stimuli they were trying to manipulate. The sites of these lesions are along the ventral and dorsal streams of information flowing from the primary visual cortex (Ungeleider and Mishkin, 1982; Figure 7.2). The conclusion was that only the *ventral stream* leads to conscious awareness of the visual environment, while the dorsal stream processes information subconsciously for the automatic guidance of movement (Milner and Goodale, 1995).

Even more precise localizations have also been proposed within these lobes. For example, on the basis of human lesion and imaging studies and single-cell recordings in monkeys, various areas in the occipital lobe have been ascribed roles in the generation of awareness about particular aspects of vision, such as the colour and motion of objects (e.g. Zeki, 1993). Similarly, the infero-temporal cortex is believed by some to be the site for object and shape awareness (e.g. Logothetis, 1998). (This issue will be discussed in more detail in section 10.2.)

The left hemisphere and/or the language centres

Other theorists ascribe consciousness to different particular regions of cortex. Let us start with Gazzaniga (1995), who has emphasized the role of the left hemisphere, based on his work on split-brain people. In these cases, the corpus callosum had been cut through, or had never grown. If such subjects fixate a point on a screen and a stimulus appears briefly to the left of fixation, the stimulus is processed by the right hemisphere, which can respond by moving the left hand, for example to point to a picture of an associated object. The left hemisphere can receive no information directly from the right hemisphere. When a split-brain subject is asked (verbally) why the left hand made that particular response, the left hemisphere responds (verbally) with a fictitious rationale, such as 'I like that picture' (i.e. it confabulates). Responses made with the right hand to stimuli on the right are, however, justified appropriately, in terms of the task. Gazzaniga concludes that there are cognitive mechanisms in the left hemisphere that interpret events and create the narrative of our lives.[10] These mechanisms give rise to consciousness because they construct our beliefs and assign affect to our cognitive acts. Consciousness comprises the feelings we have about our cognitive capacities and systems. The right hemisphere has only limited capacity in this respect; it monitors the state of the world, whereas the left hemisphere differentiates it. Note also that this division is not caused by the different abilities of the hemispheres in processing language; in those rare cases of people with right hemisphere speech, the interpreter module(s) are still in the left hemisphere. Either hemisphere may make decisions and control particular kinds of behaviour under particular circumstances, but the conscious awareness of (and post hoc justification for) *why* any given behaviour happened is generated by the interpreter module in the left hemisphere.

However, Rolls (1999, e.g. pp. 253–254) does suggest that language is the nub of consciousness and that a person has consciousness once activity reaches the linguistic stage, possibly in Broca's and Wernicke's areas in the left hemisphere. Special roles for speech in consciousness are also given by Edelman (1992), Torey (1999), Zeki (2001) and others. (This theory will be mentioned again in section 11.2.3.3.)

There are, however, critics of this idea. Thus Crick and Koch (1990) specifically excluded a crucial role for language, because higher nonhuman animals have consciousness. Damasio (1995, 1999) drew the same conclusion on the grounds that even global aphasic[11] patients do not lack consciousness, animals are conscious, verbal activity is sporadic throughout the day whereas consciousness is (more or less) continuous, and because concepts are more basic than words, which arise late, being just appended descriptions of events and ideas of which the subject has already become conscious. Panksepp (2005) has also pointed out that global aphasia leaves patients feeling fully conscious, capable of experiencing both imagistic thoughts and emotional feelings.

Now, a methodological rationale for the language approach is that it makes sense to define consciousness only in operational terms, that is, as something we can study objectively using 'scientific' techniques of third person observation. The way to study conscious experience is thus to confine ourselves to overt behavioural signs, of which a person's verbal descriptions of their inner states and feelings are a prime example – possibly the only example.[12] By restricting the study of consciousness to language behaviour, we can make progress without becoming hung up on the insoluble 'hard problem' of the nature of qualia.

So historically there have been many people who have equated thinking (and by implication consciousness) with language. At its most extreme, this follows the behaviourist 'language is thought' hypothesis, wherein thinking is regarded as nothing more than

---

10. Weiskrantz (1997) also talks about consciousness as a running 'commentary system', although he does not go into any depth and admits that this is just speculation.

11. Global aphasia involves loss of all speech functions, including understanding, production and imitation. Typically, there is widespread damage in the left hemisphere.

12. But note that more information may be conveyed via nonverbal communication (tone of voice, facial expression, body language, etc.); see, for example, Mehrabian (1969), Argyle et al. (1971) and Whitehead (2001), and, for animals, Panksepp (2005).

sub-vocal speech.[13] At the opposite extreme is the dualism of Descartes (section 2.2.1.2), in which mind = soul = consciousness = thinking = speech = humans only. Against the behaviourist theory there is a series of arguments that thought does not equal language, for example on the grounds that animals can think, and because purely visual and social thinking can occur (e.g. Weiskrantz, 1988). Against the Cartesian theory is the argument that its foundations are obsolete or at least shaky. If one starts with the dogma that only humans have souls, and includes the observation that only humans have language, then the premises all fit together into a coherent theory (soul = consciousness = thought = language = symbol processing). However, take away some of the premises (some people claim animals can acquire language; there is unconscious symbol processing; and so on) and the entire theory becomes less convincing. More moderate positions between these two extremes are of course possible, but their philosophical justification needs to be examined carefully, lest they slide towards one extreme or the other. Unfortunately, neuroscientists and psychologists all too rarely make such careful analyses.

The frontal lobes

As mentioned in the previous section on language, some researchers have argued that we must restrict ourselves to the study of overt behaviour. Thus, to enable scientific study, consciousness should be equated with motor functions, such as the events immediately preceding a movement, and planning and deciding which action to take (see also Jack and Shallice, 2001). Now, these functions are generally associated with frontal lobe activity. Hence several theorists, including Crick and Koch (1995; Koch, 2004), have proposed that for consciousness there must be activity in the frontal lobe at least.

Such a central role for the frontal lobes also follows from some parts of cognitive psychology. The mind is commonly regarded as divided into functional modules, and under homuncular functionalism (chapter 4), consciousness is seen as a high-level emergent property of a large system of sub-modules. However, several theorists have ascribed consciousness to just a limited subset of modules, perhaps only one.[14] For example, some theories postulate a '*central executive*' or '*supervisory (attentional) system*' that controls and calls up various slave subroutines, decides what to do next and uses various temporary memory stores and other subsystems to perform complex tasks (e.g. Baddeley and Hitch, 1974; Lindsay and Norman, 1977; Shallice, 1988). One theory is then to equate this central executive with the consciousness system: it is an obvious suggestion that the information being processed in the central executive is the information of which the person is

---

13. For social behaviourist theories of inner speech ('talking to oneself'), see section 6.2.2.1 and Morin (2005). The extreme 'language-is-thought' identity is not to be confused with the Sapir–Whorf hypothesis, which is that speech influences how we categorize and indeed perceive the world (Whorf, 1940; Gentner and Goldin-Meadow, 2003). Nor should it be confused with the more moderate 'language *of* thought' hypothesis that we discussed in section 2.5. The latter is to an extent metaphorical, and posits a very impoverished or simpler inner language-like system of symbols and rules (Fodor, 1975).

14. Under homuncular functionalism, any given module will always contain at least two sub-modules within it, and consciousness could emerge within that module because of the interactions between its sub-modules. When they say consciousness emerges from a single module, it therefore depends what level in the mind they are referring to as the focal level of their discussion when they use the word 'module'.

conscious (e.g. Baddeley, 1997; Andrade, 2001). In this and allied theories it is the contents of short-term memory or of ongoing '*working memory*' that are the contents of the thoughts that you are aware of.[15]

Alternatively, the *output* of the central supervisor may be identified with consciousness (Jack and Shallice, 2001).[16] The function of consciousness is regarded as to switch plans leading to *qualitative* changes in action or thought. Once initiated, such plans can continue subconsciously under the control of subroutines (these can at most adjust the *quantitative* strengths or rates of activity). Phenomenologically, we notice the unexpected and make decisions between alternative courses of action, but once any non-routine situation has been dealt with, minimal further attention is required and automated subconscious routines take over. Nevertheless, consciousness arises necessarily whenever such switching processes occur; it is not an optional add-on that may or may not be applied to inner representational states to make them conscious. This, they claim, avoids some of the problems with conventional philosophical accounts, such as how to describe qualia (sections 2.4.3.2 and 2.5.2.2) and whether we have unused phenomenal states (sections 5.2.5 and 5.3.5); consciousness arises from the process and not from the state.[17] Jack and Shallice, following Weiskrantz (1997), simply assert that becoming available for commentary, whether overt or covert, is both necessary and sufficient for consciousness to arise.[18]

Although cognitive or functional modules are not necessarily identical with anatomical modules, several neural theories have posited cerebral loci for these modules. Recent scanning studies have confirmed previous work on brain-damaged patients that suggest the

15. Confusingly, in the working memory model, the central executive is a sub-module, along with phonological/articulatory and visuo-spatial slave memory sub-modules. A multitude of processes have since come to be associated with the putative executive and working memory mechanisms (e.g. Vogeley et al., 1999; Faw, 2003) that are posited to perform a wide variety of tasks including short-term memory (with separate stores for object location and identity), decision making, response switching, response inhibition, recall from long-term memory, forward planning and self-monitoring. Thus the terms 'executive functions' and 'working memory' are both used loosely nowadays to refer to a ragbag of functions, underlain by various brain regions, including most of the frontal lobes. The latter in fact have a fine-grained anatomical substructure with many divisions, while the functional modularity has not yet been analysed to a corresponding degree (Goldman-Rakic, 2000). Any specific link postulated between a particular function or module with consciousness is thus easily lost in this confusion.

16. The supervisory module can process information from any source and is thus reminiscent of Fodor's (2000) central module, discussed in chapter 4. However, Jack and Shallice (2001) point out that their module is unlike Baar's global workspace (section 7.2.3), which is a passive disseminator of information, whereas the supervisory system is an active decision maker and controller of other modules within the brain.

17. Jack and Shallice (2001) do not go into details as to how content is determined and how intentionality is acquired. They describe their position as a variety of type functionalism (section 2.5).

18. Another reason for defining consciousness in this way is that the only variety of consciousness we can study objectively involves the awareness of our own states, making choices and intending to act (volition, free will). A problem is that all this involves introspection, which is an unreliable procedure because the judgements we make about our inner states are indirect (interpretations or constructions; see Side-box 11.2). Jack and Shallice (2001) suggest we could develop a more scientific method to study consciousness by introspection, for example by guiding and constraining the types of theory that our subjects can use to describe their own experiences.

executive functions are located in the frontal lobes (Stuss and Levine, 2002; Fassbender et al., 2004), and the same is true of working memory (Belger et al., 1998; Levy and Goldman-Rakic, 2000; Fletcher and Henson, 2001; Wager and Smith, 2003; Passingham and Sakai, 2004) – although, in both cases, networks of interaction with temporal and parietal lobes may also be emphasized. A more specific hypothesis has, however, been proposed by Jack and Shallice (2001), who argue first that consciousness may be equated with the processes that encode information into episodic memory (since conscious processes are the only ones that enable later recall of information about one's plans, percepts and thoughts, accompanied by the subjective feelings of recollection and familiarity). Second, these processes take place in the left dorso-lateral prefrontal cortex (as shown by brain scanning studies). Meanwhile, the right frontal lobe monitors ongoing events and alerts the supervisory system if anything untoward occurs, and the anterior cingulate cortex (also in the frontal lobes) implements the switching of sub-modules on and off.[19]

So what can we conclude about the frontal lobe hypothesis? There seem to be several good lines of argument and evidence linking consciousness with frontal lobe activity. However, in view of the fact that a network of areas is activated in scanning studies, Hommel et al. (2004) interpret the unity of the 'executive' system as merely apparent – as an emergent property arising from a system or network of interacting modules. This is surely a clear example of the homuncular functionalist approach (chapter 4), and raises again the issue of whether we can distinguish a nexus from a locus (sections 4.3.5–4.3.7).

Also against the localizationist thesis is the observation that lesions to the frontal areas do not knock out consciousness *tout court*. Patients have deficits, for example in attention, planning, temporal sequencing, pain perception and so on, but have every appearance of being aware (e.g. Bogen, 1995b).

The parietal lobes

Damage to the inferior parietal lobe can lead to loss of subjective awareness of various aspects of the self ('*hemineglect*': Side-box 4.5; see also section 11.3.2.2). Schacter (1989, 1990) therefore envisages the existence of a special 'conscious awareness system', located in the inferior parietal lobes (Figure 7.3). Connections from this module to the frontal lobes then enable executive decisions to be made based on the contents of conscious awareness.

Note that the inferior parietal lobes have also been linked with short-term memory. Thus electrical stimulation of part of the inferior parietal lobe (or adjacent parts of the temporal lobe) during brain surgery interferes with the short-term memory of the subject (Ojemann, 1978, 2003), and parietal lesions can cause reductions in the span of short-term memory (Warrington and Shallice, 1969). Single-cell recording in humans also shows that short-term storage and encoding functions may be mediated there (while cells in the frontal areas subserve retrieval; Ojemann, 2003). The left hemisphere is for verbal material and the right hemisphere for visuo-spatial material. So the idea of equating short-term memory with consciousness (e.g. Baddeley, 1997) is also consistent with the idea that the inferior parietal lobes may be crucial for consciousness.

---

19. Jack and Shallice (2001, p. 187) state that consciousness is of mismatches with expectation or goal state, rather than of continuing confirmatory evidence; compare section 9.3. For more on the role of the anterior cingulate cortex, see section 8.4.

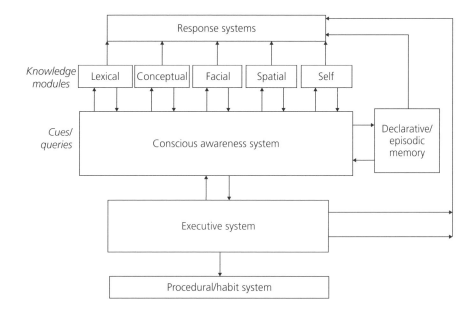

Figure 7.3 Schacter's module for consciousness is part of the DICE (dissociable interactions and conscious experience) model. From Schacter (1989).

In accordance with these views, Taylor (2001) has suggested that since the parietal lobes contain a map of our own body (remember, the somatosensory cortex is in this lobe), this makes them likely candidates for the origins of consciousness. The reasoning is that our sensory awareness at least is egocentric; that is, we experience the world from a viewpoint that is centred on our own bodies. Earlier, Damasio (1995, 1999) had included the parietal maps of the body (along with autobiographical memory and representations of the internal milieu of the body located in the hypothalamus, insula, brainstem and basal forebrain) as foundational for self-consciousness. This theory was proposed to account for the stability and uniqueness of our experiences.

Finally, Driver and Mattingley (1998) and Driver and Vuilleumier (2001) reviewed studies of damage to the parietal lobes and concluded that the inferior parietal lobes also play a part in constructing the stable representation of extrapersonal space that we see despite the occurrence of eye and body movements. The same region also integrates information from the ventral (what) and dorsal (where or how) streams, directs attention and even helps select and plan for motor action. It therefore plays a dominant role in perceptual awareness. Similarly, Robertson (2004) analysed the effects of parietal damage and concluded that spatial skills in general depend on these structures. These abilities include not just seeing the world from one point of view but also body positioning – indeed, our whole awareness of extrapersonal space and our ability to become aware of objects within it. Even ventral stream lesions do not destroy those abilities (cf. Milner and Goodale, 1995; see earlier in this section). (The same point has been made by Jacob and Jeannerod, 2003.) Since the sense of space is so central to our subjective experience (Kant, 1781/7), Robertson concludes that the parietal lobes are the relevant locus for consciousness.

7.2.2.4 Interim conclusion

The cortex is undoubtedly important, although there seem to be conflicting opinions as to the crucial site. This might be because different areas give rise to different aspects of consciousness – after all, there are many types that need to be explained (perception, emotion, action and so on).[20] Alternatively, the uncertainty may result from our poor understanding of what makes the difference between conscious and unconscious representations. Is this simply a matter of finding out the intrinsic properties held by an area that enable it to generate consciousness directly, or are areas necessarily components of a more widespread system, for example one that fulfils the vital function of integrating and disseminating information from numerous sources? In the next section we look at a set of theories that take the latter approach.

7.2.3 Global workspace theories

A recent group of theories suggests that consciousness depends upon a single location in the brain, but that to generate consciousness it needs a particular kind of relationship/ connectivity with the rest of the brain. This functionalist model will be described in section 7.2.3.1. The first neural version of the theory postulated a single fixed locus (see section 7.2.3.2), but more recent versions either describe the site as movable, in that different places may subserve the same function at different times (section 7.2.3.3), or see it as more diffusely distributed across several areas of cortex (section 7.2.3.4). A general critique will be given in section 7.2.3.5.

7.2.3.1 Functional workspace theory

This cognitive theory follows homuncular functionalism (chapter 4) in seeing the mind as composed of multiple modules, each of which subserves a different functional role. But unlike homuncular teleological functionalism, which sees the modules as self-organizing into a network of mutually interacting units, global workspace theory proposes that they are organized around a single central module whose sole function is to distribute information among all the other modules (Baars, 1988, 1997; see Figure 7.4a).

To revise: cognitive psychology has for a long time viewed the mind as containing many functional sub-units; it is a collection of mechanisms and subroutines that process information in different ways (e.g. Miller et al., 1960; Lindsay and Norman, 1977; Minsky, 1985; Shallice, 1988; chapter 4; section 6.3.1). But how do these different subroutines get access to information? Well, the reasoning now goes, there must be some kind of single universal broadcasting system, which is a bit like having a blackboard at the front of a class. Any functional unit that receives information then proceeds to process it and finally writes the result up on the blackboard. Then all the other units can access that blackboard and 'see' what has been written up, and thus 'know' what is going on. If the information is relevant to them, then they can process that information and put their own results back up on the

---

20. Even within vision, to give a specific example, Jacob and Jeannerod (2003) argue there are two types of perceptual experience – of objects and of their spatial relations – subserved by the ventral (temporal) and dorsal (parietal) streams respectively.

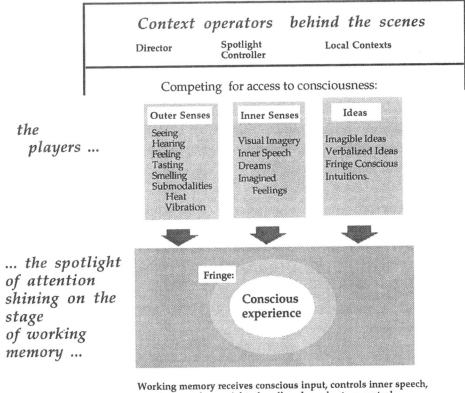

the
players ...

... the spotlight
of attention
shining on the
stage
of working
memory ...

Working memory receives conscious input, controls inner speech,
uses imagery for spatial tasks, all under voluntary control.

the   unconscious   audience...

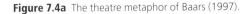

Memory systems:

Lexicon
Semantic networks
Autobiographical
& declarative memory
Beliefs, knowledge
of the world, of
oneself and others.

Interpreting conscious contents:

Recognizing objects, faces, speech,
events. Syntactic analysis. Spatial
relationships. Social inferences.

Automatisms:

Skill memory.
Details of language,
action control, reading,
thinking, and
thousands more ...

Motivational systems:

Is the conscious event relevant to my goals?   Emotional responses, facial
expressions, preparing the body for action. Managing goal conflicts.

Figure 7.4a The theatre metaphor of Baars (1997).

Figure 7.4b The blackboard metaphor of Lindsay and Norman (1977). The various demons (modules) are trying to understand a sentence that is being read ('take this sentence as an example').

blackboard, so all the other units can see the new conclusions and if they want they can process these new ideas even further (Lindsay and Norman, 1977; Figure 7.4b).[21]

Baars (1988, 1997) also developed a blackboard-like analogy for his distribution system, which he called a 'global workspace' (or a short-term 'working memory'). Most importantly for us, he said that consciousness arises when information is made available by being placed in the workspace. The workspace carries the instantaneous contents of consciousness, while the modules in the rest of the brain intrinsically carry out their information processing unconsciously. These modules may communicate directly with each other, but only when some kind of integration of their results takes place in the correct location (the workspace) does consciousness exist.[22]

Baars (1997, 1998) is also famous for using the metaphor of a theatre, in which the central distribution point is likened to the stage in a theatre and the functional modules are cast as the audience (see Figure 7.4a and Side-box 7.4). Moreover, having argued that our cognitive systems function like a theatre, he then suggests how the processes might be mapped onto brain mechanisms. Indeed, he presents not one but two different neural theories: one that the stage is thalamic and the other that it is cortical.

7.2.3.2 The thalamus as workspace

First, as we saw in section 7.2.1.2 and in Side-box 7.2, within the thalamus are several sub-nuclei that appear to have fairly diffuse connections with wide regions of the brain. These form what therefore used to be called the 'thalamic reticular system' – outposts or extensions of the brainstem reticular formation (Jasper, 1949, 1954; see section 7.2.1.3). Baars (1988) coined the acronym ERTAS ('extended reticulo-thalamic activating system') for the whole system reaching up from the brainstem via the thalamus to arouse the cortex. He presents this structure as isomorphic to the cognitive theatre; for example: 'The ERTAS as a whole can be interpreted as a functional global workspace or perhaps as an increasingly global set of workspaces. ERTAS has many properties reminiscent of global workspaces including connections in both input and output with all sensory and motor systems, and with almost all areas of the brain; known competition between different inputs and the possibility of "global broadcasting" of information through the diffuse thalamic projection system' (Baars and Newman, 1994, p. 217). The natural conclusion is that the ERTAS, and in particular the 'thalamic reticular system' (i.e. the intralaminar nuclei) is acting as a

21. Another good analogy is the hardware 'bus' in a computer. A computer has a bus (a set of wires) that is accessible by all the different sub-mechanisms that are attached to it: the memory, the logic unit, the input and output units and so on. (In older computers these were physically built on cards that slotted into connectors linked by the bus.) Each such unit can both receive and transmit information via that same bus. (They each have an address and can direct information to particular modules by putting the target's address at the head of a message. The address is received by all the modules, but it is only recognized by the relevant module, which then proceeds to read the rest of the message.) See section 4.3.7 and Side-box 4.6 for further discussion of communication between modules. A similar problem is faced within the World Wide Web or internet, where packages of information have to be routed to specific target sites. The solution used is somewhat different, in that multiple routes can be used at different times. (Essay topic: Is there is a lesson for brain science here?)

22. As Figure 7.4a shows, there is a separation on the blackboard/workspace between information within a 'spotlight' of focal attention, and that outside the spotlight, in the 'fringe' of background working memory. We will discuss the spotlight metaphor in more detail in section 8.3.1.

SIDE-BOX 7.4 THE THEATRE

It is common to picture mental functioning as being like the workings of a theatre. Let me quote exten-sively from Jung (1954), whose paper (clearly influenced by James, 1890, though without citing him) described several concepts that have since been 'rediscovered' by more recent theorists:

> Attention is a co-ordinating aid for conscious perception and may be compared to a spotlight which illuminates details in the dark unconscious field of the internal and external world (Weber and Jung, 1940). . . . consciousness should be considered together with attention: both functions are co-ordinated and selective so that consciousness will contain only very few things in a focus of attention with a fringe representing the half-conscious background . . . the searchlight of attention assists consciousness by selecting inner experiences and outer perceptions from the sense organs, so illuminating a sector of the internal and external world. The beam of light is focused on the cen-tral spot giving brightness and clarity. A surrounding fringe or 'sphere' allows a peripheral field with a more hazy picture. The searchlight is movable and can change for selection of objects. It can be concentrated or broadened to illuminate a narrow or a wide field. This . . . does not show the more dynamic side of the 'stream of consciousness'. Another metaphor may be more useful for this purpose: 15 years ago, when working on the epileptic aura (Weber and Jung, 1940) we used a further illustration for consciousness and attention and their relation to other psychological func-tions: following a suggestion of K. Jaspers (1923) we compared conscious activity with a play on a stage. On this stage various actors appear for a limited time as the actual selected contents of consciousness, illuminated by the spotlight of attention. After a short performance the actors of conscious thinking and feeling disappear behind in the unconscious background of the stage. The spotlight of attention may be broad and shine with a diffuse light on the whole stage or it may be concentrated on one actor with a small but very bright spot as when we focus our attention on one object. (Jung, 1954, pp. 310–313).

Now enter the philosophers. The metaphor of attention as a searchlight was also used by the phe-nomenologist Merleau-Ponty (1945). More recently, Dennett (1991) has agreed that many people imagine that mental functioning is like having a little theatre in the head, and that what we are aware of is the set of events happening on the stage. One or more little men comprise the audience and are looking at events on the stage of the theatre. Dennett has popularized the term 'Cartesian theatre' as a way of dramatizing the fact that this image demonstrates the continuing influence of Descartes on modern thinking. It is really a caricature of the theory put forward by Descartes (see section 7.2.1.1), of the soul looking at events in the pineal body. Although Descartes said it is wrong to think there is another pair of eyes inside the head looking at the pineal, nevertheless Dennett and others still use his name as the archetype for this kind of approach. According to such theories, what you see on stage are the qualia (which we talked about in chapter 2); these sensory elements are the actors that/who are re-enacting events in the outside world. Then there is some kind of mechanism looking at this activity, like an audience at a theatre. For modern theories, however, this mechanism is a physical one and does not involve a supernatural soul, hence it is called Cartesian 'materialism'.

Most people, including Dennett (1991, 1998), have lampooned this view and said that this is the type of theory we need to get away from, but Baars (1997, 1998) is one of the few people who says overtly that he thinks this is a good model and we should support it (see further details under the discussion of qualia and imagery in section 10.2). He says that not all theatres are dimensionless, and moreover that parts of the brain actually act like a theatre stage in that (at times) they broadcast information to the rest of the brain.

theatre stage or a blackboard, receiving from and broadcasting information to various cortical and subcortical modules.

However, Baars and Newman do not exclude other possibilities, and indeed they then proceed to argue that these may be more valid. Thus they recognize that, as they put it, the bandwidth of the ERTAS must be very limited. The number of cells in the reticular formation and in the 'reticular nucleus' of the thalamus[23] is quite small compared to the size of the cortex and certainly to the rest of the brain, so the large amount of information that (putatively) flows through the ERTAS and carries the contents of our conscious awareness would need to be very compressed. However, it is difficult to accept that so much information is actually passing through so few cells.

7.2.3.3 A cortical shifting workspace

Therefore Baars and Newman went on to say, well, the high volume of precise information must be transmitted through cortico-cortical connections, which are there in profusion. The role of blackboard or stage is then played by one of the cortical areas – for example, it might be area V1 if consciousness is currently dominated by visual stimuli. Several different areas of cortex could act as stages at different times, each mediating the global integration and dissemination of information (Baars, 1998). The function of the ERTAS is then left as that of a global switching system that turns the various cortical modules on and off, and thus controls selective attention and determines the dominance of one cortical area as the ongoing centre or stage of the global workspace.[24]

However, this new version of the theory contradicts the cognitive structure given by Baars (Figure 7.4), in which there is a separate module that is the stage (working memory) and other modules that subserve the remaining functions of the mind. Baars would have it that many modules can act as working memories at different times, while functioning as unconscious modules for the remaining times. Although such a model is consistent with the ideas of many other theorists, as we shall see later in this book, it does not sit well with the static, black-box diagrams that Baars and other cognitive psychologists have presented. The relationship between function and anatomical location may well shift from time to time, but functional modules are not supposed to swap their functions around!

7.2.3.4 A large multimodal cortical workspace

In another self-proclaimed 'global workspace theory' (Dehaene et al., 1998, 2003), the anatomical locus of the workspace is far more extensive and complicated (full details are given in Side-box 7.5). It involves many cortical regions, and places particular emphasis on the integration of sensory information in the 'multimodal' (also known as 'polymodal') areas of cortex, where visual, auditory and somatosensory information (for example) converges.[25] This

23. I presume they meant the intralaminar nuclei rather than the reticular nucleus.

24. This function for the thalamus has also been introduced by many others, e.g. Purpura and Schiff (1997) and Taylor (1999); see also sections 7.2.1.2 and 8.3.

25. Beware: 'multimodal' areas may contain (1) cells that each respond to stimuli via two or more sensory modalities, (2) cells responding via one modality whose activity is modulated by stimuli from another modality, but which do not give overt responses to the modulating modality alone (i.e. there is nonlinear interaction, not just algebraic summation of the inputs from the two modalities), or (3) a mixture of cells, each of which is unimodal. It is often unclear which arrangement is being designated when the term 'multimodal' is used to refer to an area or region of brain tissue.

SIDE-BOX 7.5 IS ALL THE BRAIN A STAGE?

Dehaene et al.'s (1998, 2003) workspace differs from Baars' (1988, 1997) in that it is more like an original Hebbian cell assembly (section 6.4.1). Its neural basis is scattered widely throughout the brain, being composed of layer 2 and 3 pyramidal cells interconnecting with each other via long cortico-cortical fibres (Figure SB 7.5.1). Such cells lie preponderantly in 'higher association areas' such as the dorso-lateral prefrontal and inferior parietal cortices. Their connections (via lower cortical layers) with thalamic nuclei are included as part of the workspace architecture. Strictly, the anatomical workspace is the total network within which all the assemblies can exist, each of the latter being some combination or pattern of active neurons in the workspace. Cells within such an assembly reinforce each other through mutual excitation, while lateral inhibition ensures only one assembly can be active at any one time.

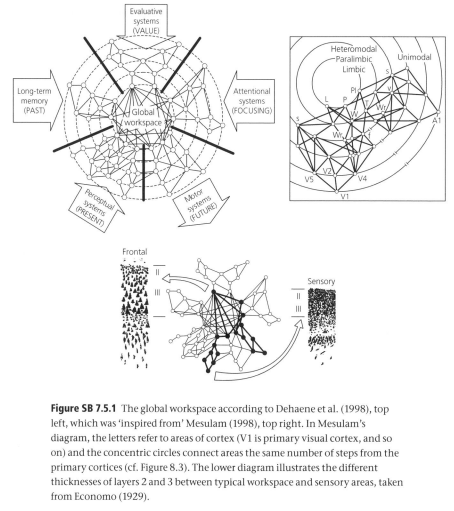

Figure SB 7.5.1 The global workspace according to Dehaene et al. (1998), top left, which was 'inspired from' Mesulam (1998), top right. In Mesulam's diagram, the letters refer to areas of cortex (V1 is primary visual cortex, and so on) and the concentric circles connect areas the same number of steps from the primary cortices (cf. Figure 8.3). The lower diagram illustrates the different thicknesses of layers 2 and 3 between typical workspace and sensory areas, taken from Economo (1929).

continues

SIDE-BOX 7.5 continued

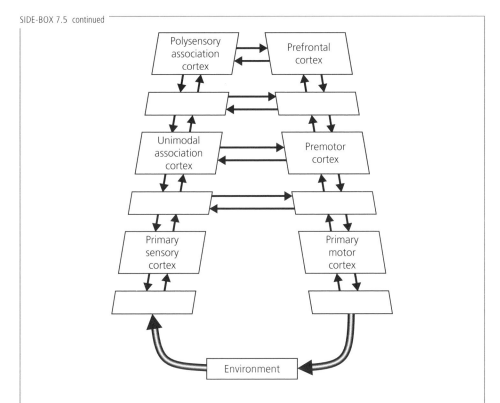

Figure SB 7.5.2 Division of the cortex into sensory and motor systems (after Fuster, 1993).

In fact, Mesulam's (1998) and Dehaene et al.'s (1998) diagrams (Figure SB 7.5.1) bear similarities to that of Fuster (1995), shown in Figure SB 7.5.2 (and also used by Crick and Koch, 1998a, Rolls, 1999, and others). Fuster's has a more behaviourist division into sensory and motor halves, whereas Mesulam's just covers the visual and auditory systems, but in both cases the connectivity is very extensive. It would appear that the 'global workspace' fills almost the entire brain! As such, the term 'global' is appropriate, but the 'workspace' is not really a workspace. It may be a universal connectivity matrix, whereby every part of the brain communicates more or less directly with every other part, or it might be Fodor's (2000) massive cognitive module, but it is not a single, central, limited capacity focus where the input and output pathways of all modules converge. The brain areas that light up *only* when consciousness is present are not the same in all tasks (Baars, 2002), as they should be if there is a single bottleneck or common pathway that carries the contents of consciousness (Baars' stage). Indeed, one review that sought a common site that is always activated when subjects are aware of a visual stimulus found just two such areas, limited to small regions in the superior parietal and the dorsolateral prefrontal cortices (Rees et al., 2002; Figure 4.8b; see also section 10.2).[a]

[a] I could also point to evidence of polymodal activity even in primary sensory cortices (e.g. Sauvan, 1998), but that would be kicking a dead donkey.

arrangement allows cells to fire as temporary coalitions or assemblies that constitute working memories and coordinate information from a wide range of sources, that is from different functional modules (that are presumed to be scattered around the brain in the various anatomical modules).

Critique

One problem is that the functional division between the global workspace and the specialist modules is central to these theories. Yet the anatomical basis proposed by Dehaene et al. is clearly not dichotomous (Side-box 7.5). The different cortical areas would *all* appear to participate in the global workspace, albeit to varying degrees, corresponding to the thickness and prominence of their layers 2 and 3.

Even if one takes Dehaene et al.'s other criterion for belonging to the workspace, namely that the specialist modules are modality specific and the global workspace is polymodal, their adoption of Mesulam's (1998) plan for cortical architecture means there are at least two 'levels' within the workspace.[26] (The term 'levels' here is allied to that of Felleman and Van Essen, 1991, and refers to how many stages of processing are applied to sensory messages as they pass through the cortex. So you need to beware of yet another terminological confusion: a 'stage of processing' – see Side-box 4.4 – is not the same notion as the stage in the theatre metaphor! For present purposes, let's call them 'tiers'.) Further analysis is therefore needed to elucidate how these tiers differ, and indeed how a multi-tier 'blackboard' or 'stage' is supposed to operate.

7.2.3.5 General critique

It is difficult to keep in sight what consciousness actually is in global workspace theories, let alone its source: the integration of information into a working memory (blackboard or stage), the distribution of activity from that stage to other parts of the brain, or just the coming into existence of the stage per se? For example, Baars often adopts a dualistic tone when he says 'consciousness is the gateway to the brain' (2003, p. 22), 'consciousness is the primary agent of such a global access function' and 'conscious perception . . . enables access to widespread brain areas' (2002, p. 47), 'conscious information enables many types of learning' and 'consciousness enables widespread access in the brain' (2002, p. 50). Confusingly, 'working memory depends on conscious elements . . . each mobilizing widespread functions' (2002, p. 49), yet 'conscious perceptual input to frontal regions might lead to executive interpretation and control, which enables working memory . . . . attention and accurate report' (2002, p. 51); so which comes first: working memory or consciousness? On attention: 'all implicit learning paradigms ask the subjects to pay conscious attention to a set of stimuli', yet 'selective attention can be defined as selection among potentially conscious contents' (2002, p. 50). The terminology used by Baars (and the other authors he approvingly cites as supportive of his approach) is so loose and jumps between levels of description so often (category errors – e.g. 'conscious information') that the whole

26. Dehaene et al. (1998) actually have one level for communication between the modules for long-term memory, attention, evaluation and perceptuo-motor functions, but they have three between the perception and motor modules (see Figure SB7.5.1 in Side-box 7.5).

theory seems to disappear in an attempt to claim his approach is supported universally.[27] Of course, 'conscious information' is shorthand for 'information of which the person is conscious' – the contents of their experience. However, the question at issue is how that information (how any information) becomes conscious. It begs the question if you have to start with conscious information to explain how consciousness arises subsequently.

Similar confusion arises when, on their opening page, Dehaene et al. (2003, p. 8520, my italics) write: 'Our model focuses on the issue of conscious access: the fact that a piece of information, *once conscious*, becomes selectively available for multiple processes of attention, intention, memory, evaluation, and verbal report.... *when* a piece of information such as the identity of a stimulus accesses a sufficient subset of workspace neurons, their activity becomes self-sustaining and can be broadcasted via long distance connections to a vast set of defined areas, *thus* creating a global and exclusive availability for a given stimulus, which is *then* subjectively experienced as conscious.'

These theorists, like Baars, are obviously failing to come to grips with the question of *when* we become aware of a stimulus, since they are unclear about when consciousness arises relative to the passage of information/activity through the global workspace. We will discuss this problem in more detail in section 10.3. There is also ambiguity over causation: is consciousness the cause or the result of access to the global workspace? Is global availability a consequence of or an explanation for consciousness?

In summary, Baars' first theory (the blackboard is part of the ERTAS, probably the intralaminar thalamus) has been replaced by a second theory (the blackboard shifts around the cortex).[28] Recent writings (Baars, 2002) have proposed that global workspace theory is supported by the fact that widespread activation of the cortex occurs during episodes of consciousness. But the problem is that these observations are actually consistent with many other theories as well (examples will be encountered below). The best we can say is that the theatre metaphor seems to have outlived its usefulness, having been subsumed into a more detailed and far more complex picture of brain function. The 'global workspace' described by Baars (1998, 2002) and Dehaene et al. (1998, 2003) is a long way from the neatly circumscribed little 'stage' or central blackboard postulated by Baars (1988).

7.2.4 Interim conclusion

How can the suggestions above all be so different in where they place the neural locus of consciousness? It is possible that these theorists may be talking about different types of consciousness (self-consciousness, language, seeing, etc.), and this might resolve some of the discrepancies between their theories – they all mean different things by 'consciousness', or different aspects of consciousness may be localized in different parts of the brain.

27. Essay topic: How many meanings of the word 'conscious' and 'unconscious' occur in the following paragraph? Explain the meaning of each. Are they consistent with one another? 'These findings support the general claim that conscious stimuli mobilize large areas of cortex, presumably to distribute information about the stimuli . . . If consciousness serves to mobilize many unconscious specialized networks, the active elements of WM [working memory] that always need to be conscious – input, recall, rehearsal, inner speech, visual imagery and report – may be widely distributed in order to recruit specific unconscious functions needed to carry out those tasks' (Baars, 2003, p. 19).

28. As such, Baars' second theory is more akin to the dynamic theories described in chapter 8.

Moreover, there are various (usually implicit) fundamental assumptions about what consciousness itself actually is (raw feelings, inner language, thought, awareness of ourselves thinking and so on) that are downright philosophical in nature (see, for example, section 5.2.5). This is just one reason why it is important to know a lot about the philosophy of mind when studying neuroscience (chapters 1–5)!

One general problem with the above theories is that they don't explain how or why that particular piece of brain gives rise to consciousness. They may narrow down the search, but how does awareness arise out of a single brain area, and why should it be that particular area; and why (importantly) *not* the other areas? For vision it may seem reasonable to propose that visual cortex should generate visual qualia, or for theories of self-awareness, that the map of one's own body may be a source of primary data upon which foundation to build the rest of consciousness. However, many of the theories acknowledge that information is transmitted to other areas; they just don't admit this is crucial. Let us therefore look next at some pure processing theories, before combining anatomical and physiological information in chapter 8.

7.3 State/property theories

From localizationist theories, we turn now to some examples of 'state-change' theories of consciousness. These suppose that there is a special state of the neural activity or representation, involving or resulting from some particular way of processing, that is necessary and sufficient for consciousness. In principle, this special kind of activity could occur anywhere in the brain (or in a Martian's brain or in the nation of China, if you take a functionalist viewpoint; section 2.5). Hence any region of the brain could 'generate' consciousness.[29] It is just a matter of the representation being processed: transforming or changing in the right way in order to create consciousness.

7.3.1 Synchronous oscillations (40 Hz theory)

The best known theory of this type nowadays is the 40 Hz theory (see section 6.4.2). The idea is that there are oscillations in cell firing, and their exact synchrony is the crucial feature. Of course, 40 Hz oscillations could simply be the neural basis of any representation, conscious or unconscious, but several people have suggested that 40 Hz oscillations are crucial for consciousness. These include Crick and Koch (1990), Zeki (1993) and Engel and Singer (2001).

For example, Crick and Koch (1990) suggested that 40 Hz oscillations could arise when the thalamic reticular nucleus allowed thalamo-cortical feedback to build up into oscillations. This was linked to selective attention to certain information processing streams, in what Crick (1984) called the 'searchlight' hypothesis (which will be described in more detail in section 8.3.1). More recently, however, Crick and Koch (1998a, 2003) have retracted this as a theory of consciousness (because 40 Hz oscillations are not readily found

---

29. Some theories refer only to the cortex rather than the whole brain, but since the cortex constitutes the greatest volume of grey matter, I count cortical theories here as non-localizationalist.

in monkeys: Young et al., 1992), concentrating more on global interactionalist ideas. They suggest instead that such oscillations may be seen when representations are being constructed, especially when they have to compete with other representations (i.e. they do not arise if we are looking at a single, simple stimulus). Alternatively, or in addition, they may be the signature of the mechanisms of figure–ground (object–background) segregation.

Zeki (1993) also adopted the theory of 40 Hz oscillations, accepting that consciousness can arise from different regions within the visual areas. Consciousness depends on integration ('binding') between activity in different areas, but this integration could take place in any of those areas (though Zeki didn't explain which area on which occasion). Information does not need to be sent across to a central integrating area or theatre where all the information comes together to form one central show or display. However, he has since gone on to suggest that any one of the visual areas can give rise to visual awareness of one particular feature ('micro-consciousnesses'; Zeki, 1998; Zeki and Bartels, 1998; Zeki and ffytche, 1998). For example, areas of the visual system that analyse colour generate consciousness of colour, and areas that deal with stimulus movement give rise to awareness of stimulus movement. Zeki (2001, 2003) suggests that binding can still occur, but if so it is between stages *along* a single neural processing pathway (or between different stages along different pathways: Bartels and Zeki, 1998), rather than laterally between areas that lie at similar 'final' stages along the various parallel streams, as in his earlier (1993) theory. (The detailed evidence for this view will be discussed in section 10.3.2.1.)

In contrast, Engel and Singer (2001) review the evidence and support a global binding model, where synchronous firing is an essential property if signals are to become manifest throughout the brain. For activity to have meaning, it must fit within a wider context and be differentiated into components. Conscious brain states are reverberatory, persist briefly (within working memory) and are widespread in the brain (enabling cross-modal integration). Engel and Singer suggest that many more studies have found 40 Hz oscillations than have not, in a variety of species and brain structures (although many of the positive cases involved anaesthetized animals!).

In conclusion, the idea that synchronous firing will have a larger effect on the target cells downstream remains a valid point. The relationship with the oscillations remains to be understood, which is a pity since oscillatory firing is easier to detect empirically than is synchrony.

Interim comment

Although the number of cells engaged in synchronous 40 Hz firing can vary, this property can be regarded as an all-or-none quality, since the intensity of cell firing is not emphasized under these theories. The theories in the next group, however, use the general idea that it is the *amount* of neural activity that makes the difference between conscious and unconscious representations. This may be the activity of a single cell or the integrated activity of some group of cells.

7.3.2 Firing rate

It seems reasonable to suggest that the crucial property may simply be a matter of *intensity*: the activity levels of the nerve cells have to rise to a certain level, and once activity reaches some *threshold* then you become aware of whatever information is passing through those

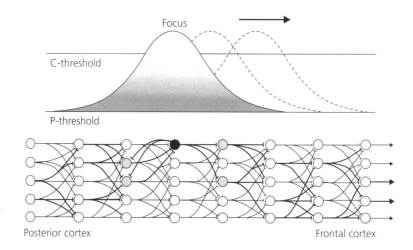

Figure 7.5 Fuster's view of the propagation of neural activity though the cortex. In the lower diagram, each circle represents a cell assembly. One (black) is sufficiently active that it exceeds the 'C-threshold' for consciousness (upper diagram) and activates recurrent connections to its input assemblies, thus setting up a persistent loop or short-term memory. The grey nodes have sufficient activity to exceed the 'P-threshold' for processing, but remain preconscious. The arrow at the top indicates the flow of representation and attention through the cortex. From Fuster (1995).

nerve cells. This is a fairly obvious theory to the extent that if you assume that activity in the brain is *necessary* for any kind of information processing, and that nothing is happening if the nerve cells are not firing, then, obviously, the firing of the nerve cells must be necessary for consciousness.[30] Firing per se may not be *sufficient*, since unconscious processing will involve firing too, but maybe with enough firing the representation transforms (more or less suddenly) into a conscious one.[31]

Let's, for example, look in detail at the theory of Fuster (1995; see Figure 7.5). He presumes that the cortex is a long-term memory store. His model of it is based on neural network theory (section 6.4.3). There is a series of layers that feed forward onto one another in a heteroassociative fashion. He regards the sensory input as being processed through these various stages, starting with the sensory cortex and moving towards the motor cortex in the frontal lobe. What Fuster suggests is that as the stimulus is processed through the various stages, the cells that are activated form a series of representations of the stimulus. This is, of course, a standard part of the serial processing model (e.g. Marr, 1982; Figure 2.4d). But Fuster (1995) calls the activated region 'active memory'. He suggests that if the activity

30. Physiologists may recognize that inhibition may still be doing something important even if the large excitatory cells (as opposed to small inhibitory interneurons) are not active (e.g. Dobson, 1975), but few theories of consciousness have reached this degree of sophistication yet.

31. Marcel (1983b, p. 250), for example, lists several psychologists who suggest that mere enhanced activation leads to consciousness, and to this list one could add Dennett (1991, p. 166), Zeki and ffytche (1998), Moutoussis and Zeki (2002) and many others. A complex and detailed neural network theory involving an activity threshold for consciousness has been given by Taylor (1999); I have summarized and reviewed that theory elsewhere (Rose, 2000b).

in a part of the network is sufficient, it may exceed a threshold for activation of recurrent connections that loop back, in what he calls 're-entrant' fashion.[32] This then serves to build up or reinforce the activity pattern and to create and increase the oscillations within it (the only recurrent connections shown in Figure 7.5 are from the single black dot). There will also be increasing persistence of this activity, making it both a form of working memory and the focus of selective attention (Fuster, 2003). Fuster then simply suggests that this reactivation threshold can be called the '*consciousness threshold*', and he just postulates that if activity reaches this level then it becomes conscious activity.[33]

So, from the point of view of theories of consciousness, first Fuster postulates that the level of activity simply has to reach a certain degree to give consciousness: it is a quantity model. Second, what is also important is that he assumes that consciousness can arise from any part of the whole neural network, at least the long-term memory network, and thus that any part of the cerebral cortex that is sufficiently active can generate consciousness. The activated part constitutes a form of short-term or working memory, but the latter is not a fixed module, as short-term memory is in many cognitive theories. As the wave of analysis of the stimulus passes through the system, so awareness of the different aspects of the stimulus as they are processed changes correspondingly.[34]

Critique

The problems are, first, that Fuster (1995) does not go into any detail as to how exceeding threshold leads to consciousness and what determines the level of that threshold. The picture presented is still a simplistic, serial processing, behaviourist one (chapter 3), albeit with a slightly more complicated feedback mechanism than the old stimulus–response reflex models. In his later book (Fuster, 2003) he puts forward a more sophisticated, hierarchical interpretation of the functionality of the network, and allows for a richer pattern of connectivity between different areas of the cortex (e.g. any given memory may depend on cells distributed across many areas; p. 125); however, it remains a network of associations (pp. 113, 142). Yet it still does not account for the different qualitative experiences that accompany activation of the different parts of the cortical network: sensory awareness, emotional feeling, abstract thought and so on. Why is it like what it is like when that particular part of the network is active rather than any other part (cf. section 2.4.3.3)?

---

32. The term 're-entry' was popularized by Edelman (1989, 1992) and has since been used by several theorists to describe a variety of functional processes: it seems, any which involve connections descending a serial or hierarchical pathway in the brain.

33. Dehaene et al. (2003) also posit a threshold for triggering consciousness, which they couch in terms of a phase transition in a dynamic network (see section 6.4.3.3) that leads to the ignition of activity becoming distributed widely throughout the brain (in a 'global workspace'; section 7.2.3). Edelman and Tononi (2000, p. 119) have a similar conception, emphasizing the self-sustaining nature of activity once it has been initiated (see also section 7.3.4).

34. Although his diagram is drawn as though the wave of activity spreads across the surface of the cortex, this is not necessarily so. The connections could be U-fibres going down into the depths of the hemisphere and up again, and could in principle hop from anatomical place to place irregularly in between the sensory and motor ends of the pathway.

Some other general problems with threshold theories are that they do not allow for the demonstrations that there are *qualitative* differences between conscious and non-conscious processes (Marcel, 1983b), that high levels of activity can occur in the cortex without consciousness arising (Goebel et al., 2001) and that consciousness does not develop suddenly although neural firing can increase very rapidly (Bachmann, 2000; Meier et al., 2003).

7.3.3 Size and duration

Other theories posit that it is the quantity of brain tissue involved – the physical size of the representation – that is the crucial factor. Two theories will be given as representative: those of Greenfield and of Calvin.

First, Greenfield (1995) proposes that activity in the brain is generated from a number of sources, such as sensory stimuli coming in, and that these act as what she calls 'epicentres' or foci. She presents an analogy with drops of water falling into a pond: the ripples spread out from these epicentres, e.g. from the sites in the brain where activity is aroused by external stimuli.[35] The activity then spreads through associative connections into other regions of the brain to form an 'ensemble' around the epicentre. There can be several of these ensembles at any instant in time – patches or collections of activity in the brain. Thus you can have several representations existing simultaneously as you receive multiple sensory inputs, internal inputs from your hormones, and so on. Now, the larger an ensemble gets, the longer lasting it is as well, so they tend to increase both in anatomical size and in duration. The longer lasting and more stable the thought, the longer lasting and more stable the neural ensemble (the collection of nerve cells that are active and connected).

Greenfield then just posits that the degree of awareness or consciousness is proportional to the size of the activated ensemble. The more brain that is devoted to some particular meaningful activity pattern, the more the individual is subjectively aware of its content. There is no sharp threshold for consciousness; instead there is a continuum.[36] We can be aware of several things at once, but to different degrees, reflecting the different amounts of neural tissue that are devoted to processing and holding those thoughts. So we may have at any moment a set of ensembles or collections of co-active linked nerve cells. Then, she says that consciousness is an emergent property of these ensembles. It is just a higher-order property.

Calvin (1996) holds what is in many ways a similar principle. He also envisages activity as spreading through the brain. He uses a more detailed knowledge of the anatomy and physiology of the forebrain than Greenfield. He extrapolates an idea based on the cellular anatomy of the visual cortex, that there actually are reciprocal connections between nerve cells (Figure 7.6). Certain kinds of neurons in the cortex, large pyramidal cells, appear to be connected directly with one another as though they are spreading activity amongst themselves. Calvin suggests that such cells would form into stable systems, and he uses dynamic systems theory to back this up (see section 6.4.3.3). Stability is enhanced if the system contains three mutually excitatory cells in an equilateral triangle; if two fire simultaneously,

---

35. Greenfield's notion of ripples spreading through the brain resembles that of Pavlov's old theory of irradiation, described in Side-box 8.4.

36. This obviates the problems of when consciousness arises in ontogeny and evolution.

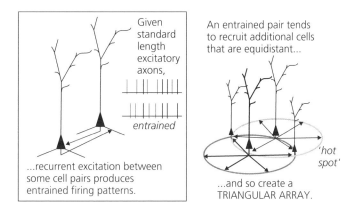

Figure 7.6 How the formation by mutual reinforcement of cell pairings can lead to triangular arrays of pyramidal cells in cerebral cortex. The potential for the subsequent generation of hexagonal arrays is also evident. From Calvin (1996).

then they are most likely to discharge the third, which then gives excitation back. Thus there arises a stable system of positive feedback within such triangular arrangements of connections (Figure 7.6) – three cells with mutual reinforcement form a stable circuit. The original triangle of active cells will then recruit others to extend into a hexagon, and then activity may continue to spread in similar fashion through the cortex. The stronger and more stable the originating pattern, the further the spread will be. Thus, looking at the brain overall, you get patches of active cells, each patch trying to spread throughout the cortex.

Then Calvin says that what you are conscious of is determined by the single 'dominant' pattern: the largest patch is the focus of consciousness. At any instant you can have several patches of different sizes in different regions of the cortex, and these are all competing with one another for space in the cortex. The more space that a patch occupies, the greater the chance that it will be the dominant pattern and thus be in control of behaviour.

Greenfield (1995) argues also that the magnitude and spread of neural ensembles depends on the nonspecific arousal systems. This is the most scientific part of her theory: her depiction of how the reticular formation and the various neurotransmitter systems based in the brainstem (see section 8.2.2.3) control the overall level of activity in the forebrain. When an organism is in a state of reasonable alertness, the nonspecific inputs are modulating the activity of cells in the forebrain in such a way as to facilitate the firing of those cells – firing that is initiated through their specific synaptic inputs. The nonspecific inputs are thus enhancing the speed with which each of these ensembles forms and spreads, its size and its persistence – and thus the spread and stability of each of the conscious thoughts in your head.[37]

It is well known that arousal needs to be at an intermediate level for optimal function (Yerkes and Dodson, 1908). Greenfield thus suggests that too much arousal will lead to one epicentre becoming too dominant, making thoughts inflexible. This happens, for

37. She does not give any details on how the arousal systems are controlled and what determines when arousal level is high or when low.

example, in obsessive-compulsive disorders and in depression. In contrast, too little arousal occurs (1) in Alzheimer's disease, where there are impoverished thinking processes, (2) in childhood, before you develop adult thinking skills, (3) in schizophrenia, where you get hopping from one thought to another very rapidly, with much distractibility and the inability to concentrate on particular thoughts for a long time, (4) in dreams, where you experience rapid illogical shifts of scene and scenario, (5) under hallucinogenic drugs, where percepts become shifting and unstable, and (6) possibly in animals, she suggests, where minds would be like this as well. Greenfield (2000, p. 182) has more recently differentiated some of these states on the basis that the strength of sensory inputs and the density of neuronal connections varies between them (for example, neural connections have not developed in childhood and have atrophied in Alzheimer's disease). She still likens schizophrenic states to those in stressful emergency situations like bungee jumping, however![38]

Note that the intensity of firing in an epicentre might contribute to the size of the ensemble that forms around it (with a given level of arousal input), but it is the size not the intensity of the ensemble firing that determines the degree of consciousness.

Critique

The mechanism here is essentially behaviourist in that the activity is said to spread through 'associative connections'. Obviously this gives rise to all the criticisms of theories that associations comprise activity running along axonal pathways between idea-bearing neurons or assemblies (section 6.4.1). This model has problems, first on anti-behaviourist grounds (section 3.5.2), and second on functionalist grounds (section 2.5.1.2): it is far too simple.

The brain is treated as a homogeneous medium (or at least, the 'association cortex', which has 'no clear function': Greenfield, 1995, p. 153). It is a Lashley-type theory (see Sidebox 6.3) that assumes that vast regions of the brain are equipotential, and the more brain activity involved in an ensemble the more conscious you are. This is just treating the brain as homogeneous porridge, as isotropic. This is not only inconsistent with empirical research (e.g. Felleman and Van Essen, 1991; Zeki, 1993; Banich, 2004), but it also leaves the question of how any particular ensemble represents any particular object such as an orange, as Greenfield (1995, p. 160) admits. She suggests it depends on the hard-wired connections normally activated by that object;[39] but then what about the new cells recruited as

---

38. In her later work Greenfield (2000, p. x) suggests 'it is the iteration between body and brain that *is* consciousness'. The body signals to the brain via hormones, and the brain releases peptides that affect the body. Each neural ensemble will release a cocktail of peptides giving a unique signature. (Curiously, peptide release from nerve cells is described as occurring only at high firing levels: Greenfield, 2000, p. 178. Hence there is a threshold for consciousness, in contradiction to her theory that there is none: pp. 167–168.) In place of her previous theory that ensemble size co-varies simply with the degree of consciousness per se, there is now a continuum of content as well. The small ensembles are the bases of emotions and raw feelings, and the large ensembles of deep meaningful rational thoughts.

39. Compare this theory with Hebb's (1949) view that it is associations that give meaning to a stimulus; even earlier, James (1890) had described the 'fringe' as the source of a thought's meaning. This idea has been rediscovered recently by Crick and Koch (2003), who ascribe the meaning of the neural correlate of consciousness to a 'penumbra' of associations, expectations and motor plans. The use of associations in this way is of course holistic. Meaning is given by links to other thoughts, but where do these thoughts get their meaning from? There develops an infinite regress of links to other

the ensemble grows larger? Are they intentionally 'uncommitted' cells whose meaning is flexible, or redundant parts of the orange-representing memory trace that are normally only activated when the sensory input is intense? In either case, conscious awareness of an orange would always be centred on one particular part of the brain (where the object's long-term memory is laid down) – a theory Greenfield has been strenuously trying to deny as it would imply a type of Cartesian theatre.

There is also another criticism: that the cortex does not normally work by spreading activity sideways within itself (Side-box 7.6). Recall that in section 6.2.4, experiments were described where cuts were made in the visual cortex and no effects were found on visual functioning. These supported the idea that if information needs to be transmitted from one point in the cortex to another, it is first sent down into the white matter and then up again via U-fibres, or down to some subcortical structure and up again. Calvin's ensembles are therefore not likely to spread very far, because the lateral spread of axons within the cortex does not carry activation sideways. Such lateral passage happens only in pathological states such as migraine (fortification illusions) and epilepsy (Jacksonian march), when there are waves of excitation (followed by depression) passing across the brain ('spreading depression'). Normally, the dominant spread of excitation is vertically within cortical columns, with lateral inhibition between columns (Colonnier, 1966; Hess et al., 1975; Szentágothai, 1978; Crook et al., 1998). Although recent work has emphasized that both excitation and inhibition pass in both directions (McGuire et al., 1991; Weliky et al., 1995; Tucker and Katz, 2003a,b; Tucker and Fitzpatrick, 2004), the point is that lateral excitation cannot be the only relevant component of one's model (Side-box 7.6).

Interestingly, Baars (2002) has recently collated evidence from a variety of experiments with the common finding that conscious events occur when wider areas of brain tissue are active (or more cells fire in certain areas[40]), as compared with the unconscious processing of (similar) information. The activated areas are not necessarily contiguous, as Greenfield's and Calvin's theories imply, however. Although Greenfield (1995, p. 120) does mention briefly that the parts of an ensemble might not be contiguous (citing work showing the existence of synchronized 40 Hz oscillations spread over wide distances; see section 6.4.2), this seems to be having it both ways. Are the ensembles spread by local connections within the cortex (in Greenfield, 2000, she cites Grinvald et al., 1988, 1994, in support) or by long-range loops between areas? She denies the latter (1995, pp. 126–133), implying this arrangement would constitute a Cartesian theatre (see Side-box 7.4).

So both Calvin's and Greenfield's theories are problematic. Both suggest the volume of active tissue determines consciousness. Hmm... intuitively reasonable, but one wants to know more – about mechanisms, for example, and about how consciousness is supposed to emerge from ensemble activity (e.g. Greenfield, 1995, p. 113). Also, do grand mal epileptic

---

thoughts – some of which will be required, no doubt, to derive their meaning from links back to the original thought you started with. Holism does not explain the origin of meaning, which must be grounded in a source of 'original' intentionality. Such sources might include sensory input or motor output, or events at lower or higher levels of description (chapter 5).

40. Although in many cases individual areas also appear larger, note that brain scanning techniques do not give accurate information about the size of an active area, since blood flow tapers off gradually at the edges of a focus of activity.

SIDE-BOX 7.6 THE PHYSIOLOGY OF HORIZONTAL ACTIVITY IN CORTEX

Does activity spread sideways in the cerebral cortex? Pavlov proposed an 'irradiation' of excitation away from the point of entry of stimulus activation in the brain (Side-box 8.4), and Greenfield (2000) theorizes that ensembles grow around their epicentres (section 7.3.3). She cites experiments by Grinvald et al. (1988, 1994) in support of the assumption that such patches of active tissue are anatomically continuous and grow sideways. Grinvald et al. applied optical dye to brain tissue to make active cells light up (literally). They found a measurable spread of activity (for similar conclusions, see Bringuier et al., 1999; Metherate and Cruikshank, 1999).

However, Grinvald's group are aware of the specific functional roles played by connections between cortical columns, and the existence of inhibition in controlling the spread of excitation and in cortical function itself (Grinvald et al., 1994; Seidemann et al., 2002; Derdikman et al., 2003; Jancke et al., 2004a). One cannot ignore the role of such lateral inhibition (Tremere et al., 2003) and it cannot be presumed that the cells which light up are exclusively excitatory: they very likely include inhibitory interneurons. Moreover, inhibition does not always reveal itself by changes in active firing, for example if spontaneous activity is low (e.g. Frégnac et al., 2003).

The lateral spread of activity actually subserves particular computational processes rather than the mere accumulation of representational or subjective weighting: it builds content rather than vehicle. Thus, although some horizontal connections do make excitatory contacts within the cortex, these are clustered and seem to be targeted at cells that have similar receptive field properties. The axons pass straight through columns of cells dealing with other properties (e.g. intermediate orientations, in visual cortex) and synapse only with functionally related cells (Gilbert and Wiesel, 1983; Weliky et al., 1995; Tucker and Fitzpatrick, 2004).

The psychophysical evidence for the effect of these connections is that they facilitate or modulate the activation of neighbouring cells rather than exciting them to the point where they fire; their effects are too weak and too slow. Functionally, they are specifically targeted and play particular roles in stimulus processing – for example, tracking an object moving through the retinal image (Georges et al., 2002; Jancke et al., 2004a,b) or tracing a long contour (Field et al., 1993; Hess et al., 2003; Roelfsema, 2005) – and they are affected by selective attention (Freeman et al., 2003, 2004). See also Li (2002) and Raizada and Grossberg (2003) for simulation studies, and Wilson et al. (2001) and Pessoa and De Weerd (2003) for additional examples of functional slow-spreading effects within particular domains of vision.

Reviewing the neurophysiology, Seriès et al. (2003, p. 461) comment: 'Surprisingly, most existing models [of area V1] ignore the functional diversity expressed at the single cell level, and are implicitly based on an hypothesis of cortical homogeneity of structure and function. They aim at providing a "canonical microcircuit" that could account for all aspects of [centre/surround] modulations. However, that such a universal circuit should exist is not obvious both at the experimental and at the theoretical levels. Indeed, recent results show that local circuits exhibit marked heterogeneities, depending for instance on their position in the [stimulus] orientation map or in the different cortical layers.'

Once again, what starts as a simple image (Greenfield's ripples on a pond, Calvin's reverberating hexagons) disappears as soon as we look into the details of how the brain actually works.

seizures or slow-wave sleep generate heightened states of consciousness? No, they generate unconsciousness. This is a problem for intensity/magnitude theories in general.

7.3.4 **Complexity**

In an attempt to break out of the impasse about how it is that one particular location or one particular neural state or property gives rise to consciousness,[41] Tononi and Edelman (1998; Edelman and Tononi, 2000) have formulated an approach couched more at the informational or functional level of description. Their postulated neural substrate is still localized (to the whole cortex and thalamus) and requires a specific type of processing ('re-entry') but the crucial factor is the 'complexity' of the information carried within the whole thalamo-cortical network in a globally distributed, self-sustaining 'dynamic core' of activity. To understand this theory, we need to look at the meanings of each of the technical terms they have coined.

First, 're-entry' was introduced by Edelman (1989, 1992) to describe the effects of the recurrent anatomical pathways from 'higher' centres to 'lower' within the cortical mantle. These early theories will be described further in section 9.3.2.3, but for now we just need to note that re-entry is not just feedback in the cybernetic sense (Edelman and Tononi, 2000, p. 48). Instead, it involves a more active process of synchronizing and coordinating the activities of different areas. It acts via multiple parallel pathways and integrates the information within the areas in such a way as to bind them into a categorical unit.[42] In their later papers, the term has come to be used more generally for the multi-way interactions occurring at any instant between a large set of functional units engaged in the processes supporting consciousness. In contrast, pathways lacking re-entry, such as those passing through the basal ganglia, support only unconscious processing.

Crucially, 'complexity' is a measure of the mutual information shared by the sub-modules within a system.[43] Edelman's background in evolutionary theory and immunology led him to see the development of the brain as involving the gradual separation of the mass of neurons into distinct functional groups competing with each other under the guidance of experience (hence the title of his book: *Neural Darwinism*, 1987). Now, the argument continues, imagine there are only two groups. The information that one group can have about the state of the other group depends upon how many different states each group can be in.

41. Tononi and Edelman accuse workers such as Crick, Koch, Zeki and Bartels of making a Ryle (1949) style 'category error' (section 2.3.2.1) in trying to explain consciousness in terms of neural anatomy or physiology.

42. The question of what 'categorization' means will be returned to in chapter 9. Note that the point is not that consciousness is associated with widespread activity in the brain (Baars, 2002); such activity could indeed be unrelated to consciousness, as Koch (2004, p. 102) points out. No, the crucial factor according to Tononi and Edelman is that such activity is synchronized.

43. Note that I am using the words 'sub-module' and 'system' to ease comparison with the analysis of modularity given in chapter 4. Tononi and Edelman actually use the term 'subset', treating the brain (for mathematical purposes) as composed of a single set of elements, all at one level of description. Whether those elements are single nerve cells or functionally integrated groups of cells is not always clear, but this gives their mathematical analysis a flexibility that might allow their technique to be applied at more than one level in a hierarchical system.

Let's put it crudely, assuming nerve cells are binary switches and can be in only one of two states – on and off – and the state of each group is a pattern of activity across all the cells in it (section 6.4.3).[44] If one group consists of only a single cell, there can be only one bit of 'mutual information' between the groups. With the brain divided into two groups of equal size there is maximal possibility for mutual information, since each can be in an equally large set of states. (This may seem trivial, but when there are many groups instead of just two the principle becomes important. Each group is considered in turn and its mutual information with the rest of the brain is calculated; the result is then averaged across all the groups to give a measure of the complexity of the whole brain.)

The complexity of the system also depends on the degree to which these groups are able to communicate their states to each other; in other words, to affect each other's state. If a change in one automatically produces a change in the other, there is redundancy of information between them.[45] If (at the other extreme) a change in one produces no effect on the other, there is no mutual information – in fact they do not even form a system. Complexity is thus maximal when there is partial interaction; that is, the subsystems can operate independently to a degree, but their activities are also (incompletely) integrated. An example of such a system is one with patchy connectivity, that is, each group has high connectivity with some of the other groups but not with all, and not with the same others in each case.

For such a system, the groups which are co-active change over time as activity flows around the whole system. This 'dynamic core' does not persist in the same set of connected locations for more than a few hundred milliseconds at most, and this set can be distributed anywhere within the entire thalamo-cortical system.[46] Other parts of this system that are inactive (or participating in non-conscious processing) at any one moment may be part of the neural substrate of the core at a later time. There is thus no 'location for consciousness' or particular 'magical' process necessary. In fact, the relevant active locations can vary from individual to individual, which is consistent with the differences found in localization studies (Tononi and Edelman, 1998).

Thus complexity depends on two factors, the relative sizes of the groups and the degree of interaction between them. There needs to be a multitude of groups, each capable of sustaining a number of different states, and their organization needs to be somewhere between randomness (complete independence) and perfect orderliness (homogeneity). The development of such a system depends upon its interactions with a complex environment, whose statistical structure[47] becomes built in to the system (as mutual information

---

44. The full argument depends on measures of entropy and degeneracy that we don't need to follow here; for more details, see Tononi et al. (1996, 1998, 1999).

45. They are also likely to enter a state of constant synchronous oscillations. A corollary is that in slow-wave sleep, anaesthesia or epilepsy, the complexity of the brain is reduced.

46. In Tononi and Edelman's 1998 paper, they seem to accept that some cortical areas may not take part in consciousness, or that 'higher' areas may play a relatively prominent role, but this is not emphasized in their book (Edelman and Tononi, 2000).

47. The 'statistical structure' of the environment reflects the fact that we do not live in a completely random world. Certain things (features, objects, elements) co-occur with others more or less systematically. The correlations are not always simple (of the type taught in first year statistics classes) but may involve higher-order 'chaotic' factors (such as correlations between an item and the co-occurrence of two other items, and so on).

between the brain and the rest of the world). The system is continually active internally as the subsystems 'talk' to one another, and it does not require incoming stimuli for its activation (cf. most of the other theories in this book!). Such stimuli merely modulate the intrinsic activity. Therefore most of the information flowing around the brain is 'memory' rather than representations of current 'perceived' environmental stimuli (this idea too is consistent with much work in cognitive psychology, as will be described in chapter 9). Hence what we are aware of is principally determined by what we already know: consciousness is memory (the 'remembered present', as Edelman, 1989, put it).

That consciousness is underlain by the 'dynamic core' of activity is supported by listing some of the properties of both and showing they match (Edelman and Tononi, 2000, pp. 145–152). These properties include integrity (unity), privateness, informational richness (complexity), global accessibility and distribution of information, global and flexible adaptability, serial and limited capacity of processing, and subjective continuity (James' 'stream of consciousness').[48]

Qualia are explained in terms of points in a multi-dimensional state space (cf. section 6.4.3.3). Tononi and Edelman eschew any simple equation of a quale with the firing of a particular group or type of nerve cell (e.g. 'red' cells), but assert that the whole dynamic core must be taken into account. In other words, the state-space has as many dimensions as there are nerve cells (or nerve cell groups?) in the core. Given that the core is mobile and dynamic, no particular cells are always involved in seeing red, for example. Indeed, there are no sensory atoms (qualia); instead, experiences are complex wholes. For example, we would not only see an object of a particular colour, texture, place, shape and motion with a particular visual context and background, but also be experiencing environmental sounds, bodily sensations, mood and so on. These all reflect the activity of a particular functionally connected dynamic core that is anatomically distributed in a large set of locations scattered throughout the brain. Moreover, the meaning of the experience derives from the discriminability of the particular experience from other experiences, each of which would lead to different consequences (with the degree of discriminability depending on the informational 'complexity' of the core).

Critique

The mathematical approach to the informational complexity and connectedness of the brain and its various sub-modules is interesting, and may provide a useful lead towards developing some long needed quantitative models of consciousness (or at least, of whole brain dynamics). Also, although Edelman and Tononi are opposed to Fodor-style symbolic representationalist approaches (who is interpreting the symbols?), their method might shed some light on the questions raised by Fodor (2000) about how connected the various modules actually are and to what degree and how they communicate (sections 4.3.4 and 4.3.7).

48. The tactic seems to follow Leibniz's law (if two things are identical their properties must be identical), following examples such as: the urea synthesized from inorganic compounds has identical properties to those of urea from organic sources, therefore they are identical and vitalism is false. Here, the properties of consciousness and of a brain process are proposed to be identical, therefore the problem of consciousness is solved . . . that is to say, dualism is false. Another example of the same implicit tactic is found in Taylor (1999, pp. 280–284).

The explanation of subjective experience is, however, somewhat vague and does not really provide any advance over the state space theory of Churchland, which was discussed in section 6.4.3.3. The problem that was highlighted there is how to attribute functional meaning to the dimensions of the state space. Whether there are only a few dimensions (such as red, green and blue, for colour experiences) or a much larger number (as in Edelman and Tononi's theory) does not matter in principle. The similarity and discriminability of two stimuli may well be related, as suggested, to their closeness in n-dimensional space, but this still does not explain why it is like what it is like. Why are particular points in the space associated with red versus pink versus middle C versus hungry, or blue versus feeling blue? There needs to be at least one anchor to stop the whole state space being rotatable (allowing the inverted spectrum: section 2.5.2.1), arbitrary or indeed indeterminate as to the subjective correlate of any point in it.

Putting the same point in neural terms, why does the particular set of cell groups active (and forming the dynamic core) at any one instant lead to the particular experience that it does (and not to another), if there is no link between a given cell group and some specific aspect of awareness? If an experience such as seeing a red balloon against a blue sky on a windy day is instead related purely to the functional interactions going on within the core, and in principle any part of the brain (or a computer, or the people of China: section 2.5.2.2) might be subserving that functional role, then Tononi and Edelman have many of the problems of computational functionalism described in section 2.5.2 to contend with.[49] Could the set of cell groups forming the core be 'rotated' among the various cell groups in the brain, so that at one instant some particular neuron's activity in occipital area V4 underlies a visual experience such as seeing the colour red, but at another time the same cell's firing can become part of the experience of smelling coffee or of wondering whether the starving millions will ever find justice? No, surely this flies in the face of the evidence. Tononi and Edelman have not avoided the problem faced up to by Crick, Koch, Zeki, Bartels and others, of how certain cells are related to particular subjective experiences.

Now, Edelman and Tononi (2000, p. 174) hint that there may be something special about inputs from the somatosensory systems, in that they are the first to arise during ontogeny and comprise the 'initially dominant axes' of the phenomenal state space. Like Panksepp (1998, 2005), Damasio (1999) and Taylor (2001), they develop a theory of the embodied self as a basic reference upon which layers of 'higher-order thought' may be added which enable us eventually to be 'conscious of being conscious' (Edelman and Tononi, 2000, pp. 104, 175). However, they do not explain the bodily sources as anchoring the overall adult state space, not even recognizing that this is necessary, let alone by what mechanism it happens. Nor do they relate their theory of higher-order thought with that of the dynamic core; the latter is a unitary and single state composed of many neuronal groups scattered throughout the brain, and there is no dichotomy into lower- and higher-order components

---

49. Tononi and Edelman deny that symbols and representations exist in the sense used within computational functionalism (section 2.5), and instead rely more on a dynamic neural network approach (section 6.4.3). However, the issue of phenomenality within state spaces still exists (section 6.4.3.3), as does the issue of how (by what mechanism) a pattern of activity across a neural network (i.e. a point in state space) gives rise to the particular experience (quale) that it does, or indeed to consciousness at all.

as there is in Edelman's earlier theory (1992; see section 11.2.3.2 for more on Edelman's theory of higher-order thought).

One may wonder by what mechanism complexity per se and the establishment of a dynamic core within a few hundred milliseconds should engender consciousness. Although it is obvious that human conscious states carry much information, the theory does not exclude the possibility that other complex information-carrying systems such as computers could be conscious too. That may be credible, but it is also not clear how much complexity is necessary for consciousness to exist in a system. At one extreme, a room containing a thermostat that switches the room heater on and off has only two states (heating on or off) and thus has minimal complexity. In addition, Tononi and Edelman describe brain complexity as being low in slow-wave sleep, anaesthesia, epilepsy and when carrying out automated (highly practised) tasks. But in those states Tononi and Edelman say there is *no* consciousness. The possibility that there is a continuum of degrees of consciousness, right down to a system with only one bit of mutual information such as a room with a thermostat (Chalmers, 1996, chapter 8) is not allowed. It seems then that there is a threshold level of complexity, but it is not stated what that threshold is and what determines it.

7.4 Conclusion

Searching for the difference between conscious and unconscious neural representations seems an intuitive approach. Theories based on the idea that only certain special brain locations give rise to consciousness do not seem satisfactory, because (1) the brain is dynamic and (2) the theories do not address the local circuitry and its dynamics within the crucial region. Also they assume a sharp dichotomy between conscious and unconscious processing that may be unwarranted. Needless to say, none of them has yet gone on to explain how or why that particular region as opposed to some other region generates consciousness. Of course these theories may only be a first step towards grounding consciousness in some special property of that one location, but so far no theory has taken that next step, and it is not obvious how they might do so. In addition, it seems problematic why percepts (vision, smell, etc.), emotions (fear, depression, etc.), actions (moving, planning) and so on seem so different; the theories tend to offer only a single solution for a supposed unitary mechanism of 'consciousness', whereas there may be a need for different mechanisms to account for each of these different types of experience.

Their philosophical position is also usually not made clear (identity, functionalism, man-in-the-head dualism?). There seems most often to be an implicit acceptance of behaviourism and/or eliminativism (see chapter 3). They all leave unsolved the hard problem of why qualia feel like they feel, and how the representational content relates to the outside world (i.e. they assume narrow content; section 2.4.3.1 and chapter 5).

Similar problems arise with state/property theories. However, these do have the merit of emphasizing the dynamic aspect of brain function. Nevertheless, there still remains the question of why dynamics per se should or could give us consciousness. For this, we need more particular models of specific functions (and since these may not all work the same way, we need to consider a range of putative mechanisms for each). There are numerous dynamic activities, both actual and possible, that could be linked to consciousness, and some theories have already been given here that attempt to do just that. Except for a few, however, most are very general and lack any sort of detailed attempt to describe how neural activities might actually explain consciousness at the psychological and philosophical levels (cf. chapter 10).

Some more specific theories of brain dynamics will therefore be examined in the next chapter.

■ **RECOMMENDED READING**

There are a number of brief surveys of models, of varying degrees of comprehensiveness, which are useful for getting a quick introduction to the field. I can recommend Scott **Stairway to the Mind** (1995, chapter 7), Palmer **Vision Science** (1999b, chapter 13), Sun (1999; **Duality of the Mind**, 2002, chapter 7), Taylor **The Race for Consciousness** (1999, chapter 5), Bachmann **Microgenetic Approach to the Consciousness Mind** (2000, pp. 211–231), Zeman (2001; **Consciousness**, 2002, chapter 8), Churchland **Brain-wise** (2002, chapter 4), Blackmore **Consciousness: An Introduction** (2003, chapters 5, 16–18), and Gray **Consciousness** (2004, chapters 11–13, 16).

Brain dynamics, attention and movement

OBJECTIVES

The main skill to be gained from this chapter is the ability to envisage brain function as the flow of activity around the cerebrum on a large scale. Although many dynamic processes take place locally within particular nuclei and areas, the majority of current theories of consciousness postulate that action potentials need to be transmitted over distances between nuclei and/or cortical areas. This is because consciousness often seems to involve (1) the integration of information from well-separated parts of the brain, and/or (2) the integration into a single system of the processing carried out by diverse functional sub-mechanisms which are, it is assumed, mediated by widely scattered loci. The implication is often that consciousness per se is generated by the fact that those long-distance connections exist, and indeed might even arise, in a sense, 'within' those connections. Given that self-sustaining dynamic processes require reciprocal interactions among the component parts of the system, we look initially at loops around which activity might circulate. Then, examples of large-scale dynamics are given, starting with the reactions to incoming stimuli: arousal and attention. A complementary analysis, of activity starting with the motor system, is also included. This chapter thus provides an introduction to the thesis that recurrence and/or cycling are crucial aspects of brain function, a theme that also crops up in the following two chapters.

8.1 Introduction

Cognitive processing is intrinsically dynamic, as was made explicit nearly half a century ago in a foundational model put forward by Miller et al. (1960; see Side-box 8.1).[1] At the neural level, we also know that activity is flowing around the brain all the time. We should therefore ask what role such dynamism plays in consciousness. Is there some crucial aspect of the flow of information and activity, or a crucial site or circuit of flow activity, that is responsible for consciousness? In the previous chapter we examined site theories and found them too simple. In this chapter we therefore first examine in more detail the various circuits that exist within the brain, and then give exemplars of some (increasingly complex) theories of consciousness based on activity within those circuits.

8.2 Dynamic brain systems

In this section we look at the anatomy and physiology of brain circuits. This is necessary to get a feel for the possibilities for a theory of dynamic consciousness. The diagrams of neuroanatomical loci and their connections given in introductory textbooks tend to give too static a picture of the brain. They also obscure the level of detail that exists within the often millions of axons running between two areas, each containing tens of millions of locally interacting neurons; all is typically reduced to two boxes connected by a line (a practice common in the reductive simplifications of neuronal behaviourism: see chapter 3). Since I cannot include moving pictures of such complex systems in this book, it is important to make the effort to try to envisage the myriad of events happening every second within the brain. One attempt to depict the sheer scale of the matter was given in section 3.5.5.1. In this section we start by looking within the cortex, before going on to study the loops and interactions between cortical areas and then between cortical and subcortical structures.

8.2.1 Local circuits

There are characteristically many feedback pathways within the cortex and, to a lesser extent, within some other brain nuclei. We can see many recurrent collaterals (axons that run back towards their origin) and various kinds of circuit that appear capable of sustaining,

---

1. Miller et al.'s (1960) model is useful because it introduces us to several important concepts that crop up elsewhere: cortico-cortical loops (between the frontal and the posterior – parietal/temporal/occipital – lobes; section 8.2.2.1), dynamic resonance (cycling and settling onto a final state; cf. autoassociative nets: section 6.4.3), the distinction between match and mismatch between input and expectation (section 9.3) and the existence of at least two types of representation/consciousness (perception and action/imagination; cf. chapter 11).

SIDE-BOX 8.1 ACTION–PERCEPTION DYNAMICS

In their classic book *Plans and Structure of Behavior*, Miller et al. (1960) first drew a distinction between what you want the world to be like and what you think the world actually is like now. Human life is a dynamic between these two sets of ideas. At any given moment, your knowledge about the current state of the world is the result of '*tests*' you have performed on the world to discover its state. These tests may be as simple as making sensory observations of your immediate environment. If the state of the world is not the way you want it to be, then you have to '*operate*' on the world – you must do something to change the world around you. This might involve carrying out actions that alter the environment, or you can move yourself into a different part of the environment. Acting involves downloading and executing plans from your stored repertoire of motor behaviour patterns. Finally, after action, you test the world again – that is, you look again to see whether it is now in the state you want it to be (Figure SB 8.1.1).

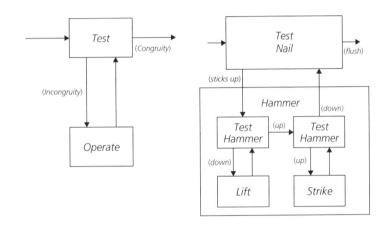

Figure SB 8.1.1 Miller et al.'s (1960) basic test–operate–test–exit circuit (left) and a hierarchical plan for hammering nails (right).

One example Miller et al. used was hammering a nail into a piece of wood. You first observe that the nail is not yet in the desired state (hammered fully home). So you hit the nail with a hammer. Then you look to see if the nail is still sticking out, and if it is, then you hit it again. This continues until one of your observations shows you that the head of the nail is now completely flush with the surface of the wood. At this point you stop hammering and go off to make a cup of tea. (Oh, and to make a cup of tea you have to see whether there is any water in the kettle, and if there isn't you have to fill the kettle until there is enough water . . . .) So the model can be seen as a general paradigm for all cognitively guided behaviour. (for more, see Shallice, 1972; Cooper and Shallice, 2000.)

Thus Miller et al. introduced the notion of repetitive test–operate–test–operate '*cycles*', in which there is a process of continuous looping between checking what state the world is in and then acting on it to change it in the desired way. If there is a mismatch between your percepts and your desires then you operate upon the world; but if there is a match and the situation is as you want it to be, then there is no need for further work, and your cognitive machinery can exit from its programme of action. Hence their model was given the acronym 'TOTE', which stands for 'test–operate–test–exit'.[a] It was designed

continues

SIDE-BOX 8.1 continued

to contrast with the serial processing models stemming from behaviourism that proposed a one-way, reflex-like flow of causation between stimulus and response.

A relevant part of their model is the distinction between '*images*' and '*plans*'. The 'image' is the internal representation of the way the world is, including the sensory awareness of the state of the immediate environment and our long term memories about the world. This function is linked with the posterior regions of cortex in general – the parietal, occipital and temporal lobes – as being the sites where the main sensory analyses take place. In contrast, the frontal lobes are responsible for holding the current 'plan', which is an action schema to implement the necessary changes, and the sequencing of relevant behaviours. First you must imagine the way you want the world to be – some possible future state of the world, that you like – and then you have to work out how to manipulate the world in order to get it into that state. This latter process is mediated by what we would now call 'executive' processes, that call up various subroutines or sub-modules to carry out the many detailed plots and plans (sections 4.2 and 7.2.2.3). The test–operate–test–exit cycle must thus involve the looping of information between posterior and frontal parts of the cortex, and the limbic system, especially the hippocampus (since it is here that Miller et al. suggested '*comparison*' takes place between the currently incoming information and the desired or expected states of the world).

This neural speculation about the localization of the elements of the TOTE model was, of course, based on the relatively simple evidence about brain function that was available at that time, and nowadays we have more complicated models. Nevertheless, it is a useful introduction to the examination of brain circuitry, and you will often see it embedded within those more elaborate theories that followed and were influenced by it.

[a] By the way, note that it emphasizes the active nature of the existence of humans (and other motile animals), so making a refreshing change from the passive sensory view of our existence that is the impression one gets from all the research on sensory systems that dominates much of this book.

at least within small regions, some kind of persisting activity (Figure 8.1; see also Figures 3.2 and 6.2). These local circuits may not just consist of simple reverberatory circles; we have seen more complex local circuits in autoassociative networks, for example (section 6.4.3.2). But these local circuits may be doing other things: whatever information processing the particular region of the brain is supposed to be doing – such as analysing the nature of the stimulus, in the sensory cortex, and controlling the gain-function and sensitivity of the information channels (see the inhibitory cell in the associative nets described in section 6.4.3, Figures 6.7 and 6.9). But possibly they are generating consciousness as well or instead. There are many local circuits in the microanatomy of brain tissue: it is very, very complicated (as demonstrated in section 3.5.5.1). So it is possible that consciousness depends on some kind of local circuit, even within a small region of the brain, in principle.[2]

2. Research on local circuits has been in relative abeyance recently (Sherman and Guillery, 2001; Rockland, 2004), perhaps because the dramatic results obtained from brain scanners have shifted emphasis to the activity levels of whole areas and regions. Thus almost all current theories of consciousness apply to interactions between areas – yet it is not clear a priori why circuits between areas should be different in kind from circuits within an area. If a particular kind of circuit is needed to generate consciousness, the wiring diagram could in principle be the same; it's just the lengths of the connections that would be different.

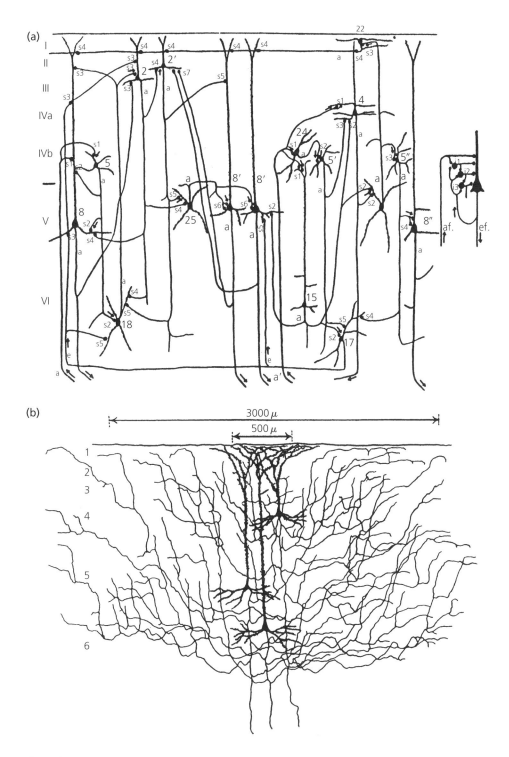

Figure 8.1 Recurrent axons in the cerebral cortex. **a.** From Lorente de Nó (1938). **b.** From Scheibel and Scheibel (1970).

Beyond simple reverberatory models, however, there is no specific theory as to how this happens.

8.2.2 Long-range loops

There are also many long-range (and often reciprocal) connections between different regions of the brain that, potentially, are available to subserve a dynamic mechanism that might be generating consciousness. We therefore need to go through some of these anatomical pathways.

8.2.2.1 Cortico-cortical

The cerebral hemispheres are full of connections running between regions of the brain: U-fibres running from one gyrus to the next, longitudinal fibre bundles running the length of the brain and commissures between the left and right sides of the brain (Figure 8.2). Any of these could be generating complete circuits, feedback loops or reverberatory pathways.

For example, Figure 8.3 (Felleman and Van Essen, 1991; Van Essen et al., 1992) summarizes anatomical evidence about connections between the cortical areas, giving a complete map of one hemisphere of the rhesus monkey cerebral cortex[3]. Each cortical area is shown as a box, and the lines show the connections between them. The diagram has the retina at the bottom, and above it the LGN, primary visual cortex V1, and the other visual areas V2, V3 and so on. The areas on the upper left lie in the parietal lobe and those on the

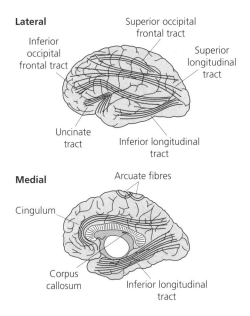

Figure 8.2 Long fibre bundles running through the white matter of the cerebral hemispheres. From Kolb and Whishaw (1980).

3. Similar analyses have also been made in some other species (Kaas, 2004; Van Essen, 2004). Indeed one could say that the attempt to map the complete mosaic in humans dominates current brain scanning studies – it is the neuroscience equivalent of the human genome project.

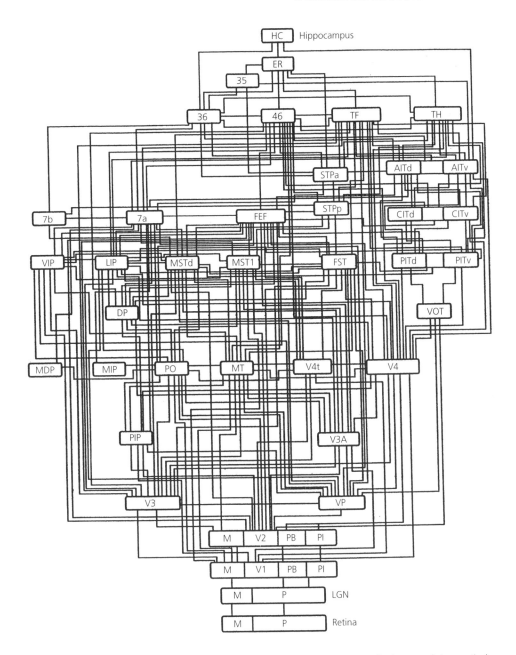

Figure 8.3 Complete wiring diagram of the visual areas of the macaque cortex. Each rectangle is a cortical area, and about two-thirds of the connections between them are reciprocal, that is to say, they include fibres running in both directions. The retina is at the bottom and the hippocampus at the top, with approximately eleven levels or stages of areas between them. The areas are labelled by their visual number (V1, etc.), Brodmann number (areas 7, 46, etc.) or location (for example, the parietal areas at mid left end in 'P' and the infero-temporal areas at upper mid right include 'IT'). The mid-temporal area MT (near the centre of the diagram) is also known as V5, the motion area. The retina, LGN, V1 and V2 are further subdivided into magno (M) and parvo (P) streams. Modified from Koch (2004) after Felleman and Van Essen (1991).

upper right in the temporal lobe. At the top is the hippocampus (HC), and just below are a couple of areas in the frontal lobes (the frontal eye fields, FEF, for example). The areas are arranged in 'levels' (i.e. stages, as defined in Side-box 4.4), based on details of the anatomy that the authors speculated indicated the degree of processing at each stage. There are about eleven levels of cortex in the monkey's visual system.[4]

All these areas are widely thought to correspond to functional black boxes performing different visual tasks, such as colour, motion and object perception (e.g. Zeki, 1993; see also sections 4.2.7 and 7.2.2, and Side-box 6.2). However, there is still some debate about how true this is (Side-box 8.2).

Now, students tend to freak out when they see Figure 8.3, presumably because they assume they are expected to memorize the entire thing. However, the points to be made from this diagram are much simpler. One is that, yes, the brain is indeed complicated, but it still deserves our love nevertheless (chapter 3)! We need to beware of overly simple theories. Other points from the diagram are that there are several dozen areas, and these form a mosaic that covers the entire cortex (Figure 8.4).

Note in addition that at least two thirds of the connections in Figure 8.3 are reciprocal, that is to say there are not only fibres running forwards but also other fibres running backwards, so influences pass in both directions between the different areas. The information flow is not just one way, as serial-processing models assume: from primary sensory cortex deeper and deeper into the system, until it eventually ends up at grandmother cells (section 6.2.6.1) that connect onto the hippocampus, which lays down into long-term memory the fact that they fired. Instead, there is a lot of feedback and bidirectional trafficking of messages (including many that pass sideways).

Also, within some of these areas at least, there is even finer anatomical substructure: columns, laminae and sub-areas (blobs, barrels, etc.). For example, in Figure 8.3 you can see that V1 and V2 are divided up into M (magno-cellular) and P (parvo-cellular) sub-units that indicate that different functional groups of nerve cells pass through those areas. One theory is that the M system is carrying information about movement and the P system is carrying information about colour (Livingstone and Hubel, 1987; but cf. Gegenfurtner and Kiper, 2003).

This obviously gives us enormous scope for tracing different circuits. The cortex is very complicated, there are vast numbers of connections, and so there is no shortage of scope for theories about how information might flow between them.

As for consciousness, Mesulam (1998), Zeki (1993, 2001) and others suggest it is the close integration between activity in some of these areas and levels that gives rise to consciousness, particularly those that receive input from several modalities. (Dehaene et al., 1998, 2003, interpret Mesulam's as a form of global workspace theory; see section 7.2.3.4.) This enables binding of the different modalities into a unified self (Side-box 4.5; but see section 11.3.4 for alternative views that such binding does not necessarily have to happen).

---

4. We should note that there have been some disputes about the above picture. For example, Mesulam (1998) uses only six levels in his model instead of eleven (Side-box 7.5), while Young (1992) has analysed the anatomical data statistically and argued that they are very indeterminate: thus many models, with anything from thirteen to twenty-four levels, would all provide equally optimal fits to the data (Hilgetag et al., 1996).

SIDE-BOX 8.2. IS THERE REALLY FUNCTIONAL LOCALIZATION IN THE VISUAL CORTEX?

The cortex is commonly thought to consist of a mosaic of functional areas that map at least partially onto the anatomical areas discovered a century ago (section 4.2.7; see Shallice, 1988, and Zeki, 1993, for historical reviews, Henson, 2005, for discussion, and Uttal, 2001, for a contrary view). For example, for the visual system, Zeki has V4 as the colour area, V5 as analysing motion and so on.

This theory has a lot of evidence for it, based not just on physiological research on monkeys but also on human brain scanning and lesion studies. The latter show that there are areas in the posterior temporal, posterior parietal and occipital lobes where lesions can cause specific deficits, for example in colour vision, face processing or movement perception (e.g. Zeki, 1993). Also, there are particular areas that light up in brain scans in normal people when you show them colour, movement or faces as stimuli to be processed. So there is much converging evidence for functional parcellation of the human cerebral cortex.

However, Lennie (1998), Gegenfurtner and Kiper (2003) and others (as mentioned in section 4.3.6) have disputed that the anatomically defined areas are specialized for different functions. For example, physiological recordings in monkeys show colour is analysed across many areas, and area V4 does not deal only with colour information. Although Zeki (1978) originally said V4 merely emphasizes colour, not that it deals exclusively with colour, the theory usually does get presented nowadays simply as 'V4 is the colour area', and so on for the other area–function links (e.g. Zeki, 1993). Lennie, Gegenfurtner and Kiper reach the opposite conclusion and suggest that most visual areas are performing similar processing, and there is less functional difference between them than Zeki likes to make out. For example, Lennie concludes V4 mediates the recognition of shape from any cue: the edges of shapes can be defined by a difference in colour, luminance, texture, motion, and so on, and it does not matter for function purposes which cue is used, just that the shape is recognized correctly. (An exceptional case is V5/MT, which may lie on a separate parallel pathway responsible for dealing with the optic flow induced by self-motion.[a]) Figure SB 8.2.1 summarizes Lennie's picture, which takes account of the numbers of fibres that run along each pathway.

As for human brain scanning, the issue of specificity has been challenged, for example by Haxby et al. (2001); see Side-box 6.2. Most studies show a network of areas lighting up on any given task. (Of course, this may be because, in the absence of correct knowledge about what the particular function of a given area is, we cannot yet design a task that uses that function and only that function.) Many studies have concluded that activity must be integrated between areas, at least for the generation of consciousness. Thus Zeki (1993) supported the binding of activity at 40 Hz between areas or (Zeki, 2001) along processing streams (section 7.3.1). Also adding to their theory (section 7.2.2.3), Goodale and Milner (2004; Goodale and Westwood, 2004) note that there must be lateral interchange between the dorsal and ventral streams. We are conscious of where things are as well as what they are, and our knowledge of object shape and function guides how we grasp an object with our hand.

So, the theory that functions map onto particular cortical locations, and that cortical areas perform particular functions, has been a guiding light for many years, but is still the subject of much dispute. It is possible to state with some certainty that a small number of gross modules exist, such as the visual, auditory and somatosensorimotor, along with the anatomical fronto-limbic (as yet functionally vague), or conversely, the functional associative (polymodal cortex? global workspace?), as even Uttal (2001) has to admit; see also Mesulam (1998) and Dehaene et al. (2003). To this extent Fodor's (2000) emphasis on the paucity of modules, particularly for 'higher' cognitive functions, is supported (section 4.3). The debate centres on to what extent we can carry the same principle down into smaller and smaller parts of the hierarchy.

continues

SIDE-BOX 8.2 continued

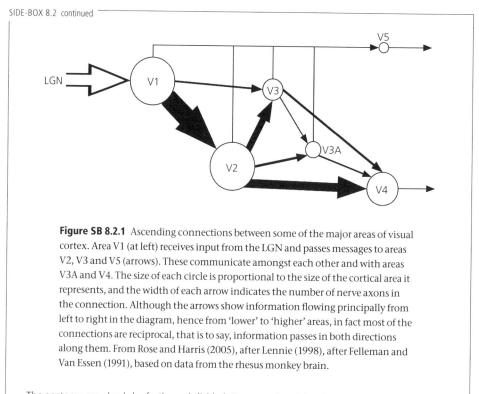

Figure SB 8.2.1 Ascending connections between some of the major areas of visual cortex. Area V1 (at left) receives input from the LGN and passes messages to areas V2, V3 and V5 (arrows). These communicate amongst each other and with areas V3A and V4. The size of each circle is proportional to the size of the cortical area it represents, and the width of each arrow indicates the number of nerve axons in the connection. Although the arrows show information flowing principally from left to right in the diagram, hence from 'lower' to 'higher' areas, in fact most of the connections are reciprocal, that is to say, information passes in both directions along them. From Rose and Harris (2005), after Lennie (1998), after Felleman and Van Essen (1991), based on data from the rhesus monkey brain.

The anatomy can clearly be further subdivided. For example, within the visual system, Hilgetag et al. (2000) and Sporns et al. (2000) used mathematical techniques to show that cortical areas form clusters such as the dorsal and ventral streams. Within each cluster there are further well-known subdivisions (into cytoarchitectonic areas, cytochrome oxidase blobs, columns and mini-columns, for instance). The functional hierarchy may also be subdivisible hierarchically (section 4.2). But the mapping between anatomy and function is proving more difficult to establish at these various levels. This may be because it is difficult to know at what level of the anatomical hierarchy a given function is carried out (Bechtel and Richardson, 1993) and at what level of the functional hierarchy we should search for the function of any given anatomical structure. Denials of the functional specificity of a particular cortical area or cell type, for example, may occur because the researchers are trying to map (impose a reductive identity) between inappropriately different levels in the two hierarchies.

[a] The V1 to V5 pathway is notable for having an unusually large axon diameter (Rockland, 2002) supporting its having a special role. But note that in humans the 'motion area' is very lateral (Orban and Vanduffel, 2004) and well below the 'dorsal stream' (normally attributed a role in visuo-motor functions: Milner and Goodale, 1995) that runs very superior in the occipital and parietal lobes.

8.2.2.2 **Thalamo-cortical**

Another major set of connections runs between the thalamus and the cortex (Figure 8.5). These circuits have been implicated recently in generating the basic states or modes of consciousness itself, particularly sleep and waking. We therefore need to look at them in some detail here.

Almost all areas of cortex are connected reciprocally with the thalamus, both with specific sub-nuclei within the thalamus (e.g. the LGN for primary visual cortex), and with

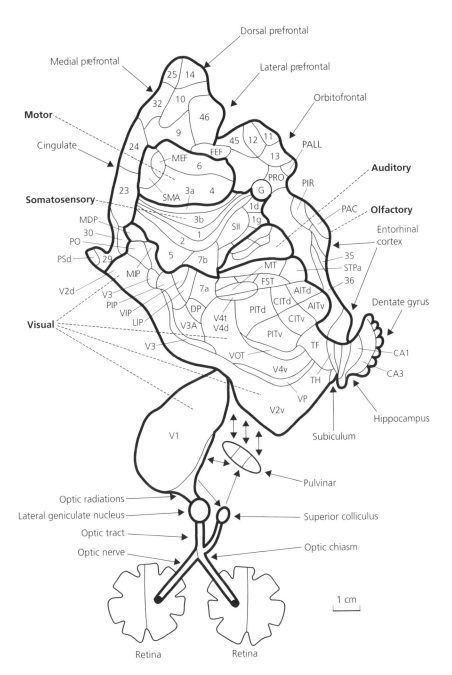

Figure 8.4a Functional cortical areas: Macaque monkey, showing flattened surface of complete cortex and retinae (from Cotterill, 1998, after Felleman and Van Essen, 1991).

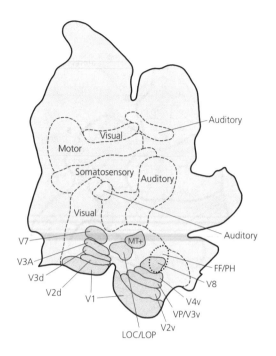

Figure 8.4b Human, showing flattened surface of cortex in one hemisphere, and some of the visual areas identified so far (bold outlines) and modality-specific regions (dashed outlines). The face and place areas (FF/PH) are indicated by the dotted line. Data from Van Essen (2004, Figures 32.4 and 32.5).

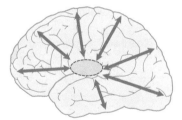

Figure 8.5 Thalamo-cortical connections are ubiquitous (except for the temporal pole).

what have been called 'nonspecific' thalamic nuclei (especially the *intralaminar* nuclei). Some further details of this connectivity are included in Side-Box 7.2 and Figure 8.6.

Recent theories have argued that reciprocal cycling interactions occur between the thalamus and cortex (e.g. Llinás et al., 1998; Steriade, 2000; Llinás and Ribary, 2001). These may form the basis for the rhythmical potentials recorded with electrodes on the scalp (Berger, 1929). Remember that in electroencephalograph (EEG) recordings we see low frequency (0.5–8 Hz) oscillations during sleep and in certain pathologies such as petit mal epilepsy (absence seizures). These oscillations become faster with general arousal, being in the alpha band (8–13 Hz) in states of relaxed alertness, and the beta band (13–30 Hz) when actively processing information. More recently, the gamma band (30–80 Hz) has been associated with states of consciousness (section 6.4.2). Previous theories attributed such '40 Hz'

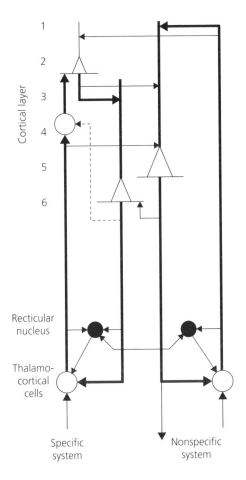

Figure 8.6 Simplified circuit of thalamo-cortical loops. The two main circuits are indicated by thick black lines. Inhibitory cells are shown filled in black, pyramidal cells as triangles and multipolar cells as circles. Note there is cross-talk between the two thalamo-cortical loops (thin lines) and additional loops within the cortex (e.g. dashed); there are also several inhibitory feedback and feed-forward loops within the cortex (not shown). After Llinás and Ribary (1993, 2001) and Jones (2002), with additional data from Douglas et al. (2004) and Rodriguez et al. (2004).

oscillations to interactions within the cortex itself (e.g. Engel et al., 1991; Zeki, 1993), but suggestions that they are generated thalamo-cortically (Crick and Koch, 1990; Crick, 1994) have been supported by recent evidence.

Critique

Interestingly, 40 Hz oscillations can also occur in bursts during rapid eye movement ('dreaming')[5] sleep as well as in wakefulness, and are coherent across the thalamus and cortex. Llinás and Ribary (1993) describe the oscillation as 'scanning' the brain from rostral to caudal.[6] Under waking conditions, incoming stimuli reset the scan/oscillation, but in

5. Note that dreams do not actually occur only in rapid eye movement sleep (e.g. Hobson, 2002). This fact poses a problem for the 40 Hz theories of consciousness. Vanderwolf (2000) and Destexhe and Sejnowski (2001), however, describe brief periods of fast oscillations that can be detected even during slow-wave sleep.

6. The theory that brain rhythms reflect a scanning mechanism actually goes back to Pitts and McCulloch (1947); see also Lindsley (1955) and Shevelev et al. (1991).

dreaming sleep the rhythms free-run, presumably driven by intrinsic activity or noise within the brain.

In contradiction, however, Llinás et al. (1998) and Steriade (2000) also hold that the 40 Hz oscillations can occur at isolated anatomical foci, that is, for loops between particular thalamic nuclei and their corresponding columns in the cortex. This is presumed to happen when we are aware of certain stimuli but not others, and is the neural basis of selective attention (see section 8.3 below; some empirical evidence in support is given by MacDonald et al., 1998).[7]

Another problem with this group of theories is that the same circuits and mechanisms are postulated, often in different papers, to underlie all the different types and frequencies of oscillation seen in the thalamo-cortical system. Thus Llinás and Ribary (2001) describe the whole system entirely in terms of 40 Hz oscillations, and Lytton and Thomas (1999) and Destexhe and Sejnowski (2001) in terms of low frequencies, while Steriade (2000) claims both can be explained. Sherman and Guillery (2001, 2002) avoid any talk of 40 Hz oscillations and emphasize that in the waking condition, thalamo-cortical cell firing becomes 'tonic' rather than oscillatory, and information transfer becomes linear (an important requirement for the correct functionality of sensory, if not all, neural processing).

Also the various hypotheses as to *the* origin of any particular rhythm have proved difficult to sustain. For example, Llinás and Ribary (2001) claim the 40 Hz properties are 'intrinsic' to several types of cell in the circuit, yet also to the whole thalamo-cortical loop. But the changes between fast (40 Hz) and slow (0–15 Hz) burst forms in individual cells as waking turns to sleep cannot be reflected in changed thalamo-cortical anatomy and transmission delays. That the system is capable of firing in complete synchrony is an emergent property, and we have to presume that the effects of the conduction latencies along the axons are obviated by the emergent property. Thus it makes much more sense to admit that an intact functional system cannot be dissected to find single 'causes', since emergent properties are generated by the interactions within the system (section 2.2.2.1; Lytton and Thomas, 1999, p. 504) and the mechanisms need to be described at many levels simultaneously (section 4.2; Lytton and Thomas, 1999, pp. 499–500).

In sum, the attempt to explain such a wide range of phenomena (from sleep to selective attention) as reflecting variations in the functioning of just a single anatomical circuit, albeit a complex one, is perhaps too ambitious. On the positive side, these theories are rare (though not unique) among those covered in this book in that they do at least consider the entire range of sleep, dreaming and waking states.

8.2.2.3 Nonspecific systems

There are various 'nonspecific' systems that originate in the brainstem and the thalamus and send axons widely throughout large regions of the brain (see section 7.2.1.2). For example,

---

7. The theory is that, for full consciousness/cognition to occur, both the specific and nonspecific thalamic inputs to cortex must be resonating in synchrony. Under those conditions, the apical dendrites of cortical pyramidal cells are receiving coincident inputs from both types of thalamic nucleus (Llinás et al., 1998; Jones, 2002); see Figure 8.6 for a circuit diagram. This also revisits older theories that specific and nonspecific inputs must coincide: see sections 8.2.2.3 and 8.3.1.

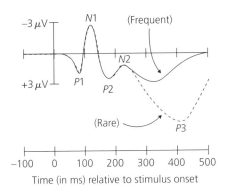

Figure 8.7 Evoked potentials recorded from the human scalp following frequent versus rare stimuli (idealized data). From Vogel et al. (1998).

electrical stimulation of the brainstem reticular formation increases the frequency of the EEG waves and increases the arousal level (Moruzzi and Magoun, 1949); hence the *'ascending reticular activating system'* or ARAS.[8] The cortex may be affected by axons running there directly from the brainstem, or affected indirectly via alterations in the thalamus and thalamo-cortical oscillations, as described in the previous section. Further illumination comes from the study of the potentials evoked by particular external events, rather than steady-state oscillation frequencies in the EEG. Following presentation of a stimulus there is a sequence of perturbations in the electrical potential (Figure 8.7), including a 'P300' wave (Side-box 8.3), and for unexpected intense events (such as someone banging a paper bag behind your head) there may be a 'startle' response (Side-box 8.4). These processes were postulated to be vital signs of the mechanisms by which we become consciously aware of the stimulus.

Now, since its initial formulation, the notion of the ascending reticular activating system has been elaborated in a number of ways.

One is that in the brainstem there are in fact several separate mechanisms with such ascending axons. These are characterized by the release of different neurotransmitters, such as noradrenaline, serotonin (5-HT), dopamine and acetylcholine. As an example, Figure 8.8 shows the cholinergic pathways in some detail. These various neurotransmitters are each to a greater or lesser extent released in the forebrain in a nonspecific fashion by cells that have their cell bodies down in the lower parts of the brain. At least some of the general phenomena previously associated with reticular stimulation or lesions are probably due to altering the various particular effects of these neurotransmitter systems. These systems play important roles in learning, pleasure, mood, dreaming and so on. We cannot pursue these ideas here, but there are several good psychopharmacology texts introducing the subject, such as McKim (2003) and Julien (2004). For more details of their roles in attention and consciousness, see Marrocco and Davidson (1998), Mentis et al. (2001) and Perry et al. (2002).

Second, the arousal system has been divided into the brainstem and thalamic portions. There are parts of the thalamus (see section 7.2.3, and Side-box 7.2) that were originally

---

8. Conversely, lesions to the reticular formation may lead to permanent coma, and lesions to the thalamus to persistent vegetative state (e.g. sections 7.2.1.2 and 7.2.1.3).

SIDE-BOX 8.3 CONSCIOUSNESS AND AROUSAL

One idea that arose during the 1950s and 1960s was that the early parts of the 'evoked' potentials (Figure 8.7), of the order of 100–200 milliseconds following the stimulus, reflect the information processing activity of the sensory systems following transduction, the transmission of information up the afferent nerves, through the thalamus and up to the sensory cortex. But what is interesting is that, under some circumstances, there is a large positive wave roughly 300 milliseconds after the stimulus (commonly known as the P300 or P3 wave[a]). This wave has quite a long latency relatively to the primary sensory processing and some of its characteristics suggest that it is an indicator of activity coming up through the arousal systems. One of these observations is that if you present a stimulus repetitively and predictably at regular intervals, say a flash of light or a click once a second, then the initial 100–200 millisecond waves remain of constant size but the amplitude of the P300 wave fades – it reduces with exposure to a repetitive stimulus, i.e. it *habituates*. So what happens as you receive a repetitive stimulus like the ticking of a clock is that it appears to fade into the background; in other words, your awareness of it declines, as your attention to it wanes. At the same time, the P300 wave becomes smaller. If, however, you present the stimuli irregularly, instead of at exactly predictable intervals, then you do not get this attenuation: instead the P300 wave stays the same amplitude and the subject continues to notice the stimulus.[b]

So the theory was developed that, when the stimulus comes in, it is processed in the sensory cortex, and then the P300 comes up as the reticular formation kicks in slightly later, and gives some kind of

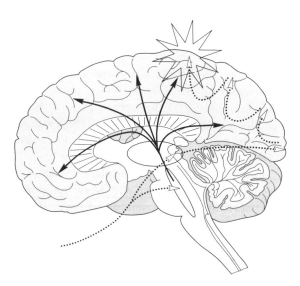

Figure SB 8.3.1 Theory of reticulo-cortical interaction. Specific inputs (dotted arrows) are processed in stages across the cortex, but also activate the reticular arousal system (black arrows), which affects the cortex after a delay. When and where these afferent influences coincide, consciousness arises (star).

continues

SIDE-BOX 8.3 continued

boost to the information processing in the cortex (Figure SB 8.3.1; see Jasper, 1966, Goff, 1969, and Boddy, 1978, for reviews). (The delay is due in part to the slow conduction velocity of the fibres, and in part to the indirectness of the route through the brainstem.[c]) The reticular input to the cortex may just be modulating the cortex so the cortex is better able to process this information, rather than simply adding linearly to the level of activation. But as information is processed in and across the various regions of cortex in turn, there has to be persisting activity, in each area, because otherwise when the reticular arousal comes up, after a delay, the cortical activity would just have faded away and the reticular input would have nothing to affect. So there must be some kind of short-term memory trace left behind as activity moves outward across[d] the cortex from the primary sensory area. Moreover, you need *both* the presence of the information passing through the cortex *and* the reticular arousal in order to become consciously aware of the stimulus. If you don't have arousal then some information processing still goes ahead, as revealed by the early waves in the evoked potential, but you don't become aware of the outside event that triggered that activity. You may be processing information unconsciously or just not attending (see also section 8.3; also section 9.2 for the effects of reticular arousal on learning).[e]

a. The P3 strictly refers to the third positive wave; its peak latency may be from 300 to 600 milliseconds.
b. The P300 wave also attenuates in conditions of drowsiness, sleep or coma. It drops out in schizophrenia as well, a condition that is characterized by attentional problems.
c. An earlier argument to this effect came from Piéron and Segal (1939), who could only reason that the slower inputs must come via polysynaptic pathways – the reticular inputs to cortex not having been discovered at that time.
d. This movement is not laterally through the cortex but via U-fibres passing down into the white matter and then up again (see section 7.3.3).
e. What if you only have the arousal? This can actually happen if an expected stimulus does not occur: there is a P300 without the earlier evoked waves (e.g. Sutton et al., 1967; Weinberg et al., 1970). You notice something has changed, but what? The clock has stopped ticking! Yet at first there is just a void in your awareness of what exactly has changed, and you need to search memory before you can analyse what has happened. Indeed, these workers interpreted the phenomenon as indicative of memory read-out (so too John et al., 1973). But secondary effects on reticular arousal cannot be excluded, as descending influences from the cortex also affect the reticular formation's activity. More modern theories also take the P300 as signifying more cognitive processes than just a stimulus-driven, behaviourist-style mechanism of 'arousal' (Dien et al., 2004). Of interest too is the observation that P300 waves can be evoked by stimuli so weak that they are only processed subconsciously (Bernat et al., 2001).

SIDE-BOX 8.4 STARTLING

The startle response or orienting reflex (or any combination of these words) has long been known as the reaction to any novel, intense, unexpected stimulus. A typical example of such a stimulus is banging a paper bag behind someone's head, but the range of contexts in which such stimuli occur can be broader. For example, even an unexpectedly weak or absent stimulus can make the hairs on the back of your neck stand up. The earliest studies also did not just involve simple stimuli such as a loud bang. For example, a nervous animal will react strongly to the approach of any unknown human, even one bringing the animal's dinner. After several such events the animal gets used to the situation and learns that the arrival of the human means 'food coming'. Then the animal greets the human and salivates rather than trying to escape (Pavlov, 1927, 1955).

Pavlov theorized that such novel stimuli cause a general 'irradiation' of excitation throughout the animal's cortex, centred on the (in this case) visual 'analyser' (i.e. the visual cortical areas). With learning, the irradiating waves come to be inhibited throughout all areas except those leading to the appropriate motor response (in this case, salivation). A beam of excitatory waves thus becomes focused from

continues

SIDE-BOX 8.4 continued

the sensory to the motor areas, forming the basis of the 'conditioned reflex' (see Pavlov, 1955; cf. Greenfield's theory of ripples spreading from an 'epicentre': section 7.3.3).

Later, Berlyne (1960), Sokolov (1963) and others developed the idea of orienting (turning towards a novel stimulus to point all your receptors at it) and alerting (allocating all your processing resources to analysing the stimulus and formulating an appropriate response) as leading to the construction of a '*representation*' of the stimulus and its context. With learning, the representation becomes installed in long-term memory and can be used as a template for fast, effortless identification of the stimulus whenever it appears again. The initial generalized startle habituates as the coping response becomes automatized.

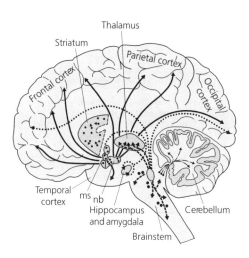

Figure 8.8 Modern map of cholinergic pathways. From Perry et al. (1999).

considered to be a kind of front-end outpost of the reticular formation, because they seem to have a moderately nonspecific projection pattern in their axonal branching pattern and targets, their axons conduct slowly and they play a role in general arousal (Morison and Dempsey, 1942; Moruzzi and Magoun, 1949; Jasper, 1949, 1954). Later (Jasper, 1960), these structures became associated with 'phasic' arousal (such as occurs when someone bangs a paper bag behind your head), in contrast to the 'tonic' arousal controlled by the brainstem (principally concerning the sleeping and waking states, including sustained vigilance and alertness level). As described elsewhere in this chapter and in section 7.2.3, modern researchers have continued to develop theories of the functional roles of the reticular and intralaminar nuclei of the thalamus. Some attribute sleep as well as phasic arousal mechanisms to the thalamus (see previous section), and almost all postulate that these nuclei contain at least some of the mechanisms of selective attention (but since this is such an important topic it requires a separate section on its own: see section 8.3 below).

A third way in which the situation has become more complex since the original studies is in showing that the P300 waves are conglomerates of several components, at least some of which have multiple, cortically localized origins (e.g. Squires et al., 1975; Johnson, 1986, 1993; Dien et al., 2004).

A fourth qualification of the original theory is that the early waves in the evoked potential (Figure 8.7) can be affected by attention, particularly to space. Stimuli in unattended locations evoke smaller early potentials than stimuli in attended or expected positions (reviewed by Luck and Girelli, 1998). For more on the evidence that attention can affect the early stages of processing, see section 8.3.

8.2.3 Interim conclusion

There seems little doubt that the brain is dynamic at many levels, and should be analysed as such.[9] The processing theories discussed in chapter 7 should merge naturally into the dynamic theories introduced in this section. However, processing theories normally demand that a particular type of processing be specified, and the term 'dynamic' is too all-encompassing to suffice (though some workers clearly seem to think it is enough). It is a truism to say the brain is dynamic, and so this solves little by itself, except to warn us against simple static theories. What we need are more specific theories and models that relate to particular phenomena and make use of some of the ideas about how the brain can be dynamic that were introduced in this section. Therefore we turn now to attention and, in the next two chapters, to memory and then back to perception.

8.3 Selective attention

A common idea is that attention and consciousness can be equated, in that to be conscious of something is to be paying attention to it, and the contents of our focus of attention are the things we are conscious of (e.g. Jung, 1954; Baars, 1988; Crick and Koch, 1990; He et al., 1996; Cavanagh, 1998).[10] If these are identical, does this mean one can be reduced to the other, and if so, which to which (in the sense of section 2.4)? Psychological theories of attention are well developed, and it might therefore be fruitful to attempt to subsume consciousness research within this well-established body of theory and data. Physiological research into the brain mechanisms of attention is also well under way, and might then be regarded as research on the neural bases of consciousness. The contrast between the

9. Consciousness itself can also be described as essentially dynamic (e.g. the 'stream of consciousness'), although, as we shall see in section 10.3.1, moments of stasis can also be argued for on empirical and phenomenological grounds.

10. Note, however, that equating attention with consciousness may be an oversimplification. Many workers have dichotomized perceptual mechanisms into a central focus of awareness and a surrounding background or fringe: for example, Trevarthen (1968) made a distinction between focal and ambient awareness, and Crick and Koch (1990, 1998a), following Neisser (1967), referred to an iconic 'fleeting awareness'. However, James' (1890) famous use of the term 'fringe' referred more to the transitional aspects of consciousness across time (the nascent processes by which thoughts tend to move towards a conclusion), rather than the spatial surround to the centre of attention. The contents of each are qualitatively different, so the background is not just a diffuse or weaker form of consciousness. For some empirical evidence, see Rock et al. (1992), Braun and Julesz (1998), Hardcastle (2003) and Lamme (2003).

processing of attended and unattended stimuli would then be the same as the contrast between conscious and unconscious processing. We have already met the idea that certain brain mechanisms, such as the reticular nucleus of the thalamus (Side-box 7.2), can control attention to particular types of stimuli (such as visual versus auditory). Here, we examine in more detail some further theories; a refresher on the psychology of attention is given in Side-box 8.5.

SIDE-BOX 8.5 SELECTIVE ATTENTION: PSYCHOLOGICAL RESEARCH

The beginnings of modern research on selective attention are normally attributed to Cherry (1953). It is an everyday observation that you can attend selectively: in other words, you can solve the 'cocktail party problem'. When you are in a crowded room with a lot of people yakking away, you can somehow concentrate on following a conversation between two people on the other side of the room, and you may then be totally oblivious to the contents of the other conversations going on, which reduce phenomenologically to a background buzz. Empirical research throughout the 1950s and 1960s confirmed and quantified this phenomenon in laboratory conditions, and led to the conclusion that only some of the sensory information received is processed by the brain, and a lot of the information is ignored or suppressed. There can be 'selective' analysis of information and the rest of the stimulation that you receive is not processed.

A recent revival of this idea has come from the study of 'change blindness'. We are sometimes surprisingly oblivious to a large change in our environment. One example involves comparing two pictures. There can be quite a clear difference between the two pictures but it is surprisingly difficult to notice what that difference is. (You can either have the pictures side by side and look backwards and forwards between them or you can present them in alternation on a screen. In the latter case, the phenomenon only works if there is a temporal gap between the pictures, analogous to what happens to the retinal image when you blink your eyes, or if there is a distracting flash somewhere else in the display at the same time as the change you are supposed to detect.) The change can involve people appearing or disappearing, or buildings or objects moving up and down in the background or even in the foreground (e.g. Figure SB 8.5.1). Striking empirical studies show that what are clearly detectable changes in the sensory stimulus – they are not below threshold or subtle at all – can go unnoticed. Until you notice these major changes, or they are pointed out to you, you are not conscious of them. This suggests that what we are conscious of is only a very small fraction of the sensory input that we receive. It is another demonstration that we don't process everything. (For further demonstrations, see Mack and Rock, 1998.)

Another argument comes from the fact that the entire visual scene in front of us appears phenomenologically to be detailed and in colour, despite the fact that our visual systems do not provide us physiologically with detailed colour vision beyond the central part of our visual field (Dennett, 1991). Our peripheral vision seems to be 'filled in', possibly by using stored knowledge, perhaps gained on previous foveations of the other parts of the scene, or by extrapolation from what is in the centre of our retinae (the explanation is a matter of intense debate; see Noë, 2002). Some workers go so far as to suggest that we do not store knowledge of the visual scene at all. Information about the outside world is always present in the external world, and so we do not need to internalize it. When needed, we can gain more knowledge by acting on the world, for example by moving our eyes to foveate putatively relevant places. We use the world as an 'outside memory' (O'Regan, 1992). We pay attention by acting on the world, and thus our consciousness is intimately tied up with motor behaviour (O'Regan and Noë, 2001).[a]

_____ continues

SIDE-BOX 8.5 continued

Figure SB 8.5.1 Change blindness. The difference between these two pictures is not easily noticed, even if they are shown in alternation on the same spot, provided a grey gap separates the two. From Rensink's web site: <http://www.psych.ubc.ca/~rensink/flicker/download/index.html>

However, this does not mean that we possess only instantaneous information about events happening immediately in the outside world. Other research demonstrates that stimuli are often processed without our becoming aware of them. This processing can be to varying depths, and of course it takes time. Throughout the 1960s and 1970s there had been much argument about to what extent non-attended information is actually processed. One of the classic experiments was done by Moray (1959), who showed that if your name is mentioned in an unattended stream of speech, then it captures your attention (for an update, see Harris et al., 2004). So there is a degree of quite sophisticated unconscious processing going on, even when you are not paying attention. This led to the idea of 'late' selection of stimuli rather than early. Assuming a serial processing model, the unattended stimuli were 'filtered out' after they had been processed in quite some depth, rather than before any analysis had been done.

continues

SIDE-BOX 8.5 continued

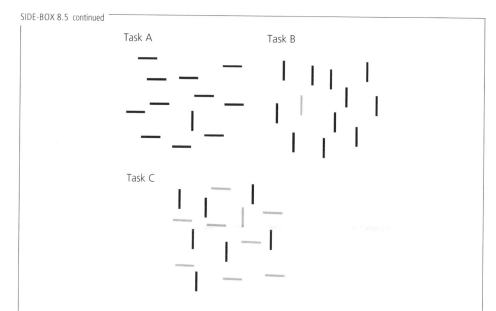

Figure SB 8.5.2 Search tasks. Find the target: in task A it is a vertical line, in task B a grey line, and in task C a vertical grey line. Only in tasks A and B does the target pop out; in task C you have to search each item serially.

Further research investigated the nature of what then became known as 'pre-attentive' processing (Neisser, 1967; Julesz, 1981; section 4.3.6). One paradigm is the 'visual search' task. Thus if you search for one item in a collection of many similar items, sometimes the target item will just 'pop out' at you immediately, and sometimes it won't. For example, if you look for a black dot among white dots, or a red dot amongst green dots, or a horizontal line among verticals, then the different stimulus will immediately pop out, that is to say, you notice it straight away and without effort or concentration (e.g. Figure SB 8.5.2, tasks A, B). The number of background stimuli can vary from one to dozens with hardly any effect on the time it takes to detect the target (Treisman and Gormican, 1988). The implication is that many, if not all, stimuli are processed in parallel and automatically. On the other hand, attentive processing is required when the target can only be identified because it possesses a combination of two characteristics. For example, the stimuli might consist of lines, randomly positioned on a screen, that are of two luminances, black and grey, and two orientations, horizontal and vertical (Figure SB 8.5.2, task C). All the vertical lines are black and all the horizontal lines are grey. The subject then has to say whether or not there is a grey vertical line (sometimes there is one of these in the display, sometimes there isn't). This is not easy and subjects cannot do the task immediately; they have to look at each individual line and decide whether it is a grey vertical line or not, and to continue doing this until the target is found (if one is present at all). Reaction time increases linearly with the number of lines in the display (typical rates of search are 20–50 milliseconds per item; Treisman and Gormican, 1988[b]). Subjects thus have to use what is called 'attentive' processing. Each of the stimuli present in the environment is analysed one at a time by focusing attention on it and then analysing it in depth using concentrated processing resources. It takes a measurable length of time to shift attention from one item to another.

Indeed, demonstrations that attention behaves like a 'spotlight', and can be moved around the visual scene, had earlier been given by, for example, Shulman et al. (1979), Posner (1980) and Remington and

continues

Pierce (1984). Subjects were required to shift attention from one location to another, without moving their eyes, and probe stimuli were presented at various points and times along the route between these locations. By measuring the subjects' ability to detect these probes, the movement and size of the spotlight of attention could be charted. (For more recent views on this searchlight or spotlight metaphor, see Cave and Bichot, 1999, and Fernandez-Duque and Johnson, 1999.)

Treisman's work also led to the idea that attention just *is* the integration of different features (Treisman and Gelade, 1980; for a review, see Quinlan, 2003). There are many aspects to any stimulus, such as its colour and orientation, that are analysed in different modules (see also section 4.3.6). Treisman and Gelade's theory is also a solution to the binding problem (section 4.3.7), which is the question of how information about the various features that make up an object – its colour, shape, location and so on – are kept together. The theory suggests that a spatial map is used as a master reference base through which the information being processed in separate functional modules across the visual system is linked together.[c] This contrasted with the older, serial processing theories that posited convergence onto a higher stage in which one would find representations of particular complex stimuli (and their current locations).[d]

More recent theories of attention have moved on to incorporate 'top-down' influences, that is, they try to explain *how* a choice is made as to which stimuli are attended, and how that choice is implemented in the sensory pathways. Purely 'bottom-up' mechanisms cannot be understood on their own. A groundbreaking study was that of Chaudhuri (1990), who showed that directing attention to a stream of characters and away from a drifting grating pattern reduces the strength of the motion after-effect induced by the pattern. Since motion after-effects are normally attributed to quite low-level visual mechanisms, it would seem that the module for early vision is 'penetrable' (section 4.3.6) by cognitive activity. Similar effects occur for several stimulus dimensions (for references, see Rose et al., 2003). A second common paradigm is that of 'cueing'. Here, the processing of a target is found to be affected by previous stimuli that provide a clue as to the nature or location of the target. For example, presenting a red spot in the centre of fixation a few hundred milliseconds before flashing a target shape on a red spot among a group of other colour spots (set at some distance from fixation) enhances one's reaction to the target (Barrett et al., 2003). Interestingly, Wolfe and Horowitz (2004) review evidence showing that not all aspects of cognitive knowledge can affect the deployment of attention, although some clearly can do so: colour, motion and others can, faces and line intersections are among those that can't. For recent general reviews on how attention is controlled, see Spekreijse (2000), Braun et al. (2001), Wolfe (2003) and Burr et al. (2004). The neural bases of these effects are introduced in Side-box 8.6.

In summary, there is evidence from empirical psychology for a distinction between information that you pay attention to and information that you don't. Only the former is conscious (or enters consciousness, or influences it, or becomes conscious . . . how you word this depends on your theory of consciousness). If we can elucidate the mechanisms of attention, and the difference between the processing of attended versus non-attended stimuli, we will have some ideas on the mechanisms of consciousness itself.

[a] There is a similarity here to the motor chauvinist theory of consciousness, which asserts that awareness is tied to preparation for action (e.g. section 8.4). O'Regan and Noë's theory is directed more at the phenomenology as originating in sensorimotor contingencies, i.e. the sensory changes that follow from particular movements. One problem with this theory is that it doesn't deal very well with how there can be different smells, for example.
[b] Wolfe (1998), however, found there is actually no set rate. Across many studies, the values found are distributed evenly from zero to several hundred milliseconds per item.
[c] Given that the highest-resolution spatial information about the visual scene is in the primary visual cortex (Barlow, 1979, 1981), this map could be located there and accessed via recurrent pathways to that area (see chapters 9 and 10).
[d] Zeki (1993), for example, argued against such a higher stage and proposed binding directly between the modules using a 40 Hz code (section 6.4.2), or between the modules at various stages along a processing pathway (Zeki, 2001).

Note that there are two types of attention that must be differentiated: 'bottom-up' atten-tion is captured automatically by stimulus onset transients (Egeth and Yantis, 1997), whereas 'top-down' attention is internally directed by cognitive or conative mechanisms. Bottom-up attention is attracted by, for example, someone waving their hand at you across a crowded cocktail party – something you may catch sight of 'out of the corner of your eye' – whereas top-down processes come into play when you are told to 'look for someone car-rying a newspaper and wearing a red carnation'. The latter process can thus be cued by sym-bolic and cross-modal stimuli such as verbal commands and task instructions and contexts, and must therefore require cognitive mechanisms. In contrast, bottom-up processes are more akin to the 'orienting reflexes' discussed in Side-box 8.4. Empirical stud-ies have revealed many functional differences between these two types of attention, and the neural mechanisms of control are correspondingly related to posterior (especially right parietal) and anterior (cingulate) cortex respectively (Posner and Dehaene, 1994).[11] Side-box 8.5 gives a quick revision of the psychological research on selective attention and Side-box 8.6 presents some of the neuroscience evidence.

8.3.1 Searchlight theories

How does attention work at the neural level? Let's begin with a simple theory – one steeped in reductionist identity theory and neuronal behaviourism. Then, we will examine how research based on this theory developed, and hopefully we will learn as we go what is wrong with this approach.

The psychological evidence for a 'searchlight' type of process (see Side-boxes 7.4 and 8.5) leads naturally to the search for a homologous mechanism at the neural level. The exist-ence of the thalamic reticular nucleus (Side-box 7.2), a sheet of inhibitory neurons sur-rounding the thalamus, leads naturally to the simple image of this nucleus as a mask that blocks activation of the cortex by the thalamus, except in one or more small regions (e.g. Yingling and Skinner, 1977; Scheibel, 1980; Taylor, 1999). Activation passes through these small 'holes' like a beam of light shining up onto the cortex, where it illuminates whatever processes are going on there. Neurally, the beam may be composed of nonspecific modula-tion, perhaps from the intralaminar nuclei, while the activity in the illuminated region of cortex might originate from cortico-cortical inputs or from specific thalamo-cortical fibres running along the same beam. Where nonspecific modulation coincides with information processing in the cortex, *there* is the source of consciousness.

Of course, this theory presents a gross oversimplification of what actually happens.

The best-known recent development from this basic idea is Crick's (1984) 'searchlight hypothesis'. Crick was concerned to explain the psychophysical conclusions (a spotlight of attention, movable through visual space) and in particular Treisman's theory that a master map of space is used to bind together information (about colour, shape, etc.) scattered across several cortical areas (e.g. Treisman and Gelade, 1980). He therefore emphasized the distributed nature of object representation: cell assemblies form that extend across the visual areas (V1, V2, V3 and so on). These assemblies are transitory coalitions; their

---

11. Recent studies have actually implicated a network of regions in the frontal and parietal cortices in top-down control (e.g. Corbetta and Shulman, 2002; Kastner, 2004).

SIDE-BOX 8.6 SELECTIVE ATTENTION: HOW LOW CAN IT GO?

What can neurophysiological studies tell us about the mechanisms of selective attention? Early work demonstrated that at higher stages in the processing pathway neuronal responses to a stimulus were enhanced if the subject was paying attention to that stimulus. For example, in unanaesthetized monkeys, Chelazzi et al. (1993) found that infero-temporal cortical cells responded more vigorously to a target stimulus that had been cued than to one that hadn't (considering the period beyond 200 milliseconds after stimulus onset). However, the consensus was that the more posterior in the brain, the smaller the effects (for vision), and no alteration of V1 responses at all could be induced by varying attention.

In the 1990s however, the tide turned. In parallel with psychophysical studies of early penetrability (Chaudhuri, 1990; see Side-box 8.5), scattered reports of neurophysiological changes appeared (e.g. Motter, 1993). Around the turn of the millennium there was a sudden plethora of works that together probably constitute a revolution or paradigm shift (in the terminology of Kuhn, 1962). These included studies of single neurons, intracortical evoked potentials and metabolic activity in monkey V1 (e.g. Vidyasagar, 1998; Posner and Gilbert, 1999; Mehta et al., 2000a, b; Vanduffel et al., 2000) and of human brain scans[a] and evoked potentials (e.g. Rees et al., 1997; Büchel et al., 1998; Watanabe et al., 1998a, b; Posner and Gilbert, 1999; Somers et al., 1999; Kastner and Ungerleider, 2000; Smith et al., 2000; Martínez et al., 2001). Perhaps the most convincing experiment was that of Olson et al. (2001). They placed electrodes directly on the surface of conscious humans' visual cortex during surgery and recorded the potentials evoked by stimuli that were or were not attentionally cued. The early parts of the evoked potentials were unaffected, but later components (more than 200 milliseconds) were enhanced if the stimulus was cued. The conclusion was that the effects of attention arrive relatively late in area V1 – but arrive they do. Feedback from higher centres was suggested as the mechanism.

Attention is thus known to influence the first anatomical stages of cortical analysis (and, moreover, at least one study has even found effects in the human LGN: O'Connor et al., 2002). The effects of attention in V1 are still smaller than in higher centres and of longer latency (e.g. Kastner and Ungerleider, 2000), but they are nevertheless real. Indeed, a recent study demonstrated that large effects can be obtained in V1 when attention is directed towards its optimally encoded stimuli, namely grating orientation and spatial frequency (Kamitani and Tong, 2005). But one need not rely only on the evidence about V1: the clear effects in V2 and V3 also indicate that 'early' vision is affected. In the auditory system, the evidence is also clear: area A1 is affected by selective attention to one ear or the other (see Luck and Girelli, 1998).

The theoretical counterpart of the recent conceptual revolution was that many detailed reviews and models of attention appeared that integrated psychophysical and neurophysiological evidence for top-down feedback from higher to lower stages in the sensory pathways (e.g. Deco and Schürmann, 2000; Lamme and Roelfsema, 2000; Lamme and Spekreijse, 2000; Spivey and Spirn, 2000; Suder and Wörgötter, 2000; Schroeder et al., 2001). This is not to exclude earlier theories – Desimone and Duncan's (1995) attack on searchlight theories was particularly influential – but to point to a sudden rise in the popularity of this approach. Further good general reviews of the new paradigm for attention can be found in Di Lollo et al. (2000, 2001), Driver and Frackowiak (2001), Friston (2002), Hochstein and Ahissar (2002), Paradiso (2002), Wolfe (2003), Deco and Lee (2004), Shipp (2004) and Spratling and Johnson (2004). For more on the neural mechanisms, see Corbetta and Shulman (2002) and Reynolds and Chelazzi (2004). Note, however, that additional theories about the functional roles of feedback pathways are central topics in chapters 9 and 10.

continues

SIDE-BOX 8.6 continued

To summarize, there is evidence that attention is not just like a filter that is high up along the serial processing pathway after complete and automatic 'pre-attentive' (and hence preconscious) processing, as in the previous generation of psychological theories. Instead, attention can modulate, if not restructure,[b] information processing quite early in the sensory systems, possibly through recurrent connections passing back down towards the 'early' regions of sensory cortex. These effects may be delayed in time by a couple of hundred milliseconds, but they nevertheless affect the 'early' stages of stimulus analysis. This will be taken up further in chapter 9. See also Side-box 4.5 for studies of attentional deficits with parietal lesions, and Side-box 11.1 for the effects of frontal malfunction on attention.

[a] Koch (2004) has argued that blood flow measures do not reflect functional activity accurately (see also Logothetis and Wandell, 2004), so some of this evidence may need to be re-evaluated. However, many theories of attention posit nonlinear modulatory rather than additive effects of feedback or selective arousal, so the cellular effects of paying attention cannot be expected to sum linearly with the afferent responses to stimuli. Most theories of attention are still qualitative, so Koch's arguments about the brain scanning evidence are not (yet) decisive. For additional discussion see Side-box 10.1.
[b] Current models of attention have moved away from simple neuronal summation ideas (e.g. that the modulatory inputs facilitate or inhibit the responses of cells that carry the sensory signal). That idea reduces the mechanism of attention to too low a level of description (chapter 3). Instead, functional theories stress the reorganization of processing to enable more efficient execution of the current task (e.g. Di Lollo et al., 2000, 2001). The field merges with the study of the phenomenon of rapid, early, perceptual learning (Fahle and Poggio, 2002; Fahle, 2004; Ghose, 2004). The outputs of the various sensory filters, channels or processing modules can be recombined rapidly and flexibly as needed, to make maximal use of the information they are providing in the current context. The neuronal changes that underlie such reorganization must involve more than just the injection of current into a few 'relay' cells along a simple chain of connections forming a reflex-like transmission route through the brain. For further relevant psychophysical studies, see Freeman et al. (2004).

existence coincides with our awareness of the stimulus object, and they dissolve and reassemble as we move our attention to another stimulus. Cells in an assembly all fire in synchrony (perhaps oscillating at 40 Hz; Crick and Koch, 1990).

So where is the searchlight? Crick (1984) suggests there may be several: for example, one for area V1 and another for the other visual areas. Crick admits, however, that the number and size of the searchlights will depend upon the extent and strength of lateral inhibition in the thalamic reticular nucleus, and we just do not have enough data as yet to be able to establish these values.[12]

Now, a priori there might in fact be a hierarchical arrangement of searchlights. At one level, we can simply pay attention to vision as opposed to hearing or touch. Within vision, however, we may pay attention to (search for) colour versus shape, and within colour, to red versus green. So when people propose searchlight theories, at which level do they envisage the searchlight as operating? (This is something to watch out for in the subsequent discussion of neural theories in the next few subsections!)

12. In fact recent data suggest that in adults the number of short-range collaterals that run within the reticular nucleus may be very low, and there is no clear evidence that these form conventional GABA-ergic synapses onto nearby cells (Pinault, 2004, p. 17). However, lateral inhibition can be mediated indirectly via descending connections into the thalamus and then up to neighbouring regions of the reticular nucleus, and perhaps also via dendro-dendritic contacts within the reticular nucleus. Immediately neighbouring reticular cells can, however, behave almost independently, and Pinault therefore suggests that each individual cell can act as an independent searchlight in the Crick sense! Their action is, however, more integrative in that they act by engaging and coordinating cells in various thalamic nuclei rather than just by inhibiting a halo of spatially surrounding thalamo-cortical projections (although Pinault says that may happen too).

Let us imagine in more detail what happens as we shift our attention from one object to another simultaneously visible on a screen, say from a red triangle to a green circle. There has to be movement of the searchlight(s) across a spatial map, a colour map and a shape map. According to Treisman, the spatial map is dominant. So as the person decides to move attention from one object to the other, their executive systems in the frontal lobes (section 7.2.2.3) direct the thalamic reticular nucleus to move the spot of disinhibited thalamo-cortical projections from the location of the first object to that of the second. Now, one possibility is that V1 is the main spatial map (this is likely because, of all areas within the cortex, it contains the highest resolution information about the spatial detail in the retinal image: Barlow, 1979, 1981; Lee et al., 1998; Pollen, 1999).[13] As the spotlight moves across V1, does a second spotlight move simultaneously across V4 from the red to the green represen-tation, and a third across infero-temporal cortex from triangle to circle representations? If so, how are these searchlights coordinated? How does the controlling mechanism know where to direct the second and third beams? Surely the anatomy of the reticular nucleus and its outputs are too diffuse, and there is no possibility of a highly specific linking con-nection that would make all three spotlights move in such a precisely coordinated fashion?

Alternatively, suppose there is a single spotlight that is directed to move across the master saliency map[14] (of space); this will necessarily cause a subsequent change in the stimulus information that flows forward from V1 to the other visual areas. If the new target is a green circle, the green and circle representations will automatically become activated in the relevant areas via cortico-cortical connections. However, this then leaves the question: why have a reticular nucleus interposed between the thalamus and those areas, if it is not used to control and direct selective attention?

Perhaps the pre-striate areas (V2 and upwards) receive a diffuse spotlight that facilitates the processing of any visual stimulus and is active just so long as you pay attention to vision per se. However, the large cortical extent of all those areas put together (Felleman and Van Essen, 1991; Van Essen, 2004) makes this unlikely, since the anatomy of the reticular nucleus surrounding the pulvinar (the thalamic nucleus projecting to those areas) is not so coarsely divided that it would function as a single unit in this way (e.g. Pinault, 2004).[15]

13. See Li (2002) for an account of bottom-up attentional selection in area V1.

14. Theorists often talk about a 'saliency map' that represents the importance of each stimulus, (for reviews see Itti and Koch, 2001; Shipp, 2004); a very intense stimulus, for example, will be salient and can capture attention. Salience can also be a matter of colour or shape and so on, not just brightness. One of the functions of pre-attentive vision is to establish stimulus salience in a rough map of the world that expresses the 'gist' of what is happening out there (Biederman, 1972; Hochstein and Ahissar, 2002; Wolfe, 2003). (Of course, you might say this term is defined circularly: how do you know a stimulus is salient? Because it captures attention. How does it capture attention? By virtue of the fact it possesses the quality 'salience'.) Koch (2004, pp. 161–162) defines saliency as an attribute that is constant across the range of behavioural tasks demanded of the subject, but also as a *relational* property, proportional to the difference between the object's 'intrinsic attributes' and those of its surroundings. So it is not an object that is salient; rather, the display or scene contains various objects that may be of differing relative saliencies.

15. However, this is a judgement on my part, not definitive fact. Pinault (2004) thinks each reticular nucleus cell may be able to act independently. At the opposite extreme, some theories treat the whole reticular nucleus as a single functional unit; see section 8.3.2. Such uniformity of activity may occur during sleep – see section 8.2.2.2 – but surely not in waking (a point also made by LaBerge, 2000).

What other possibilities are there? There are actually several maps of space in the brain (Gross and Graziano, 1995). Scheibel (1980) suggested the mesencephalic reticular formation (merging with the 'deep layers' of the superior colliculus) could control the directing of attention, since it contains a polymodal map of extrapersonal space and has direct inputs to the thalamic reticular nucleus. Crick and Koch (1990) suggest the pulvinar contains the saliency map, since it is in an excellent position to coordinate all the necessary information and to synchronize the oscillations in the various parts of the cortical assemblies representing each object. One relevant input to the pulvinar is from the superior colliculus, which determines the saliency of stimuli that attract eye movements (see also Side-box 8.7). In addition, lesions to the pulvinar have a profound effect on attention (e.g. Rafal and Posner, 1987; Posner and Dehaene, 1994; Ward et al., 2002). The circuitry involved in accessing the map, and in using it to control (activate, inhibit or modulate) particular parts of the rest of the thalamus and the cortex selectively, remains to be worked out. Shipp (2004) has recently reviewed possible circuits and has suggested how multiple functional searchlights could be coordinated. This can happen because the pulvinar

---

SIDE-BOX 8.7 TOPOGRAPHIC MAPS

It is natural to imagine that the topographic maps of the world that exist in the visual system are topographic because this enables them to be scanned to obtain information about the spatial locations of the stimuli. However, to do so without having to assume some prior inbuilt 'knowledge' of space – what it is and how it is scaled quantitatively – is another matter (Rose, 1999a).

One example is the superior colliculus, which contains a nice map of extrapersonal space, activated polymodally in its 'deep' layers. This site directs eye movements, if not all orienting of attention through space (Scheibel, 1980; Blakemore, 1990). Indeed, Blakemore (1990) defends a functional role for topographic maps in general by suggesting that processes such as attention may use a spatial mechanism to activate or address parts of topographic maps that encode colour or orientation (for example).

But this is not necessary: functional connections can form whatever the anatomical layout, as neural network simulations have shown. Perhaps extended experience may ultimately refine the network to minimize axonal lengths, and as a by-product generate a systematic anatomical organization of the functional dimension (e.g. Cowey, 1979; Koenderink, 1984; van de Grind, 1984; Durbin and Mitchison, 1990), but this topography does not cause or enable the function: it is the other way round. (People tend to assume that the anatomy of the brain is given a priori, and then whatever functions can emerge from that structure may do so. This ignores, however, the priority of functional need in guiding both phylogenetic and ontogenetic growth of the brain, and evidence for brain plasticity.)

Imagine, to adapt an example of Dennett (1988), that an evil demon comes along during the night and rearranges the cells in one of your topographic maps. The cells are now randomly arranged in, say, your superior colliculus. But none of the synapses has been disconnected: the dendrites and axons have been stretched by the demon so that the connectivity remains as it was before. Do you notice any difference? Does space appear distorted? Do your eye movements become chaotic? Surely (assuming that axon/dendrite length has no functional importance, so that, for example, changing the temporal delays has no effect on the coding), if the functional connectivity is unaltered then the function of the superior colliculus will be unaffected.

contains within it parallel slabs of tissue, each corresponding to one of the cortical areas along the ventral pathway and thus representing a different feature map (colour, shape, etc.). The spatial locations of the stimuli represented within each slab are aligned, so a single narrow 'beam' of neural activation directed along an axis through the body of the pulvinar, normal to the slabs, will activate all the maps at the same (real-world) spatial coordinate.[16] Each locus in the pulvinar then affects its corresponding locus in the cortex via the normal mechanisms of thalamo-cortical projection. The beam within the pulvinar can be controlled by the superior colliculus, and salience mapping then emerges from the collective activity of the whole system (cortex, colliculus, pulvinar) rather than being the function of a special module within it.

In conclusion, therefore, the notion of a searchlight, while easily understood at a functional level, does not translate directly into the obvious neural analogue, namely, an internal searchlight centred on the thalamus, selectively activating parts of the cerebral cortex and focused and directed by the reticular nucleus under the control of the frontal lobe (for top-down attention) or a saliency map of space (for bottom-up attention). Nevertheless, scientists do not give up easily on a good analogy, so in the next section we will look at another detailed attempt to make it work.

8.3.2 **Top-down control circuitry**

How does the frontal lobe transmit its influences to the posterior cortices in such a precise manner that we can attend so selectively?[17] In this section we look at one detailed explanation of how such a process could be taking place at the neuronal level.

To account for the results of his empirical studies of selective attention, LaBerge (1995, 1997, 2000) proposed that attention is mediated by what he calls a 'triangular circuit'. The basic loop involves two regions of cortex (one for the attentional content and one for the control of attention) and the thalamus. Embedded within this circuit are representations of content, each of which is assumed to be mediated by a cortical column (or, more properly, a cluster of columns in several different areas, representing, for example, a seen object's colour, shape and location), plus, for each column, a closely linked part (a 'sector') of specific thalamus. The circuit itself may also be embedded within a set of circuits that together give full-blown awareness.[18] LaBerge gives a fairly detailed account of these circuits, so let us begin with the columnar structures and work our way up in scale.

First, LaBerge posits that the specific connections that exist between a given column in cortex and its corresponding sector in a thalamic nucleus (e.g. in the LGN for a column in

---

16. Naturally, this is not settled yet: Sherman and Guillery (2002, p. 1704) challenge how exact the topography is in the pulvinar.

17. Diffuse attention is more easily explained, for example as transmitted via the cholinergic basal nucleus of Figure 8.8 (Nelson et al., 2005).

18. LaBerge carefully defines the term 'awareness', i.e. awareness of one's own senses and thoughts, and distinguishes it from mere wakefulness, which is the basic meaning of 'consciousness'. The terminology in the literature is, as he says, ambiguous and vague. In this book I am mainly talking about what LaBerge calls 'awareness', and my ubiquitous use of 'consciousness' should not be taken to indicate an alternative concept to 'awareness' (see section 7.1); the exception occurs in sections 7.2.1.2 and 8.2.2.2 on thalamo-cortical interactions, where I mention sleep–waking differences.

area V1) act to amplify the activity within the column, and to extend its duration. However, they only do so when 'modulated' by feedback connections from the controlling centre, which lies in the frontal lobes. Otherwise, activity in the column decays rapidly. Attention is thus a matter of amplifying signals from attended stimuli, rather than filtering out or suppressing unwanted signals, as in most other theories of attention.

The circuits that mediate this part of the mechanism are shown in Figure 8.9. They are in fact part of a network of similar circuits throughout the cortex. In posterior regions these mediate sensory states and in anterior cortex their function pertains more to action plans. They mediate automatic fast processing of inputs and potential actions. Their links form what I shall call 'mini-triangles', each of which carries information from one area of cortex to another. Throughout the visual areas, for example, there is a chain of such mini-triangles carrying information up from the optic nerve (starting on the left in Figure 8.10). This aspect of the theory stems from Guillery (1995; see also Sherman and Guillery, 1996, 2001, 2002, 2004, and Crick and Koch, 1998b; but cf. Shipp, 2003) and provides an alternative interpretation of the way that information passes from one cortical area to another (Side-box 8.8).

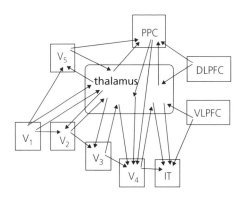

Figure 8.9 LaBerge's (1997, p. 161) 'schematic diagrams of some of the triangular circuits in the visual system'.

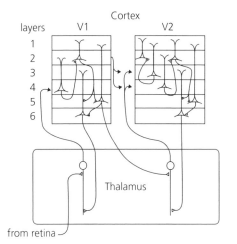

Figure 8.10 Flow of excitatory influences from the retina to higher cortical areas, here exemplified as far as V2. Both direct cortico-cortical and indirect cortico-thalamo-cortical connections run from the column in area V1 to that in V2, forming a (mini-)triangular circuit. From LaBerge (1997).

SIDE-BOX 8.8 THE CORTICO-THALAMO-CORTICAL THEORY

The normal interpretation of the functioning of cortical areas (as mapped by Felleman and Van Essen, 1991; see Figure 8.3) is that activity entering from the senses passes mainly to primary sensory cortex and thence via cortico-cortical fibres across to other areas of cortex. Sherman and Guillery (e.g. 2001) argue that this does not explain the function of the 'higher' nuclei in the thalamus, such as the pulvinar, that have traditionally been assumed merely to transmit ascending information from subcortical centres such as the superior colliculus, or play a role in sleep. Instead, it is proposed that the higher nuclei are driven mainly by collaterals of descending axons issuing from layer 5 pyramidal cells in the cortex and carrying 'motor' commands to subcortical centres (Guillery and Sherman, 2002). The information reaching each of these nuclei is then transmitted to its corresponding 'higher' area of cortex (Figure SB 8.8.1). They admit, however, that the anatomical evidence we have so far does not really allow a definitive conclusion (Sherman and Guillery, 2001, pp. 240–245; Casagrande et al., 2005).

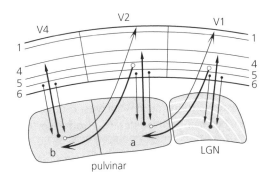

Figure SB 8.8.1 Cortico-thalamo-cortical theory of ascending connections in the visual system. Strong excitatory 'driving' connections are shown as thick arrows, modulatory feedback paths by thin lines. From Shipp (2003).

However, Jones (2002) describes the fibres from cortical layer 5 as projecting 'diffusely' to the thalamus, by which he means they usually form synapses in more than one thalamic sub-nucleus (including sometimes the intralaminar nuclei). His view is that these induce synchronous 40 Hz oscillations across wide regions of the cortex, which have been proposed as the basis of perceptual binding and consciousness (see the discussion of this idea in sections 6.4.2 and 8.2.2.2, and Shipp, 2003, for support). On the other hand, Sherman and Guillery (2002) deny that the layer 5 connections are diffuse and claim they provide the main excitatory drive carrying specifically targeted information to the higher regions of cortex.

On the basis of the anatomical and physiological evidence, Casanova (2004) takes a third view: that the cortico-pulvinar-cortical connections are 'active partners' with the direct cortico-cortical connections in passing influence from lower to higher visual areas. The pulvinar, he points out, is engaged in several different functions, including the transmission of visual information and the control of both attention and eye movements, as well as in several aspects of visual processing and analysis per se.

How far the information about a stimulus penetrates into the brain depends both on stimulus strength/salience and on top-down attention. The latter can modulate the thalamic parts of selected mini-triangles in such a way as to amplify the activity entering the mini-triangle from the senses (or perhaps already circulating up and down within the side of the mini-triangle formed by the connection between the cortical column and its specific thalamic nucleus).[19]

This modulation is switched on by descending fibres from certain centres in the frontal lobe, which LaBerge says can connect directly onto the relevant sectors in the thalamic nuclei (right side of Figure 8.9). For example, for visual stimuli, the areas V2 to V5 are reciprocally connected with the pulvinar nucleus in the thalamus, and this nucleus is the target of axons running from prefrontal cortex (Selemon and Goldman-Rakic, 1988). LaBerge mentions as examples of directing centres the dorso-lateral part of prefrontal cortex (DLPFC) for the control of attention to stimulus location, and the ventro-lateral prefrontal cortex (VLPFC) for the control of attention to colour and shape.[20] A second triangle for such connections also runs from prefrontal cortex to dorso-medial thalamus to posterior cortex (Schmahmann and Pandya, 1990). There are also direct axons running from the control centres in the prefrontal cortex to the posterior parietal (PPC) and infero-temporal (IT) regions of cortex. These connections determine exactly which columns are to be activated in the lower areas, while the indirect connections via the thalamus determine by how much these columns are to magnify their signals (LaBerge, 1997, p. 159).

This then is the mechanism of attention, in what we should call the 'triangle proper'. For example, one such circuit is between ventro-lateral prefrontal cortex, pulvinar and area V4, for attention to colour.

Stimuli are analysed serially through the various sensory areas of cortex, and if they are salient they may affect the frontal lobe centres of control. If the stimulus is salient it may interrupt ongoing processing of other stimuli, or if it is relevant to current desires and goal states it will continue to be processed and in fact be given priority by having its neural effects amplified. In that case, top-down attentional mechanisms emit action potentials back to the relevant part of the thalamus to strengthen and prolong the activity in the relevant analysis pathway, i.e. the route along which information about the stimulus is currently coming in.

The prefrontal centres are normally protected from distraction from the current behavioural task (for example, by irrelevant background stimuli) by having their thalamic

---

19. LaBerge (2000) states that the thalamo-cortical circuits may or may not generate 40 Hz oscillations; his theory is neutral in this regard. This implies there may be oscillatory or looping activity. However, the specific connections from the cortical layer 6 cells (i.e. the ones that project to the thalamic sector that provides driving input to layer 4 in the same column) are known to form modulatory synapses rather than excitatory 'driving' synapses (McCormick and Von Krosigk, 1992). Nevertheless, it appears that the thalamo-cortical circuit may still act as a self-sustaining loop, at least when embedded within the rest of the thalamic circuitry (Von Krosigk et al., 1993; Llinás et al., 1994). Certainly, however, LaBerge thinks the activity decays quickly unless maintained by the mechanism of attention.

20. Later (LaBerge et al., 2000) he changes the details: the prefrontal area instead contains columns that 'select' which stimulus to attend to. These control columns are in the premotor cortex, and it is these that are the 'modulatory' centres that actually send their axons to the pulvinar to implement attention.

counterparts tonically inhibited by inputs from the basal ganglia. To the latter, together with the hypothalamus, LaBerge ascribes the function of 'motivation'. It is they that control the prefrontal centres that control attention. Stimuli that are strong enough (such as someone shouting at you) may distract you from a task by punching through this inhibition along a connection from posterior cortex to dorso-medial thalamus (LaBerge, 2000). Normally, however, weaker activations in posterior cortex have to pass into the basal ganglia for assessment of their motivational relevance. Any stimulus that is of current or chronic 'interest' then activates a local inhibitory interneuron within the basal ganglia, that in turn suppresses the ganglia's tonic inhibitory output to the dorso-medial thalamus. This enables takeover of attention by the stimulus, via direct cortico-cortical inputs to the prefrontal centres and/or (?) the posterior cortex to dorso-medial thalamus to frontal cortex route.

Finally, LaBerge adds a mechanism for awareness, which is distinguished from mere attentional processing (involving feedback modulation via the thalamus) and from mere automatic processing (involving cortico-cortical connections only). There are regions of posterior parietal cortex that deal with representations of the body, and other (unspecified) regions that store 'verbal representations' of autobiographical memories. LaBerge takes these to be the bases of the 'self' (as do Damasio, 1999, and Taylor, 1999, 2001; see 'Parietal lobes' in section 7.2.2.3, and section 11.3). Thus attention can be directed towards the self, by modulating the relevant parts of the pulvinar and hence arousing activity in posterior parietal cortex.

Now, the important twist is that the attentional circuits need not be activated singly: it is possible to pay attention to more than one thing at a time. If one of those things is the self, then you will be thinking of yourself at the same time as you are thinking of the other object(s) represented by the cortical columns in the other activated triangular circuit(s). This is how you become aware of yourself perceiving those objects, LaBerge says. This synchronicity of activation can occur when a single control centre in the frontal lobe turns on the relevant triangular circuits at the same time. Under these circumstances, LaBerge (1997, p. 173) states, attention is being directed to a self that is controlling its own attention to the external object. There is thus a qualitative uniqueness to this situation that is beyond merely mechanical attention. This is LaBerge's explanation for awareness.

Critique

There is some basis to this theory in empirical evidence from neurophysiology and anatomy and in LaBerge's own neural network simulations and experiments on selective attention. The latter are restricted mainly to studies of visual shape and location, from which the rest of the theory is inductively generalized. Empirical support for activation of a distributed network of regions, including frontal and parietal cortex and the pulvinar (and other areas), in attention to location, has subsequently been obtained (e.g. Pessoa and Ungerleider, 2004).

Despite LaBerge's ambiguous use of the term 'triangle' to refer to loops at more than one level in a hierarchical arrangement, we can see how several functional mechanisms can be assigned to the various circuits within the brain. There is a touch of neuronal behaviourism (chapter 3) to such theories, which merely assign representational content to activity in certain circuits (here, cortical columns and cortico-thalamic loops[21]) without explaining why the associated phenomenology and function vary between the various columns.[22] Thus LaBerge (1997, p. 168) sees the progressive analysis of incoming stimuli as like a chain of dominoes falling over, in that each thalamic sector just has to be triggered by activity in the preceding cortical area (e.g. V1 merely activates the pulvinar sector that drives V2 and so on). He denies that stimulus analysis involves the transformation or processing of the information passing from one cortical area to another. This view is thus antithetical to the functionalism described in section 2.5, to the neural network theories described in section 6.4.3 and so on. As far as I can tell, it is a form of reductive identity theory, and liable to the same problems (section 2.4.3).

The putative representational bases (columns and cortico-thalamic loops) have been selected for emphasis in this theory, and several known links are missing from LaBerge's diagrams. For example, the connections between the cortical areas, and between the cortex and the thalamus, are reciprocal. In addition, direct connections run from retina to pulvinar, between V1 and V3, V4 and V5, and so on (e.g. Figure 8.3). Also, as Selemon and Goldman-Rakic (1988) report, there are more than two dozen other regions of brain, both cortical and subcortical, in which posterior parietal and dorso-lateral prefrontal outputs converge. What are all these connections doing, and do they interfere with the mechanisms LaBerge postulates?

LaBerge's theory depends crucially on the connections from frontal lobe to pulvinar (and from frontal cortex to dorso-medial thalamus to parietal cortex) to mediate highly selective effects. But how precise and tightly focused are such long-range anatomical connections? For example, the frontal input to the thalamus terminates in a different part of the pulvinar from the parietal input (Selemon and Goldman-Rakic, 1988; Cavada et al., 1995; Grieve et al., 2000) and the dorso-medial nucleus also receives frontal and parietal inputs in different sub-nuclei (Cavada et al., 1995). There are thus gaps (or at least unproven links) across these thalamic nuclei in the proposed chains of connections between the frontal and posterior cortices.[23]

Even if there is precise connectivity between pulvinar and cortex,[24] how does the frontal lobe activate single representations selectively? It seems there is a triangle proper connecting,

---

21. LaBerge says there may be a set of columns scattered around the parietal lobe representing the various aspects of the stimulus, but for simplicity of exposition I will continue to refer here to just a single column.

22. Ramachandran and Hubbard (2003), for example, suggest phenomenology must arise from the whole set of active areas in the brain. See section 10.2.3 for more details on this issue.

23. As Sherman and Guillery (2001, p. 240), Rockland (2002) and Shipp (2003) admit, however, the anatomy of the pulvinar has not been worked out in sufficient detail for us to be able to decide one way or the other on the issue. Further, when we consider the projections from thalamus to cortex, the various sub-nuclei within both the dorso-medial nucleus and the pulvinar project to different cortical areas within each of the frontal and parietal lobes (Asanuma et al., 1985; Schmahmann and Pandya, 1990; Grieve et al., 2000). Moreover, it is a simplification to regard each projection pathway as homogeneous: there are at least two types of axon projecting from cortex to pulvinar and similarly from pulvinar to cortex. To resolve the situation we need more detailed tracing of individual axonal connections, not just averaging across whole tracts of fibres (Rockland, 2002, 2004).

24. Shipp (2004) argues that the pathway from frontal lobe to pulvinar can carry precise information (about spatial location) if it is indirect, running from frontal cortex to superior colliculus to pulvinar.

say, the parietal V4 representation of red with a single column in frontal lobe and a single sector in pulvinar, while there exist in parallel separate triangles for each of green, blue and so on. Therefore, the frontal lobe must contain a duplicate set of representations of that contained within the parietal lobe. These are, however, LaBerge says, more closely spaced than those in the parietal lobe, hence lateral inhibition between frontal columns can explain the selectivity of attention to, in this case, colour. Perhaps the functional precision of the posterior lobe activations is augmented by the thalamic reticular nucleus, which is seen as sharpening the transmission of the information passing through it, since it introduces lateral inhibition between neighbouring points of activation (Side-box 7.2; Taylor, 1999). However, this mechanism would not cope well when the spatial separation between two stimuli is increased, especially when they appear in opposite visual fields and hence are processed in opposite hemispheres of the brain. In those cases, lateral inhibition in the thalamic reticular nucleus cannot aid selectivity (LaBerge, 1995, pp. 197–198).

Note that in LaBerge's theory the reticular nucleus does not act as a unified unit, for example to transmit selective attentional control functions from frontal to posterior regions of the brain, as in the theories of Yingling and Skinner (1977), Crick (1984) and Baars and Newman (1994). LaBerge's argument is based on the lack of evidence for direct connections from frontal lobe to posterior reticular nucleus. This is a refreshing touch of evidence-based reasoning, but leaves open the possibility of indirect connections, for example, influences might be carried within the reticular nucleus itself or via some other locations such as the intralaminar nuclei. Although there is physiological evidence that frontal inputs to rostral reticular nucleus can affect information transmission between posterior thalamus and cortex (Skinner and Yingling, 1977),[25] LaBerge (2000) argues this occurs only in deep sleep, when uniform activity spreads across the entire reticular nucleus and thus sets up synchronous oscillations throughout the cortex. In the waking brain, he says, the reticular nucleus acts purely locally on the information being transmitted through it along particular tracts between a thalamic sector and a cortical column.[26]

On the other hand, the intralaminar thalamic nuclei are hardly mentioned at all by LaBerge, who merely assigns to them the function of general wakefulness or alertness. This role agrees with that cast by Newman et al. (1997) and Jones (2002), but contrasts with the more central role in selective consciousness ascribed to those nuclei by Bogen (1995a), Purpura and Schiff (1997) and Cotterill (1998; next section).

25. Claims have been made more recently that information can spread across the entire thalamus, for example from rostral intralaminar nuclei to thalamic reticular nucleus to caudal intralaminar (Crabtree and Isaac, 2002) or through the entire reticular nucleus per se (Zhang and Jones, 2004). However, these are rather overstated generalizations drawn from data obtained from *in vitro* slices of immature rodent brain.

26. Recall from section 8.2.2.2 that 40 Hz oscillations have been posited to occur across the thalamo-cortical mantle in the awake state that are both uniform (scanning; Llinás and Ribary, 1993) and focal (selective; Llinás et al., 1998, and Steriade, 2000). We should also note that close anatomical inspection reveals variations in the internal structure of the thalamic reticular nucleus in different parts of the thalamus. This diversity implies the nucleus may not be performing the same function upon all the thalamo-cortical connections that pass through it (Guillery et al., 1998; Sherman and Guillery, 2001, pp. 223–224.).

LaBerge's use of the frontal cortex as the only source of top-down attentional control may be too limited. Thus Kastner (2004) regards both the frontal and parietal cortices as control centres for attention (remember, LaBerge just had the frontal cortex for control and the parietal for the 'expression' of attention to a particular object). Kastner says, based on her fMRI studies of changes in blood flow during attention, that attention is instead expressed in the visual areas along the ventral stream, including V1, which the frontal and parietal cortices control via a top-down mechanism. Vidyasagar (1999) has also argued for parietal control of the ventral stream. (See also chapters 9 and 10 for more about top-down effects on visual cortex.)

The mechanisms suggested for the bottom-up capture of attention and the screening of stimuli for relevance are also somewhat vague. LaBerge asserts without justification that the screening is carried out in the basal ganglia, but these are normally ascribed a role in motor functions.[27] The complexities of their circuitry (e.g. Cotterill, 2001) are not described in sufficient detail by LaBerge. Nor is it explained how stimuli are assessed there in comparison to representations of currently expected, let alone all possible, motivationally interesting stimuli.

Finally, LaBerge's explanation of how we actually become aware (rather than merely paying attention) is interesting but needs far more exposition and elaboration, particularly with regard to its philosophical position. In the terminology of Side-box 7.1, it is a theory of representation with added qualities: there are thresholds of intensity and duration that neural representations have to exceed. To this extent it resembles the theories of Greenfield and Calvin (section 7.3.3), although LaBerge considers these thresholds merely to determine when we are paying 'attention', which falls short of full 'awareness'. In addition to attention, a further quality is required: simultaneous activity in the representation of the self.[28] However, LaBerge's account does not make clear exactly how his two foci of attention relate to one another. Instead, he assumes first that mere activity in a particular cortical area generates the particular content of consciousness (e.g. a quale or idea), and second that simultaneous activation of the self-concept somehow makes one aware that one is paying attention to that particular content (1997, p. 173). His exposition of this crucial point is frustratingly brief.[29]

Thus how is it that activation of the self-concept at the same time as the concept of, say, a cat, makes one aware that one is *paying attention to* the cat, rather than simply being aware of oneself (I exist) at the same time as *being aware of* the cat (it exists)? Compare activation of two other representations, say, a cat and a mouse; one would then be paying attention to these two animals. But how would one represent (at the neural level) a cat paying attention to a mouse? And *how would I represent a cat paying attention to me?* My self-representation would need to be activated twice: once to give my consciousness and once as object of the

27. Although atrophy of the basal ganglia can also be accompanied by cognitive executive difficulties (Banich, 2004), these seem to be independent effects caused by transmitter depletion in frontal cortex or by striato-frontal diaschisis (Woods and Troster, 2003; Monchi et al., 2004).

28. A similar idea has also been put forward by Kihlstrom (1993) and Pollen (2003).

29. Worse, it is extrapolated into sweeping explanations that compare how we savour the sound of a Bach cadence (our attentional triangles intensify and prolong activity in the relevant cortical columns: LaBerge, 1997, pp. 171–172) and at other times we may lose ourselves 'enraptured' in the music (because no self-representation is receiving attentional activation: 1997, p. 175).

cat's consciousness. There seems to be no explanation in LaBerge's theory for the link 'paying attention to'. His reductive identity theory implies that the attentional load is simply the sum of the activated representations of objects in the world. The relationships between the objects are not explained. Perhaps there is a mechanism that can add such relationships (e.g. frontal lobe action plans), but why is the self-concept so different in its effects from the other representations, such that when activated there emerges a new property – awareness – that does not arise from the co-activation of the representations of a cat and a mouse, or a cat looking at me?

His depiction of the representation of the self as based on the map of the body in the somatosensory cortex is also too simple (even if it is supported by others such as Damasio, 1995, 1999, and Taylor, 2001). We will cover the model of the self in more detail in section 11.3.2, but for now note that, according to LaBerge, a lesion to this region should leave us with attention without awareness. However, (1) why does blindsight, in which one can orient to a stimulus without perceiving it, follow from area V1 lesions, (2) why is hemineglect predominantly obtained following right parietal lesions but rarely left and (3) why can anosognosia (loss of self-awareness) follow from lesions to any higher area of cortex, and occur for some deficits but not others within the same patient (Prigatano, 1999; Marcel et al., 2004)? None of these facts is accounted for by LaBerge's theory of awareness.[30]

8.3.3 Interim conclusion

So far, neural theories of attention have adopted the searchlight metaphor and tried to find a neural homologue in which particular neurons and connections can be mapped one-to-one onto the functional diagrams. The problems with these theories seem to be that they are reducing too far: from psychology directly to the level of single neurons. The complexities of the neural machinery at this level are far too great to fit the simple metaphors of searchlight and focusing within the phenomenological realm. The biological data underconstrain the psychological theories and indeed it seems still more data are to come before the neural connection patterns are fully known. Some further intermediate level explanations are required to bridge the gap between single cells and phenomenology. Research into the questions of amplification of sought signals versus suppression of the unwanted and

---

30. More recently, LaBerge (2001) has put forward another speculation about consciousness. This time, he simply equates consciousness with 'waves' of activity in the apical dendrites of cortical pyramidal cells. These waves must repeat at a fast rate (presumably, around 40 Hz) and exist across many columns. Despite the pure reductive identity of this theory, there is an almost dualistic twist: 'a subjective experience can itself be the goal of brain activity' (2001, p. 15), and does not need to lead to an adaptive response to the environment. He contrasts this role for apical dendrites with that of the basal dendrites, which are supposed to mediate 'pulse' transmission and the processing of information. The latter is unconscious and the results are passed to other regions of the brain (in the case of cortical areas, via the direct cortico-cortical fibres). Apical dendritic waves in primary sensory areas, generated by incoming stimuli and of brief duration, are proposed as being the 'background' consciousness, while the more persisting bursts of waves generated in higher sensory cortices by the triangular circuits of attention form the conscious contents of our attentional focus. Mysteriously, no role is proposed for the apical dendrites in frontal cortex, and it is conjectured, again without justification or logic (though presumably as an ad hoc explanation for hemineglect data), that 'experiences are produced mainly in columns of the right hemisphere' (2001, p. 22).

distracting, and the identities of the broad areas of the brain involved (e.g. the networks seen to become active in brain scanning work), may channel future theorizing better towards the neuronal bases.

At the same time, our understanding of attention must include how it fits into action, memory and perception. Let us therefore look at another theory of brain dynamics within which attention is just one integrated part.

8.4 **Motor efference copy**

Recall from Side-box 8.1 that Miller et al. (1960) put forward a general scheme in which plans for action are central to the operation of the mind. A recent revival of belief in the primacy of action has come to be known as 'motor chauvinism'. This school of thought believes that the motor system is the single central integrative system of the mind, and indeed more generally that life is about movement. Supporters include Humphrey (1992), Hurley (1998), Burkitt (1999), Núñez and Freeman (1999), Sheets-Johnstone (1999), Llinás (2001), O'Regan and Noë (2001), Ellis and Newton (2004), Shadlen and Gold (2004), Lethin (2005) and Noë (2005); see also Cohen (1986) for historical roots.[31] It is proposed that the motor system is the basis for the unity of consciousness, and in section 11.3 I will say more on how it tries to explain the unity of the self.

In this section I will describe a detailed neural theory of how the flow of information between various parts of the brain and the outside world serves to integrate the mind with the environment (Cotterill, 1998, 2001). Although the centre of dynamics is the motor system in the frontal lobes of the brain, the mechanisms of perception and attention in the posterior lobes are also included within the overall schema. At first blush Cotterill's theory resembles LaBerge's (section 8.3.2), to the extent that it again involves a triangular circuit between the thalamus, frontal and posterior cortical regions. However, Cotterill's view is rather different from LaBerge's, from his understanding of overall brain function through to his theory of the difference between conscious and unconscious processing.

Thus Cotterill sees the premotor cortex as the conceptual origin of consciousness (in contrast to the traditional view that the stimulus is the origin). The brain learns about the environment by posing questions to it. As Cotterill puts it: 'each walking stride is effectively a question: is the ground still there?' (1998, p. 389). In other words, the brain learns what is 'out there' by formulating hypotheses and testing them, which it can only do by moving the body and seeing what happens.[32] The results of each movement are monitored through

---

31. An earlier, more behaviourist, manifestation asserted that all thinking is motor preparation or subvocal speech (see also Cohen, 1986). Neisser (1967, p. 191) attributes this idea to Bergson (1911) but pithily remarks (p. 197) that one can recognize and imagine the tone of a familiar person's voice without necessarily being able to mimic that tone.

32. In behaviourist terms, this is 'response–stimulus' associationism. An alternative nomenclature is 'sensorimotor contingency' (e.g. O'Regan and Noë, 2001). In contrast, however, Jacob and Jeannerod (2003, pp. 170–172) say that some aspects of perception involve stimulus–stimulus covariations, and, moreover, lesions to the dorsal and ventral pathways can dissociate perception from action.

SIDE-BOX 8.9 EFFERENCE COPY

The existence of an internal system to monitor motor output was first noted by Helmholtz (1866). For example, if someone's eye muscles are paralysed and the person voluntarily tries to move their eyes (for instance, to the left) then the visual scene appears to swing wildly in the opposite direction (that is, to the right) even though there is no physical movement. Conversely, even without paralysis, pushing your eyeball with your finger can make the visual world appear to move. The movement of the image across the retina may be exactly the same as it is when you move your eye naturally, but in the latter case the world appears stable (Ross et al., 2001). It is as if the visual system 'knows' that you have moved your eye and compensates for it when interpreting the movement of the image across the retina.

Helmholtz postulated an 'efference copy' of the motor command. When a command is sent from the brain to the eye muscles, a copy is passed internally within the brain back to the visual system. This process (also sometimes called 'corollary discharge') has since been generalized to all motor commands (Holst and Mittelstaedt, 1950; Sperry, 1952; see Cotterill, 1998, p. 389, for strict terminological definitions, and Webb, 2004, Box 2, for a summary). For example, if you move your whole body to the left the image on the retina will change, even if your eyes remain stationary within the head; yet you still perceive the world as stable and yourself as having moved. To give an additional example module, if you reach out your hand to pick up a cup of coffee, your touch module needs to know it is your hand that has moved and not the cup, and how hard your fingers should be pressing on the cup in order to lift it without letting it slip.

Malfunctions of the efference copy system have been postulated to have a profound effect; for example, they may be the primary cause of schizophrenia (see Side-boxes 4.5 and 11.1).

the posterior, sensory regions of cortex. The sensory feedback received after movement can be compared with that expected, given knowledge of the nature of the movement, and the truth of the hypothesis is thus ascertained.

But how and where is this comparison made between the knowledge of movement and its results? Note first that the presence of such a system was demonstrated long ago, in studies of 'efference copy' (Side-box 8.9). A whole raft of evidence has since accumulated that the sensory systems are affected by prior knowledge of the stimulus that is to be expected. This phenomenon is variously known as set, expectancy, pre-cueing, priming, forward masking, anticipation, top-down attention, search, vigilance, etc., depending on the exact experimental context. Not all of these appear to be linked closely to motor execution or preparation, but Cotterill and the other motor chauvinists declare that all thought is based around motor functions (e.g. 'a dog recognizes a bone by gnawing it': Young, 1978, p. 57; 'we know with our muscles': Cotterill, 2001, p. 22).

It is on the question of where this efference copy goes that Cotterill really shines. He describes in fact not one but three relevant circuits. Yes, three. (I told you in chapter 3 that the brain was complicated!)

Figure 8.11 shows the first of his circuits. Here, like Miller et al. (1960), Fuster (1995, 2003), LaBerge (1995), Taylor (1999) and Crick and Koch (2003), he has made a broad distinction between the frontal cortex and the posterior cortex, i.e. the occipital, parietal and temporal lobes. The latter process incoming sensory information, whereas the frontal cortex

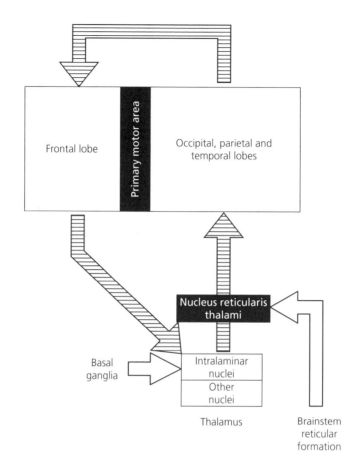

Figure 8.11 Flow of activity between the posterior cortex, anterior cortex and thalamus (stripey arrows), which is 'the basic circuit underlying awareness and thought' (Cotterill, 1998, p. 348).

generates the outputs of the brain. When the frontal lobe orders movement or 'decides' to make a movement, not only does it send commands out ultimately to the muscles but there is also a message sent to the sensory cortices via the intralaminar nuclei of the thalamus. This message has to pass through the reticular nucleus, a shell that surrounds the thalamus and appears to 'gate' traffic passing up to the cortex (see Side-box 7.2 concerning the relevant thalamic nuclei, and section 8.3 above). Here, general arousal and emotional factors are, according to Cotterill, able to interact with the messages, through inputs from the brainstem and anterior cingulate cortex respectively.

It is this circuit (the stripey arrows in Figure 8.11) that Cotterill suggests underlies all thought, and is thus the basis of consciousness. The contents of awareness are given by the particular areas of sensory cortex involved. Activity would circulate around the loop (perhaps at gamma band frequencies: Cotterill, 1998, p. 349), giving a form of short-term memory that can persist for several seconds (p. 351).[33]

33. As we shall see later (Side-box 9.1), 'record' might be a better term than short-term memory. Cotterill also ascribes blackboard-like working memory functions to the prefrontal cortex.

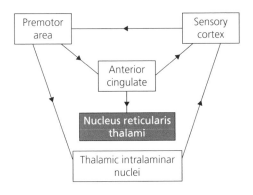

Figure 8.12 The anterior cingulate cortex is located so as to be able to control activity flowing round the first circuit, which it can do by blocking the corticopetal output of the thalamus. From Cotterill (1998).

The second circuit is shown in Figure 8.12, nestled inside the previous triangular loop. It runs between the premotor, anterior cingulate and sensory cortices. This loop does not sustain consciousness on its own, but instead has a controlling function over the other loop. It is responsible for blocking and redirecting activity in the first circuit, which it does by activating the thalamic reticular nucleus through which the first messages have to pass. This gives firstly a power of 'veto', which Cotterill follows Libet (1985) in seeing as the 'free will' aspect of consciousness. Awareness of danger, for example, can inhibit the automatic responses that might be maladaptive in certain situations. It is obviously useful for survival that one can anticipate danger, and so checking one's 'plans for future action' (generated in the frontal lobe) to see if they might lead to pain would be a useful function carried out by the anterior cingulate. This region is known to be important for the registration of feedback from pain, so it may well be the source of the emergency signals that halt and divert ongoing information processing in the brain. Secondly, the redirecting of activity in the thalamus gives selective attention – about which more below.

Cotterill's third circuit is direct cortico-cortical feedback from premotor cortex to sensory cortex. It is shown as the thick, double-headed arrow in the centre of Figure 8.13. This figure (which was presented also as Figure 3.6b) shows the previous two circuits in medium-thick lines, and a lot of non-conscious processing connections as thin lines (mainly in the subcortical motor system; see Cotterill, 2001, for even more). The thick lines show a rapid feedback pathway from movement via the environment, that is, when the premotor cortex (PMC) issues a command the muscles and limbs move, and there is a more or less immediate alteration in the pattern of sensory inflow. The latter rapidly affects the sensory cortices and hence the input to premotor cortex becomes changed. The messages running back from premotor to sensory cortex mediate unconscious expectations: we are able to walk without noticing the pressure on the soles of our feet induced by every footfall, as we move our eyes the image of the entire world swings rapidly across the retina without our noticing a blur, and when we move our limbs we are not distracted by the drag of clothing against our skin. Cotterill (1998, pp. 432–433) describes the presence of this back pathway as reflecting the correlations between motor output and sensory input that have been built up by long-term experience. The hippocampus may play a role in installing this correlational information as long-term memory.

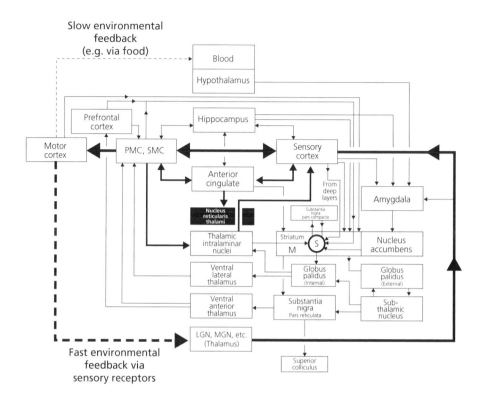

Figure 8.13 Location of some of the feedback loops within the forebrain. The thick arrows constitute a rapid feedback loop involving the environment, and the medium arrows show Cotterill's first and second internal circuits. From Cotterill (1998).

Now how does this all work? It seems that when expectations are not met (e.g. your foot does *not* encounter the ground when you are walking) then consciousness becomes engaged. In other words, an alerting or arousal response occurs (section 8.2.2.3; Sidebox 8.4). Thus under routine circumstances the efference copy operates unconsciously via the direct fronto-posterior connections (Cotterill's third circuit), but there is another route for efference copy, via the intralaminar nuclei (the first circuit), that does sustain conscious awareness and is engaged in emergencies. This switching is mediated via the anterior cingulate gyrus (in the second circuit).

Critique

Upon reflection, Cotterill's theory is, as theories of consciousness go, one of the most well informed. It gives an exceptionally acute depiction of the complexity of the neural circuitry involved in brain function. It not only has an extensive empirical basis in brain physiology and anatomy but provides interesting philosophical arguments for the primacy of motor function. However, the theory still has behaviourist overtones. Thus Cotterill talks about 'association cortex', the learning of associations between different stimuli being the function of the brain, and stimulus–response (or movement–stimulus) associations as the basis of perception. Proposing that seeing red is just preparation for saying the word 'red' (Cotterill, 1997, p. 237) is surely going too far.

Although comprehensive, Cotterill's diagrams have some important omissions. For example, the sensory cortices also project backwards, down to the thalamic nuclei that provide their input. Both pathways pass through the thalamic reticular nucleus and make synapses there (e.g. Side-box 7.2 and Figure 8.6). This arrangement for regulating the flow along the specific pathways has been postulated to mediate the switching of attention between different sensory stimuli (or at least to be part of the arrangement; for example, see sections 8.2 and 8.3 on attention). If so, the selectivity is not just the result of gating the output of the intralaminar nuclei, as Cotterill would have it. Of course, both the specific and the nonspecific (intralaminar) outputs of the thalamus may be gated by the reticular nucleus, but the relative importance of the control of each pathway, and the exact functional roles of both gates, remain to be clarified.

Further, the input to the reticular nucleus from the anterior cingulate may well control the ascending inputs from the thalamus to the anterior cingulate and nearby regions of frontal cortex, but there is controversy over whether it regulates the transmission of information through more posterior parts of the thalamus and up to the sensory cortices (see previous section). Moreover, if there is a single control centre, other workers argue that it is the premotor cortex not the anterior cingulate (LaBerge, 1995: see section 8.3.2; however, both centres might work together: Cohen et al., 2000). In addition, all regions of cortex are able to turn the reticular gates on and off, at least within restricted regions of the nucleus, so the control centre, if there is one, cannot be in complete command of the nucleus.

The central position of the intralaminar nuclei in the crucial first circuit implies that the content of consciousness passes through this nucleus. However, the relatively small size of this structure must surely restrict the range of ideas that can be carried. As Baars and Newman (1994) put it, the bandwidth of information transmission through nonspecific structures must be limited, and prima facie that would apply to the intralaminar nuclei too. So the nature of the signals passing through this first circuit, which Cotterill (1998, p. 433) describes as 'an essential participant' in conscious mental processing, may be too restricted to subserve the full range of conscious experiences. Cotterill would have the messages be predictions of sensory changes caused by the currently active motor plan (or the motor sequence 'associated with every thought': p. 433), yet the full range of sensory experiences we have is also determined by which area of posterior cortex is involved (e.g. p. 372). So consciousness in all its glory and complexity depends on several regions of brain, and the circuits emphasized are merely necessary but not sufficient causes of our subjective experiences. This still leaves a gap in the explanation we require.

Cotterill admits there is a lack of data about what happens at the within-area scale of processing, and certainly, not much detail is given about the specific local circuits within each of the cortical and subcortical areas referred to. His theory is thus like the other current theories that involve large-scale movements of information around the brain; these tend to ignore the fact that there is very complex circuitry within each of the little boxes in their diagrams. Although Cotterill explains very clearly how the circuitry within each area works in principle as a 'neural network' (section 6.4.3), that internal circuitry is not suggested as giving rise to consciousness per se.

The theory also falls into the class which emphasize novel or unexpected stimuli as evoking arousal and hence awareness (sections 8.2.2.3 and 9.3.3). For example, it attributes the switching between thoughts (i.e. plans for motor action) to the anterior cingulate gyrus (in what I have been calling Cotterill's 'second' triangular circuit: Figure 8.12). These switches are triggered by pain or the expectation of pain.[34] However, I am not sure where and how the switching occurs in the more general case, since Cotterill (2001, p. 24) lists several subcortical sites as being involved in 'novelty detection', including the hippocampus, basal ganglia, thalamus, cerebellum and both premotor and prefrontal cortices. Indeed, in that paper he even adds another (fourth) major pathway for efference copy, which passes via the cerebellum! Although I am in favour of complexity when appropriate, and there are indeed many different situations in which discrepancies from expectation may occur (and over many different timescales!), this plethora of potentially relevant brain areas makes it difficult to see how to test any particular prediction.

Another problem is that expectation can facilitate, not suppress, the perception of anticipated stimuli (and vice versa for novel stimuli). One must distinguish Cotterill's proposed role for efference copy as a mechanism to check the success of predictions/ hypotheses (in which success leads to lack of awareness and failure to arousal), from the idea of anticipation as selective attention to a stimulus whose appearance is desired and sought (in which success leads to enhanced awareness and the wrong stimuli are ignored and their perception inhibited).

In fact, as we will see in the next two chapters, the feedback pathways of the brain have been attributed many different functional roles, including not just anticipation and selective attention, but also the consolidation of memories, stimulus recognition, read-out from memory, imagery, gain control, noise reduction, hypothesis testing, contextual guidance, binding and consciousness itself. The choice between these theories is one of the biggest questions facing current research on the brain.[35]

8.5 Conclusion

The brain is dynamic throughout, and this cannot be ignored when theorizing about consciousness. The basic mechanisms of arousal, sleep and waking involve subcortical structures such as the brainstem and thalamus that have a variety of complex interactions with the cortex. Oscillatory activity occurs at all times, as witness the EEG, but the mechanisms by which shifts of frequency occur remain to be clarified. So too does the question of

---

34. The functions of the anterior cingulate cortex have been variously suggested to include the control of attention, the monitoring of errors and the selection of appropriate responses and actions; they can also be divided into cognitive and emotional aspects (Bush et al., 2000) and control may also be expressed via the prefrontal cortex and the brainstem (Cohen et al., 2000). Frith and Frith (2003) argue that part of this area mediates the perception or belief about how strong or stressful a pain is – or, in general, the attitude towards any stimulus.

35. However, note that any given mechanism can in principle subserve several functional roles (multiplexing), depending on its evolutionary history (chapter 5)!

why particular frequencies subserve particular states of alertness, and how come any frequency at all should be related to consciousness.

One fruitful approach considered in this chapter is to compare attended and non-attended processes.[36] Although it would indeed be useful and promising to be able to reduce consciousness to a well-researched empirical field such as attention, the latter has undergone rapid advances recently as to the psychological mechanisms and the gross brain areas involved. Yet the theories we have looked at include detailed proposals about the neuroanatomical connections (e.g. around the human thalamus) and their physiological functions (e.g. modulation versus driving) that we are just unable to evaluate at present owing to lack of relevant data. Moreover, the psychological revolution points to reorganizational principles operating at a functional level of description (Side-box 8.5) that do not translate obviously into single-cell terminology.[37] There is a discrepancy between the states of research at the various levels of description, a state which makes for poor theorizing about both attention and consciousness. Theories need to integrate our knowledge across many levels of description (chapter 4), so we need comparably sophisticated models at all these various levels.

Action-oriented theories such as those of Miller et al. (1960) and the motor chauvinist school address the *origin* of top-down attention, as well as other willed or cognitive 'executive' decisions. These theories regard the control of movement as the final common pathway through which all processing is channelled, and thus as the central locus for switching and guiding functions. Being thus in control, the motor modules have to connect extensively and with detailed precision onto the other internal functional modules. Therefore both attentional and motor chauvinism theories involve 'feedback' to the 'early' regions of the cortex, and indeed information flowing along these 'descending' pathways is known to affect sensitivity and functioning in the sensory processing regions. But to understand what information is carried in that feedback, we have to know how the system 'decides' what is important, or what should be paid attention to. To avoid treating the motor or executive module as a full homunculus we have to look at how it interacts dynamically with other modules, such as those handling the concurrent sensory inflow. For example, how well does the current sensory input match what is expected (is inflow what the motor modules suggest it *should* be, as communicated via their efferent copy connections to the sensory modules), and how well does inflow match what is in the long-term memory? To that end, in the next chapter we will look at how memory interacts with sensory input, and how memory, perception and attention have to be considered together to understand how the

36. This presupposes there is a dichotomy between the two that is identical to an equally clear separation into conscious and unconscious processing. The divisions might be sharp or blurry, and there could be qualitative or quantitative differences across the boundary. However, the definitions of the boundaries and the phenomena considered to lie on either side are often not clear, and may not even be discussed by the theory's protagonists. Some have disputed that the divisions are identical, and it is quite possible that the various phenomena of attention (focal versus ambient, pre-attentive versus effortful, gist versus filled-in, isolated features versus conjoined object files) and consciousness (focal versus fringe, raw qualia versus intentional representations, lower- versus higher-order) are a genuine menagerie and not just two sides of the same simple dichotomy!

37. But see Meese and Georgeson (1996), Freeman et al. (2004) and Reynolds and Chelazzi (2004) for some relevant progress.

system as a whole is functioning (for example, how the system settles into a new steady state, with implications for sensory experience arising out of that). Such switches of perceptual state bear on changes in the entire mind, including (self-)consciousness (chapter 11).

■ RECOMMENDED READING

Brain dynamics are covered partially by the readings given at the end of chapter 6, and their implications for consciousness by the readings for chapter 7. Cotterill's Enchanted Looms (1998) contains a comprehensive overview of the relevant brain anatomy and physiology.

A brief introduction to the psychology and neurophysiology of attention is given by Koch in The Quest for Consciousness (2004, chapters 9 and 10). Specialist tomes on the topic include the edited volumes by Parasuraman The Attentive Brain (1998), Humphreys et al. *'Brain Mechanisms of Selective Perception and Action'* (1998) and Attention, Space, and Action (1999), Braun et al. Visual Attention and Cortical Circuits (2001), Leclercq and Zimmerman Applied Neuropsychology of Attention (2002) and Kanwisher and Duncan Functional Neuroimaging of Visual Cognition (2004). Three specialist volumes also worth looking at are Robertson and Halligan Spatial Neglect (1999), Karnath et al. The Cognitive and Neural Bases of Spatial Neglect (2002) and Robertson Space, Objects, Minds and Brains (2004).

Memory and perception

OBJECTIVES

In this chapter, the interaction between incoming stimuli and the fabric of the brain will be explored. The rationale for this is that much of the brain's dynamic involves such interaction, and although much of this interplay is for the purposes of learning about the world (and how to survive and reproduce in it), we again have to consider the two possibilities for the basis of consciousness: either stable or dynamic end states may be the crucial foundation. We start with neural and cognitive theories as separate strands of research development, but the need for multi-level theories that connect such realms takes us into some detailed attempts to bridge the gap. This necessitates that we go through some well-developed theories of neural network dynamics. Although I have not given any quantitative descriptions here, the ability (of some of these models) to be simulated on a computer or analysed mathematically represents a necessary step towards differentiating and testing the various possibilities. You need to see how such in-depth run-throughs are useful; the devil is in the details, and meticulous analyses are necessary if you want to understand the complex system that is the brain. In addition, some of the more general ideas that emerge from these analyses will prove surprisingly useful for our further investigation of consciousness.

9.1 **Introduction**

In section 8.3 we considered the relationship between attention and perception, and to what extent we are in fact studying consciousness when we talk about these concepts, since they are loosely defined and often used in an overlapping fashion. In this chapter, we will consider the relationship between top-down processes, memory and conscious perception.

One of the first lessons we learn in psychology is that long-term memory is distinct from short-term or working memory, as evidenced, for example, by the effects of brain damage. Lesions to the hippocampus or hippocampal region lead to loss of the ability to form new long-term memories but leave short-term memory intact, so that people are able to remember things by rehearsal and repetition without loss of the normal 7 ± 2 item span. Conversely, lesions to the parietal lobe can reduce short-term span without affecting the formation, retention or recall of long-term memories. This is often cited as a textbook example of a double dissociation (see Side-box 4.2). A putative relationship between consciousness and short-term memory was introduced in section 7.2.2.3.

A more elaborate example postulating that consciousness may depend on not one but a series of short-term stores is described in Side-box 9.1. This model introduces a number of concepts that will be elaborated later in this chapter and in the next as to how the recurrent cycling described in sections 6.4.3 and 8.2 may manifest itself at the functional level. In the next section, we will look at where long-term memory is stored and what exactly is stored, preparatory to studying how it interacts with sensory input in creating our conscious awareness of the state of the world (section 9.3).

SIDE-BOX 9.1 PRECONSCIOUS MEMORY

Can we be influenced without being aware of it? Psychologists have long debated whether this is possible. Here, I will describe a set of experiments that purport to show that we can recognize words presented briefly on a screen without being aware that we have seen anything. These studies lead to a model of preconscious processing that summarizes and typifies much of the standard cognitive approach to perception (Marcel, 1983a,b).

In these experiments, each word was presented for a brief period before being replaced by a mask (a random pattern of letter fragments). Marcel tested three different kinds of processing. One was simple sensitivity to the presence of any stimulus at all. For this, he asked the subject whether a word was visible before the mask. As the gap (stimulus onset asynchrony or s.o.a) between the word and mask increased, so the percentage of correct responses increased (Figure SB 9.1.1).

On other trials the procedure was the same, but after the trial he presented two words on a card, and the subject had to say which of the two words was most similar to the word that had been flashed on the screen. In one condition, the criterion for similarity was *graphemic*, in other words, how similar the words appeared in their physical structure: the shape of the word and the letters. The results were that graphemic similarity judgements were possible with shorter s.o.a.s on the whole than in the detection task (see Figure SB 9.1.1). The other criterion used was *semantic* similarity. After the trial Marcel asked which word on the card had the most similar meaning to the flashed word. So if the word 'moral' was

_____ continues

SIDE-BOX 9.1 continued

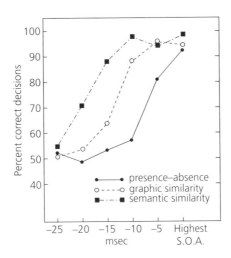

Figure SB 9.1.1 Effects of varying the separation between a target word and a mask (stimulus onset asynchrony) on successful word analysis. Subjects were required to choose which of two probe words was most like the target word, using three different criteria. Each subject's data have been normalized to the level at which the subject detected the word on just under 100% of trials ('Highest S.O.A.' = 0). Modified from Marcel (1983a).

flashed and the subject had a choice of 'ethical' or 'cloud', then 'ethical' should be the correct answer (as opposed to the graphemic similarity criterion, where 'moral' is more closely related to 'molar' than to 'cloud'). The empirical curve this time was even further to the left (Figure SB 9.1.1), showing that semantic information was extractable with even shorter s.o.a.s.

Now, this pattern of findings was somewhat paradoxical because at the time it was assumed that the information that comes into the visual system is processed through a series of stages – sequential analysis. For reading words, for example, first the system analyses the shapes of the words – their features (vertical and horizontal lines, etc.), then the structures of the individual letters, and then it goes on to link these together as words (e.g. Selfridge, 1959; Lindsay and Norman, 1977). Then, once the system has identified the words, they are associated with their various meanings and related concepts. Finally, you have awareness of the content of the message you are reading, and behavioural responses to it. So it should actually take longer to extract the semantic representation than the graphemic – and (presumably) even longer for conscious awareness.

But Marcel's results went in the opposite direction. As a result of this and a complex series of other similar experiments, he came up with the model shown in Figure SB 9.1.2. The idea is that as the sensory input comes in, it is analysed through a series of stages, and at each of these stages the information is encoded in what Marcel called '*representations*'. These representations in some way contain relevant information about the stimulus. There is a series of encoding and recoding or analysing stages between each of the representations, e.g. A to B to C in Figure SB 9.1.2. (We know, for example, that lexical information can be encoded as the shape of the word, or the sound of the word or the meaning of the word: e.g. Baddeley, 1966a,b). At the same time, each of these stages gives rise to what Marcel called a '*record*', which is a kind of short-term memory store, a briefly lasting trace of the information encoded.

continues

SIDE-BOX 9.1 continued

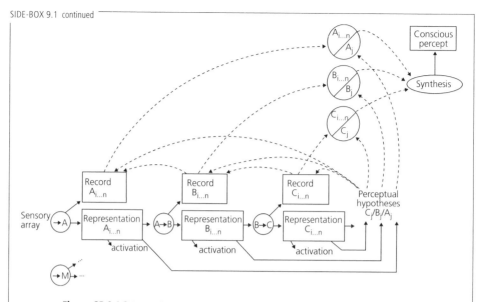

Figure SB 9.1.2 Marcel's constructivist model of preconscious processing. Input at lower left is transformed into a series of representations and records (A, B, C . . .). The former evoke hypotheses that are checked back against the original records; verification leads to synthesis of the successful hypotheses into a coherent percept (top right). Solid lines show automatic processes, dashed lines show intentional/selective processing. From Marcel (1983b).

The representations also give rise to what he called '*activations*'. Although only briefly described by Marcel, these apparently include the priming of similar concepts and 'motor adjustments' (1983b, p. 246).

And the representations also give rise to what Marcel called '*perceptual hypotheses*'. What he meant by a perceptual hypothesis was a long-term memory for a particular object: a file or structure of knowledge based on previous experience of a category of stimuli. The idea is that the representations are usually incomplete: the information coming in may be only partial, containing just a few features, cues or clues to what the stimulus is. But the perceptual hypothesis will contain (relatively) full knowledge about any given real-world object. Thus if the visual system extracts some cues, for example that 'it looks roughly like a horse', then some kind of file in long-term memory would be aroused that might include a stereotyped image of what a horse looks like.[a] This file can fill in the gaps of what is missing from the stimulus, e.g. if the horse is half hidden behind a tree (Gregory, 1970; section 9.3.1).

So according to Marcel's model, because the cues are partial and thus ambiguous, various perceptual hypotheses might be evoked by the multiple stages of representation. What the system then needs to do is find out whether those perceptual hypotheses are correct, which it does by checking them against the incoming information. Each hypothesis includes a specification as to which features are needed to verify it, and these can be sought by going back to the records – the traces of the earlier stages of processing – and 'recovering' more information from them. For example, if the perceptual hypothesis says it is a horse then the input should contain certain key features (which may not all be the features that evoked that particular hypothesis). Moreover, the various fragmentary and incomplete cues in the input may have evoked several different hypotheses, so the system has to check back and find out which of them is most consistent with the incoming data. The system then has to choose, from

continues

among the perceptual hypotheses, the long-term memory that is most consistent with the data. In many cases, however, there would be various degrees of consistency between the various perceptual hypotheses and the inputs, and indeed there may genuinely be several stimulus objects that are present simultaneously. Then, the system must somehow integrate and synthesize these various hypotheses into a unified percept that is the final decision about what it must be that is present in the outside world. This then leads to conscious perception of the stimulus object or array of objects, and awareness of what it is you are looking at (top right of Figure SB 9.1.2).

There are several points to note about Marcel's model. One is that sensory analysis is automatic: it proceeds through all the stages of representation and the input is analysed as fully as it possibly can be at this preconscious level. So all possible representations of the stimulus are generated, along with a corresponding short-term record or memory. Now, what we are aware of is not identical to those representations. This is an *indirect* theory of perception, in that there are processes of inference and synthesis that mediate between the incoming stimulus and conscious awareness. The process of synthesis is one of imposing structure: of segmenting or parsing the input stream into separate events or figures. Different perceptual hypotheses compete with one another via inhibition so as to generate only one final interpretation of the input. This model thus fits in with the traditional indirect perception theories that suggest that what we are aware of is some kind of internal construct or 'model' that is based on the incoming data but also on our knowledge or long term memory derived from previous experiences with the world (e.g. Craik, 1943; Neisser, 1967; Gregory, 1970; Johnson-Laird, 1983; Rock, 1983).

Critique

On the positive side, the notion of multiple memory stores is reasonable and finds support elsewhere. For example, Vogel et al. (1998) present evidence in favour of a similarly multi-staged model – although rather than seeing sensory analysis as automatic, they propose that attention is needed to transfer information from certain stages to the next. Moreover, they propose two types of selective attention: one operates spatially at early stages and the other is a more general, late selection mechanism. In support of lasting traces, Supèr et al. (2001) have shown that even the earliest cortical stage (visual area V1) can act as a temporary memory store.

Marcel himself does not say anything about the anatomical locations of the mechanisms he proposes, although he does discuss the effects of brain damage with regard to dyslexia, visual agnosia and blindsight. He argues that these syndromes support his division into different functional modules, and that they can be interpreted in terms of his theory.

It is also not clear why semantic and graphemic analyses drop out in the order they do (Figure SB 9.1.1). It makes sense under his theory that conscious detection should be lost first as s.o.a. decreases. As Marcel puts it, the mask comes increasingly to be within the same segment of time as the word and is thus taken as 'the' event that occurred, hence dominating the percept; yet the priming or arousing effects of the preconscious 'activations' created by the graphemic and semantic representations would still be intact and available to bias behaviour at the time of testing (when the subjects had to choose between two words shown on a card after the trial). However, it is still not clear why grapheme-based behaviour should go next and semantic last, as s.o.a. is reduced. Marcel's (1983b, p. 270) explanation is based on the assertion that the two types of information are carried by different spatial frequencies; but his argument is ad hoc and unconvincing.

continues

SIDE-BOX 9.1 continued

There has also been controversy over whether the 'subliminal perception' demonstrated by Marcel (1983a) and others (e.g. Dixon, 1981) actually occurs (e.g. Holender, 1986; Erdelyi, 2004; Kouider and Dupoux, 2004). Can someone genuinely fail to detect a stimulus consciously despite showing evidence of preconscious processing (cueing, priming, implicit learning)? Specifically, were Marcel's tests of semantic and graphemic associations more sensitive because he was using a forced-choice task, whereas the conscious detection test merely required a present-versus-absent choice and subjects may have been setting a high criterion in the signal detection sense (i.e. they were reluctant to claim they saw the word unless they were absolutely sure)? More recent studies using improved methods have, on the whole, supported the conclusion that subliminal or preconscious processing occurs (e.g. Groeger, 1988; Bachmann, 2000, pp. 93–96; Bernat et al., 2001; Jack and Shallice, 2001; Ortells et al., 2003; Hutchinson et al., 2004; Kihlstrom, 2004; Snodgrass, 2004) but the debate rumbles on (Dehaene, 2001; Snodgrass et al., 2004).

Marcel's model (Figure SB 9.1.2) also leaves consciousness sitting at the top, like an epiphenomenon, floating above the system where it does not seem to have any active role. There is no explanation for top-down effects such as attention and expectancy (knowing what it is that might appear next; sections 8.3 and 8.4). How does searching for a particular stimulus bias the interpretation of incoming sensory stimuli? Perhaps the simple addition of some extra top-down connections could explain such phenomena, although this might constitute an ad hoc addition to the model.

Nevertheless, the late generation of consciousness in this model is typical of 'indirect' theories of perception, in which much interpretation and analysis proceeds before we become aware of a stimulus.

[a] The typical view of an object is known as a 'canonical view' or prototype. There has been a long debate over whether our memories store a single such view that is then transformed (e.g. mentally rotated and scaled) to match the input or to enable us to 'imagine' the view from another angle (what does a horse look like from behind?), or whether we store several typical views (exemplars) and take the closest – or indeed whether memory for a sensory stimulus is imagistic at all (e.g. see Lamberts and Shanks, 1997; for more discussion see section 9.3.2).

9.2 Long-term memory formation

What is the physical basis of long-term memory (LTM)? It was found, most famously by Bliss and Lømo (1973), that activating synapses intensively leads to subsequent facilitation of transmission across those synapses. This is support for Hebb's idea that usage of synapses leads to enhancement of their efficiency (section 6.4.1). As a simulation of repeated trials in learning experiments, the inputs to a synapse are repeatedly stimulated by electric shocks at a rapid rate for a minute or so; this activates a biochemical mechanism that causes the synapses to transmit information more strongly on subsequent occasions. The effect can persist for hours at least, so is known as *'long-term potentiation' (LTP)*. The general theory is that, with use, the engram is being written in, in the form of an enhancement of the ability of those synapses to transmit information. The training causes permanent anatomical changes in the structures of the synapses.

Long-term potentiation is prevalent in the hippocampus, although it can be demonstrated in just about all neural tissues, including the cerebral cortex (Buonomano and Merzenich, 1998; Frégnac and Shulz, 1999; Song and Abbott, 2001; Teyler et al., 2005). But it has been mainly studied in the hippocampus because that structure seems to show long-term potentiation most easily and over the longest period.

In serial processing models of sensory analysis, the hippocampus is depicted as the most advanced stage, as though incoming information flows all the way through the cortical systems and ends up in the hippocampus (right at the top of Figure 8.3). The assumption is that sensory information is analysed and identified, its ramifications and implications are somehow thought through and then, at the end, if it is important, it goes to the hippocampus where it is fed through into the memory store(s). The hippocampus acts as a gateway to this separate module, a filing cabinet of memories. Long-term potentiation is part of the process of '*consolidation*' by which anatomical changes occur that may persist for the rest of the individual's life.

The hippocampus is also part of the limbic system, so there is the possibility of motivation, values and emotional goal criteria being used there to judge whether a stimulus is important and thus memorable. If something is important it is put through into the memory system, or if it is unimportant then it is forgotten. This is the old behaviourist model (see chapter 3 and section 6.4.1).

The modern development of this model emphasizes the fact that most of the connections in the cortex are two-way, and there is also backward flow of information from the hippocampus to the cerebral cortex. Figure 9.1 gives a more detailed illustration of how the two-way connections between the various neural networks within the hippocampus and

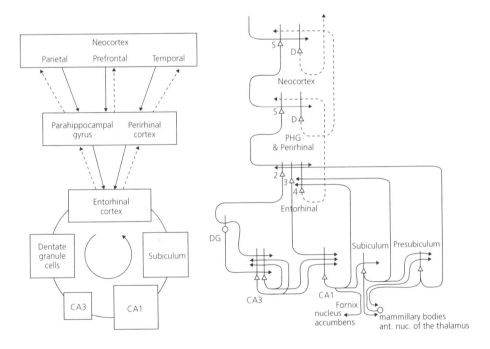

Figure 9.1 Interactions between hippocampus and cortex. At left is the functional flow diagram and at right the neural network equivalent (where each connection and cell represents a large number of parallel processing units). At the top, input enters and flows between successive cortical areas (solid lines), eventually entering the entorhinal cortex–hippocampal complex where it circulates through the various substructures and returns through the cortical areas (dashed lines). Only excitatory units are shown. Within the cortex, S and D represent superficial and deep layer pyramidal cells, and the entorhinal cortical layers are indicated by numbers (2–4). Modified slightly from Rolls (2000).

cortex are arranged. This returning flow of information must be doing something, and one of the central ideas is that long-term memories are not stored in a special module, but are located throughout these areas of the cerebral cortex. What happens when learning occurs is that information comes in through the lower stages (see Figure 8.3), leaving short-term traces at each of them ('records', in Marcel's terminology – Side-box 9.1; e.g. Supèr et al., 2001). Following some kind of 'higher' process of evaluation or association or whatever, if the memory is deemed important enough to be laid down, the hippocampus then sends signals back down into these earlier regions of cortex to initiate the process of consolidation, i.e. the laying down of long-term memories by physical synaptic anatomical alterations. The formation of long-term memory is thus initiated or controlled in this top-down fashion from the hippocampus (Rolls, 1990, 2000; Mishkin, 1993; Eichenbaum et al., 1996; Squire and Zola, 1996). Further supporting evidence has come from studies of brain damage or atrophy (Murre et al., 2001; Kopelman, 2002; Eustache et al., 2004; Westmacott et al., 2004a,b; see Side-box 9.2) and from brain scanning studies in normals (Haist et al., 2001; Piefke et al., 2003).

SIDE-BOX 9.2 LONG-TERM MEMORY: MODULES OR GRADIENTS?

In Side-box 6.3, Lashley's idea of mass action was described, in which all areas of brain tissue were ascribed equal status in contributing to any given memory. In support of this, no small lesion in humans causes total retrograde amnesia (the loss of all long-term memory for things learned before the onset of brain damage). (I will restrict this discussion to declarative memories and the cerebral cortex, omitting procedural memories that rely more on the basal ganglia and/or cerebellum).

Many types of brain damage can cause amnesia, and one old rule of thumb (Ribot, 1881) is that the older the memory, the more resistant it is to damage (Ribot's law: e.g. Kopelman, 2002). Amnesia is the commonest complaint among people with even mild head injury (Brandt, 1988), and yet vocabulary learned in childhood is almost never lost (indeed it is often tested in the clinic to give an idea of what the person had been capable of before the head injury; Nelson and Willison, 1991). Instead, a gradient of loss is often seen, with memories for the most recent events being the most profoundly affected. In accordance with this, as the person recovers from their amnesia, the most recent events are reinstated last. A typical clinical test is to present the faces or names of people who were famous within the last ten years, 10–20 years ago, 20–30, and so on. Patients with amnesia show a shallower gradient of loss than normals, that is, their recollections may be as good for old stimuli as for new, or even better, whereas normal people show a progressive loss with age. Such findings are taken to show that older memories are somehow more deeply 'inscribed' into the brain, although whether that is due to their age alone (perhaps some intrinsic biochemical process continues indefinitely) or to the frequent repetition or recall of the stimuli is difficult to decide. Whatever the processes involved, they certainly continue for many years (e.g. Haist et al., 2001; Kopelman, 2002; Piefke et al., 2003).

Are all areas of the brain equipotent, as Lashley suggested? Many lesions affect specific functions: for example, occipital lesions affect various visual functions (Side-box 6.2), and deficits in the recognition of objects have often been divided into 'apperceptive' and 'associative' agnosias (e.g. Banich, 2004). These differ in that the former involve perceptual difficulties, whereas the latter are characterized by loss of understanding of the identity and purpose of a stimulus object. The simple, serial processing

continues

conclusion is that perceptual and mnemonic functions in the brain are separate. Farah (2000, 2004), however, argues for a continuum of disability between these two conditions: associative visual agnosics can copy drawings accurately (e.g. Humphreys and Riddoch, 1987), but they take an extremely long time to do so, while apperceptive agnosics are only impaired when presented with artificial degraded stimuli. She concludes that damage can occur at various stages in a serial processing multi-layer neural network, in which there is no sudden change in function from perceptual to semantic (Farah, 2004, pp.153–154).

Several types of brain atrophy are also characterized by a differential loss of memories. Thus, semantic dementia is a specific loss of semantic memory with (relatively) intact episodic/autobiographical memory (Graham, 1999; Murre et al., 2001; Grossman, 2002). Patients may, for example, recognize the faces of their personal acquaintances but not those of famous people. The primary locus of atrophy is the lateral anterior temporal cortex (though with disease progression the effects spread). More medial temporal atrophy leads to loss of episodic memory (Westmacott et al., 2004a,b). There is continuing controversy over (1) whether the hippocampus is involved in the storage of old episodic memories as well as new,[a] and (2) whether the semantic–episodic distinction is merely due to the connectivity of the areas involved with other regions of cortex that deal with 'perceptual' processing, which connections enable links to be made with the context in which stimuli occurred (see Graham et al., 1999; Snowden et al., 1999; Garrard et al., 2002; Shastri, 2002; Eustache et al., 2004; Piolino et al., 2004). It is these links to perceptual regions that may create the vivid sense of being there that we get when recalling an episodic memory (Tulving, 2001, 2002), perhaps by top-down reconstitution of a previous pattern of sensory input (see section 9.3.4).[b]

As dementias progress, category-specific deficits in semantic knowledge may develop, for example for faces, places, tools, animals and so on, if atrophy extends into the ventral occipito-temporal areas. These deficiencies match those studied as 'visual agnosias' and that light up in brain scans when the appropriate stimuli are applied (Side-box 6.2; Forde and Humphreys, 2002). This implies that memory and perception for any given category are subserved by the same neural structure, strengthening the idea that perception and memory reflect the activity and anatomy respectively of the same neural net (section 6.4.1). Whether or not these categories and the neural mechanisms that deal with them are modular remains a matter of debate (see above, and Side-box 6.2). Certainly, the gradient model of memory does not necessarily imply a smooth linear gradation over cortex. There are many stages, areas and modules in the cortex and the model simply requires that these be monotonically ordered.

The areas implicated by semantic dementia are restricted to the temporal lobe, which counts against the theory (see section 9.2) that the *entire* cortex contains a gradient of stimulus frequency, with the longest-established and most hard-wired memories stored closest to the primary sensory cortices, and the rare episodic memories closest to the hippocampus. However, the deficits seen clinically are stimulus-specific (e.g. they show hemisphere differences, dependent on whether topographic or autobiographical materials and tasks are used) and the tests used clinically so far rarely aim to test the kinds of processing that occur nearer the primary sensory cortices. For the moment, suffice it to say that some dementias can affect visual cognitive functions (e.g. Hof et al., 1997; Pringle and Davies, 2001; Cronin-Golomb and Hof, 2004) and, of course, the effects of localized lesions to such cortices can also be interpreted as consistent with this scheme.

In addition, the gradient model does not necessarily mean that memories are distributed along a straight course between the hippocampus and sensory cortex: the routes available between these

continues

SIDE-BOX 9.2 continued

stations are many and various. For instance, there is evidence that small regions of the frontal lobes are involved in episodic memory storage too (although retrieval may be the principal role of these areas: Maguire, 2001; Piolino et al., 2004). Wide regions of the posterior half of the brain are also engaged nevertheless. Thus Conway and Pleydell-Pearce (2000) suggest that the right frontal lobe stores life-story themes, the posterior temporal lobes store schemas for particular general scenarios and the parietal and occipital lobes store images of particular events – including vivid flashbulb memories (Brown and Kulik, 1977; Conway, 1995, 2001).

[a] Recent evidence suggests that this controversy may stem in part from hemisphere differences, since the right hippocampus but not the left is engaged progressively less as the memory becomes more remote in time (Maguire and Frith, 2003b). It also varies with the age of the subject (Maguire and Frith, 2003a).

[b] The issues are very difficult to resolve, in view of the complexity of the system. Episodic/autobiographical memories vary not just in their age but also in the vividness of the visual imagery they evoke, whether the imagery is of scenes seen as though from one's own viewpoint (which happens for recent memories) or from that of an external observer (for distant memories), how emotional they are, how familiar they feel and their content (memory for items versus the context in which they were encountered – and 'context' can mean location in space, time or one's life story). There are also methodological confounds such as the difficulty of testing the state of the memory store independently of the state of the encoding and/or retrieval mechanisms, the fact that memories are likely to be re-encoded when they are recalled (thus: older memories are more rarely retrieved, so the act of recall counts as a novel event, hence enhancing the re-encoding) and the degree to which memories incorporate general knowledge about oneself (e.g. 'knowing' you have been to Paris; hence, semantic) rather than of specific incidents ('remembering' being in Paris: hence, episodic). All of these factors may vary between studies and may rely on different brain regions (e.g. Baddeley et al., 2001; Tulving, 2002; Piolino et al., 2004).

Taking the theory forward, one can imagine a wave of effect passing from the hippocampus and outwards over the cortex. The more frequently a stimulus is encountered, and the more over-learned the stimulus is, the further back down into the cortex the effect of that experience will reach. Thus the most commonly occurring stimuli or features will have had their memory traces pushed progressively further and further back towards earlier and earlier stages of sensory analysis (i.e. lower and lower in Figure 8.3). This makes sense because the more frequently a feature occurs, the better it is for this feature to be picked up early and analysed quickly by these lower stages. The higher regions of the cortex would be left containing memories of stimuli that are less frequent, including perhaps complex conjunctions of features. For example, many people think that the infero-temporal cortex contains memories of complex objects (section 6.2.6.1) and the medial temporal cortex relates to autobiographical events (Side-box 9.2); these might both include the sight of your grandmother! According to the same model, memories of simpler visual features like colours and straight lines are stored in the earlier parts of the visual system. So the idea is of a gradient of frequency and expectancy across the cerebral cortex, where the rarest items are dealt with at the highest stages.

An interesting wrinkle is that numerous studies have found a link between learning and sleep. An old theory of why we sleep is that it consolidates learning. For example, Wilson and McNaughton (1994) found evidence that during slow-wave sleep, hippocampal activity reproduces the patterns experienced during the day, and Karni et al. (1994) showed that perceptual skill learning is facilitated by REM sleep. These findings support the idea that there is a read-out from the hippocampus to the cortex during sleep, which presumably mediates the consolidation of memories into long term storage.[1] For further details, see Side-box 9.3.

1. Dreaming might then be a side effect of this writing-in process.

SIDE-BOX 9.3 SLEEP AND MEMORY FORMATION

A great deal of research has tended to confirm the existence of a link between sleep and memory formation. The findings have suggested in addition that slow-wave and REM sleep play complementary roles at different phases of consolidation, and that procedural and declarative skills both benefit (e.g. Stickgold, 1998; Sejnowski and Destexhe, 2000; Maquet, 2001; Stickgold et al., 2001; Fenn et al., 2003; Maquet et al., 2003; Huber et al., 2004; Rauchs et al., 2005; Walker, 2005).[a] Moreover, relatively direct evidence for a progressive spread of the effects of hippocampal long-term potentiation (LTP) across several synapses (i.e. as far as motor cortex, in the rat) during successive sleep episodes has recently been provided by Ribeiro et al. (2002).

These sleep studies show that information is stored in the hippocampus for several hours, i.e. from day until night, before being transferred out to the cortex. (Similar 'intermediate-term memories' in the hippocampus have been postulated before: Marr, 1971; Rawlins, 1985; Eichenbaum et al., 1994.) Most importantly, they show that the information transmitted from the hippocampus *is contentful*, rather than just being a 'write now' signal to store the information that is actually contained within the short-term 'records' in the cortex.[b]

[a] Siegel (2001) sounded a cautionary note in remarking, for example, that across species there is no correlation between the amounts of REM sleep and learning. However, the total amount of sleep taken by different species varies notoriously from a few hours to most of the day, making 'the' function of sleep difficult to pin down. For the moment, theorists have to accept that the amount of sleep does not vary linearly with any of its putative functions.

[b] Livingston (1967a,b) suggested that the effect of (limbically-triggered) reticular arousal might be a 'now print' signal to write recent activity into the cortex. In contrast, Marr (1971, p. 54) posited that during sleep, the memories of strong emotional experiences of personal significance would act as cues triggering the downloading – to use modern terminology – of the rest of the hippocampal database (of the day's input of raw data) to the cortex, where it would be analysed and processed into long-term memory (which consists of categorized knowledge).

Now, declarative memories can be divided into semantic and episodic types (Tulving, 1972). Episodic memories are for particular events, scenarios and happenings that you experienced personally (such as a visit you made to Paris two years ago), and semantic memories are for general knowledge (e.g. Paris is the capital of France; the formula for salt is NaCl) that have become separated from any particular episode (such as your school-teacher telling you that Paris is the capital of France, your reading it in a book, and so on). The difference between the two types of memory is often referred to as the '*remember–know*' distinction: we 'remember' episodes and events but we 'know' general knowledge. More recently, Tulving (2001, 2002; Wheeler et al., 1997) has redefined the division to emphasize the different types of consciousness that are involved in each case. Semantic recall (knowing) is often accompanied by 'noetic' experience – a feeling of familiarity with the material and awareness that one knows it. Episodic recall, however, is an 'autonoetic' (self-knowing) experience; it is a process by which particular perceptual experiences are linked to the self and to time, to give a sense of the self as reliving a particular occasion from the past.[2]

---

2. The same mechanism can also give introspection about the state of one's self in the present, plus imagination of actions in the future. It may be related to internal monitoring operations in right frontal cortex (Side-box 4.5 and Side-box 11.1). Tulving seems almost to treat future planning as a fortuitous side effect of the evolution of autonoetic consciousness; yet surely the ability to think ahead is patently advantageous for survival (and may even be the source of consciousness itself, according

Indeed, it seems the essential property of 'autonoetic consciousness' is not self-knowledge but the sense or awareness of time (or perhaps the *binding* of the two to give a sense of a continuing self-identity). Unfortunately, the origins of these vital senses, particularly that of time, are not explained. (Is there a special representation of time? How is time encoded? How do we become aware of it?) And how do the mechanisms also locate and/or bind in the particular phenomenal content that is appropriate to a given time and self?[3]

The dichotomy between episodic and semantic memories contrasts with the old – and perhaps more intuitive – idea that these are just extremes of a continuum (Tulving, 2001). Remember, the gradient model introduced above assumes only one type of memory, characterized in terms of the frequency of stimulus occurrence or generality as opposed to the specific contents. Episodic memories are assumed to be those stored nearest the hippocampus, while semantic memories are stored nearer the primary sensory regions.[4] In support of the dual-process (episodic ≠ semantic) hypothesis, however, there is evidence that the brain regions responsible are not organized in that fashion. Instead, Wheeler et al. (1997) say that for episodic memory, the frontal lobe organizes and gives a sense of time and of the self (especially the most anterior region of the lobe). However, at recall, the content and imagery of the memory are expressed in the posterior lobes (so also Conway, 2001). It is also well established that for episodic memory the left frontal cortex is the more involved in encoding and the right in retrieval, whereas for semantic memory the left frontal cortex is the one engaged during retrieval (for a review of evidence, see Tulving, 2002).[5] These frontal sites may, however, be for executive and control functions rather than

to some theorists: section 8.4)! Episodic recollection of the past then becomes the side effect (chapter 5). However, Conway (2001) provides a rationale for the evolution of episodic memory for past events. Such a mechanism enables us to make rational decisions based on experiences we can be sure we had in actuality rather than in a dream or fantasy.

3. The relationship between acts of remembering and consciousness is unclear (my italics throughout): 'autonoetic consciousness . . . is *expressible* . . . [as] episodic remembering' (Wheeler et al., 1997, p. 350), yet 'autonoetic awareness of the subjective past *constitutes* episodic retrieval' (p. 350) and 'autonoetic consciousness . . . *makes* episodic memory what it is' (p. 349). Earlier, 'autonoetic consciousness is the *capacity* that allows adult humans to mentally represent and to become aware of their protracted existence across subjective time' (p. 335) and it is likened to James' (1890) 'stream of consciousness'. Moreover, autonoesis is a 'special kind of consciousness that *allows* us to be aware of subjective time in which events happen. Autonoetic awareness . . . is *required* for remembering' (Tulving, 2002, p. 2) and 'three clues – sense of subjective time, autonoetic awareness, and self – point to three central *components* of a neurocognitive (mind/brain) system that makes mental time travel possible.' (pp. 2–3). Essay questions: Does autonoetic consciousness cause or enable episodic recall (or vice versa; or are they the same)? Are the definitions of autonoetic consciousness and of episodic recall circular? Does autonoetic consciousness depend on *representations* of the self and of time?

4. Also, episodic memories for recent events might be stored nearer the hippocampus than memories from childhood. There is, however, an active debate as to whether this occurs, or whether episodic memories remain permanently in the hippocampus as well as being incorporated into the cortex (Nadel and Moscovitch, 1997; Shastri, 2002; Eustache et al., 2004; Piolino et al., 2004). For semantic memories the evidence is more consistent with the transfer hypothesis (Side-box 9.2).

5. Jack and Shallice (2001) propose that output from the left frontal executive region is crucial for consciousness, since subjective experiences from our own point of view are the ones remembered as episodic memories (section 7.2.2.3). What is encoded into episodic memory in some sense is or contains (information about or a representation of) a conscious experience.

the storage of content, which could well be read out from another location under frontal control. (See also Side-box 9.2.)

Critique

One problem is how the system is controlled, that is, how the hippocampus 'decides' what to write into the cortex as long-term memory and how the hippocampus evaluates what is important. It seems that the hippocampus has a lot to do; it acts almost like a full person-in-the-head (cf. chapter 4), since it has to be able to solve the frame problem (section 4.3.4) and to make highly complex and sophisticated decisions. Now, it can be argued that the hippocampus has many connections with the frontal and the temporal lobes, and so it is just part of a complex system of decision making, goal evaluation and the strategic planning of behaviour. It also has strong connections with other limbic structures, including cholinergic input from the septum and a substantial output to the hypothalamus and anterior thalamus. So it is not just sitting at the top of the brain in isolation as shown in Figure 8.3; it actually comes under the control of large regions of the brain and is just one of the mechanisms that is used by those regions. At the very least it is an integral part of an executive network of regions.

The notion that memories are 'written into' the cortex from the hippocampus is also misleadingly behaviourist. It implies that the information is transferred across the brain without processing or transformation, like a thing that can just be moved unaltered. The memory 'trace' is just presumed to carry its intentionality along with it. In contrast, cognitive theories emphasize the structure and organization of the knowledge base. There could still be a wave of effect emanating from the hippocampus and spreading progressively across the cortex, but it would be a wave of restructuring and reorganization, not the movement of fixed items of information or templates from one place to another (see also section 9.3.4).

These theories all treat learning as the only source of knowledge; in other words they ignore the possibility of innate and prenatal structuring of the cortex and hence of the long-term memory base. Whether such inbuilt structure is merely scaffolding preparatory to learning, or whether it already includes contentful representations, is an ancient debate that I will not repeat here (see the discussions of teleological functionalism and intentionality in chapter 5, and of modularity in chapter 4 and sections 7.2.2.3, 7.2.3 and 7.3.4). The points can nevertheless still be made that cortical areas do show consistency in their order of development and vulnerability to genetic modification, both anatomically and physiologically, and that even neonates possess specific neuronal functionality, such as orientation selectivity in area V1 (O'Leary and Nakagawa, 2002; Sengpiel and Kind, 2002; Grove and Fukuchi-Shimogori, 2003; Kaas, 2004; Kennedy and Burkhalter, 2004).

The gradient theory is supported by two types of evidence. One is for transfer from hippocampus to cortex over a period of hours to days (the consolidation of memory during sleep) and the other is for changes over years (the conversion of episodic into semantic memory, and the increasing resilience of older memories; Side-box 9.2). However, it is almost certainly a simplification to lump the episodic and semantic memory systems together, particularly when we consider the underlying mechanisms (Side-box 9.2). For example, Conway (2001) breaks the episodic system up further. He reserves the term 'episodic' for memories up to twenty-four hours old that may be consolidated during sleep, and 'autobiographic' for the lifelong memory that provides a context or frame for individual acts of episodic recall. The former are supported by posterior parts of the cortex, the latter by anterior (see also Conway and Pleydell-Pearce, 2000).

Another problem for the theory is that it leaves open the role of arousal and the reticular formation (sections 7.2.1.3 and 8.2.2.3). Evidence that these mechanisms play a role in memory may come from the flashbulb effect (Side-box 9.4).

SIDE-BOX 9.4 AROUSAL AND THE FLASHBULB EFFECT

One question about the memory theories described in Side-box 9.2 is what role is played by arousal and the reticular formation (sections 7.2.1.3 and 8.2.2.3).[a] Witness, for example, the flashbulb effect. When we suddenly receive some dramatic and unexpected news we remember the entire episode as a unitary whole (Livingston, 1967a,b; Brown and Kulik, 1977; Conway, 1995). The memory is unusually vivid and long-lasting. The original example is: 'Where were you when you heard that President Kennedy had been shot?', but this has been superseded by more recent tragedies. For the next generation, the typical questions will include: 'Where were you when you heard about the destruction of the World Trade Center in New York?' and 'Where were you when you heard about or saw the pictures of the effects of the tsunami in the Indian Ocean?'. You can remember the place you were in, who was there, what they said, and even the colour of their clothes and other background details. The quality of that memory is somehow much more complete than those for most of the other incidents in your life. As well you know, when you sit in an exam trying to remember what you heard in a lecture or what you read on this page, you will not be able to evoke such clear and detailed images as given by flashbulb memories.

Could this effect be a consequence of generalized reticular arousal affecting the whole cortex (Livingston, 1967a,b; see side-box 8.3)? One might postulate that the reticular arousal is a consequence of a hippocampal decision;[b] yet that would leave the direct hippocampo-cortical pathways without a functional role. The same applies if the amygdala is the control centre rather than the hippocampus – a suggestion made by LeDoux (1998) to explain how we react to stimuli that evoke the emotion of fear. Certainly, fear-inducing stimuli are memorable and emotional arousal augments learning about those stimuli. LeDoux (e.g. pp. 296–299) suggests that while the cortex is processing the stimulus in working memory, the amygdala-cortical connections determine the identity of the emotional feeling, and the amygdala's activation of the reticular system (particularly the cholinergic mechanisms: section 8.2.2.3) creates and maintains arousal and attention to the stimulus. It therefore seems that the brainstem arousal systems could well play a role as necessary components permitting and amplifying cortical processing, presumably including the encoding of stimuli into memory.[c]

[a] In general, Kahneman (1973) argued, arousal determines the total amount of processing resources available for use in attention and allied cognitive processing.
[b] Livingston's (1967a,b) original speculation was that *limbic* structures evaluating the significance of an event for the self would activate the reticular formation and thus the forebrain. Later, Gray (1995), in reply to Newman, also added a connection from the hippocampal system onto the ERTAS (section 7.2.3.2), both at the reticular and the intralaminar levels. This, however, was merely postulated to switch attention to novel stimuli, rather than carrying content per se. See section 9.3.3.3 for more on Gray's model.
[c] As Panksepp (2005) points out, LeDoux's (1998) theory is neuronal behaviourist (see chapter 3). Some more sophisticated theories of emotion and its relationship to memory are reviewed by Conway and Pleydell-Pearce (2000).

9.2.1 Interim conclusion

The gradient model seems acceptable when applied to semantic memory, but the situation is less certain for episodic. Recent research has distinguished between several sub-types of episodic memory (imagistic versus conceptual, autobiographical general knowledge versus particular event memory, and so on) and the brain locations of the mechanisms involved are still hotly debated.

Overall, the cognitive modular and reorganizational models discussed so far operated initially purely at the psychological level, and have more recently become linked via brain imaging to particular regions and areas of the brain. Meanwhile, cellular research on long-term potentiation has elucidated the low-level mechanisms of plasticity and learning. What is lacking, however, is an intermediate or integrative theory as to how the cognitive and the cellular levels are linked. We need to be able to relate cellular models of synaptic growth and neural network circuit dynamics to the emergent properties of stimulus recognition and memory recall, plus their associated phenomenology. To this end, in the remainder of this chapter we need to go through some detailed ideas as to how pattern recognition could be achieved – by integrating memory with perception. These ideas carry implications first for the type of memory retrieval system we need, and second for the mechanisms of consciousness. In the next chapter we will thus be able to look at both the where and when of sensory awareness.

9.3 Long-term memory in perceptual awareness

9.3.1 Top-down knowledge in perception

The role of top-down knowledge in perception is well known and well established (e.g. Anderson et al., 1997). For example, Figure 9.2 shows Kanizsa's triangle and the Dalmatian dog to remind you of the standard demonstrations that long-term memory does interact with perception and aids the interpretation of sparse or inadequate sensory stimuli (which arguably we receive all the time, not just in black/white diagrams). Veridical perception depends upon our previous experience of Dalmatian dogs, triangles and such like. Gregory (1970) and Rock (1983) have supported this 'indirect' perception view that 'intelligent' processes of preconscious interpretation and synthesis pre-process the sensory stimuli before we become aware of them (let alone what they are or what they mean). This is one side of a long debate in psychology and philosophy. It can also be called 'constructivism', and is tied to cognitive theories that our minds build 'mental models' of the world.[6]

Where in the brain is the knowledge built in? In the previous section it was proposed that memory location may vary with the commonness of the stimulus. For example, visually

---

6. The opposite point of view is usually cited as Gibson's (though the Gestalt theorists were also non-constructivists), and is usually known as 'direct' perception. It states there is enough information in the input to guide us, and indeed that we do not need internal memory in order to perceive ('the world as an outside memory': O'Regan, 1992: see Side-box 8.5).

Figure 9.2 Examples of top-down knowledge in perception: the Kanizsa triangle and the Dalmatian dog.

seen edges would be represented (anatomically) in or near visual cortex and grandmothers and Paris nearer the hippocampus. Now, a common sight is of one object occluded by another nearer object. This may be the basis of the Kanizsa effect shown in Figure 9.2. Indeed, 'illusory contours' of the type that form the triangle can activate cells in area V2, and possibly in V1 as well (Peterhans and von der Heydt, 1991; Grosof et al., 1993; Sugita, 1999; Seghier et al., 2000; Lee and Nguyen, 2001; Ramsden et al., 2001). In addition, with prolonged training at detecting and analysing simple stimuli, long-lasting perceptual learning can occur at very early stages of sensory analysis, possibly including the primary cortices (Fahle and Poggio, 2002; Sowden et al., 2002; Fahle, 2004; Ghose, 2004). With training on complex objects, however, more anterior occipito-temporal areas are involved (Gauthier et al., 1999; Tarr and Gauthier, 2000; Side-box 6.2). The evidence so far is thus consistent with the gradient theory that 'memory' is inextricably built in to the 'perceptual' systems at multiple stages, the location depending on the complexity/rarity of the input.

9.3.1.1 Implications: two theories of consciousness

What, however, do we become aware of? There seem to be two views on this, known as the '*match*' and '*mismatch*' theories. These depend on presuppositions about what the sensory systems are doing, and why we have consciousness at all. Thus, according to the match theories, if we need to identify objects, people and situations in the outside world then matches between stimuli and memory will count as successes, and we should become aware of those. On the other hand, there are various limitations to this strategy. One is that an exhaustive identification of everything 'out there' would often take an enormous amount of processing. It therefore becomes more efficient to reduce the load by analysing only the most highly informative aspects of the sensory input. These include changes – across time, space and any other sensory dimensions (mathematically, the first derivatives) – and perhaps active suppression of redundant information about constant background conditions (Attneave, 1954; Barlow, 1959; Helson, 1964). Second, surprising stimuli are often the most important, so should be detected as quickly as possible (imagine a tiger jumping out from behind a tree). Third, if it becomes easier to see a common stimulus every time we perceive it, there will be positive feedback, that is, those memories will become ever-increasingly strong.

The alternative, mismatch theories – that we become aware only of the unusual events – are therefore emphasized by some thinkers, and are supported by much empirical evidence. If you encounter something new you stop to examine it, and if you hear a sudden noise (or if the clock stops ticking) you notice it (section 8.2.2.3). Let us therefore look next at some of the theories of both types: match and mismatch.

9.3.2 Sensory–LTM matching

First, we will briefly revise the historical origin of match theories in studies of cognition and pattern recognition. Then we examine some evidence, and in the final subsections, two types of putative mechanism will be examined and contrasted.

9.3.2.1 Template matching

The basic principle of template matching is that the input activates (somehow) certain parts of long-term memory that are, in some ways, similar: congruent, isomorphic or resonant.[7] This match may be in terms of critical features or overall Gestalt structure. The system then checks back down again to see which of the activated long-term memories is most similar to the input (cf. Marcel's theory: Side-box 9.1), and the result is then fed back up to correct the choice of long-term memory structures, stereotypes or templates.

This idea – that perception involves matching between sensory input and the existing long-term memory base – is fairly old. It goes back at least to MacKay (1956), Miller et al. (1960) and Milner (1974), while Mumford (1992), Ullman (1995), Grossberg (1999), Friston (2003) and others have put it forward more recently; for a brief but comprehensive historical

---

7. Early work in cognition emphasized that template matching is unlikely to occur because objects can be recognized from many perspectives, under different lighting conditions, from various distances and so on. The pattern of activity on the receptors will almost never match any single image held in memory. Therefore, some kind of analysis by component features (e.g. lines and edges) is more likely to work (Selfridge, 1959; Lindsay and Norman, 1977) – although this needs to be supplemented by creative synthetic mechanisms (Neisser, 1967, p. 190). Later, Fourier encoding theories were proposed (see Cavanagh, 1985; Daugman, 1985; MacKay, 1985; Pollen et al., 1985), as was analysis into higher-order shape primitives (Marr, 1982; Biederman, 1987) or surfaces (Marr, 1982; Koenderink, 1990). These all went some way towards meeting the original problems of template theory, which basically presumed a two-stage architecture for perception (a receptor array feeding directly into a memory store). Multi-stage models have now given us a more sophisticated understanding of pattern recognition mechanisms (section 6.4.3; Figure 8.3). Nevertheless, the term 'template theory' persists in some areas of research despite the questions of what is matched and how.

review see Pollen (1999). Some of these theories will be explicated in more detail below. For the moment, remind yourselves of some of the basic principles. For instance, even a simple closed loop (Figure 6.2a) resonates to inputs at a particular frequency, and could thus be described as constituting a long-term memory template for that frequency of input, physically embodied as the delay around the loop. More sophisticated examples were given in section 6.4.3 where we introduced autoassociative neural nets, chaos theory and attractors, and showed the way trained networks can settle down into a stable state. They may cycle around their final state for a while before reaching it, or approach it asymptotically, and indeed the end condition may be static or oscillatory. In all cases, the principle is the same: if a learned input appears the system 'reverberates' to it; the final state of the system depends on what is in the long-term memory (which under neural network theories just is the network's anatomical structure). In autoassociative nets, the template is built into a single neural net, but in heteroassociative nets it can exist at a higher stage of processing. Heteroassociative nets sometimes include a descending pathway carrying an 'error signal', at least during training ('back propagation'), and these multi-layer arrangements of cells therefore form a system that can also settle onto a single stable solution that exists across all the layers in the network.[8]

As for consciousness, one view is that the process of settling down is the process of becoming conscious, in other words, you are not fully aware of the stimulus until after the system has settled down to a stable state. What you are conscious of may then, under different theories, be the memory, the input, or some synthesis of the two. Alternatively, the process of settling down may require consciousness, since the effort involved in identifying the stimulus, particularly a novel or obscure stimulus, may demand it be the focus of attention.

9.3.2.2 Top-down knowledge affects area V1

One argument for template-matching is that templates stored in long-term memory affect perception. Neurophysiological evidence for such top-down signalling in perception has been given by Lee et al. (1998, 2002) and Lee and Nguyen (2001), building on the theory of Mumford (1991, 1992). They studied the activity of cells in the primary visual cortex of the monkey and demonstrated that the receptive fields change over time in the first few hundred milliseconds after the appearance of a stimulus. It is well known that Hubel and Wiesel (1959, 1962, 1968) demonstrated the existence of orientation-selective receptive fields, but current research in this field has emphasized the rapid adaptability of the properties of receptive fields, which change over a very short timescale (receptive fields are *dynamic*: e.g. Ringach et al., 1997, 2003; Gilbert, 1998). In this vein, Lee et al. (1998) report that the cells in V1 respond initially (forty milliseconds post-stimulus) with local feature and edge detection properties, à la Hubel and Wiesel (1968). However, twenty milliseconds later the cells start to show 'higher' properties, such as sensitivity to the surface borders and regional axes within which the local features are embedded. Thus these higher aspects are

---

8. One must distinguish the 'settling' that takes place during learning, where error signals adjust the weights of synapses until the whole network matches (in the sense of teleological functionalism: chapter 5) the environment, from the settling that takes place during testing, when instantaneous signals induce potentially resonant activity within the system.

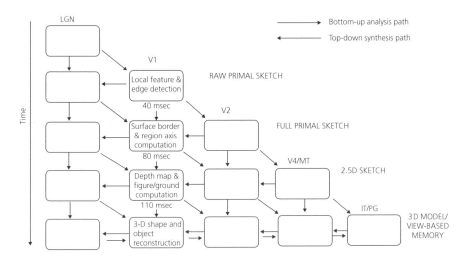

Figure 9.3 Development over time of an integrated pattern of activity across visual cortical areas. As a new stimulus is progressively analysed by successive areas, feedback alters the receptive field characteristics of cells in earlier stages, as explicated here for area V1. Time flows down the figure and spatial location from left to right. On the right are shown functional equivalents in the terminology of Marr (1982). From Lee et al. (1998).

computed after the local features. Then a little later arise depth maps and figure–ground segregation, and then three-dimensional effects. Thus, finally, the responses of the cells in V1 are influenced by the entire visual context, and not just by an independent feature, such as a vertical edge within what is traditionally called the 'receptive field', regardless of what is going on in the rest of the visual scene.

Thus Lee et al. found empirically that there are sensitivities in early visual cortex to aspects of the stimulus that are normally (i.e. according to serial models) regarded as analysed by higher regions where 'knowledge' of complex objects is stored, such as the sight of your grandmother or a cube. These medium and higher stages contain fundamental knowledge about the properties of the world such as figure–ground segregation, three-dimensional structure, and so on. This information feeds back down in the course of the first few hundred milliseconds to appear in V1 as well.

The model that Lee et al. (1998) put forward is summarized in Figure 9.3. Information about a new stimulus spreads progressively into the visual system over time (upwards in Figure 8.3, downwards in Figure 9.1, top left to bottom right in Figure 9.3!), but it also feeds back from V1 to LGN, V2 to V1 and so on at all stages. Over time the activities (i.e. the response properties) of cells in any area are influenced not only by the stimulus but also by activity coming back down from higher and higher regions in the system. For example, V1 cell properties change over a timescale of 40–110 milliseconds and more after their initial response (see Figure 9.3).[9]

9. The values obtained by Lee et al. were taken from studies of monkey brain, which is much smaller than human brain. To allow for the longer axon lengths and hence conduction latencies in humans, a good rule of thumb is to double the given time values to obtain estimates of the equivalent processing times in humans.

On the right of their diagram, Lee et al. have added Marr's (1982) terms for the different stages of vision, which Lee et al. try to map onto their model. Marr's is a bottom-up model (e.g. Figure 2.4d); he simply said that the image is analysed through a series of stages, which he called the raw primal sketch, full primal sketch, 2.5-D sketch and 3-D sketch.[10] It is now obvious that Marr's model needs to be improved by adding the top-down influences that guide and correct the earlier sketches. Note that Lee et al. also call the effects of the top-down influences 'synthesis', which ties their model in with the cognitive tradition of Neisser, Marcel and others (see Side-box 9.1 and section 9.3.4.2).

Critique

Lee et al.'s theory synthesizes a number of strands of research: into the physiology of single cells, the theory of dynamic oscillating systems, cognitive theories of memory–perception interaction and Marr's theory of how the visual scene has to be analysed. You have to picture the whole region from V1 right up to the infero-temporal cortex as settling down over the first few hundred milliseconds onto a complex and distributed state.[11] The representation of the entire stimulus object is a complex: a whole pattern of activity across all of the areas in the visual cortex (Figure 8.3). You cannot just say that a grandmother is represented by the firing of a single cell in the infero-temporal cortex (section 6.2.6.1)!

It is, however, confusing to see yet another function reduced to activity in the feedback connections, to which roles have now been attributed in carrying top-down signals from stores of (rarer) memories for use in stimulus recognition (this section), consolidation of learning (section 9.2), verification of short-term memories held at earlier stages (Side-box 9.1), top-down attention (Side-box 8.6), predictions about imminent input (section 8.4), and so on and so on (and we have yet to come to recall of memories in section 9.3.4 and imagery in section 10.2.1.2). Essay topic: do a theory reduction/unification (section 2.4.2.1) on these and show that they are really all aspects of a single underlying function!

There is also some debate over the relative roles of the feedback connections and the horizontal connections within a given area. The latter also create a network, which can settle onto a stable state and change the properties of individual cells over short time periods (for references see Side-box 7.6; Li, 2002; Raizada and Grossberg, 2003). These too may contain information that constitutes a relevant long-term memory for some property of the information entering that area of cortex.

9.3.2.3 Consciousness as synthesis between memory and input

Another famous theory that incorporates cycling between stages of analysis has been put forward by Edelman (1989, 1992; see Figure 9.4, taken from his 1992 volume summarizing

---

10. Curiously, we only become aware of the (contents of the) 2.5-D sketch, according to Jackendoff (1987); see section 10.2.1.3. This sketch describes the surfaces that we see and their orientations. The fundamental mechanisms of such a function are located by Grossberg in area V4 (section 9.3.2.4), but Lee et al. emphasize that their influence becomes distributed across the visual areas.

11. Koch (2004) says the frontal lobe must be involved too.

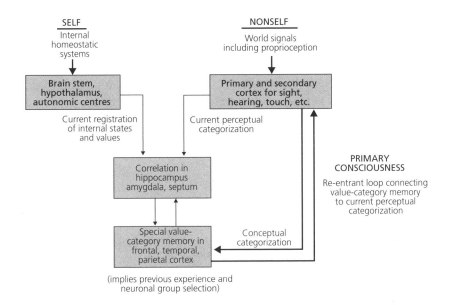

Figure 9.4 Edelman's scheme for the generation of 'primary' consciousness of the world. Inputs are given preliminary processing in the sensory cortices (top right) and then compared with memories stored in higher regions of cortex. If these 'correlate' then consciousness arises (thick lines at lower right). Meanwhile, limbic structures check whether the inputs correlate with internal needs and goals (top left), and if they do then new learning takes place. From Edelman (1992).

his previous three books).[12] His model of consciousness involves the idea that there are what he calls 're-entrant' loopings. Here let us just consider his explanation of 'primary' consciousness, which is awareness of the immediate sensory stimulus: of colours, edges, objects and so on. (His theory of 'secondary' consciousness will be covered in section 11.2.3.2.) He describes the primary and secondary sensory cortices as being surrounded by higher areas that, in some way, 'categorize' the stimuli. Higher regions store memories of these categories that are filtered according to their value. Value comes from the limbic/autonomic system. In the hippocampus a 'correlation' is calculated between the internal needs of the self and the external incoming stimuli, and these correlations determine the 'value category memory'. These memories are stored in the frontal, temporal and parietal cortex, broadly speaking, meaning the 'higher' regions of the cortex. These then have 're-entrant' feedback connections back down to the primary sensory cortices.

Edelman says that what the brain looks for is a correlation between the established memories and the incoming information. When there is a correlation, there follows some sort of reinforcement, a positive cycling, that may show up as 40 Hz oscillations (1989, p. 52). These rhythms involve the binding of information in the higher and lower parts and reflect

12. Edelman was an immunologist and has used analogous principles to explain the development of the brain (see his *Neural Darwinism*, 1987, concerning how the structure of the brain grows analogously to the way the immune system and species both develop – through competition between different functional groupings of units – here, nerve cells – which come to perform particular tasks). For his more recent ideas, see section 7.3.4.

synchronized firing across different regions of the brain. The re-entrant connections may be direct cortico-cortical, or they may go via the thalamus and/or the thalamic reticular nucleus – Edelman (1989, pp. 162–166) leaves the question open. But what he asserts clearly is that the synchronous, correlated firing *is* the physical basis of conscious awareness of the particular sensory stimuli. He is one of the few people to claim he has a mechanism that is not only necessary but is also sufficient for consciousness. He argues that *this* is the physical basis and all that is necessary is the re-entrant loop between the regions of higher and lower cortex.

Critique

Edelman's theory brings a welcome sense of the dynamic, adaptive and biological nature of brain function, and attempts to integrate many aspects of mental and neural activity. Yet there are still some problems with it. One is a lack of clarity over what is meant by the crucial processes of 'categorization' and 'correlation'. These terms seem to be based on an extended analogy with how the immune system grows to recognize antigens, and how cells recognize and compete or cooperate with each other in the developing body and brain. However, at the psychological, functional, informational level of object recognition – how memories arise and 'compete' with each other to find the best match to a stimulus – Edelman does not explain in any detail how the processes work.

Also, it is not obvious why mere correlation between memories and incoming input should lead to consciousness. Edelman asserts this is not just necessary but also sufficient for consciousness (e.g. 1989, pp. 151, 154; 1992, p. 119), but the reasoning behind this – how it explains what we now call the hard problem, for example – is obscure.[13] In addition, consciousness depends in part on the arousal systems (see sections 9.3.3 and 10.3). But Edelman does not mention these at all, merely stating that failed matches, or identified dangers, lead to a shift of attention via the basal ganglia and motor planning mechanisms (1992, p. 143).[14]

The title of his book, *The Remembered Present* (1989), also confuses, in that it seems to suggest we are aware in the present of memories of previous present instants. This implies that consciousness comprises the activated memories or templates in the long-term memory base (cf. sections 7.2.2.1 and 7.3.2). However, Edelman explicitly denies this (1989, p. 249) and claims his model explains the 'synthesis' of percepts (1989, pp. 82–86). Edelman regards the interaction between memory and input as generative of consciousness – indeed, he approvingly cites Marcel's (1983a,b) papers (see Side-box 9.1). As such he is part of the Neisser, Marcel, Mumford, Gregory and Rock tradition that posits that a new pattern is synthesized by the joint action of the incoming sensory input and the established knowledge base. We become aware of the new synthesis, which is not necessarily identical to anything already present in the memory store.

---

13. He probably just means to exclude homuncular or dualist explanations, but he overtly eschews any attempt to explain qualia (Edelman, 1989, p. 299).

14. His theory of attention (Edelman, 1989, pp. 201–207) bears resemblances to those of LaBerge and Cotterill (sections 8.3.2 and 8.4).

9.3.2.4 **Consciousness as resonance between memory and input**

Another deep analysis of the possible ways memory might interact with ongoing sensory input has been given by Grossberg. He has written at great length about how cognitive systems need to be organized to explain a wide variety of phenomena in perception, attention, memory and so on (e.g. 1980, 1987a,b, 1999, 2004). Although couched in neural terms, his central ideas are consonant with much that is commonplace in cognitive psychology. I will describe just one of his models, and then how he relates it to consciousness (Grossberg, 1999).

The basic circuit of Grossberg's 'adaptive resonance theory' is shown in Figure 9.5. The two rectangles F_1 and F_2 demarcate sets of neural units or nodes, each of which can carry a pattern of activity for a short period (hence they each act as short-term memories, STM). They are joined by adaptable connections; the semicircular terminals indicate plastic synapses that can be modified by learning. Indeed, long-term memory exists as the pattern of those synapses: in other words, as the connections between modules, rather than within any single module itself. The excitatory feedback connections from F_2 to F_1 are proposed to mediate expectancy and top-down attention. There is also an inhibitory circuit (shown on the left) that controls threshold and suppresses non-attended items in F_1. On the right of figure 9.5 is a comparator that compares the input with the current content of F_1 and initiates an arousal response if the correspondence is too low (for further explanation of its function, see below).

The aim of the circuit is to establish a stable state where there is resonance between F_1 and F_2. The goal is for positive feedback to set up a self-perpetuating excitatory loop, which can happen if the patterns of activity in the two rectangles, transformed through the patterns of connections between them, reinforce each other. This indicates a successful identification of the input, in that the codes for the stimulus are consistent throughout. The process is described as 'template matching' and implements the mechanism of preconscious inference first postulated by Helmholtz (Grossberg, 1980, pp. 2–3).

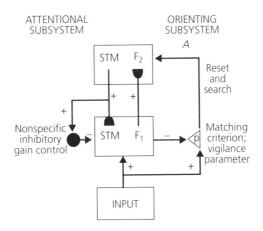

Figure 9.5 Basic adaptive resonance circuit of Grossberg (1999). The two short-term memory (STM) modules F are linked by adaptable synapses (semicircles). The gain control mechanism (at left) acts as a top-down attentional system, and the orienting system (at right) evokes a nonspecific arousal response if the contents of F_1 deviate too much from the input. From Grossberg (1999).

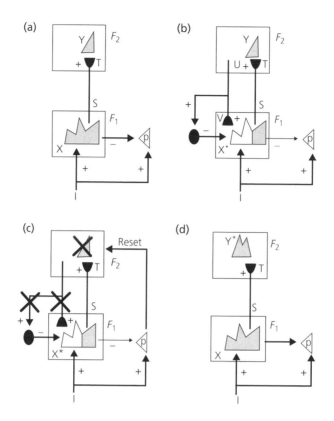

Figure 9.6 Operation of the adaptive resonance circuit of Grossberg (1999). In panel **a** an input evokes a template or prototype in F_2 that does not exactly match that in F_1. In panel **b** the descending process of verification alters the representation in F_1. In panel **c**, the new pattern in F_1 does not match the input sufficiently closely and the orienting system (Figure 9.5) cancels the content of F_2 – and hence the descending influences (crosses) – and a new search for a match is initiated. In panel **d** a new hypothesis has appeared in F_2 and the original pattern reinstated in F_1. The cycle then continues until a sufficiently close match is found and a state of resonance sets in. From Grossberg (1999).

Once established, the resonance enables learning to take place along the connection pathways; hence the system is self-organizing and adapts to its environment. If there is no other input, spontaneous habituation terminates the activity (Grossberg, 1999, pp. 15–16).

Figure 9.6 traces the course of events during recognition of a stimulus. The pattern of activity in F_1 evokes a pattern in F_2, where higher categories of entity are coded (Figure 9.6a). This is a first approximation or guess as to the identity of the stimulus. It is then (Figure 9.6b) fed back down to see if it evokes a pattern in F_1 that is consistent with the pattern already there. Grossberg (1999, pp. 10, 27) uses strikingly cognitive terminology here, saying that F_2 patterns can be interpreted as 'hypotheses' or prototypes that must be verified or tested against the earlier stages of processing (see Side-box 9.1 and section 9.3.4.2).

In Figure 9.6a and b, there is a mismatch. For small mismatches, resonance may still be established, but for large mismatches the drop in activity in F_1 disinhibits the arousal mechanism (on the right in the diagrams). This causes the contents of F_2 to be wiped out ('reset') and a new search through the hypothesis base is initiated (Figure 9.6c). The original pattern is reinstated in F_1 and a new pattern is produced in F_2 (the previous pattern still being suppressed; Figure 9.6d). The cycle then continues in the search for a sufficiently close match.

The two-layer schematic shown in Figures 9.5 and 9.6 is just a building block, and the principles can extend through an indefinite number of layers, corresponding to successive stages in cortical processing (Figures 8.3 and 9.3). Top-down influences can extend to very early stages of vision, possibly including V1 and the LGN (Grossberg, 1999, pp. 24, 33). Other anatomical localizations proposed by Grossberg include the infero-temporal cortex for attention (presumably because it is the end point of the ventral pathway) and the hippocampus for the detection of mismatch and the triggering of arousal.[15] The amnesia symptoms caused by hippocampal lesions can be explained by loss of the mismatch and resetting system (1999, pp. 32–33).[16]

An important contrast is with models in which the ascending or descending branches of the loop carry 'error signals' (e.g. back propagation models). Grossberg opposes this idea and emphasizes resonance as neural excitation. As a consonant match becomes established between the patterns in the two short-term stores F_1 and F_2, any error signal would decrease to zero, not persist!

Also, the top-down signals are interpreted purely as 'attention'. The effects of a stimulus feature's context (e.g. aiding figure–ground segregation, in early visual cortex) are implemented via the *horizontal* connections within a cortical area. This separation is necessary to enable both learning (which occurs when there is resonance with higher areas) and perception (dependent on lateral connections) to occur in the same network without new inputs overwriting the existing memory traces too easily (see Raizada and Grossberg, 2003). The theory is thus consistent with feedback models of attention such as those listed in Side-box 8.6, but not with the models of feedback as contextual guidance or template matching given in section 9.3.2.2.

To explain the phenomenology of visual perception, Grossberg (e.g. 1987a,b; 2004) has also developed a theory that two processes are necessary. One delimits the boundaries of objects (subsequent to figure–ground segregation and depth extraction) while the other fills in the surface colours and textures of the objects (subsequent to colour and brightness constancy mechanisms). The former may involve areas as early as V2, while the filling-in mechanism is attributed to V4. The latter resonates with infero-temporal cortex when complex shapes are recognized, since the latter area contains the codes for whole objects.

In general, conscious states are underlain by persisting resonant states in the neural architecture, of the type described above. Consciousness therefore (1) takes some time to develop, (2) persists for a period of time and (3) involves relatively intense neural activity. (The first two properties will be supported in section 10.3 and the last has been discussed in chapter 7.) However, not all resonant states are conscious ones, as exemplified by Grossberg's theory of vision. The startling truth is that we perceive the surfaces of objects but not their

15. Of course, other arguments point to the parietal and frontal lobes as the control centres for attention (section 8.3). The hippocampal reset proposal is similar to that made in some mismatch theories, as described in section 9.3.3.

16. This theory contrasts with the conventional wisdom that the hippocampus has a more executive function in controlling consolidation in the cortex: section 9.2.

boundaries. Edges are always invisible, unless there are different surface colours or luminances on either side of the edge; but even then we don't directly 'see' a contour tracing the edge. As Grossberg (e.g. 1999, pp. 37–39; 2004) says, Kanizsa triangles (Figure 9.2) have edge segments that are not visible[17] and the occluded segments of objects partially hidden behind other objects are not seen (although we can reach out and grasp them correctly, so the information is present in our brains). Grossberg explains why this may be useful (so we do not try to reach through solid objects to grasp those behind) but does not account for why the boundary resonances do not engender conscious perception. He admits there is still something extra needed for awareness, as well as resonance, but cannot say at this time what that is.

Critique

Grossberg's work is perhaps the most ambitious attempt to explain an enormous range of phenomena in vision and in psychology generally. I have only mentioned the central themes here, and leave his numerous long papers for you to peruse further. The price of such an explanatory range is a degree of neuronal behaviourism (chapter 3), in that functions are explained in terms of simple neuronal circuits without it being clear where and how phenomenology arises. The 1999 paper usefully makes clear the limitations in this regard and includes further relevant arguments such as why procedural memory does not involve consciousness (it is based on detecting mismatches, not matches). Grossberg's scientific method, however, veers between reasoning as to (1) how the brain must function in order for us to survive and learn in the world and (2) how the brain must be in order to generate the phenomena scientists have observed empirically, such as visual illusions. There is thus a mixture of rationalist and empiricist argumentation, with the latter giving the theory an ad hoc feel, as yet another bit of circuitry is tacked on to explain yet another illusion, over and over.[18]

The reader is still left wondering how the whole system functions after all the detailed circuits have been put into place. The principles of adaptive resonance theory are supposed to apply at more than one scale. Thus at times the whole visual system is treated as a single entity: the F_1 boxes in Figures 9.5 and 9.6 are said to hold 'feature detectors' and the F_2 boxes the hypotheses or prototypes. So far so good, but the 'attentional subsystem' (on the left of Figure 9.5) is related to the infero-temporal cortex and the 'orienting subsystem' to the hippocampus (1999, p. 32). Indeed the reset signal might be visible as the P300 wave in the EEG (Grossberg, 1980, pp. 24–25; section 8.2.2.3). All this implies a single global system. However, it is also proposed that the theory applies at a more micro-level, between successive areas of visual cortex. Resonances can be set up between areas V1 and V2, V2 and V3,

17. In support of the theory, there is evidence that illusory contours are analysed in V2 and perhaps V1: section 9.3.1.

18. In the terminology of philosophy of science, Grossberg is attempting a theory reduction (see section 2.4.2.1) from perception, attention, pattern recognition and memory to his adaptive resonance theory. In addition, he is proposing an ontological reduction (see section 2.2.2.1) of attention to activity in top-down pathways – but also of the transmission or transformation of a template pattern to activity in those same pathways. (He also reduces figure–ground segregation to the action of horizontal connections within an area.)

and so on (1999, pp. 24, 33; see also Raizada and Grossberg, 2003). That also makes sense; the 'attentional subsystem' is then duplicated at each stage, mediated by recurrent connections to earlier areas. These contacts modulate the gain of neurons in the target area's layer 4 (via top-down connections synapsing in its layer 6 and then a vertical relay up to layer 4). Presumably, global top-down attention can be transmitted to the earliest stages in a series of steps through all the cortical areas in the chain. But what happens to the orienting subsystem? It turns out that there is no separate feed-forward mismatch signal between successive areas of visual cortex in the model (see Raizada and Grossberg, 2003; Grossberg, 2004, p. 1630). Does this mean that any mismatch between any pair of cortical areas will result in a global reset signal being sent from the hippocampus to every area in the brain? This would surely be inefficient, since many pairs of areas might have settled correctly onto a locally resonant match. And how would the signal reach the hippocampus? Grossberg's assumption seems to be that the entire visual system must converge onto a stable state, else reset signals will blank the whole system and start the process of object recognition all over again. This is surely inconsistent with the incompleteness of the losses of visual function that can be found after localized lesions (visual agnosias, prosopagnosia, etc.) and with evidence for successful partial analysis along the visual pathways under many different experimental circumstances (e.g. from Marcel, 1983a, to Zeki, 2001).

The effect of the feedback signals is also ambiguous. First, the notion of 'resonance' between two systems means to most people their reciprocal excitation, such as in the simple loop of Figure 6.2a; system A excites system B and vice versa. This positive feedback makes their activity build up and persist. Indeed, Raizada and Grossberg (2003, p. 107) actually state: 'Mutual excitation between the top-down feedback and the bottom-up signals that they match strengthens, synchronizes and maintains existing neural activity'. Such loops were, however, explicitly frowned upon by Crick and Koch (1998b) as liable to go out of control (see chapter 8). At least one 'modulatory' synapse was demanded somewhere in the loop. Now, Grossberg does indeed describe the descending connections in his 'adaptive resonance theory' as modulatory! What exactly does this mean, however? They should not arouse the lower-stage cells to the point where they fire – or at most the cells should fire too weakly to interact effectively through horizontal connections with other cells in the same area (Raizada and Grossberg, 2003, p. 102). At times their effect is described as weakly facilitatory and at others multiplicative.[19] Yet these are not the same thing. Crucially, multiplicative synapses will not sustain activity in a loop once the stimulus is removed; they will only enhance the responses to a steady input (by increasing the gain of the cells).[20] Additive inputs may, however, be strong enough to sustain activity without a persisting stimulus (following a brief flash of light, for example). It is therefore important to be clear which type of 'modulation' is meant.

Finally, it is proposed that the reset signal in Figures 9.5 and 9.6 not only initiates a new search for a template in F_2 but also resets the F_1 pattern to its original form. How is this to be

19. The model enhances responses at an attentional focus and suppresses those in a surround, so subtractive or divisive effects are also called for.

20. Think of a straight line passing through the origin of a graph of response as a function of input: $y = kx + b$, where b is initially 0. Response to a given input can be increased by shifting the line up (increasing the value of b, i.e. adding a constant to all responses) or by increasing the slope factor k (i.e. multiplying all responses to positive inputs). When the multiplication factor is very high, the

done if the stimulus was brief, and so is no longer available to reset F_1 (and what stops the input resetting F_1 if it is persistent)? No allowance is made for the storage and re-readout of the original input pattern into F_1. Such a process may be possible in a chain of short-term stores, but even Marcel (1983b) recognized the need for separate additional persisting 'records' at each stage along the pathway (Side-box 9.1).

9.3.2.5 Interim conclusion

There is a commonality among template matching theories, not only in that they all propose that stimulus object recognition is mediated by top-down matching between input and long-term memory, but also in their incorporation of reverberant or iterative cycling towards a steady state and (in most theories) the postulation that an interpretation or compromise must be made between input and long-term memory, at least when there is a (sufficiently small) discrepancy between them. However, there are major differences between these theories that should not be glossed over. Although this is not the place to review the mechanisms in detail, it is worth noting that they vary along a number of parameters (see Side-box 9.5).

SIDE-BOX 9.5 TEMPLATE MATCHING THEORIES

Template matching theories can be characterized by the assumptions that have been made as to the settings or values of a number of 'parameters' that together constitute the theories. These N parameters are analogous to the N axes of an N-dimensional search space within which the solution to a problem is to be found (here, the problem is to find the correct theory).[a]

For template matching theories, some of the relevant parameters are:

1. Is the end state stable (i.e. unit activity level is constant) or oscillatory – in other words, what exactly does 'reverberation' mean? Some systems oscillate for a while before settling into the end state; so how is that state defined? In other words, how stable does the network have to be to be 'stable'? For example, is settling into a stable state necessarily 'reverberation'? Consider Figures 6.10 and 6.11; a network can settle into a singularity or it can enter a closed cycling loop. Both are 'stable', but in one the cells do not change their firing over time and in the other there is a rhythmic oscillation or a binary alternation of activity. Both may maximize the match (minimize the error) between the template and input; but these two outcomes have different implications. For example, how can rapidly flickering stimuli be represented (Blake and Yang, 1997; Shadlen and Movshon, 1999)? Also, are slowly oscillatory states the basis for our alternating perception of ambiguous stimuli such as the Necker cube and Rubin vase? The meaning of the term 'reverberation' is thus ambiguous and needs to be specified each time it is used, at least as regards the frequency of oscillation.[b] (There are implications here for the latency of perceptual awareness: see section 10.3.)

continues

---

effect is similar to a logic gate: the cell might fire, for example, only when both inputs, the driver and the multiplier, are active. In this case the cell would function as an AND gate (McCulloch and Pitts, 1943). Multiplicative synapses could facilitate the effects of any spontaneous activity in the input. But the cortex is notoriously almost silent when no stimuli are present, so such a mechanism would not have much effect beyond the LGN to V1 step.

2. Is the comparison between input and stored template carried out at the higher or the lower stage, or both? In other words, which locus's contents change in order to form and hold the compromise or synthesized solution if the match is not exact? In Figure 9.6, for example, the higher location holds LTM templates that do not change in the short term (though they adapt gradually, with learning). Most importantly for us, *which site determines the content of consciousness* (or if awareness and performance are based on a blend of the contents of both stores, where and how does that happen)?

3. Are the 'templates' or stimulus categories stored as prototypes, a set of exemplars, or what (Lamberts and Shanks, 1997; section 9.2)? Do they have information about the variance within the category, or examples of extreme or borderline cases that define the boundaries of the category (Mumford, 1992)?

4. Are there short-term memory stores alongside each of the processing stages (e.g. Marcel, 1983b; Mumford, 1991, 1992) or not (Grossberg, 1999)?[c]

5. Are the messages that are transmitted between the stages full contentful representations, or just 'residuals' (i.e. the differences between input and memory, unexplained features of the input, errors in the match)? Some theorists call the top-down signals 'predictions'[d] and the bottom-up 'residuals' (Mumford, 1992; Rao and Ballard, 1999; Friston, 2003; Kersten et al., 2004), and the network is supposed to converge onto a state where the bottom-up signals disappear.[e] This, however, seems inconsistent with physiological observations of rapid-onset sustained firing at stages high along the sensory pathways (Koch and Poggio, 1999), and other theorists prefer a reverberatory model in which presumably the bottom-up and top-down signals are both full representations, even if these are in some way 'complementary' rather than simply echoic (Grossberg, 1999; Pollen, 1999), perhaps with a separate pathway for a one-bit error signal (Grossberg, 1999).[f]

6. Are the connections between stages simply transmitting representations or actually processing them? For example, Mumford (1992) says they translate between the (Fodor-style) languages spoken in each of the two modules they connect, and Ullman (1995) refers to them as performing transforms or mapping functions. In the terminology of computational functionalism (section 2.5), they implement rules applied to the symbols held in the stages. Grossberg (1999), however, says that the pattern of connections actually contains the long-term memory templates (in accordance with neural network theory: section 6.4.3).

7. Are the connections between stages transmitting information or just activation? Is the functionally important factor the pattern of (predictive or residual) activity held in the processing stages and travelling along the pathways between them, or merely the amount of excitation (neural facilitation or modulation) passing along the connections? It seems to me that many theorists are trying to gloss over the gap between explanations couched at the psychological level and those at the physiological. Everyone seems a bit too ready and eager to make reductive identities across levels. Thus top-down connections are said to carry predictions, hypotheses, templates and other information-bearing representations, yet at the same time they are supposed to excite the target areas and may set up reverberatory activity (presumably in proportion to their 'strength'). Now in principle they could do both: the cells carrying a pattern of activity can all co-vary in how strongly they fire (within their dynamic ranges), and indeed Grossberg (1999) claims that the messages are both informationally structured (patterned) and excitatory so that they can set up resonance. But there are two different mechanisms here: if the stimulus is identified it is because the patterns match, not because there is resonance. Under some

continues

SIDE-BOX 9.5 continued

theories a pattern match will also set up an excitatory resonance loop – and speculatively that resonance might even give the system an extra quality or property such as generating (or being the neural basis for) conscious awareness. But under other theories the match is sought by using an error-cancelling mechanism and reverberation does not occur after identification has been successfully completed – although other properties may arise then, such as prolonged stability (constant firing), that might instead be the basis of awareness we are looking for (section 10.3.1). Therefore it makes a difference to theories of consciousness exactly how the top-down matching mechanism works.

[a] The classification of models according to their location in such a theory space is explained further in Rose and Dobson (1985, 1989).
[b] For example, it has been suggested that the cycles might occur within the gamma range ('40 Hz'), either at steady state (Edelman, 1989) or during settling onto a final state (Crick and Koch, 1998a, 2003). It would then seem natural to assume that each cycle is an iteration of activity between the higher and the lower area. However, 40 Hz oscillations are emphatically synchronous, that is, in exact phase with each other, over large regions of cortex, including between anatomically defined areas (e.g. Engel et al., 1991; Engel and Singer, 2001). They are therefore not generated by alternating interaction between the input and template as described in the matching models in section 9.3.2. Such an arrangement would be revealed by the lower and higher areas firing in antiphase.
[c] In this book I am using the word 'stage' to refer to a stage of processing. Obviously, this should not be confused with the very different notion of a stage held by the global workshop theories (section 7.2.3), but most importantly these stages should not be confused with the records or short-term stores that might run alongside the main processing stream, as in Marcel's theory (Side-box 9.1). The problem is that some theorists assume a single chain of processing with persisting representations at each stage; therefore the representations may each be described as existing within a short-term store. There is no consistent terminology for distinguishing between these two possibilities. I will use the word 'stage' to refer to the container of a representation that is along the main processing stream, and 'store' or 'short-term memory' for the container of a persisting representation. These may be the same thing, depending on the theory!
[d] These predictions are about the details that will be found within the present input if the current hypothesis as to its identity is correct. They should not be confused with the 'predictions' about the effects of current motor outputs on future sensory input mediated by efference copy (section 8.4).
[e] For example, Rao and Ballard (1999) and Deco and Schürmann (2000) posit that the descending connections are inhibitory, thus implementing a subtractive form of negative feedback.
[f] Ullman (1995) argues that as there is a series of stages between the top and the bottom of the analysis pathway, the whole system can settle onto the most stable state possible (a local entropy optimum) without necessarily iterating cyclically.

Finally, it is instructive to compare these theories of object recognition with those of attention, which were described in section 8.3. In both, recurrent or feedback pathways were ascribed functional roles that at first seem very different. Yet there may be a common theme, particularly for bottom-up attention (a novel stimulus 'catching your eye') and object recognition (what is that novel stimulus?). The same processes of checking back to verify hypotheses or choices of template may also be used in top-down attention, where the complete idea or search target is initially generated internally (by the ongoing flow of thought, or by a verbal command such as 'look for the Dalmatian dog' that evokes an internally stored image of what input the sensory system should be receiving) rather than by an initial upward sweep of analysis of a new sensory signal that has to stimulate by itself a preliminary guess as to the identity of the object. In all cases, the subsequent top-down checking of the input may be a common mechanism. Indeed, several theorists have tried to explain both attention and object recognition as manifestations or emergent properties of the same neural model (e.g. Grossberg, 1999; Deco and Schürmann, 2000; Deco and Rolls, 2004; Hamker, 2004a,b). How successful they are remains another topic for an essay (see Side-box 9.6 for a preliminary discussion)!

SIDE-BOX 9.6 TOP-DOWN PROCESSES: ATTENTION OR RECOGNITION?

How do the roles for feedback posited in this chapter relate to those ascribed in section 8.3, where they were suggested as the neural bases for selective attention? The reductive identity suggested by top-down attentional (e.g. searchlight) theories (section 8.3.1) was that higher stages could predict (facilitate, seek) input by excitatory modulation of particular places in the brain. This might be, for example, a locus within a saliency map (or in, say, area V1 directly) if the location of the stimulus in extrapersonal space was its defining feature, or a locus in area V4 if a particular colour (e.g. 'red') was the relevant attribute, and so on. The searchlight beam could be broad or narrow, but it is *non-specific* in activating cells within its focus. On the other hand, bottom-up attention seems similar to the recognition mechanisms discussed in this chapter. In both, a first sweep up the system has to drive some kind of identification mechanism that can be used for evaluation of the stimulus. This may then have further effects, that could include those leading to conscious awareness of the stimulus.[a] The criteria used by the evaluation mechanism differs, however, between the two theories.

In bottom-up attention theories, the criterion is stimulus salience or importance.[b] If salience is high, there follows further allocation of processing resources that could have a variety of top-down effects, such as amplifying the input and/or extracting more detail from earlier stages. There may also be analysis of the representation to further depth at 'higher' stages such as executive mechanisms and motor planning and output.

In recognition theories, the evaluation criterion is identifiability (the accuracy of a template or preliminary hypothesis). Whether the stimulus is 'important' or not is another matter (one dealt with in section 9.3.3). The evoked hypothesis may (either automatically or attentively) be checked back top-down, i.e. the input may be amplified and analysed in further detail. This may lead to sustained activity, either throughout the system (resonance) or only at the stage where the successful representation is held (e.g. at a high stage if an error-suppressing algorithm is used to cancel the input[c]).

Despite this difference in evaluation criteria, are the subsequent effects so similar that we could effect a theory reduction, equating bottom-up attention and template matching models of recognition? After all, in both cases a sudden stimulus enters the system and recurrent top-down pathways may subsequently be activated. But there is at least one difference. Recurrent attention (i.e. any late top-down cycles evoked by bottom-up stimuli) is a relatively blunt instrument, having a *non-specific* effect on its target (at the neural level); thus it is typically described as modulating or facilitating the responses to any activity coming into its target area of brain along the afferent axons to that area.[d]

Identification theories, however, require more precise effects, since the *content* of the template must be transmitted and received (either verbatim or transformed in some way). Suppose for the sake of argument that a template/hypothesis is a pattern of activity within a small neural network (i.e. assuming a low-level neural net is the appropriate level at which to describe the representation; section 6.4.3). Sending this down the sensory pathway involves cell-by-cell accuracy in turning some cells on and others off in the lower, target area.

Thus attention cannot use the same top-down processing system as object recognition by template matching, as some workers have suggested it does (e.g. Grossberg, 1999; Deco and Schürmann, 2000; Deco and Rolls, 2004; Hamker, 2004a,b). Note, however, that in principle these functions might be extremes of a continuum: attentional modulation could be more or less selective for particular cells or cell types within its focus, rather than totally nonspecific in its effect.

In sum, there are philosophical, psychological, cybernetic and neural issues that remain to be solved in comparing the theories of attention and stimulus recognition by template matching.

continues

SIDE-BOX 9.6 continued

[a] One theory is that *primitive* awareness can arise from the bottom-up sweep. For vision, this comprises the 'gist' of the scene (Hochstein and Ahissar, 2002; Koch, 2004, p. 165), i.e. the basic layout and feature groupings/bindings, parsed and summarized in a preliminary way. The gist could also be called the initial 'hypothesis'. Later, awareness of additional aspects arises as recurrent processing converges the system to a more precise and more stable interpretation of the input (Bachmann, 2000; Hochstein and Ahissar, 2002; Kitazawa, 2002; section 10.3.2.2). This process of interpretation continues to separate and crystallize the input into independent 'stimuli' (objects, background, etc.) and then to analyse sub-components and features if necessary.

[b] Koch (2004) says that salience is contrast between whatever stimuli are incoming at the time – the most different is the most salient. A saliency map might lie at a stage in the sensory system at which retinotopic coding exists; but other mechanisms may exist, for example to compute salience between object representations. If common stimuli are analysed early, as suggested by the gradient model of memory given in Side-box 9.2, then perhaps important common stimuli will be picked out at low stages of processing but important rare stimuli will be selected at high stages.

[c] In some theories the top-down signal is designed to *inhibit* the lower stages (e.g. Rao and Ballard, 1999; Deco and Schürmann, 2000), rather than excite them as in many attention theories (e.g. LaBerge, 1995; Koch, 2004). Other attentional theories emphasize the inhibition of unwanted signals rather than or as well as facilitation of the wanted ones. The object recognition theories do not have this distinction between focus and surround – although 'competition' may exist between templates at the higher level – so the subtractive effects postulated by Rao and Ballard and Deco and Schürmann should presumably be compared with events postulated for the 'focus' described in attentional theories.

[d] Top-down attention theories seem to assume that what is needed is activation (priming, modulation) of a single locus in the target area. This might be in the saliency map for location, a visual categorization area (Side-box 6.2) for objects such as Dalmatian dogs, or V4 for a colour such as red. Such theories assume that stimuli are encoded by their location within the brain (e.g. Koch, 2004, thinks columns of like-firing cells are the relevant form of 'explicit' encoding), or by particular cells firing (not necessarily grandmother cells, but a small group: section 6.2.6.1). However, the assumption that content is given by brain locus is a major philosophical trap. It is by no means clear why particular cells, columns and areas underlie the phenomenology that they do (sections 6.4.3.3 and 7.3.4; Rose, 1999a).

9.3.3 Sensory–LTM mismatching

In contrast to the theories in the previous section, others see consciousness as evoked when there is a mismatch between stimulus and expectation or previous experience. Novel events and objects in the world are clearly of more interest – potentially of greater significance – than steady-state situations.

9.3.3.1 The orienting response

To begin, revise section 8.2.2.3 where we looked at the classical idea that unexpected or rare stimuli cause arousal, activating the reticular system (e.g. Sokolov, 1963) and generating a P300 wave. If the background is boring and is always there, like the sound made by a ticking clock, the touch of your clothes on your skin or the sight of the walls of your room, then it fades from your awareness as the relevant sensory system habituates to the predictably repeated stimuli or continuous level of input. Those theories lead to the idea that consciousness correlates with or comes in after a mismatch. What you become particularly aware of are the unexpected stimuli or changes in stimulus intensity.[21]

So where are the relevant templates stored and where is consciousness generated? Some theories suggest that the templates of common stimuli are stored in the sensory systems,

21. Indeed, constant levels of stimulation are filtered out very early: the retina, for example, where lateral inhibition acts to reduce low-frequency transmission (e.g. Enroth-Cugell and Robson, 1966). This accords with the general trend for redundancy reduction (Attneave, 1954; Barlow, 1959; Helson, 1964).

perhaps even built in to them, as described in sections 9.2 and 9.3.2. Other theories suggest that templates are transmitted backwards from high stages such as the frontal lobes, as in motor chauvinist theories that the motor system is the central formulator of top-down hypotheses about the stimulus (section 8.4). In the next two subsections I describe a couple of other interesting models, both of which suggest it is the *hippocampus* whose top-down effects play a role in determining conscious awareness. The first theory suggests that the hippocampus predicts sensory inflow and is part of a network containing the site of consciousness. The second says that the hippocampus both predicts the effects of actions and chooses the next action to take, and although it does not generate consciousness within itself, it directs the cortical mechanisms of subjective experience.

9.3.3.2 Hippocampal memory maps as predictors of input

Imagine you are strolling along the path from your favourite watering hole back towards your cave. Suddenly the hairs on the back of your neck stand up, and you realize there are tiger footprints heading in the same direction along the path. These have attracted your attention much more forcefully than any of the normal and familiar sights along your routine route. Such a role for spatial memory in keeping track of your location within the environment and detecting deviations from the norm is fundamental, and may be the primary function of the hippocampus (O'Keefe, 1985). The 'place cells' there fire whenever an animal is at a certain point in its environment, at least in a familiar locale such as the animal's home territory (O'Keefe and Nadel, 1978; O'Keefe, 1993). Given a background knowledge of what to expect, novelty will be more easily detectable and discriminable from the humdrum. Even the effects of self-movement can be predicted: the response of the hippocampal population of cells indicates where a moving animal will be in the near future (Wilson and McNaughton, 1993; Frank et al., 2000; cf. also Maguire et al., 1997).[22] In humans, such spatial mapping functions may be restricted to the right hippocampus while the left performs a more semantic or narrative role.

O'Keefe (1985) went on to suggest that such maps of the environment, held in the hippocampus, are responsible for our background awareness of the world. Most importantly, it is mismatches or failed predictions that become the focus of attention. (His conception follows quite closely the distinction between focal and ambient or fringe attention discussed in section 8.3.) O'Keefe went on to suggest a holographic field theory of consciousness (see section 6.2.4) based around the local theta rhythms generated in the

---

22. Arbib (1972) introduced an analogy between vision and making an animated cartoon. First a 'cel' (a transparent sheet of celluloid) is laid down on which the background is drawn: the sky, ground, clouds, trees and so on. Then other cels are overlaid on which are drawn objects closer and closer to the foreground: particularly characters and other objects that move – in other words, that change from frame to frame. The same background can remain in place throughout any given scene, and only the foreground cels have to be redrawn to express each instantaneous change in the movie. Now imagine moving from one room in your house into another room: there is a change of background cel, slotted into your hippocampus as the change of environment occurs. If someone has placed a new object in the room, or hung a new picture on the wall, it draws your eye towards it. Even when you know the new object is there, it still takes several days to become used to the new layout and to cease noticing it every time you go into that room.

septo-hippocampal system. However, he did not give any detail as to how this field gives rise to the particular contents of any instant of awareness.

9.3.3.3 The hippocampus as comparator

Gray (1995, 2004; Gray and McNaughton, 2000) has also emphasized the mismatch aspect of brain function, and in particular identified the hippocampus as mediating this overall role. He describes the fundamental role of the hippocampus as associating items of memory with their contexts (items become 'tagged' with where and when, i.e. under what circumstances, they occurred: Gray, 2004, p. 207). The context has both spatial and temporal dimensions that give us (1) awareness of an image-like visual scene, but also the ability to imagine navigation in 3-D allocentric space (i.e. in coordinates centred on the world rather than only on one's own point of view), (2) the recall of episodic memories (which may also involve imagery: section 9.2) and (3) the meaningfulness of the items in memory.

A role for the hippocampus in anxiety is also added. The linking together of stimuli, responses and goals is central to brain function, but often there will be conflict between alternative courses of action. A '*comparator*' mechanism is therefore necessary to decide which action plan will be the one put into effect. The hippocampus does this by inhibiting all but one of the candidate sensorimotor plans. If necessary (i.e. if the choice is difficult to resolve because more than one goal is equally important), the hippocampus can also enhance negative associations (I presume this means increasing 'anxiety') so that the action associated with the least negative outcomes can be discovered and chosen. There may also be an increase in general exploratory behaviour to try to find another way of resolving the conflict.

At the same time, Gray describes the comparator's function as to detect the occurrence of errors, that is to say, failed predictions, or mismatches between the effects that the internal mechanisms 'expected' motor activity to bring about and the actual feedback from the environment (e.g. Gray, 2004, p. 77; cf. section 8.4). Gray emphasizes the latency of this feedback and the parcellation of processing (perhaps by the hippocampal theta rhythms) into units of at least a hundred milliseconds; thus information about errors is substantially delayed relative to the emitting of behaviour.

Consciousness is posited to depend on the output of the hippocampal comparator mechanism. This output will be increased if there is conflict between equally strong demands for action, or mismatch between expectation and the result of action. (Activity important for ongoing motor programs can also be allowed through even if there is no conflict: Gray, 2004, p. 80.) The output is not all-or-none: there are degrees of mismatch and corresponding degrees of attention and awareness to the relevant situation. Consciousness is correspondingly delayed relative to stimulus onset (by at least a hundred milliseconds after the arrival of sensory activity at the hippocampus? See also section 10.3).

Gray's theory of conscious experience is more cognitive than his neural theory. He supports constructivist approaches, seeing qualia as elements in a virtual reality display – a 'sketch' inside the head. Just as someone might make a sketch of St Mark's Square in Venice that can be used to aid recall of the cathedral, so conscious images are constructed to help our brain mechanisms to recall events and items.[23] The man-in-the-head problem is avoided because it is unconscious brain mechanisms that are looking at the sketch, not a conscious homunculus. He suggests a kind of dual-aspect monism[24] in that phenomenology is the result of our unconscious modules looking at the sketch, and physical brain processes are what outsiders see when looking at the same sketch.[25]

How does this relate back to his neural theory of hippocampal function? Although he starts by equating consciousness with (some of) the outputs of the hippocampal comparator system, his arguments lead him to conclude that these merely determine and select the contents of consciousness, which are actually generated in other areas, such as sensory cortex.[26] He makes the provocative assertion that 'the contents of consciousness are purely and entirely perceptual' (e.g. Gray, 2004, p. 89) and seems to support Zeki's (1998) hypothesis that individual areas of visual cortex such as V4 can generate qualia such as colours on their own.[27] In addition he suggests the hippocampus may generate experiences of episodic recall (although, as mentioned in section 9.2, perceptual imagery is an important part of episodic recall, especially in acts of 'remembering' as opposed to 'knowing').

Critique

Gray's theory is based on empirical as well as philosophical arguments, and as such it is broad, eclectic and innovative. Although much of the introduction to hippocampal function is based on rat behaviour and couched in the terminology appropriate for describing experiments on rats, the inclusion of data from human lesion studies and perceptual experiments broadens the database from which the theory is derived. It is especially refreshing to see honest attempts at self-criticism, with the theory's weaknesses, inconsistencies and failures pointed out and discussed. For example, Gray attacks functionalism

---

23. Qualia are generated automatically, bottom-up, without attention or other top-down processes. Qualia do not need to be integrated into complex wholes to have intentionality. Gray admits changing his mind about this in the course of writing his last book, however (2004, p. 318; on pp. 90–91 he assumed qualia always have intentionality, but by the time he wrote the final chapter he concluded they need not). See also sections 11.2.1.1 and 11.2.1.2.

24. His dual aspect theory (Gray 2004, p. 111) is not the same as that classically defined, where matter and mind are two aspects of the same thing that manifest themselves as different substances under different circumstances (section 1.2). See also Panksepp (2005) for another dual-aspect stance similar to Gray's.

25. Following Velmans (2000), Gray describes the inner point of view as that taken by 'the experiencing subject' (2004, p. 111), but I think it makes more sense to say it is taken by unconscious mechanisms – especially since that is the point Gray makes two pages earlier (p. 109)!

26. Hippocampal lesions do not destroy conscious experience. However, they may induce attentional lability because the comparator mechanism cannot switch sensorimotor schemata appropriately – as happens also in schizophrenia.

27. Gray criticizes Zeki on the grounds that blindsight and hemineglect involve losses of perceptual awareness (2004, pp. 227–228). However, Zeki's (2001) theory that interactions along a processing stream are necessary obviates, I think, Gray's criticism without detracting from Gray's hypothesis that consciousness is generated in the sensory cortices and not just in the hippocampus.

vituperously, but admits there is a functionalist basis to his comparator theory. The existence of consciousness in patients with hippocampal lesions leads him to modify his theory to say that the comparator depends on a wider system of structures than just the hippocampus. Qualia were initially assumed to be generated top-down by the hippocampal output, but later came to be viewed as bottom-up products of sensory cortex. Although these changes may seem confusing and inconsistent, they do reflect the state of uncertainty in this field, where there is a lot to learn and theories are underconstrained by data.

The metaphor of consciousness as an internally constructed 'sketch' of the world is designed to avoid dualism and epiphenomenalism, but is presented modestly, without the dogmatism common in this field. The idea is intriguing, and fits with modern metaphors for brain science,[28] but the notion that the sketch is constructed in a 'medium' does leave questions about the nature of that medium, which is left unexplained.

Gray does not mention the arousal systems, and indeed he criticizes brainstem theories (section 7.2.1.3) and concentrates on cortical involvement in phenomenology. He instead posits that the hippocampus directs the cortical generation of experience via hippocampo-cortical fibres or via the basal ganglia and thalamic reticular nucleus (2004, p. 211). Nevertheless, his emphasis on mismatch as the prerequisite for much of our conscious experience fits with much empirical evidence as well as common sense.

9.3.3.4 Interim conclusion

In sum, there are a number of arguments pointing to the conclusion that when incoming information does *not* match the structure that is built in as memory, *that* is what initiates the genesis of conscious awareness of the sensory stimulus. How those subsequent processes give rise to awareness is, however, left open and remains to be explained. The most obvious compromise would be that after mismatch signals have initiated and directed arousal and attention, the content of consciousness is settled by another method. However, this cannot be one of the match-seeking methods, because these only really explain the perception of items for which there exists already a sufficiently similar template or long-term memory. Instead, some creative process would appear to be called for, perhaps one that combines fragments or features in some novel way. Such processes are often hinted at in the match theories, but little by way of detail is given about how this works for immediate perception of the never-before-encountered stimulus (although an explanation may be given of how long-term learning is initiated, leading to the formation of a new template).

However, immediate perception of new and of old stimuli does not seem so different, at least in terms of sensory awareness. Consider meeting a stranger and a familiar person; their faces appear the same, visually speaking. The familiar person has an extra 'aura', because they evoke in us additional knowledge (what we know about them), emotional

---

28. Metaphors have guided our understanding of the brain through the ages (Side-box 3.5). The most complex technology of the day has normally provided the current model for neuroscience. For instance, in modern times we have seen hydraulics (Descartes), telephone switchboards (behaviourism), computers (cognitivism) and now virtual reality games (Revonsuo, 1995). One should perhaps add that consciousness as a fictional narrative is also a metaphor, as in the multiple drafts model (Dennett, 1991) and in social and linguistic constructivist theories (section 6.2.2.1).

reactions (whether we like or dislike their personalities) and so on, but their skin, eyes, and indeed the general appearance of their visage are not *qualitatively* different. Accordingly, might it be the case that *all* purely sensory awareness is based on a single mechanism, namely, creative construction? Indeed, there are theories that all cognition (including acts of recognition and recall) – and thus perhaps all of consciousness – are constructions. This will be the topic of the next section.

9.3.4 Recall as reconstruction of perception

9.3.4.1 The effort after meaning

Many of the theories presented previously as to the role and mechanisms of top-down memory in perception claim to be consistent with the idea that memory is reconstructed. The principle source for this idea is the work of Bartlett (1932) on memory recall itself. He gave people stories to remember, and asked them to reproduce them later – not once, but at more than one interval. The main finding was that, over time, the stories transmuted in certain ways: they became shorter and they distorted in such a way as to increase the sense of the story – sense as understood by the teller (Bartlett called this process of rationalization 'effort after meaning'). For instance, one of the stories was a native American folk tale about a war between ghosts that included many cultural references that were unfamiliar to the British subjects in his studies. It contained elements that were not understood (such as 'something black' coming out of the mouth of someone as they died), but upon recall these details were either omitted or were replaced by more familiar ideas (such as blood or breath coming out of the person's mouth).

Bartlett (1932) concluded that 'the description of memories as "fixed and lifeless" is merely an unpleasant fiction' (p. 311) and that remembering is 'an affair of construction rather than one of mere reproduction' (p. 205).[29] The act of remembering involves first the formation of an 'attitude' (Bartlett also described this as a feeling, affect or general impression) about what happened, followed by a process of constructive rationalization aimed at justifying that 'attitude'.

9.3.4.2 Analysis by synthesis

In his book *Cognitive Psychology* – regarded one of the milestones in the foundation of cognitive psychology – Neisser (1967, pp. 280–284) also lays into the empiricist, behaviourist, Gestalt and folk psychological conception of memory as the storage of items that can reappear over and over again. He asserted that this notion is totally 'misguided' and such entities are (as James, 1890, said) 'mythological'. This means that neither perceiving nor remembering can be simply a matter of (passively) finding and downloading from your long-term memory one or more pre-existing templates or prototypes of objects that you know about, like opening a drawer in your filing cabinet and digging out the right copy. Perception is not just finding a match with the incoming sensory information.

Neisser's theory is far more radical. First, stored information and incoming stimuli are both preconscious. They are cues, used as a basis for the construction of new thoughts and

---

29. As I type these words I wonder how I arrive at the same spelling for a given word on each occasion; but Bartlett's aim was at our higher levels of cognition.

percepts. This generative act allows for 'adaptive variation' in the finished product.[30] But what is the actual content of the stored information, if a memory is not an image or reproduced simulacrum of the outside world? It must consist of 'traces of *prior processes of construction*' (Neisser, 1967, p. 285; his italics). He continues: 'all learning is . . . learning to carry out a coordinated system of acts' that may be internal, not just overt movements. Therefore '*we store traces of earlier cognitive acts, not the products of those acts*' (p. 285; my italics).[31]

Instead, Neisser supported the idea that perception utilizes a process of 'analysis by synthesis'.[32] The theory is that, for each stimulus, the system actually manufactures some new internal construct from, perhaps, fragments or features of previous acts.[33] When reading quietly, for example, the components are recombined within the mind to form a 'deep cognitive structure . . . a continuing silent stream of thought' (1967, p. 136). This structure should account as closely as possible for the worldly causes of the sensory inflow. The act of synthesis is the act of perception, which is a process of *thinking*, leading to understanding. Another, more blatantly functionalist (section 2.5), way of describing the process is 'silent calculation . . . One makes a hypothesis about the original message, applies rules to determine what the input would be like if the hypothesis were true, and checks to see whether the input really is like that' (p. 194). The process of hypothesis generation is pre-attentive and depends upon context, whereas the subsequent testing is synthetic, detailed and attentive.

Neisser, like Bartlett, did not speculate on the neural bases of these processes. It is fun to try to do so (another essay topic for you) but important to distinguish (1) the idea that the contents of the brain (whether we call them traces, templates, representations or just plain memories) do not resemble the outside world (because they are *constructs* rather than images, icons or simulacra) from (2) the idea that they contain information about previous instances of *processing* (acts, recipes for *how to construct* a meaningful schema about the world or a plan of action, *rules* to be applied to representations) rather than static representations (whatever the degree of resemblance between these representations and the outside world).[34]

---

30. I think Edelman (section 9.3.2.3) and Millikan and Dennett (chapter 5) would all like the Darwinian flavour of this!

31. What appear to be repetitive products of memory, such as skilled behaviours, knowledge learned by rote, invariant facts and spelling, perhaps depend more closely on the stored traces and less on new constructive processes at retrieval; there could be a continuum of degrees of reliance on the two. Neisser himself (1967, p. 170) was more reluctant to give up on his theory, however, merely making the vague suggestion that 'the principles and mechanisms of construction are different' in these cases.

32. The term and the theory are not Neisser's own, though he developed them, provided evidence and made them famous within psychology. See his book (1967) for the original sources. He does not cite MacKay (1956), who gave a cybernetic justification for the internal synthesis of a matching template.

33. The notion of an 'act' should not be equated with motor preparation or imagery, although there are functional parallels. See section 8.4 for discussion of the theory that perception is covert action.

34. The italics here are designed to suggest how this theory might relate to functionalism; see section 2.5 and chapter 5, especially section 5.2.5. For another argument that rules need to be applied to representations in perception, see Gregory (1970; 1994, chapter 17; 1998, p. 251).

9.3.4.3 **Recall as retroactivation**

The neural theories in sections 9.3.2 and 9.3.3 proposed explanations of creative perception by postulating that the final percept is some kind of compromise between a static template and the input. It might be a nearest neighbour match (generalization, categorization), a distortion of a template or a 'correlation' between the template and the input – it is not always clear which. In all cases, however, the contents of memory are object representations rather than rules.[35] But to map onto the cognitive theories described so far in this section (9.3.4), can we find a genuinely constructivist *neural* theory?

One candidate for such a theory is the 'retroactivational' model of memory recall and stimulus recognition (Damasio, 1989; Damasio and Damasio, 1994). In this theory it is asserted that there is a series of processing stages or 'zones' in the brain. The primary stage is sensory analysis of the input and its features. A second-order stage involves related concepts – semantic information, organized into categories (cf. section 6.4.3). Then there is a third-order stage, at which there is convergence between such second-stage concepts that have become related or associated to form unique constellations of items representing particular people, places or events.

The evidence on which this model is based first involves brain damage. The Damasios found, for example, that lesions to the anterior left temporal lobe would cause a syndrome in which patients have problems linking people or places with their names. The patients would understand who a person was and what they had done, but they could not think of the right name. They were also unimpaired in naming common objects, so this was not just a general deficit in finding the right word. The anterior infero-temporal cortex is thus a tertiary zone, in their terminology, in that its loss removed the ability to link knowledge about specific people and their names. Other evidence comes from brain scanning studies, that is, from seeing which areas of cortex are activated when identifying or using particular kinds of information. For example, Damasio et al. (1996) support the idea that information about different kinds of objects is stored in different parts of the brain (see Side-box 6.2). They found that relating images of faces to names activates the anterior part of the temporal lobe, and also that naming animals depends on the middle section of the infero-temporal cortex and naming tools on the posterior infero-temporal cortex.

The higher stages are called 'convergence zones': information from the first-order analyses converges onto particular anatomical loci in the cerebral cortex. A second stage of convergence then exists from the secondary to the tertiary zones. These highest zones do not, however, themselves contain representations of higher-order or complex concepts (such as grandmother cells: section 6.2.6.1). Instead, they contain *links* between the representations of the constituent parts of those complex concepts. These might include, for example, a particular item's name, a visual image, understanding of its functional use – in other words, various aspects of the semantic network of knowledge that is pertinent to (associated with, or constitutive of) the concept. These aspects are, however, 'stored' in the next lower areas of the cortex. For example, to get from a facial image to a name (or vice versa), messages have to go up from a second- to a third-order zone and then back down again.

---

35. Grossberg's theory (section 9.3.2.4) has both: representations held in the short-term memory buffers, and transformations (rules) in the pattern of connections between them. Ullman (1995) also stresses the transformational aspect of the relationships between stages of analysis.

Similarly, the secondary, categorical zones link features represented directly by information-bearing nodes in the lower, primary zones. Put another way, a higher zone contains 'records' of the patterns of active records in the next lower zones.

Neurally, the connections between zones are correspondingly two-way: there is convergence of neural activity when ascending zones and divergence when descending. The connections in both directions are excitatory (no mention of modulatory synapses here!). This is because the functions of the recurrent axons are essentially reconstructive. During recall, the top-down process constructs a pattern of activity in the lower parts of the system, and this pattern is similar if not identical to the pattern of activity that was induced by the actual sensory stimulus (in primary zones) and/or the concept (in secondary zones) when it occurred in the past. For example, when you look at a comb (or a grandmother or a horse) it invokes a particular pattern of activity across the sensory and other regions of the brain, which is the concomitant of the ongoing information processing. But when you recall that stimulus, or imagine it or see a fragment of it and then mentally complete the whole, what happens is that information is fed back from the higher zones that reconstructs the original pattern of activity across the same regions of the brain.

Conscious awareness of the item depends on a sufficient level of activity being aroused in the lower zones. Moreover, this activity needs to be bound into a coherent whole by being synchronized across all the lower areas activated (as suggested by others: see section 6.4.2). The top-down connections are proposed by the Damasios as responsible for orchestrating such synchrony.

Critique

So, like the cognitive approaches, this is a reconstructive and a top-down theory of memory (and by implication perception). However, in part it incorporates conventional ideas about the storage of representations (at least at lower stages) and consciousness – such as its depending on the amount of neural activity (Side-box 7.1) and its synchrony across areas (section 6.4.2). The novel aspect is the recursive role of the 'higher' stages of cortex, which avoids the problem of having a single integration area (section 7.2) and the man-in-the-head problem (section 4.2.1) by returning activity towards lower levels and implementing an iterative loop between higher and lower zones. Indeed, they say that a number of recursions may take place, implying the settling down of the system onto a stable state. As such, this theory sounds like the template matching theories described in section 9.3.2; but instead, here each template is distributed across many areas. The lower areas contain the detailed fragments (e.g. features, components) of a template and the higher areas store the knowledge that these are bound together into a particular whole. In contrast, the matching theories have complete templates stored at one stage and the sensory input at another; the two are then compared in various ways requiring complex circuitry for the processes of comparison, evaluation, error signalling and correction, gain control and so on.

But beware: reconstruction is not reconstitution. Although many theories describe memories as 'reconstructions', there are two meanings to this term. Bartlett and Neisser emphasized that *all* acts of recall are novel, and the original pattern of activity and experience is never reproduced exactly. The Damasios also say that cognitive functions are constructive ('fabrications': Damasio and Damasio, 1994, p. 61), but they state that at root the *aim* of the higher zones is replication of the activation patterns in lower zones (Damasio, 1989, p. 47).[36] Reproduction is never exact, however, because a higher zone has to handle many links simultaneously and these interact with each other within the zone. There are often multiple inputs to the zone and this may cause the production of 'blends' containing new 'fragments' of previous patterns in the lower zones. They also suggest that weak and transient activity may generate novel combinations (Damasio and Damasio, 1994, p. 72). No doubt there are always differences between the original pattern and the recalled one due to change of context (the Damasios are particularly keen on homeostatic drives and emotions as causative: Side-box 9.7), the aging of the subject, internal noise (Rose, 1999b) and so on.

SIDE-BOX 9.7 EMOTION

The role of motivation and emotion in deciding what is important has long been neglected. Rather than regarding these as separate modular functions, some workers now see them as integrated more widely into brain dynamics. For example, in his book *Descartes' Error* (which starts off by saying it is not about Descartes at all or about Descartes making an error), Damasio (1995) says Descartes' error was being too rational, in that he concentrated on explaining how we think logically and indeed saw the mind as primarily the (human-only) seat of language and reasoning. Damasio argues instead that the most fundamental factor in determining how the brain develops and learns is not the rational logical analysis of sensory information (which so much research concerns, because for practical reasons it is easy for us to control the input), but what he calls 'gut feelings' (see also Damasio, 1999). Damasio supports the argument that intuitions or basic instincts are the primary and primitive guiding principles behind the growth of the brain both through evolution and ontogeny. It is traditional to argue that, somewhere in the limbic system, instincts or feelings do play a role (the 'motives' of behaviourist psychology), but Damasio emphasizes that these are the primary determinants of what you learn and remember: whether they bring positive reward or negative reward, pleasure or pain. The brain is not just sitting there analysing every single stimulus with equanimity, as though all inputs were equally valid, and just remembering the most frequent (as many researchers think: e.g. Barlow, 1959; Gallant, 2004; Olshausen, 2004). Instead, Damasio argues that the growth of sensory and long-term memory is controlled in some way by the basic emotional systems in the limbic system and brainstem. Echoes of this role are seen in the fact that brainstem structures are active during emotional experiences (Damasio et al., 2000).

Panksepp (1998, 2005) also regards the monitoring of bodily homeostatic functions as foundational for emotional experiences, and indeed for all consciousness. He places emphasis solely on the subcortical mechanisms for these functions, which he places in the periaqueductal grey matter (PAG), known to be important in pain and other basic euphorias and dysphorias. The PAG is a region of tissue surrounding the cerebral aqueduct, a fluid-filled tunnel joining the third and fourth ventricles. It runs through the brainstem close to the reticular formation and to the deep layers of the superior colliculus,

continues

---

36. Theories that memory recall involves the reconstitution of earlier patterns of activity in the brain have a long history: for example, Weinberg et al. (1970) and John et al. (1973). These, however, did not emphasize the novel constructional nature of those memories, as have more modern theories: for example, Schacter et al. (1998) and Conway and Pleydell-Pearce (2000).

SIDE-BOX 9.7 continued

from which the PAG can receive information from the external senses. It is closely integrated with the arousal systems (Panksepp, 1998, cites the ERTAS theory of Newman and Baars: section 7.2.3.2) and the modulatory neurotransmitter systems (section 8.2.2.3) enabling the visceral interoceptive PAG system to 'tune' the perceptual exteroceptive systems in the thalamus and cortex (1998, p. 571; for a brief summary, see Watt, 2005).

In his review of these theories, however, Gray (2004, chapter 18) emphasizes the cortical components of the underlying mechanisms that subserve the phenomenology in adults. The insula and the anterior cingulate cortices in particular appear to have roles in the expression of emotion and pain. LeDoux (1998) also proposed a cortical origin for experience, under the direction and orchestration of subconscious subcortical mechanisms.

For further readings, see Lane and Nadel (2000), Thompson and Colombetti (2005) and the journals *Consciousness and Emotion* and *Cognition and Emotion*.

The fundamental point, however, is that the higher convergence zones are described as containing 'linkages' in a neuronal associative sense, rather than optionally applied rules in a cognitive functionalist sense. There is an important philosophical distinction here between creative construction and slavish replication as the proper function of memory.[37] The former sees original thoughts as normal and desirable (for example, so we can cope with our ever-changing environment by generating and selecting ever-better plans via a Darwin-like winnowing mechanism). The latter view takes original thoughts as failures or aberrations (misrepresentations; see the discussion of this important issue in chapter 5).[38]

9.4 Conclusion

Top-down processes are important for perception but also for controlling the formation of long-term memories. As sensory inputs arrive, their effects ascend the processing systems but also activate top-down signals that aid stimulus recognition and can also play a part in attention and learning.

Thus, looking first at what happens over a long timescale, the top-down effects build into the system the memories of an event or input – in other words, they have the teleological function of restructuring the neural nets to accommodate future inputs that might be similar. This leads to further reinforcement of the incoming pathways, strengthening the synapses along them to build in the analytical mechanisms that were successful or useful in the past. Thus processing becomes hard-wired in – automatized – so the system can detect

37. Millikan (chapter 5) defines 'proper function' as what a system is supposed to do, and why it operates the way it does, at least under normal circumstances.

38. In both cases, maladaptive hallucinations or delusions may result if too much originality occurs, or too inflexible (stereotyped, obsessive, perseverative) behaviour and thought if too little, and a balanced middle way seems obviously desirable. But understanding both normal and abnormal psychology, and being able to cure the latter, requires a correct appreciation of which of these basic strategies is actually implemented in the brain.

and analyse that stimulus faster and more easily if it occurs subsequently. There may be a gradient of such reconstructional effects across the cortex, with the commoner stimuli dealt with or 'represented' earlier in the sensory pathways.

What are the implications of this model for the immediate processing of sensory inflow? One is that stimulus recognition may require penetration of its effects into the brain to various distances, depending on task demand (cf. Craik and Lockhart, 1972; section 2.5; Side-box 4.4) and on the stimulus. For example, Pollen (1999) suggests colour and motion may be identifiable purely in the early areas of cortex (V4 and V5), whereas shape and object recognition may require engagement of higher areas such as infero-temporal cortex; the latter are subserved by the more prolonged iterative procedures described by template matching models (section 9.3.2). Building 'memories' into progressively earlier stages may enable recognition to proceed via bottom-up mechanisms only, or via iteration between early areas only, and implies we perceive common stimuli more quickly than rare. In fact there is some evidence that fast processing can give good recognition of natural scenes (VanRullen and Thorpe, 2001a,b; 2002). These authors attribute this ability purely to the feed-forward, bottom-up, ascending wave of action potentials. However, Hochstein and Ahissar (2002) suggest that the feed-forward sweep through the system just gives 'vision at a glance' (the 'gist' of a scene; see Biederman, 1972, Wolfe, 2003; Koch, 2004, p. 165) and top-down processes are necessary to extract further details if these are required ('vision with scrutiny'). The primary role ascribed to the hippocampus by mismatch theories (section 9.3.3) might relate to this scene-based process of preliminary evaluation of whether a stimulus is new and therefore deserves further 'attentive' analysis (and this can then be carried out via recurrent top-down signals that initiate or continue the further processing of the information held in the temporary records persisting in 'earlier' areas of cortex).

In general, models of object perception try to account for the interplay between the incoming stimulus and top-down effects. These effects on lower centres in turn alter the ascending signals, so there is an iterative or cycling dynamic to the mechanisms that underlie perception. There are two kinds of theory as to what happens. One set of theories emphasizes positive feedback between well-established memories and the currently incoming sensory stimulus. These theories stress that if a stimulus comes in that is consistent with the knowledge base, that is to say if it is the kind of stimulus that has been seen many times before, then this will lead to reverberatory activity, perhaps persisting for hundreds of milliseconds.

The other set of theories sees the feedback as more negative, leading to suppression of information that becomes redundant once a successful recognition has occurred. The higher stages contain coding mechanisms that enable a known stimulus to be represented more efficiently than merely by reproducing the full pattern of sensory input, so activity in the earlier stages of the sensory pathways then becomes unnecessary and is suppressed. This has the bonus of leaving the early stages ready to deal with new incoming information. It also obviates the requirement for a man-in-the-head to inspect and interpret the reproduced pattern.

On the other hand, rare stimuli are not dealt with in similar fashion. There is, first of all, a mismatch between the higher and lower stages. If a sensory pattern occurs that has never been met before, then a number of perceptual hypotheses might be evoked, that is, a number of parts of the long-term memory base may be activated in a search for the nearest match to the pattern of the incoming stimulation. In dynamic systems terminology, the system will have to search through its state space to find a locus of at least locally optimum entropy (section 6.4.3.3). The arousal systems may well not be necessary for this process. If a match is not readily found, a new concept may need to be actively synthesized; the system may need to 'think' creatively. In fact, given the continuously novel nature of the total sensory flux entering our senses, it is probably never the case that an exact match occurs, and our sensory and cognitive experiences may therefore all be original creations.

These studies have drawn out several questions and assumptions about consciousness that remain unanswered. How far into the brain do the effects of a stimulus have to penetrate? Does awareness arise during settling of the system onto a final state, or after that state has been reached? Is the neural basis of consciousness a stable, reverberatory, oscillating or transient state? These questions can be couched in another way, namely, what is the latency of awareness? How long after a stimulus occurs do we realize something has happened and know what it is? This is the main topic of the next chapter, which also begins with a reconsideration of the allied question as to where in the brain sensory awareness arises.

■ RECOMMENDED READING

Introductory psychology texts on memory and cognition abound (for example, I found Groeger, 1997, and Eysenck and Keane, 5th edn, 2005, helpful), but specialized neurally-oriented texts are rarer: Eichenbaum's The Cognitive Neuroscience of Memory (2002) is the most obvious choice.

More advanced sets of readings are easier to find: Anderson et al.'s 'Knowledge-based vision in man and machine' (1997) is good on top-down processing in vision, and Forde and Humphreys (eds) Category Specificity in Brain and Mind (2002) on the analysis of seen objects into categories and types in different brain areas. For more on hippocampal function and place cells, see Burgess et al. The Hippocampal and Parietal Foundations of Spatial Cognition (1999) and Jeffery The Neurobiology of Spatial Behaviour (2003). Baddeley et al.'s 'Episodic Memory' (2001; reprinted by Oxford University Press, 2002) covers . . . episodic memory. Neuropsychological studies are central to Parker et al. The Cognitive Neuroscience of Memory (2002) and Squire and Schachter Neuropsychology of Memory, 3rd edn (2002). A good set of general chapters is available in Tulving and Craik The Oxford Handbook of Memory (2000), more advanced chapters in Tulving Memory, Consciousness, and the Brain (2000), and for a very detailed general text see Eichenbaum and Cohen From Conditioning to Conscious Recollection (2001). Finally, a reference work that explains much of the terminology in elementary terms is Dudai's Memory from A to Z (2002).

10 The where and when of visual experience

OBJECTIVES

Several of the lessons from previous chapters need to be brought together to reveal how a particular instance of consciousness, namely visual awareness, arises within the context of the complex system that is the brain. In addition, by making explicit the importance of timing, we add a dimension that is missing from many previous theories. In the cases of both space and time, you should note how investigations that start with simple questions lead almost invariably toward complex answers. Indeed, the sophisticated theories that we end up with then entail a re-evaluation of the meaning of the premises from which we started, and may thus bring about a revolution in our common-sense understanding of our own minds.

10.1 **Introduction**

In this chapter, we will examine in depth the neural bases of sensory phenomenality. We focus on this problem because, first, perceptual experience seems (initially) to be a relatively circumscribed case through which we can study the question of where and how awareness arises in the brain in general. Vision is a very highly researched topic across many levels of description, which makes it the best topic for an in-depth integrative treatment. Also, studying the neural bases of sensory phenomenality brings us to the important issue of the localization of neural and phenomenal events in time as well as space. The 'where' of consciousness has already been dealt with in some depth in section 7.2. The conclusion was that ascribing consciousness to a single location is far too simple.[1] However, by concentrating on sensory awareness we can also introduce 'time of experience' as a variable. So one new idea we will discuss in this chapter is that when a stimulus appears, a wave of activity sweeps up the sensory nerves and into the brain, and we can in principle ask *when* this wave arrives at the crucial site (if there is only one). After all, we become aware of that stimulus at a particular point in time, at least subjectively. So why not find out *where* the wave is at that point and then we will be able to infer where consciousness arises . . . won't we? But we will discover that to answer this question we may need to revise our conception of consciousness rather than simply to collect empirical data.

The second reason for concentrating on sensory phenomenality is to continue our series of analyses of the possible roles for top-down processes. In chapter 8, these were introduced as implementing (selective) attention, and in chapter 9, they were characterized as central to recognition, recall and learning. Note that the reconstructive theories of memory described in chapter 9, particularly for episodic memory, suggest that recall may actually involve the re-evocation of a previous instance of conscious experience. Since some experiences are visual, it would be instructive if we could come to understand the mechanisms by which the brain/mind reconstructs the subjective appearance of a previously seen object. Knowing how visual imagery works should help us understand how consciousness, attention, memory and perception fit together.

10.2 Where is visual awareness generated?

10.2.1 A single site

First I need to give a reminder of the localizationist thesis. In chapter 7, we used the term 'Cartesian theatre' to refer to the idea that there is one site in the brain where consciousness is generated. This is analogous to Descartes' idea that there must only be one site where the unitary soul communicates with the brain. Dennett (1991) characterized such a site as functioning like a theatre, where an audience is looking at events on the stage. This is in fact a parody of the way many people think: the various sensory pathways convey information up into the brain where it is processed progressively through the sensory areas until it

---

1. Reasons why a single locus is too simple a possibility include, first, that there are many types of consciousness (sensory experience, thinking, emotion, self-awareness and so on) that may rely on different brain substrates. Second, brain structures do communicate with one another rather than working in isolation. Third, cortical areas broadly resemble each other so it is not clear why some areas would and others would not give rise to consciousness. Fourth, experiences themselves are not unitary but instead have several aspects, depending on the 'depth of processing', the task they are intended to subserve ('what is this object for' versus 'what colour is this object', for example), and the degree of attention paid to them (section 8.3).

reaches one particular region of the brain, and this is where, as Dennett puts it, 'it all comes together'. There, all the different ongoing environmental stimuli are reconstructed, more or less accurately, to form a complete, unified scene. This depiction of the entire outside world is displayed in this location for other parts of the brain to inspect, like an audience watching a play in a theatre.

Another way to characterize this site is as a 'blackboard' or 'global workspace', mediating the communication between all the various anatomical and functional modules in the rest of the system.

A range of putative locations for such a singular site was described in section 7.2 – and turned out to include most regions of the brain![2]

A simple way of categorizing these ideas is in terms of *where* along the sensory pathways they locate the crucial site. In some theories it is the highest stage of processing, and integrates information from all sensory modalities, motor decisions, emotional overtones and, indeed, every aspect of consciousness. Other theories, however, are more modest and simply attempt to account for the phenomenal experience generated within a single modality, such as vision. Yet even within vision there are many stages[3] of processing up the visual pathway and across a large region of the cortex (Figure 8.3). Can we narrow down the crucial locus within this system?

10.2.1.1 The lateral geniculate nucleus (LGN)

Probably the earliest stage of processing at which the theatre has been located is the LGN to area V1 loop. Harth (1993), for example, has suggested that the LGN is used like a sketch pad or screen where images can be formed – not only by sensory input but also by the cortex, which can 'draw' what it is looking for. By a process of positive feedback and bootstrapping ('cyclic reactivation'; Harth, 1993, p. 142) the thalamo-cortical system settles on a single stable state that represents the best match between the sensory input and the cortical knowledge store.[4] According to Harth, consciousness arises in this 'echoic' interaction between thalamus and cortex. Harth sees the sketch pad as holding literally a picture or a mental image that is inspected by the cortex as in a Cartesian theatre. However,

---

2. A number of parameters characterize the possibilities for such a locale:
    i) It may always be in the same place or it may move around.
    ii) It may be large or small.
    iii) It may be able to generate consciousness within itself, intrinsically, or it may need to link to other places in the brain. In the latter case, these areas might function together:
       • as a stage plus audience (the locus broadcasts to the audience)
       • as a blackboard (the locus broadcasts to and receives input from the audience)
       • as a distribution centre (the locus transmits to specific key places rather than to all, and perhaps receives from them too – either selectively or non-selectively)
       • as a whole network bound together by resonance (or some other, perhaps very sophisticated, transformation) – but within the network one locus is vital for the whole to generate visual consciousness even though connectivity-wise they form an integrated system and all or several loci may speak directly to all or several others.

3. Remember: I am using the term 'theatre stage' to refer to the stage of a Cartesian theatre, and the term 'stage' alone to refer to a stage of processing along a serial pathway.

4. This theory is thus similar to the general template matching approach to pattern recognition discussed in section 9.3.2. Look also at section 8.2.2.2 on the properties of thalamo-cortical loops.

the homuncular fallacy is avoided because the loops are self-referent and 'the signaler and the perceiver are one' (p. 106). Harth simply asserts that: 'The neural message does not have to be read by any homunculus. It reads itself' (p. 71).

Importantly, Harth includes an element of randomness, noise or chaos in his model. This functions to prevent the system from settling into a non-optimal state, and it also prevents the system from hanging if there is no detectable input at all. For example, Harth suggests that dreams and hallucinations occur when the cortex paints a picture in the LGN and then interprets it as though it had come from the retina. The images experienced are not realistic, however, because the element of randomness has a creative effect. In situations of reduced sensory input there is little to prevent the positive feedback loop between cortex and LGN from making the image drift further and further from its original, meaningful pattern, once it is deflected from such by the random noise inherent in the visual system. For further discussion of this theory of creativity see Rose (1999b) and Side-box 5.2.

Harth also takes the odd but interesting view that activity passing from one area of cortex to another is not part of consciousness (Harth, 1993, p. 142). It is operating at a symbolic level of processing (the higher level of activity in which meaningful units of semantic information pass from module to module) and is part of the unconscious information processing that underlies thinking. So his theory inverts the usual, serial-processing idea that preconscious processing of stimuli occurs first and conscious processing happens later, at higher stages. Instead, Harth has consciousness occurring early in the sensory pathway.

Critique

It is not obvious how the LGN would act as a sketch pad. The LGN is highly structured: it contains six layers of cells, three of which are driven by the left eye and three by the right. It is therefore not clear how the visual image would be reconstructed there, given this laminar architecture. Nor is it clear how stereoscopic depth could be represented, since this is an essentially binocular process. LGN cells are fairly strictly monocular: each responds to stimuli in one eye or the other and is not influenced by what is seen via the other eye (except for some slight inhibition). There is no evidence for any kind of depth representation there, whereas the scene we experience subjectively has a clear three-dimensional structure. Similarly, there is no evidence of colour, shape or orientation constancy in LGN cells.

Another problem is that the LGN is a fairly small part of the thalamus anatomically, yet phenomenologically vision seems to play by far the most prominent role, at least for humans. Although we are aware of sounds, touch, smell, etc., vision is the most dominant sense. Anatomically there are multiple nuclei within the thalamus dealing with somatosensation, body movement and so on, yet the phenomenology associated with these other modalities is not as prominent as their anatomical size would suggest, relative to vision. Although there is a large 'visual' nucleus alongside the LGN, namely the pulvinar, Harth's theory excludes it from the mechanisms of consciousness (hence 'blindsight' – including, obviously, subjective blindness – occurs after V1 lesions only; Harth, 1993, p. 142). Although Harth mentions the existence of 'self-referent' loops and projection screens in the other sensory pathways (pp. 109, 142), he does not elaborate on them, and he certainly does not attribute to the rest of the thalamus any direct role in consciousness.

Damage to the optic radiation severs the connections between the LGN and the visual cortex, and causes blindness in the affected part of the visual field. According to Harth's theory, direct electrical stimulation of the visual cortex should not then be able to induce conscious experiences in the blind field, since no messages can pass to and from the LGN. Yet there is evidence that such subjects do experience visual 'phosphenes' (flashes of light) when their primary visual cortex is shocked (Dobelle and Mladejovsky, 1974). Although the exact neurological lesions in these patients were not detailed, the study seems sufficiently clear to pose a problem for Harth's theory.

Finally, of course, it is not obvious why consciousness should arise purely from the interactions between cortex and thalamus (and between LGN and V1 in particular), but not from, say, cortico-cortical loops. Harth's explanation of consciousness as arising from 'self-referent' loops is not explained in sufficient detail to be convincing.

10.2.1.2 The primary visual cortex

The next simple theory would be that consciousness can arise within primary sensory cortex alone. For vision this would be area V1,[5] and the idea is supported prima facie by the loss of subjective vision after V1 lesions. This by itself is not, of course, conclusive (retinal lesions also cause blindness!), as discussed in Side-box 7.3. There is, however, an active debate over the hypothesis that it is worth becoming familiar with. Thus Crick, Koch and Braun have argued that primary visual cortex is the only area of cortex that does *not* give rise to awareness directly (see Side-box 10.1 and section 10.2.3.1).

More direct evidence for the role of the primary sensory cortices in generating awareness comes from studies that examine which areas of the brain are engaged when subjects use imagery (Side-box 10.2). For not only can we use stored sensory information to aid perception, as we saw in chapter 9, we can also recall it voluntarily to evoke what seem to be 'pictures' in our minds. Such images affect sensory processing (Finke, 1986) and therefore may well use the same neural mechanisms, at least in part. So if we can locate the brain activity evoked in imagery, we may find a clue to the normal site of consciousness. For example, Kosslyn et al. (1993) and Le Bihan et al. (1993) asked subjects to imagine particular visual stimuli while they were in a brain scanner. Of course, as with all brain scanning studies, several areas were activated. However, these areas included the primary visual cortex, area V1, and moreover, there were topographic resemblances between the image and the pattern of activity in V1. Thus using imagery can activate V1 in a top-down fashion (Miyashita, 1995; Kosslyn and Thompson, 2003, pp. 724–725). Although these results are the topic of a continuing debate (see Side-box 10.2), they support a role for the primary visual cortex in visual experience, particularly for high-resolution images of object shapes.[6]

---

5. For example, Baars and Newman (1994, p. 223) suggested the theatre stage can be V1 – although Baars (1998, pp. 59, 61) later said that anterior infero-temporal cortex is the origin of consciousness for vision, on the basis of the work of Logothetis (e.g. 1998).

6. Note that these studies do not prove that V1 is the only area involved in any instance of consciousness, nor that other areas can operate without V1; but exactly how this area feeds into, integrates with or receives feedback from other areas is an open question. Remember also that closing one's eyes makes a big difference to the quality of visual experience (Gregory, 1996); qualia normally only arise for current sensory input. What about hallucinations, dreams and synaesthetic experiences? Perhaps these involve anomalous activation of the mechanisms that generate proper qualia that mere volitional imagery does not, since the latter works by nonlinear facilitation.

SIDE-BOX 10.1 CAN AREA V1 GENERATE CONSCIOUSNESS?

In discussing visual consciousness, Crick and Koch (1995, 1998a; see also Koch and Braun, 1996; Rees et al., 2002) have claimed that area V1, the primary visual cortex, is the only one of the visual cortical areas that does not generate consciousness itself.[a] Their reasoning is, first, that the neural basis of consciousness must have access to motor planning and control. These abilities are mediated in the frontal lobes. Second, there may need to be feedback from the frontal lobes to amplify the activity in the relevant neural assembly. The primary visual cortex does not have the direct anatomical connections necessary for either of these functions.[b]

Indirect transmissions through other areas cannot suffice, because they would acquire the properties of those intermediate areas, which do not merely relay information unchanged. As Crick and Koch put it, information is recoded at each stage in the visual hierarchy. This is demonstrated most obviously by the changes in receptive field properties along the visual pathway. (Note, however, Gegenfurtner and Kiper's, 2003, conclusion that colour information is not altered along the V1 to V4 pathway.)

More recently, empirical evidence consistent with Crick and Koch's proposal has been obtained. For example, area V1 seems able to respond to stimuli that are nevertheless not consciously perceived (He et al., 1996). In addition, V1 does not appear to be active during dreaming (Braun et al., 1998) or hallucinations (ffytche et al., 1998). See Crick and Koch (1998a) and Koch (2004) for reviews, and Gray (2004, chapter 13) for further support.

Critique

It is difficult to prove a negative, and further research may alter the conclusion (cf. the susceptibility of V1 to attention, which was long denied, until more sensitive techniques came along; see Side-box 8.6). For example, although the brain scanning studies of Braun et al. (1998) and ffytche et al. (1998) found little activity in V1 under conditions of internally generated visual experiences, this might simply reflect the lack of synaptic input from the LGN in those conditions. It seems that the blood flow in a cortical area is mainly determined by the area's synaptic inputs and intracortical processing, rather than by its large output neurons (Logothetis and Wandell, 2004). Thus a zero change in blood flow does not exclude the occurrence of neural output from an area (perhaps generated intrinsically by the large pyramidal cells). Second, eye movements depress blood flow in area V1, hence perhaps nullifying any increase that may occur due to neural activity during REM sleep (Kosslyn and Thompson, 2003). Third, some studies have actually found area V1 to become active during REM sleep (Lövblad et al., 1999). Finally, area V1 contains within it some serial processing (cf. Hubel and Wiesel's, 1968, model of simple and complex cells); the preconscious processing studied by He et al. (1996) and Haynes and Rees (2005) might well exist at an early stage, and consciousness per se could arise at a later stage – yet still within V1 itself.

Crick and Koch's conclusion is based on an assumption of purely serial processing that may not be warranted given the recurrent nature of processing illustrated in chapters 7–9. Indeed, some resonance/feedback theorists argue that V1 can be a vital part of the network that generates certain types of consciousness, and in this respect V1 is no different from any other visual area of cortex (e.g. Pollen, 1999; Lamme et al., 2000). Further, Goebel et al. (2001) hint that V1 may always be necessary, since without it there is no visual awareness even when pre-striate areas are highly active.[c]

More direct empirical evidence that V1 is involved comes from studies in which transcranial magnetic stimulation (TMS) is applied to stimulate the visual pathways directly and transiently. For example, if pre-striate area V5 is activated 5–45 milliseconds before area V1, then awareness is blocked (Pascual-Leone and Walsh, 2001). Moreover, a blindsight patient with a lesion restricted to area V1 in

continues

SIDE-BOX 10.1 continued

his left hemisphere has visual experiences when his right V5 is activated by TMS, but not when his left V5 is activated (Cowey and Walsh, 2000).[d]

Yet, Ro et al. (2003) applied TMS to area V1 and found that this both enhanced the masking of one visual stimulus by another that preceded it in time, and enhanced the perception of the stimulus that occurred first. When the TMS was timed so that it impaired processing of the second stimulus, this allowed the feedback effects of the first stimulus to re-occupy V1's functioning. The authors thus also concluded that awareness depends normally upon intact mechanisms of feedback to early cortical stages.

Further, Ro et al.'s results are consistent with Bullier's (2001) earlier suggestion that the first wave of feedback comes from magno system input, since Breitmeyer (1984) had earlier linked such inter-stimulus ('metacontrast') masking functions to the different latencies of magno and parvo cells (remember: magno cells conduct action potentials faster than parvo cells). Bullier concludes that the early processing areas of cortex act like Mumford-style 'blackboards' (see section 10.2.2) to integrate, bind and distribute the results of processing in the pre-striate areas.

See Stoerig (2001) and Tong (2003) for good reviews in favour of a role for V1 in consciousness.

[a] Curiously, Eccles (1990, p. 442) also opined, without supporting evidence, that 'It is generally believed that activation of primary sensory areas of the neocortex . . . does not directly deliver conscious experiences.'
[b] This contrasts with Crick's (1994) earlier suggestion that consciousness, being tied up with short-term memory, might originate in persisting reverberatory loops between the thalamus and cortex. These loops, from layer 6 to thalamus and back to layers 4 and 6, will be too weak to sustain reverberations in areas where layer 4 is small (1994, pp. 240–241, 251). But in primary sensory cortex, layer 4 is extremely thick, so we should expect it to generate consciousness! Crick and Koch (1998b) now deny that there can be such simple reverberatory loops.
[c] Stoerig and Barth (2001) established that genuinely visual awareness can arise in these blindsight cases, albeit of an impoverished kind. However, Stoerig (2001) suggests that such experience may only arise in patients who have had extensive practice performing visual tasks as experimental subjects.
[d] Commenting, Pollen (2003, pp. 807–808) says that we cannot yet tell if these results mean that consciousness depends upon 'the entire recursive loop back to V1, upon more local feedback from V5 to V1 and/or to V2 or that a reactivated V1 is essential for perception to provide concurrent activation of the parietal lobe and other areas, in addition to the activation of afferent pathways by the direct stimulation of V5.'

10.2.1.3 Intermediate areas

A couple of other theories have placed the relevant locus at intermediate levels along the processing pathway. Thus Jackendoff (1987) made an interesting point based partly around Marr's theory of vision (section 9.3.2.2).[7] Jackendoff points out that *what we are aware of phenomenologically is the 2.5-D sketch*. We actually experience the intermediate level in Marr's model – surfaces, seen from our own viewpoint – and we don't 'see' objects at the 3-D level. We can imagine how the object would look from the back ('mental rotation')

7. As a reminder: Marr (1982) proposed a bottom-up theory in which incoming information is analysed first in terms of simple primitives, for example the brightnesses in different parts of the image, in what is called the primal sketch. This leads on to what he called the 2.5-D sketch and then on to the 3-D sketch. In the 2.5-D sketch, the scene is mapped out or parsed into surfaces and areas at different distances and orientations, with different surface textures and so on. These are all encoded as seen from the viewer; it is a viewer-centric representation of the image. The 3-D sketch, however, includes a model of each object you are looking at. Each of those objects is three-dimensional, so you can mentally rotate it and imagine what it would look like from the rear, you can describe it as seen from another person's point of view, and you know what it would feel like if you put your hand round it to touch the back. The representation is now object-centred. One recent, parallel-processing alternative is that viewer-centred ('egocentric') representations are generated in the dorsal stream and object-centred ('allocentric') in the ventral stream (Rolls and Deco, 2002, p. 464; Jacob and Jeannerod, 2003).

SIDE-BOX 10.2 THE NEURAL BASES OF IMAGERY

There are two relevant empirical issues we need to cover here, and one theoretical. The first is whether imagery engages the same mechanisms as are usually involved in the processing of sensory input. The second is whether these include primary visual cortex, area V1.[a] Finally, what does imagery tell us about the nature of representation?

Imagery and perception

Psychological studies have supported the idea that imaging a stimulus alters the perception of similar incoming stimuli, even for simple stimuli such as line and grating patterns (Perky, 1910; Finke, 1986; Ishai and Sagi, 1995; Craver-Lemley and Arterberry, 2001). The general principle, however, seems to be that this overlap is only partial, and there are some differences in the underlying mechanisms activated (for introductory reviews, see Miyashita, 1995; Behrmann, 2000; Farah, 2000, chapter 9). Much of the recent evidence brought to bear on this issue comes from comparisons between the brain areas activated during both types of task. These studies indeed show overlap to a large degree (e.g. O'Craven and Kanwisher, 2000; see also Kreiman et al., 2000b, who used single unit recording in conscious humans), although with discrepancies. For example, the earlier areas along the visual pathway have been found to light up less than the more anterior areas when comparing imagery with normal perception (e.g. Goebel et al., 1998; Ganis et al., 2004). However, the anterior areas of the brain must function during imagery to hold task demand in working memory, recall the image from long-term memory and focus sustained attention on the task; these functions probably do not need to be activated so intensely during passive viewing of a real stimulus.

Imagery and area V1

The specific question of whether area V1 is engaged by imagery relates to the general issue about whether that area plays a role in consciousness at all (see Side-box 10.1). Psychophysical studies provide strong support, in that the effects of imagery can be selective for line orientation and eye of origin, qualities mainly restricted to area V1 cells (Ishai and Sagi, 1995; Miyashita, 1995). Several brain scanning studies have found that area V1 is aroused during imagery,[b] and, moreover, to an extent that correlates with the topographic content of the imagery. Thus larger images evoke activity in areas correspondingly further from the foveal representation in V1 (Kosslyn et al., 1993, 1995). The failures of some studies to activate area V1 are attributed to methodological factors, such as lack of task demand for high-resolution imagery, a requirement to visualize spatial relations instead of shapes and the use of insensitive scanning techniques (Kosslyn and Thompson, 2003), the use of poor imagers as subjects (Behrmann, 2000) and monitoring of sustained instead of transient changes in blood flow (the latter effects are more reliable in V1: Klein et al., 2000). The most direct demonstrations are, perhaps, that transcranial magnetic stimulation (TMS) of area V1 affects imagery as well as perception (Kosslyn et al., 1999) and the cortex is more easily activated by TMS during visual imagery (Sparing et al., 2002).

The imagery debate

An important theoretical rationale for all these studies of imagery is to discover whether visual representations are pictorial and image-like or consist of abstract logical proposition-like symbols (cf. the grounding problem: section 2.5.2.4).[c] This is known as 'the imagery debate' and has been rumbling on for years (see Tye, 1991). On one side, Kosslyn (1983, 1994) argued that mental images are held in a 'visual buffer' that consists of an analogue spatial medium – although the images it holds are merely

continues

SIDE-BOX 10.2 continued

treated as pictures by the mechanisms of processing, rather than being (literally) pictures in the head (see also Dennett, 1991).[d] On the other hand, Pylyshyn (1984) agreed that there is an implicit or analogue medium, but argued that mental imagery involves processes at a higher cognitive/semantic level of description. At one time this debate was considered a draw, since all experimental data could be accounted for by both theories. However, recent brain imaging studies have revived hope of a resolution of the issue (e.g. Kosslyn and Thompson, 2003; Pylyshyn, 2002, 2003, 2004) – some hope!

[a] Analogous investigations have taken place on imagery in the other sensory modalities (e.g. Yoo et al., 2001; Zatorre, 2003; Djordjevic et al., 2004a,b).
[b] At least one study also reports LGN activation during imagery: Chen et al. (1998).
[c] The fundamental debate here is between analogue and propositional codes. Analogue coding and computing involve representations that are continuously variable. The representation of an object may or may not be isomorphic to the object (i.e. the same shape), but there is a functional if not physical basis to the representation that is in some way directly mappable onto the stimulus and vice versa. In contrast, propositional codes are discrete and symbolic, like linguistic statements or mathematical formulae. Under some theories, these symbols are arbitrary descriptions of the stimulus, so the mapping between the code and the stimulus or idea is indirect: it requires a decoder or reader to interpret the symbols. It also needs some kind of processor to write or generate the symbols. Thus there has to be a set of cognitive processes to encode or inscribe the propositions into the brain and another set to decode these things. Both processes require a key to what the symbols mean (see also section 2.5). Support for analogue coding has been given by Gregory (1968), and for the simultaneous existence of both types by Paivio (1986). One interesting suggestion is that the left hemisphere uses propositional codes (ordinal scales, such as whether objects are to the left or right of each other) while the right hemisphere uses more analogue, metrical codes, such as how far away from each other two objects are (Kosslyn et al., 1989).
[d] Visual phenomenality behaves in many ways *as though* the brain maintains a topographic, picture-like representation of the visual field, in which visible surfaces are 'filled in' with colour and texture, but in which occluded surfaces are not (Pessoa and De Weerd, 2003). See also sections 7.3.3 and 9.3.2.4.

and we can imagine how to reach round behind it and what it will feel like to grasp – but we don't experience the back visually in the sense of having qualia about it. Similarly, if an object is partially hidden behind another one, we don't see phenomenologically the occluded part of the half-hidden object, even if we are very familiar with its full appearance. This implies that, if we assume that the visual system is a serial-processing system with the 3-D model up in the infero-temporal cortex and the primitives analysed down in the primary visual cortex, what we experience is generated at some intermediate level, where we have the image parsed into figures and surfaces. Jackendoff (1987) made the same point about other functional systems too, such as speech. We 'hear' words, not sound frequencies and harmonics, and not pure meaning.

Grossberg (1987a,b; 2004; section 9.3.2.4) has made the related point that we are only aware of surfaces, colours and brightnesses. He posits two processes, one of which (the 'boundary contour system') finds the edges of objects and divides the visual scene up into separate objects. The other process (the 'feature contour system') '*fills in*' the colour and the surface qualities within each object. The boundary system does not directly give rise to phenomenology; we don't actually experience edges in the same way that we experience surfaces. So visual awareness is related only to the feature system, which may be the function of area V4.

10.2.1.4 Infero-temporal cortex

The serial processing model leads us to the assumption that the point where conscious awareness of stimuli arises is at the ending of 'sensory' processing. We become aware of objects and events once they have been identified by the various mechanisms of preconscious analysis. Some evidence in favour of such a high-level origin comes from studies of binocular rivalry. In this paradigm, different images are presented to the two eyes, yet subjects experience the sight of only one image at a time, while the other image is suppressed. Every few seconds the percepts spontaneously swap over, so the previously invisible image appears and dominates phenomenal awareness for the next few seconds (Blake, 1989; Alais and Blake, 2005). Yet where in the brain does this alternation arise? The most obvious possibility is that a mutually suppressive interaction occurs between the monocular signals reaching the cortex from each eye. This happens most probably in area V1, since cells beyond that stage can be driven by either eye (e.g. Hubel and Wiesel, 1968).

Is it the content or the vehicle that is suppressed, in other words, is suppression selective for the particular pattern in one eye, or is that entire eye's input suppressed? Most evidence suggests the latter (Blake, 1989), yet there remain indications that cognition can influence rivalry and that similarly timed alternations of perception can occur between object representations, as in the Rubin vase and other well-known ambiguous figures (reviewed by Logothetis, 1998). So Logothetis and colleagues studied cell behaviour along the visual pathway in monkeys viewing binocular rivalry displays, to find where the brain's activity correlates with the percept rather than the stimulus. They concluded that this happens in infero-temporal cortex, i.e. at a late stage in processing, and rivalry therefore occurs between the representations of whole objects. As such, the traditional idea that rivalry arises between monocular signals arriving from the two eyes cannot be correct. These results are commonly taken as supporting a late (infero-temporal) origin of visual awareness (e.g. Baars, 1998, pp. 59, 61; Gray, 2004, p. 69; Koch, 2004, chapter 16).

Critique

The stimuli used by Logothetis' group (Logothetis, 1998) were inappropriate in two ways. First, they flickered them rapidly, a manoeuvre that inevitably obscures interocular rivalry, which is switched by transients in the stimulus to one eye. With other types of stimulus, rivalry can easily be demonstrated to occur at the interocular stage (e.g. Lee and Blake, 1999, 2002, 2004; Polonsky et al., 2000; Tong, 2003). Second, in some experiments Logothetis mixed stimuli of different types, such as a face in one eye and a striped pattern in the other (so too Lumer et al., 1998, and Lumer and Rees, 1999, who also presented different colours and motions to each eye). This is guaranteed to give results that are not straightforward, since colour, motion, faces and straight lines are dealt with in different areas of the brain. The psychophysical evidence clearly shows that rivalry can occur at many stages in a hierarchical system, and the results you get depend on where along the processing system you tap into, which in turn depends on the attentional demands of the task and the stimulus parameters (e.g. Ooi and He, 1999, 2003; Bonneh et al., 2001; Blake and Logothetis, 2002; Wilson, 2003; Pearson and Clifford, 2004).

Moreover, Logothetis (1998) based his conclusion on the *percentage* of cells in each area whose firing correlates with the percept. Yet the *absolute* number of cells in each area tends to decrease as the visual pathway is ascended (Lennie, 1998). Taking the figures from Felleman and Van Essen (1991), monkey areas V1 and V2 each constitute about 12% of the entire neocortex, while the infero-temporal areas sampled by Logothetis together total only 2.7%. This fivefold decrease approximately offsets the fivefold increase Logothetis found in the *proportion* of cells in those areas whose activity mirrors the percept. The number of cells changing their firing as perception changes was therefore about the same in V1 as in infero-temporal cortex, and there is no clear reason why we should consider the relative rather than the absolute number of cells firing within an area as the important factor.[8]

Finally, if competition exists only between object representations, then we should only be able to see one thing at a time (simultanagnosia) when their images are optically superimposed; yet we do not. It is only with dichoptic presentation (a different object viewed by each eye) that rivalry occurs, which ties the phenomenon incontrovertibly to eye of origin.[9]

10.2.1.5 Interim conclusion

These several attempts to locate 'the' origin for visual awareness may demonstrate the inadequacy of treating consciousness as a simple unitary entity that arises instantaneously when activation occurs at a particular and single point in the brain. This conclusion has already been reached by Dennett, for example (e.g. 1991, 1998), who has emphasized that when a stimulus occurs the information is processed widely throughout the brain. Both parallel and serial analyses occur through a vast network of areas (e.g. Figure 8.3) and there is no single site at which the results of all the processing come together. Such a 'Cartesian theatre' would require converging input from all the modalities and from the other analytical mechanisms in all the modules, and there is just no such location. This view is broadly supported also by brain scanning studies, which show that whenever you perform any particular task, many widely scattered regions of the brain are activated. It is very rare, almost nonexistent, to find that only one region of the brain lights up when the subject has to perform a task or to analyse any particular type of stimulus (see section 4.3.6).

10.2.2 Multiple independent sites

One compromise to the Cartesian theatre metaphor would be if the brain contains several such theatres (e.g. Baars, 1998, p. 61). For example, there could be separate mechanisms of this type for vision, hearing, feeling sad, wanting to drink coffee and so on. This would explain why there is no single site that carries all aspects of conscious experience.[10] Although this does not obviate the logical problem of how any such theatre gives rise to consciousness, it might break the problem up into smaller and more specific questions, each of which might be more tractable on its own (section 4.2.2).

For example, Mumford (1991) proposed that the thalamus contains an entire set of blackboards, one for each area of cortex with which it is reciprocally connected. Each such blackboard is used much as Harth (1993) suggests the LGN is used (Harth and Mumford cite

---

8. A similar point was made qualitatively by Pollen (1999).

9. The alternation between seeing a vase and seeing two faces in the Rubin figure, or alternative interpretations of the Necker cube and other ambiguous figures, probably pertains to competition at the level of cues or cue integration, rather than whole object representations (e.g. Gregory, 1970, 1998).

10. It implies consciousness is not a single unified entity, and there may be many independent streams. The ramifications of this alternative will be discussed more fully in chapter 11.

each other's work) – except that Mumford leaves pattern recognition (template matching) functions to cortico-cortical loops (Mumford, 1992; see section 9.3.2). The thalamic blackboards have an active processing role, with important contents encoded in an efficient symbolic format and irrelevant or noisy information suppressed. They hold temporary data upon which iterative computations are being made by the cortex, and they integrate bottom-up (sensory) and top-down (cortical) sources to synthesize 'ideas'. Interestingly, Mumford hints at a homuncular functionalist approach (chapter 4) when he says: 'Each area of cortex is like a homunculus which has a certain narrow view of the world' (1991, p. 139). On the negative side, however, he is vague about the thalamic anatomy, wanting both a specific relationship between each blackboard and its corresponding area of cortex, and a diffuse broadcasting system whereby a blackboard can be used to coordinate the activity of many areas of cortex and broadcast information to them (see section 8.2.2 for details of the real thalamic anatomy).[11]

Another prominent theory states that the multiple areas of cortex each subserve a different aspect of consciousness (Zeki, 1998; Zeki and Bartels, 1998). These aspects are called 'micro-consciousnesses' and include, for the case of vision, the experiences of colour, motion, shape and so on. This position derives from Zeki's (1993) arguments that area V4, for example, subserves colour vision, area V5 motion, and so forth. Zeki does not regard these locations as theatres, suggesting instead that activity within an area, plus input from the reticular formation, is the (sufficient) physical basis of visual awareness (Zeki and ffytche, 1998; see section 10.3.2.1 for more details).[12]

10.2.3 Distributed sites

Although the Cartesian theatre is normally defined such that its anatomical location mimics its functionality, it is conceivable that the theatre stage could be distributed across many

11. If we look back at Figure 8.10, and especially Figure SB 8.8.1 in Side-box 8.8, we can see how a theory might be developed of partial broadcasting, which might be easier to sustain than the 'global workspace' models described in section 7.2.3. If, following Mumford (1991), we regard each thalamic nucleus as a 'blackboard', it would appear that each can be written to by two cortical areas along each stream, and can in turn broadcast to those same two areas. (Of course there are more complex lateral, converging and diverging connections between processing streams, as is apparent from Figure 8.3, and there may also be diffuse connections as described in Figure 8.6, but for argument's sake we can allow the simplified story.) Now look again at Side-box 9.1. Marcel's (1983b) theory proposes that along a processing stream there must be two kinds of functional unit at each stage: representations (for further processing) and records (for later checking back of hypotheses). Can we map these two theories onto one another? The thalamic nuclei could be acting as short-term stores (as in Mumford's 1991 theory) while the cortico-cortical connections execute functional processing; or it could be vice versa, with the cortex retaining traces for longer (Supèr et al., 2001) while the main processing stream passes from cortex to thalamus to cortex (Guillery, 1995; LaBerge, 1997). Such a mapping of function to structure would of course be a very simplistic reduction, and even reductive theories would allow that both retention of the original copy and its processing might take place within the same anatomical locus, but nevertheless this might provide a compromise between the extremes of global access and narrow theatre spotlight theories.

12. O'Brien and Opie (1999) take a similar position, in postulating that individual neural networks can generate consciousness within themselves. This happens whenever an area's intrinsic state is stable (see section 10.3.1). Stability facilitates the communication of a representation's contents to other networks in the hierarchy, but that process of transmission is not what generates consciousness.

brain areas. For purely sensory phenomenology, two types of theory postulate that a neural representation is widely distributed. One is that each representation is an integrated unit despite being spatially smeared, and the second is that each representation has a multi-levelled structure, with each level linked in some way with a different brain area.[13]

10.2.3.1 Integrated wholes

There have been several suggestions that activity must be bound, coordinated or related in some way across brain areas. This idea is, in particular, part of the 40 Hz theory and of resonance theories in general (chapters 6–9). At root is a presupposition that brain areas do not generate consciousness for its own sake, since this would be dualism or epiphenomenalism. Nor do they exist in isolation from the rest of the brain, but instead, neural activity must be transmitted somewhere and must do something, else consciousness would not have any efficacious function.

For example, the 40 Hz theory had originally postulated that representations are distributed across cortical areas, with each area containing cells firing at 40 Hz in synchrony with those in other cortical areas, so an object's colour, motion, shape, etc., are bound together (see section 4.3.7, section 6.4.2 and section 7.3.1). Later, Crick and Koch (1995) argued that there must be direct communication between a sensory cortical area and the frontal lobe for the contents of that area to correlate with awareness. There need to be resonant or standing wave patterns between the front and back of the brain (Koch, 2004, pp. 124, 216, 245, 301, 324). Controversially, they also suggested that these can arise from any sensory area except V1 (see Side-box 10.1). However, in reply, Pollen (1999), citing Grossberg (section 9.3.2.4), pointed out that resonance can occur between V1 and other cortical areas. A direct link between V1 and frontal lobe is not necessary, and the arguments offered by Koch and Crick are not conclusive (for details see Side-box 10.1).[14]

Also postulating integrated wholes, some field theories propose a unified physical entity spread across several areas of brain; see, for example, the quantum theory of Woolf and Hameroff (2001) and the electric field theories described in section 6.2.4.

10.2.3.2 Complex layered structures

Another set of theories also proposes that representations involve multiple sites within the brain, but these are not unified wholes (either in that their content is a singularity such as a structureless 'quale', or because they are closely bound features of a single stimulus such as a moving red triangle). Instead, they have a layered or hierarchical structure (see Side-boxes 4.4 and 8.2). For example, a seen object can be analysed to different depths,

---

13. There may be several actors on the Cartesian theatre stage at any one time, so – assuming the spatial dimension to be relevant – the neural theatre stage would be correspondingly as large as or larger than a neural representation.

14. For example, Crick and Koch (1995) propose that frontal areas must be involved because people can report their conscious experiences (and if there can be no report, we cannot study qualia scientifically). Yet as Pollen (1999) points out, phenomenal qualia are indescribable ('ineffable'): you cannot describe the experience of 'green' to a person blind from birth (see also Dennett's 1988 discussion of the sound of an osprey call in the next section). Yet subjective experiences are still real and we need to accept and study first person accounts of so-called 'qualia' even if they cannot be articulated (see chapter 1).

into its surface features (colour, size, location, motion), shape and structure, identity, purposes, animateness, name, origin, mass, hardness and so on. A full representation of that object must include all these aspects of it, and these must be integrated together to form a unified representation. This entity will probably be distributed across many stages of brain processing from primary sensory cortex at least as far as infero-temporal cortex (for the perceptual aspects) and perhaps as far as the hippocampus and/or frontal lobe for its cognitive qualities (chapter 9).

A variation is that consciousness arises when there is integration anchored at the highest stages (for vision, infero-temporal and/or prefrontal areas) rather than the lowest (Hochstein and Ahissar, 2002). In this theory, the initial forward sweep of activity elicits preliminary hypotheses in the highest stages along the visual pathway, and these can then become integrated with lower stages – though exactly how low varies, depending on how much stimulus detail needs to be perceived.[15] This contrasts with the more traditional integration theory developed from the bottom-up serial processing model, in which the degree of understanding of the stimulus is proportional to how many stages up the pathway become integrated with the earliest stage.

Now, the idea of hierarchically structured neural representations is tied (by identity theory) to the idea that experiences are similarly structured. The phenomenology of perception, for example, shows that we can focus in on colour and edge details, recognize faces or read the expression on them. We should therefore go back to the (some would say, logically prior) question of the nature of sensory experience.

Remember, the traditional conception is that qualia are atomic or quantal units, the elements of experience – basic, primitive or raw feelings such as seeing red or above or moving to the left and so on (see also section 2.5.2.1). Deriving from Locke (1690) and Hume (1739), the theory was that complex 'ideas' are built up through association, by combining different basic elements of sensation and experience, that we learn as we grow. This is the empiricist, associationist view in psychology.

An alternative view has been described briefly in section 4.3.1. For example, Dennett (1988) supports the idea that experiences are complex wholes. He put forward a number of examples of how experiences are not unitary, indivisible atoms. For instance, we may come to acquire connoisseurship for particular real-world stimuli, such as wine, coffee or particular musical sounds. What at first seems a blurry, single experience becomes, with practice and training, divisible into sub-parts, like a scene coming into focus revealing the presence of one or more separate figures against a background. Thus one can learn to detect different components in a complex taste – for example, experienced cooks can tell what ingredients there are in a casserole or a sauce. A note or chord on a guitar can be broken down into its fundamental and harmonics – by listening to the different components, musicians learn to analyse further what seems at first to be a single stimulus.

How do we come to make fine categorizations of stimuli? Another example Dennett (1988) uses is that of an osprey call. He asks: how do you know what an osprey sounds like? People can tell you ospreys make a sort of repeating 'cheep' noise – but that does not

---

15. Although there are formal similarities with Marcel's (1983b) functionalist theory (Side-box 9.1), for Hochstein and Ahissar (2002) visual consciousness arises as soon as recurrent activity occurs, whereas Marcel took such processes to be preconscious.

really pin it down. Perhaps they may say: well, a merlin instead has a repeated 'screech' – but still, this leaves many kinds of bird call uncategorized, not even into birds of prey versus other birds. It is not until you actually hear an osprey call that you know: *that* is what an osprey call sounds like.[16] However, this still leaves you with the question of exactly what features of that sound define and categorize it as an osprey call rather than a merlin or some other kind of bird's call. Because these sounds are complex, you do not initially experience them as basic primitives that you later learn to build up together by association into complex wholes. Instead, experience begins as a complex whole – a blooming buzzing confusion – that you then learn to analyse into smaller and smaller parts and categories.[17]

The point (that Dennett should have then made, although to my knowledge he didn't) is that there is no principled end to this process of categorization and sub-categorization. Throughout our lives we can go on and on learning to make finer and finer distinctions, breaking phenomenal experience into more subtle and precise fragments. There is no point at which one can say: these at last are the qualia, and we can go no further.[18]

As such, this view represents an inversion of the traditional empiricist mechanism of perception, in which simple qualia or atomistic representations are built up into complexes through associative learning during ontogeny. Instead, our representation of the world starts as a complex whole, within which nuggets of knowledge progressively condense or crystallize. Or better: our representations begin as diffuse formless entities that then acquire increasingly more structure within them (and boundaries between them).[19]

In the terminology of homuncular functionalism (chapter 4), there is a progressive modularization of the hierarchy of representation, semantic knowledge and functional role. Experience too thus becomes a nested hierarchical structure (as described – for the adult case – by Metzinger, 1995, Lycan, 1996, O'Brien and Opie, 1999 and Brown, 2002). For example, Lycan (1996, pp. 144–151) argued that there can be representations with many levels of intentional content. An experience may be of a patch of red, a patch of red leather,

---

16. You can experience one yourself by logging on to
<http://www.twingroves.district96.k12.il.us/Wetlands/Osprey/OspreySound/Osprey.aiff>, and compare this with a merlin call at <http://www.buteo.com/merlin.html>.

17. To my knowledge, Dennett was not aware that the same argument had earlier been made by Gibson and Gibson (1955). It is also regrettable that Dennett did not cite any of the extensive literature on the psychology of categorization, particularly that on colour (Berlin and Kay, 1969; Hardin and Maffi, 1997) or concepts in general (see Lamberts and Shanks, 1997). Bachmann (2000) adds that the nature of perception – as progressive analysis and differentiation of an initial whole, rather than as the integration and binding of elemental units – is demonstrated in the global-to-local order of processing that is well established in the psychophysical literature.

18. Although one defining characteristic of qualia is their 'homogeneity', i.e. the green-ness of green has *no sub-structure* (see section 1.1.3 on the definition of qualia), one can still continue to subcategorize greens into different shades of green.

19. Essay topic: How does the theory of categorical learning as continual differentiation relate to the biological theories of memory described in chapter 9? Refer particularly to the notion of a progressive shift of representation across the cortex with repeated experiences, and also to the work on visual categorization areas described in Side-box 6.2.

a red leather armchair or your grandmother's armchair (section 4.3.1).[20] He suggests that perhaps there are Cartesian theatres – but if so, there are many, not just one. Within each of them is some kind of scanning mechanism that monitors the output of the theatre's stage. (His ideas on this architecture will be dealt with in section 11.2.2.3.) Because there are many different theatre mechanisms, the experiences we have are not necessarily all synthesized on a single stage. There is still a stage–audience metaphor, but each theatre is smaller and contains only a part of the entire range of (potential) experiences (Lycan, 1987, p. 13; 1996, p. 32).

10.2.4 Interim conclusion

What are the implications of the hierarchically structured, multi-level nature of experience for theories of the neural bases of awareness? The traditional picture of perception regards processing levels as correlated with locations along a serial analysis pathway. The early stages would give rise to the more primitive, qualia-like aspects of the experience such as brightness, location, colour and movement, while the higher levels would give rise to more complex aspects such as seeing an armchair or a face – or knowing that it is a face at all, or a particular person's face, or that you hate that particular person.[21] With such a presupposition, distributed representations could involve any combination of brain areas along the pathway, in accordance with the nature of the particular stimulus. Each aspect or level of awareness would depend on a different stage of the pathway, and several such stages could be active at any one time.[22]

Under pure localizationist theories, such as Zeki's theory of micro-consciousnesses, activity in an individual area underlies each of those aspects of awareness more or less independently from activity in other areas. In contrast, according to resonance or binding theories (Pollen, 1999; section 9.3.2), the areas must be integrated with each other, and

---

20. Hebb (1949) made a similar point about our ability to attend to a triangle versus each of its sides in turn. Hinton (1990; section 6.4.2.2) emphasized how representations must be structured, for example, that of a face must also include its features (eyes, nose, mouth, etc.) and sub-features (eyelashes, iris, pupil, etc.).

21. Under serial processing models, the higher stages are assumed to be more embued with meaning, i.e. intentionality. It is arguable how far back down intentionality goes, or whether the higher stages only deal with the meaningfulness of the stimuli while the lower stages generate qualia. Some philosophers, for example, regard all experiences as intentional, even that of seeing a pure white square (e.g. Merleau-Ponty, 1945; Lycan, 1996). See also Side-box 4.4 and section 11.2.1.1.

22. Also beware: becoming aware of a change and being aware of the steady state conditions in the world may involve different neural sites. For example, different areas light up in brain scanning studies when there is a change in percept rather than a steady state (Kleinschmidt et al., 2002; Eriksson et al., 2004; see also Lumer et al., 1998, Lumer and Rees, 1999, Klein et al., 2000, and Polonsky et al., 2000). Some argue that we are not aware of the transitions, for example between interpretations of ambiguous figures, or in binocular rivalry (Pollen, 1999; Koch, 2004, chapters 15 and 16); yet others emphasize the importance of transients, for example in capturing attention (Egeth and Yantis, 1997). No doubt different functional mechanisms are activated in each case: awareness of external changes will relate to mechanisms of arousal, for example, whereas that of stimulus constancy and stability will involve working memory. Conclusions about the localization of awareness therefore depend on the type of awareness.

perhaps also with some higher centre such as the long-term or the working memory store, the hippocampus, the frontal lobe, a convergence zone and/or a control centre for attention (there are many theories under this category!). The content of an experience (e.g. of seeing red, or red leather, or a red leather armchair) depends on how far up or down the pathway binding or resonance is occurring between the different stages.

So by adopting an adaptive resonance or binding theory (chapter 9), and combining it with a top-down attentional theory (chapter 8), one can suggest that as you attend to different aspects of the stimulus you are modulating or varying both the location and the anatomical range of the resonance within the network of cortical areas (Figures 8.3 and 8.4). In this flexible model, many different regions of the brain can give rise to awareness, and as you attend to different aspects of the stimulus so those various regions are becoming differentially engaged and integrated into the whole representation.[23]

10.3 When is visual awareness generated?

One way to test the issue of localization of sensory awareness is to look at the temporal domain. There are two aspects to discuss: one is whether there is a persistence threshold for consciousness, and the other is when experiences occur relative to events in the outside world.

All physicalist theories accept that there is a delay between stimulation and consciousness, if only because the sensory nerves take time to convey action potentials into the brain. What happens there is the crucial point. Is the wave of activity evoked by the stimulus all that underlies conscious awareness – for example, could a single action potential be enough (or exactly synchronous potentials in several neurons in parallel)? In addition, is there then some preconscious processing that further delays the experience? As if this is not enough, some theories posit that it is not the processing per se, but an eventual steady state of neural activity that generates the subjective state. Consciousness may thus be delayed until (1) the messages have arrived in the brain, (2) a representation is constructed and (3) that representation has been stable for a certain period of time. The question is whether this third stage exists, and if so, exactly how much time it requires.

10.3.1 Is there a persistence threshold?

A simple theory of consciousness is that the crucial aspect of a representation is not its elaboration, or any magical quality or process added to it (section 7.1), but merely the fact that it continues for a period of time. Several theorists simply suggest that persistence of activity, or at least of some particular kind of activity (perhaps repetition of the same activity), creates consciousness.

For example, both Greenfield and Calvin (section 7.3.3) said that the more brain tissue is activated by a stimulus and the more persistent the particular cluster of activity, so the

---

23. The connection between these areas need not be simple resonance in the Grossberg sense (section 9.3.2.4), or binding in the sense of 40 Hz theory (section 6.4.2) – there could be some quite complex functional interplay of processing between the several areas involved.

more consciously aware you are of the contents represented within those brain regions. A corollary is that there is not a single threshold but a continuum: the degree of consciousness or the salience of the thought is proportional to or grows with the duration of the brain activity that underlies it. The duration and the size are always correlated in their theories, so it is not immediately obvious whether one aspect alone could (in principle) 'cause' consciousness or whether both are necessary.

Next, several theorists, including Grossberg and Koch (see section 9.3.2.4) propose that resonance has to be set up before consciousness occurs. Thus Grossberg (1999) suggests that resonance between the memory and the input has to be established through a positive feedback mechanism between the higher and lower regions, and once such resonance is set up, *then* you become consciously aware of the stimulus. Koch (2004) locates the frontal lobe and the posterior lobe cortices as the poles of the resonant system. In both cases there is a delay before consciousness while (in the terminology of dynamic systems theory: section 6.4.3.3) the network is settling into its attractor state.

Philosophical support for the basic notion has been given by O'Brien and Opie (1999), who reason that stable representations are necessary and sufficient for conscious awareness of the contents carried by the (stable) vehicle. The underlying mechanism, however, is a neural net (lying within a single cortical area) in which the cells each fire at a constant rate (while the spatial pattern of activity carries the content) for a brief period of time. The representation they envisage is thus not 4-D (spatio-temporal) in the sense given in section 6.4.

A more 4-D view was given by Rose (1999b), in suggesting that consciousness occurs when there is recurrence of the same spatial pattern (in dynamic systems terms: returning to or cycling round an attractor point, or completing a traversal of a circular attractor; Figures 6.10 and 6.11), even a single oscillation. Also, Newton (1991, 2001) proposed that consciousness originates in the superimposition ('blending', 'merging') of activity representing events happening at different times. Thus 'phenomenal consciousness essentially involves synchronous activations of representations, with distinct temporal tags, of more or less "identical" intentional content' (Newton, 2001, p. 51). It may arise from resonance between current input and short-term working memory (p. 56), with the stimulus represented as occurring at the present time.[24]

These are all attempts to explain consciousness as arising from the temporal aspects of neural processing. We might almost say that '*binding across time*' is the mechanism that generates consciousness. (I will return to this idea in chapter 12.)

Does all this map onto the phenomenology of consciousness? Several phenomenologists have indeed concluded that there is a 'thickness' to the experienced present (e.g. James, 1890; Husserl, 1928; Newton, 1991, 2001; Humphrey, 1992; Varela, 1999). A mental state thus has a temporal duration.[25] Husserl (1928), in particular, saw time as the

---

24. This makes an interesting contrast with the theories described in section 9.3.2.4 of resonance between input and long-term memory. The notion of 'temporal tags' is an old one (e.g. Yntema and Trask, 1963) and of course requires further explanation: how, and in what medium, is time of occurrence assigned to a representation?

25. Naturally, identity theorists (section 2.4) would like to explain this as following from and indeed mimicking the duration of some brain event – the event that just is consciousness. Other theorists such as Dennett (and perhaps Marcel, Libet, Zeki and others) would not require the brain event to have the same duration as the apparent duration of experience, since the latter is a construct.

crucial source of subjective experience. He partitioned it into three aspects: anticipation ('protention'), present and memories ('retention'), all of which are necessary.

The phenomenologists do not put quantitative labels on their diagrams, but psychologists typically estimate the duration is about 100–200 milliseconds – although figures from twenty milliseconds up to several seconds in length have also been proposed (the value perhaps varying with attention: Pockett, 2003). This diversity reflects the multiplicity of experiences that may be categorized as 'conscious'. For example, simultaneity thresholds (the ability to tell if two stimuli occurred at exactly the same time or not) give a lower bound on what has been called the 'perceptual moment' (Stroud, 1955).[26] Yet expectation or set, and short-term memory, may have durations spanning several seconds.

Such longer timespans for the present 'now' might therefore be possible if, as Newton (1991) and Humphrey (1992), suggest the memory traces of recent stimuli are essential for the awareness of those stimuli, and if the anticipation (expectancy, protention) of experience is also a crucial part of consciousness (James, 1890; Husserl, 1928; Varela, 1999; Newton, 2001).

But is the brain ever truly stable? At neural levels of description, it is clear that many processes happen much faster. A neural network, in a single cortical area, takes fifteen milliseconds to settle on a new attractor (Panzeri et al., 2001), synchronous correlated firing establishes itself in three milliseconds (von der Malsburg, 2002), individual action potentials (plus refractory period) last one millisecond, and each ion channel opening, chemical reaction, electrical current flow and quantal wave collapse is even briefer[27] (Figure 10.1).

So, during each moment of experience, an enormous number of physical events is happening in the brain, and that number increases as we look at lower and lower levels of description (Side-box 4.4). In accordance with multi-levellist philosophy (chapter 4), the mind–body problem is about how to solve the relationships between each pair of adjacent levels, by understanding how the phenomena at one level emerge from the interactions between the subsystems at the next lower level. If phenomenology is also multi-levelled, then perhaps we can use identity theory to equate neural and phenomenal events on a

---

26. The perceptual moment hypothesis is that subjective time is divided into discrete, quantal units. Stimulus events within the same unit are perceived as simultaneous, and only if stimuli occur in different units is a sensation of sequentiality generated. Some variants see the moment as sliding continuously through objective/external time (the 'travelling moment': Allport, 1968), while others see each moment as defined by successive cycles of the brain's EEG rhythm (e.g. stimuli occurring within the same cycle of the alpha rhythm are perceived as simultaneous: Pitts and McCulloch, 1947; Harter, 1967; Varela et al., 1981; VanRullen and Koch, 2003; see also Gray, 2004, pp. 211–212, who links moments to the hippocampal theta rhythm). See Patterson (1990) for a critical review of the hypothesis.

27. At the quantum level, Woolf and Hameroff (2001) claim it takes time for a wave field to build up over the visual areas. A wave function grows and then collapses every twenty-five milliseconds or so as successive cortical areas are recruited (hence the 40 Hz oscillations), giving rise to 'rudimentary' consciousnesses, akin to Zeki's micro-consciousnesses. This continues until the entire visual system is engaged in an integrated 'Gestalt' that collapses to give a vivid 'moment' of consciousness. Why this final collapse constitutes closure of the moment and onset of the next is not clear (why does the moment end when it does; for example, why don't more anterior areas of cortex also become integrated into the Gestalt, thus prolonging the moment?). However, under this theory it is the near instantaneous collapse of the wave function that is the actual generator of consciousness, not the steady build-up of the wave.

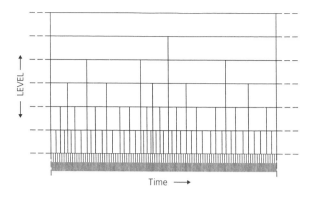

Figure 10.1 Higher-level states last longer. Imagine a thread passing vertically through a nested hierarchy such as that shown in Figure 4.1 or Figure 4.2. The transitions taking place at each level along that thread are indicated schematically here by the vertical lines.

level-by-level basis. Since high-level events proceed more slowly (Side-box 4.4), prolonged experiences would be underlain by steady-state or slow neural processes or states; and at progressively lower levels the timescale would speed up.

10.3.1.1 Interim conclusion

The conclusion is that if consciousness is underlain/subvened by a prolonged neural state, it is not a matter of there being a threshold, and/or of a steadily increasing degree of awareness as time passes while the brain is in that state. Instead, there may arise qualitative differences in experience as time allows the development/unfolding/organization of new processes at successively higher levels. The duration and persistence of awareness thus depends on the type and level of awareness you are talking about. The distinction made above between a processing stage and a steady-state stage thus breaks down, since it is not at a single level that the stream of events in time generates a singular event of consciousness.[28]

10.3.2 What is the latency of awareness?

It is common to think that there must be a delay between an external event and our consciousness of it, if only because there is some conduction delay before the news reaches the brain. However, in addition, it might be that some further processing must occur before consciousness arises. For example, consider Marcel's theory (Side-box 9.1), in which various preconscious processes analyse information (through a series of stages with short-term

---

28. Supposing the neural basis of consciousness is a prolonged neural state, of whatever length, suggests that awareness that a stimulus has occurred does not arise until after a correspondingly long delay. Now, in chapter 9, resonance state theories were contrasted with those suggesting it is discrepancy between memory and perception that leads to arousal and hence to consciousness. These mismatch theories, however, also imply that consciousness arises late – for example, at the time of the P300 wave (section 8.2.2.3). The latency of awareness is thus a question that applies in all cases, and is dealt with in the next section.

memory traces at each stage), perceptual hypotheses are evoked that are then checked back to the original input and it is all then synthesized before leading on into consciousness. So there is a delay that is not simply a conduction delay as information passes up the sensory nerves to the brain – there is some more or less elaborate kind of processing that has to occur before consciousness arises.

So, how long after a stimulus occurs do you become aware of it? This is a very obvious and basic question, and one could argue that research on it dates back more than a hundred years, in the form of reaction-time studies. Obviously there are conduction delays between an event's occurring and the information reaching certain parts of the brain, but one allied question is: which part of the brain? In principle, it is possible to follow the wave of activity up the sensory nerves into the brain, and to track the disturbance caused by the stimulus throughout the system. This method assumes, of course, that the first wave of action potentials (e.g. VanRullen and Thorpe, 2001a,b, 2002; Koch, 2004) determines the latency of awareness, rather than the time taken to process the message once it has arrived, as just discussed.[29]

10.3.2.1 There may be several latencies

Moutoussis and Zeki (1997a,b), for example, examined the issue by presenting a stimulus that suddenly changed in some of its characteristics. They used a set of moving squares generated on a computer screen. The squares all changed direction of movement repeatedly (every 268.5 or 358 milliseconds) between upwards and downwards motion. The squares also changed colour at the same rate, from red to green and back again, and, as for movement, they all changed colour at the same time. However, the changes in colour occurred after a delay relative to each change in direction, and the experimenters varied the amount of the delay. The question they asked the subjects was: which colour were the squares during each direction of motion? It was found that if the squares changed colour exactly halfway between each change in direction of motion, the subjects consistently reported each colour as clearly linked to one of the two directions (e.g. red = up and green = down), rather than there being a fifty-fifty connection between the two features. For the subjects to have equal associations, the colour had to change 60–100 milliseconds after the squares reached the halfway point along the motion trajectory. The authors concluded that there are 60–100 millisecond differences in the relative latencies of awarenesses of colour change and of motion change, with colour perceived sooner after it changes than motion is. A corollary is that each feature is perceived independently of the other, without binding, in the form of what they called 'micro-consciousnesses' (sections 7.3.1 and 10.2.2).

Critique

These studies do not claim to give the absolute latencies of awareness – in other words, they do not answer the question of 'when' we become aware. However, they do suggest that the

29. An alternative is that the bottom-up wave is not enough to generate awareness and some recurrent influence must be added (Lamme and Roelfsema, 2000; Thorpe et al., 2002). The simplest possibility is that a single act of feedback to a centre such as area V1 is enough for consciousness (e.g. Pascual-Leone and Walsh, 2001; Ro et al., 2003; see Side-box 10.1), but several iterations in a reverberatory pattern could be required (section 9.3.2).

latency of awareness differs depending on what the event is: awareness of colour change and awareness of motion change may not occur simultaneously even if the changes in stimulus colour and motion are simultaneous. Other studies, in fact, indicate that this is a general result: for example, reaction times for hearing and vision are different, and our awareness of touch does not occur at equal delays after touch to the toe and touch to the forehead (in fact, this is how Helmholtz measured nerve conduction velocity a hundred and fifty years ago; see also Klemm, 1925; Halliday and Mingay, 1964).

It is odd that colour should be perceived before motion, given that the neural delays are actually shorter for motion (ffytche et al., 1995; Schmolesky et al., 1998). Also, the relative latencies of V1 and V5 responses vary with stimulus velocity; yet curiously Zeki et al. (Moutoussis and Zeki, 1997a; Zeki and Moutoussis, 1997) did not find any appreciable or systematic difference in their data with change in stimulus velocity between 3 and 67 degrees per second.

Moutoussis and Zeki's data are also not easy to replicate. Some workers have found subsequently that a relative delay between colour and motion awarenesses only occurs if there are rapid repetitive oscillations in the stimulus qualities. If these are slower, or there is only a single change of colour and a single change of motion, then the relative timings are perceived veridically: in other words, simultaneous changes appear simultaneous (Rose, 2001; Nishida and Johnston, 2002).[30] It is not obvious from the theory of micro-consciousnesses why that should be so. The same applies to the observation that the relative timing depends on how large a change in direction of motion occurs (Arnold and Clifford, 2002; Bedell et al., 2003) and to the disappearance of the lag when the subject has to move a computer mouse in time with the stimulus rather than reporting the phenomenal appearance with button presses, or when the subject has to make judgements of temporal order (Nishida and Johnston, 2002). Although one could argue it is only necessary to establish that a dissociation can occur under some conditions in order to demonstrate the independence of micro-consciousnesses, the lack of any explanation within the hypothesis as to why the dissociation disappears under many experimental conditions leaves it with an unsatisfactory status.[31]

The original experiments certainly initiated a great deal of work and discussion. Alternative theories have suggested the effects may be caused by (1) adaptation to the stimulus (Clifford et al., 2003), (2) the fact that three samples must be taken at successive instants to detect whether the stimulus has changed motion direction, whereas only two are needed for colour changes, which can lead to differences in their salience and thus attentional mis-matching of the markers for each type of change (Nishida and Johnston, 2002),[32] and (3) the more rapid conduction of signals about stimulus changes

---

30. Another group found no delay either at high or at low frequencies of change (Holcombe and Cavanagh, 2001).

31. For other demonstrations that dissociation can occur see Arnold et al. (2001), Viviani and Aymoz (2001) and Kerzel (2003).

32. Zeki (2003) has repudiated this explanation on the grounds that Moutoussis and Zeki (1997b) found the percept of a change of line orientation also to be lagged in time relative to colour. Nevertheless, such changes also involve motion, so spatio-temporal explanations may still turn out to be the most generally applicable here too.

SIDE-BOX 10.3 THE FLASH-LAG EFFECT

Recent studies have tried to integrate the timing issue with research into the general spatio-temporal aspects of perception, such as how to predict or intercept a moving target. In the latter case, a subject might be asked to indicate where a spot of light is at a particular time, for example by adjusting the location of a briefly flashed probe so that it coincides with the moving target at a particular point in space and time. These studies have, however, revealed interesting errors in performance. The most famous illusion is the 'flash-lag effect', wherein the subject sees the flash as located behind a moving stimulus with which it is actually in spatio-temporal alignment. The stimuli typically appear as though there is about 40–80 milliseconds offset in real time between them. The most obvious explanation is that the processing of flashed stimuli is delayed relative to that of moving stimuli. This might not be surprising if the various features of a stimulus can be processed asynchronously, as some reports suggest (section 10.3.2.1).

   However, there are several competing proposals as to the underlying mechanism of the relative delay, and even claims that the delay is itself a delusion – merely apparent – for example, since processing time does not determine perceived time (sections 10.3.2.2 and 10.3.2.3). One proposed mechanism is a 'deblurring' process that shortens the perceived duration and trajectory length of moving stimuli. Another suggested mechanism extrapolates along a motion trajectory so that a moving target is seen at the location where it will be a short time into the future. Alternatively, a flash stimulus may initiate a resampling of the inputs from all stimuli; the perceived location of a moving stimulus may jump when this occurs as its previously accumulated positional uncertainty is resolved. Another related idea is that representations are completed only after a delay during which the information received over some (short) preceding interval of time is analysed. In addition, perceived extrapersonal space may be being distorted by the presence of the moving stimulus, and/or by the mechanisms that prepare for an eye movement. Finally, attentional factors cannot be excluded: (1) focusing attention shortens the latency of perception, and the flash and the tracked object may not receive equal attention; and (2) shifting attention between stimuli in order to compare them also takes time.

   Note that these explanatory factors are not mutually exclusive, so several (or none) could be relevant! Unfortunately, the current empirical evidence does not fit neatly into any one of these hypotheses. For introductory reviews, see Krekelberg and Lappe (2001), Nijhawan (2002) and Pockett (2002b); further ideas and evidence continually appear in the current literature. An explanation in terms of delayed thalamo-cortical modulation being necessary for consciousness (see section 8.2.2.3) is given by Bachmann et al. (2003) and some physiological evidence is reported by Jancke et al. (2004b).

(transients) than about the steady-state properties of the stimulus, and the flexible recombination of channel outputs to suit different task demands (Bedell et al., 2003). Side-box 10.3 introduces another approach to the empirical investigation of the timing of perception.

   The conclusion is that the cognitive complexity of the original task (asking subjects to judge an association between rapidly alternating changes along two different dimensions: Moutoussis and Zeki, 1997a,b) makes an interpretation in terms of simple processing latencies highly inadequate.

10.3.2.2 **There is a long latency**

In what has now become a famous series of experiments,[33] Libet also investigated the latency of consciousness (for summaries, see Libet, 1993, 2003a). In these experiments he activated the somatosensory cortex directly, in the way Penfield and Rasmussen (1950) had done earlier, applying electric shocks directly to the exposed cortex of patients with their skulls open under local anaesthetic. When the cortex is stimulated in this way, the person reports a feeling of touch – numbness, buzzing or a tingling feeling on the skin of a contralateral part of the body, such as the hand. In one experiment, for comparison, Libet also directly stimulated the skin of the person's other hand (the one on the same side as the brain activation), at the same time as he stimulated the brain (Libet et al., 1979). He asked the subjects: given that you are aware of a buzzing feeling in one hand and a real touch on the other, did those occur simultaneously? Well, the answer was 'no'. What Libet found was in fact paradoxical: when stimulated at the same time, the real stimulus to the hand appeared to come first, despite the fact that there were conduction delays while the information ran up the nerve from the hand to the brain and was then registered in the brain. By varying the stimulus onset asynchrony, Libet discovered that a 300–500 millisecond latency difference was necessary for subjective simultaneity of the percepts of the two stimuli. It was as though direct stimulation of the cortex did not give rise to awareness until it had been continuing for 300–500 milliseconds. From these and his earlier experiments Libet concluded that this is how long it takes for consciousness to arise from cortical activity. Moreover, it is the duration that is the necessary and sufficient property for generating consciousness.

But why was awareness of the external stimulus not subject to the same kind of latency, so that it did not arise until 300–500 milliseconds after the action potentials arrived from the skin? Well, Libet proposed that, normally, when a stimulus comes in it is subject to some kind of process that backdates its time of occurrence. Although our conscious awareness is delayed – it takes almost half a second to develop – subjectively, we refer the time of occurrence back, so that we think that the stimulus event happened half a second earlier, or in real time. The initial arrival of a natural pattern of neural input to the cortex sets up some kind of 'time marker' to which the perceived time is later referred (but direct electrical stimulation of the cortex does not create such a marker). So although if we could detect the brain mechanisms of consciousness directly we would find them physically delayed, our subjective awareness is (for natural stimuli) corrected for this delay.

It is obviously necessary – for catching a ball, or getting out of the way if somebody throws a rock at you – to be able to operate in real time. The brain needs to work out what is happening and then somehow to extrapolate our experience back, once consciousness has arisen. But how can our consciousness make decisions about how to cope with events that happen within less than half a second and are therefore over before awareness has arisen? What of our free will and choice of action? Libet also did a series of experiments on these questions.

Note that the latency question can also be posed for motor output. How long does it take between your making a decision to move your arm and the actual physical movement? Libet and colleagues (1983) asked subjects to bend their finger or wrist voluntarily

---

33. Eccles, Penrose and others have admitted being influenced by Libet's work.

whenever they chose, while he measured their brain activity (these were normal subjects, with electrodes on the scalp). He also asked them to estimate when it was that they made the decision to move their finger, which they reported by noting the position of a spot of light that was moving around the circumference of a circular screen the subject was looking at. Libet et al. found that they were able to detect changes in the potential on the scalp anything up to 300–500 milliseconds before the subjects made the decision (or claimed that was when they made the decision). Again, Libet suggested that there was activity in the brain for anything up to half a second before subjects were subjectively aware (of having made the decision), so consciousness was following after a delay (Libet et al., 1983; see Haggard and Eimer, 1999, Haggard et al., 2002, and Trevena and Miller, 2002, for recent developments).

The ability to make decisions more quickly than this, as when ducking to avoid an approaching missile, happens preconsciously. Our choices of action have to be made rapidly, because the read-out and execution of motor plans takes time, but the mechanisms of consciousness do still have a say: they are able to *veto* plans that would lead to disadvantage in the long run, and to permit only the beneficial ones to proceed. 'Free will' is thus expressed in the form of selective permission of automatically generated actions, rather than as the (Cartesian) initiation of action by an independent mind (Libet, 1985).[34] As one wag put it: 'We don't have free will but we do have free won't' (Gregory, cited in Blackmore, 2003, p. 129). Libet's (1994) philosophical conclusion is that consciousness exists as a dualistic mental field.

Critique

Libet's experiments and interpretations have generated a controversy that has persisted for decades. For criticisms, see, for example, Churchland (1981), Dennett (1991), Glynn (1991), Gomes (1998), Pollen (2004) and the series of papers introduced by Banks (2002). Libet has defended himself repeatedly; see, for example, Libet (1985, 2003b) and his articles in Banks (2002).[35] This long dispute is perhaps not surprising, given that the conclusions are somewhat bizarre and rather counter-intuitive. Although the brain activity underlying

34. See also section 8.4 on Cotterill's (1998) proposed mechanism for how a 'sense of danger' can prevent actions that may lead to pain.

35. Many of the objections are on technical grounds. For example, stimulating the cortex electrically does not make the cortex work properly; the spatio-temporal pattern of activity does not mimic that induced by natural stimuli. Indeed, the normal processes that give rise to consciousness might have occurred only after the offset of stimulation in Libet's experiments (Glynn, 1991; Gomes, 1998, Figure 5). Alternatively, Libet's stimuli may have been of such low intensity that they took a few hundred milliseconds to build up to the threshold for any neural activity in the cortex, or for such activity to reach a 'threshold for sensation' (Gomes, 1998; Pockett, 2004; Pollen, 2004). In either case, the time when the cortex was relevantly active was not what Libet thought it was. The arguments on both sides, however, implicitly assume that there are activation thresholds (section 7.3.2) and ignore the possible involvement of other regions of brain (such as the thalamic arousal system: Churchland, 1981; section 8.2.2.3). On this last point, if the P300 wave is the correlate of consciousness (Sidebox 8.3), then long latencies might indeed be expected. However, Bachmann et al. (2003) estimate a delay of only 40–70 milliseconds between the arrival times of the specific and nonspecific thalamic inputs, so total latency for consciousness should still be shorter than Libet suggests.

action may well build up for a long period preconsciously,[36] the late genesis of awareness of sensory events seems difficult to reconcile with our ability to make both strategic and sensorimotor decisions rapidly, for example while driving, playing sports or in hand-to-hand combat.

An additional point is that consciousness is not an all-or-none phenomenon that arises suddenly and fully formed. As described above (section 10.2.3.2), representations, even of apparently simple stimuli, have many components. Thus micro-awarenesses of the location, intensity, identity and other qualities of the stimulus are not necessarily all achieved simultaneously, but develop over perhaps as many as several hundred milliseconds (Kitazawa, 2002; see also Bachmann, 2000; Hochstein and Ahissar, 2002).

10.3.2.3 **There is no answer in principle**

Dennett's (1991; Dennett and Kinsbourne, 1992) alternative theory to Libet's and Descartes' is the 'multiple drafts model'. I mentioned before the emphasis of this theory on the spatially distributed processing of the stimulus over multiple sites in the brain (section 10.2.1.5). Dennett argues that it does not make sense to point either to any single instant in time or to any single location in the brain that is the crucial point in time or the crucial site at which we become aware. He suggests that information processing is an evolving continual process that goes on over the course of a few hundred milliseconds and in wide regions of the brain.

Because, like most philosophers, he thinks verbally rather than visually, he tends to favour linguistic metaphors, so his overall metaphor here is with writing.[37] He likens brain function to the preparation of a manuscript: writing, editing, rewriting and re-editing the manuscript bit by bit, over and over again. This is the origin of his model's name: many drafts are prepared before a final form is settled on. Each draft comprises a narrative: a story about what is happening (out there in reality). Each act of editing is an attempt to improve the story in the light of some new evidence or some further process of internal reasoning.

Dennett's main aim is to counter the Cartesian model, which proposed what he calls a 'Cartesian theatre'. This was introduced above, when we discussed the spatial spread of activity in the brain (section 10.2.1), but Dennett makes it more obvious by attacking the temporal aspect of the theatre metaphor. A corollary of the metaphor is that the events on the stage of the theatre are not just spatially isomorphic in some way to the outside world, but also temporally. That is, events on the stage take place in strictly the same order as in the outside world, including similar delays separating each event. There might be a constant latency, due to nerve conduction delay, but other than that the relative timings are intact (on an interval scale of measurement). I call this *'isochronic'* processing, by analogy with 'isomorphic' spatial representation.

In Dennett's model, there can be a post hoc synthesis as to when a stimulus event actually occurred, for example, there may be written into the story a particular instant in time at which it is decided retrospectively that the stimulus must have occurred (because this maximizes the sense the story makes). However, that particular instant is not necessarily

---

36. Witness the 'readiness potential', which is a negative shift in the EEG that builds up for a few hundred milliseconds before someone makes a movement (e.g. Deeke, 1987).

37. However, he has also likened thinking to re-editing a film (Dennett, 1996).

directly related to the instant of time at which the re-editing occurs, i.e. at which a particular kind of brain activity occurs or at which activity reaches some particular spot in the brain. The order in which we see stimuli is not directly physically determined in any one-to-one fashion – there is no perfect correlation between activity in the brain and the sub-jective order of stimuli in time – at least within the range of a few hundred milliseconds.[38] (How we perceive the temporal order of events separated by more than a few hundred milliseconds is not explained by Dennett.)

Now, we could take the findings of Moutoussis and Zeki (1997a,b) as supporting Dennett's theory, in that they show different latencies for colour and motion awarenesses, and lead to the idea that small regions of tissue can generate independent 'micro-consciousnesses' (Zeki, 1998; Zeki and Bartels, 1998; see section 10.3.2.1). However, this hypothesis operates within a conceptual framework that assumes neural processing time determines time of perception: the time taken for a brain area to receive information and complete its processing determines when we become aware of the corresponding aspect of the stimulus.[39] The importance of neural latency is indeed a common assumption, and one with recent empirical support (e.g. Clifford et al., 2003). In contrast, more direct support for Dennett's view – that perceived time does not correspond to brain processing time, but is instead a construction and can be post-dated so we may sometimes think an external event happened at a time before our brain had actually done the relevant computations – has come from Eagleman and Sejnowski (2000, 2003) and Nishida and Johnston (2002).[40]

But Dennett originally used some other empirical studies in support of his theory. One is an old experiment by Kolers and Von Grünau (1976) (although their conclusion too is con-tentious because neither I nor anyone I've spoken to can replicate it). The stimulus was a basic phi motion display in which there were just two nearby spots of light, one of which came on and then went off and then the other one came on then disappeared.[41] What Kolers and Von Grünau did in addition was to change the colour of the lights: the first light might be red and the second one green. In these displays, one still sees smooth phi movement as usual, but what happens to the colour? In fact, Kolers and Von Grünau had originally asked what intermediate states the colour goes through – does it desaturate to grey or white before turning green, does it go round the rainbow (e.g. red to orange to

---

38. To this extent at least, Dennett is in agreement with Libet (section 10.3.2.2)!

39. The completion of neural processing may be the instant of awareness, but there might also be a constant additional factor, for example if messages then have to be transferred to another brain centre such as the frontal lobe. The theory does not specify the absolute latency of awareness, only its timing relative to other similar ongoing processing.

40. Whether we detect a stimulus or not can be influenced retrospectively by subsequent events, as in backwards masking (Breitmeyer, 1984; Bachmann, 2000; Pascual-Leone and Walsh, 2001) or facilitation (Piéron and Segal, 1939; Ro et al., 2003). This, however, is a different issue from retrospective adjustment of the perceived time of an event.

41. Phi motion is a well-studied phenomenon in perception. Observers experience the illusion of a single dot physically moving between the locations of the dots, rather than seeing one light go off and the other come on. The movement is an emergent phenomenon, since it does not exist physically within the stimulus. Hence this attracted the interest of the Gestalt psychologists (e.g. Wertheimer, 1912): the whole is greater than the sum of its parts.

yellow to green), or what exactly does it do? Instead, their subjects reported that the spot changed colour from red to green suddenly, roughly halfway along its trajectory. Subjects saw a continuous red streak that then just altered into a similar but green streak moving across. (In fact Dennett's argument would hold just as well – even better, given the contentious nature of the colour change phenomena claimed by Kolers and Von Grünau – about phi motion itself, with the same colour throughout. But let's carry on with the original argument as presented.)

Dennett asks: if what you experience across time is simply a match with the temporal sequence of events in the outside world, how come you experience the change of colour before the dot has reached its new position? What physically occurs is: a red light comes on and goes off 150 milliseconds later, then nothing occurs for fifty milliseconds, and then a green light comes on for 150 milliseconds. The brain must be reconstructing the movement and the colour changes, if you take the visual system as simply presenting a strictly linear, serial picture of what happens in the world. There is no real movement, so the brain must be creating and backdating this apparent movement, filling it in across the gap in time between the dot transients. The same also applies to the colour: the idea that the dot changes colour halfway along the trajectory must be some kind of cognitive reconstruction, a hypothesis that has been generated to try to explain the pattern of sensory stimulation that occurred earlier. What real-world events could possibly have caused that pattern of stimulation? Well, the most likely explanation is that there was a dot that changed colour halfway along.

Note that Kolers and Von Grünau also did experiments with phi motion between two different shapes, and they found that the change of shape appeared smooth rather than sudden. So why do location and shape seem to change smoothly but colour changes abruptly? Dennett does not go into that, but whatever the answer, the point is that there must be some backwards reconstruction.[42]

Dennett argues that, if the serial model is true, then there are two possibilities for what is happening in the brain. One is what he calls a 'Stalinist show trial'. The decisions about what happened, all the perceptual hypothesis formation and preconscious processing, occur first, and then, at the end, after a decision is made – after the network has settled onto some new attractor state – *then* you become aware of the events. Everything is decided beforehand and the visible events presented on the stage of the Cartesian theatre are final and determine exactly what it is that you perceive. There is no possibility for any further or alternative interpretation of the evidence, which is unambiguous as presented at the trial. So according to this possibility, decision making is preconscious and there is a long delay before awareness occurs.

The second possibility is what Dennett calls an 'Orwellian revision of history' (so named because analogous events were depicted in Orwell's book *1984*). You do experience the events as they occur in real time: you see the red dot going off and the green dot coming on, after a delay, some distance away. But what happens is that the brain then reconsiders what

---

42. One can argue that objects often move position smoothly in the environment, but rarely change colour gradually (moving into a shadow does not alter colour, merely luminance). Although in nature squares do not morph steadily into triangles, an irregularly shaped object that rotates can alter its outline gradually. So perhaps the particular percepts reported by Kolers and Von Grünau result from reasonable guesses by the brain; but these arguments are all highly speculative!

it was that must have happened and the memory traces of the original experiences are then overwritten. Thus, all you remember is experiencing the dot moving and changing colour halfway along. You have no memory of the original experience, although you did actually have that original experience of seeing what happened in reality, in real time (or at least after a fixed delay due to conduction latency in the nervous system).

Dennett then says that there is no way in principle to tell whether the Stalinist or the Orwellian mechanism is the correct one. Therefore the whole idea of having a Cartesian theatre, comprising a single site and a single time at which consciousness occurs, is incoherent. He regards his argument as a *reductio ad absurdum* of the theatre model. Other people, of course, disagree and have suggested that you could tell the difference (e.g. Rosenthal, 1995; Christie and Barresi, 2002). Perhaps you can think of some experiments that would enable you to differentiate between these two scenarios. Write essays on this hot topic!

As a result of Dennett's (1991, 1994, 1998) motive to exclude the Cartesian theatre from theories of the mind, he has tried to describe brain processes as all of one type. Remember, with the theatre metaphor there are preconscious mechanisms determining events on the stage, and post-conscious mechanisms in the audience. Rather than talk about perception versus cognition, Dennett prefers to describe what happens in the brain as acts of belief fixation, judgement, interpretation, elaboration, categorization, decision, recognition, discrimination and identification.[43] What this list of terms has in common is that *our inner processes are more akin to thinking than to perception.* Although there are many loci in the brain, their effects in rewriting and editing the various draft beliefs we have about 'what is happening out there' are all of this single type.

Critique

Widely discussed and influential, Dennett's multiple drafts model is a sincere attempt to come to grips with the problem of mind – body relations, informed by some experimental data as well as a mixture of behaviourist and eliminative reasoning. However, the model is frustratingly vague and qualitative ('a superficial metaphor', according to Wilks, 2002, p. 261). It does not explain particular details, such as why Kolers and von Grünau's (1976) subjects saw a sudden red–green transition, or how we compare the timing of stimuli separated by more than a couple of hundred milliseconds.

Dennett has been so concerned to counter the prevailing tendency to assume a Cartesian theatre that he has tried to compress all relevant processing into a single type (belief fixation, or the selecting and re-editing of drafts). Although we may accept his point that there is not a second type that happens only in a separate 'mental' realm,[44] we cannot deny

43. Akins and Winger (1996, p. 184) interpret Dennett's 'judgements' as 'conclusions'. Compare Lennie's (1998) theory that cortical areas make 'perceptual decisions' which are passed to higher areas as summaries.

44. Dennett (1988, 1991) has also tried to achieve the same aim by denying the existence of qualia. For example, he said: 'Philosophers have adopted a variety of names for the things in the beholder (or properties of the beholder) that have been supposed to provide a safe home for the colors and the rest of the properties that have been banished from the "external" world by the triumphs of physics: "raw feels," "sensa," "phenomenal qualities," "intrinsic properties of conscious experiences," "the

that there are numerous kinds of psychological process that happen in perception, memory, reasoning, emotion and so on, and many types of neural processing that happen in different brain areas and nuclei (see also Akins, 2002). Dennett simply describes all these processes as 'judgments' about what just happened in the external world, but many commentators (e.g. Rosenthal, 1995) have pointed out that this at least implies a division between the results of a judgement and the evidence upon which it is based, which in most cases is also an internal representation or preliminary draft (see also section 5.3.5). Many modern philosophers therefore continue to take a dual-process view, and we will look at some of their ideas in the next chapter.

10.4 **Conclusion**

At the end of section 10.2, we developed a picture of representation and of brain activity as a multi-levelled complex, so asking where consciousness arises is asking too simple a question. The same applies to the question of when it arises. For instance, the obvious model – in which action potentials arrive at a particular time and place to give us an imme-diate instance of subjective illumination – ignores the diffuse nature of the wave of activity coming up the sensory nerves (not all axons carry impulses at the same speed), the wide-spread array of processing modules waiting to analyse each aspect of the input, the lateral and recurrent interactions between the neurons in the cortex and thalamus, and the lateral and recurrent interactions between the functional mechanisms needed to create a moment of consciousness (attention, memory recall, verification, etc.). Bottom-up processing produces little awareness on its own (Lamme and Roelfsema, 2000; Thorpe et al., 2002) or only a basic kind of awareness (Hochstein and Ahissar, 2002), and the full ramifications of a new input may take a long time to manifest themselves. (When do you understand a sentence? How often have you suddenly got the point of a joke hours after you heard it?). In addition, higher-level experiences have longer durations. So the answer to the question of when we become aware depends on the type or level of awareness you mean. Consciousness is not a singularity or a unit phenomenon – a conclusion we elaborate upon in the next chapter.

---

qualitative content of mental states," and, of course, "qualia," the term I will use . . . I *am* denying that there are any such properties.' (Dennett, 1991, p. 372). The inclusion of 'phenomenal qualities' and 'qualitative content' in this list of eliminanda certainly implies that all qualitative phenomenal experience is to be denied. Dennett has of course denied this (e.g. 1995, p. 289). Indeed, at the end of his original paper (1988) he still had to use the terms 'experience' (p. 73) and 'subjective experience' (p. 74) to explain what changes during perceptual learning. In a later paper (1998) he changed the terminology of his attack to a denial of 'double transduction', the idea that at some stage (!) brain events have to be transduced into mental events. Nowadays, the consensus seems to be that Dennett's attack was a matter of underlying assumptions and definitions rather than a denial of subjective experience. The term 'qualia' continues to be used by modern writers, although (usually) without the Cartesian connotations it might once have had. See Brook (2002) and Akins (2002) for recent evaluations.

■ RECOMMENDED READING

On imagery, good overviews can be found in Farah's The Cognitive Neuroscience of Vision (2000, chapter 9) and Palmer's Vision Science (1999b, section 12.2).

Research on the timing of awareness is so new that few texts cover it, although a brief introduction can be found in Koch's The Quest for Consciousness (2004, chapter 15), and Blackmore's Consciousness: An Introduction (2003, chapters. 4, 5 and 9) is good on Libet and Dennett. Whole issues of journals have also been dedicated to the current debates, such as Banks (2002); see also Pockett (2004).

Dennett's original writings are themselves very readable (e.g. Consciousness Explained, 1991, chapters 5 and 6). Some recent volumes containing reviews of his work are Ross et al. Dennett's Philosophy (2000; see especially chapter 11 and parts of chapter 15) and Brook and Ross Daniel Dennett (2002; especially chapters 2, 8 and parts of 1).

11 Multiple types of consciousness

OBJECTIVES

In this penultimate chapter, we step back from some of the simplifying assumptions we have adopted so far, in particular to consider that there may be a variety of types of representation. We look at theories that consciousness may arise from the interactions between particular different types of intentional representation, and the possibility that there are multiple types of consciousness. One issue we deal with in depth is the nature of 'the self' and what role it may play in consciousness. The questions to bear in mind are whether it is logical that consciousness itself can be explained by the differences between the various types of representation at the same level. Alternatively, is it necessary for the types to be at different levels, and is there an implicit crossing of levels as the various types are defined (revise Sideboxes 4.1 and 4.4 on levels)? In other words, in what sense are the representations different, and is this difference merely a postulated magic something that does not actually explain anything?

The student should also obtain from this chapter a renewed sense of the complexity of the mind/brain as a system of interrelated components, and the fact that simple unitary models of representation by themselves do not account for the full range of phenomena found within the mind.[1]

11.1 **Introduction**

In this book I have taken the philosophical stance that consciousness is a matter of representation (section 2.5, chapters 4 and 5). In the previous chapters, I adopted the simplifying assumption that there is only one kind of representation and I thus pursued a single answer to the question: what is the neural basis of consciousness? However, by now it should be obvious that there may well be different types of consciousness, different types of representation and no doubt correspondingly different types of underlying neural substrate. The diversity of existing definitions of consciousness was introduced briefly in chapter 1, but now we can begin to analyse these more systematically. First, we need to list some distinctions at several levels.[2] Starting at the finest, these are:

1. seeing red versus a different shade of red

2. seeing red versus green

3. seeing colour versus movement

4. seeing versus hearing

5. sensation versus perception, features versus objects

6. sensation/perception versus cognition/thinking (versus emotional feeling, moving the body, etc.)

7. awareness of self versus the world.

In section 11.2, I will be elaborating on the dichotomies at levels 5 and 6, because it is often suggested that the very difference between types at these levels is fundamental to the mechanism of consciousness. As we shall see, several theories posit that some kind of link between these different types of representation is the basis for consciousness. Such a link

1. One may also learn something here about the strategy of theory formation. Thus, for clarity, it is often necessary to begin with simple dichotomies marking out the extremes of each theoretical dimension. Now, the two defined alternatives may indeed represent qualitatively separated categories. Yet, on the other hand, they might instead demarcate the ends of a continuum of possibilities; if so, we need to fill in between them. In either case, if there are many relevant dichotomies/dimensions, we also need to combine them to form a multi-dimensional space of possible theories (Rose and Dobson, 1985, 1989). Then, we can envisage the search for the answer we seek as one of exploring a state space, where the space circumscribes all the possible states of the final theory (cf. Figure 6.11). In section 11.2 we begin, for example, by discussing whether qualia and intentionality are two separate dimensions of consciousness, opposite extremes of a single one, or identical. Then we add further dichotomies that expand the number of dimensions to the theory space.

2. There are also distinctions between the type of coding used in representations at any one level, such as analogue versus propositional (Side-box 10.2) and explicit versus implicit (Koch, 2004), that I will not be going into in this chapter. Revise also the distinction between plans and images given in Side-box 8.1.

may be one of direct connection (analogous to the binding problem at lower levels: section 4.3.7) or one of indirect inference (construction, or functionalist processing; see also sections 5.3.4 and 5.3.5).

In section 11.3, I will then cover level 7, dealing first with the representation of the self (is it just another representation or in some way unique?) and whether its linking to other representations is the crucial step responsible for generating consciousness (analogous to the interaction described in section 11.2).[3] As part of this discussion, we also need to consider the metaphysical nature of the 'self' as an entity.

Finally, section 11.4 will reassess whether there really is a diversity of types of representation.[4]

11.2 Two types of representation

11.2.1 Serial processing

It seems natural to assume a serial processing model, since sensory input clearly enters the mind/brain and behavioural output is, at least on occasions, subsequently emitted. As chapters 7–10 have emphasized, however, there is more to it than just a single feed-forward sweep! Nevertheless, it still remains common to postulate that the first arrivals in the mind/brain set up representations that differ in some fundamental and crucial way from those that arise later via subsequent internal processing. For example, some philosophers see the input-driven states as mere 'indicators', perhaps with primitive raw qualia, whereas only the later inferentially generated states have true 'meaning' (see Side-box 5.1; sections 5.2.5, 5.3.4 and 5.3.8). Here, we will examine what light neural considerations can throw on this issue.

11.2.1.1 Qualia or intentionality?

As stated in chapter 1, some people define consciousness in terms of qualia (or 'how it feels') and others define it as a state with intentionality (consciousness is always about something, i.e. meaningful). Does consciousness always possess both characteristics, or are these properties separable?[5]

First, can we make a case for there being identity between the neural substrates of qualia and intentionality? Some philosophers particularly have argued that qualia cannot exist

3. At a higher level, this may also be analogous to the generation of consciousness by the linking between 'selves' in social interaction: section 6.2.2.1; see further in section 12.2.3.

4. Essay topic: In chapter 5 the notion of broad content was introduced, which suggests that a link between a representation and the world gives intentionality and hence consciousness. Internal links may also transfer intentionality from one representation to another. Are the theories described in this chapter broad or narrow content theories?

5. Essay topic: Is the question of whether qualia and intentionality are separable meaningless, since qualia and intentionality can be considered two logically different categories? Or might there be (if only contingently) states with one or the other property alone? Give examples of the ways in which the answer varies with the definitions of qualia and intentionality.

without intentionality, in that all experiences have some kind of meaning. For example, Merleau-Ponty (1945) has argued that even if you see a patch of white, there is still meaning linked with it (such as: it is a figure, with shape, intensity and function), and qualia cannot be experienced in an elemental, abstract, isolated fashion. We could then suggest the same applies vice versa: there is 'something it is like' to hate someone, feel blue (!), believe in God, want to understand Kant, think you understand Kant, imagine the future and so on. Thus meaning and experience always occur together.[6] The recurrent and tightly coupled activity patterns seen in the brain during object recognition, recall and imagery (chapters 9 and 10) are consistent with this integrated picture. Perhaps we can differentiate the early phase of activity (the first few tens of milliseconds after a stimulus) from the later phases (chapters 7–10),[7] but the *anatomical* stages of analysis do not mirror any simple dichotomy.

On the other hand, the dichotomy between qualia and intentionality may be supported. First, it is common sense: as Hume (1739, Book 1, Part 1, Section 1, §1) put it, 'Every one of himself will readily perceive the difference betwixt feeling and thinking'. Note also that some restrict qualia to states indicating the present sensory input (Gregory, 1996), while another contrast describes qualia as resulting from processes of 'filling in' whereas intentionality comes from the logical reasoning processes of 'finding out' (Ramachandran, 2003b). Although the very possibility of neural approaches to this problem may seem simplistic to many philosophers, support can be taken from the data presented by Penfield (1958, 1975) showing that electrical stimulation of primary sensory cortex evokes experiences of simple flashes of light, buzzing sounds and so on, whereas stimulation of cortex away from the primary regions can engender more complex experiences, of a deeper and more meaningful nature, such as feelings of familiarity accompanying evoked memories. A similar division was also created historically within neuropsychology from comparison between the apperceptive and associative agnosias (see Zeki, 1993; Banich, 2004; Farah, 2004; Side-box 9.2).[8] Briefly, the losses of ability caused by damage to sensory parts of the cortex could be divided broadly into two types. The apperceptive agnosias are those in which the patients have problems with perceptual analysis per se, such as in perceiving the relationships between the different parts of objects. They may have problems with copying, drawing and integrating details into wholes (in the case of vision). The associative agnosias are cases in which people have problems more with understanding. They cannot tell the uses of an object, identify what the object is, know what it is for – for example, knowing that a comb is used to comb your hair, a pen is for writing, or that a door is hard and you will hurt yourself if you walk into it. Thus perceptual and conceptual processing are separable anatomically as well as functionally.

6. This may be partly a matter of definition. For example, in clarifying this issue, Crane (2001, sections 22–25) had to make distinctions between qualia, qualitative states and phenomenal states, between states and properties, between intentional content and mode, and between weak and strong intentionalism. Here, I have simply used 'qualia' (what it is like) and 'intentionality' (meaning) in broad brush ways, which should be sufficiently clear for the present purposes.

7. If qualia indicate the present (Gregory, 1996), then one might suggest they are generated by the early, ongoing analysis of current input only. However, this cannot just be the first bottom-up sweep; some recurrent processing is necessary (see section 10.4).

8. This classification arose about a hundred years ago, when the term 'associative' agnosia fitted into the picture they had at that time that 'higher' areas of the cerebral cortex were responsible for association

---

SIDE-BOX 11.1 ANOSOGNOSIA

Anosognosia is loss of knowledge about yourself, and occurs in a range of neurological and psychiatric syndromes. Following brain damage, for instance, people are often unaware of their altered condition and the fact that they are in some way disabled or different from what they were before. In some cases they may simply deny a physical change such as the loss of a limb or the inability to move properly; at other levels they may lack awareness of a cognitive problem such as having a poor memory; and in some cases their sense of who they are seems impaired. Patients may think they can go home and back to work at any time, and they are only staying in hospital because they want to help out or they are being kept there against their will. Such confabulations are common in these cases; people make up elaborate stories or excuses to rationalize their situation (for examples, see Feinberg, 2001b, and Hirstein, 2004). Generally, some recovery occurs, but in a few cases a degree of anosognosia may be permanent (Prigatano, 1999).

Numerous types of localized brain damage can lead to anosognosia (Vuilleumier, 2004). For example, in hemineglect, right parietal damage may lead to denial of left hemiplegia and unawareness that one is not moving the left limbs when asked to (see Side-box 4.5 for more details). In Anton's (1899) syndrome, occipital damage results in objective blindness, but patients deny that they are blind, and instead claim that they can see perfectly normal scenes in front of them (if they move around they bump into things, but they then confabulate about what happened, such as 'you moved that chair before I had time to react'). In frontal lobe syndrome, social graces may be lost and intrusive or offensive behaviour is carried out without the person realizing that there is any contravention of normal etiquette (Stuss and Levine, 2002). We could also add the split-brain cases here, since when separated the hemispheres do not each understand what the other is doing and why, and the left may confabulate freely about what its partner is up to (see sections 7.2.2.3 and 11.2.3.1).

More generalized conditions may also involve anosognosia as a component. For example, schizophrenics may display a variety of behaviours linked with loss of conscious self-control and awareness that anything is wrong (see Side-box 4.5). Frith's (1992) theory is that the feedback generated both internally and via the outside world as a result of actions should coincide (cf. Side-box 8.9). In schizophrenia there is malfunction of this comparison process, and sensory input is no longer bound correctly to the current internal model of the world (including the model of the self). This may apply at the social level, too, with discrepancies between social behaviour and feedback (other people reacting negatively or disapprovingly) not altering one's models of the world; hence one's understanding of oneself (the self-model) and of others may drift progressively away from reality, leading perhaps to belief that one is someone else and/or the subject of a conspiracy (delusions of grandeur, paranoia). See also Feinberg and Guazzelli (1999), Vogeley et al. (1999), Blakemore et al. (2000), Turken et al. (2003), Ford and Mathalon (2004), Vuilleumier (2004) and the papers in Sedvall and Terenius (2000).

In Cotard's syndrome, people believe they are dead, or that life is an unreal dream (depersonalization or derealization). According to Ramachandran (2003a), this results from disconnection between the parts of the brain that generate cognitive and emotional reactions to a stimulus. The right temporoparietal region may be damaged and the patient is usually depressed (Young et al., 1992; Gardner-Thorpe and Pearn, 2004). The person experiences a complete loss of the gut feelings that normally occur whenever one meets people and situations, and consequentially confabulates a rationale to explain why that is. The willingness to believe these bizarre conclusions may also indicate a failure of rational thinking, in that too much credence is given to one's perceptual experiences rather than to one's internal web of knowledge (Stone and Young, 1997).

_____ continues

SIDE-BOX 11.1 continued

Finally, in multiple personality disorder, people may at times be unaware that they are unable to access memories of past experiences (Side-box 4.5 and section 11.3.1).

So there are many different types of case where anosognosia occurs. These indicate that there may be numerous specialist mechanisms in the brain to mediate self-awareness of your various aspects, including awareness of the body, of your own cognitive processing capacities and of yourself as an individual.

However, there is another dimension that cuts across the dichotomy between sensory and ideational states, namely that of the complexity of the representation. Thus the empiricist-associationist philosophers Locke (1690) and Hume (1739) suggested a division into simple versus complex states.[9] Simple states are in some way related to what we now call qualia: they are sense 'impressions' or simple 'ideas', and serve as building blocks or elements of awareness. These simple entities become associated together, through experience, to form complex ideas or concepts. These more complicated, holistic ideas differ from simple in the (lower) vividness of the imagery accompanying them (this particularly applies to old memories or imaginings), and in their (completely learned) origins.[10]

In the standard serial analysis model, then, processing generates more sophisticated ideas about the stimulus, so the representation can be said to become increasingly complicated as extra associations are added and more information-rich conclusions are reached. At the neural level, many workers, such as Baars (section 7.2.3), Greenfield and Calvin (section 7.3.3) assume analogously that 'consciousness' arises as the brain builds up an enlarged, globally linked or bound region of activity.[11] However, none of these proposals explicitly incorporates a distinction between qualia and intentionality.

---

formation and were used for interpreting stimuli (see Zeki, 1993, for a historical review). In between the primary sensory cortices and the motor cortex was a large region that could not be activated easily in experiments (on animals) and was largest in humans; hence this was assumed to be the source of human intelligence by virtue of its subserving a massive ability to form associations.

9. Thus Locke distinguished 'sensations' from 'ideas' (which could be simple or complex). Hume also contrasted 'impressions' with 'ideas', which were possibly ends of a continuum; but *both* could be simple or complex. Simple ideas were linked by (vaguely specified) principles of correspondence to the primitive sense input states, while complex ideas were built from simple by association.

10. More recent workers in this tradition moved the boundary to allow more scope for preconscious processing. Thus Helmholtz (1866) concluded that there must be 'unconscious inference' to transform sensory input before consciousness arises, and Russell (1912) called the input 'sense data'. These arguments have come through to influence the indirect perception theorists such as Gregory (1970), Marcel (1983b) and Rock (1983), who propose that elementary sensory inputs are processed preconsciously to construct the substrates of conscious awareness.

11. On the other hand, it has recently been suggested that serial analysis progressively leads to 'conclusions' or 'decisions', such as to which category the stimulus belongs, and thus to increasingly simple representations. Thus, what is sent to 'higher' stages is a more condensed summary of what is happening in the outside world (e.g. Lennie, 1998). High-information representations are not necessarily complex in structure (if only because the amount of information carried depends on how many alternatives the message distinguishes between; e.g. Dretske, 1981).

11.2.1.2 **Continua?**

Thus, one variation on the theme, implicit in previous chapters, is that qualia and intentionality might each constitute a continuum rather than being all-or-none.

According to the serial processing view, the purest qualia would be generated in the primary regions of sensory cortex, and then progressively less vivid percepts would arise as neural activity moves away from the primary regions. For instance, thinking about your grandmother's personality (let alone justice, or 'what Kant really meant') evokes relatively weak mental images. (Stronger images can be evoked by these thoughts if we make an effort to engage imagery, which involves concomitant activation of lower sensory cortex by top-down recurrent mechanisms: Side-box 10.2.) However, in section 10.2 we asked whether there are particular stages of processing at which qualia are generated, such as the primary sensory regions, the intermediate stages, the higher areas, or all of them. The answer turned out to be not so simple, since interactions between areas are typically involved in most kinds of brain activity. A recurrent model, with activity becoming coordinated across several stages, seems better than the unidirectional serial processing model.

Let's therefore approach the question from the angle of complexity rather than intensity. To take an everyday example, in what way does your grandmother's face look different from the face of some similar old lady, a stranger who is not your grandmother? Superficially, the appearances (of skin, eyes, wrinkles, etc.) are not different phenomenologically; yet you do experience a different feeling when you see a familiar face versus an unfamiliar one – particularly if you know what type of personality the familiar person has, and even more especially if you are emotionally involved with that person.[12] The better you 'know' someone, the more these emotional/motivational feelings dominate over superficial appearance. Again, it would seem consciousness is not all-or-none; at least in the sense that it always comprises collections of feelings (e.g. seeing a hostile face, feeling fear and wanting to run away). The number in that collection can vary, and any given experience does not consist of just an isolated quale.[13] To this extent, then, there is a more or less continuous gradation in sensory experience.

What about intentionality? The serial model says a new wave of neural activity spreading from the sensory areas is increasingly assessed for significance or meaningfulness (whether the stimulus is good or bad, familiar or unfamiliar, dangerous, edible, a potential mate, etc.). Thus intentionality 'arises' progressively towards the 'higher' centres as there is increasing 'depth of processing'. According to the serial processing model, then, the neural origins of intentionality are inversely related to those of qualia: as one rises the other falls.

Similarly, under behaviourist psychology, meaning arises from the associations evoked by a stimulus (e.g. Hebb, 1949; Crick and Koch, 2003). As a stimulus is analysed progressively through several stages, so the brain derives more and more meaning from the stimulus as the number of associative connections activated in the semantic network of long-term memory increases (cf. depth of processing: sections 2.5 and 9.4). And so there is no single point or stage where the meaningfulness starts – it is a matter of degree.

---

12. Some people's lovers are ugly, but they are not *seen* as such – unless they become ex-lovers; photographs of such people just do not look like them (perhaps this is an everyday form of Capgras or Cotard delusion: see Side-box 11.1 and Ramachandran, 2003a).

13. Reading a word, however, may be an all-or-none event (Sergent and Dehaene, 2004).

Also, as mentioned in Side-box 9.2, for example, recent empirical research into neuropsychology casts doubt on the simple dichotomous nature of the deficits that follow damage to the posterior regions of the brain (Farah, 2000, 2004). The syndromes are never purely of one type or the other (apperceptive or associative), and alternative, more complex classification schemes have been developed that better match the diversity of cases that occur (e.g. Warrington, 1982; Humphreys and Riddoch, 1987; Bradshaw and Mattingley, 1995).

From philosophy, too, Lyons (1995) suggests how intentionality develops ontogenetically through several levels or layers, first by the formation of associations between sensory experiences, and between these and the sensory consequences of actions. Later, other people become involved in the causal loops that link our own experiences, and so arise symbolic representations, beliefs, propositional attitudes and public language. In addition, from a teleological stance (chapter 5), Millikan argues that intentionality is a matter of degree (1984, e.g. chapter 7). It depends upon the extent to which a signalling system interacts properly with other co-evolved systems, and to what extent their contents correlate with the real-world states they are supposed to signify.

There are thus numerous lines of argument for continuum theories.

11.2.1.3 Interim conclusion

Since the behaviourist background has shifted, the simple serial associative model need not dominate our interpretation of how processing proceeds, with its corollary of a division into qualia and intentionality or simple and complex states as characterizing two successive stages of analysis. At the very least we should say there are several stages, if not a continuum. These matters are certainly not all or none.[14]

Nevertheless, there remains the problem of how different neural loci – of basically similar anatomical structure (Rockel et al., 1980) – could possibly 'give rise to' qualia as opposed to intentionality if these are logically different categories. Although there may well be qualitative differences between what happens at lower and higher stages or at early and late times of sensory processing, there does not appear to be a single and sharp division between them. Given the complex nature of the underlying pathways involved (Figure 8.3) and the recurrent dynamics of the system (chapters 7–10) this may not be surprising. However, other ways of categorizing mental states exist that (try to) go beyond the simple serial processing model, and we turn to some of these next.

11.2.2 Modern philosophical dichotomies

In modern philosophy of mind another group of distinctions has arisen that are presented as sharp dichotomies. Some of these were briefly introduced in section 5.3.5 and Side-box 5.1, but here we can go into more detail.

---

14. Although there is a trivial logical distinction between one versus two, three, four . . . parts in a collection, this may not be so trivial if all the parts are interacting to form a system. Remember, even two mutually linked elements can give rise to new emergent properties (Figure 3.2). However, as system complexity increases so the numbers of possible phase transitions between states can grow disproportionately. Thus, since there can be more and more categories of function emerging as a system becomes ever more elaborate, the simple–complex dimension can hold more than just a dichotomy (one versus many) of properties.

11.2.2.1 **Phenomenal versus access consciousness**

For example, Block (1995) introduced the distinction between phenomenal and access consciousness.[15] By 'access consciousness' he refers to higher executive processes: the representational states that occur in everyday thinking and comprise the 'functional' aspects of cognitive processing that are 'poised' to affect reasoning and overt behaviour. These can be elucidated by using the range of methods available in cognitive neuroscience, psychology and functionalist philosophy. 'Phenomenal consciousness' then includes the subjective qualia of our experience, or 'what it is like'. Although some workers see this aspect as mysterious and the subject of the intractable 'hard problem' of how feelings arise from the material brain (section 2.2.2.1), interestingly, Block (2005) has recently suggested that it can be studied by using signal detection theory. Further, he suggests such phenomenality arises from recurrent processing between the sensory areas of cortex (as we described in chapters 7–10) while access consciousness involves information transfer to the 'global workspace' for widespread broadcasting throughout the brain (see section 7.2.3). There is thus a dichotomy between the (qualitatively different) neural substrates underlying the two types of consciousness.

11.2.2.2 **Creature versus state consciousness**

Perhaps comparably to the traditional division, Dretske (1995) and Rosenthal (1997, 2002) have contrasted creature versus state consciousness (cf. Side-box 5.1). 'Creature consciousness' is the kind of consciousness that might readily be ascribed to animals or young children. It is a primitive consciousness that would be roughly equivalent to qualia or sensory awareness. It is distinguished from 'state consciousness', which entails propositional encoding and knowledge or awareness of those sensory states. One of the examples Dretske gives is of a mouse listening to somebody playing a piano (1995, p. 9). The mouse can hear the piano but the mouse does not know, think, believe or understand that it is a piano. The mouse can hear the sounds and be conscious of them, but does not know their meaning. So there is a distinction between being aware of the incoming stimuli and having knowledge or beliefs about those experiences. There are qualitative differences between the two types of consciousness. Sensory experiences are in some way more primitive: they are built in to the mind in the same way that the sensory systems are built in to the body and brain. The sensory experiences we have are generated by our hard-wired neural connections, whereas the beliefs we have are learned, cognitive states. The sensory states are (accompanied by?) phenomenal experiences – qualia – whereas beliefs are (may be?) propositional.[16]

15. The term 'access' is unfortunate in that it raises questions such as 'access to/by whom/what?'. The dichotomy was also challenged by Dennett, who claimed Block was merely defining two extremes of a continuum of states with varying informational content; see section 11.4 for more on Dennett's views.

16. Thus believing that you are seeing something is like believing that the capital of France is Paris or knowing that the formula for salt is NaCl. It does not seem the same kind of experience as you get when you look at the white page in front of you or actually hear the sound of a piano. For one thing, it is all or none; you may be uncertain about the name of the capital of France, but beliefs do not vary in intensity or vividness the way the perceived brightness of a light varies, over a large continuum. Also, it is certainly wrong to believe the capital of France is Lyon, whereas the senses may generate indeterminate representations (see the discussion of bug detectors in sections 5.2.6 and 5.3.8).

11.2.2.3 Lower versus higher order representation

The analysis then becomes more subtle. Notice the contrast between beliefs about experiences and beliefs about the world. There are thus two problems to solve: how you know you are experiencing, and how you know what you are experiencing – whether there is any representation at all versus the content of the representation. For example, you wake up suddenly and open your eyes – is it day or night? If you can *detect* light, it is day. But where are you? To *identify* the stimulus requires analysis of the content of the representations. The first is the more basic problem, and indeed the foundation of the mind–body problem: how do we become aware of anything at all?[17] To solve this problem (although, as we shall see, it is not always clear exactly which one is being tackled, or whether they can actually be separated), some philosophers posit the existence of 'higher-order' mental states. There are two analogies used here. One is that of higher-order *perception* (HOP) or *experience* (HOE) and the other is of higher-order *thought* (HOT).[18]

Higher-order perception

The first theory is that higher states are in some way analogous to perceptual states, where perception is defined as the relationship between the lower-order states and the outside world. So just as lower-order representations – sensory impressions, phenomenal, creature consciousnesses – are in some way determined by events in the outside world, so higher-order beliefs are determined in a similar way by lower-order states.

Recall from section 7.2.3 that Baars (1988, 1997) adopted the Cartesian theatre idea. In this, events in the outside world are depicted on the stage of the theatre, and there is then an audience consisting of the various cognitive processing modules. There are many of these and they can all receive information from the stage – from the global workspace, as Baars calls it. Each module sits there like a student looking at a blackboard, and 'perceives' what is on the blackboard. The audience is necessary for consciousness and thus comprises an internal perception mechanism. Baars, however, states that the audience modules are not conscious in themselves (the issue of where and when consciousness arises in Baars' model is rather unclear: see section 7.2.3). How does his theory compare in this respect with the philosophical HOP model?

In discussing the Cartesian theatre model, Lycan (1987, p. 13; 1996, pp. 31–34; as mentioned in section 10.2.3.2) claims that some of the pitfalls of Cartesianism would be avoided if there were multiple theatres rather than just one. He uses the words 'scanning' or 'monitoring' rather than perceiving. One internal module can scan another module (where a homuncular 'module' is defined functionally rather than anatomically) without the scanner having to be conscious or intelligent in itself. Each scanner only acquires

---

17. In psychophysics, the tasks of detection versus identification ('which one of this set of stimuli do you perceive on the screen over there?') have long been distinguished. Although some work has shown that stimuli can be identified as soon as they can be detected (e.g. whether lines that are only just detectable on a screen are vertical or horizontal; Watson and Robson, 1981), this is not always the case. Some stimuli can be detected but not identified (e.g. Lindsey and Teller, 1990), while in pathological cases the reverse might be true – although the latter is controversial (cf. Weiskrantz et al., 1995; Weiskrantz, 1997; Zeki and ffytche, 1998; Cowey, 2004).

18. Essay topic: Are these divisions between two stages in a serial processing model, or two levels in the sense defined in chapter 4?

information for local use within the homunculus to which it belongs, rather than broad-casting to the whole brain globally. This homuncular functionalist approach avoids the man-in-the-head problem of full Cartesianism (section 4.2.1).

There may well be instances in which functional systems within the brain scan or moni-tor activity going on in other systems. A similar idea can be found in some scientific writ-ings; for example, implicit in Levi and Klein (1990) and many other papers is the assumption that the location of a stimulus is encoded by the location of activity within the primary visual cortex, and that this location is then detected by scanning mechanisms in some other part of the system. Similar ideas have been expressed about the superior col-liculus and other areas where there are topographic maps (e.g. Harris and Jenkin, 1997). Some models of attention are also very like this. They assume some parts of the brain can 'focus' on other parts of the brain (e.g. Crick, 1984; Blakemore, 1990), and/or selectively accept only parts of the information broadcast to them ('ideal observers'; e.g. Deneve et al., 1999; Rose and Pardhan, 2000). When attending to a particular stimulus, or expecting or watching out for something, it is as though the subject is turning some kind of internal searchlight or scanner onto the relevant module (or channels within that module). For example, if you are told to look out for a red object, you might 'tune into' the colour module, or even to the red channels within that module. This is also like constructing a template in short-term memory that the sensory input has to match.[19] There is indeed much recent empirical evidence that selective attention does sensitize the parts of the brain that deal with stimuli of the expected type (and it also desensitizes the other parts) – see chapter 8, especially Side-boxes 8.5 and 8.6.

Critique

Güzeldere (1995; see also Dretske, 1995, pp. 108–109) asks what it is that the higher-order states are supposedly perceiving. If a higher-order process is looking at the content of the lower-order representation, then the content of the higher-order representation will be the same as the content of the lower-order representation and the difference between the two representations disappears.[20] But if the higher-order representation is looking at the lower-order representation itself rather than its content, it is looking at the vehicle (cf. Side-box 2.2). This would not make sense, because higher-order thoughts are not about the contents of the brain – for example, which parts of your primary sensory cortex are active. Instead, the higher-order representations are about the outside world. People are not aware of the mechanisms that convey sensory information in the brain, i.e. the vehicles of the lower-order representations. The only way that could happen would be if the vehicles resemble their contents, in other words if representations were isomorphic to the objects they represent – but this is not on (see section 6.2.4 on isomorphism). Lycan's internal scanner hypothesis is not specified in any neurophysiological detail (but see the papers

---

19. Fans of theory reduction and the unity of science (sections 2.4.2.1 and 2.4.3.6) will be impressed by the unification of the theories of recognition by template matching, perceptual learning, selective attention and psychophysical channelling that Deneve et al. (1999) have proposed.

20. But maybe the vehicles have different properties, or the perceiving process is selective. Lycan says they are *used* differently within the rest of the mind.

cited in the previous paragraph) and anyway it is not obvious how such scanning would generate higher-order consciousness. So whether it is the lower-order content or vehicle that is perceived, the higher-order perception theory cannot be correct.[21]

Higher-order thought

The alternative philosophical position is the higher-order *thought* theory. In this, the higher-order states are more like propositions than percepts, and are related to the lower-order states inferentially.

Rosenthal (1993, 1995, 1997, 2002) is one of the main proponents of this theory. He argues that higher-order thoughts are necessary for consciousness and that you don't get awareness from lower-order representations alone. You have to *think* (know, believe . . .) that you are seeing red, hearing a whistle or looking at your grandmother in order to be conscious. Consciousness is knowing that you have (or are 'in') a lower-order perceptual state; simply having that state on its own does not render its contents conscious. Rosenthal (1997) suggests it will be easier if we learn how to explain non-conscious mental states first, as an intermediate step towards explaining conscious ones. For example, higher-order thoughts are of fewer types (perhaps just 'thinking') as opposed to the multitude of lower-order sensings (of red, middle C, pain, etc.) and thus have more universal function. He also suggests that a HOT could exist without a corresponding LOT (lower-order thought), hence explaining confabulation, filling-in of the visual scene, and (presumably) other delusions and hallucinations (although we may wonder where consciousness then arises, since there is no LOT to provide the content that becomes conscious). Moreover, higher-order thoughts are about things and can be reported verbally, whereas sensory states (qualia) are ineffable. Non-conscious sensory states clearly exist, however, as witness their effects on our behaviour (as in body language, scratching ourselves and unexpressed motives such as those shown by Nisbett and Wilson, 1977).[22] More recently, Rosenthal (2002, pp. 413–414) has added that you cannot be conscious without a HOT because, for example, you cannot think you are seeing 'red' unless you already have the concept or category 'red' (and the same, more obviously, for 'triangle', 'grandmother' and so on). More remarkably, in addition you need the prior concept of 'visual' to distinguish sights from other modalities of stimulus input. His point is that, since concepts are not percepts, LOTs cannot be experienced in isolation from a HOT (although LOTs may exist in isolation). Gennaro (2005) makes the theory clearer when he gives an example of a HOT more simply as 'I am seeing a red triangle now', rather than 'I think I am seeing a red triangle now'. He suggests that a conscious state is always a 'complex' system consisting of both a LOT and a HOT in combination (rather than the mere presence of the HOT making the LOT conscious).[23]

21. There is a third possibility – that the higher-order state represents whether there is a lower-order representation at all (as described in the introduction to this section). However, Güzeldere (1995) says this would be a higher-order thought, not a percept.

22. Philosophers often cite Nisbett and Wilson (1977) as evidence that we have unconscious states controlling our behaviour, and that we do not have direct knowledge of our own mental states. They never cite descriptions of the methodological flaws in that study (see Smith and Miller, 1978; Ericsson and Simon, 1980).

23. One of the examples often presented is that of a long-distance driver (Armstrong, 1980). Anybody who drives a lot knows that once you have practised driving you can continue on 'autopilot'; in fact,

Dretske (1995), while agreeing that higher-order representations are thoughts rather than percepts, argues that you can be aware of first-order primitives without their having to have higher-order states linked to them. The lower-order states may count as a type of consciousness (creature consciousness). Even if you are paying attention somewhere else and not having HOTs about them, you can be aware of red traffic lights without knowing that you are looking at a red traffic light – just as a mouse can be aware of the sound of a piano without knowing that it is aware of the sound of a piano (see also Nelkin, 1995; Block, 2005). The higher-order thoughts represent not the outside world but the fact that you are having an experience, and that the (lower-order) representation is a conscious experience/percept rather than an unconscious representation.

Critique

Rosenthal posits that the higher-order state is not conscious (unless one is introspecting: see section 11.3); its function is to make the lower-order state conscious. He thus treats consciousness as an intrinsic quality that can be added to a mental state by attaching an external (higher-order) state to it (cf. Side-box 7.1 concerning attaching qualities to representations to make them conscious ones).

Yet the exposition is not always so clear; for example: 'HOTs result in conscious qualities because they make us *conscious of ourselves as being in certain qualitative states*, which results in the subjective impression of conscious mental qualities' (Rosenthal, 2002, p. 414; his italics). Similarly with Dretske, for example: 'what makes an experience (the sort of mental state we are concerned with here) conscious is that the creature whose experience it is believes, knows, or somehow conceptually represents this experience (or itself as having this experience)' (Dretske, 1995, p. 106), and 'HOT theories require, not sensory awareness of an experience, but a conceptual awareness of it, some thought or judgement *that it is an experience* (perhaps, an experience of such-and-such kind)' (Dretske, 1995, p. 109; my italics).

Expressed in this way, we may ask how a (higher-order) thought (or the creature as a whole?) represents something (a lower-order, representational experience) as being an experience, in other words, a conscious state. How does the higher-order thought represent experience? How does it even 'know' that there is such a phenomenon as experience, let alone what it is? Where does it get the concept?[24] Does it possess some inbuilt (Kant-style

---

once any skill is practised and automated it can be carried out without paying much attention (e.g. Lindsay and Norman, 1977). You can drive along a familiar route, stopping at red lights, turning corners and avoiding the other traffic, but then at the end of the journey you realize you have been thinking about shopping, exams, what excuse you will give if you arrive late, or whatever. You have no awareness – or certainly no memory – of having stopped at the red lights and so on. The question is: were you actually conscious of the red lights at the time you encountered them? Rosenthal's argument is that you are not conscious of such sensory inputs if you are thinking of something else: daydreaming or whatever it is you do when you are operating on autopilot. You are only conscious of a red light if you think about it.

24. I am drawing an analogy here with Rosenthal's point about needing to have conceptual categories (i.e. thoughts not percepts), such as 'oboe' and 'hearing' in order to hear an oboe consciously (2002, pp. 413–414). Perhaps it is Rosenthal's third-order thoughts that must include the categories 'I' and 'am' and 'conscious/experiencing'. The question still remains as to how these categories are acquired – a soluble one, perhaps, but needing an explicit answer.

'a priori') knowledge that such a thing is possible? *It begs the question as to how consciousness arises if the HOT (or the creature) has to possess knowledge that consciousness exists before consciousness can arise.* It sounds as though the HOT theory is merely positing some mysterious extra something that can be added to representations to make them conscious – a magical step in processing – and as such it does not present any advance in solving the mind–body problem (section 7.1).

Additionally, this theory may be confused with that of introspection, in other words, with representing the self as being aware of the (existence or content?) of the lower-order representation. Again: 'what makes an experience . . . conscious is that the creature whose experience it is believes, knows, or somehow conceptually represents this experience (*or itself as having this experience*)' (Dretske, 1995, p. 106; my italics). As such, the representation of the self comes into play, introducing a (potentially) qualitatively novel element (possibly, an unexplained magical conferrer of consciousness). In section 8.3.2 we saw how LaBerge ran into trouble with this approach, and in section 11.3 below we will return to the notions of introspection and the self in more detail. Meanwhile, a variety of recent arguments for and against the HOT theory may be found in Gennaro (2004).

11.2.3 Modern neural dichotomies

There are also a number of neurally based theories that differentiate higher- from lower-order representations, but in ways that do not follow a simple serial model. Some of these depend on the idea that *language* is in some way special, and have been introduced in section 7.2.2.3.

11.2.3.1 Hemisphere differences

For example, Gazzaniga (1995) concluded from his studies of split-brain patients that the right hemisphere is only capable of generating raw, primal, emotional feelings about events in the world, whereas the left hemisphere is responsible for the fine discrimination of feelings, for labelling or categorizing them and for rational thinking: making inferences about cause and effect, executive decisions and the strategic control of behaviour. The left hemisphere monitors the actions of unconscious cognitive modules, rationalizes and creates an explanatory narrative. It synthesizes consciousness by integrating feelings and cognition. This left hemisphere ability is not dependent on its linguistic processing module, since it remains there even in individuals whose language function is located in the right hemisphere.

11.2.3.2 Categories of categories

A more specifically language-based neural theory is that of Edelman (1989, 1992). In section 9.3.2.3, I introduced his theory that primary consciousness arises in the re-entrant looping connections between the frontal, temporal and parietal lobe memories and the primary and secondary sensory cortices. These generate phenomenal experience of the instantaneous sensory environment (1992, p. 115). However, Edelman also tacks on a higher-order consciousness that is generated in a set of secondary loops through the language areas of the cortex: Broca's and Wernicke's areas (Figure 11.1). The language cortices organize and encode in symbolic/linguistic formats the lower-order category memories in

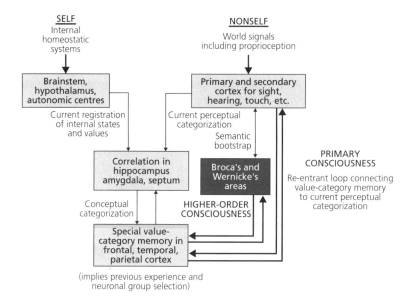

Figure 11.1 Edelman's (1992) complete schema for primary and secondary types of consciousness (extending that shown in Figure 9.4).

the frontal, parietal and temporal cortices. Edelman relates the generation of these meta-categories to language. There is a social component in that one learns language through interpersonal experiences and rewards, for example by ostensive definitions – someone saying 'that is a duck' (1992, p. 129). Such episodes guide the formation of the higher-area categories, that are then used for planning: for building models of the world and the self, and projecting into the past and the future. Curiously, Edelman uses the word 'qualia' to refer to higher-order categories only, so qualia ('recategorizations . . . of value-laden perceptual relations . . . or their conceptual combinations with each other'; 1992, p. 136) are limited to humans. Moreover, Edelman does not go into any specific details as to how the higher-level categories are used or processed internally to generate awareness of the self and time.

11.2.3.3 **Internal monitoring**

Finally, Rolls (1999) also links higher-order thought with language, but his inspiration follows Rosenthal (section 11.2.2.3) and he calls it 'higher order linguistic thought' (HOLT). This involves a kind of mentalese (an impoverished internal language; section 2.5) – that is, higher-order thought is not identical to human verbal language. The crucial point is that propositions or symbols are processed according to syntactic rules. The objects of processing are the operations of the lower-order thinking processes, particularly those responsible for the planning of behaviour.

The computational function of the internal monitoring system is debugging. When something you do does not work, you obviously need to know what went wrong, so that you can correct your actions and do it right next time. In many real-world tasks, the action taken depends on a complex chain of reasoning made internally – an elaborate plan formulated on the basis of a complex model of the outside world and perhaps a series of choices between several ideas as to how to change it. If your action does not work properly you need to be able to scan the entire internal plan, like looking through a computer program and finding where the bug or error is. So you have to be able to become 'aware' of your internal thinking processes, in the sense that you can recall, re-analyse, re-evaluate and alter them as necessary. This is how consciousness is generated. It also explains why consciousness evolved: one needs some kind of internal self-analysing mechanism. It might even additionally help us to understand and predict the actions that others take based on their own lower-order thinking processes (Humphrey, 1983; section 6.2.2.1).

Rolls suggests an anatomical location for the HOLTs: they are linked to the language cortices in the left hemisphere that are the primary origins of all types of consciousness. This is because qualia are generated only to the extent that lower-order states are subject to higher-order monitoring, in other words, that other areas of the brain (including primary sensory cortices) communicate with the language areas. This process need not be via direct axonal connections, but must to be able to bypass intermediate stages of cortical processing so that the functioning of the early cortices can be monitored, as well as that of all the intermediate stages independently.[25]

11.2.4 Interim comment

There are thus numerous ways of formulating dichotomies between different types of mind/brain state. Although all those based on serial processing may be variations on the same underlying principle, the modern alternatives introduce orthogonal new ideas (unless language is merely regarded as the final stage in a serial processing pathway). The existence of parallel and recurrent pathways in the brain suggests that any theoretical dichotomy will turn out to be artificially sharp. On the contrary, one could certainly argue that the brain is filled with such a multitude of different types of consciousness-generating process, with varying degrees of qualia and intentionality, that no single dichotomy suffices to characterize them all.

11.3 Is the self special?

In this section we introduce another putative difference: between representations of the self versus those of the outside world. Several theories we have met in earlier chapters posit not merely that the representation of the self is qualitatively different from other representations, but that this is the actual key to how consciousness arises (e.g. sections 7.2.2.3 and 8.3.2). However, before we can discuss this idea we need to clarify several issues about the notion of 'the self'.

25. Rolls points out that the dependence of qualia on higher-order thoughts implies that qualia (including emotional and motivational states as qualia – feelings) did not evolve first. His position thus contrasts with those of Damasio (1995, 1999), Edelman and Tononi (2000) and others.

First is the ontological question: what is the self? Is there a metaphysical entity that just is the individual person's self, like a soul or spirit? This makes the topic a religious issue, as discussed in chapter 1. The crucial point here is that many people believe in the existence of this 'self' – we certainly believe that we exist as individual selves. (Essay topic: Are we aware of ourselves or of our selves?) There is thus a reflexive component within the self, and this raises interesting epistemological questions as to the origins of consciousness. How is it that we are self-aware (or as Descartes asked: how do we know that we exist?)? If there is a self then there must be non-self, that is, something we may call here 'the outside world'. The question of self-awareness thus has a mirror: how do we come to be aware of the external world (in other words: how do we know the rest of the world exists)? It is not clear which comes first: self-awareness or awareness of external entities. Most modern theories posit the latter has priority and that self-awareness develops later.[26] Many current theories of self-awareness are thus offshoots or extensions of theories of consciousness in general. For example, representational theories may posit a special representation of the self that may or may not have properties similar to those of representations of trees, triangles, truth, grandmother or the colour 'red'. We may or may not become conscious of our selves (ourselves) in the same way that we become conscious of trees, etc. Other theories say we can only become conscious of trees because we have selves to be conscious, or to make (somehow) the contents of tree-representations conscious.

The properties of 'the self' include having a unity (each of us is a single entity) and persisting as the same entity over time (Blackmore, 2003, p. 94). Moreover, our awareness has what is often called a 'point of view', that is to say, we are aware of being in the world, at a particular place and time. Awareness of the world from that point of view is thus intimately tied up with awareness of being a single entity and of being able to move through space over time within that perceived world. The latter also involves a sense of free will – of being in control of our actions.

So now, bearing in mind the many meanings of the term, we can approach what has been written about the self from a number of viewpoints. I will start with the neural bases of its unity, then list some hypotheses about its neural representation, and then go on to some higher-level theories at the cognitive and social levels. Next I will deal with the issue of whether introspection is the same as self-awareness, and finally the question of whether there is a unified self at all. (Many of these ideas have already been introduced in earlier chapters, so I will just summarize briefly here and give back-references to relevant sections.)

11.3.1 Unification of the self

The first question we need to cover is the (apparent) unity of the self. Some people explain this as a form of 'binding', since all our senses, thoughts, and actions seem to be linked to each other in some way and experienced by a single individual (e.g. Cleeremans, 2003; section 4.3.7). There may not be a single convergently generated self; instead the self is just a closely connected network of functional modules. In various disorders this unity may break down, and manifestations of self-unawareness are postulated to result from disconnections between the units (e.g. Side-box 4.5).

---

26. This is the opposite of Descartes' reasoning: I think therefore I am; I exist therefore the world must exist.

For example, Forrest (2001) describes the development of cognitive models of the self during infancy. Each model arises from the social relationship the child forms with a person the child interacts with (see section 6.2.2.1 for more on the social origins of consciousness). Normally, the child's actions affect those of the caregiver and vice versa, so a mutually adaptive fit develops between the individual and their (social) environment. Successive experiences with different people then lead to a generalized model of 'the self'. However, in some cases inconsistent, inflexible or painful social interactions occur that prevent the formation of such a unified model. Therefore several 'personalities' (systems of behaviour) may develop that can be used to cope with different social contexts ('multiple personality disorder' or 'dissociative identity disorder'). Forrest attributes the independence of the various self/world models in such people, rather reductively, to lateral inhibition between patterns of activity across neural network modules, with particular emphasis on the orbito-frontal cortex as the crucial neural site of control.

Another, lower-level approach to unification assumes that there is neural convergence, which is necessitated by the fact that although we have several different sensory input modalities we only have one motor output (in the sense that there is only one direction you can move your arm in at any time or one direction you can walk in). So there has to be some kind of funnelling-down of decisions to a single centre, a unitary process, that decides what the next movement is going to be. This system then feeds the decision back internally to all the other regions of the brain through 'efference copy' (recurrent) pathways. Thus copies of the motor output are sent to all the sensory regions to coordinate and unify the activity of different parts of the brain (section 8.4; Side-box 8.9; Churchland, 2002, pp. 70–90).[27] Malfunctions of this system may lead to schizophrenia, in which there are disorders of 'the self' (Side-boxes 8.9 and 11.1).

Unification is also implicit in field theories, which see the entire mind as a single continuous entity in a medium such as an electromagnetic gradient or a quantum probability wave (section 6.2.4).

11.3.2 **Representation of the self**

11.3.2.1 **Memory-based models**

A second major aspect of the self is its continuity over time. This can include extrapolation into the future and the planning of actions to achieve goals (e.g. Rolls, 1999, p. 255), but even more obvious is memory of the past, and in particular autobiographical memory (Neisser and Fivush, 1994; Fivush and Haden, 2003). Episodic memories are normally seen from the same point of view as our current experience: we recall images of events as they were seen at the time (most dramatically in 'flashbulb' memories) and this is especially so for recent events (the more distant ones may be seen as happening from the point of view

---

27. This is useful because when you move this should create a particular change in the sensory inflow as a result. For example, if the motor system decides to move the eyes to the right, the entire visual image will swing suddenly across the retina a few hundred milliseconds or so later. By knowing ahead of time what the movement will be, the sensory systems can prepare for the change, in a way that speeds up their processing and reduces the need for a full re-analysis of the entire sensory inflow after the event (Side-box 8.9).

of a third person, who is watching us from outside our own body[28]). For more see section 9.2 and Side-box 9.2 (particularly, the ideas of Tulving and Conway).

For example, Taylor (1999, chapter 11) ascribes the self to autobiographical memory. The parahippocampal cortex stores cues[29] that can activate action/behaviour memories stored in the medial orbito-frontal cortex. Taylor also uses this model to explain multiple personality disorder. In these cases, segments of the parahippocampal cortex can be inhibited if there is strong emotionally driven input from the amygdala. This inhibition suppresses whole sections of the person's autobiographical memory while releasing others. The striatum also (somehow) plays a role in mediating competition between these alternative personalities and switching between expressing the behaviours based on one set of memories or another. This theory compares interestingly with that of Forrest (2001), which posits inhibition between whole networks within the orbito-frontal cortex in mediating such switches of personality. This area of brain normally functions to suppress behaviour driven by the ongoing sensory input in favour of actions based on internally stored information, including cognitive models of the self and world based on autobiographical experience (see preceding section).[30]

Recent brain imaging evidence supports a role for the medial prefrontal cortex in 'metacognition', i.e. knowledge about one's own cognitive abilities, including an individual's own personality and hence at least one type of self-awareness. But it is not still clear to what extent these studies tap into autobiographical memory rather than personal semantic memory, emotional or retrieval processes (see Schmitz et al., 2004). An argument against the self being entirely based on autobiographical memory is given by Churchland (2002, p. 65), who describes a patient with bilateral temporal lobe damage and almost global retrograde amnesia but who maintains at least a certain degree of self-representation.

11.3.2.2 Body-based models

Another common idea is that the sense of self originates from representation of the body (e.g. Bermúdez et al., 1995; Taylor, 2001; Churchland, 2002; Kinsbourne, 2002) or the body plus autobiographical memory (Damasio, 1995, 1999; LaBerge, 1997, p. 174). The feeling that we can deliberately control the behaviour of our bodies is central to the experience of self (voluntary 'free will'). But before we move our bodies we need to know where our limbs are, so we can initiate movements in the right direction. It would appear that we can obtain such knowledge easily, since there are innate and often topographic neural connections giving the brain proprioceptive and kinaesthetic data about limb locations, and also several internal monitors of blood ion and hormone levels. The brain's main centre for mapping body location in space is the parietal lobe, particularly inferiorly in the right hemisphere (section 7.2.2.3). Thus lesions there may result in spatial agnosias, including hemineglect wherein patients ignore the left side of their body, and even deny the

---

28. This implies a change from egocentric to world-centred coding within the representation of the scenario.

29. These are what Morton et al. (1985) called 'headings', which function like the labels on files, guiding our search for bundles of information in our memories.

30. While both Taylor's (1999) and Forrest's (2001) models are reductive and of course vague on details, the latter paper presents a far more detailed and well-supported case.

existence of their left limbs (Side-box 4.5). Conversely, after amputation of a limb a person may continue to feel that the limb is still there ('phantom limb' syndrome), as though a mental model of it remains in existence.[31] Abnormalities of the egocentre (point of view) and of the perceived size, shape and location of one's own body have been related to neurological problems in the parieto-temporal region (Blanke et al., 2004) – although other medial parietal and frontal regions are also involved in generating the egocentric self-view in normals (Vogeley and Fink, 2003).[32]

One way to test the right parietal hypothesis is to look for hemisphere differences in the representation of the self, which might thus be stronger in the right side of the brain. In split-brain patients, Sperry (1984), however, concluded there were two selves, one in each hemisphere. For example, each hemisphere can recognize and respond appropriately to pictures of itself (Sperry et al., 1979). On the other hand, Gazzaniga (1995; Turk et al., 2003) concluded that the left hemisphere 'interpreter' (section 7.2.2.3) is the basis of the self-concept. Moreover, Gazzaniga's group found a split-brain patient who recognized pictures of himself better with the left hemisphere, and those of familiar other people with the right (Turk et al., 2002).[33] In contrast to both groups, MacKay (1987) and Sergent (1987) disputed that the evidence was sufficient to demonstrate the existence of two 'free wills'. They were able to show cooperative goal-seeking behaviour between the hemispheres of split-brain patients, presumably mediated by descending connections to regions of the brain where left-right cross-talk is possible or where some unified mechanism exists.

11.3.2.3 Multi-level models

Baars (1997, chapter 7) adopted a multi-level model of the self, with narrative interpreter and body schema mechanisms superimposed over a 'deep context' that comprises one's long-term expectations and goals in life. These are stable aspects of one's existence that are so invariant they are not thought about consciously, 'just as we take for granted the stability of the ground on which we walk' (1997, p. 145). Presumably, they are built up through experience and inscribed deeply within memory. Consciousness arises when this self 'accesses' (receives information from?) other parts of the system (modules, memories, via the theatre stage), and it is thus part of the 'audience' in Baars' theatre model (section 7.2.3).

Another multi-level structure for the self has been suggested by Damasio (1999). He distinguished three levels, of which only the second and third are conscious:

1. A proto-self built around brainstem, hypothalamic, insular and right parietal structures monitoring the internal condition of the body.

2. A core self based in thalamic and cingulate cortical activity (perhaps together with superior colliculus and prefrontal lobe), which generates an account of how objects in

---

31. Single neurons in the more superior parts of the parietal lobes can encode and recode spatial relationships between objects and various parts of the self, transforming retinocentric to hand-centric and body-centric coordinates (e.g. Colby and Duhamel, 1996; Wolpert et al., 1998; Carey, 2004; Scherberger and Andersen, 2004). In the ventral stream there is recoding into allocentric (object-centred) and world-centred coordinates (Rolls and Deco, 2002, p. 464).

32. See Mandik (2001) for a defence of point of view as an important – not to say intrinsic – component of many representations.

the world are interacting with the proto-self. Each such interaction gives a stream of current consciousness and the feeling of knowing.

3. An autobiographical self that is responsible for the 'extended consciousness' that spans our past and future. This modifiable self includes dispositions to produce actions and imagery and is based in prefrontal and temporal cortices and basal ganglia. (The sensory cortices are where imagery is generated by both the core and autobiographical selves – the latter reconstructing images under the direction of what Damasio had earlier called 'convergence zones': see section 9.3.4.3.)

The idea of multi-level selves follows naturally from homuncular functionalism (chapter 4) and means we should consider all the levels at which such an entity or entities could possibly emerge (section 6.2). For example, many well-supported theories exist in developmental and social psychology as to how individuals acquire their sense of identity and personality. Some of these ideas are described in section 6.2.2.1 as possible origins for conscious awareness in general, and more specifically self-awareness. For example, consider social narrative theories, which see the self as a social construct (Harré and Gillett, 1994; Neisser and Fivush, 1994; Harré, 1998; Fireman et al., 2003). Part of the dialogue we have with one another requires us to create ourselves (and others) as characters taking part in a plot within a context (Clocksin, 1998, p. 115). We give accounts to each other about what we are doing and why. These social and cultural constructs are themselves the context (metasystem) within which our internal cognitive and neural models of the self must be embedded, and we cannot understand the latter without knowing the former.

What might be the neural structures created along with the social-level constructs? We can only speculate. Some might point to the 'mirror neurons' in the premotor cortex that fire when an action is performed voluntarily but also when another individual is observed performing the same action (e.g. eating, scratching, gesturing; for reviews, see Gallese et al., 2004, Keysers and Perrett, 2004, and Rizzolatti and Craighero, 2004; but for a critical appraisal, see Jacob and Jeannerod, 2005).[34] Such a mirroring mechanism has been suggested as the basis for the evolution of language in humans (e.g. Rizzolatti and Arbib, 1998; Stamenov and Gallese, 2002) and of self-awareness too (e.g. Metzinger and Gallese, 2003). Another possibility is a special 'theory of mind' module involving the medial frontal lobes and other structures (Frith and Frith, 2003; Bird et al., 2004; Lee et al., 2004). The growth of such mechanisms obviously depends on life experiences as well as neural processes, and this remains a fruitful area for investigating how the 'self', brain and environment come to be coordinated (see also Frith and Wolpert, 2003).[35]

33. In view of the antisocial behaviour sometimes shown by the left hand in split-brain patients, one psychiatrist I heard at a conference stated that the Freudian 'id' is in the right hemisphere and the 'ego' in the left hemisphere!

34. Mead (1934) made the important point that our behaviour is not just imitative of what other people do. We modify and select our behavioural responses to others with the aim of affecting or controlling their behaviour.

35. Feinberg (2001b) gives a nice account of such a multi-level embedded model. The psychoanalytic theory of the existence of a variable 'ego boundary' between self and other can also be explicated in this way. People you know well ('significant others') – especially those you love – are part of your self,

11.3.3 **Self versus self-awareness and introspection**

Knowing yourself – that you exist, that you have certain inner feelings, memories, properties, a 'character' and so on – can be contrasted with introspection, or the immediate sense of watching yourself and of being aware of how you feel right now. Although controversy exists historically as to whether introspection distorts the mechanisms that are observed, so providing unreliable evidence about our inner states (Side-box 11.2), the only question we need to deal with here is what mechanisms have been proposed for introspection and how these relate to other suggestions as to how self-awareness is generated.

SIDE-BOX 11.2 SELF-AWARENESS AND INTROSPECTION

Introspection is direct

The notion of self-awareness is related to the philosophical theories of higher-order thought and higher-order perception, and of course it is also partly about introspection. The traditional view is that introspection is direct. We are aware of our own mental states and we have direct infallible knowledge of our own minds. This goes back to Descartes or earlier: the one thing that Descartes decided he could be sure of was that he was thinking.

The arguments in favour of direct introspection are as follows:

1. Direct awareness avoids an infinite regress. Consider the indirect awareness model. First, note that knowledge of the outside world is often imperfect, unreliable, distorted and illusory and possibly even, in principle, not ever giving us any accurate picture of external reality (Kant, 1781/7). Also, many of our experiences are of the type 'secondary qualia': our depictions and representations of colour, heat, smell, taste and so on do not in any direct way resemble the outside world, which is just chemicals, electromagnetic radiation and so on. The argument then proceeds that you must have a little man in the head, or a little pair of eyes in the head, to *interpret* these representations of the world, because the latter may not be accurate. The homunculus must contain within it 'intelligent' mechanisms, and these require inner, second-order representations to work on. However, the homunculus may also be fallible or not very bright, so its representations (of the representations (of the world)) may not be accurate either. So then you need another inner, inner homunculus to interpret or 'understand' the second-order representations. Continuing the logic, you must have representations of representations of representations, ad infinitum; for example, 'I think I think I think am looking at something red'. In the end, this picture, of an infinite chain of internal perceptions, is unhelpful, unlikely and unrealistic.

But if introspection is direct, there is a stopping point. Instead of having fallible representations of representations (of representations . . .), we must have an infallible stage somewhere in the process. The obvious solution is for there to be an internal mechanism of consciousness that includes accurate

continues

---

or at least of your self-model. The (integrated cognitive plus emotional) concepts of yourself and of others come to be locked together via the (system-forming) interactions people have with each other. An individual's 'ego boundary' thus extends out into the world. Changes to the (experience of) self that occur in schizophrenia, Capgras and Cotard (depersonalization) syndromes, anosognosia (Side-box 11.1), bereavement and even being robbed of our possessions, can all be understood as attritions to our extended selves, or as losses of awareness of parts of those selves.

SIDE-BOX 11.2 continued

knowledge of our (first-order) representations of the world. The latter and the latter only necessarily may be inaccurate, thus explaining our susceptibility to illusions and perceptual errors. Thus having the sure and certain ability to identify our inner states is logically a sounder model, since otherwise we would have to postulate an infinite list (R→R→R→R→R . . ., where R is a representation).

2. It seems intuitively obvious that we know how we feel (Descartes). How can we be mistaken about our own mental states? If I think I am seeing something red, then I am experiencing a sensation of redness. The object I see (if any exists – it might be a hallucination or a dream) may not be red, but it certainly looks red to me. I know this is how I am feeling, I know my own internal states and I know my own mind.

There are also some arguments against direct introspection:

1. According to Churchland (1988), representation of the outside world evolved first – whether the outside world is red, hot, dangerous or whatever. Self-awareness must have evolved secondarily to these representations, so knowledge of our own internal states is a later evolutionary step. However, the mechanisms of evolution would be the same in each case, so the kind of process at both stages would probably be the same, i.e. using the same principles. Both stages would thus be prone to error. However, this argument does not get round the infinite regress question.

2. Stronger arguments come from the notion that introspection can be incorrect. We can have illusions and delusions about ourselves and we do not know our own mental states perfectly; we don't know our own motives (Nisbett and Wilson, 1977; but cf. Smith and Miller, 1978; Ericsson and Simon, 1980). In some cases we are mistaken even about the state of our own bodies (for example, anorexics think they are fatter than they really are). Most obviously, do we really know what mental states we are in when we are drugged or asleep? Brain damage can also give rise to some obvious cases. The most interesting one is *anosognosia*, a collection of syndromes where people are not aware of their own condition (see Side-box 11.1).

3. Psychological evidence and theory suggests that there is actually a long chain of processing of representations (cf. retina–LGN–cortex, or Marcel's theory: Side-box 9.1). Consciousness might arise at the end of this long chain of preconscious processing. This is the serial model, which suggests that what we are aware of is just the final outcome of a long series of processes. However, even alternative models posit that there are lots of mental states and processes which are unconscious or preconscious (see chapter 7). To that extent our introspection cannot gain access to all of our mental states.

4. Introspection is not something you do all the time. Indeed, if you start thinking about yourself and the mental states you have in any particular situation, then this distorts those mental states. The act of 'looking' at them affects them, perhaps directly, perhaps indirectly via the changes in the higher-level processing you are using to introspect with. The whole pattern of internal feedback is altered. In contrast, when you are simply behaving – moving through life without introspecting – then your thoughts proceed differently.

Introspection is indirect

A central theme in modern cognitive psychology is that you have only fallible knowledge of the outside world and so you construct hypotheses about and mental models of the way the outside world is. Now, by analogy, your self-knowledge arises in the same way as your knowledge of the outside world. Through individual growth you build up knowledge about yourself – your self-identity, behaviour patterns, likes and preferences, what you do, how you think and so on. The unity of your self centres

continues

SIDE-BOX 11.2 continued

around the single concept or model you thus form of yourself. This model is no different in kind from the mental models you have of other people and objects in the environment. It is qualitatively similar in the sense that it is just another mental model, and when you think of yourself, you are gaining access to that mental model. Your consciousness or awareness of yourself involves processing information in that mental model of yourself. (This theory may or may not have alongside it the notion that awareness of their outside world is direct or indirect.)

As such, the model is not necessarily an accurate reflection of yourself: errors, mistakes and illusions about yourself can creep into the model (for examples, see Side-box 11.1).

The model is a special part of your mind that is derived from the rest of your mind (rather than 'looking at' the rest of your mind), and so the knowledge you have of yourself is not directly linked to the main functional states. It is a special functional module, a collection of mental states that you have built up. But each state is the same type as any other representation.

In sum, there are two stages, so in a sense you have two categories of mental states: mental states that you use when you are navigating the world, seeing red, feeling sad, etc.; and then another level that may represent what you think of yourself, what you are aware of within yourself.

In section 11.2.2.3, Rosenthal's (1997, 2002) higher-order thought theory was presented, according to which higher- or second-order thoughts are those creating consciousness of the contents of first-order, sensory experiences ('I think I am seeing red'). This theory is easily extended to account for introspection, which occurs when there are third-order thoughts. These are thoughts or knowledge about second-order states – for example, they may contain the content 'I know that I think I am seeing red'. Thus there is a third layer of representation that is about the existence of second-order representations. Note that Rosenthal denies that any further, fourth-order and so on, layers exist, so there is no infinite regress of higher and higher thoughts. Although one can state 'I know I know I know I know I am hearing a piano', this does not describe how the mind actually works. We can at times think we are now conscious of seeing something red or hearing a piano, but we do not introspect our introspections.

Lycan (1987, pp. 71–72; 1996, chapter 1), however, merely treats introspection as voluntarily directed attention to one's inner psychological states. His basic theory is that a higher-order perception (HOP) mechanism is the basis of consciousness (see section 11.2.2.3), but he also describes HOP as a type of introspection (1996, p. 13) and thus does not distinguish the two mechanisms. Awareness depends on our paying attention to our inner sensory and perhaps higher-order states, and is like perceiving ('self-scanning'; Lycan, 1996, pp. 30, 48).

11.3.4 Against a unified self

11.3.4.1 A non-unified self (many independent parts)

In many clinical cases there is loss of self-awareness, known as 'anosognosia' (Side-box 11.1). What can we learn about the neural representation of the self from such cases? Prigatano (1999, chapter 12) points out that there are many different aspects of self-awareness that may be lost in any one person. These losses can be restricted to one narrow area of self-knowledge, such as the fact that the subject has a paralysed left arm, poor social skills or aphasia. The anosognosic symptoms can also be multiple, vary from person to person and recover to varying extents over different timescales. Prigatano concludes by classifying the symptoms into four syndromes, each centred on damage to regions of 'higher' integrative and polymodal cortices in the four lobes. Self-awareness depends on the integration of thinking and feeling that occurs in those regions, and there is thus no single self-representation in the brain.

To a first approximation, then, the relative independence of the mental blind spots that can occur in self-awareness suggests a polymodular basis for the self in neurologically intact people. Multiple mechanisms exist, each of which monitors the activity of a restricted domain of the brain to generate self-awareness of the functioning of that subset of neural mechanisms and that subset alone.

11.3.4.2 Many selves – or many self-awarenesses

Other studies have suggested that there can be more than one self within a single person's head. For example, Sperry's (1984) analysis of split-brain patients led him to conclude that they have two selves, one in each hemisphere (but see section 11.3.2).

Further, Marcel's (1993) survey of various kinds of anosognosia and blindsight, as well as his psychophysical investigations of intact subjects, led him to suggest that multiple self-consciousnesses can occur commonly. Any single sensory quale can drive several parallel mechanisms, each leading to behavioural outcomes that are empirically identifiable as independent (by asking the subject to respond in different ways, such as blinking, speaking or pressing a key, different sensitivities to the stimulus are demonstrable). Because they are cognitively penetrable (the experimenter tells the subject to respond when the subject 'sees' the stimulus), these higher-order mechanisms each involve conscious awareness of the stimulus (the content of the lower-order phenomenal sensation). There can thus be several independent consciousnesses about the same stimulus at any one time. This multiplicity, however, only applies when paying attention to one's self, or when asked to introspect about one's own sensations or inner states. If attention is directed outwards, such as in performing some complex skill (like driving along a busy street), then consciousness is more unified. There may be a single 'self' (though Marcel is vague about what exactly that is), but self-awareness comes via multiple mechanisms.[36]

11.3.4.3 Unified but not a self

There are many theorists who argue against the idea of there being any special or qualitatively different representation of the self. Dennett (1991), for example, in his theory of multiple drafts (section 10.3.2.3), sees the various threads of activity passing round the brain as processes of creating and continually re-editing fragments of narrative about what is happening. When it comes to the 'self', Dennett describes it as merely the 'centre of narrative gravity'. It is not a specific entity, in the same way that the centre of gravity of a

---

36. Marcel (1993) says that the self is not autobiographical memory, because memories are like sensations in that they can become separated from the self in conditions such as anosognosia, or from all but one of the selves in multiple personality disorder. Further evidence for the multiplicity of self-representation, at least of the bodily self, is given in Marcel et al. (2004) and Vuilleumier (2004).

physical object is not a real thing. The latter is a useful shorthand for describing the behaviour of a mass such as a planet or a piece of metal – it has certain functional uses, but it is just a convenient fiction to describe and predict the behaviour of the object. Similarly, when it comes to people, the self or centre of narrative gravity is a convenient fiction to summarize a person's behaviour, feelings and thoughts. It is a central character in the narrative that is made up through the multiple drafts – the central theme in the story that is that person's mental life.[37]

11.3.4.4 **Neither unified nor a self**

Another allied view is bundle theory, the view of the Buddha, Hume (1739), Parfit (1984, 1987) and Varela et al. (1991); see also Blackmore (2003) and Carruthers (2003). It says that there is no such thing as the self as postulated in the atomist, Platonist–Christian idea of a soul or 'ego' (Murphy, 2003). Instead, you are just a bundle of various feelings, thoughts, abilities, processes, mental states and so on. Your self is just the collection of abilities you have at any particular time.

Hume asked what gives a person, a growing tree or a flowing river its individual continuity over time, given their continually changing constituent parts. An analogy given by Parfit is with membership of a club: over time, some members may leave and other new people may join, but it remains the same club. Thus there is unity over time although the constituents may change as the membership changes. A club is not a physical thing, it is the sum total of the individual members. Likewise, the self is just the sum total of all an individual's various faculties, modules, properties and experiences, and there is no special one internal to that collection that is the 'real' self. Over time a person may learn new skills and forget many things too, but the continuity of self is maintained. The self is a higher-level category – the total set of all one's mental states, rather than a subset or a particular member of them.

One may wonder what binds these elements into a whole. For Hume, the feeling of personal identity was merely an illusion based on the memory's production of a sequence of similar ideas of successive instants in time. For Buddhists, it is the continuity of the pattern of habits, accumulated through ontogeny and phylogeny (Varela et al., 1991, pp. 116, 121). Modern theories of binding suggest more mechanistic or real-emergent explanations, in which 'the self' is a distributed representation (distributed across many if not all the representations in the brain, or among all the people who know you) or an integrated network of lower-level constituent representations or subsystems (chapter 4 and section 11.3.1).

The point here may be that there is no 'self' within the person, although there may be an individual person. The terminology easily becomes confusing. For example, it is common to find even philosophers asking 'How am I conscious?' or 'How am I aware of my mental states (or of the world)?' or declaring 'I know my mental states, they are my own and belong only to me; and I do not know anyone else's states in that way'. But who is this 'I' who possesses those states, and how does it 'possess' them? There is a circularity in many of the discussions of the self; they seem to explain self-awareness by presuming the existence of a self who/that can then become aware of its self (itself?). As with so many aspects of the

---

37. Llinás (2001, p. 128) similarly describes the self as a vector, and says it is like 'Uncle Sam': a useful symbol but not a real person.

mind–body problem, the answer may come from moving up or down a level of description (chapter 4). Thus social constructionists may see the 'self' as existing at a higher, societal level, whereas reductionists prefer to look to lower levels, such as the constituent mental states all having their neural bases in common in the same brain.[38]

11.4 Against multiple types of representation

Parfit's and Dennett's theories of the self incorporate the notion that there is no such thing as a 'self', or at least nothing special about the representation of oneself.[39] In this section, we consider more general arguments against the idea that more than one type of representation exists.

One philosophical argument against the possibility of a special kind of representation is that this might lead into an infinite regress. Thus if you need second-order representations to explain how the first-order ones become conscious, then third-order to explain how second-order become conscious and so on, then where does it end? Also, why should having a higher-order process generate consciousness?[40]

Restriction of representation to a single type is also implicit in several neural theories, like those of Calvin and Greenfield (section 7.3.3). In their theories of consciousness, the activity in any part of the cortex can generate consciousness, and you are aware of experiences in proportion to the amount of activity, either in each of those active regions (Greenfield) or only in the largest, which comes to dominate all the others (Calvin).

In similar vein, Dennett (1994) talks about 'fame in the brain'. Dennett's drafts are rather like Pandemonian demons (Selfridge, 1959; Lindsay and Norman, 1977): they 'tell' other regions of brain what they think, rather than passively showing their products (Dennett, 1991, chapter 10). Each acts to influence the redrafting processes that occur in other parts of the brain, so its contents become as widely known as possible throughout the brain, rather than just fading away and dying. The most successful draft becomes the most dominant, or famous, and has the most effect over overt behaviour (therefore Dennett, 2000, says 'influence in the brain' would be a better term than 'fame in the brain'). The point here, however, is that all the drafting mechanisms belong to the same kind of process. There are not separate kinds of process for self-awareness versus awareness of the outside

---

38. In the latter case, the states would be unified at minimum by their having the same intracranial basis, even if it turns out they do not interact or bind directly with each other to form a single whole network.

39. Lycan (1987, pp. 80–81; 1996, chapter 3) also argues there is nothing special about self-representation. What happens when you think of yourself is that the representations that are active are simply representations whose subject or content is your self. They are self-referential, bearing intentionality toward themselves; 'self-regarding (propositional) attitudes'. They may be used differently within the mind, but their intentionality-fixing conditions are the same as for any other representation. 'What it is like' depends on the functional role played by a representation, not on its referent. Essay topic: Do representations of the self have narrow or broad content? (See sections 2.4.3.1 and 5.3.4.)

40. In reply, Rosenthal just says: well, you don't go on like this ad infinitum; third order is as high as you need to go to explain human consciousness (section 11.3.3).

world, or lower- versus higher-order, or phenomenal versus belief/access awareness, or preconscious versus conscious. Thus Dennett refers to this process as making 'beliefs', 'judgements', 'categorizations', 'thinking', 'deciding' (1991, p. 364), 'micro-takings' (of information; 1996, pp. 160, 171), acts of content-fixation, and lists as synonyms 'categorization, recognition, discrimination and identification' (1995, p. 513).

I think what Dennett is trying to say is that it is all right to use the metaphor that parts of the brain 'think', but not that they 'perceive'. Homunculi (chapter 4) can perform acts of logical reasoning, however simple and impoverished, but only a complete person can perceive. This fits in with his eschewal of the Cartesian theatre (section 10.3.2.3) and of qualia as internal phenomenal states.[41] As part of his denial that there are qualia (Dennett, 1988, 1991), he tries to reduce everything in the mind to beliefs and dispositions, in the behaviourist sense (section 2.3). He argues that when you are experiencing red, in fact you are actually believing that you are experiencing red (just like the subjects in Kolers and Von Grünau's, 1976, experiments believed a moving spot changed colour halfway along its trajectory: see section 10.3.2.3). That mental state is just the same kind as any other belief state, in terms of the processes going on within it. As a behaviourist Dennett then tries to reduce beliefs to dispositions or tendencies to behave in certain ways.

Several philosophers, however, regard Dennett's 'belief that you are experiencing red' as a clear example of a higher-order thought (HOT) (Dennett, 1991, pp. 372–373; Botterill and Carruthers, 1999, pp. 266–271; Erik Myin, personal communication, 2000; Heil, 2004a, pp. 160–169; see also section 5.3.5). Dennett was fundamentally trying to deny a dichotomy between mental and physical states, or between events on and off the stage of a Cartesian theatre. The fact that many different types of process exist in the brain might not surprise him, but these would all need to be types that can be reduced to dispositions.

11.5 Conclusion

The question of whether there are different 'types' of mental state therefore depends on your criteria for classifying types. Looked at in sufficient detail, all states are unique; but by using coarser criteria for categorizing them we could decide that there are commonalities among them. Under a multi-level homuncular functionalist philosophy (chapter 4), for example, the groupings might be larger at higher levels. Gerry's social narrative self is a representation that exists throughout a group of people, emerging at successive levels from the verbal interactions between their various bodies and their cognitive models of Gerry's self – including the one within Gerry, which emerges from knowledge-containing models of Gerry's body, life history, goals, etc., each of which may involve both experiences/feelings and propositional knowledge, and is built from neural underpinnings – of types which might even include one if not several of those described in chapters 6–10!

41. Visual phenomenology is about 'finding out', rather than 'filling in' some image-like view of a theatre stage or cinema screen (Dennett, 1991, pp. 344–356) as many think (for example, see Ramachandran, 2003b).

Under this homuncular philosophy, consciousness is not generated within a single level by virtue of the differences between the types of interacting representation. Several systems of the same type may interact (such as two people talking to one another, or two intracranial modules transmitting patterns of nerve firings), but this is not the key to consciousness; that is a matter of the organization of the systems (all of one type) to generate new emergent properties at a higher level. So a 'higher-level thought' may emerge from a configuration of two or more lower-level representations. The contents of the thought need not include those of all the lower-level thoughts involved,[42] and one of those may (or may not) need to represent the self or the body in some way.[43] The emergence of consciousness is also not just a matter of creating links between representations within the brain, activating and binding them, mediated by some non-selective broadcasting or connecting via a 'global workspace' (Baars, 2002; Block, 2005), but requires instead that the lower-level representations self-organize into a particular pattern.[44]

Of course, homuncular functionalism is not the only philosophical stance, and you will accept or reject this conclusion in accordance with your own preferred position. But in all cases, to understand the issues it is necessary to know your metaphysical presuppositions overtly so you can see what kind of link may exist between the phenomenology of consciousness and the empirical data of psychology and neuroscience.

■ RECOMMENDED READING

Introductions to higher-order representation may be found in Botterill and Carruthers's **The Philosophy of Psychology** (1999, chapter 9) and Cunningham's **What is a Mind?** (2000, pp. 71–79). For more advanced treatments, see Rowlands' **The Nature of Consciousness** (2001, chapters 4 and 5), Droege's

42. Hence the objections of Güzeldere (1995; see section 11.2.2.3) may be obviated, since these assume a one-to-one linking between a HOT and a LOT (which is the standard assumption everyone makes).

43. Let's construct a crude analogy by treating thoughts as being like sentences. Thus, 'I am seeing something red now' is a HOT expressed by a sentence of six words; but each of these words roughly corresponds to one of the six LOTs that together (and in that arrangement) make up the HOT. It would be interesting to go into more depth here, by explaining, for example, how each of the LOTs requires some prior, inbuilt knowledge (such as that there exist: a division between the self and non-self; time; colour; and so on), and the syntax by which they are arranged also needs to be clarified (but I leave this for an essay topic!).

44. Consider another linguistic analogy: compare English, and Latin. In English the word order is crucial, but this is not necessarily so in Latin. For example, 'men like women' has a different meaning from 'women like men', whereas 'viri amant feminas' has pretty much the same meaning as 'feminas amant viri' or any other sequence of these three words. In Latin, the words contain suffixes (i.e. they have 'intrinsic properties') that indicate the number, case and gender of nouns and the number and person of verbs, and these syntactic features can be used to discover which words are linked to which others and in what ways. The semantic structure of the whole sentence is determined by these features, which in English are replaced by word order, i.e. relative location in time. Now, the question is: do neural representations combine to give a higher-order thought by virtue of their having intrinsic (syntactic) features or by their having relative location along some dimension (and if so, what dimension might that be: location in the brain? sequence of firing? frequency of synchronous firing?)?

Caging the Beast (2003) and Gennaro's Higher-order Theories of Consciousness (2004). On metacognition, see Nelson and Rey, '*Metacognition and consciousness*' (2000). An account of the multiplicity of representations in vision, reviewing and integrating the various philosophical, psychological and neurological classification schemes, is given by Jacob and Jeannerod in Ways of Seeing (2003).

On the self, good introductions may be found in Cunningham's What is a Mind? (2000, chapter 5), Churchland's Brain-wise (2002, chapter 3) and Blackmore's Consciousness: An Introduction (2003, chapters 7–9). Both Cockburn in An Introduction to the Philosophy of Mind (2001, chapter 8) and Maslin in An Introduction to the Philosophy of Mind (2001, chapter 10) also give clear elementary explanations of bundle theory. Feinberg's Altered Egos (2001b) gives a readable and wide-ranging account of how the self is constructed, including many descriptions of pathological cases. Further details and discussions can be found in the edited volumes by Gallagher and Shear Models of the Self (1999), Varela and Shear The View from Within (1999), Zahavi Exploring the Self (2000), Knoblich et al. '*Grounding the self in action*' (2003), Zahavi et al. The Structure and Development of Self-consciousness (2004) and the – excellently eclectic – LeDoux et al. The Self: From Soul to Brain (2003). The book by Brook and DeVidi, Self-reference and Self-awareness (2001), is very advanced. An extended monograph in support of the self as a cognitive model but not an ontological entity is Metzinger's Being No One (2003), while Carruthers' The Nature of the Mind (2003) readably discusses the metaphysical nature of the self and the soul.

12 | Conclusion

12.1 Retrospect

We would all like there to be some simple answer to the question of what consciousness is and how it is related to the brain and to the wider world. In the course of this book, we have travelled from simple theories to complex, and from general principles to detailed expositions, surveying the theoretical and the empirical realities of consciousness. It has become apparent that the answer to the puzzle of consciousness is not a simple one. However, although there are many facts about the brain that must be known, there are many philosophical guidelines and principles we can use to structure our search, and these should in the long run enable us to build a realistic understanding of the phenomena.

I have warned you that the simple paths that promise to lead straight to a solution usually turn out to rely on miracles occurring along the way (Figure 7.1). For example, a special brain site, synchronous oscillation, higher-order thought, self-representation, language and so on may all prove important, but each on its own does not provide the single Right Answer that we think should exist for us to find.[1] At the end of chapter 11, it was suggested instead that new types of representation may arise at higher levels. These would emerge as the result of interactions between lower-order representations, and this internal structuring

---

1. Perhaps instead there are numerous simple solutions, one for each of the various types of consciousness. Alternatively there might be a more complicated theory that can account for all aspects of our conscious life. More pessimistically, we may need different complex explanations for each type of consciousness – including perhaps even for each modality of sensory awareness (I call this the 'hard solution'). Whichever the case, there is no evading the need to become familiar with the several academic disciplines involved.

is crucial for consciousness. This theory demands, of course, further development to specify how such complex structuring makes these representations the basis of consciousness. To avoid the accusation of being just another miracle theory, specific proposals must be made. However, these will not be simple proposals, since they will involve detailed accounts of the organizations and properties of the entities that exist through perhaps several such levels of emergence. Indeed, homuncular functionalism suggests that the magic that would be introduced if there were a man-in-the-head somewhere in the system can be eliminated if there is an appropriately structured hierarchy of functional/representational units with many levels of (as we descend) increasingly simple but still highly organized elements (chapter 4).

12.2 **Prospect**

12.2.1 **Empirical**

From one direction, analysing the structure of consciousness can begin at the phenomenological level. Although various traditions of studying and decomposing the mind from the Buddha to Husserl are well-established, further modern developments are also in prospect (see Blackmore, 2003, chapter 25), including 'interpretative phenomenological analysis' (Smith, 2006; Brown et al., submitted; see also Jack and Shallice, 2001).

Psychological investigations will of course continue, with clever new techniques becoming available (for example, those of Debner and Jacoby, 1994, and Gosselin and Schyns, 2003). The analysis of time experience is another area of particular importance, as already recognized within both phenomenology and psychology (section 10.3.1).[2] (I will return to the importance of time again in section 12.2.3.)

At the levels studied by neuroscience there is no end to the data that need to be collected. Among the many unanswered questions that have been highlighted in this book are the connectivity of the thalamus (section 8.3.2) and the local (columnar) intracortical circuitry.[3]

12.2.2 **Theoretical**

Better theories are always needed, and in this field there are many particular areas in which theory development seems especially crucial. I will mention just a few here, and in the next section generate a few putative lines of advance of my own.

2. There is a sub-field of psychology already studying the ability to judge duration and timing. The most popular functional model posits that somewhere inside us a pulse-generator is feeding into an accumulator that eventually reaches a threshold for discharge. At least three different mechanisms operate over different timescales (Fraisse, 1984; Pöppel, 1997). The physiological mechanisms are currently unknown, but the cerebellum, basal ganglia, frontal and parietal lobes all seem important in various types of time-related task (Ivry and Spencer, 2004; Mauk and Buonomano, 2004; Meck, 2005).

3. For example, after more than forty years of research, we still don't understand how the wiring of area V1 generates the physiological properties it does (e.g. Seriès et al., 2003; Olshausen and Field, 2005).

One direction in which we have a long way to go is in understanding qualia, or the subjective feelings and experiences we have. Of course, many will say this is obviously the Big Problem, but remember that under some definitions of consciousness it is the intentionality or contentfulness of mental states that is what we need to explain (chapter 1); yet progress has been made in that area (chapter 5). However, there are some more specific sub-problems into which we can break the qualia issue and in which advances can be predicted. One is the relative contributions of bottom-up and top-down activity flow in the brain. Thus some workers suggest that sensory awareness can arise with the first arrival of information into the brain, while others regard recurrent flow as essential, and some take an in-between position, with primitive awareness arising from bottom-up activity and more detailed knowledge arising later (e.g. section 9.4). One way to attack the question is to ask what the flow of activity from hippocampus to cortex during sleep tells us about the origins of dream experiences: does phenomenology arise because of this recurrent flow or because the bottom-up pathways are also becoming activated?

The terminology we use is also much in need of refinement. I have gone to quite some trouble to explicate my use of the word 'level', for example (Side-box 4.4). However, there are many other commonly occurring terms I have used in this book (for brevity and simplicity of exposition) that appear throughout the research literature as well, but that are all in need of refinement. Such commonly used expressions as 'conscious representation', 'meaning', 'qualia', 'stage', 'workspace' and 'consciousness/awareness' itself (see also my comments on 'conscious information' in section 7.2.3) are multiply ambiguous (polysemous) or at least open to many interpretations that depend in part on which theoretical stance you take or on your disciplinary background (the same words often have different technical meanings in philosophy, psychology and neuroscience, and yet again in common speech). Indeed, we also need many new labels to be defined. Within the kind of multi-level scheme advocated in chapter 4, for example, the names for the intermediate levels and their denizens are still unclear (information, patterns, symbols, knowledge, homunculi...). How should we describe them, and the structures of the representations that span all the levels? What is clear is that we need to perform an analysis such as this; we cannot remain stuck with the idea that there are only two levels (mental and physical) separated by a gap, as many philosophies have it, and nor can we be satisfied with the reduction to a single level as neuronal behaviourism believes appropriate, a conclusion that can only be arrived at by ignoring the phenomenology of consciousness, not to mention cognition, information processing and so on (chapter 3).

12.2.3 Speculative

12.2.3.1 Multi-levellism

The consequences of embracing multi-levellist functionalism have been explained at several points in this book. I have adopted that point of view and, in the spirit of Side-box 0.1, I have sometimes taken it to its logical conclusion to see where we ended up. Some of the proposals may therefore have seemed weird to anyone who does not subscribe to this particular research programme; but as we have seen throughout the book, whatever your pet theory or evidence, there is always an orthogonal point of view from which it can be disputed. Thus we each have to make a decision as to what we think is the best way forward. Mine is through taking the stance that the mind/brain is a nested hierarchical system, and attempting to interpret the empirical and theoretical research accordingly. To the extent this turns out to be successful, the basic programme will have been justified. However, I would not want to be described as 'believing' that this approach is the right one: it is my best guess as to the best way forward, and I think it will help organize and structure future research and understanding optimally. But I also hope my mind is still open on this issue (after all, I don't think it is just confined within my brain, as it can be changed by events in the outside world).

Throughout the book we have seen several attempts to apply metaphorical descriptions to the intermediate levels. These best originate at high levels and are taken downwards to see if they shed light on the functions that might be being subserved by the mechanisms at lower levels. Let me give one speculative example of how this process might work.

Let us begin with the suggestion that consciousness originates in social interactions and in linguistic interchanges (section 6.2.2.1). These may become internalized, and as Mead (1934), for instance, then put it, consciousness is an 'internal conversation' between what he called the 'I' (the executive, choosing between actions and aware of those actions) and the 'me' (autobiographical memory; the model of the self). Next, compare this with more recent formulations of interactions between plans and images (Side-box 8.1), the updating of models of the self via feedback from the effects of behaviour (Side-boxes 4.5 and 11.1), the internal prediction of the effects of behaviour on subsequent sensory inflow (section 8.4) and the hypothesis that modules communicate via a 'language of thought' (section 2.5), and we see perhaps that there is a common theme. We could further say that these conversations are constituted at an even lower level by the frontal lobes and the posterior half of the cortex talking to one another (both directly and indirectly). Then at lower levels still there are conversations going on – to give three examples: between the higher and lower areas of sensory cortex to generate the phenomenon of stimulus representation and recognition, between areas within the frontal lobe to give working memory, and perhaps between hippocampus and cortex to implement learning (chapter 9). But in all these cases the 'conversations' would actually be somewhere between mere mechanistic resonance and a higher-level language of thought. (Essay topic: what name would you give to such interactions, and why?)

Starting from the social level again: if self-awareness comes from a socially-constructed narrative or a reflection of the mental models that others have of our minds (sections 6.2.2.1 and 11.3.2.3), then, analogously, internal consciousness might be constructed from the communications between modules within our own brains (section 4.3.7.1). Now, I don't think anyone has yet gone on to repeat this principle at lower levels, that is, to suggest that modules have internal models of other modules that might then include models of the original module, hence generating a self-model and hence self-awareness within an individual module. These models are of course impoverished (relative to an entire person's self-understanding), because they are built using information derived via an impoverished communication medium or language of thought. Each is restricted to the domain, modality or whatever the system of modules deals with; that is, at lower levels the models will be correspondingly simpler and more restricted in scope and intentionality. Nevertheless, we can see how in this way, homunculi could have partial consciousness (assuming you accept the premise we began with, that interpersonal interactions are capable of creating full consciousness!). If this is so, we will have achieved the aim of homuncular functionalism: the Big Problem will have been diffused by being broken down progressively into smaller and more comprehensible units.

12.2.3.2 Time

Another major problem for future research is the phenomenon of time 'perception' and awareness. What is the medium of temporal coding and awareness, what are temporal tags or markers and how do they work? More needs to be done on this baffling problem. As for the phenomenology of time, the thickness of the temporal present was mentioned in section 10.3.1; but should we think of this merely as spread diffusely around the present? Should its neural substrate be similarly seen merely as the persistence of a representation (analogous to the spatio-temporally blurring growth of neural ensembles discussed in section 7.3.3)? Or does temporal awareness depend rather upon a structured system of representations, each intending a different moment or period in time? (The analogy would be with the way that modules or subsystems existing in space are organized to form higher-level systems in a hierarchical scheme: chapter 4.) The phenomenologists would support the latter, because there are qualitative differences between the leading, central and trailing aspects of the experienced present (Varela, 1999). Under this view, the connections across time (or perhaps better, between representations of events as occurring at different times) are not merely implemented in the form of a diffuse spread in time but by a structured and selective connectivity. Arguably, our representations of the past, present and future come to mean something in virtue of this selectivity (rather than merely implementing a continuous reflex-like reactivity to ongoing current inputs). The growth of a person's consciousness (its development during individual ontogeny) would stem from the increasing sophistication of these links, enabled by the greater range of available representations, an increasing skill in selecting among them and the growing ability to construct elaborate structures from them. The more meaningful these structures, the longer they persist and vice versa.[4]

Moreover, there could be several levels of consciousness. Note first that if there is a level that is foundational, i.e. the absolute lowest, this could be where simple blurring in time gives the experience of raw feeling (remember, traditional qualia are supposed to be homogeneous, i.e. to have no substructure). But at all higher levels, consciousness would be formed by binding (defined here as system-forming interactions or 'conversations' between two or more entities).[5] Such binding might variously be between (1) current input representations, short-term records and current motor efference to give the retention and protention of the phenomenologists' 'thickness' of experience, (2) various durations of

4. This is not circular reasoning because the causal basis of this correlation is how well the structures fit into their environment or context (see chapter 5). Thus remember that in Side-box 4.4 it was pointed out that there is a correlation between level in the hierarchies of Nature and the temporal stability (persistence) of the systems, with higher-level systems maintaining homeostatic equilibrium for longer periods. The longer the persistence of systems in interaction (including representational states) the more a stable metasystem is likely to be formed, and thus a new higher level will have emerged.

5. Husserl had a similar conception, though he used the term 'associations' – a term that is now obsolete, having been replaced with a variety of types of more active functional interchange (section 2.5).

longer-term memory (either semantic or episodic) to generate conscious awareness of the identity and meaning of a stimulus, and (3) long-term autobiographical memory and long-term plans, desires and life-goals (derived from both semantic and autobiographical memory) – our memories of the most significant events in our life so far, and imagined goals we want to reach in the future – to give us who we are and our sense of self. The occurrence of such bindings at many levels simultaneously would give phenomenal experiences with depth and structure.

In sum, binding across time to form systematic structures connecting memory, current inflow and plans for the future may be the key process in the genesis of phenomenology. Recurrence of this principle across several timescales could create multi-levelled experiences. As these hierarchical representational structures shift, so our mind changes.[6]

12.3 **Knowing about knowing about knowing (reprised)**

One has to commit oneself to a particular theoretical stance, as was stated in the Preface (Side-box 0.1). This is true for one's philosophical, psychological and neurological theories. So after considering the options, are you a dualist, a functionalist, a reductionist or what? Do you belong with the behaviourists, cognitivists, phenomenologists or whom? Do you think we should look for our answers among single neuron properties, neural networks and dynamics, quantum mechanics or where? Are your three choices consistent with one another? In this book, I have leaned toward multi-level homuncular functionalism as a philosophy, which enables me to be eclectic about research going on across the entire field, since all levels have to be analysed and integrated. This approach seems to me to hold the most promise for steadily and progressively building up an answer to the mind–body problem, without relying on a miracle occurring that we can never explain. But your choice may be different, and I hope if you have read all this you are now better equipped to make that choice.

6. By 'mind' I here mean current mental state: see section 1.1.1.

■ REFERENCES

Adams, F. (2003) Thoughts and their contents: naturalised semantics. In Stich, S.P. and Warfield, T.A., eds., *The Blackwell Guide to Philosophy of Mind*. Blackwell, Malden, pp. 143–172.

Adjamian, P., Holliday, I.E., Barnes, G.R., Hillebrand, A., Hadjipapas, A. and Singh, K.D. (2004) Induced visual illusions and gamma oscillations in human primary visual cortex. *European Journal of Neuroscience* **20**, 587–592.

Adolphs, R. (2003) Cognitive neuroscience of human social behavior. *Nature Reviews Neuroscience* **4**, 165–178.

Akins, K. (2002) A question of content. In Brook, A. and Ross, D., eds., *Daniel Dennett*. Cambridge University Press, Cambridge, pp. 206–249.

Akins, K.A. and Winger, S. (1996) Ships in the night: Churchland and Ramachandran on Dennett's theory of consciousness. In Akins, K., ed., *Perception*. Oxford University Press, Oxford, pp. 173–197.

Alais, D. and Blake, R. (2005) eds. *Binocular Rivalry*. MIT Press, Cambridge, MA.

Aleksander, I. (2000) *How to Build a Mind*. Weidenfeld and Nicolson, London.

Allen, C., Bekoff, M. and Lauder, G.V. (1998) eds. *Nature's Purposes: Analyses of Function and Design in Biology*. MIT Press, Cambridge, MA.

Allen, T.F.H. and Starr, T.B. (1982) *Hierarchy: Perspectives for Ecological Complexity*. University of Chicago Press, Chicago.

Allport, D.A. (1968) Phenomenal simultaneity and perceptual moment hypothesis. *British Journal of Psychology* **59**, 395–406.

Amundson, R. and Lauder, G.V. (1994) Function without purpose: the uses of causal role function in evolutionary biology. *Biology and Philosophy* **9**, 443–469.

Andersen, P.B., Emmerche, C., Finnemann, N.O. and Christiansen, P.V. (2000) eds. *Downward Causation: Minds, Bodies and Matter*. Aarhus University Press, Århus.

Andersen, R.A. and Buneo, C.A. (2002) Intentional maps in posterior parietal cortex. *Annual Review of Neuroscience* **25**, 189–220.

Anderson, J., Barlow, H.B. and Gregory, R.L. (1997) eds. Knowledge-based vision in man and machine. *Philosophical Transactions of the Royal Society of London, Series B* **352**, 1117–1290.

Andjus, R.K., Knopfelmacher, F., Russell, R.W. and Smith, A.U. (1955) Effects of hypothermia on behavior. *Nature* **176**, 1015–1016.

Andrade, J. (2001) The contribution of working memory to conscious experience. In Andrade, J., ed., *Working Memory in Perspective*. Psychology Press, Hove, pp. 60–78.

Anton, G. (1899) Über die Selbstwahrnehmung der Herderkrankungen des Gehirns durch den Kranken bei Rindenblindheit und Rindentaubheit. *Archiv für Psychiatrie und Nervenkrankheiten* **32**, 86–127.

Arbib, M.A. (1972) *The Metaphorical Brain: An Introduction to Cybernetics as Artificial Intelligence and Brain Theory*. Wiley-Interscience, New York.

Arbib, M.A. (2002) ed. *The Handbook of Brain Theory and Neural Networks, 2nd edn*. MIT Press, Cambridge, MA.

Arbib, M.A., Érdi, P. and Szentágothai, J. (1997) *Neural Organization: Structure, Function, and Dynamics*. MIT Press, Cambridge, MA.

Argyle, M., Alkema, F. and Gilmour, R. (1971) Communication of friendly and hostile attitudes by verbal and non-verbal signals. *European Journal of Social Psychology* **1**, 385–401.

Ariew, A., Cummins, R. and Perlman, M. (2002) eds. *Functions: New Essays in the Philosophy of Psychology and Biology*. Oxford University Press, Oxford.

Armstrong, D.M. (1980) What is consciousness? In Armstrong, D.M., ed., *The Nature of Mind*. University of Queensland Press, St. Lucia, pp. 55–67.

Arnold, D.H. and Clifford, C.W. (2002) Determinants of asynchronous processing in vision. *Proceedings of the Royal Society of London, Series B* **269**, 579–583.

Arnold, D.H., Clifford, C.W. and Wenderoth, P. (2001) Asynchronous processing in vision: color leads motion. *Current Biology* **11**, 596–600.

Arrow, H., McGrath, J.E. and Berdahl, J.L. (2000) *Small Groups as Complex Systems: Formation, Coordination, Development and Adaptation*. Sage, Thousand Oaks, CA.

Asanuma, C., Andersen, R.A. and Cowan, W.M. (1985) The thalamic relations of the caudal inferior parietal lobule and the lateral prefrontal cortex in monkeys: divergent cortical projections from cell clusters in the medial pulvinar nucleus. *Journal of Comparative Neurology* **241**, 357–381.

Ashby, W.R. (1952) *Design for a Brain*. Chapman and Hall, London.

Attneave, F. (1954) Some informational aspects of visual perception. *Psychological Review* **61**, 183–193.

Attneave, F. (1961) In defense of homunculi. In Rosenblith, W.A., ed., *Sensory Communication*. MIT Press, Cambridge, MA, pp. 777–782.

Ayala, F.J. and Dobzhansky, T. (1974) eds. *Studies in the Philosophy of Biology: Reduction and Related Problems*. Macmillan, London.

Baars, B.J. (1986) *The Cognitive Revolution in Psychology*. Guilford Press, New York.

Baars, B.J. (1988) *A Cognitive Theory of Consciousness*. Cambridge University Press, Cambridge.

Baars, B.J. (1997) *In the Theater of Consciousness: The Workspace of the Mind*. Oxford University Press, New York.

Baars, B.J. (1998) Metaphors of consciousness and attention in the brain. *Trends in Neurosciences* **21**, 58–62.

Baars, B.J. (2002) The conscious access hypothesis: origins and recent evidence. *Trends in Cognitive Sciences* **6**, 47–52.

Baars, B.J. (2003) Working Memory requires consciousness, not vice versa: a Global Workspace account. In Osaka, N., ed., *Neural Basis of Consciousness*. Benjamins, Amsterdam, pp. 11–26.

Baars, B.J., Banks, W.P. and Newman, J.B. (2003) eds. *Essential Sources in the Scientific Study of Consciousness*. MIT Press, Cambridge, MA.

Baars, B.J. and Newman, J. (1994) A neurobiological interpretation of global workspace theory. In Revonsuo, A. and Kamppinen, M., eds., *Consciousness in Philosophy and Cognitive Neuroscience*. Erlbaum, Hillsdale, pp. 211–226.

Bachmann, T. (2000) *Microgenetic Approach to the Conscious Mind*. Benjamins, Amsterdam.

Bachmann, T., Luiga, I., Põder, E. and Kalev, K. (2003) Perceptual acceleration of objects in stream: evidence from flash-lag displays. *Consciousness and Cognition* **12**, 279–297.

Bacon, F. (1620) *Novum Organon*. Johannem Billium, London.

Baddeley, A.D. (1966a) The influence of acoustic and semantic similarity on long-term memory for word sequences. *Quarterly Journal of Experimental Psychology* **18**, 302–309.

Baddeley, A.D. (1966b) Short-term memory for word sequences as a function of acoustic, semantic and formal similarity. *Quarterly Journal of Experimental Psychology* **18**, 362–365.

Baddeley, A.D. (1997) *Human Memory, 2nd edn*. Psychology Press, Hove.

Baddeley, A.D., Aggleton, J. and Conway, M. (2001) eds. Episodic memory. *Philosophical Transactions of the Royal Society of London, Series B* **356**, 1343–1515. Reprinted by Oxford University Press, Oxford, 2002.

Baddeley, A.D. and Hitch, G. (1974) Working memory. In Bower, G.H., ed., *The Psychology of Learning and Motivation*. Academic Press, New York, pp. 47–89.

Baddeley, A.D. and Lieberman, K. (1980) Spatial working memory. In Nickerson, R.S., ed., *Attention and Performance VIII*. Erlbaum, Hillsdale, pp. 521–539.

Balkin, T.J., Braun, A.R., Wesensten, N.J., Jeffries, K., Varga, M., Baldwin, P., Belenky, G. and Herscovitch, P. (2002) The process of awakening: a PET study of regional brain activity patterns mediating the re-establishment of alertness and consciousness. *Brain* **125**, 2308–2319.

Banich, M.T. (2004) *Cognitive Neuroscience and Neuropsychology, 2nd edn*. Houghton Mifflin, Boston.

Banks, W.P. (2002) ed. On timing relations between brain and world. *Consciousness and Cognition* **11**, 141–374.

Barlow, H. (1953) Summation and inhibition in the frog's retina. *Journal of Physiology* **119**, 69–88.

Barlow, H. (1959) Sensory mechanisms, the reduction of redundancy and intelligence. In *Mechanisation of Thought Processes*. Her Majesty's Stationery Office, London, pp. 535–574.

Barlow, H. (1972) Single units and sensation: a neuron doctrine for perceptual psychology? *Perception* **1**, 371–394.

Barlow, H. (1979) Reconstructing the visual image in space and time. *Nature* **279**, 189–190.

Barlow, H. (1981) Critical limiting factors in the design of the eye and visual cortex. *Proceedings of the Royal Society of London, Series B* **212**, 1–34.

Barlow, H. (1985) Cerebral cortex as model builder. In Rose, D. and Dobson, V.G., eds., *Models of the Visual Cortex*. Wiley, Chichester, pp. 37–46.

Barlow, H. (1995) The neuron doctrine in perception. In Gazzaniga, M.S., ed., *The Cognitive Neurosciences*. MIT Press, Cambridge, MA, pp. 415–434.

Barlow, H. (1998) The nested networks of brains and minds. In Bock, G. and Goode, J.A., eds., *The Limits of Reductionism in Biology*. Wiley, Chichester, pp. 142–159.

Barnden, J.A. (1997) Consciousness and common sense metaphors of mind. In Ó Nualláin, S., Mc Kevitt, P. and Mac Aogáin, E., eds., *Two Sciences of Mind*. Benjamins, Amsterdam, pp. 311–340.

Barrett, D.J.K., Bradshaw, M.F. and Rose, D. (2003) Endogenous shifts of covert attention operate within multiple coordinate frames: evidence from a feature-priming task. *Perception* **32**, 41–52.

Barsalou, L.W. (1999) Perceptual symbol systems. *Behavioral and Brain Sciences* **22**, 577–660.

Bartels, A. and Zeki, S. (1998) The theory of multistage integration in the visual brain. *Proceedings of the Royal Society of London, Series B* **265**, 2327–2332.

Bartha, G.T. and Thompson, R.F. (1995) Cerebellum and conditioning. In Arbib, M.A., ed., *Handbook of Brain Theory and Neural Networks*. MIT Press, Cambridge, MA, pp. 169–172.

Bartlett, F.C.S. (1932) *Remembering*. Cambridge University Press, Cambridge.

Baylis, G.C., Rolls, E.T. and Leonard, C.M. (1985) Selectivity between faces in the responses of a population of neurons in the cortex in the superior temporal sulcus of the monkey. *Brain Research* **342**, 91–102.

Baylis, G.C., Rolls, E.T. and Leonard, C.M. (1987) Functional subdivisions of the temporal lobe neocortex. *Journal of Neuroscience* **7**, 330–342.

Bechtel, W. (1986) Teleological functional analyses and the hierarchical organization of nature. In Rescher, N., ed., *Current Issues in Teleology*. University Press of America, Lanham, MD, pp. 26–48.

Bechtel, W. (1988a) *Philosophy of Mind: An Overview for Cognitive Science*. Erlbaum, Hillsdale.

Bechtel, W. (1988b) *Philosophy of Science: An Overview for Cognitive Science*. Erlbaum, Hillsdale.

Bechtel, W. and Graham, G. (1998) eds. *A Companion to Cognitive Science*. Blackwell, Malden.

Bechtel, W., Mandik, P., Mundale, J. and Stufflebeam, R.S. (2001) eds. *Philosophy and the Neurosciences: A Reader*. Blackwell, Malden.

Bechtel, W. and Richardson, R.C. (1993) *Discovering Complexity: Decomposition and Localization as Strategies in Scientific Research*. Princeton University Press, Princeton.

Beck, D.M., Rees, G., Frith, C.D. and Lavie, N. (2001) Neural correlates of change detection and change blindness. *Nature Neuroscience* **4**, 645–650.

Beck, F. and Eccles, J.C. (2003) Quantum processes in the brain: a scientific basis of consciousness. In Osaka, N., ed., *Neural Basis of Consciousness*. Benjamins, Amsterdam, pp. 141–166.

Bedell, H.E., Chung, S.T., Ogmen, H. and Patel, S.S. (2003) Color and motion: which is the tortoise and which is the hare? *Vision Research* **43**, 2403–2412.

Behrmann, M. (2000) The mind's eye mapped onto the brain's matter. *Current Directions in Psychological Science* **9**, 50–54.

Belger, A., Puce, A., Krystal, J.H., Gore, J.C., Goldman-Rakic, P. and McCarthy, G. (1998) Dissociation of mnemonic and perceptual processes during spatial and nonspatial working memory using fMRI. *Human Brain Mapping* **6**, 14–32.

Bem, S. and Looren de Jong, H. (1997) *Theoretical Issues in Psychology*. Sage, London.

Bennett, M.R. and Hacker, P.M.S. (2003) *Philosophical Foundations of Neuroscience*. Blackwell, Malden.

Berger, H. (1929) Über das Elektrenkephalogramm des Menschen. *Archiv für Psychiatrie und Nervenkrankheiten* **87**, 527–570.

Bergson, H. (1911) *Matter and Memory*. Macmillan, New York.

Berkeley, G. (1707) *An Essay Towards a New Theory of Vision*. Pepyat, Dublin.

Berlin, B. and Kay, P. (1969) *Basic Color Terms: Their Universality and Evolution*. University of California Press, Berkeley.

Berlyne, D.E. (1960) *Conflict, Arousal and Curiosity*. McGraw-Hill, New York.

Bermúdez, J.L., Marcel, A.J. and Eilan, N. (1995) eds. *The Body and the Self*. MIT Press, Cambridge, MA.

Bernat, E., Shevrin, H. and Snodgrass, M. (2001) Subliminal visual oddball stimuli evoke a P300 component. *Clinical Neurophysiology* **112**, 159–171.

Bertalanffy, L. von (1968) *Organismic Psychology and Systems Theory*. Clark University Press, Worcester, MA.

Bickle, J. (1998) *Psychoneural Reduction: The New Wave*. MIT Press, Cambridge, MA.

Bickle, J. (2003a) Philosophy of mind and the neurosciences. In Stich, S.P. and Warfield, T.A., eds., *The Blackwell Guide to Philosophy of Mind*. Blackwell, Malden, pp. 322–351.

Bickle, J. (2003b) *Philosophy and Neuroscience: A Ruthlessly Reductive Account*. Kluwer, Dordrecht.

Biederman, I. (1972) Perceiving real-world scenes. *Science* **177**, 77–80.

Biederman, I. (1987) Recognition-by-components: a theory of human image understanding. *Psychological Review* **94**, 115–147.

Biederman, I. and Shiffrar, M.M. (1987) Sexing day old chicks: a case study and expert systems-analysis of a difficult perceptual learning task. *Journal of Experimental Psychology: Learning, Memory and Cognition* **13**, 640–645.

Bigelow, J. and Pargetter, R. (1987) Functions. *Journal of Philosophy* **84**, 181–196.

Bird, C.M., Castelli, F., Malik, O., Frith, U. and Husain, M. (2004) The impact of extensive medial frontal lobe damage on 'Theory of Mind' and cognition. *Brain* **127**, 914–928.

Blackmore, S. (1999) *The Meme Machine*. Oxford University Press, Oxford.

Blackmore, S. (2003) *Consciousness: An Introduction*. Hodder and Stoughton, London.

Blackmore, S. (2005a) *Consciousness: A Very Short Introduction*. Oxford University Press, Oxford.

Blackmore, S. (2005b) *Conversations on Consciousness: Interviews with Twenty Minds*. Oxford University Press, Oxford.

Blake, R. (1989) A neural theory of binocular rivalry. *Psychological Review* **96**, 145–167.

Blake, R. and Logothetis, N.K. (2002) Visual competition. *Nature Reviews Neuroscience* **3**, 13–21.

Blake, R. and Yang, Y. (1997) Spatial and temporal coherence in perceptual binding. *Proceedings of the National Academy of Sciences of the United States of America* **94**, 7115–7119.

Blakemore, C. (1973) The language of vision. *New Scientist* **58**, 674–677.

Blakemore, C. (1990) Understanding images in the brain. In Barlow, H., Blakemore, C. and Weston-Smith, M., eds., *Images and Understanding*. Cambridge University Press, Cambridge, pp. 257–283.

Blakemore, S.-J., Smith, J., Steel, R., Johnstone, C.E. and Frith, C.D. (2000) The perception of self-produced sensory stimuli in patients with auditory hallucinations and passivity experiences: evidence for a breakdown in self-monitoring. *Psychological Medicine* **30**, 1131–1139.

Blanke, O., Landis, T., Spinelli, L. and Seeck, M. (2004) Out-of-body experience and autoscopy of neurological origin. *Brain* **127**, 243–258.

Bliss, T.V. and Lømo, T. (1973) Long-lasting potentiation of synaptic transmission in the dentate area of the anaesthetized rabbit following stimulation of the perforant path. *Journal of Physiology* **232**, 331–356.

Block, N. (1978) Troubles with functionalism. In Savage, C.W., ed., *Perception and Cognition: Issues in the Foundations of Psychology. Minnesota Studies in the Philosophy of Science, vol. 9*. University of Minnesota Press, Minneapolis, pp. 261–325.

Block, N. (1986) Advertisement for a semantics for psychology. *Midwest Studies in Philosophy* **10**, 615–678.

Block, N. (1995) On a confusion about a function of consciousness. *Behavioral and Brain Sciences* **18**, 227–287.

Block, N. (2005) Two neural correlates of consciousness. *Trends in Cognitive Sciences* **9**, 46–52.

Block, N., Flanagan, O.J. and Güzeldere, G. (1997) eds. *The Nature of Consciousness: Philosophical Debates*. MIT Press, Cambridge, MA.

Bloor, D. (1976) *Knowledge and Social Imagery*. Routledge and Kegan Paul, London.

Boddy, J. (1978) *Brain Systems and Psychological Concepts*. Wiley, Chichester.

Bogdan, R.J. (2000) *Minding Minds: Evolving a Reflexive Mind by Interpreting Others*. MIT Press, Cambridge, MA.

Bogen, J.E. (1995a) On the neurophysiology of consciousness: I. An overview. *Consciousness and Cognition* **4**, 52–62.

Bogen, J.E. (1995b) On the neurophysiology of consciousness: Part II. Constraining the semantic problem. *Consciousness and Cognition* **4**, 137–158.

Bohm, D. (1980) *Wholeness and the Implicate Order*. Routledge and Kegan Paul, London.

Bonneh, Y., Sagi, D. and Karni, A. (2001) A transition between eye and object rivalry determined by stimulus coherence. *Vision Research* **41**, 981–989.

Botterill, G. and Carruthers, P. (1999) *The Philosophy of Psychology*. Cambridge University Press, Cambridge.

Bowers, J.S. and Marsolek, C.J. (2003) eds. *Rethinking Implicit Memory*. Oxford University Press, Oxford.

Braak, H. (1976) On the striate area of the human isocortex. A Golgi- and pigmentarchitectonic study. *Journal of Comparative Neurology* **166**, 341–364.

Bradshaw, J.L. and Mattingley, J.B. (1995) *Clinical Neuropsychology*. Academic Press, San Diego, CA.

Brandt, J. (1988) Malingered amnesia. In Rogers, R., ed., *Clinical Assessment of Malingering and Deception*. Guilford Press, New York, pp. 65–83.

Braun, A.R., Balkin, T.J., Wesensten, N.J., Gwadry, F., Carson, R.E., Varga, M., Baldwin, P., Belenky, G. and Herscovitch, P. (1998) Dissociated pattern of activity in visual cortices and their projections during human rapid eye movement sleep. *Science* **279**, 91–95.

Braun, J. and Julesz, B. (1998) Withdrawing attention at little or no cost: detection and discrimination tasks. *Perception and Psychophysics* **60**, 1–23.

Braun, J., Koch, C. and Davis, J.L. (2001) eds. *Visual Attention and Cortical Circuits*. MIT Press, Cambridge, MA.

Breakwell, G.M. and Rose, D. (2000) Research: theory and method. In Breakwell, G.M., Hammond, S. and Fife-Schaw, C., eds., *Research Methods in Psychology, 2nd edn*. Sage, London, pp. 5–21.

Breidbach, O. (2001) The origin and development of the neurosciences. In Machamer, P.K., Grush, R. and McLaughlin, P., eds., *Theory and Method in the Neurosciences*. University of Pittsburgh Press, Pittsburgh, pp. 7–30.

Breitmeyer, B.G. (1984) *Visual Masking: An Integrative Approach*. Clarendon, Oxford.

Brennan, J.F. (2003) *History and Systems of Psychology,* 6th edn. Prentice Hall, Upper Saddle River.

Brentano, F.C. (1874) *Psychologie vom empirischen Standpunkt, Band 1*. Duncker und Helmblot, Leipzig.

Bringuier, V., Chavane, F., Glaeser, L. and Frégnac, Y. (1999) Horizontal propagation of visual activity in the synaptic integration field of area 17 neurons. *Science* **283**, 695–699.

Brodmann, K. (1909) *Vergleichende Lokalisationslehre der Großhirnrinde in ihren Prinzipien dargestellt auf Grund des Zellenbaues*. Barth, Leipzig.

Brook, A. (2002) The appearance of things. In Brook, A. and Ross, D., eds., *Daniel Dennett*. Cambridge University Press, Cambridge, pp. 41–64.

Brook, A. and DeVidi, R.C. (2001) eds. *Self-Reference and Self-Awareness*. Benjamins, Amsterdam.

Brook, A. and Ross, D. (2002) eds. *Daniel Dennett*. Cambridge University Press, Cambridge.

Brook, A. and Stainton, R. (2000) *Knowledge and Mind: A Philosophical Introduction*. MIT Press, Cambridge, MA.

Brown, D., Lyons, E. and Rose, D. (submitted) The self after brain injury: finding the missing bits of the puzzle.

Brown, R. and Kulik, J. (1977) Flashbulb memories. *Cognition* **5**, 73–99.

Brown, S.R. (2002) *Structural phenomenology: a top-down analytic method*. Paper presented at: Association for the Scientific Study of Consciousness 6 (Barcelona). ⟨http://www.ub.es/grc_logos/assc6/prog/abstracts/ASSC6-P1-04.html⟩

Bruce, V. and Young, A. (1986) Understanding face recognition. *British Journal of Psychology* **77**, 305–327.

Büchel, C., Josephs, O., Rees, G., Turner, R., Frith, C.D. and Friston, K.J. (1998) The functional anatomy of attention to visual motion: a functional MRI study. *Brain* **121**, 1281–1294.

Buller, D.J. (1998) Etiological theories of function: a geographical survey. *Biology and Philosophy* **13**, 505–527.

Buller, D.J. (1999a) ed. *Function, Selection, and Design*. State University of New York Press, Albany, NY.

Buller, D.J. (1999b) Natural teleology. In Buller, D.J., ed., *Function, Selection, and Design*. State University of New York Press, Albany, NY., pp. 1–27.

Buller, D.J. (2005a) Evolutionary psychology: the emperor's new paradigm. *Trends in Cognitive Sciences* **9**, 277–283.

Buller, D.J. (2005b) *Adapting Minds: Evolutionary Psychology and the Persistent Quest for Human Nature*. MIT Press, Cambridge, MA.

Bullier, J. (2001) Feedback connections and conscious vision. *Trends in Cognitive Sciences* **5**, 369–370.

Bunnin, N. and Tsui-James, E.P. (1996) eds. *The Blackwell Companion to Philosophy*. Blackwell, Oxford.

Buonomano, D.V. and Merzenich, M.M. (1998) Cortical plasticity: from synapses to maps. *Annual Review of Neuroscience* **21**, 149–186.

Burgess, N., Jeffery, K.J. and O'Keefe, J. (1999) eds. *The Hippocampal and Parietal Foundations of Spatial Cognition*. Oxford University Press, Oxford.

Burkitt, I. (1991) *Social Selves: Theories of the Social Formation of Personality*. Sage, London.

Burkitt, I. (1999) *Bodies of Thought: Embodiment, Identity and Modernity*. Sage, London.

Burr, D., Kowler, E., Reeves, A. and Verghese, P. (2004) eds. Visual attention. *Vision Research* **44**, 1189–1492.

Bush, G., Luu, P. and Posner, M.I. (2000) Cognitive and emotional influences in anterior cingulate cortex. *Trends in Cognitive Sciences* **4**, 215–222.

Bushara, K.O., Hanakawa, T., Immisch, I., Toma, K., Kansaku, K. and Hallett, M. (2003) Neural correlates of cross-modal binding. *Nature Neuroscience* **6**, 190–195.

Buxhoeveden, D.P. and Casanova, M.F. (2002) The minicolumn hypothesis in neuroscience. *Brain* **125**, 935–951.

Cacioppo, J.T. (2002) Social neuroscience: understanding the pieces fosters understanding the whole and vice versa. *American Psychologist* **57**, 819–831.

Cacioppo, J.T., Berntson, G.G., Adolphs, R., Carter, C.S., Davidson, R.J., McClintock, M.K., McEwen, B.S., Meaney, M.J., Schacter, D.L., Sternberg, E.M., Suomi, S.S. and Taylor, S.E. (2002) eds. *Foundations in Social Neuroscience*. MIT Press, Cambridge, MA.

Cahill, L., McGaugh, J.L. and Weinberger, N.M. (2001) The neurobiology of learning and memory: some reminders to remember. *Trends in Neurosciences* **24**, 578–581.

Calvin, W.H. (1996) *The Cerebral Code: Thinking a Thought in the Mosaics of the Mind*. MIT Press, Cambridge, MA.

Campbell, F.W. and Kulikowski, J.J. (1966) Orientational selectivity of the human visual system. *Journal of Physiology* **187**, 437–445.

Campbell, F.W. and Robson, J.G. (1968) Application of Fourier analysis to the visibility of gratings. *Journal of Physiology* **197**, 551–566.

Capra, F. (1996) *The Web of Life: A New Scientific Understanding of Living Systems*. Anchor Books, New York.

Carey, D. (2004) Neuropsychological perspectives on sensorimotor integration: eye-hand coordination and visually guided reaching. In Kanwisher, N. and Duncan, J., eds., *Functional Neuroimaging of Visual Cognition*. Oxford University Press, Oxford, pp. 481–502.

Carpenter, R.H.S. (1990) *Neurophysiology, 2nd edn*. Edward Arnold, London.

Carruthers, P. (2003) *The Nature of the Mind: An Introduction*. Routledge, London.

Carruthers, P. (2004) The mind is a system of modules shaped by natural selection. In Hitchcock, C.R., ed., *Contemporary Debates in Philosophy of Science*. Blackwell, Oxford, pp. 293–311.

Casagrande, V., Sherman, S.M. and Guillery, R.W. (2005) eds. *Cortical Function: A View from the Thalamus. Progress in Brain Research, vol. 149*. Elsevier, Amsterdam.

Casanova, C. (2004) The visual functions of the pulvinar. In Chalupa, L.M. and Werner, J.S., eds., *The Visual Neurosciences*. MIT Press, Cambridge, MA, pp. 592–608.

Cavada, C., Compañy, T., Hernández-González, A. and Reinoso-Suárez, F. (1995) Acetylcholinesterase histochemistry in the macaque thalamus reveals territories selectively connected to frontal, parietal and temporal association cortices. *Journal of Chemical Neuroanatomy* **8**, 245–257.

Cavanagh, P. (1985) Local log polar frequency analysis in the striate cortex as a basis for size and orientation invariance. In Rose, D. and Dobson, V.G., eds., *Models of the Visual Cortex*. Wiley, Chichester, pp. 85–95.

Cavanagh, P. (1989) Multiple analyses of orientation in the visual system. In Lam, D.M.-K. and Gilbert, C.D., eds., *Neural Mechanisms of Visual Perception*. Portfolio, Woodlands, pp. 261–279.

Cavanagh, P. (1998) Attention: a peaceful haven for studies of conscious information processing. *Perception* **27** (Supplement), 23.

Cave, K.R. and Bichot, N.P. (1999) Visuospatial attention: beyond a spotlight model. *Psychonomic Bulletin and Review* **6**, 204–223.

Chalmers, A. (1999) *What is This Thing Called Science? 3rd edn*. Open University Press, Maidenhead.

Chalmers, D.J. (1996) *The Conscious Mind*. Oxford University Press, New York.

Chalmers, D.J. (2002) ed. *Philosophy of Mind: Classical and Contemporary Readings*. Oxford University Press, New York.

Charles, E.S. and d'Appolonia, S.T. (2004) *Developing a conceptual framework to explain emergent causality: overcoming ontological beliefs to achieve conceptual change*. Paper presented at: Cognitive Science Society (Chicago). ⟨http://www.cogsci.northwestern.edu/ cogsci2004/papers/paper405.pdf⟩

Chaudhuri, A. (1990) Modulation of the motion aftereffect by selective attention. *Nature* **344**, 60–62.

Chelazzi, L., Miller, E.K., Duncan, J. and Desimone, R. (1993) A neural basis for visual search in inferior temporal cortex. *Nature* **363**, 345–347.

Chen, W., Kato, T., Zhu, X.H., Ogawa, S., Tank, D.W. and Ugurbil, K. (1998) Human primary visual cortex and lateral geniculate nucleus activation during visual imagery. *Neuroreport* **9**, 3669–3674.

Cherry, E.C. (1953) Some experiments on the recognition of speech, with one and with two ears. *Journal of the Acoustical Society of America* **23**, 915–919.

Chomsky, N. (1957) *Syntactic Structures*. Mouton, The Hague.

Chomsky, N. (1959) Verbal behavior: Skinner, B.F. *Language* **35**, 26–58.

Chomsky, N. (1980) *Rules and Representations*. Blackwell, Oxford.

Christie, J. and Barresi, J. (2002) Using illusory line motion to differentiate misrepresentation (Stalinesque) and misremembering (Orwellian)

accounts of consciousness. *Consciousness and Cognition* **11**, 347–365.

Churchland, P.M. (1985) Reduction, qualia and the direct introspection of brain states. *Journal of Philosophy* **82**, 8–28.

Churchland, P.M. (1988) *Matter and Consciousness: A Contemporary Introduction to the Philosophy of Mind, rev. edn*. MIT Press, Cambridge, MA.

Churchland, P.S. (1981) On the alleged backwards referral of experiences and its relevance to the mind–body problem. *Philosophy of Science* **48**, 165–181.

Churchland, P.S. (1986) *Neurophilosophy: Toward a Unified Science of the Mind–Brain*. MIT Press, Cambridge, MA.

Churchland, P.S. (1996) Do we propose to eliminate consciousness? In McCauley, R.N., ed., *The Churchlands and their Critics*. Blackwell, Cambridge, MA, pp. 297–300.

Churchland, P.S. (2002) *Brain-wise: Studies in Neurophilosophy*. MIT Press, Cambridge, MA.

Churchland, P.S. and Churchland, P.M. (2002) Neural worlds and real worlds. *Nature Reviews Neuroscience* **3**, 903–907.

Churchland, P.S. and Sejnowski, T.J. (1992) *The Computational Brain*. MIT Press, Cambridge, MA.

Clapin, H. (2002) ed. *Philosophy of Mental Representation*. Oxford University Press, Oxford.

Clapin, H., Staines, P.J. and Slezak, P.P. (2004) eds. *Representation in Mind: New Approaches to Mental Representation*. Elsevier, Amsterdam.

Clark, A. (1993) *Sensory Qualities*. Oxford University Press, Oxford.

Clark, A. (1997) *Being There: Putting Brain, Body, and World Together Again*. MIT Press, Cambridge, MA.

Clark, A. (2000) *A Theory of Sentience*. Oxford University Press, Oxford.

Clark, A. (2001) *Mindware: An Introduction to the Philosophy of Cognitive Science*. Oxford University Press, New York.

Clarke, M. (2004) *Reconstructing Reason and Representation*. MIT Press, Cambridge, MA.

Cleeremans, A. (2003) ed. *The Unity of Consciousness: Binding, Integration, and Dissociation*. Oxford University Press, Oxford.

Clifford, C.W., Arnold, D.H. and Pearson, J. (2003) A paradox of temporal perception revealed by a stimulus oscillating in colour and orientation. *Vision Research* **43**, 2245–2253.

Clocksin, W.F. (1998) Artificial intelligence and human identity. In Cornwell, J., ed., *Consciousness and Human Identity*. Oxford University Press, New York, pp. 101–121.

Cockburn, D. (2001) *An Introduction to the Philosophy of Mind*. Palgrave, Basingstoke.

Cohen, B.H. (1986) The motor theory of voluntary thinking. In Davidson, K.J., Schwartz, G.E. and Shapiro, D., eds., *Consciousness and Self-Regulation, vol. 4*. Plenum, New York, pp. 9–54.

Cohen, J.D. and Blum, K.I. (2002) eds. Reward and decision. *Neuron* **36**, 193–332.

Cohen, J.D., Botvinick, M. and Carter, C.S. (2000) Anterior cingulate and prefrontal cortex: who's in control? *Nature Neuroscience* **3**, 421–423.

Colby, C.L. and Duhamel, J.R. (1996) Spatial representations for action in parietal cortex. *Cognitive Brain Research* **5**, 105–115.

Collins, A.M. and Quillian, M.R. (1969) Retrieval time from semantic memory. *Journal of Verbal Learning and Verbal Behavior* **8**, 240–247.

Colonnier, M.L. (1966) The structural design of the neocortex. In Eccles, J.C., ed., *Brain and Conscious Experience*. Springer-Verlag, New York, pp. 1–23.

Coltheart, V. (1999) Modularity and cognition. *Trends in Cognitive Science* **3**, 115–120.

Connors, B.W. and Long, M.A. (2004) Electrical synapses in the mammalian brain. *Annual Review of Neuroscience* **27**, 393–418.

Conway, M.A. (1995) *Flashbulb Memories*. Erlbaum, Hove.

Conway, M.A. (2001) Sensory-perceptual episodic memory and its context: autobiographical memory. *Philosophical Transactions of the Royal Society of London, Series B* **356**, 1375–1384.

Conway, M.A. (2003) ed. *Levels of Processing 30 Years On*. Psychology Press, Hove. (First published in *Memory* **10** (5–6), 2002).

Conway, M.A. and Pleydell-Pearce, C.W. (2000) The construction of autobiographical memories in the self-memory system. *Psychological Review* **107**, 261–288.

Cooley, C.H. (1902) *Human Nature and the Social Order*. Scribner, New York.

Cooper, R. (2001) The role of object-oriented concepts in cognitive models. *Trends in Cognitive Sciences* **5**, 333.

Cooper, R. and Shallice, T. (2000) Contention scheduling and the control of routine activities. *Cognitive Neuropsychology* **17**, 297–338.

Corbetta, M., Kincade, J.M. and Shulman, G.L. (2002) Neural systems for visual orienting and their relationships to spatial working memory. *Journal of Cognitive Neuroscience* **14**, 508–523.

Corbetta, M. and Shulman, G.L. (2002) Control of goal-directed and stimulus-driven attention in the brain. *Nature Reviews Neuroscience* **3**, 201–215.

Cosmides, L. and Tooby, J. (1992) Cognitive adaptations for social exchange. In Barkow, J.H., Cosmides, L. and Tooby, J., eds., *The Adapted Mind: Evolutionary Psychology and the Generation of Culture*. Oxford University Press, New York, pp. 163–227.

Cotterill, R. (1998) *Enchanted Looms: Conscious Networks in Brains and Computers*. Cambridge University Press, Cambridge.

Cotterill, R.M.J. (2001) Cooperation of the basal ganglia, cerebellum, sensory cerebrum and hippocampus: possible implications for cognition, consciousness, intelligence and creativity. *Progress in Neurobiology* **64**, 1–33.

Cowey, A. (1979) Cortical maps and visual perception. *Quarterly Journal of Experimental Psychology* **31**, 1–17.

Cowey, A. (2004) Fact, artefact, and myth about blindsight. *Quarterly Journal of Experimental Psychology* **57A**, 577–609.

Cowey, A. and Walsh, V. (2000) Magnetically induced phosphenes in sighted, blind and blindsighted observers. *Neuroreport* **11**, 3269–3273.

Cowey, A. and Walsh, V. (2001) Tickling the brain: studying visual sensation, perception and cognition by transcranial magnetic stimulation. In Casanova, C. and Ptito, M., eds., *Vision: From Neurons to Cognition. Progress in Brain Research, vol. 134*. Elsevier, Amsterdam, pp. 411–425.

Crabtree, J.W. and Isaac, J.T.R. (2002) New intrathalamic pathways allowing modality-related and cross-modality switching in the dorsal thalamus. *Journal of Neuroscience* **22**, 8754–8761.

Craik, F.I.M. and Lockhart, R.S. (1972) Levels of processing: a framework for memory research. *Journal of Verbal Learning and Verbal Behavior* **11**, 671–684.

Craik, K.J.W. (1943) *The Nature of Explanation*. Cambridge University Press, Cambridge.

Crane, T. (2001) *Elements of Mind: An Introduction to the Philosophy of Mind*. Oxford University Press, Oxford.

Craver, C.F. (2001) Role functions, mechanisms, and hierarchy. *Philosophy of Science* **68**, 53–74.

Craver-Lemley, C. and Arterberry, M.E. (2001) Imagery-induced interference on a visual detection task. *Spatial Vision* **14**, 101–119.

Crick, F. (1984) Function of the thalamic reticular complex: the searchlight hypothesis. *Proceedings of the National Academy of Sciences of the United States of America* **81**, 4586–4590.

Crick, F. (1994) *The Astonishing Hypothesis: The Scientific Search for the Soul*. Simon and Schuster, London.

Crick, F. and Koch, C. (1990) Towards a neurobiological theory of consciousness. *Seminars in the Neurosciences* **2**, 263–275.

Crick, F. and Koch, C. (1995) Are we aware of neural activity in primary visual cortex? *Nature* **375**, 121–123.

Crick, F. and Koch, C. (1998a) Consciousness and neuroscience. *Cerebral Cortex* **8**, 97–107.

Crick, F. and Koch, C. (1998b) Constraints on cortical and thalamic projections: the no-strong-loops hypothesis. *Nature* **391**, 245–250.

Crick, F. and Koch, C. (2003) A framework for consciousness. *Nature Neuroscience* **6**, 119–126.

Cronin-Golomb, A. and Hof, P.R. (2004) eds. *Vision in Alzheimer's Disease*. Karger, Basel.

Crook, J.M., Kisvarday, Z.F. and Eysel, U.T. (1998) Evidence for a contribution of lateral inhibition to orientation tuning and direction selectivity in cat visual cortex: reversible inactivation of functionally characterized sites combined with neuroanatomical tracing techniques. *European Journal of Neuroscience* **10**, 2056–2075.

Cummins, R. (1975) Functional analysis. *Journal of Philosophy* **72**, 741–765.

Cummins, R. and Cummins, D.D. (2000) eds. *Minds, Brains, and Computers: The Foundations of Cognitive Science. An Anthology*. Blackwell, Malden.

Cunningham, S. (2000) *What Is a Mind? An Integrative Introduction to the Philosophy of Mind*. Hackett, Indianapolis.

Damasio, A.R. (1989) Time-locked multiregional retroactivation: a systems-level proposal for the neural substrates of recall and recognition. *Cognition* **33**, 25–62.

Damasio, A.R. (1995) *Descartes' Error: Emotion, Reason and the Human Brain*. Picador, London.

Damasio, A.R. (1999) *The Feeling of What Happens: Body and Emotion in the Making of Consciousness*. Harcourt Brace, New York.

Damasio, A.R. and Damasio, H. (1994) Cortical systems for the retrieval of concrete knowledge: the convergence zone framework. In Koch, C. and Davis, J.L., eds., *Large-Scale Neuronal Theories of the Brain*. MIT Press, Cambridge, MA, pp. 61–74.

Damasio, A.R., Grabowski, T.J., Bechara, A., Damasio, H., Ponto, L.L.B., Parvizi, J. and Hichwa, R.D. (2000) Subcortical and cortical brain activity during the feeling of self-generated emotions. *Nature Neuroscience* **3**, 1049–1056.

Damasio, H., Grabowski, T.J., Tranel, D., Hichwa, R.D. and Damasio, A.R. (1996) A neural basis for lexical retrieval. *Nature* **380**, 499–505.

Darden, L. (1980) Theory construction in genetics. In Nickles, T., ed., *Scientific Discovery: Case Studies*. Reidel, Dordrecht, pp. 151–170.

Darden, L. and Maull, N. (1977) Interfield theories. *Philosophy of Science* **44**, 43–64.

Daugman, J.G. (1985) Representational issues and local filter models of two-dimensional spatial visual encoding. In Rose, D. and Dobson, V.G., eds., *Models of the Visual Cortex*. Wiley, Chichester, pp. 96–107.

Daugman, J.G. (1990) Brain metaphor and brain theory. In Schwartz, E.L., ed., *Computational Neuroscience*. MIT Press, Cambridge, MA, pp. 9–18.

Davidson, D. (1987) Knowing one's own mind. *Proceedings and Addresses of the American Philosophical Association* **61**, 441–458.

Davies, M. and Stone, T. (1995) eds. *Folk Psychology: The Theory of Mind Debate*. Blackwell, Oxford.

Davies, P.S. (2001) *Norms of Nature: Naturalism and the Nature of Functions*. MIT Press, Cambridge, MA.

Dawkins, R. (1976) *The Selfish Gene*. Oxford University Press, Oxford.

Dawkins, R. (1982) *The Extended Phenotype: The Gene as the Unit of Selection*. Freeman, San Francisco.

Dayan, P. and Abbott, L.F. (2001) *Theoretical Neuroscience: Computational and Mathematical Modeling of Neural Systems*. MIT Press, Cambridge, MA.

De Gelder, B., De Haan, E.H.F. and Heywood, C.F. (2001) eds. *Out of Mind: Varieties of Unconscious Processes*. Oxford University Press, Oxford.

Debner, J.A. and Jacoby, L.L. (1994) Unconscious perception: attention, awareness, and control. *Journal of Experimental Psychology: Learning, Memory and Cognition* 20, 304–317.

deCharms, R.C. and Zador, A. (2000) Neural representation and the cortical code. *Annual Review of Neuroscience* 23, 613–647.

Deco, G. and Lee, T.S. (2004) The role of early visual cortex in visual integration: a neural model of recurrent interaction. *European Journal of Neuroscience* 20, 1089–1100.

Deco, G. and Rolls, E.T. (2004) A neurodynamical cortical model of visual attention and invariant object recognition. *Vision Research* 44, 621–642.

Deco, G. and Schürmann, B. (2000) A hierarchical neural system with attentional top-down enhancement of the spatial resolution for object recognition. *Vision Research* 40, 2845–2859.

Deeke, L. (1987) Bereitschaftspotential as an indicator of movement preparation in supplementary motor area and motor cortex. In Porter, R., ed., *Motor Areas of the Cerebral Cortex. Ciba Foundation Symposia, vol. 132*. Wiley, Chichester, pp. 231–250.

Dehaene, S. (2001) ed. The cognitive neuroscience of consciousness. *Cognition* 79, 1–237. Also published by MIT Press, Cambridge, MA.

Dehaene, S., Kerszberg, M. and Changeux, J.P. (1998) A neuronal model of a global workspace in effortful cognitive tasks. *Proceedings of the National Academy of Sciences of the United States of America* 95, 14529–14534.

Dehaene, S., Sergent, C. and Changeux, J.P. (2003) A neuronal network model linking subjective reports and objective physiological data during conscious perception. *Proceedings of the National Academy of Sciences of the United States of America* 100, 8520–8525.

Deneve, S., Latham, P.E. and Pouget, A. (1999) Reading population codes: a neural implementation of ideal observers. *Nature Neuroscience* 2, 740–745.

Dennett, D.C. (1978) *Brainstorms: Philosophical Essays on Mind and Psychology*. Bradford, Montgomery, VT.

Dennett, D.C. (1983) Artificial intelligence and the strategies of psychological investigation. In Miller, J., ed., *States of Mind*. British Broadcasting Corporation, London, pp. 66–81.

Dennett, D.C. (1987) *The Intentional Stance*. MIT Press, Cambridge, MA.

Dennett, D.C. (1988) Quining qualia. In Marcel, A.J. and Bisiach, E., eds., *Consciousness in Contemporary Science*. Oxford University Press, Oxford, pp. 42–77.

Dennett, D.C. (1991) *Consciousness Explained*. Little, Brown and Co., Boston.

Dennett, D.C. (1994) Real consciousness. In Revonsuo, A. and Kampinnen, M., eds., *Consciousness in Philosophy and Cognitive Neuroscience*. Erlbaum, Hillsdale, pp. 55–63.

Dennett, D.C. (1995) *Darwin's Dangerous Idea: Evolution and the Meanings of Life*. Allen Lane, London.

Dennett, D.C. (1996) Granny versus Mother Nature: no contest. *Mind and Language* 11, 263–269.

Dennett, D.C. (1998) The myth of double transduction. In Hameroff, S.R., Kaszniak, A.W. and Scott, A., eds., *Toward a Science of Consciousness II: The Second Tucson Discussions and Debates*. MIT Press, Cambridge, MA, pp. 97–107.

Dennett, D.C. (2000) With a little help from my friends. In Ross, D., Brook, A. and Thompson, D., eds., *Dennett's Philosophy: A Comprehensive Assessment*. MIT Press, Cambridge, MA, pp. 327–388.

Dennett, D.C. and Kinsbourne, M. (1992) Time and the observer: the where and when of consciousness in the brain. *Behavioral and Brain Sciences* 15, 183–247.

Derdikman, D., Hildesheim, R., Ahissar, E., Arieli, A. and Grinvald, A. (2003) Imaging spatiotemporal dynamics of surround inhibition in the barrels somatosensory cortex. *Journal of Neuroscience* 23, 3100–3105.

Descartes, R. (1637) *Discours de la méthode pour bien conduire sa raison et chercher la verité dans les sciences*. Jan Maire, Leyden.

Descartes, R. (1641) *Meditationes de Prima Philosophia*. Michel Suly, Paris.

Desimone, R. and Duncan, J. (1995) Neural mechanisms of selective visual attention. *Annual Review of Neuroscience* 18, 193–222.

Destexhe, A. and Sejnowski, T.J. (2001) *Thalamocortical Assemblies: How Ion Channels, Single Neurons, and Large-scale Networks Organize Sleep Oscillations*. Oxford University Press, Oxford.

Devlin, J.T., Moore, C.J., Mummery, C.J., Gorno-Tempini, M.L., Phillips, J.A., Noppeney, U.,

Frackowiak, R.S., Friston, K.J. and Price, C.J. (2002) Anatomic constraints on cognitive theories of category specificity. *Neuroimage* **15**, 675–685.

DeVries, S.H. (1999) Correlated firing in rabbit retinal ganglion cells. *Journal of Neurophysiology* **81**, 908–920.

Di Lollo, V., Enns, J.T. and Rensink, R.A. (2000) Competition for consciousness among visual events: the psychophysics of reentrant visual processes. *Journal of Experimental Psychology: General* **129**, 481–507.

Di Lollo, V., Kawahara, J., Zuvic, S.M. and Visser, T.A.W. (2001) The preattentive emperor has no clothes: a dynamic redressing. *Journal of Experimental Psychology: General* **130**, 479–492.

Diamond, I.T. (1979) The subdivisions of the neocortex: a proposal to revise the traditional view of sensory, motor, and associational areas. *Progress in Psychobiology and Physiological Psychology* **8**, 1–43.

Dien, J., Spencer, K.M. and Donchin, E. (2004) Parsing the late positive complex: mental chronometry and the ERP components that inhabit the neighborhood of the P300. *Psychophysiology* **41**, 665–678.

Dixon, M.J., Desmarais, G., Gojmerac, C., Schweizer, T.A. and Bub, D.N. (2002) The role of premorbid expertise on object identification in a patient with category-specific visual agnosia. *Cognitive Neuropsychology* **19**, 401–419.

Dixon, N.F. (1981) *Preconscious Processing*. Wiley, Chichester.

Djordjevic, J., Zatorre, R.J. and Jones-Gotman, M. (2004a) Effects of perceived and imagined odors on taste detection. *Chemical Senses* **29**, 199–208.

Djordjevic, J., Zatorre, R.J., Petrides, M. and Jones-Gotman, M. (2004b) The mind's nose: effects of odor and visual imagery on odor detection. *Psychological Science* **15**, 143–148.

Dobelle, W.H. and Mladejovsky, M.G. (1974) Phosphenes produced by electrical stimulation of human occipital cortex, and their application to the development of a prosthesis for the blind. *Journal of Physiology* **243**, 553–576.

Dobson, V. (1975) Pattern learning and the control of behaviour by all-inhibitory neural network hierarchies. *Perception* **4**, 35–50.

Dobson, V.G. and Rose, D. (1985) Models and metaphysics: the nature of explanation revisited. In Rose, D. and Dobson, V.G., eds., *Models of the Visual Cortex*. Wiley, Chichester, pp. 22–36.

Douglas, R., Markram, H. and Martin, K. (2004) Neocortex. In Shepherd, G.M., ed., *The Synaptic Organization of the Brain, 5th edn*. Oxford University Press, New York, pp. 499–558.

Dretske, F. (1981) *Knowledge and the Flow of Information*. MIT Press, Cambridge, MA.

Dretske, F. (1986) Misrepresentation. In Bogdan, R.J., ed., *Belief: Form, Content, and Function*. Clarendon, Oxford, pp. 17–36.

Dretske, F. (1988) *Explaining Behavior: Reasons in a World of Causes*. MIT Press, Cambridge, MA.

Dretske, F. (1995) *Naturalizing the Mind*. MIT Press, Cambridge, MA.

Driver, J. and Frackowiak, R.S.J. (2001) eds. Imaging selective attention in the human brain. *Neuropsychologia* **39**, 1255–1371.

Driver, J. and Mattingley, J.B. (1998) Parietal neglect and visual awareness. *Nature Neuroscience* **1**, 17–22.

Driver, J. and Vuilleumier, P. (2001) Perceptual awareness and its loss in unilateral neglect and extinction. *Cognition* **79**, 39–88.

Droege, P. (2003) *Caging the Beast: A Theory Of Sensory Consciousness*. Benjamins, Philadelphia.

Dudai, Y. (2002) *Memory from A to Z: Keywords, Concepts, and Beyond*. Oxford University Press, Oxford.

Durbin, R. and Mitchison, G. (1990) A dimension reduction framework for understanding cortical maps. *Nature* **343**, 644–647.

Eagleman, D.M. and Sejnowski, T.J. (2000) Motion integration and postdiction in visual awareness. *Science* **287**, 2036–2038.

Eagleman, D.M. and Sejnowski, T.J. (2003) The line-motion illusion can be reversed by motion signals after the line disappears. *Perception* **32**, 963–968.

Eccles, J. (1986) Do mental events cause neural events analogously to the probability fields of quantum mechanics? *Proceedings of the Royal Society of London, Series B* **227**, 411–428.

Eccles, J. (1990) A unitary hypothesis of mind–brain interaction in the cerebral cortex. *Proceedings of the Royal Society of London, Series B* **240**, 433–451.

Economo, C. von (1929) *The Cytoarchitectonics of the Human Cerebral Cortex*. Oxford University Press, London.

Edelman, G.M. (1987) *Neural Darwinism: The Theory of Neuronal Group Selection*. Basic Books, New York.

Edelman, G.M. (1989) *The Remembered Present: A Biological Theory of Consciousness*. Basic Books, New York.

Edelman, G.M. (1992) *Bright Air, Brilliant Fire: On the Matter of the Mind*. Allen Lane, London.

Edelman, G.M. and Tononi, G. (2000) *Consciousness: How Matter Becomes Imagination*. Allen Lane, London.

Egeth, H.E. and Yantis, S. (1997) Visual attention: control, representation, and time course. *Annual Review of Psychology* **48**, 269–297.

Eichenbaum, H. (2002) *The Cognitive Neuroscience of Memory: An Introduction*. Oxford University Press, New York.

Eichenbaum, H. and Cohen, N.J. (2001) *From Conditioning to Conscious Recollection: Memory Systems of the Brain*. Oxford University Press, Oxford.

Eichenbaum, H. and Davis, J.L. (1998) eds. *Neuronal Ensembles: Strategies for Recording and Decoding*. Wiley-Liss, New York.

Eichenbaum, H., Schoenbaum, G., Young, B. and Bunsey, M. (1996) Functional organization of the hippocampal memory system. *Proceedings of the National Academy of Sciences of the United States of America* **93**, 13500–13507.

Eliasmith, C. and Anderson, C.H. (2003) *Neural Engineering: Computation, Representation, and Dynamics in Neurobiological Systems*. MIT Press, Cambridge, MA.

Ellis, A.W. and Young, A.W. (1996) *Human Cognitive Neuropsychology: A Textbook with Readings, augmented edn*. Psychology Press, Hove.

Ellis, R.D. and Newton, N. (2004) *Consciousness and Emotion: Agency, Conscious choice, and Selective Perception*. Benjamins, Amsterdam.

Engel, A.K., Konig, P., Kreiter, A.K. and Singer, W. (1991) Interhemispheric synchronization of oscillatory neuronal responses in cat visual cortex. *Science* **252**, 1177–1179.

Engel, A.K. and Singer, W. (2001) Temporal binding and the neural correlates of sensory awareness. *Trends in Cognitive Sciences* **5**, 16–25.

Enroth-Cugell, C. and Robson, J.G. (1966) The contrast sensitivity of retinal ganglion cells of the cat. *Journal of Physiology* **187**, 517–552.

Enç, B. (2002) Indeterminacy of function attributions. In Ariew, A., Cummins, R. and Perlman, M., eds., *Functions: New Essays in the Philosophy of Psychology and Biology*. Oxford University Press, Oxford, pp. 291–313.

Enç, B. and Adams, F. (1992) Functions and goal directedness. *Philosophy of Science* **59**, 635–654.

Erdelyi, M.H. (2004) Subliminal perception and its cognates: theory, indeterminacy, and time. *Consciousness and Cognition* **13**, 73–91.

Ericsson, K.A. and Simon, H.A. (1980) Verbal reports as data. *Psychological Review* **87**, 215–251.

Eriksson, J., Larsson, A., Ahlstrom, K.R. and Nyberg, L. (2004) Visual consciousness: dissociating the neural correlates of perceptual transitions from sustained perception with fMRI. *Consciousness and Cognition* **13**, 61–72.

Erlanger, J. and Gasser, H.S. (1937) *Electrical Signs of Nervous Activity*. Milford, London.

Eustache, F., Piolino, P., Giffard, B., Viader, F., De La Sayette, V., Baron, J.C. and Desgranges, B. (2004) 'In the course of time': a PET study of the cerebral substrates of autobiographical amnesia in Alzheimer's disease. *Brain* **127**, 1549–1560.

Eysenck, M.W. and Keane, M.T. (2005) *Cognitive Psychology: A Student's Handbook, 5th edn*. Psychology, Hove.

Fahle, M. (2004) Perceptual learning: A case for early selection. *Journal of Vision* **4**, 879–890.

Fahle, M. and Poggio, T. (2002) eds. *Perceptual Learning*. MIT Press, Cambridge, MA.

Fairén, A. and Valverde, F. (1979) Specific thalamo-cortical afferents and their presumptive targets in the visual cortex. A Golgi study. *Progress in Brain Research* **51**, 419–438.

Farah, M.J. (2000) *The Cognitive Neuroscience of Vision*. Blackwell, Oxford.

Farah, M.J. (2004) *Visual Agnosia, 2nd edn*. MIT Press, Cambridge, MA.

Farber, I. (2005) How a neural correlate can function as an explanation of consciousness. Evidence from the history of science regarding the likely explanatory value of the NCC approach. *Journal of Consciousness Studies* **12** (4–5), 77–95.

Fassbender, C., Murphy, K., Foxe, J.J., Wylie, G.R., Javitt, D.C., Robertson, I.H. and Garavan, H. (2004) A topography of executive functions and their interactions revealed by functional magnetic resonance imaging. *Cognitive Brain Research* **20**, 132–143.

Faw, B. (2003) Pre-frontal executive committee for perception, working memory, attention, long-term memory, motor control, and thinking: a tutorial review. *Consciousness and Cognition* **12**, 83–139.

Feinberg, I. and Guazzelli, M. (1999) Schizophrenia – a disorder of the corollary discharge systems that integrate the motor systems of thought with the sensory systems of consciousness. *British Journal of Psychiatry* **174**, 196–204.

Feinberg, T.E. (2001a) Why the mind is not a radically emergent feature of the brain. *Journal of Consciousness Studies* **8** (9–10), 123–145.

Feinberg, T.E. (2001b) *Altered Egos: How the Brain Creates the Self*. Oxford University Press, Oxford.

Felleman, D.J. and Van Essen, D.C. (1991) Distributed hierarchical processing in the primate cerebral cortex. *Cerebral Cortex* **1**, 1–47.

Fenn, K.M., Nusbaum, H.C. and Margoliash, D. (2003) Consolidation during sleep of perceptual learning of spoken language. *Nature* **425**, 614–616.

Fernandez-Duque, D. and Johnson, M.L. (1999) Attention metaphors: how metaphors guide the cognitive psychology of attention. *Cognitive Science* **23**, 83–116.

Feyerabend, P. (1970) Consolations for the specialist. In Lakotos, I. and Musgrave, A., eds., *Criticism and the Growth of Knowledge*. Cambridge University Press, Cambridge, pp. 197–230.

ffytche, D.H., Guy, C.N. and Zeki, S. (1995) The parallel visual motion inputs into areas V1 and V5 of human cerebral cortex. *Brain* **118**, 1375–1394.

ffytche, D.H., Howard, R.J., Brammer, M.J., David, A., Woodruff, P. and Williams, S. (1998) The anatomy of conscious vision: an fMRI study of visual hallucinations. *Nature Neuroscience* **1**, 738–742.

Field, D.J., Hayes, A. and Hess, R.F. (1993) Contour integration by the human visual system: evidence for a local "association field". *Vision Research* **33**, 173–193.

Finke, R.A. (1986) Mental imagery and the visual system. *Scientific American* **254** (3), 76–83.

Fireman, G.D., McVay, T.E. and Flanagan, O.J. (2003) eds. *Narrative and Consciousness: Literature, Psychology, and the Brain*. Oxford University Press, New York.

Fivush, R. and Haden, C.A. (2003) eds. *Autobiographical Memory and the Construction of a Narrative Self: Developmental and Cultural Perspectives*. Erlbaum, Mahwah.

Flanagan, O.J. (1992) *Consciousness Reconsidered*. MIT Press, Cambridge, MA.

Fletcher, P.C. and Henson, R.N. (2001) Frontal lobes and human memory: insights from functional neuroimaging. *Brain* **124**, 849–881.

Flohr, H. (1991) Brain processes and phenomenal consciousness: a new and specific hypothesis. *Theory and Psychology* **1**, 245–262.

Fodor, J. (1968) The appeal to tacit knowledge in psychological explanation. *Journal of Philosophy* **65**, 627–640.

Fodor, J. (1975) *The Language of Thought*. Harvester Press, Hassocks.

Fodor, J. (1983) *Modularity of Mind: An Essay on Faculty Psychology*. MIT Press, Cambridge, MA.

Fodor, J. (1987) *Psychosemantics*. MIT Press, Cambridge, MA.

Fodor, J. (1990) *A Theory of Content and Other Essays*. MIT Press, Cambridge, MA.

Fodor, J. (1994a) Fodor, Jerry A. In Guttenplan, S., ed., *A Companion to the Philosophy of Mind*. Blackwell, Oxford, pp. 292–300.

Fodor, J. (1994b) *The Elm and the Expert*. MIT Press, Cambridge, MA.

Fodor, J. (1996) Deconstructing Dennett's Darwin. *Mind and Language* **11**, 246–262.

Fodor, J. (1998a) *Concepts: Where Cognitive Science Went Wrong*. Oxford University Press, Oxford.

Fodor, J. (1998b) *In Critical Condition: Polemical Essays on Cognitive Science and the Philosophy of Mind*. MIT Press, Cambridge, MA.

Fodor, J. (2000) *The Mind Doesn't Work That Way: The Scope and Limits of Computational Psychology*. MIT Press, Cambridge, MA.

Fodor, J. and Lepore, E. (1992) *Holism: A Shopper's Guide*. Blackwell, Oxford.

Fodor, J. and Lepore, E. (1999) All at sea in semantic space: Churchland on meaning similarity. *Journal of Philosophy* **96**, 381–403.

Fodor, J. and Pylyshyn, Z.W. (1981) How direct is visual perception? Some reflections on Gibson's "ecological approach". *Cognition* **9**, 139–196.

Fodor, J. and Pylyshyn, Z.W. (1988) Connectionism and cognitive architecture: a critical analysis. *Cognition* **28**, 3–71.

Ford, J.M. and Mathalon, D.H. (2004) Electrophysiological evidence of corollary discharge dysfunction in schizophrenia during talking and thinking. *Journal of Psychiatric Research* **38**, 37–46.

Forde, E.M.E. and Humphreys, G.W. (2002) eds. *Category Specificity in Brain and Mind*. Psychology, Hove.

Forrest, K.A. (2001) Toward an etiology of dissociative identity disorder: a neurodevelopmental approach. *Consciousness and Cognition* **10**, 259–293.

Foster, J. (1991) *The Immaterial Self: A Defence of the Cartesian Dualist Conception of the Mind*. Routledge, London.

Fraisse, P. (1984) Perception and estimation of time. *Annual Review of Psychology* **35**, 1–36.

Frank, L.M., Brown, E.N. and Wilson, M. (2000) Trajectory encoding in the hippocampus and entorhinal cortex. *Neuron* **27**, 169–178.

Freeman, A. (2003) *Consciousness: A Guide to the Debates*. ABC–Clio, Santa Barbara.

Freeman, E., Driver, J., Sagi, D. and Zhaoping, L. (2003) Top-down modulation of lateral interactions in early vision: does attention affect integration of the whole or just perception of the parts? *Current Biology* **13**, 985–989.

Freeman, E., Sagi, D. and Driver, J. (2004) Configuration-specific attentional modulation of flanker – target lateral interactions. *Perception* **33**, 181–194.

Freeman, W.J. (2000) *Neurodynamics: An Exploration in Mesoscopic Brain Dynamics*. Springer, London.

Frégnac, Y., Monier, C., Chavane, F., Baudot, P. and Graham, L. (2003) Shunting inhibition, a silent step in visual cortical computation. *Journal of Physiology – Paris* **97**, 441–451.

Frégnac, Y. and Shulz, D.E. (1999) Activity-dependent regulation of receptive field properties of cat area 17 by supervised Hebbian learning. *Journal of Neurobiology* **41**, 69–82.

Friston, K. (2002) Beyond phrenology: what can neuroimaging tell us about distributed circuitry? *Annual Review of Neuroscience* **25**, 221–250.

Friston, K. (2003) Learning and inference in the brain. *Neural Networks* **16**, 1325–1352.

Friston, K.J. and Price, C.J. (2001) Dynamic representations and generative models of brain function. *Brain Research Bulletin* **54**, 275–285.

Frith, C. (1992) *The Cognitive Neuropsychology of Schizophrenia*. Erlbaum, Hove.

Frith, C. and Gallagher, S. (2002) Models of the pathological mind. *Journal of Consciousness Studies* **9** (4), 57–80.

Frith, C. and Wolpert, D.M. (2003) eds. *The Neuroscience of Social Interactions: Decoding, Imitating, and Influencing the Actions of Others*. Oxford University Press, Oxford.

Frith, U. and Frith, C.D. (2003) Development and neurophysiology of mentalizing. *Philosophical Transactions of the Royal Society of London, Series B* **358**, 459–473.

Fuster, J.M. (1993) Frontal lobes. *Current Opinion in Neurobiology* **3**, 160–165.

Fuster, J.M. (1995) *Memory in the Cerebral Cortex: An Empirical Approach to Neural Networks in the Human and Nonhuman Primate*. MIT Press, Cambridge, MA.

Fuster, J.M. (2003) *Cortex and Mind: Unifying Cognition*. Oxford University Press, New York.

Galarreta, M. and Hestrin, S. (2001) Electrical synapses between GABA-releasing interneurons. *Nature Reviews Neuroscience* **2**, 425–433.

Gallagher, S. and Shear, J. (1999) eds. *Models of the Self*. Imprint Academic, Thorverton.

Gallant, J.L. (2004) Neural mechanisms of natural scene perception. In Chalupa, L.M. and Werner, J.S., eds., *The Visual Neurosciences*. MIT Press, Cambridge, MA, pp. 1590–1602.

Gallese, V., Keysers, C. and Rizzolatti, G. (2004) A unifying view of the basis of social cognition. *Trends in Cognitive Sciences* **8**, 396–403.

Ganis, G., Thompson, W.L. and Kosslyn, S.M. (2004) Brain areas underlying visual mental imagery and visual perception: an fMRI study. *Cognitive Brain Research* **20**, 226–241.

Gardner-Thorpe, C. and Pearn, J. (2004) The Cotard syndrome. Report of two patients: with a review of the extended spectrum of 'délire des négations'. *European Journal of Neurology* **11**, 563–566.

Garfield, J.L. (2000) The meanings of "meaning" and "meaning": dimensions of the sciences of mind. *Philosophical Psychology* **13**, 421–440.

Garrard, P., Lambon Ralph, M.A. and Hodges, J.R. (2002) Semantic dementia: a category-specific paradox. In Forde, E.M.E. and Humphreys, G.W., eds., *Category Specificity in Brain and Mind*. Psychology, Hove, pp. 149–179.

Gauthier, I., Tarr, M.J., Anderson, A.W., Skudlarski, P. and Gore, J.C. (1999) Activation of the middle fusiform 'face area' increases with expertise in recognizing novel objects. *Nature Neuroscience* **2**, 568–573.

Gazzaniga, M.S. (1995) Consciousness and the cerebral hemispheres. In Gazzaniga, M.S., ed., *The Cognitive Neurosciences*. MIT Press, Cambridge, MA, pp. 1391–1400.

Gazzaniga, M.S. (2004) ed. *The Cognitive Neurosciences III*. MIT Press, Cambridge, MA.

Gegenfurtner, K.R. and Kiper, D.C. (2003) Color vision. *Annual Review of Neuroscience* **26**, 181–206.

Gegenfurtner, K.R. and Kiper, D.C. (2004) The processing of color in extrastriate cortex. In Chalupa, L.M. and Werner, J.S., eds., *The Visual Neurosciences*. MIT Press, Cambridge, MA, pp. 1017–1028.

Gennaro, R.J. (2004) ed. *Higher-Order Theories of Consciousness: An Anthology*. Benjamins, Amsterdam.

Gennaro, R.J. (2005) The HOT theory of consciousness: between a rock and a hard place? *Journal of Consciousness Studies* **12** (2), 3–21.

Gentner, D. and Goldin-Meadow, S. (2003) eds. *Language in Mind: Advances in the Study of Language and Thought*. MIT Press, Cambridge, MA.

Georges, S., Seriès, P., Frégnac, Y. and Lorenceau, J. (2002) Orientation dependent modulation of apparent speed: psychophysical evidence. *Vision Research* **42**, 2757–2772.

Ghose, G.M. (2004) Learning in mammalian sensory cortex. *Current Opinion in Neurobiology* **14**, 513–518.

Gibson, J.J. (1979) *The Ecological Approach to Visual Perception*. Houghton Mifflin, Dallas.

Gibson, J.J. and Gibson, E.J. (1955) Perceptual learning: differentiation or enrichment? *Psychological Review* **62**, 32–41.

Gilbert, C.D. (1998) Adult cortical dynamics. *Physiological Reviews* **78**, 467–485.

Gilbert, C.D., Das, A., Ito, M., Kapadia, M. and Westheimer, G. (1996) Spatial integration and cortical dynamics. *Proceedings of the National Academy of Sciences of the United States of America* **93**, 615–622.

Gilbert, C.D. and Wiesel, T.N. (1983) Clustered intrinsic connections in cat visual cortex. *Journal of Neuroscience* **3**, 1116–1133.

Gilinsky, A.S. (1984) *Mind and Brain: Principles of Neuropsychology*. Praeger, New York.

Glynn, I.M. (1991) Conscious vs neural time. *Nature* **352**, 27–28.

Godfrey-Smith, P. (1994) A modern history theory of functions. *Nous* **28**, 344–362.

Godfrey-Smith, P. (1996) *Complexity and the Function of Mind in Nature*. Cambridge University Press, Cambridge.

Goebel, R., Khorram-Sefat, D., Muckli, L., Hacker, H. and Singer, W. (1998) The constructive nature of vision: direct evidence from functional magnetic resonance imaging studies of apparent motion and motion imagery. *European Journal of Neuroscience* **10**, 1563–1573.

Goebel, R., Muckli, L., Zanella, F.E., Singer, W. and Stoerig, P. (2001) Sustained extrastriate cortical activation without visual awareness revealed by fMRI studies of hemianopic patients. *Vision Research* **41**, 1459–1474.

Goff, W.R. (1969) Evoked potential correlates of perceptual organization in man. In Evans, C.R. and Mulholland, T.B., eds., *Attention in Neurophysiology*. Butterworth, London, pp. 169–193.

Goldberg, S. and Pessin, A. (1997) *Gray Matters: An Introduction to the Philosophy of Mind*. M.E. Sharpe, Armonk, NY.

Goldman-Rakic, P. (2000) Localization of function all over again. *Neuroimage* **11**, 451–457.

Gomes, G. (1998) The timing of conscious experience: a critical review and reinterpretation of Libet's research. *Consciousness and Cognition* **7**, 559–595.

Goodale, M.A. and Milner, A.D. (2004) *Sight Unseen: An Exploration of Conscious and Unconscious Vision*. Oxford University Press, Oxford.

Goodale, M.A. and Westwood, D.A. (2004) An evolving view of duplex vision: separate but interacting cortical pathways for perception and action. *Current Opinion in Neurobiology* **14**, 203–211.

Goode, R. and Griffiths, P.E. (1995) The misuse of Sober's selection for/selection of distinction. *Biology and Philosophy* **10**, 99–108.

Gosselin, F. and Schyns, P.G. (2003) Superstitious perceptions reveal properties of internal representations. *Psychological Science* **14**, 505–509.

Gould, S.J. (1980) *The Panda's Thumb: More Reflections in Natural History*. Norton, New York.

Gould, S.J. (1996) *Life's Grandeur*. Jonathan Cape, London.

Gould, S.J. and Lewontin, R.C. (1979) The spandrels of San Marco and the Panglossian paradigm: a critique of the adaptationist programme. *Proceedings of the Royal Society of London, Series B* **205**, 581–598.

Graham, K.S. (1999) Semantic dementia: a challenge to the multiple-trace theory? *Trends in Cognitive Sciences* **3**, 85–87.

Graham, K.S., Lambon Ralph, M.A. and Hodges, J.R. (1999) A questionable semantics: the interaction between semantic knowledge and autobiographical experience in semantic dementia. *Cognitive Neuropsychology* **16**, 689–698.

Gray, C.M. and Singer, W. (1989) Stimulus-specific neuronal oscillations in orientation columns of cat visual cortex. *Proceedings of the National Academy of Sciences of the United States of America* **86**, 1698–1702.

Gray, J.A. (1995) The contents of consciousness: a neurophysiological conjecture. *Behavioral and Brain Sciences* **18**, 659–722.

Gray, J.A. (2004) *Consciousness: Creeping up on the Hard Problem*. Oxford University Press, Oxford.

Gray, J.A., Buhusi, C.V. and Schmajuk, N. (1997) The transition from automatic to controlled processing. *Neural Networks* **10**, 1257–1268.

Gray, J.A. and McNaughton, N. (2000) *The Neuropsychology of Anxiety: An Enquiry into the Function of the Septo-hippocampal System,* 2nd edn. Oxford University Press, Oxford.

Grayling, A.C. (1998) ed. *Philosophy 1: A Guide Through the Subject*. Oxford University Press, Oxford.

Greenfield, S. (1995) *Journey to the Centers of the Mind: Toward a Science of Consciousness*. Freeman, New York.

Greenfield, S. (2000) *The Private Life of the Brain: Emotions, Consciousness, and the Secret of the Self*. Wiley, New York.

Gregory, R.L. (1959) Models and the localization of function in the central nervous system. In *Mechanisation of Thought Processes*. Her Majesty's Stationery Office, London, pp. 669–690.

Gregory, R.L. (1961) The brain as an engineering problem. In Thorpe, W.H. and Zangwill, O.L., eds., *Current Problems in Animal Behaviour*. Methuen, London, pp. 547–565.

Gregory, R.L. (1968) Perceptual illusions and brain models. *Proceedings of the Royal Society of London, Series B* **171**, 279–296.

Gregory, R.L. (1970) *The Intelligent Eye*. Weidenfeld and Nicolson, London.

Gregory, R.L. (1974) Choosing a paradigm for perception. In Carterette, E.C. and Friedman, E.P., eds., *Handbook of Perception. Vol. 1. Historical and Philosophical Roots of Perception*. Academic, New York, pp. 255–283.

Gregory, R.L. (1981) *Mind in Science: A History of Explanations in Psychology and Physics*. Weidenfeld and Nicolson, London.

Gregory, R.L. (1985) Premature reductions and mythical productions. *Perception* **14**, 1–4.

Gregory, R.L. (1994) *Even Odder Perceptions*. Routledge, London.

Gregory, R.L. (1996) What do qualia do? *Perception* **25**, 377–379.

Gregory, R.L. (1998) *Eye and Brain: The Psychology of Seeing, 5th edn*. Oxford University Press, Oxford.

Gregory, R.L. (2004) ed. *The Oxford Companion to the Mind, 2nd edn*. Oxford University Press, Oxford.

Grice, H.P. (1957) Meaning. *Philosophical Review* **66**, 377–388.

Grieve, K.L., Acuna, C. and Cudeiro, J. (2000) The primate pulvinar nuclei: vision and action. *Trends in Neurosciences* **23**, 35–39.

Grill-Spector, K., Knouf, N. and Kanwisher, N. (2004) The fusiform face area subserves face perception, not generic within-category identification. *Nature Neuroscience* **7**, 555–562.

Grill-Spector, K., Kourtzi, Z. and Kanwisher, N. (2001) The lateral occipital complex and its role in object recognition. *Vision Research* **41**, 1409–1422.

Grinvald, A., Frostig, R.D., Lieke, E. and Hildesheim, R. (1988) Optical imaging of neuronal activity. *Physiological Reviews* **68**, 1285–1366.

Grinvald, A., Lieke, E.E., Frostig, R.D. and Hildesheim, R. (1994) Cortical point-spread function and long-range lateral interactions revealed by real-time optical imaging of macaque monkey primary visual cortex. *Journal of Neuroscience* **14**, 2545–2568.

Groeger, J.A. (1988) Qualitatively different effects of undetected and unidentified auditory primes. *Quarterly Journal of Experimental Psychology* **40A**, 323–339.

Groeger, J.A. (1997) *Memory and Remembering: Everyday Memory in Context*. Longman, Harlow.

Groome, D., Dewart, H., Esgate, A., Gurney, K., Kemp, R. and Towell, N. (1999) *An Introduction to Cognitive Psychology: Processes and Disorders*. Psychology Press, Hove.

Grosof, D.H., Shapley, R.M. and Hawken, M.J. (1993) Macaque V1 neurons can signal illusory contours. *Nature* **365**, 550–552.

Gross, C.G. (2002) Genealogy of the "grandmother cell". *The Neuroscientist* **8**, 512–518.

Gross, C.G. and Graziano, M.S.A. (1995) Multiple representations of space in the brain. *The Neuroscientist* **1**, 43–50.

Gross, C.G., Rocha-Miranda, C.E. and Bender, D.B. (1972) Visual properties of neurons in inferotemporal cortex of the macaque. *Journal of Neurophysiology* **35**, 96–111.

Grossberg, S. (1980) How does a brain build a cognitive code? *Psychological Review* **87**, 1–51.

Grossberg, S. (1987a) Cortical dynamics of three-dimensional form, color, and brightness perception: I. Monocular theory. *Perception and Psychophysics* **41**, 87–116.

Grossberg, S. (1987b) Cortical dynamics of three-dimensional form, color, and brightness perception: II. Binocular theory. *Perception and Psychophysics* **41**, 117–158.

Grossberg, S. (1999) The link between brain learning, attention, and consciousness. *Consciousness and Cognition* **8**, 1–44.

Grossberg, S. (2004) Visual boundaries and surfaces. In Chalupa, L.M. and Werner, J.S., eds., *The Visual Neurosciences*. MIT Press, Cambridge, MA, pp. 1624–1639.

Grossman, M. (2002) Frontotemporal dementia: a review. *Journal of the International Neuropsychological Society* **8**, 566–583.

Grove, E.A. and Fukuchi-Shimogori, T. (2003) Generating the cerebral cortical area map. *Annual Review of Neuroscience* **26**, 355–380.

Guillery, R.W. (1995) Anatomical evidence concerning the role of the thalamus in corticocortical communication: a brief review. *Journal of Anatomy* **187**, 583–592.

Guillery, R.W., Feig, S.L. and Lozsádi, D.A. (1998) Paying attention to the thalamic reticular nucleus. *Trends in Neurosciences* **21**, 28–32.

Guillery, R.W. and Sherman, S.M. (2002) The thalamus as a monitor of motor outputs. *Philosophical Transactions of the Royal Society of London, Series B* **357**, 1809–1821.

Gurney, K. (1997) *An Introduction to Neural Networks*. UCL Press, London.

Guttenplan, S. (1994) ed. *A Companion to the Philosophy of Mind*. Blackwell, Oxford.

Güzeldere, G. (1995) Is consciousness the perception of what passes in one's own mind? In Metzinger, T., ed., *Conscious Experience*. Schöningh, Paderborn, pp. 335–359.

Hacking, I. (1983) *Representing and Intervening*. Cambridge University Press, Cambridge.

Haggard, P., Clark, S. and Kalogeras, J. (2002) Voluntary action and conscious awareness. *Nature Neuroscience* **5**, 382–385.

Haggard, P. and Eimer, M. (1999) On the relation between brain potentials and the awareness of voluntary movements. *Experimental Brain Research* **126**, 128–133.

Haier, R.J., Siegel, B.V., Jr., MacLachlan, A., Soderling, E., Lottenberg, S. and Buchsbaum, M.S. (1992) Regional glucose metabolic changes after learning a complex visuospatial/motor task: a positron emission tomographic study. *Brain Research* **570**, 134–143.

Haist, F., Gore, J.B. and Mao, H. (2001) Consolidation of human memory over decades revealed by functional magnetic resonance imaging. *Nature Neuroscience* **4**, 1139–1145.

Haken, H. (1978) *Synergetics: an Introduction. Nonequilibrium Phase Transitions and Self Organization in Physics, Chemistry and Biology*, 2nd edn. Springer, Berlin.

Halliday, A.M. and Mingay, R. (1964) On the resolution of small time intervals and the effect of conduction delays on the judgment of simultaneity. *Quarterly Journal of Experimental Psychology* **16**, 35–46.

Hameroff, S.R. (1998) 'Funda-Mentality': is the conscious mind subtly linked to a basic level of the universe? *Trends in Cognitive Sciences* **2**, 119–127.

Hameroff, S.R., Kaszniak, A.W. and Chalmers, D.J. (1999) eds. *Toward a Science of Consciousness* III: *The Third Tucson Discussions and Debates*. MIT Press, Cambridge, MA.

Hameroff, S.R., Kaszniak, A.W. and Scott, A. (1996) *Toward a Science of Consciousness: The First Tucson Discussions and Debates*. MIT Press, Cambridge, MA.

Hameroff, S.R., Kaszniak, A.W. and Scott, A. (1998) eds. *Toward a Science of Consciousness* II: *The Second Tucson Discussions and Debates*. MIT Press, Cambridge, MA.

Hamker, F.H. (2004a) Predictions of a model of spatial attention using sum- and max-pooling functions. *Neurocomputing* **56**, 329–343.

Hamker, F.H. (2004b) A dynamic model of how feature cues guide spatial attention. *Vision Research* **44**, 501–521.

Hanson, N.R. (1958) *Patterns of Discovery: An Inquiry into the Conceptual Foundations of Science.* Cambridge University Press, Cambridge.

Hardcastle, V.G. (1999a) ed. *Where Biology Meets Psychology: Philosophical Essays.* MIT Press, Cambridge, MA.

Hardcastle, V.G. (1999b) Understanding functions: a pragmatic approach. In Hardcastle, V.G., ed., *Where Biology Meets Psychology: Philosophical Essays.* MIT Press, Cambridge, MA, pp. 27–43.

Hardcastle, V.G. (2003) Attention versus consciousness. In Osaka, N., ed., *Neural Basis of Consciousness.* Benjamins, Amsterdam, pp. 105–121.

Hardin, C.L. and Maffi, L. (1997) eds. *Color Categories in Thought and Language.* Cambridge University Press, New York.

Harnad, S. (1990) The symbol grounding problem. *Physica D* **42**, 335–346.

Harnish, R.M. (2002) *Minds, Brains, Computers: An Historical Introduction to the Foundations of Cognitive Science.* Blackwell, Malden.

Harré, R. (1998) *The Singular Self: An Introduction to the Psychology of Personhood.* Sage, London.

Harré, R. and Gillett, G. (1994) *The Discursive Mind.* Sage, London.

Harris, C.R., Pashler, H.F. and Coburn, P. (2004) Moray revisited: high-priority affective stimuli and visual search. *Quarterly Journal of Experimental Psychology* **57A**, 1–31.

Harris, L. and Jenkin, M. (1997) Computational and psychophysical mechanisms of visual coding. In Jenkin, M. and Harris, L., eds., *Computational and Psychophysical Mechanisms of Visual Coding.* Cambridge University Press, Cambridge, pp. 1–19.

Harris, L. and Jenkin, M. (2003) eds. *Levels of Perception.* Springer, New York.

Harter, M.R. (1967) Excitability cycles and cortical scanning: a review of two hypotheses of central intermittency in perception. *Psychological Bulletin* **68**, 47–58.

Harth, E. (1993) *The Creative Loop: How the Brain Makes a Mind.* Addison-Wesley, Reading, MA.

Hatfield, G.C. (1988) Representation and content in some (actual) theories of perception. *Studies in the History and Philosophy of Science* **19**, 175–214.

Hatfield, G.C. (1991) Representation in perception and cognition: connectionist affordances. In Ramsey, W., Stich, S.P. and Rumelhart, D.E., eds., *Philosophy and Connectionist Theory.* Erlbaum, Hillsdale.

Hatfield, G.C. (1999) Mental functions as constraints on neurophysiology: biology and psychology of vision. In Hardcastle, V.G., ed., *Where Biology Meets Psychology: Philosophical Essays.* MIT Press, Cambridge, MA, pp. 251–271.

Haxby, J.V., Gobbini, M.I., Furey, M.L., Ishai, A., Schouten, J.L. and Pietrini, P. (2001) Distributed and overlapping representations of faces and objects in ventral temporal cortex. *Science* **293**, 2425–2430.

Haynes, J.-D. and Rees, G. (2005) Predicting the orientation of invisible stimuli from activity in human primary visual cortex. *Nature Neuroscience* **8**, 686–691.

He, S., Cavanagh, P. and Intriligator, J. (1996) Attentional resolution and the locus of visual awareness. *Nature* **383**, 334–337.

Heatherton, T.F. (2004) ed. Social cognitive neuroscience. *Journal of Cognitive Neuroscience* **16**, 1681–1863.

Hebb (1949) *The Organization of Behavior.* Wiley, New York.

Heil, J. (2004a) *Philosophy of Mind: A Contemporary Introduction,* 2nd edn. Routledge, London.

Heil, J. (2004b) ed. *Philosophy of Mind: A Guide and Anthology.* Oxford University Press, Oxford.

Heil, J. and Mele, A. (1993) eds. *Mental Causation.* Oxford University Press, Oxford.

Heilman, K.M., Nadeau, S.E. and Beversdorf, D.O. (2003) Creative innovation: possible brain mechanisms. *Neurocase* **9**, 369–379.

Helmholtz, H.L.F. von (1866) *Handbuch der Physiologischen Optik, Dritter Band.* Leopold Voss, Leipzig.

Helson, H. (1964) *Adaptation-Level Theory: An Experimental and Systematic Approach to Behavior.* Harper and Row, New York.

Henson, R. (2005) What can functional neuroimaging tell the experimental psychologist? *Quarterly Journal of Experimental Psychology* **58A**, 193–233.

Hermer, L. and Spelke, E. (1996) Modularity and development: the case of spatial reorientation. *Cognition* **61**, 195–232.

Hernández, A., Zainos, A. and Romo, R. (2002) Temporal evolution of a decision-making process in medial premotor cortex. *Neuron* **33**, 959–972.

Hess, R., Negishi, K. and Creutzfeldt, O. (1975) The horizontal spread of intracortical inhibition in the visual cortex. *Experimental Brain Research* **22**, 415–419.

Hess, R.F., Hayes, A. and Field, D.J. (2003) Contour integration and cortical processing. *Journal of Physiology – Paris* **97**, 105–119.

Heywood, C.A., Milner, A.D. and Blakemore, C. (2003) eds. *The Roots of Visual Awareness. Progress in Brain Research, vol. 144*. Elsevier, Amsterdam.

Hiley, B.J. and Pylkkänen, P. (2001) Naturalizing the mind in a quantum framework. In Pylkkänen, P. and Vadén, T., eds., *Dimensions of Conscious Experience*. Benjamins, Amsterdam, pp. 119–144.

Hilgetag, C.-C., Burns, G.A.P.C., O'Neill, M.A., Scannell, J.W. and Young, M.P. (2000) Anatomical connectivity defines the organization of clusters of cortical areas in the macaque monkey and the cat. *Philosophical Transactions of the Royal Society of London, Series B* **355**, 91–110.

Hilgetag, C.-C., O'Neill, M.A. and Young, M.P. (1996) Indeterminate organization of the visual system. *Science* **271**, 776–777.

Hinton, G.E. (1990) Mapping part–whole hierarchies into connectionist networks. *Artificial Intelligence* **46**, 47–75.

Hirstein, W. (2004) *Brain Fiction: Self-Deception and the Riddle of Confabulation*. MIT Press, Cambridge, MA.

Hitchcock, C.R. (2004) ed. *Contemporary Debates in Philosophy of Science*. Blackwell, Oxford.

Hobson, J.A. (2002) *Dreaming: An Introduction to the Science of Sleep*. Oxford University Press, Oxford.

Hochstein, S. and Ahissar, M. (2002) View from the top: hierarchies and reverse hierarchies in the visual system. *Neuron* **36**, 791–804.

Hof, P.R., Vogt, B.A., Bouras, C. and Morrison, J.H. (1997) Atypical form of Alzheimer's disease with prominent posterior cortical atrophy: a review of lesion distribution and circuit disconnection in cortical visual pathways. *Vision Research* **37**, 3609–3625.

Hofstadter, D.R. (1995) *Fluid Concepts and Creative Analogies: Computer Models of the Fundamental Mechanisms of Thought*. Basic Books, New York.

Holcombe, A.O. and Cavanagh, P. (2001) Early binding of feature pairs for visual perception. *Nature Neuroscience* **4**, 127–128.

Holender, D. (1986) Semantic activation without conscious identification in dichotic listening, parafoveal vision, and visual masking: a survey and appraisal. *Behavioral and Brain Sciences* **9**, 1–66.

Holland, J.H. (1995) *Hidden Order: How Adaptation Builds Complexity*. Addison-Wesley, Reading, MA.

Holland, J.H. (1998) *Emergence: From Chaos to Order*. Oxford University Press, Oxford.

Holst, E. von and Mittelstaedt, H. (1950) Das Reafferenzprinzip. Wechselwirkungen zwischen Zentralnervensystem und Peripherie. *Die Naturwissenschaften* **37**, 464–476.

Hommel, B. (2004) Event files: feature binding in and across perception and action. *Trends in Cognitive Sciences* **8**, 494–500.

Hommel, B., Daum, I. and Kluwe, R.H. (2004) Exorcizing the homunculus, phase two: editors' introduction. *Acta Psychologica* **115**, 99–104.

Hommel, B., Müsseler, J., Aschersleben, G. and Prinz, W. (2001) The theory of event coding (TEC): a framework for perception and action planning. *Behavioral and Brain Sciences* **24**, 849–937.

Honderich, T. (2005) ed. *The Oxford Companion to Philosophy*, 2nd edn. Oxford University Press, Oxford.

Hopfield, J.J. (1982) Neural networks and physical systems with emergent collective computational abilities. *Proceedings of the National Academy of Sciences of the United States of America* **79**, 2554–2558.

Howard, D. (1997) Language in the human brain. In Rugg, M.D., ed., *Cognitive Neuroscience*. Psychology Press, Hove, pp. 277–304.

Hubel, D.H. and Wiesel, T.N. (1959) Receptive fields of single neurones in the cat's striate cortex. *Journal of Physiology* **148**, 574–591.

Hubel, D.H. and Wiesel, T.N. (1962) Receptive fields, binocular interaction and functional architecture in the cat's visual cortex. *Journal of Physiology* **160**, 106–154.

Hubel, D.H. and Wiesel, T.N. (1965) Receptive fields and functional architecture in two nonstriate visual areas (18 and 19) of the cat. *Journal of Neurophysiology* **28**, 229–289.

Hubel, D.H. and Wiesel, T.N. (1968) Receptive fields and functional architecture of monkey striate cortex. *Journal of Physiology* **195**, 215–243.

Huber, R., Ghilardi, M.F., Massimini, M. and Tononi, G. (2004) Local sleep and learning. *Nature* **430**, 78–81.

Hull, C.L. (1943) *Principles of Behavior: An Introduction to Behavior Theory*. Appleton-Century, New York.

Hull, D.L. and Ruse, M. (1998) eds. *The Philosophy of Biology*. Oxford University Press, Oxford.

Hume, D. (1739) *A Treatise of Human Nature*. John Noon, London.

Humphrey, N. (1983) *Consciousness Regained: Chapters in the Development of Mind*. Oxford University Press, Oxford.

Humphrey, N. (1992) *A History of the Mind*. Chatto and Windus, London.

Humphrey, N. and Dennett, D.C. (1989) Speaking for ourselves: an assessment of multiple personality disorder. *Raritan: A Quarterly Review* **9**, 68–98.

Humphreys, G.W., Duncan, J. and Treisman, A. (1998) eds. Brain mechanisms of selective perception and action. *Philosophical Transactions of the Royal Society of London, Series B* **353**, 1241–1393.

Humphreys, G.W., Duncan, J. and Treisman, A. (1999) eds. *Attention, Space and Action: Studies in Cognitive Neuroscience*. Oxford University Press, Oxford.

Humphreys, G.W. and Riddoch, M.J. (1987) *To See But Not to See: A Case Study of Visual Agnosia*. Erlbaum, Hillsdale.

Hurley, S.L. (1998) *Consciousness in Action*. Harvard University Press, Cambridge, MA.

Hurley, S.L. and Chater, N. (2005) eds. *Perspectives on Imitation: From Neuroscience to Social Science*. MIT Press, Cambridge, MA.

Hurvich, L.M. and Jameson, D. (1957) An opponent-process theory of color vision. *Psychological Review* **64**, 384–404.

Husserl, E. (1928) Vorlesungen zur Phänomenologie des inneren Zeitbewusstseins. *Jahrbuch für Philosophie und Phänomenologische Forschung* **9**, 367–498.

Hutchinson, K.A., Neely, J.H., Neill, W.T. and Walker, P. (2004) Lexical and sub-lexical contributions to unconscious identity priming. *Consciousness and Cognition* **13**, 512–539.

Ishai, A. and Sagi, D. (1995) Common mechanisms of visual imagery and perception. *Science* **268**, 1772–1774.

Itti, L. and Koch, C. (2001) Computational modelling of visual attention. *Nature Reviews Neuroscience* **2**, 194–203.

Ivry, R.B. and Spencer, R.M.C. (2004) The neural representation of time. *Current Opinion in Neurobiology* **14**, 225–232.

Jack, A.I. and Shallice, T. (2001) Introspective physicalism as an approach to the science of consciousness. *Cognition* **79**, 161–196.

Jackendoff, R. (1987) *Consciousness and the Computational Mind*. MIT Press, Cambridge, MA.

Jackson, F. (1982) Epiphenomenal qualia. *Philosophical Quarterly* **32**, 127–136.

Jackson, F. (1986) What Mary didn't know. *Journal of Philosophy* **83**, 291–295.

Jackson, F. and Rey, G. (1998). Mind, philosophy of. In Craig, E., ed., *Routledge Encyclopedia of Philosophy*. Routledge. London. ⟨http://www.rep.routledge.com/article/V038⟩

Jacob, P. (1997) *What Minds Can Do*. Cambridge University Press, Cambridge.

Jacob, P. and Jeannerod, M. (2003) *Ways of Seeing: The Scope and Limits of Visual Cognition*. Oxford University Press, Oxford.

Jacob, P. and Jeannerod, M. (2005) The motor theory of social cognition: a critique. *Trends in Cognitive Sciences* **9**, 21–25.

Jacobs, J. (1986) Teleology and reduction in biology. *Biology and Philosophy* **1**, 389–399.

Jacobson, M. (1993) *Foundations of Neuroscience*. Plenum, New York.

Jacobson, M.J. (2001) Problem solving, cognition, and complex systems: differences between novices and experts. *Complexity* **6**, 41–49.

James, W. (1890) *The Principles of Psychology*. Holt, New York.

Jancke, D., Chavane, F., Naaman, S. and Grinvald, A. (2004a) Imaging cortical correlates of illusion in early visual cortex. *Nature* **428**, 423–426.

Jancke, D., Erlhagen, W., Schoner, G. and Dinse, H.R. (2004b) Shorter latencies for motion trajectories than for flashes in population responses of cat primary visual cortex. *Journal of Physiology* **556**, 971–982.

Jasper, H.H. (1949) Diffuse projection systems: the integrative action of the thalamic reticular system. *Electroencephalography and Clinical Neurophysiology* **1**, 405–419.

Jasper, H.H. (1954) Functional properties of the thalamic reticular system. In Delafresnaye, J.F., ed., *Brain Mechanisms and Consciousness*. Blackwell, Oxford, pp. 374–401.

Jasper, H.H. (1960) Unspecific thalamocortical relations. In Field, J., ed., *Handbook of Physiology, Section 1: Neurophysiology, vol. II*. American Physiological Society, Washington, pp. 1307–1321.

Jasper, H.H. (1966) Brain mechanisms and states of consciousness. In Eccles, J.C., ed., *Brain and Conscious Experience*. Springer, Berlin, pp. 256–282.

Jaspers, K. (1923) *Allgemeine Psychopathologie*. Springer, Berlin.

Jeffery, K.J. (2003) ed. *The Neurobiology of Spatial Behaviour*. Oxford University Press, Oxford.

Jenkin, M. and Harris, L. (1997) eds. *Computational and Psychophysical Mechanisms of Visual Coding*. Cambridge University Press, Cambridge.

Jibu, M. and Yasue, K. (1995) *Quantum Brain Dynamics and Consciousness: An Introduction*. Benjamins, Amsterdam.

John, E.R. (2001) A field theory of consciousness. *Consciousness and Cognition* **10**, 184–213.

John, E.R., Bartlett, F., Shimokochi, M. and Kleinman, D. (1973) Neural readout from memory. *Journal of Neurophysiology* **36**, 893–924.

Johnson, R., Jr. (1986) A triarchic model of P300 amplitude. *Psychophysiology* **23**, 367–384.

Johnson, R., Jr. (1993) On the neural generators of the P300 component of the event-related potential. *Psychophysiology* **30**, 90–97.

Johnson-Laird, P.N. (1983) *Mental Models: Towards a Cognitive Science of Language, Inference, and Consciousness*. Cambridge University Press, Cambridge.

Jones, E.G. (2002) Thalamic circuitry and thalamocortical synchrony. *Philosophical Transactions of the Royal Society of London, Series B* **357**, 1659–1673.

Jordan, G. and Mollon, J.D. (1993) A study of women heterozygous for colour deficiencies. *Vision Research* **33**, 1495–1508.

Juarrero, A. (1999) *Dynamics in Action: Intentional Behavior as a Complex System*. MIT Press, Cambridge, MA.

Julesz, B. (1981) Textons, the elements of texture perception, and their interactions. *Nature* **290**, 91–97.

Julien, R.M. (2004) *A Primer of Drug Action: A Concise, Nontechnical Guide to the Actions, Uses, and Side Effects, 10th edn*. Worth, New York.

Jung, R. (1954) Correlation of bioelectrical and autonomic phenomena with alterations of consciousness and arousal in man. In Delafresnaye, J.F., ed., *Brain Mechanisms and Consciousness*. Blackwell, Oxford, pp. 310–344.

Kaas, J.H. (2004) The evolution of the visual system in primates. In Chalupa, L.M. and Werner, J.S., eds., *The Visual Neurosciences*. MIT Press, Cambridge, MA, pp. 1563–1572.

Kahneman, D. (1973) *Attention and Effort*. Prentice-Hall, Englewood Cliffs.

Kamitani, Y. and Tong, F. (2005) Decoding the visual and subjective contents of the human brain. *Nature Neuroscience* **8**, 679–685.

Kant, I. (1781/7) *Critik der reinen Vernunft*. Hartknoch, Riga.

Kant, I. (1790) *Critik der Urtheilskraft*. Lagarde und Friederich, Berlin.

Kanwisher, N. and Duncan, J. (2004) eds. *Functional Neuroimaging of Visual Cognition*. Oxford University Press, Oxford.

Karnath, H.O., Milner, A.D. and Vallar, G. (2002) eds. *The Cognitive and Neural Bases of Spatial Neglect*. Oxford University Press, Oxford.

Karni, A., Tanne, D., Rubenstein, B.S., Askenasy, J.J. and Sagi, D. (1994) Dependence on REM sleep of overnight improvement of a perceptual skill. *Science* **265**, 679–682.

Kastner, S. (2004) A neural basis for human visual attention. In Chalupa, L.M. and Werner, J.S., eds., *The Visual Neurosciences*. MIT Press, Cambridge, MA, pp. 1514–1523.

Kastner, S. and Ungerleider, L.G. (2000) Mechanisms of visual attention in the human cortex. *Annual Review of Neuroscience* **23**, 315–341.

Kauffman, S.A. (1993) *The Origins of Order: Self Organization and Selection in Evolution*. Oxford University Press, New York.

Kauffman, S.A. (1996) *At Home in the Universe: The Search for Laws of Self-organization and Complexity*. Penguin, London.

Kauffman, S.A. (2000) *Investigations*. Oxford University Press, Oxford.

Kelso, J.A.S. (1995) *Dynamic Patterns: The Self-organization of Brain and Behavior*. MIT Press, Cambridge, MA.

Kennedy, H. and Burkhalter, A. (2004) Ontogenesis of cortical connectivity. In Chalupa, L.M. and Werner, J.S., eds., *The Visual Neurosciences*. MIT Press, Cambridge, MA, pp. 146–158.

Kersten, D., Mamassian, P. and Yuille, A. (2004) Object perception as Bayesian inference. *Annual Review of Psychology* **55**, 271–304.

Kerzel, D. (2003) Asynchronous perception of motion and luminance change. *Psychological Research* **67**, 233–239.

Keysers, C. and Perrett, D.I. (2004) Demystifying social cognition: a Hebbian perspective. *Trends in Cognitive Sciences* **8**, 501–507.

Kihlstrom, J.F. (1987) The cognitive unconscious. *Science* **237**, 1445–1452.

Kihlstrom, J.F. (1993) The psychological unconscious and the self. In Bock, G.R. and Marsh, J., eds., *Experimental and Theoretical Studies of Consciousness. CIBA Foundation Symposium 174*. Wiley, Chichester, pp. 147–167.

Kihlstrom, J.F. (2004) Availability, accessibility, and subliminal perception. *Consciousness and Cognition* **13**, 92–100.

Kim, J. (1993) *Supervenience and Mind: Selected Philosophical Essays*. Cambridge University Press, Cambridge.

Kim, J. (1996) *Philosophy of Mind*. Westview, Boulder.

Kim, J. (1998) *Mind in a Physical World*. MIT Press, Cambridge, MA.

Kinomura, S., Larsson, J., Gulyas, B. and Roland, P.E. (1996) Activation by attention of the human reticular formation and thalamic intralaminar nuclei. *Science* **271**, 512–515.

Kinsbourne, M. (2002) The brain and body awareness. In Cash, T.F. and Pruzinsky, T., eds., *Body Image*. Guilford Press, New York, pp. 22–29.

Kirsh, D., Altman, J.S., Changeux, J.-P., Damasio, A.R., Durbin, R., Engel, A.K., Hillis, W.D., Premack, D., Rivest, R., Roland, P.E., Rosenbloom, P.S., Stent, G. and Stoerig, P. (1993) Architectures of intelligent systems. In Poggio, T. and Glaser, D.A., eds., *Exploring Brain Functions: Models in Neuroscience*. John Wiley, Chichester, pp. 293–321.

Kitazawa, S. (2002) Where conscious sensation takes place. *Consciousness and Cognition* **11**, 475–477.

Kitchener, K.S. (1983) Cognition, metacognition and epistemic cognition: a three-level model of cognitive processing. *Human Development* **26**, 222–232.

Kitcher, P. (1993a) *The Advancement of Science: Science without Legend, Objectivity without Illusions*. Oxford University Press, New York.

Kitcher, P. (1993b) Function and design. *Midwest Studies in Philosophy* **18**, 379–397.

Klein, I., Paradis, A.-L., Poline, J.-B., Kosslyn, S.M. and Le Bihan, D. (2000) Transient activity in the human calcarine cortex during visual–mental imagery: an event-related fMRI study. *Journal of Cognitive Neuroscience* **12**, 15–23.

Kleinschmidt, A., Buchel, C., Hutton, C., Friston, K.J. and Frackowiak, R.S. (2002) The neural structures expressing perceptual hysteresis in visual letter recognition. *Neuron* **34**, 659–666.

Klemm, O. (1925) Über die Wirksamkeit kleinster Zeitunterschiede im Gebiete des Tastsinns. *Archiv für die gesamte Psychologie* **50**, 205–220.

Knoblich, G., Elsner, B., Aschersleben, G. and Metzinger, T. (2003) eds. Grounding the self in action. *Consciousness and Cognition* **12**, 487–782.

Knott, R. and Marslen-Wilson, W. (2001) Does the medial temporal lobe bind phonological memories? *Journal of Cognitive Neuroscience* **13**, 593–609.

Koch, C. (1997) Computation and the single neuron. *Nature* **385**, 207–210.

Koch, C. (1998) *Biophysics of Computation: Information Processing in Single Neurons*. Oxford University Press, New York.

Koch, C. (2004) *The Quest for Consciousness*. Roberts, Englewood.

Koch, C. and Braun, J. (1996) The functional anatomy of visual awareness. *Cold Spring Harbor Symposia on Quantitative Biology* **61**, 49–57.

Koch, C. and Poggio, T. (1985) The synaptic veto mechanism: does it underlie direction and orientation selectivity in the visual cortex? In Rose, D. and Dobson, V.G., eds., *Models of the Visual Cortex*. Wiley, Chichester, pp. 408–419.

Koch, C. and Poggio, T. (1999) Predicting the visual world: silence is golden. *Nature Neuroscience* **2**, 9–10.

Koenderink, J.J. (1984) The concept of local sign. In van Doorn, A.J., Koenderink, J.J. and van de Grind, W.A., eds., *Limits in Perception*. VNU Science Press, Utrecht, pp. 495–547.

Koenderink, J.J. (1990) *Solid Shape*. MIT Press, Cambridge, MA.

Koestler, A. (1967) *The Ghost in the Machine*. Hutchinson, London.

Kohler, E., Keysers, C., Umiltà, M.A., Fogassi, L., Gallese, V. and Rizzolatti, G. (2002) Hearing sounds, understanding actions: action representation in mirror neurons. *Science* **297**, 846–848.

Köhler, W. (1925) *The Mentality of Apes*. K. Paul, Trench, Trubner & Co., London.

Köhler, W. (1940) *Dynamics in Psychology*. Liveright, New York.

Köhler, W. (1958) The present situation in brain physiology. *American Psychologist* **13**, 150–154.

Kohonen, T. (1984) *Self-organization and Associative Memory*. Springer, Berlin.

Kolak, D., Hirstein, W., Mandik, P. and Waskan, J. (2006) *Cognitive Science*. Routledge, London.

Kolb, B. and Whishaw, I.Q. (1980) *Fundamentals of Human Neuropsychology*. Freeman, San Francisco.

Kolers, P.A. and Von Grünau, M. (1976) Shape and color in apparent motion. *Vision Research* **16**, 329–335.

Kolinsky, R., Fery, P., Messina, D., Peretz, I., Evinck, S., Ventura, P. and Morais, J. (2002) The fur of the crocodile and the mooing sheep: a study of a patient with a category-specific impairment for biological things. *Cognitive Neuropsychology* **19**, 301–342.

Konorski, J. (1967) *Integrative Activity of the Brain: An Interdisciplinary Approach*. University of Chicago Press, Chicago.

Kopelman, M.D. (2002) Disorders of memory. *Brain* **125**, 2152–2190.

Kosslyn, S.M. (1983) *Ghosts in the Mind's Machine: Creating and Using Images in the Brain*. Norton, New York.

Kosslyn, S.M. (1994) *Image and Brain: The Resolution of the Imagery Debate*. MIT Press, Cambridge, MA.

Kosslyn, S.M., Alpert, N.M., Thompson, W.L., Maljkovic, V., Weise, S.B., Chabris, C.F., Hamilton, S.E., Rauch, S.L. and Buonanno, F.S. (1993) Visual mental imagery activates topographically organized visual cortex. *Journal of Cognitive Neuroscience* **5**, 263–287.

Kosslyn, S.M., Koenig, O., Barrett, A., Cave, C.B., Tang, J. and Gabrieli, J.D. (1989) Evidence for two types of spatial representations: hemispheric specialization for categorical and coordinate relations. *Journal of Experimental Psychology: Human Perception and Performance* **15**, 723–735.

Kosslyn, S.M., Pascual-Leone, A., Felician, O., Camposano, S., Keenan, J.P., Thompson, W.L., Ganis, G., Sukel, K.E. and Alpert, N.M. (1999) The role of area 17 in visual imagery: convergent evidence from PET and rTMS. *Science* **284**, 167–170.

Kosslyn, S.M. and Thompson, W.L. (2003) When is early visual cortex activated during visual mental imagery? *Psychological Bulletin* **129**, 723–746.

Kosslyn, S.M., Thompson, W.L., Kim, I.J. and Alpert, N.M. (1995) Topographical representations of mental images in primary visual cortex. *Nature* **378**, 496–498.

Kouider, S. and Dupoux, E. (2004) Partial awareness creates the "illusion" of subliminal semantic priming. *Psychological Science* **15**, 75–81.

Kourtzi, Z., Tolias, A.S., Altmann, C.F., Augath, M. and Logothetis, N.K. (2003) Integration of local features into global shapes: monkey and human fMRI studies. *Neuron* **37**, 333–346.

Krauskopf, C.J. (1978) On identifying detectors. In Armington, J.C., Krauskopf, J. and Wooten, B.R., eds., *Visual Psychophysics and Physiology*. Academic Press, New York, pp. 283–295.

Kreiman, G., Koch, C. and Fried, I. (2000a) Category-specific visual responses of single neurons in the human medial temporal lobe. *Nature Neuroscience* **3**, 946–953.

Kreiman, G., Koch, C. and Fried, I. (2000b) Imagery neurons in the human brain. *Nature* **408**, 357–361.

Krekelberg, B. and Lappe, M. (2001) Neuronal latencies and the position of moving objects. *Trends in Neurosciences* **24**, 335–339.

Kuhn, T.S. (1962) *The Structure of Scientific Revolutions*. University of Chicago Press, Chicago.

LaBerge, D. (1995) *Attentional Processing: The Brain's Art Of Mindfulness*. Harvard University Press, Cambridge, MA.

LaBerge, D. (1997) Attention, awareness, and the triangular circuit. *Consciousness and Cognition* **6**, 149–181.

LaBerge, D. (2000) Clarifying the triangular circuit theory of attention and its relations to awareness. Replies to seven commentaries. *Psyche* **6**.

⟨http://psyche.cs.monash.edu.au/v6/psyche-6-06-laberge-html⟩

LaBerge, D. (2001) Attention, consciousness, and electrical wave activity within the cortical column. *International Journal of Psychophysiology* **43**, 5–24.

LaBerge, D., Auclair, L. and Sieroff, E. (2000) Preparatory attention: experiment and theory. *Consciousness and Cognition* **9**, 396–434.

Ladyman, J. (2002) *Understanding Philosophy of Science*. Routledge, London.

Lakatos, I. (1970) Falsification and the methodology of scientific research programmes. In Lakatos, I. and Musgrave, A., eds., *Criticism and the Growth of Knowledge*. Cambridge University Press, Cambridge, pp. 91–196.

Lakoff, G. and Johnson, M. (1980) *Metaphors We Live By*. University of Chicago Press, Chicago.

Lamberts, K. and Shanks, D.R. (1997) eds. *Knowledge, Concepts and Categories*. Psychology Press, Hove.

Lamme, V.A.F. (2003) Why visual attention and awareness are different. *Trends in Cognitive Sciences* **7**, 12–18.

Lamme, V.A.F. and Roelfsema, P.R. (2000) The distinct modes of vision offered by feedforward and recurrent processing. *Trends in Neurosciences* **23**, 571–579.

Lamme, V.A.F. and Spekreijse, H. (2000) Modulations of primary visual cortex activity representing attentive and conscious scene perception. *Frontiers in Bioscience* **5**, D232–D243.

Lamme, V.A.F., Supèr, H., Landman, R., Roelfsema, P.R. and Spekreijse, H. (2000) The role of primary visual cortex (V1) in visual awareness. *Vision Research* **40**, 1507–1521.

Landreth, A. and Richardson, R.C. (2004) Localization and the new phrenology: a review essay on William Uttal's 'The New Phrenology'. *Philosophical Psychology* **17**, 107–123.

Lane, R.D. and Nadel, L. (2000) eds. *Cognitive Neuroscience of Emotion*. Oxford University Press, New York.

Lashley, K.S. (1950) In search of the engram. In Danielli, J.F. and Brown, R., eds., *Symposia of the Society for Experimental Biology, No. 4: Physiological Mechanisms in Animal Behaviour*. Cambridge University Press, Cambridge, pp. 454–482.

Lashley, K.S., Chow, K.L. and Semmes, J. (1951) An examination of the electrical field theory of cerebral integration. *Psychological Review* **58**, 123–136.

Latour, B. and Woolgar, S. (1979) *Laboratory Life: The Social Construction of Scientific Facts*. Sage, Beverly Hills (2nd edn, 1986, Princeton University Press).

Laureys, S. (2005) ed. *The Boundaries of Consciousness: Neurobiology and Neuropathology. Progress in Brain Research, vol. 150*. Elsevier, Amsterdam.

Le Bihan, D., Turner, R., Zeffiro, T.A., Cuenod, C.A., Jezzard, P. and Bonnerot, V. (1993) Activation of human primary visual cortex during visual recall: a magnetic resonance imaging study. *Proceedings of the National Academy of Sciences of the United States of America* **90**, 11802–11805.

Leahey, T.H. (2000) *A History of Psychology: Main Currents in Psychological Thought*, 5th edn. Prentice Hall, Upper Saddle River.

Leclercq, M. and Zimmermann, P. (2002) eds. *Applied Neuropsychology of Attention: Theory, Diagnosis and Rehabilitation*. Psychology, Hove.

LeDoux, J. (1998) *The Emotional Brain: The Mysterious Underpinnings of Emotional Life*. Weidenfeld & Nicolson, London.

LeDoux, J., Debiec, J. and Moss, H. (2003) eds. The self: from soul to brain. *Annals of the New York Academy of Sciences* **1001**, 1–317.

Lee, H.Y., Yahyanejad, M. and Kardar, M. (2003) Symmetry considerations and development of pinwheels in visual maps. *Proceedings of the National Academy of Sciences of the United States of America* **100**, 16036–16040.

Lee, K.H., Farrow, T.F., Spence, S.A. and Woodruff, P.W. (2004) Social cognition, brain networks and schizophrenia. *Psychological Medicine* **34**, 391–400.

Lee, S.-H. and Blake, R. (1999) Rival ideas about binocular rivalry. *Vision Research* **39**, 1447–1454.

Lee, S.-H. and Blake, R. (2002) V1 activity is reduced during binocular rivalry. *Journal of Vision* **2**, 618–626.

Lee, S.-H. and Blake, R. (2004) A fresh look at interocular grouping during binocular rivalry. *Vision Research* **44**, 983–991.

Lee, T.S., Mumford, D., Romero, R. and Lamme, V.A.F. (1998) The role of the primary visual cortex in higher level vision. *Vision Research* **38**, 2429–2454.

Lee, T.S. and Nguyen, M. (2001) Dynamics of subjective contour formation in the early visual cortex. *Proceedings of the National Academy of Sciences of the United States of America* **98**, 1907–1911.

Lee, T.S., Yang, C.F., Romero, R.D. and Mumford, D. (2002) Neural activity in early visual cortex reflects behavioral experience and higher-order perceptual saliency. *Nature Neuroscience* **5**, 589–597.

Lehky, S.R. and Sejnowski, T.J. (1990) Neural network model of visual cortex for determining surface curvature from images of shaded surfaces. *Proceedings of the Royal Society of London, Series B* **240**, 251–278.

Leibniz, G.W. (1710) *Essais de Théodicée sur la bonté de Dieu, la liberté de l'homme et l'origine du mal*. Isaac Troyel, Amsterdam.

Lennie, P. (1998) Single units and visual cortical organization. *Perception* **27**, 889–935.

Lethin, A. (2005) Covert agency with proprioceptive feedback. *Journal of Consciousness Studies* **12** (4–5), 96–114.

Lettvin, J.Y., Maturana, H.R., McCulloch, W.S. and Pitts, W.H. (1959) What the frog's eye tells the frog's brain. *Proceedings of the IRE* **47**, 1940–1951.

Levi, D.M. and Klein, S.A. (1990) The role of separation and eccentricity in encoding position. *Vision Research* **30**, 557–585.

Levine, J. (1983) Materialism and qualia: the explanatory gap. *Pacific Philosophical Quarterly* **64**, 354–361.

Levy, R. and Goldman-Rakic, P.S. (2000) Segregation of working memory functions within the dorsolateral prefrontal cortex. *Experimental Brain Research* **133**, 23–32.

Lewis, D. (1988) What experience teaches. In Copley-Coltheart, J., ed., *Proceedings of the Russellian Society*. University of Sydney, Sydney.

Li, Z. (2002) A saliency map in primary visual cortex. *Trends in Cognitive Sciences* **6**, 9–16.

Libet, B. (1985) Unconscious cerebral initiative and the role of conscious will in voluntary action. *Behavioral and Brain Sciences* **8**, 529–566.

Libet, B. (1993) The neural time factor in conscious and unconscious events. In Bock, G.R. and Marsh, J., eds., *Experimental and Theoretical Studies of Consciousness. Ciba Foundation Symposium 174*. Wiley, Chichester, pp. 123–146.

Libet, B. (1994) A testable field theory of mind–brain interaction. *Journal of Consciousness Studies* **1**, 119–126.

Libet, B. (2003a) Cerebral physiology of conscious experience: experimental studies. In Osaka, N., ed., *Neural Basis of Consciousness*. Benjamins, Amsterdam, pp. 57–84.

Libet, B. (2003b) Timing of conscious experience: reply to the 2002 commentaries on Libet's findings. *Consciousness and Cognition* **12**, 321–331.

Libet, B., Gleason, C.A., Wright, E.W. and Pearl, D.K. (1983) Time of conscious intention to act in relation to onset of cerebral activity (readiness-potential): the unconscious initiation of a freely voluntary act. *Brain* **106**, 623–642.

Libet, B., Wright, E.W., Feinstein, B. and Pearl, D.K. (1979) Subjective referral of the timing for a conscious sensory experience: functional role for the somatosensory specific projection system in man. *Brain* **102**, 193–224.

Lindsay, P.H. and Norman, D.A. (1977) *Human Information Processing: An Introduction to Psychology,* 2nd edn. Academic Press, New York.

Lindsey, D.T. and Teller, D.Y. (1990) Motion at isoluminance: discrimination/detection ratios for moving isoluminant gratings. *Vision Research* **30**, 1751–1761.

Lindsley, D.B. (1955) Higher functions of the central nervous system. *Annual Review of Physiology* **17**, 311–338.

Livingston, R.B. (1967a) Brain circuitry relating to complex behavior. In Quarton, G.C., Melnechuk, T. and Schmitt, F.O., eds., *The Neurosciences: A Study Program*. Rockefeller University Press, New York, pp. 499–515.

Livingston, R.B. (1967b) Reinforcement. In Quarton, G.C., Melnechuk, T. and Schmitt, F.O., eds., *The Neurosciences: A Study Program*. Rockefeller University Press, New York, pp. 568–577.

Livingstone, M.S. and Hubel, D.H. (1987) Psychophysical evidence for separate channels for the perception of form, color, movement, and depth. *Journal of Neuroscience* **7**, 3416–3468.

Llinás, R. (2001) *I of the Vortex: From Neurons to Self*. MIT Press, Cambridge, MA.

Llinás, R. and Ribary, U. (1993) Coherent 40-Hz oscillation characterizes dream state in humans. *Proceedings of the National Academy of Sciences of the United States of America* **90**, 2078–2081.

Llinás, R. and Ribary, U. (2001) Consciousness and the brain: the thalamocortical dialogue in health and disease. *Annals of the New York Academy of Sciences* **929**, 166–175.

Llinás, R., Ribary, U., Contreras, D. and Pedroarena, C. (1998) The neuronal basis for consciousness. *Philosophical Transactions of the Royal Society of London, Series B* **353**, 1841–1849.

Llinás, R., Ribary, U., Joliot, M. and Wang, X.-J. (1994) Content and context in temporal thalamocortical binding. In Buzsáki, G., Llinás, R., Singer, W., Berthoz, A. and Christen, Y., eds., *Temporal Coding in the Brain*. Springer, Berlin, pp. 251–272.

Locke, J. (1690) *Essay Concerning Humane Understanding*. Bassett, London.

Lodge, D. (2001) *Thinks . . . .* Secker & Warburg, London.

Logothetis, N.K. (1998) Single units and conscious vision. *Philosophical Transactions of the Royal Society of London, Series B* **353**, 1801–1818.

Logothetis, N.K. and Wandell, B.A. (2004) Interpreting the BOLD signal. *Annual Review of Physiology* **66**, 735–769.

Lorente de Nó, R. (1938) The cerebral cortex: architecture, intracortical connections and motor projections. In Fulton, J.F., ed., *Physiology of the Nervous System*. Oxford University Press, New York, pp. 291–325.

Losee, J. (2001) *A Historical Introduction to the Philosophy of Science,* 4th edn. Oxford University Press, Oxford.

Lotze, R.H. (1879) *Metaphysik: drei Bücher der Ontologie, Kosmologie und Psychologie*. Hirzel, Leipzig.

Lövblad, K.O., Thomas, R., Jakob, P.M., Scammell, T., Bassetti, C., Griswold, M., Ives, J., Matheson, J., Edelman, R.R. and Warach, S. (1999) Silent functional magnetic resonance imaging demonstrates focal activation in rapid eye movement sleep. *Neurology* **53**, 2193–2195.

Lovelock, J. (1982) *Gaia: A New Look at Life on Earth*. Oxford University Press, Oxford.

Lowe, E.J. (2000) *An Introduction to the Philosophy of Mind*. Cambridge University Press, Cambridge.

Luck, S.J. and Girelli, M. (1998) Electrophysiological approaches to the study of selective attention in the human brain. In Parasuraman, R., ed., *The Attentive Brain*. MIT Press, Cambridge, MA, pp. 71–94.

Ludlow, P., Nagasawa, Y. and Stoljar, D. (2004) eds. *There's Something about Mary: Essays on Phenomenal Consciousness and Frank Jackson's Knowledge Argument*. MIT Press, Cambridge, MA.

Lumer, E.D., Friston, K.J. and Rees, G. (1998) Neural correlates of perceptual rivalry in the human brain. *Science* **280**, 1930–1934.

Lumer, E.D. and Rees, G. (1999) Covariation of activity in visual and prefrontal cortex associated with subjective visual perception. *Proceedings of the National Academy of Sciences of the United States of America* **96**, 1669–1673.

Lycan, W.G. (1987) *Consciousness*. MIT Press, Cambridge, MA.

Lycan, W.G. (1996) *Consciousness and Experience*. MIT Press, Cambridge, MA.

Lycan, W.G. (1999) ed. *Mind and Cognition: An Anthology*, 2nd edn. Blackwell, Malden.

Lycan, W.G. (2001) The case for phenomenal externalism. In Tomberlin, J.E., ed., *Philosophical Perspectives, 15, Metaphysics*. Blackwell, Malden, pp. 17–35.

Lynch, M. (1985) *Art and Artifact in Laboratory Science: A Study of Shop Work and Shop Talk in a Research Laboratory*. Routledge & Kegan Paul, London.

Lyons, W. (1995) *Approaches to Intentionality*. Oxford University Press, Oxford.

Lyons, W. (2001) *Matters of the Mind*. Edinburgh University Press, Edinburgh.

Lytton, W.M. and Thomas, E. (1999) Modeling thalamocortical oscillations. In Ulinski, P.S., Jones, E.G. and Peters, A., eds., *Cerebral Cortex, vol. 13: Models of Cortical Circuits*. Kluwer, New York, pp. 479–509.

MacDonald, K.D., Fifkova, E., Jones, M.S. and Barth, D.S. (1998) Focal stimulation of the thalamic reticular nucleus induces focal gamma waves in cortex. *Journal of Neurophysiology* **79**, 474–477.

Machamer, P.K. (2002) A brief historical introduction to the philosophy of science. In Machamer, P.K. and Silberstein, M., eds., *The Blackwell Guide to the Philosophy of Science*. Blackwell, Oxford, pp. 1–17.

Machamer, P.K., Grush, R. and McLaughlin, P. (2001) eds. *Theory and Method in the Neurosciences*. University of Pittsburgh Press, Pittsburgh.

Mack, A. and Rock, I. (1998) *Inattentional Blindness*. MIT Press, Cambridge, MA.

MacKay, D. (1956) Towards an information-flow model of human behaviour. *British Journal of Psychology* **47**, 30–43.

MacKay, D. (1980) The interdependence of mind and brain. *Neuroscience* **5**, 1389–1391.

MacKay, D. (1985) The significance of 'feature sensitivity'. In Rose, D. and Dobson, V.G., eds., *Models of the Visual Cortex*. Wiley, Chichester, pp. 47–53.

MacKay, D. (1986) Vision: the capture of optical covariation. In Pettigrew, J.D., Sanderson, K.J. and Levick, W.R., eds., *Visual Neuroscience*. Cambridge University Press, Cambridge, pp. 365–373.

MacKay, D. (1987) Divided brains – divided minds? In Blakemore, C. and Greenfield, S., eds., *Mindwaves: Thoughts on Intelligence, Identity and Consciousness*. Blackwell, London, pp. 5–16.

Maffei, L. and Fiorentini, A. (1973) The visual cortex as a spatial frequency analyser. *Vision Research* **13**, 1255–1267.

Maguire, E.A. (2001) Neuroimaging studies of autobiographical event memory. *Philosophical Transactions of the Royal Society of London, Series B* **356**, 1441–1451.

Maguire, E.A., Frackowiak, R.S. and Frith, C.D. (1997) Recalling routes around London: activation of the right hippocampus in taxi drivers. *Journal of Neuroscience* **17**, 7103–7110.

Maguire, E.A. and Frith, C.D. (2003a) Aging affects the engagement of the hippocampus during autobiographical memory retrieval. *Brain* **126**, 1511–1523.

Maguire, E.A. and Frith, C.D. (2003b) Lateral asymmetry in the hippocampal response to the remoteness of autobiographical memories. *Journal of Neuroscience* **23**, 5302–5307.

Mandik, P. (2001) Points of view from the brain's eye view: subjectivity and neural representation. In Bechtel, W., Mandik, P., Mundale, J. and Stufflebeam, R.S., eds., *Philosophy and the Neurosciences: A Reader*. Blackwell, Malden, pp. 312–327.

Mandler, G. (2002) Organization: what levels of processing are levels of. *Memory* **10**, 333–338.

Mangan, B. (2001) Sensation's ghost: the non-sensory "fringe" of consciousness. *Psyche* **7** (18). 〈http://psyche.cs.monash.edu.au/v7/psyche-7-18-mangan.html〉

Maquet, P. (2001) The role of sleep in learning and memory. *Science* **294**, 1048–1052.

Maquet, P., Schwartz, S., Passingham, R. and Frith, C. (2003) Sleep-related consolidation of a visuomotor skill: brain mechanisms as assessed by functional magnetic resonance imaging. *Journal of Neuroscience* **23**, 1432–1440.

Marcel, A.J. (1983a) Conscious and unconscious perception: experiments on visual masking and word recognition. *Cognitive Psychology* **15**, 197–237.

Marcel, A.J. (1983b) Conscious and unconscious perception: an approach to the relations between phenomenal experience and perceptual processes. *Cognitive Psychology* **15**, 238–300.

Marcel, A.J. (1993) Slippage in the unity of consciousness. In Bock, G.R. and Marsh, J., eds., *Experimental and Theoretical Studies of Consciousness. CIBA Foundation Symposium 174*, pp. 168–186.

Marcel, A.J., Tegner, R. and Nimmo-Smith, I. (2004) Anosognosia for plegia: specificity, extension, partiality and disunity of bodily unawareness. *Cortex* **40**, 19–40.

Marcus, G.F. (1999) Connectionism: with or without rules? Response to J.L. McClelland and D.C. Plaut (1999). *Trends in Cognitive Sciences* **3**, 168–170.

Marcus, G.F. (2001) *The Algebraic Mind: Integrating Connectionism and Cognitive Science*. MIT Press, Cambridge, MA.

Margolis, E. and Laurence, S. (2003) Concepts. In Stich, S.P. and Warfield, T.A., eds., *The Blackwell Guide to Philosophy of Mind*. Blackwell, Malden, pp. 190–214.

Marr, D. (1971) Simple memory: a theory for archicortex. *Philosophical Transactions of the Royal Society of London, Series B* **262**, 23–81.

Marr, D. (1982) *Vision: Computational Investigation into Human Representation and Processing of Visual Information*. WH Freeman, San Francisco.

Marrocco, R.T. and Davidson, M.C. (1998) Neurochemistry of attention. In Parasuraman, R., ed., *The Attentive Brain*. MIT Press, Cambridge, MA, pp. 35–51.

Marshall, W.H. and Talbot, S.A. (1942) Recent evidence for neural mechanisms in vision leading to a general theory of sensory acuity. *Biological Symposia* **7**, 117–164.

Martínez, A., DiRusso, F., Anllo-Vento, L., Sereno, M.I., Buxton, R.B. and Hillyard, S.A. (2001) Putting spatial attention on the map: timing and localization of stimulus selection processes in striate and extrastriate visual areas. *Vision Research* **41**, 1437–1457.

Maslin, K.T. (2001) *An Introduction to the Philosophy of Mind*. Polity, Cambridge.

Mather, G. (2001) Object-oriented models of cognitive processing. *Trends in Cognitive Sciences* **5**, 182–184.

Mauk, M.D. and Buonomano, D.V. (2004) The neural basis of temporal processing. *Annual Review of Neuroscience* **27**, 307–340.

Maxwell, N. (1984) *From Knowledge to Wisdom: A Revolution in the Aims and Methods of Science*. Blackwell, Oxford.

Maxwell, N. (1985) Methodological problems of neuroscience. In Rose, D. and Dobson, V.G., eds., *Models of the Visual Cortex*. Wiley, Chichester, pp. 11–21.

Maxwell, N. (2001) *The Human World in the Physical Universe: Consciousness, Free Will, and Evolution*. Rowman and Littlefield, Lanham.

Maynard Smith, J. (1978) Optimization theory in evolution. *Annual Review of Ecology and Systematics* **9**, 31–56.

McCormick, D.A. and Von Krosigk, M. (1992) Corticothalamic activation modulates thalamic firing through glutamate metabotropic receptors. *Proceedings of the National Academy of Sciences of the United States of America* **89**, 2774–2778.

McCulloch, W. and Pitts, W. (1943) A logical calculus of the ideas immanent in nervous activity. *Bulletin of Mathematical Biophysics* **5**, 117–128.

McFadden, J. (2002a) Synchronous firing and its influence on the brain's electromagnetic field: evidence for an electromagnetic theory of consciousness. *Journal of Consciousness Studies* **9** (4), 23–50.

McFadden, J. (2002b) The conscious electromagnetic field theory: the Hard Problem made easy. *Journal of Consciousness Studies* **9** (8), 45–60.

McGinn, C. (1989) Can we solve the mind–body problem? *Mind* **98**, 349–366.

McGuire, B.A., Gilbert, C.D., Rivlin, P.K. and Wiesel, T.N. (1991) Targets of horizontal connections in macaque primary visual cortex. *Journal of Comparative Neurology* **305**, 370–392.

McKim, W.A. (2003) *Drugs and Behavior: An Introduction to Behavioral Pharmacology,* 5th edn. Prentice Hall, Upper Saddle River.

McLeod, P., Plunkett, K. and Rolls, E.T. (1998) *Introduction to Connectionist Modelling of Cognitive Processes*. Oxford University Press, Oxford.

McMillan, T. (1997) Neuropsychological assessment after extremely severe head injury in a case of life or death. *Brain Injury* **11**, 483–490 and 775.

McMillan, T. (2000) Will to live? *New Scientist* **165** (2229), 50–51.

McMillan, T. and Herbert, C.M. (2000) Neuropsychological assessment of a potential "euthanasia" case: a 5 year follow-up. *Brain Injury* **14**, 197–203.

McMillan, T. and Herbert, C.M. (2004) Further recovery in a potential treatment withdrawal case 10 years after brain injury. *Brain Injury* **18**, 935–940.

McNaughton, B.L. and Morris, R.G.M. (1987) Hippocampal synaptic enhancement and information storage within a distributed memory system. *Trends in Neurosciences* **10**, 408–415.

Mead, G.H. (1934) *Mind, Self and Society from the Standpoint of a Social Behaviorist*. University of Chicago Press, Chicago.

Meador, K.J., Ray, P.G., Echauz, J.R., Loring, D.W. and Vachtsevanos, G.J. (2002) Gamma coherence and conscious perception. *Neurology* **59**, 847–854.

Meck, W.H. (2005) ed. Neuropsychology of timing and time perception. *Brain and Cognition* **58**, 1–147.

Meese, T.S. and Georgeson, M.A. (1996) Spatial filter combination in human pattern vision: channel interactions revealed by adaptation. *Perception* **25**, 255–277.

Mehrabian, A. (1969) Significance of posture and position in the communication of attitude and status relationships. *Psychological Bulletin* **71**, 359–372.

Mehta, A.D., Ulbert, I. and Schroeder, C.E. (2000a) Intermodal selective attention in monkeys: I. Distribution and timing of effects across visual areas. *Cerebral Cortex* **10**, 343–358.

Mehta, A.D., Ulbert, I. and Schroeder, C.E. (2000b) Intermodal selective attention in monkeys: II. Physiological mechanisms of modulation. *Cerebral Cortex* **10**, 359–370.

Meier, B., Morger, V. and Graf, P. (2003) Competition between automatic and controlled processes. *Consciousness and Cognition* **12**, 309–319.

Mentis, M.J., Sunderland, T., Lai, J., Connolly, C., Krasuski, J., Levine, B., Friz, J., Sobti, S., Schapiro, M. and Rapoport, S.I. (2001) Muscarinic versus nicotinic modulation of a visual task: a PET study using drug probes. *Neuropsychopharmacology* **25**, 555–564.

Merleau-Ponty, M. (1945) *Phénoménologie de la perception*. Gallimard, Paris.

Mesulam, M.-M. (1998) From sensation to cognition. *Brain* **121**, 1013–1052.

Metherate, R. and Cruikshank, S.J. (1999) Thalamocortical inputs trigger a propagating envelope of gamma-band activity in auditory cortex in vitro. *Experimental Brain Research* **126**, 160–174.

Metzinger, T. (1995) Faster than thought: holism, homogeneity and temporal coding. In Metzinger, T., ed., *Conscious Experience*. Schöningh, Paderborn, pp. 425–461.

Metzinger, T. (2000) ed. *Neural Correlates of Consciousness: Empirical and Conceptual Questions*. MIT Press, Cambridge, MA.

Metzinger, T. (2003) *Being No One: The Self-model Theory of Subjectivity*. MIT Press, Cambridge, MA.

Metzinger, T. and Gallese, V. (2003) The emergence of a shared action ontology: building blocks for a theory. *Consciousness and Cognition* **12**, 549–571.

Midgley, M. (1989) *Wisdom, Information and Wonder: What is Knowledge For?* Routledge, London.

Miller, G.A., Galanter, E. and Pribram, K.H. (1960) *Plans and Structure of Behavior*. Holt, Rinehart and Winston, New York.

Miller, J.G. (1978) *Living Systems*. McGraw-Hill, New York.

Millikan, R.G. (1984) *Language, Thought, and Other Biological Categories: New Foundations for Realism*. MIT Press, Cambridge, MA.

Millikan, R.G. (1993) *White Queen Psychology and Other Essays for Alice*. MIT Press, Cambridge, MA.

Millikan, R.G. (2004) *Varieties of Meaning*. MIT Press, Cambridge, MA.

Milner, A.D. and Goodale, M.A. (1995) *The Visual Brain in Action*. Oxford University Press, Oxford.

Milner, P.M. (1957) The cell assembly: Mark II. *Psychological Review* **64**, 242–252.

Milner, P.M. (1974) A model for visual shape recognition. *Psychological Review* **81**, 521–535.

Minamimoto, T. and Kimura, M. (2002) Participation of the thalamic CM-Pf complex in attentional orienting. *Journal of Neurophysiology* **87**, 3090–3101.

Mingers, J. (1995) *Self-producing Systems: Implications and Applications of Autopoiesis*. Plenum, New York.

Minsky, M. (1985) *The Society of Mind*. Simon and Schuster, New York.

Mishkin, M. (1993) Cerebral memory circuits. In Poggio, T.A. and Glaser, D.A., eds., *Exploring Brain Functions: Models in Neuroscience*. Wiley, Chichester, pp. 113–125.

Mitchell, S.D. (2003) *Biological Complexity and Integrative Pluralism*. Cambridge University Press, Cambridge.

Mitroff, S.R., Scholl, B.J. and Wynn, K. (2005) The relationship between object files and conscious perception. *Cognition* **96**, 67–92.

Miyashita, Y. (1995) How the brain creates imagery: projection to primary visual cortex. *Science* **268**, 1719–1720.

Monchi, O., Petrides, M., Doyon, J., Postuma, R.B., Worsley, K. and Dagher, A. (2004) Neural bases of set-shifting deficits in Parkinson's disease. *Journal of Neuroscience* **24**, 702–710.

Moody, T.C. (1994) Conversations with zombies. *Journal of Consciousness Studies* **1**, 196–200.

Moray, N. (1959) Attention in dichotic listening: affective cues and the influence of instructions. *Quarterly Journal of Experimental Psychology* **11**, 56–60.

Morin, A. (2005) Possible links between self-awareness and inner speech: theoretical background, underlying mechanisms, and empirical evidence. *Journal of Consciousness Studies* **12** (4–5), 115–134.

Morison, R.S. and Dempsey, E.W. (1942) A study of thalamocortical relations. *American Journal of Physiology* **135**, 281–292.

Morowitz, H.J. and Singer, J.L. (1995) eds. *The Mind, the Brain, and Complex Adaptive Systems*. Addison-Wesley, Reading, MA.

Morton, J., Hammersley, R.H. and Bekerian, D.A. (1985) Headed records: a model for memory and its failures. *Cognition* **20**, 1–23.

Moruzzi, G. and Magoun, H.W. (1949) Brain stem reticular formation and the activation of the EEG. *Electroencephalography and Clinical Neurophysiology* **1**, 455–473.

Motter, B.C. (1993) Focal attention produces spatially selective processing in visual cortical areas V1, V2, and V4 in the presence of competing stimuli. *Journal of Neurophysiology* **70**, 909–919.

Mountcastle, V.B. (1957) Modality and topographic properties of single neurons of cat's somatic sensory cortex. *Journal of Neurophysiology* **20**, 408–434.

Moutoussis, K. and Zeki, S. (1997a) A direct demonstration of perceptual asynchrony in vision. *Proceedings of the Royal Society of London, Series B* **264**, 393–399.

Moutoussis, K. and Zeki, S. (1997b) Functional segregation and temporal hierarchy of the visual perceptive systems. *Proceedings of the Royal Society of London, Series B* **264**, 1407–1414.

Moutoussis, K. and Zeki, S. (2002) The relationship between cortical activation and perception investigated with invisible stimuli. *Proceedings of the National Academy of Sciences of the United States of America* **99**, 9527–9532.

Müller, J. (1826) *Zur vergleichenden Physiologie des Gesichtsinnes des Menschen und der Thiere.* Cnobloch, Leipzig.

Mumford, D. (1991) On the computational architecture of the neocortex: I. The role of the thalamo-cortical loop. *Biological Cybernetics* **65**, 135–145.

Mumford, D. (1992) On the computational architecture of the neocortex: II. The role of cortico-cortical loops. *Biological Cybernetics* **66**, 241–251.

Murphy, N. (2003) Whatever happened to the soul? Theological perspectives on neuroscience and the self. *Annals of the New York Academy of Sciences* **1001**, 51–64.

Murre, J.M.J., Graham, K.S. and Hodges, J.R. (2001) Semantic dementia: relevance to connectionist models of long-term memory. *Brain* **124**, 647–675.

Nadel, L. and Moscovitch, M. (1997) Memory consolidation, retrograde amnesia and the hippocampal complex. *Current Opinion in Neurobiology* **7**, 217–227.

Nagel, T. (1974) What is it like to be a bat? *Philosophical Review* **83**, 435–450.

Naghavi, H.R. and Nyberg, L. (2005) Common fronto-parietal activity in attention, memory, and consciousness: shared demands on integration? *Consciousness and Cognition* **14**, 390–425.

Nakayama, K. (2001) Modularity in perception: its relation to cognition and knowledge. In

Goldstein, E.B., ed., *Blackwell Handbook of Perception.* Blackwell, Malden, pp. 737–759.

Nauta, W.J.H. and Feirtag, M. (1986) *Fundamental Neuroanatomy.* Freeman, San Francisco.

Neander, K. (1991a) Functions as selected effects: the conceptual analysts defense. *Philosophy of Science* **58**, 168–184.

Neander, K. (1991b) The teleological notion of a function. *Australasian Journal of Philosophy* **69**, 454–468.

Neander, K. (1995) Misrepresenting and malfunctioning. *Philosophical Studies* **79**, 109–141.

Neander, K. (1999) Fitness and the fate of unicorns. In Hardcastle, V.G., ed., *Where Biology Meets Psychology.* MIT Press, Cambridge, MA, pp. 3–26.

Neisser, U. (1963) Multiplicity of thought. *British Journal of Psychology* **54**, 1–14.

Neisser, U. (1967) *Cognitive Psychology.* Appleton-Century-Crofts, New York.

Neisser, U. and Fivush, R. (1994) eds. *The Remembering Self: Construction and Accuracy in the Self-narrative.* Cambridge University Press, New York.

Nelkin, N. (1995) The dissociation of phenomenal states from apperception. In Metzinger, T., ed., *Conscious Experience.* Schöningh, Paderborn, pp. 373–387.

Nelson, C.L., Sarter, M. and Bruno, J.P. (2005) Prefrontal cortical modulation of acetylcholine release in posterior parietal cortex. *Neuroscience* **132**, 347–359.

Nelson, H.E. and Willison, J.R. (1991) *National Adult Reading Test: Test Manual (2nd edn.) NART II.* NFER-Nelson, Windsor.

Nelson, T.O. and Rey, G. (2000) eds. Metacognition and consciousness: a convergence of psychology and philosophy. *Consciousness and Cognition* **9**, 147–326.

Nemirow, L. (1980) Review of Thomas Nagal, Mortal Questions. *Philosophical Review* **89**, 473–477.

Newell, A. (1982) The knowledge level. *Artificial Intelligence* **18**, 87–127.

Newman, J., Baars, B.J. and Cho, S.-B. (1997) A neural global workspace model for conscious attention. *Neural Networks* **10**, 1195–1206.

Newton, N. (1991) Consciousness, qualia, and reentrant signaling. *Behavior and Philosophy* **19**, 21–41.

Newton, N. (2001) Emergence and the uniqueness of consciousness. *Journal of Consciousness Studies* **8** (9–10), 47–59.

Newton-Smith, W.H. (2000) ed. *A Companion to the Philosophy of Science*. Blackwell, Malden.

Niebur, E., Hsiao, S.S. and Johnson, K. (2002) Synchrony: a neuronal mechanism for attentional selection? *Current Opinion in Neurobiology* **12**, 190–194.

Nijhawan, R. (2002) Neural delays, visual motion and the flash-lag effect. *Trends in Cognitive Sciences* **6**, 387–393.

Nirenberg, S., Carcieri, S.M., Jacobs, A.L. and Latham, P.E. (2001) Retinal ganglion cells act largely as independent encoders. *Nature* **411**, 698–701.

Nisbett, R.E. and Wilson, T.D. (1977) Telling more than we can know: verbal reports on mental processes. *Psychological Review* **84**, 231–259.

Nishida, S. and Johnston, A. (2002) Marker correspondence, not processing latency, determines temporal binding of visual attributes. *Current Biology* **12**, 359–368.

Nitecki, M.H. (1988) ed. *Evolutionary Progress*. University of Chicago Press, Chicago.

Noë, A. (2002) ed. Is the visual world a grand illusion? *Journal of Consciousness Studies* **9** (5–6), 1–202.

Noë, A. (2005) *Action in Perception*. MIT Press, Cambridge, MA.

Núñez, R. and Freeman, W.J. (1999) eds. Reclaiming cognition: the primacy of action, intention and emotion. *Journal of Consciousness Studies* **6** (11–12), 1–284.

O'Brien, G. and Opie, J. (1999) A connectionist theory of phenomenal experience. *Behavioral and Brain Sciences* **22**, 127–196.

Ochsner, K.N. (2004) Current directions in social cognitive neuroscience. *Current Opinion in Neurobiology* **14**, 254–258.

Ochsner, K.N. and Lieberman, M.D. (2001) The emergence of social cognitive neuroscience. *American Psychologist* **56**, 717–734.

O'Connor, D.H., Fukui, M.M., Pinsk, M.A. and Kastner, S. (2002) Attention modulates responses in the human lateral geniculate nucleus. *Nature Neuroscience* **5**, 1203–1209.

O'Connor, T. and Robb, D. (2003) eds. *Philosophy of Mind: Contemporary Readings*. Routledge, London.

O'Craven, K.M. and Kanwisher, N. (2000) Mental imagery of faces and places activates corresponding stimulus-specific brain regions. *Journal of Cognitive Neuroscience* **12**, 1013–1023.

Odling-Smee, F.J. (1988) Niche-constructing phenotypes. In Plotkin, H.C., ed., *The Role of Behaviour in Evolution*. MIT Press, Cambridge, MA, pp. 73–132.

Ojemann, G.A. (1978) Organization of short-term verbal memory in language areas of human cortex: evidence from electrical stimulation. *Brain and Language* **5**, 331–340.

Ojemann, G.A. (2003) The neurobiology of language and verbal memory: observations from awake neurosurgery. *International Journal of Psychophysiology* **48**, 141–146.

Okasha, S. (2003) Fodor on cognition, modularity, and adaptationism. *Philosophy of Science* **70**, 68–88.

O'Keefe, J. (1985) Is consciousness the gateway to the hippocampal cognitive map? A speculative essay on the neural basis of the mind. In Oakley, D.A., ed., *Brain and Mind*. Methuen, London, pp. 59–98.

O'Keefe, J. (1993) Kant and the sea-horse: an essay in the neurophilosophy of space. In Eilan, N., McCarthy, R.A. and Brewer, B., eds., *Spatial Representation: Problems in Philosophy and Psychology*. Blackwell, Oxford, pp. 43–64.

O'Keefe, J. and Nadel, L. (1978) *The Hippocampus as a Cognitive Map*. Oxford University Press, Oxford.

Oldroyd, D. (1986) *The Arch of Knowledge: an Introduction to the History of the Philosophy and Methodology of Science*. Methuen, London.

O'Leary, D.D. and Nakagawa, Y. (2002) Patterning centers, regulatory genes and extrinsic mechanisms controlling arealization of the neocortex. *Current Opinion in Neurobiology* **12**, 14–25.

Olshausen, B. and Reinagel, P. (2003) eds. Sensory coding in the natural environment. *Network: Computation in Neural Systems* **14**, 371–612.

Olshausen, B.A. (2004) Principles of image representation in visual cortex. In Chalupa, L.M. and Werner, J.S., eds., *The Visual Neurosciences*. MIT Press, Cambridge, MA, pp. 1603–1615.

Olshausen, B.A. and Field, D.J. (2005) How close are we to understanding V1? *Neural Computation* **17**, 1665–1699.

Olson, I.R., Chun, M.M. and Allison, T. (2001) Contextual guidance of attention: human intracranial event-related potential evidence for feedback modulation in anatomically early, temporally late stages of visual processing. *Brain* **124**, 1417–1425.

Ó Nualláin, S., Mc Kevitt, P. and Mac Aogáin, E. (1997) eds. *Two Sciences of Mind*. Benjamins, Amsterdam.

Ooi, T.L. and He, Z.J. (1999) Binocular rivalry and visual awareness: the role of attention. *Perception* **28**, 551–574.

Ooi, T.L. and He, Z.J. (2003) A distributed intercortical processing of binocular rivalry: psychophysical evidence. *Perception* **32**, 155–166.

Oppenheim, P. and Putnam, H. (1958) Unity of science as a working hypothesis. In Feigl, H., Maxwell, G. and Scriven, M., eds., *Concepts, Theories, and the Mind–Body Problem*. University of Minnesota Press, Minneapolis, pp. 3–36.

Orban, G.A. and Vanduffel, W. (2004) Functional mapping of motion regions. In Chalupa, L.M. and Werner, J.S., eds., *The Visual Neurosciences*. MIT Press, Cambridge, MA, pp. 1229–1246.

O'Regan, J.K. (1992) Solving the "real" mysteries of visual perception: the world as an outside memory. *Canadian Journal of Psychology* **46**, 461–488.

O'Regan, J.K. and Noë, A. (2001) A sensorimotor account of vision and visual consciousness. *Behavioral and Brain Sciences* **24**, 939–1031 and **27**, 904–908.

Ortells, J.J., Daza, M.T. and Fox, E. (2003) Semantic activation in the absence of perceptual awareness. *Perception and Psychophysics* **65**, 1307–1317.

Osaka, N. (2003) ed. *Neural Basis of Consciousness*. Benjamins, Amsterdam.

Paivio, A. (1986) *Mental Representations: A Dual Coding Approach*. Oxford University Press, New York.

Palmer, S.E. (1988) PDP: A new paradigm for cognitive theory. *Contemporary Psychology* **32**, 925–928.

Palmer, S.E. (1999a) Color, consciousness, and the isomorphism constraint. *Behavioral and Brain Sciences* **22**, 923–989.

Palmer, S.E. (1999b) *Vision Science: Photons to Phenomenology*. MIT Press, Cambridge, MA.

Panksepp, J. (1998) *Affective Neuroscience: The Foundations of Human and Animal Emotions*. Oxford University Press, New York.

Panksepp, J. (2005) Affective consciousness: core emotional feelings in animals and humans. *Consciousness and Cognition* **14**, 30–80.

Pantle, A. and Sekuler, R. (1968) Size-detecting mechanisms in human vision. *Science* **162**, 1146–1148.

Panzeri, S., Rolls, E.T., Battaglia, F. and Lavis, R. (2001) Speed of feedforward and recurrent processing in multilayer networks of integrate-and-fire neurons. *Network: Computation in Neural Systems* **12**, 423–440.

Papineau, D. (1996) Philosophy of science. In Bunnin, N. and Tsui-James, E.P., eds., *The Blackwell Companion to Philosophy*. Blackwell, Oxford, pp. 290–324.

Papineau, D. and Selina, H. (2000) *Introducing Consciousness*. Icon, Cambridge.

Paradiso, M.A. (2002) Perceptual and neuronal correspondence in primary visual cortex. *Current Opinion in Neurobiology* **12**, 155–161.

Parasuraman, R. (1998) ed. *The Attentive Brain*. MIT Press, Cambridge, MA.

Parfit, D. (1984) *Reasons and Persons*. Clarendon, Oxford.

Parfit, D. (1987) Divided minds and the nature of persons. In Blakemore, C. and Greenfield, S., eds., *Mindwaves: Thoughts on Intelligence, Identity and Consciousness*. Blackwell, Oxford, pp. 18–26.

Parker, A., Wilding, E.L. and Bussey, T.J. (2002) eds. *The Cognitive Neuroscience of Memory: Encoding and Retrieval*. Psychology Press, Hove.

Pascual-Leone, A. and Walsh, V. (2001) Fast backprojections from the motion to the primary visual area necessary for visual awareness. *Science* **292**, 510–512.

Passingham, D. and Sakai, K. (2004) The prefrontal cortex and working memory: physiology and brain imaging. *Current Opinion in Neurobiology* **14**, 163–168.

Patterson, R. (1990) Perceptual moment models revisited. In Block, R.A., ed., *Cognitive Models of Psychological Time*. Erlbaum, Hillsdale, pp. 85–100.

Pavlov, I.P. (1927) *Conditioned Reflexes*. Oxford University Press, London.

Pavlov, I.P. (1955) *Selected Works*. Foreign Languages Publishing House, Moscow.

Pawelzik, K. (2000) ed. Aspects of neuronal dynamics. *Journal of Physiology – Paris* **94**, 301–582.

Pearson, J. and Clifford, C.G. (2004) Determinants of visual awareness following interruptions during rivalry. *Journal of Vision* **4**, 196–202.

Pellionisz, A. and Llinás, R. (1979) Brain modeling by tensor network theory and computer simulation. The cerebellum: distributed processor for predictive coordination. *Neuroscience* **4**, 323–348.

Penfield, W. (1958) *The Excitable Cortex in Conscious Man*. Liverpool University Press, Liverpool.

Penfield, W. (1975) *The Mystery of the Mind: A Critical Study of Consciousness and the Human Brain*. Princeton University Press, Princeton.

Penfield, W.G. and Rasmussen, T. (1950) *The Cerebral Cortex of Man: A Clinical Study of Localization of Function*. Macmillan, New York.

Penner, D.E. (2000) Explaining systems: investigating middle school students' understanding of emergent phenomena. *Journal of Research in Science Teaching* **37**, 784–806.

Penrose, R. (1989) *The Emperor's New Mind: Concerning Computers, Minds, and the Laws of Physics*. Oxford University Press, Oxford.

Penrose, R. (1994) *Shadows of the Mind: A Search for the Missing Science of Consciousness*. Oxford University Press, Oxford.

Perky, C.W. (1910) An experimental study of imagination. *American Journal of Psychology* **21**, 422–452.

Perlman, M. (1997) The trouble with two-factor conceptual role theories. *Minds and Machines* **7**, 495–513.

Perlman, M. (2002) Pagan teleology: adaptational role and the philosophy of mind. In Ariew, A., Cummins, R. and Perlman, M., eds., *Functions: New Essays in the Philosophy of Psychology and Biology*. Oxford University Press, Oxford, pp. 263–290.

Perrett, D.I., Rolls, E.T. and Caan, W. (1982) Visual neurones responsive to faces in the monkey temporal cortex. *Experimental Brain Research* **47**, 329–342.

Perry, E., Walker, M., Grace, J. and Perry, R. (1999) Acetylcholine in mind: a neurotransmitter correlate of consciousness? *Trends in Neurosciences* **22**, 273–280.

Perry, E., Ashton, H. and Young, A. (2002) eds., *Neurochemistry of Consciousness: Neurotransmitters in Mind*. Benjamins, Amsterdam.

Perry, W.G. (1970) *Forms of Intellectual and Ethical Development in the College Years: A Scheme*. Holt, Reinhart and Winston, New York.

Pessoa, L. and De Weerd, P. (2003) *Filling-in: From Perceptual Completion to Cortical Reorganization*. Oxford University Press, Oxford.

Pessoa, L. and Ungerleider, L.G. (2004) Neural correlates of change detection and change blindness in a working memory task. *Cerebral Cortex* **14**, 511–520.

Peterhans, E. and von der Heydt, R. (1991) Subjective contours: bridging the gap between psychophysics and physiology. *Trends in Neurosciences* **14**, 112–119.

Piefke, M., Weiss, P.H., Zilles, K., Markowitsch, H.J. and Fink, G.R. (2003) Differential remoteness and emotional tone modulate the neural correlates of autobiographical memory. *Brain* **126**, 650–668.

Pinault, D. (2004) The thalamic reticular nucleus: structure, function and concept. *Brain Research Reviews* **40**, 1–31.

Pinker, S. (1997) *How the Mind Works*. Norton, New York.

Pinker, S. and Mehler, J. (1988) eds. Connectionism and symbol systems. *Cognition* **28**, 1–247.

Piolino, P., Giffard-Quillon, G., Desgranges, B., Chetelat, G., Baron, J.C. and Eustache, F. (2004) Re-experiencing old memories via hippocampus: a PET study of autobiographical memory. *Neuroimage* **22**, 1371–1383.

Pitts, W. and McCulloch, W.S. (1947) How we know universals: the perception of auditory and visual forms. *Bulletin of Mathematical Biophysics* **9**, 127–147.

Piéron, H. and Segal, J. (1939) Sur un phénomene de facilitation rétroactive dans l'éxcitation électrique de branches nerveuses cutanées (sensibilité tactile). *Journal of Neurophysiology* **2**, 178–191.

Place, U.T. (1956) Is consciousness a brain process? *British Journal of Psychology* **47**, 42–51.

Plotkin, H. (2004) *Evolutionary Thought in Psychology: A Brief History*. Blackwell, Malden.

Pockett, S. (2000) *The Nature of Consciousness: A Hypothesis*. Writers Club Press, San Jose.

Pockett, S. (2002a) Difficulties with the electromagnetic field theory of consciousness. *Journal of Consciousness Studies* **9** (4), 51–56.

Pockett, S. (2002b) Backward referral, flash-lags, and quantum free will: a response to commentaries on articles by Pockett, Klein, Gomes, and Trevena and Miller. *Consciousness and Cognition* **11**, 314–325.

Pockett, S. (2003) How long is "now"? Phenomenology and the specious present. *Phenomenology and the Cognitive Sciences* **2**, 55–68.

Pockett, S. (2004) Hypnosis and the death of "subjective backwards referral". *Consciousness and Cognition* **13**, 621–625.

Poincaré, H. (1908) *Science et méthode*. E. Flammarion, Paris.

Polanyi, M. (1968) Life's irreducible structure. *Science* **160**, 1308–1312.

Pollen, D.A. (1999) On the neural correlates of visual perception. *Cerebral Cortex* **9**, 4–19.

Pollen, D.A. (2003) Explicit neural representations, recursive neural networks and conscious visual perception. *Cerebral Cortex* **13**, 807–814.

Pollen, D.A. (2004) Brain stimulation and conscious experience. *Consciousness and Cognition* **13**, 626–645.

Pollen, D.A., Foster, K.H. and Gaska, J.P. (1985) Phase-dependent response characteristics of visual cortical neurons. In Rose, D. and Dobson, V.G., eds., *Models of the Visual Cortex*. Wiley, Chichester, pp. 281–291.

Polonsky, A., Blake, R., Braun, J. and Heeger, D.J. (2000) Neuronal activity in human primary visual cortex correlates with perception during binocular rivalry. *Nature Neuroscience* **3**, 1153–1159.

Pöppel, E. (1997) A hierarchical model of temporal perception. *Trends in Cognitive Sciences* **1**, 56–61.

Popper, K.R. (1934) *Logik der Forschung: zur Erkenntnistheorie der modernen Naturwissenschaft*. Springer, Wien.

Popper, K.R. (1963) *Conjectures and Refutations: The Growth of Scientific Knowledge*. Routledge & Kegan Paul, London.

Popper, K.R. and Eccles, J.C. (1977) *The Self and its Brain*. Springer, Berlin.

Posner, M.I. (1980) Orienting of attention. *Quarterly Journal of Experimental Psychology* **32**, 3–25.

Posner, M.I. and Dehaene, S. (1994) Attentional networks. *Trends in Neurosciences* **17**, 75–79.

Posner, M.I. and Gilbert, C.D. (1999) Attention and primary visual cortex. *Proceedings of the National Academy of Sciences of the United States of America* **96**, 2585–2587.

Pouget, A., Dayan, P. and Zemel, R.S. (2003) Inference and computation with population codes. *Annual Review of Neuroscience* **26**, 381–410.

Pribram, K. (1971) *Languages of the Brain: Experimental Paradoxes and Principles in Neuropsychology*. Prentice-Hall, Englewood Cliffs.

Pribram, K. (1986) The cognitive revolution and mind/brain issues. *American Psychologist* **41**, 507–520.

Pribram, K. (2003) Commentary on 'Synaesthesia' by Ramachandran and Hubbard. *Journal of Consciousness Studies* **10** (3), 75–76.

Prigatano, G.P. (1999) *Principles of Neuropsychological Rehabilitation*. Oxford University Press, New York.

Prigogine, I. and Stengers, I. (1984) *Order Out of Chaos: Man's New Dialogue with Nature*. Heinemann, London.

Pringle, H.A. and Davies, I.R. (2001) Attentional impairment in an odd case of dementia. *Perception* **30** (Supplement), 46.

Pulvermüller, F. (1999) Words in the brain's language. *Behavioral and Brain Sciences* **22**, 253–336.

Pulvermüller, F. (2001) Brain reflections of words and their meaning. *Trends in Cognitive Sciences* **5**, 517–524.

Pulvermüller, F. (2002) *The Neuroscience of Language: On Brain Circuits of Words and Serial Order*. Cambridge University Press, Cambridge.

Purpura, K.P. and Schiff, N.D. (1997) The thalamic intralaminar nuclei: a role in visual awareness. *The Neuroscientist* **3**, 8–15.

Putnam, H. (1967) The mental life of some machines. In Castañeda, H.-L., ed., *Intentionality, Minds, and Perception*. Wayne State University Press, Detroit, pp. 177–200.

Putnam, H. (1975) The meaning of 'meaning'. In Gunderson, K., ed., *Language, Mind, and Knowledge. Minnesota Studies in the Philosophy of Science, vol. VII*. University of Minnesota Press, Minneapolis, pp. 131–193.

Pylyshyn, Z. (1980) Computation and cognition: issues in the foundations of cognitive science. *Behavioral and Brain Sciences* **3**, 111–169.

Pylyshyn, Z. (1984) *Computation and Cognition: Toward a Foundation for Cognitive Science*. MIT Press, Cambridge, MA.

Pylyshyn, Z. (1999) Is vision continuous with cognition? The case for cognitive impenetrability of visual perception. *Behavioral and Brain Sciences* **22**, 341–423.

Pylyshyn, Z. (2002) Mental imagery: in search of a theory. *Behavioral and Brain Sciences* **25**, 157–237.

Pylyshyn, Z. (2003) Return of the mental image: are there really pictures in the brain? *Trends in Cognitive Sciences* **7**, 113–118.

Pylyshyn, Z. (2004) *Seeing and Visualizing: It's Not What You Think*. MIT Press, Cambridge, MA.

Quian Quiroga, R., Reddy, L., Kreiman, G., Koch, C. and Fried, I. (2005) Invariant visual representation by single neurons in the human brain. *Nature* **435**, 1102–1107.

Quine, W.V.O. (1951) Two dogmas of empiricism. *Philosophical Review* **60**, 20–43.

Quine, W.V.O. (1960) *Word and Object*. MIT Press, Cambridge, MA.

Quinlan, P.T. (2003) Visual feature integration theory: past, present, and future. *Psychological Bulletin* **129**, 643–673.

Rafal, R.D. and Posner, M.I. (1987) Deficits in human visual spatial attention following thalamic lesions. *Proceedings of the National Academy of Sciences of the United States of America* **84**, 7349–7353.

Rainville, P. (2002) Brain mechanisms of pain affect and pain modulation. *Current Opinion in Neurobiology* **12**, 195–204.

Raizada, R.D. and Grossberg, S. (2003) Towards a theory of the laminar architecture of cerebral cortex: computational clues from the visual system. *Cerebral Cortex* **13**, 100–113.

Ramachandran, V.S. (1985) The neurobiology of perception. *Perception* **14**, 97–103.

Ramachandran, V.S. (2003a) *The Emerging Mind*. Profile, London.

Ramachandran, V.S. (2003b) Foreword. In Pessoa, L. and De Weerd, P., eds., *Filling-in: From Perceptual Completion to Cortical Reorganization*. Oxford University Press, Oxford, pp. xi–xxii.

Ramachandran, V.S. and Hubbard, E.M. (2003) The phenomenology of synaesthesia. *Journal of Consciousness Studies* **10** (8), 49–57.

Ramón y Cajal, S. (1906) *Textura del Sistema Nervioso del Hombre y de los Vertebrados*. Tomás Moya, Madrid.

Ramsden, B.M., Hung, C.P. and Roe, A.W. (2001) Real and illusory contour processing in area VI of the primate: a cortical balancing act. *Cerebral Cortex* **11**, 648–665.

Rang, H.P., Dale, M.M., Ritter, J.M. and Moore, P. (2003) *Pharmacology,* 5th edn. Churchill Livingstone, Edinburgh.

Rao, R.P.N. and Ballard, D.H. (1999) Predictive coding in the visual cortex: a functional interpretation of some extra-classical receptive-field effects. *Nature Neuroscience* **2**, 79–87.

Rauchs, G., Desgranges, B., Foret, J. and Eustache, F. (2005) The relationships between memory systems and sleep stages. *Journal of Sleep Research* **14**, 123–140.

Ravenscroft, I. (2005) *Philosophy of Mind: A Beginner's Guide*. Oxford University Press, Oxford.

Rawlins, J.N.P. (1985) Associations across time: the hippocampus as a temporary memory store. *Behavioral and Brain Sciences* **8**, 479–496.

Rees, G., Frith, C.D. and Lavie, N. (1997) Modulating irrelevant motion perception by varying attentional load in an unrelated task. *Science* **278**, 1616–1619.

Rees, G., Kreiman, G. and Koch, C. (2002) Neural correlates of consciousness in humans. *Nature Reviews Neuroscience* **3**, 261–270.

Regan, B.C., Julliot, C., Simmen, B., Vienot, F., Charles-Dominique, P. and Mollon, J.D. (2001) Fruits, foliage and the evolution of primate colour vision. *Philosophical Transactions of the Royal Society of London, Series B* **356**, 229–283.

Remington, R. and Pierce, L. (1984) Moving attention: evidence for time-invariant shifts of visual selective attention. *Perception and Psychophysics* **35**, 393–399.

Revonsuo, A. (1995) Consciousness, dreams and virtual realities. *Philosophical Psychology* **8**, 35–58.

Rey, G. (1997) *Contemporary Philosophy of Mind: A Contentiously Classical Approach*. Blackwell, Cambridge, MA.

Reynolds, J.H. and Chelazzi, L. (2004) Attentional modulation of visual processing. *Annual Review of Neuroscience* **27**, 611–647.

Ribeiro, S., Mello, C.V., Velho, T., Gardner, T.J., Jarvis, E.D. and Pavlides, C. (2002) Induction of hippocampal long-term potentiation during waking leads to increased extrahippocampal *zif-268* expression during ensuing rapid-eye-movement sleep. *Journal of Neuroscience* **22**, 10914–10923.

Ribot, T.A. (1881) *Les Maladies de la mémoire*. Ballière, Paris.

Rieke, F., Warland, D., de Ruter van Steveninck, R. and Bialek, W. (1997) *Spikes: Exploring the Neural Code*. MIT Press, Cambridge, MA.

Ringach, D.L., Hawken, M.J. and Shapley, R. (1997) Dynamics of orientation tuning in macaque primary visual cortex. *Nature* **387**, 281–284.

Ringach, D.L., Hawken, M.J. and Shapley, R. (2003) Dynamics of orientation tuning in macaque V1: the role of global and tuned suppression. *Journal of Neurophysiology* **90**, 342–352.

Rizzolatti, G. and Arbib, M.A. (1998) Language within our grasp. *Trends in Neurosciences* **21**, 188–194.

Rizzolatti, G. and Craighero, L. (2004) The mirror neuron system. *Annual Review of Neuroscience* **27**, 169–192.

Ro, T., Breitmeyer, B., Burton, P., Singhal, N.S. and Lane, D. (2003) Feedback contributions to visual awareness in human occipital cortex. *Current Biology* **13**, 1038–1041.

Robertson, I.H. and Halligan, P.W. (1999) *Spatial Neglect: A Clinical Handbook for Diagnosis and Treatment*. Psychology, Hove.

Robertson, L.C. (2004) *Space, Objects, Minds, and Brains*. Psychology, New York.

Robinson, J.O. (1972) *The Psychology of Visual Illusion*. London, Hutchinson.

Rochester, N., Holland, J., Haibt, L. and Duda, W. (1956) Tests on a cell assembly theory of the action of the brain, using a large digital computer. *IRE Transactions on Information Theory* **IT-2**, 80–93.

Rock, I. (1983) *The Logic of Perception*. MIT Press, Cambridge, MA.

Rock, I., Linnett, C.M., Grant, P. and Mack, A. (1992) Perception without attention: results of a new method. *Cognitive Psychology* **24**, 502–534.

Rockel, A.J., Hiorns, R.W. and Powell, T.P. (1980) The basic uniformity in structure of the neocortex. *Brain* **103**, 221–244.

Rockland, K.S. (2002) Visual cortical organization at the single axon level: a beginning. *Neuroscience Research* **42**, 155–166.

Rockland, K.S. (2004) Connectional neuroanatomy: the changing scene. *Brain Research* **1000**, 60–63.

Rodriguez, A., Whitson, J. and Granger, R. (2004) Derivation and analysis of basic computational operations of thalamocortical circuits. *Journal of Cognitive Neuroscience* **16**, 856–877.

Roelfsema, P.R. (2005) Elemental operations in vision. *Trends in Cognitive Sciences* **9**, 226–233.

Roland, P.E., Larsen, B., Lassen, N.A. and Skinhøj, E. (1980) Supplementary motor area and other cortical areas in organization of voluntary movements in man. *Journal of Neurophysiology* **43**, 118–136.

Rolls, E.T. (1990) Theoretical and neurophysiological analysis of the functions of the primate hippocampus in memory. *Cold Spring Harbor Symposia on Quantitative Biology* **55**, 995–1006.

Rolls, E.T. (1999) *The Brain and Emotion*. Oxford University Press, Oxford.

Rolls, E.T. (2000) Hippocampo-cortical and cortico-cortical backprojections. *Hippocampus* **10**, 380–388.

Rolls, E.T. and Deco, G. (2002) *Computational Neuroscience of Vision*. Oxford University Press, Oxford.

Rolls, E.T. and Treves, A. (1998) *Neural Networks and Brain Function*. Oxford University Press, Oxford.

Rose, D. (1987) Is brain research dead? *Trends in Neurosciences* **10**, 196–197.

Rose, D. (1995) A portrait of the brain. In Gregory, R., Harris, J., Heard, P. and Rose, D., eds., *The Artful Eye*. Oxford University Press, Oxford, pp. 28–51.

Rose, D. (1996) Some reflections on (or by?) grandmother cells. *Perception* **25**, 881–886.

Rose, D. (1999a) The historical roots of the theories of local signs and labelled lines. *Perception* **28**, 675–685.

Rose, D. (1999b) Creativity, intentionality and the conscious/unconscious distinction: a neural theory. *Journal of Intelligent Systems* **9**, 407–443.

Rose, D. (2000a) Toward a multi-level theory of intentionality. *Consciousness and Cognition* **9**, s99–s100.

Rose, D. (2000b) "The Race for Consciousness" by J.G. Taylor. *Perception* **29**, 373–375.

Rose, D. (2001) *On the latency of visual perception: the role of display parameters*. Paper presented at: Applied Vision Association (London). ⟨http://www.psy.surrey.ac.uk/staff/d.rose/ AVA2001.pdf⟩.

Rose, D. (2002) *Causation runs horizontally: the stream of thought as a sequence of hierarchical event-complexes*. Paper presented at: Association for the

Scientific Study of Consciousness (Barcelona).⟨http://www.ub.es/grc_logos/assc6/prog/abstracts/ASSC6-P2-06.html⟩.

Rose, D., Bradshaw, M.F. and Hibbard, P.B. (2003) Attention affects the stereoscopic depth aftereffect. *Perception* **32**, 635–640.

Rose, D. and Dobson, V.G. (1985) Methodological solutions for neuroscience. In Rose, D. and Dobson, V.G., eds., *Models of the Visual Cortex*. Wiley, Chichester, pp. 533–545.

Rose, D. and Dobson, V.G. (1989) On the nature of theories and the generation of models of the circuitry of the primary visual cortex. In Kulikowski, J.J., Dickinson, C. and Murray, I.J., eds., *Seeing Contour and Colour*. Pergamon, Oxford, pp. 651–658.

Rose, D. and Harris, J.P. (2005) Perception. In Hewstone, M.R.C., Fincham, F.D. and Foster, J., eds., *Psychology*. Blackwell, Oxford, pp. 156–179.

Rose, D. and Pardhan, S. (2000) Selective attention, ideal observer theory and 'early' visual channels. *Spatial Vision* **14**, 77–80.

Rosenthal, D.M. (1993) Thinking that one thinks. In Davis, M. and Humphreys, G.W., eds., *Consciousness: Psychological and Philosophical Essays*. Blackwell, Oxford, pp. 198–223.

Rosenthal, D.M. (1995) Multiple drafts and the facts of the matter. In Metzinger, T., ed., *Conscious Experience*. Schöningh, Paderborn, pp. 359–372.

Rosenthal, D.M. (1997) A theory of consciousness. In Block, N., Flanagan, O. and Güzeldere, G., eds., *The Nature of Consciousness*. MIT Press, Cambridge, MA, pp. 729–753.

Rosenthal, D.M. (2002) Explaining consciousness. In Chalmers, D.J., ed., *Philosophy of Mind: Classical and Contemporary Readings*. Oxford University Press, New York, pp. 406–421.

Ross, D. (2002) Dennett and the Darwin wars. In Brook, A. and Ross, D., eds., *Daniel Dennett*. Cambridge University Press, Cambridge, pp. 271–293.

Ross, D., Brook, A. and Thompson, D. (2000) eds. *Dennett's Philosophy: A Comprehensive Assessment*. MIT Press, Cambridge, MA.

Ross, J., Morrone, M.C., Goldberg, M.E. and Burr, D.C. (2001) Changes in visual perception at the time of saccades. *Trends in Neurosciences* **24**, 113–121.

Rowlands, M. (1999) *The Body in Mind: Understanding Cognitive Processes*. Cambridge University Press, Cambridge.

Rowlands, M. (2001) *The Nature of Consciousness*. Cambridge University Press, Cambridge.

Ruchkin, D., Grafman, J., Cameron, K. and Berndt, R. (2003) Working memory retention systems: a state of activated long-term memory. *Behavioral and Brain Sciences* **26**, 709–777.

Rumelhart, D., Lindsay, P. and Norman, D. (1972) A process model for long term memory. In Tulving, E. and Donaldson, W., eds., *Organization of Memory*. Academic Press, New York, pp. 198–246.

Rumelhart, D.E. and McClelland, J.L. (1986) On learning the past tenses of English verbs. In McClelland, J.L., Rumelhart, D.E. and the PDP Research Group, eds., *Parallel Distributed Processing: Explorations in the Microstructure of Cognition. Vol.2: Psychological and Biological Models*. MIT Press, Cambridge, MA, pp. 216–271.

Ruse, M. (1986) Teleology and the biological sciences. In Rescher, N., ed., *Current Issues in Teleology*. University Press of America, Lanham, MD, pp. 54–64.

Russell, B. (1912) *The Problems of Philosophy*. Thornton Butterworth Ltd, London.

Ryle, G. (1949) *The Concept of Mind*. Hutchinson, London.

Salner, M. (1986) Adult cognitive and epistemological development in systems education. *Systems Research* **3**, 225–232.

Salthe, S.N. (1985) *Evolving Hierarchical Systems: Their Structure and Representation*. Columbia University Press, New York.

Salzman, C.D., Murasugi, C.M., Britten, K.H. and Newsome, W.T. (1992) Microstimulation in visual area MT: effects on direction discrimination performance. *Journal of Neuroscience* **12**, 2331–2355.

Sattler, R. (1986) *Biophilosophy*. Springer, Berlin.

Sauvan, X.M. (1998) Early integration of retinal and extra-retinal information: recent results and hypotheses. *Reviews in the Neurosciences* **9**, 291–299.

Schacter, D.L. (1989) On the relationship between memory and consciousness: dissociable interactions and conscious experience. In Roediger, H.L. III and Craik, F.I.M., eds., *Varieties of Memory and Consciousness: Essays in Honour of Endel Tulving*. Erlbaum, Hillsdale, pp. 355–389.

Schacter, D.L. (1990) Toward a cognitive neuropsychology of awareness: implicit knowledge and anosognosia. *Journal of Clinical and Experimental Neuropsychology* **12**, 155–178.

Schacter, D.L., Norman, K.A. and Koutstaal, W. (1998) The cognitive neuroscience of constructive memory. *Annual Review of Psychology* 49, 289–318.

Scheibel, A.B. (1980) Anatomical and physiological substrates of arousal: a view from the bridge. In Hobson, J.A. and Brazier, M.A.B., eds., *The Reticular Formation Revisited: Specifying Function for a Nonspecific System.* Raven Press, New York, pp. 55–66.

Scheibel, M.E. and Scheibel, A.B. (1967) Structural organization of nonspecific thalamic nuclei and their projection toward cortex. *Brain Research* 6, 60–94.

Scheibel, M.E. and Scheibel, A.B. (1970) Elementary processes in selected thalamic and cortical sub-systems – the structural substrates. In Schmitt, F.O., ed., *The Neurosciences: Second Study Program.* Rockefeller University Press, New York, pp. 443–457.

Scherberger, H. and Andersen, R.A. (2004) Sensorimotor transformation in the posterior parietal cortex. In Chalupa, L.M. and Werner, J.S., eds., *The Visual Neurosciences.* MIT Press, Cambridge, MA, pp. 1324–1336.

Schiff, N.D. and Plum, F. (2000) The role of arousal and "gating" systems in the neurology of impaired consciousness. *Journal of Clinical Neurophysiology* 17, 438–452.

Schmahmann, J.D. and Pandya, D.N. (1990) Anatomical investigation of projections from thalamus to posterior parietal cortex in the rhesus monkey: a WGA-HRP and fluorescent tracer study. *Journal of Comparative Neurology* 295, 299–326.

Schmitz, T.W., Kawahara-Baccus, T.N. and Johnson, S.C. (2004) Metacognitive evaluation, self-relevance, and the right prefrontal cortex. *Neuroimage* 22, 941–947.

Schmolesky, M.T., Wang, Y., Hanes, D.P., Thompson, K.G., Leutgeb, S., Schall, J.D. and Leventhal, A.G. (1998) Signal timing across the macaque visual system. *Journal of Neurophysiology* 79, 3272–3278.

Schneider, W. (1987) Connectionism: is it a paradigm shift for psychology? *Behavior Research Methods, Instruments, and Computers* 19, 73–83.

Schnitzer, M.J. and Meister, M. (2003) Multineuronal firing patterns in the signal from eye to brain. *Neuron* 37, 499–511.

Schrödinger, E. (1944) *What is Life?* Cambridge University Press, Cambridge.

Schroeder, C.E., Mehta, A.D. and Foxe, J.J. (2001) Determinants and mechanisms of attentional modulation of neural processing. *Frontiers in Bioscience* 6, D672–D684.

Scott, A. (1995) *Stairway to the Mind: The Controversial New Science of Consciousness.* Springer, New York.

Scott, A. (1998) Reductionism revisited. In Hameroff, S.R., Kaszniak, A.W. and Scott, A., eds., *Toward a Science of Consciousness II: The Second Tucson Discussions and Debates.* MIT Press, Cambridge, MA, pp. 71–78.

Scott, A. (2000) Modern science and the mind. In Velmans, M., ed., *Investigating Phenomenal Consciousness: New Methodologies and Maps.* Benjamins, Amsterdam, pp. 215–232.

Scott, A. (2004) Reductionism revisited. *Journal of Consciousness Studies* 11 (2), 51–68.

Scoville, W.B. and Milner, B. (1957) Loss of recent memory after bilateral hippocampal lesions. *Journal of Neurology, Neurosurgery and Psychiatry* 20, 11–21.

Seager, W. (1993) The elimination of experience. *Philosophy and Phenomenological Research* 53, 345–365.

Seager, W. (1999) *Theories of Consciousness.* Routledge, London.

Searle, J.R. (1980) Minds, brains, and programs. *Behavioral and Brain Sciences* 3, 417–457.

Searle, J.R. (1992) *The Rediscovery of the Mind.* MIT Press, Cambridge, MA.

Searle, J.R. (1997) *The Mystery of Consciousness.* Granta, London.

Searle, J.R. (2000) Consciousness. *Annual Review of Neuroscience* 23, 557–578.

Searle, J.R. (2002) *Consciousness and Language.* Cambridge University Press, Cambridge.

Sedvall, G. and Terenius, L. (2000) eds. Schizophrenia: pathophysiological mechanisms. *Brain Research Reviews* 31, 107–404.

Seghier, M., Dojat, M., Delon-Martin, C., Rubin, C., Warnking, J., Segebarth, C. and Bullier, J. (2000) Moving illusory contours activate primary visual cortex: an fMRI study. *Cerebral Cortex* 10, 663–670.

Seidemann, E., Arieli, A., Grinvald, A. and Slovin, H. (2002) Dynamics of depolarization and hyperpolarization in the frontal cortex and saccade goal. *Science* 295, 862–865.

Sejnowski, T.J. and Destexhe, A. (2000) Why do we sleep? *Brain Research* 886, 208–223.

Sejnowski, T.J. and Rosenberg, C. (1987) Parallel networks that learn to pronounce English text. *Complex Systems* **1**, 145–168.

Selemon, L.D. and Goldman-Rakic, P.S. (1988) Common cortical and subcortical targets of the dorsolateral prefrontal and posterior parietal cortices in the rhesus monkey: evidence for a distributed neural network subserving spatially guided behavior. *Journal of Neuroscience* **8**, 4049–4068.

Selfridge, O.G. (1959) Pandemonium: a paradigm for learning. In *Mechanisation of Thought Processes*. Her Majesty's Stationery Office, London, pp. 511–531.

Sengpiel, F. and Kind, P.C. (2002) The role of activity in development of the visual system. *Current Biology* **12**, R818–R826.

Sergent, C. and Dehaene, S. (2004) Is consciousness a gradual phenomenon? Evidence for an all-or-none bifurcation during the attentional blink. *Psychological Science* **15**, 720–728.

Sergent, J. (1987) A new look at the human split brain. *Brain* **110**, 1375–1392.

Seriès, P., Lorenceau, J. and Frégnac, Y. (2003) The "silent" surround of V1 receptive fields: theory and experiments. *Journal of Physiology – Paris* **97**, 453–474.

Shadish, W.R. and Fuller, S. (1994) eds. *The Social Psychology of Science*. Guilford Press, New York.

Shadlen, M.N. and Gold, J.I. (2004) The neurophysiology of decision making as a window on cognition. In Gazzaniga, M.S., ed., *The Cognitive Neurosciences III*. MIT Press, Cambridge, MA, pp. 1229–1241.

Shadlen, M.N. and Movshon, J.A. (1999) Synchrony unbound: a critical evaluation of the temporal binding hypothesis. *Neuron* **24**, 67–77, 111–125.

Shallice, T. (1972) Dual functions of consciousness. *Psychological Review* **79**, 383–393.

Shallice, T. (1988) *From Neuropsychology to Mental Structure*. Cambridge University Press, Cambridge.

Shastri, L. (2002) Episodic memory and cortico-hippocampal interactions. *Trends in Cognitive Sciences* **6**, 162–168.

Sheets-Johnstone, M. (1999) *The Primacy of Movement*. Benjamins, Amsterdam.

Sherman, S.M. and Guillery, R.W. (1996) Functional organization of thalamocortical relays. *Journal of Neurophysiology* **76**, 1367–1395.

Sherman, S.M. and Guillery, R.W. (2001) *Exploring the Thalamus*. Academic Press, San Diego.

Sherman, S.M. and Guillery, R.W. (2002) The role of the thalamus in the flow of information to the cortex. *Philosophical Transactions of the Royal Society of London, Series B* **357**, 1695–1708.

Sherman, S.M. and Guillery, R.W. (2004) The visual relays in the thalamus. In Chalupa, L.M. and Werner, J.S., eds., *The Visual Neurosciences*. MIT Press, Cambridge, MA, pp. 565–591.

Shevelev, I.A., Kostelianetz, N.B., Kamenkovich, V.M. and Sharaev, G.A. (1991) EEG alpha-wave in the visual cortex: check of the hypothesis of the scanning process. *International Journal of Psychophysiology* **11**, 195–201.

Shipp, S. (2003) The functional logic of cortico-pulvinar connections. *Philosophical Transactions of the Royal Society of London, Series B* **358**, 1605–1624.

Shipp, S. (2004) The brain circuitry of attention. *Trends in Cognitive Sciences* **8**, 223–230.

Shulman, G.L., Remington, R.W. and Mclean, J.P. (1979) Moving attention through visual space. *Journal of Experimental Psychology: Human Perception and Performance* **5**, 522–526.

Siegel, J.M. (2001) The REM sleep–memory consolidation hypothesis. *Science* **294**, 1058–1063.

Silberstein, M. (2001) Converging on emergence: consciousness, causation and explanation. *Journal of Consciousness Studies* **8** (9–10), 61–98.

Sillito, A. (1995) Chemical soup: where and how drugs may influence visual perception. In Gregory, R., Harris, J., Heard, P. and Rose, D., eds., *The Artful Eye*. Oxford University Press, Oxford, pp. 294–306.

Simon, H.A. (1962) The architecture of complexity: hierarchic systems. *Proceedings of the American Philosophical Society* **106**, 467–482.

Simon, H.A. (1996) *The Sciences of the Artificial, 3rd edn*. MIT Press, Cambridge, MA.

Singer, W. (1985) Activity-dependent self-organisation of the mammalian visual cortex. In Rose, D. and Dobson, V.G., eds., *Models of the Visual Cortex*. Wiley, Chichester, pp. 123–136.

Skarda, C.A. (1999) The perceptual form of life. *Journal of Consciousness Studies* **6** (11–12), 79–93.

Skinner, B.F. (1987) Whatever happened to psychology as the science of behavior? *American Psychologist* **42**, 780–786.

Skinner, J.E. and Yingling, C.D. (1977) Central gating mechanisms that regulate event-related potentials and behavior: a neural model for attention. In Desmedt, J.E., ed., *Attention, Voluntary Contraction and Event-Related Cerebral Potentials. Progress in Clinical Neurophysiology, vol. 1*. Karger, Basel, pp. 30–69.

Skrbina, D. (2003) Panpsychism as an underlying theme in western philosophy: a survey paper. *Journal of Consciousness Studies* **10** (3), 4–46.

Sloman, A. (2001) *Philosophical foundations: some key questions*. Paper presented at: IJCAI (Seattle). ⟨http://www.cs.bham.ac.uk/~axs/ijcai01/fulltut.2page.pdf⟩.

Smart, J.J.C. (1959) Sensations and brain processes. *Philosophical Review* **68**, 141–156.

Smith, A.T., Singh, K.D. and Greenlee, M.W. (2000) Attentional suppression of activity in the human visual cortex. *Neuroreport* **11**, 271–277.

Smith, E.R. and Miller, F.D. (1978) Limits on perceptions of cognitive processes: a reply to Nisbett and Wilson. *Psychological Review* **82**, 322–362.

Smith, H.J. (2005) ed. *Smith and Williams' Introduction to the Principles of Drug Design and Action*, 4th edn. Taylor and Francis, London.

Smith, J.A. (2006) Interpretative phenomenological analysis. In Breakwell, G.M., Hammond, S. and Fife-Schaw, C., eds., *Research Methods in Psychology,* 3rd edn. Sage, London (in press).

Smith, L.D. (1986) *Behaviorism and Logical Positivism: A Reassessment of the Alliance*. Stanford University Press, Stanford.

Smolensky, P. (1988) On the proper treatment of connectionism. *Behavioral and Brain Sciences* **11**, 1–74.

Snodgrass, M. (2004) The dissociation paradigm and its discontents: how can unconscious perception or memory be inferred? *Consciousness and Cognition* **13**, 107–116.

Snodgrass, M., Bernat, E. and Shevrin, H. (2004) Unconscious perception: a model-based approach to method and evidence. *Perception and Psychophysics* **66**, 846–867.

Snowden, J.S., Griffiths, H. and Neary, D. (1999) The impact of autobiographical experience on meaning: a reply to Graham, Lambon Ralph and Hodges. *Cognitive Neuropsychology* **16**, 673–688.

Sokolov, E.N. (1963) *Perception and the Conditioned Reflex*. Pergamon, Oxford.

Somers, D.C., Dale, A.M., Seiffert, A.E. and Tootell, R.B.H. (1999) Functional MRI reveals spatially specific attentional modulation in human primary visual cortex. *Proceedings of the National Academy of Sciences of the United States of America* **96**, 1663–1668.

Song, S. and Abbott, L.F. (2001) Cortical development and remapping through spike timing-dependent plasticity. *Neuron* **32**, 339–350.

Sowden, P.T., Rose, D. and Davies, I.R.L. (2002) Perceptual learning of luminance contrast detection: specific for spatial frequency and retinal location but not orientation. *Vision Research* **42**, 1249–1258.

Sparing, R., Mottaghy, F.M., Ganis, G., Thompson, W.L., Topper, R., Kosslyn, S.M. and Pascual-Leone, A. (2002) Visual cortex excitability increases during visual mental imagery: a TMS study in healthy human subjects. *Brain Research* **938**, 92–97.

Spector, L. (2002) Hierarchy helps it work that way. *Philosophical Psychology* **15**, 109–117.

Spekreijse, H. (2000) ed. Pre-attentive and attentive mechanisms in vision: perceptual organization and dysfunction. *Vision Research* **40**, 1179–1638.

Sperber, D., Premack, D. and Premack, A.J. (1995) eds. *Causal Cognition*. Oxford University Press, Oxford.

Sperry, R. (1952) Neurology and the mind–brain problem. *American Scientist* **40**, 291–312.

Sperry, R. (1980) Mind–brain interaction: mentalism, yes; dualism, no. *Neuroscience* **5**, 195–206.

Sperry, R. (1984) Consciousness, personal identity and the divided brain. *Neuropsychologia* **22**, 661–673.

Sperry, R.W. and Miner, N. (1955) Pattern perception following insertion of mica plates into visual cortex. *Journal of Comparative and Physiological Psychology* **48**, 463–469.

Sperry, R.W., Miner, N. and Myers, R.E. (1955) Visual pattern perception following sub-pial slicing and tantalum wire implantations in the visual cortex. *Journal of Comparative and Physiological Psychology* **48**, 50–58.

Sperry, R.W., Zaidel, E. and Zaidel, D. (1979) Self recognition and social awareness in the deconnected minor hemisphere. *Neuropsychologia* **17**, 153–166.

Spiridon, M. and Kanwisher, N. (2002) How distributed is visual category information in human occipito-temporal cortex? An fMRI study. *Neuron* **35**, 1157–1165.

Spivey, M.J. and Spirn, M.J. (2000) Selective visual attention modulates the direct tilt aftereffect. *Perception and Psychophysics* **62**, 1525–1533.

Sporns, O., Tononi, G. and Edelman, G.M. (2000) Theoretical neuroanatomy: relating anatomical and functional connectivity in graphs and cortical connection matrices. *Cerebral Cortex* **10**, 127–141.

Spratling, M.W. and Johnson, M.H. (2004) A feedback model of visual attention. *Journal of Cognitive Neuroscience* **16**, 219–237.

Squire, L.R. and Schacter, D.L. (2002) eds. *Neuropsychology of Memory*, 3rd edn. Guilford Press, New York.

Squire, L.R. and Zola, S.M. (1996) Structure and function of declarative and nondeclarative memory systems. *Proceedings of the National Academy of Sciences of the United States of America* **93**, 13515–13522.

Squires, N.K., Squires, K.C. and Hillyard, S.A. (1975) Two varieties of long-latency positive waves evoked by unpredictable auditory stimuli in man. *Electroencephalography and Clinical Neurophysiology* **38**, 387–401.

Staats, A.W. (1983) *Psychology's Crisis of Disunity: Philosophy and Method for a Unified Science*. Praeger, New York.

Stamenov, M. and Gallese, V. (2002) eds. *Mirror Neurons and the Evolution of Brain and Language*. Benjamins, Amsterdam.

Stanley, R.P. (1999) Qualia space. *Journal of Consciousness Studies* **6** (1), 49–60.

Star, S.L. (1989) *Regions of the Mind: Brain Research and the Quest for Scientific Certainty*. Stanford University Press, Stanford.

Stepanyants, A. and Chklovskii, D.B. (2005) Neurogeometry and potential synaptic connectivity. *Trends in Neurosciences* **28**, 387–394.

Sterelny, K. (1990) *The Representational Theory of Mind: An Introduction*. Blackwell, Oxford.

Sterelny, K. (2003) *Thought in a Hostile World: The Evolution of Human Cognition*. Blackwell, Malden.

Steriade, M. (2000) Corticothalamic resonance, states of vigilance and mentation. *Neuroscience* **101**, 243–276.

Stettler, D.D., Das, A., Bennett, J. and Gilbert, C.D. (2002) Lateral connectivity and contextual interactions in macaque primary visual cortex. *Neuron* **36**, 739–750.

Stevens, L.A. (1971) *Explorers of the Brain*. Knopf, New York.

Stich, S.P. (1983) *From Folk Psychology to Cognitive Science*. MIT Press, Cambridge, MA.

Stich, S.P. and Warfield, T.A. (2003) eds. *The Blackwell Guide to Philosophy of Mind*. Blackwell, Malden.

Stickgold, R. (1998) Sleep: off-line memory reprocessing. *Trends in Cognitive Sciences* **2**, 484–492.

Stickgold, R., Hobson, J.A., Fosse, R. and Fosse, M. (2001) Sleep, learning, and dreams: off-line memory reprocessing. *Science* **294**, 1052–1057.

Stirling, J.D. (2002) *Introducing Neuropsychology*. Psychology Press, Hove.

Stoerig, P. (2001) The neuroanatomy of phenomenal vision: a psychological perspective. *Annals of the New York Academy of Sciences* **929**, 176–194.

Stoerig, P. and Barth, E. (2001) Low-level phenomenal vision despite unilateral destruction of primary visual cortex. *Consciousness and Cognition* **10**, 574–587.

Stone, T. and Young, A.W. (1997) Delusions and brain injury: the philosophy and psychology of belief. *Mind and Language* **12**, 327–364.

Stroud, J.M. (1955) The fine structure of psychological time. In Quastler, H., ed., *Information Theory in Psychology: Problems and Methods*. Free Press, Glencoe, pp. 174–207.

Stuss, D.T. and Levine, B. (2002) Adult clinical neuropsychology: lessons from studies of the frontal lobes. *Annual Review of Psychology* **53**, 401–433.

Suder, K. and Wörgötter, F. (2000) The control of low-level information flow in the visual system. *Reviews in the Neurosciences* **11**, 127–146.

Sugita, Y. (1999) Grouping of image fragments in primary visual cortex. *Nature* **401**, 269–272.

Sumner, P. and Mollon, J.D. (2000) Catarrhine photopigments are optimized for detecting targets against a foliage background. *Journal of Experimental Biology* **203**, 1963–1986.

Sun, R. (1999) Computational models of consciousness: an evaluation. *Journal of Intelligent Systems* **9**, 507–568.

Sun, R. (2002) *Duality of the Mind: A Bottom-up Approach Toward Cognition*. Erlbaum, Mahwah.

Supèr, H., Spekreijse, H. and Lamme, V.A.F. (2001) A neural correlate of working memory in the monkey primary visual cortex. *Science* **293**, 120–124.

Sutherland, K. (1995) ed. Symposium on 'Conversations with zombies'. *Journal of Consciousness Studies* **2**, 312–372.

Sutton, S., Tueting, P., Zubin, J. and John, E.R. (1967) Information delivery and the sensory evoked potential. *Science* **155**, 1436–1439.

Syková, E. (2004) Extrasynaptic volume transmission and diffusion parameters of the extracellular space. *Neuroscience* **129**, 861–876.

Szentágothai, J. (1973) Synaptology of the visual cortex. In Jung, R., ed., *Handbook of Sensory Physiology, vol. VII/3/B*. Springer, Heidelberg, pp. 269–324.

Szentágothai, J. (1978) The neuron network of the cerebral cortex: a functional interpretation. *Proceedings of the Royal Society of London, Series B* **201**, 219–248.

Tallon-Baudry, C. and Bertrand, O. (1999) Oscillatory gamma activity in humans and its role in object representation. *Trends in Cognitive Sciences* **3**, 151–162.

Tanaka, K. (2004) Inferotemporal response properties. In Chalupa, L.M. and Werner, J.S., eds., *The Visual Neurosciences*. MIT Press, Cambridge, MA, pp. 1151–1164.

Tanifuji, M., Tsunoda, K. and Yamane, Y. (2004) Neural representation of object images in the macaque inferotemporal cortex. In Kanwisher, N. and Duncan, J., eds., *Functional Neuroimaging of Visual Cognition*. Oxford University Press, Oxford, pp. 241–256.

Tarr, M.J. and Gauthier, I. (2000) FFA: a flexible fusiform area for subordinate-level visual processing automatized by expertise. *Nature Neuroscience* **3**, 764–769.

Taylor, J. (1999) *The Race for Consciousness*. MIT Press, Cambridge, MA.

Taylor, J.G. (2001) The central role of the parietal lobes in consciousness. *Consciousness and Cognition* **10**, 379–417.

Teyler, T.J., Hamm, J.P., Clapp, W.C., Johnson, B.W., Corballis, M.C. and Kirk, I.J. (2005) Long-term potentiation of human visual evoked responses. *European Journal of Neuroscience* **21**, 2045–2050.

Thagard, P. (1998) ed. *Mind Readings: Introductory Selections in Cognitive Science*. MIT Press, Cambridge, MA.

Thom, R. (1975) *Structural Stability and Morphogenesis: An Outline of a General Theory of Models*. Benjamin, Reading, MA.

Thompson, E. (1995) *Colour Vision: A Study in Cognitive Science and the Philosophy of Perception*. Routledge, London.

Thompson, E. (2001) ed. Between ourselves. *Journal of Consciousness Studies* **8** (5–7), 1–314.

Thompson, E. and Colombetti, G. (2005) eds. Emotion experience. *Journal of Consciousness Studies* **12** (8–10), 1–262.

Thorpe, S.J., Bacon, N., Rousselet, G.A., Macé, M.J.-M. and Fabre-Thorpe, M. (2002) Rapid categorisation of natural scenes: feedforward vs feedback contribution evaluated by backward masking. *Perception* **31**, 150.

Toet, A., Blom, J. and Koenderink, J.J. (1987) The construction of a simultaneous functional order in nervous systems: I. Relevance of signal covariances and signal coincidences in the construction of a functional order. *Biological Cybernetics* **57**, 115–125.

Tong, F. (2003) Primary visual cortex and visual awareness. *Nature Reviews Neuroscience* **4**, 219–229.

Tononi, G. and Edelman, G.M. (1998) Consciousness and complexity. *Science* **282**, 1846–1851.

Tononi, G., Edelman, G.M. and Sporns, O. (1998) Complexity and coherency: integrating information in the brain. *Trends in Cognitive Sciences* **2**, 474–484.

Tononi, G., Sporns, O. and Edelman, G.M. (1996) A complexity measure for selective matching of signals by the brain. *Proceedings of the National Academy of Sciences of the United States of America* **93**, 3422–3427.

Tononi, G., Sporns, O. and Edelman, G.M. (1999) Measures of degeneracy and redundancy in biological networks. *Proceedings of the National Academy of Sciences of the United States of America* **96**, 3257–3262.

Tootell, R.B., Nelissen, K., Vanduffel, W. and Orban, G.A. (2004) Search for color 'center(s)' in macaque visual cortex. *Cerebral Cortex* **14**, 353–363.

Torey, Z. (1999) *The Crucible of Consciousness*. Oxford University Press, London.

Treisman, A. and Gelade, G. (1980) A feature integration theory of attention. *Cognitive Psychology* **12**, 97–136.

Treisman, A. and Gormican, S. (1988) Feature analysis in early vision: evidence from search asymmetries. *Psychological Review* **95**, 15–48.

Tremere, L.A., Pinaud, R. and De Weerd, P. (2003) Conclusion: contributions of inhibitory mechanisms to perceptual completion and cortical reorganization. In Pessoa, L. and De Weerd, P., eds., *Filling-in: From Perceptual Completion to Cortical Reorganization*. Oxford University Press, Oxford, pp. 295–322.

Trevarthen, C.B. (1968) Two mechanisms of vision in primates. *Psychologische Forschung* **31**, 299–348.

Trevena, J.A. and Miller, J. (2002) Cortical movement preparation before and after a conscious decision to move. *Consciousness and Cognition* **11**, 162–190.

Tucker, T.R. and Fitzpatrick, D. (2004) Contributions of vertical and horizontal circuits to the response properties of neurons in primary visual cortex. In Chalupa, L.M. and Werner, J.S., eds., *The Visual Neurosciences*. MIT Press, Cambridge, MA, pp. 733–746.

Tucker, T.R. and Katz, L.C. (2003a) Spatiotemporal patterns of excitation and inhibition evoked by the horizontal network in layer 2/3 of ferret visual cortex. *Journal of Neurophysiology* **89**, 488–500.

Tucker, T.R. and Katz, L.C. (2003b) Recruitment of local inhibitory networks by horizontal connections in layer 2/3 of ferret visual cortex. *Journal of Neurophysiology* **89**, 501–512.

Tulving, E. (1972) Episodic and semantic memory. In Tulving, E. and Donaldson, W., eds., *Organization of Memory*. Academic, New York, pp. 381–403.

Tulving, E. (2000) ed. *Memory, Consciousness, and the Brain: The Tallin Conference*. Psychology Press, Philadelphia.

Tulving, E. (2001) Episodic memory and common sense: how far apart? *Philosophical Transactions of the Royal Society of London, Series B* **356**, 1505–1515.

Tulving, E. (2002) Episodic memory: from mind to brain. *Annual Review of Psychology* **53**, 1–25.

Tulving, E. and Craik, F.I.M. (2000) eds. *The Oxford Handbook of Memory*. Oxford University Press, Oxford.

Turing, A.M. (1936) On computable numbers, with an application to the Entscheidungsproblem. *Proceedings of the London Mathematical Society* **42**, 239–265.

Turing, A.M. (1950) Computing machinery and intelligence. *Mind* **59**, 433–460.

Turk, D.J., Heatherton, T.F., Kelley, W.M., Funnell, M.G., Gazzaniga, M.S. and Macrae, C.N. (2002) Mike or me? Self-recognition in a split-brain patient. *Nature Neuroscience* **5**, 841–842.

Turk, D.J., Heatherton, T.F., Macrae, C.N., Kelley, W.M. and Gazzaniga, M.S. (2003) Out of contact, out of mind: the distributed nature of the self. *Annals of the New York Academy of Sciences* **1001**, 65–78.

Turken, A.U., Vuilleumier, P., Mathalon, D.H., Swick, D. and Ford, J.M. (2003) Are impairments of action monitoring and executive control true dissociative dysfunctions in patients with schizophrenia? *American Journal of Psychiatry* **160**, 1881–1883.

Tye, M. (1991) *The Imagery Debate*. MIT Press, Cambridge, MA.

Ullman, S. (1995) Sequence seeking and counter streams: a computational model for bidirectional information flow in the visual cortex. *Cerebral Cortex* **5**, 1–11.

Ungeleider, L.G. and Mishkin, M. (1982) Two cortical visual systems. In Ingle, D.J., Goodale, M.A. and Manstead, R.J.W., eds., *Analysis of Visual Behavior*. MIT Press, Cambridge, MA, pp. 549–586.

Uttal, W.R. (2001) *The New Phrenology: The Limits of Localizing Cognitive Processes in the Brain*. MIT Press, Cambridge, MA.

Valverde, F. (1971) Short axon neuronal subsystems in the visual cortex of the monkey. *International Journal of Neuroscience* **1**, 181–197.

van de Grind, W.A. (1984) Decomposition and neuroreduction of visual perception. In van Doorn, A.J., van de Grind, W.A. and Koenderink, J.J., eds., *Limits in Perception*. VMU Science Press, Utrecht, pp. 431–494.

Van Essen, D.C. (2004) Organization of visual areas in macaque and human cerebral cortex. In Chalupa, L.M. and Werner, J.S., eds., *The Visual Neurosciences*. MIT Press, Cambridge, MA, pp. 507–521.

Van Essen, D.C., Anderson, C.H. and Felleman, D.J. (1992) Information processing in the primate visual system: an integrated systems perspective. *Science* **255**, 419–423.

Van Gulick, R. (1980) Functionalism, information and content. *Nature and System* **2**, 139–162.

Van Gulick, R. (2001) Reduction, emergence and other recent options on the mind/body problem: a philosophic overview. *Journal of Consciousness Studies* **8** (9–10), 1–34.

Vanderwolf, C.H. (2000) Are neocortical gamma waves related to consciousness? *Brain Research* **855**, 217–224.

Vanduffel, W., Tootell, R.B. and Orban, G.A. (2000) Attention-dependent suppression of metabolic activity in the early stages of the macaque visual system. *Cerebral Cortex* **10**, 109–126.

VanRullen, R. and Koch, C. (2003) Is perception discrete or continuous? *Trends in Cognitive Sciences* **7**, 207–213.

VanRullen, R. and Thorpe, S.J. (2001a) The time course of visual processing: from early perception to decision-making. *Journal of Cognitive Neuroscience* **13**, 454–461.

VanRullen, R. and Thorpe, S.J. (2001b) Is it a bird? Is it a plane? Ultra-rapid visual categorisation of natural and artifactual objects. *Perception* **30**, 655–668.

VanRullen, R. and Thorpe, S.J. (2002) Surfing a spike wave down the ventral stream. *Vision Research* **42**, 2593–2615.

Varela, F.J. (1999) Present-time consciousness. *Journal of Consciousness Studies* **6**(2–3), 111–140.

Varela, F.J. and Shear, J. (1999) eds. The view from within: first-person approaches to the study of consciousness. *Journal of Consciousness Studies* **6**(2–3), 1–314.

Varela, F.J., Thompson, E. and Rosch, E. (1991) *The Embodied Mind: Cognitive Science and Human Experience*. MIT Press, Cambridge, MA.

Varela, F.J., Toro, A., John, E.R. and Schwartz, E.L. (1981) Perceptual framing and cortical alpha rhythm. *Neuropsychologia* **19**, 675–686.

Velmans, M. (2000) *Understanding Consciousness*. Routledge, London.

Vidyasagar, T.R. (1998) Gating of neuronal responses in macaque primary visual cortex by an attentional spotlight. *Neuroreport* **9**, 1947–1952.

Vidyasagar, T.R. (1999) A neuronal model of attentional spotlight: parietal guiding the temporal. *Brain Research Reviews* **30**, 66–76.

Viviani, P. and Aymoz, C. (2001) Colour, form, and movement are not perceived simultaneously. *Vision Research* **41**, 2909–2918.

Vizi, E.S., Kiss, J.P. and Lendvai, B. (2004) Nonsynaptic communication in the central nervous system. *Neurochemistry International* **45**, 443–451.

Vogel, E.K., Luck, S.J. and Shapiro, K.L. (1998) Electrophysiological evidence for a postperceptual locus of suppression during the attentional blink. *Journal of Experimental Psychology: Human Perception and Performance* **24**, 1656–1674.

Vogeley, K. and Fink, G.R. (2003) Neural correlates of the first-person-perspective. *Trends in Cognitive Sciences* **7**, 38–42.

Vogeley, K., Kurthen, M., Falkai, P. and Maier, W. (1999) Essential functions of the human self model are implemented in the prefrontal cortex. *Consciousness and Cognition* **8**, 343–363.

Voltaire, F.M.A. de (1759) *Candide, ou l'Optimisme, traduit de l'allemand de Mr. le docteur Ralph*. Lambert, Paris.

von der Malsburg, C. (1973) Self-organization of orientation sensitive cells of the striate cortex. *Kybernetik* **14**, 85–100.

von der Malsburg, C. (2002) How are neural signals related to each other and to the world? *Journal of Consciousness Studies* **9** (1), 47–60.

Von Krosigk, M., Bal, T. and McCormick, D.A. (1993) Cellular mechanisms of a synchronized oscillation in the thalamus. *Science* **261**, 361–364.

Vuilleumier, P. (2004) Anosognosia: the neurology of beliefs and uncertainties. *Cortex* **40**, 9–17.

Wager, T.D. and Smith, E.E. (2003) Neuroimaging studies of working memory: a meta-analysis. *Cognitive, Affective and Behavioral Neuroscience* **3**, 255–274.

Walker, M.P. (2005) A refined model of sleep and the time course of memory formation. *Behavioral and Brain Sciences* **28**, 51–104.

Walsh, D.M. (2002) Bretano's chestnuts. In Ariew, A., Cummins, R. and Perlman, M., eds., *Functions: New Essays in the Philosophy of Psychology and Biology*. Oxford University Press, Oxford, pp. 314–337.

Walsh, V. and Pascual-Leone, A. (2003) *Transcranial Magnetic Stimulation: A Neurochronometrics of mind*. MIT Press, Cambridge, MA.

Ward, R., Danziger, S., Owen, V. and Rafal, R. (2002) Deficits in spatial coding and feature binding following damage to spatiotopic maps in the human pulvinar. *Nature Neuroscience* **5**, 99–100.

Warrington, E.K. (1982) Neuropsychological studies of object recognition. *Philosophical Transactions of the Royal Society of London, Series B* **298**, 15–33.

Warrington, E.K. and Shallice, T. (1969) The selective impairment of auditory verbal short-term memory. *Brain* **92**, 885–896.

Watanabe, T., Harner, A.M., Miyauchi, S., Sasaki, Y., Nielsen, M., Palomo, D. and Mukai, I. (1998a) Task-dependent influences of attention on the activation of human primary visual cortex. *Proceedings of the National Academy of Sciences of the United States of America* **95**, 11489–11492.

Watanabe, T., Sasaki, Y., Miyauchi, S., Putz, B., Fujimaki, N., Nielsen, M., Takino, R. and Miyakawa, S. (1998b) Attention-regulated activity in human primary visual cortex. *Journal of Neurophysiology* **79**, 2218–2221.

Watson, A.B. and Robson, J.G. (1981) Discrimination at threshold: labelled detectors in human vision. *Vision Research* **21**, 1115–1122.

Watson, J.B. (1925) *Behaviorism*. Norton, New York.

Watt, D.F. (2005) Panksepp's common sense view of affective neuroscience is not the commonsense view in large areas of neuroscience. *Consciousness and Cognition* **14**, 81–88.

Watt, S. (1997) The lion, the bat, and the wardrobe. In Ó Nualláin, S., Mc Kevitt, P. and Mac Aogáin, E., eds., *Two Sciences of Mind*. Benjamins, Amsterdam, pp. 55–61.

Webb, B. (2004) Neural mechanisms for prediction: do insects have forward models? *Trends in Neurosciences* **27**, 278–282.

Weber, W.C. and Jung, R. (1940) Über die epileptische Aura. *Zeitschrift für die gesamte Neurologie und Psychiatrie* **170**, 211–265.

Weinberg, H., Grey Walter, W. and Crow, H.J. (1970) Intracerebral events in humans related to real and imaginary stimuli. *Electroencephalography and Clinical Neurophysiology* **29**, 1–9.

Weiskrantz, L. (1988) ed. *Thought without Language*. Clarendon, Oxford.

Weiskrantz, L. (1997) *Consciousness Lost and Found: A Neuropsychological Exploration*. Oxford University Press, Oxford.

Weiskrantz, L., Barbur, J.L. and Sahraie, A. (1995) Parameters affecting conscious versus unconscious visual discrimination with damage to the visual cortex (V1). *Proceedings of the National Academy of Sciences of the United States of America* **92**, 6122–6126.

Weliky, M., Kandler, K., Fitzpatrick, D. and Katz, L.C. (1995) Patterns of excitation and inhibition evoked by horizontal connections in visual cortex share a common relationship to orientation columns. *Neuron* **15**, 541–552.

Wertheimer, M. (1912) Experimentelle Studien über das Sehen von Bewegung. *Zeitschrift für Psychologie* **61**, 161–265.

Westmacott, R., Black, S.E., Freedman, M. and Moscovitch, M. (2004a) The contribution of autobiographical significance to semantic memory: evidence from Alzheimer's disease, semantic dementia, and amnesia. *Neuropsychologia* **42**, 25–48.

Westmacott, R., Freedman, M., Black, S.E., Stokes, K.A. and Moscovitch, M. (2004b) Temporally graded semantic memory loss in Alzheimer's disease: cross-sectional and longitudinal studies. *Cognitive Neuropsychology* **21**, 353–378.

Wheeler, M.A., Stuss, D.T. and Tulving, E. (1997) Toward a theory of episodic memory: the frontal lobes and autonoetic consciousness. *Psychological Bulletin* **121**, 331–354.

Whitehead, C. (2001) Social mirrors and shared experiential worlds. *Journal of Consciousness Studies* **8** (4), 3–36.

Whitehead, C. (2004) Everything I believe might be a delusion. Whoa! Tuscon 2004: Ten years on are we anywhere nearer to a science of consciousness? *Journal of Consciousness Studies* **11** (12), 68–88.

Whorf, B.J. (1940) Science and linguistics. *Technology Review* **42**, 229–231, 247–248.

Wilks, Y. (2002) Dennett and artificial intelligence: on the same side, and if so, of what? In Brook, A. and Ross, D., eds., *Daniel Dennett*. Cambridge University Press, Cambridge, pp. 249–270.

Willis, T. (1664) *Cerebri Anatome: cui accessit Nervorum descriptio et usus*. Martyn and Allestry, London.

Wilson, H.R. (1999) *Spikes, Decisions, and Actions: The Dynamical Foundations of Neuroscience*. Oxford University Press, Oxford.

Wilson, H.R. (2003) Computational evidence for a rivalry hierarchy in vision. *Proceedings of the*

National Academy of Sciences of the United States of America **100**, 14499–14503.

Wilson, H.R., Blake, R. and Lee, S.H. (2001) Dynamics of travelling waves in visual perception. *Nature* **412**, 907–910.

Wilson, M.A. and McNaughton, B.L. (1993) Dynamics of the hippocampal ensemble code for space. *Science* **261**, 1055–1058.

Wilson, M.A. and McNaughton, B.L. (1994) Reactivation of hippocampal ensemble memories during sleep. *Science* **265**, 676–679.

Wilson, R.A. and Keil, F.C. (1999) eds. *The MIT Encyclopedia of the Cognitive Sciences*. MIT Press, Cambridge, MA.

Wimsatt, W.C. (1976) Reductionism, levels of organisation, and the mind–body problem. In Globus, G.G., Maxwell, G. and Slavodnik, I., eds., *Consciousness and the Brain*. Plenum, New York, pp. 199–267.

Wimsatt, W.C. (2002) Functional organization, analogy, and inference. In Ariew, A., Cummins, R. and Perlman, M., eds., *Functions: New Essays in the Philosophy of Psychology and Biology*. Oxford University Press, Oxford, pp. 173–221.

Wittgenstein, L.J.J. (1953) *Philosophical Investigations*. Transl. Anscombe, G.E.M. Blackwell, Oxford.

Wolf, K. (2002) Visual ecology: coloured fruit is what the eye sees best. *Current Biology* **12**, R253–R255.

Wolfe, J.M. (1998) What do 1 million trials tell us about visual search? *Psychological Science* **9**, 33–39.

Wolfe, J.M. (2003) Moving towards solutions to some enduring controversies in visual search. *Trends in Cognitive Sciences* **7**, 70–76.

Wolfe, J.M. and Horowitz, T.S. (2004) What attributes guide the deployment of visual attention and how do they do it? *Nature Reviews Neuroscience* **5**, 495–501.

Wolpert, D.M., Goodbody, S.J. and Husain, M. (1998) Maintaining internal representations: the role of the human superior parietal lobe. *Nature Neuroscience* **1**, 529–533.

Woods, S.P. and Troster, A.I. (2003) Prodromal frontal/executive dysfunction predicts incident dementia in Parkinson's disease. *Journal of the International Neuropsychological Society* **9**, 17–24.

Woodward, J. and Cowie, E. (2004) The mind is not (just) a system of modules shaped (just) by natural selection. In Hitchcock, C.R., ed., *Contemporary Debates in Philosophy of Science*. Blackwell, Oxford, pp. 312–334.

Woolf, N.J. and Hameroff, S.R. (2001) A quantum approach to visual consciousness. *Trends in Cognitive Sciences* **5**, 472–478.

Wright, L. (1973) Functions. *Philosophical Review* **82**, 139–168.

Wuerfel, J., Krishnamoorthy, E.S., Brown, R.J., Lemieux, L., Koepp, M., Tebartz van Elst, L. and Trimble, M.R. (2004) Religiosity is associated with hippocampal but not amygdala volumes in patients with refractory epilepsy. *Journal of Neurology, Neurosurgery and Psychiatry* **75**, 640–642.

Yerkes, R. and Dodson, J. (1908) The relation of strength of stimulus to rapidity of habit-formation. *Journal of Comparative Neurology and Psychology* **18**, 459–482.

Yingling, C.D. and Skinner, J.E. (1977) Gating of thalamic input to cerebral cortex by nucleus reticularis thalami. In Desmedt, J.E., ed., *Attention, Voluntary Contraction and Event-Related Cerebral Potentials. Progress in Clinical Neurophysiology, vol. 1*. Karger, Basel, pp. 70–96.

Yntema, D.B. and Trask, F.P. (1963) Recall as a search process. *Journal of Verbal Learning and Verbal Behavior* **2**, 65–74.

Yoo, S.S., Lee, C.U. and Choi, B.G. (2001) Human brain mapping of auditory imagery: event-related functional MRI study. *Neuroreport* **12**, 3045–3049.

Young, J.Z. (1978) *Programs of the Brain*. Oxford University Press, Oxford.

Young, M.P. (1992) Objective analysis of the topological organization of the primate cortical visual system. *Nature* **358**, 152–155.

Young, M.P. (2000) The architecture of visual cortex and inferential processes in vision. *Spatial Vision* **13**, 137–146.

Young, M.P., Hilgetag, C.-C. and Scannell, J.W. (2000) On imputing function to structure from the behavioural effects of brain lesions. *Philosophical Transactions of the Royal Society of London, Series B* **355**, 147–161.

Young, M.P., Tanaka, K. and Yamane, S. (1992) On oscillating neuronal responses in the visual cortex of the monkey. *Journal of Neurophysiology* **67**, 1464–1474.

Young, M.P. and Yamane, S. (1992) Sparse population coding of faces in the inferotemporal cortex. *Science* **256**, 1327–1331.

Zahavi, D. (2000) ed. *Exploring the Self: Philosophical and Psychopathological Perspectives on Self-experience*. Benjamins, Amsterdam.

Zahavi, D., Grünbaum, T. and Parnas, J. (2004) eds. *The Structure and Development of Self-Consciousness: Interdisciplinary Perspectives*. Benjamins, Amsterdam.

Zatorre, R.J. (2003) Music and the brain. *Annals of the New York Academy of Sciences* **999**, 4–14.

Zeki, S. (1978) Uniformity and diversity of structure and function in rhesus monkey prestriate visual cortex. *Journal of Physiology* **277**, 273–290.

Zeki, S. (1993) *A Vision of the Brain*. Blackwell, Oxford.

Zeki, S. (1998) Parallel processing, asynchronous perception, and a distributed system of consciousness in vision. *The Neuroscientist* **4**, 365–372.

Zeki, S. (2001) Localization and globalization in conscious vision. *Annual Review of Neuroscience* **24**, 57–86.

Zeki, S. (2003) The disunity of consciousness. *Trends in Cognitive Sciences* **7**, 214–218.

Zeki, S. (2004) Improbable areas in color vision. In Chalupa, L.M. and Werner, J.S., eds., *The Visual Neurosciences*. MIT Press, Cambridge, MA, pp. 1029–1039.

Zeki, S. and Bartels, A. (1998) The autonomy of the visual systems and the modularity of conscious vision. *Philosophical Transactions of the Royal Society of London, Series B* **353**, 1911–1914.

Zeki, S. and ffytche, D.H. (1998) The Riddoch syndrome: insights into the neurobiology of conscious vision. *Brain* **121**, 25–45.

Zeki, S. and Moutoussis, K. (1997) Temporal hierarchy of the visual perceptive systems in the Mondrian world. *Proceedings of the Royal Society of London, Series B* **264**, 1415–1419.

Zeman, A. (2001) Consciousness. *Brain* **124**, 1263–1289.

Zeman, A. (2002) *Consciousness: A User's Guide*. Yale University Press, New Haven.

Zhang, L.M. and Jones, E.G. (2004) Corticothalamic inhibition in the thalamic reticular nucleus. *Journal of Neurophysiology* **91**, 759–766.

■ INDEX